Identity Theft:

Breakthroughs in Research and Practice

Information Resources Management Association
USA

www.igi-global.com

Published in the United States of America by
    IGI Global
    Information Science Reference (an imprint of IGI Global)
    701 E. Chocolate Avenue
    Hershey PA, USA 17033
    Tel: 717-533-8845
    Fax: 717-533-8661
    E-mail: cust@igi-global.com
    Web site: http://www.igi-global.com

                    Library of Congress Cataloging-in-Publication Data

Names: Information Resources Management Association, editor.
Title: Identity theft : breakthroughs in research and practice / Information
    Resources Management Association, editor.
Description: Hershey : Information Science Reference, 2017. | Includes
    bibliographical references and index.
Identifiers: LCCN 2016024525| ISBN 9781522508083 (hardcover) | ISBN
    9781522508090 (ebook)
Subjects: LCSH: Identity theft. | Identity theft--Prevention. |
    Internet--Security measures. | Internet--Safety measures. | Computer
    crimes.
Classification: LCC HV6675 .I344 2017 | DDC 364.16/33--dc23 LC record available at https://lccn.loc.gov/2016024525

British Cataloguing in Publication Data
A Cataloguing in Publication record for this book is available from the British Library.

For electronic access to this publication, please contact: eresources@igi-global.com.

List of Contributors

Table of Contents

Section 1
Fundamental Concepts and Design Methodologies

This section serves as a foundation for this exhaustive reference tool by addressing underlying principles essential to the understanding of Identity Theft and provides in-depth coverage of conceptual architecture frameworks to provide the reader with a comprehensive understanding of the emerging developments within the field of Identity Theft. With 7 chapters comprising this foundational section, the reader can learn and chose from a compendium of expert research on the elemental theories underscoring the Identity Theft discipline. Research fundamentals imperative to the understanding of developmental processes within Identity Theft are offered. Chapters found within these pages provide an excellent framework in which to position Identity Theft within the field of information science and technology. From broad examinations to specific discussions on methodology, the research found within this section spans the discipline while offering detailed, specific discussions. From basic designs to abstract development, these chapters serve to expand the reaches of development and design technologies within the Identity Theft community. Insight regarding the critical incorporation of global measures into Identity Theft is addressed, while crucial stumbling blocks of this field are explored.

Section 2
Technologies and Applications

This section presents an extensive coverage of various tools and technologies available in the field of Identity Theft and discusses a variety of applications and opportunities available that can be considered by practitioners in developing viable and effective Identity Theft programs and processes. With 7 chapters, this section offers a broad treatment of some of the many tools and technologies within the Identity Theft field. These chapters enlighten readers about fundamental research on the many tools facilitating the burgeoning field of Identity Theft and review topics from case studies to best practices and ongoing research. Further chapters discuss Identity Theft in a variety of settings. Contributions included in this section provide excellent coverage of today's IT community and how research into Identity Theft is impacting the social fabric of our present-day global village. It is through these rigorously researched chapters that the reader is provided with countless examples of the up-and-coming tools and technologies emerging from the field of Identity Theft.

Section 3
Social Implications, Critical Issues, and Emerging Trends

This section contains 6 chapters, giving a wide range of research pertaining to the social and behavioral impact of Identity Theft, and a wide variety of perspectives and advancement of the discipline on Identity Theft. The reader is presented with an in-depth analysis of research into the integration of global Identity Theft as well as the most current and relevant issues within this growing field of study in which crucial questions are addressed and theoretical approaches discussed. Chapters in this section discuss the effects of user behavior as well as future research directions and topical suggestions for continued debate.

Preface

The constantly changing landscape of Identity Theft makes it challenging for experts and practitioners to stay informed of the field's most up-to-date research. That is why Information Science Reference is pleased to offer this single-volume reference collection that will empower students, researchers, and academicians with a strong understanding of critical issues within Identity Theft by providing both broad and detailed perspectives on cutting-edge theories and developments. This reference is designed to act as a single reference source on conceptual, methodological, and technical, as well as provide insight into emerging trends and future opportunities within the discipline.

Identity Theft: Breakthroughs in Research and Practice is organized into three sections that provide comprehensive coverage of important topics. The sections are:

1. Fundamental Concepts and Design Methodologies;
2. Technologies and Applications;
3. Social Implications, Critical Issues, and Emerging Trends.

The following paragraphs provide a summary of what to expect from this invaluable reference tool.

Section 1, "Fundamental Concepts and Design Methodologies," serves as a foundation for this extensive reference tool by addressing crucial theories and presents in-depth coverage of the conceptual design and architecture essential to the understanding of Identity Theft. Introducing the book is *Privacy, Security, and Identity Theft Protection: Advances and Trends* by Guillermo A. Francia III, Frances Shannon Hutchinson, and Xavier Paris Francia; a great foundation laying the groundwork for the basic concepts and theories that will be discussed throughout the rest of the book. Through case studies, this section lays excellent groundwork for later sections that will get into present and future applications for Identity Theft. The section concludes, and leads into the following portion of the book with a nice segue chapter, *Identity Management Systems: Models, Standards, and COTS Offerings* by Reema Bhatt, Manish Gupta, and Raj Sharman.

Section 2, "Technologies and Applications," presents extensive coverage of the various tools and technologies used along with describing how the broad range of Identity Theft efforts has been utilized and offers insight on and important lessons for their applications and impact. The first chapter *The German Electronic Identity Card: Lessons Learned* by Christoph Sorge, lays a framework for the types of works that can be found in this section. This section includes the widest range of topics because it describes tools at place in the modeling, planning, and applications along with case studies, research, methodologies, frameworks, architectures, theory, analysis, and guides for implementation of Identity Theft. We conclude the section with *A Wrapper-Based Classification Approach for Personal Identification through Keystroke Dynamics Using Soft Computing Techniques* by Shanmugapriya D. and Padmavathi Ganapathi a well-rounded transitional chapter into the next section.

Section 3, "Social Implications, Critical Issues, and Emerging Trends," includes chapters discussing the organizational and social impact of Identity Theft, coverage of academic and research perspectives on tools and applications and highlights areas for future research. The section opens with *Cyber Risk: A Big Challenge in Developed and Emerging Markets* by Maria Cristina Arcuri, Marina Brogi, and Gino Gandolfi. This section focuses on how these technologies affect human lives, discusses theoretical approaches and offer alternatives to crucial questions, and looks at what might happen in the coming years that can extend the applications for Identity Theft. The final chapter of the book looks at an emerging field within Identity Theft, in the excellent contribution, *User Authentication based on Dynamic Keystroke Recognition* by Khaled Mohammed Fouad, Basma Mohammed Hassan, and Mahmoud F. Hassan.

Although the primary organization of the contents in this work is based on its three sections, offering a progression of coverage of the important concepts, methodologies, technologies, applications, social issues, and emerging trends, the reader can also identify specific contents by utilizing the extensive indexing system listed at the end. As a comprehensive collection of research on the latest findings related to using technology to providing various services, *Identity Theft: Breakthroughs in Research and Practice*, provides researchers, administrators and all audiences with a complete understanding of the development of applications and concepts in Identity Theft. Given the vast number of issues concerning usage, failure, success, policies, strategies, and applications of Identity Theft in countries around the world, *Identity Theft: Breakthroughs in Research and Practice* addresses the demand for a resource that encompasses the most pertinent research in technologies being employed to globally bolster the knowledge and applications of Identity Theft.

Section 1
Fundamental Concepts and Design Methodologies

This section serves as a foundation for this exhaustive reference tool by addressing underlying principles essential to the understanding of Identity Theft and provides in-depth coverage of conceptual architecture frameworks to provide the reader with a comprehensive understanding of the emerging developments within the field of Identity Theft. With 7 chapters comprising this foundational section, the reader can learn and chose from a compendium of expert research on the elemental theories underscoring the Identity Theft discipline. Research fundamentals imperative to the understanding of developmental processes within Identity Theft are offered. Chapters found within these pages provide an excellent framework in which to position Identity Theft within the field of information science and technology. From broad examinations to specific discussions on methodology, the research found within this section spans the discipline while offering detailed, specific discussions. From basic designs to abstract development, these chapters serve to expand the reaches of development and design technologies within the Identity Theft community. Insight regarding the critical incorporation of global measures into Identity Theft is addressed, while crucial stumbling blocks of this field are explored.

Chapter 1
Privacy, Security, and Identity Theft Protection:
Advances and Trends

Guillermo A. Francia III
Jacksonville State University, USA

Frances Shannon Hutchinson
ITEL Laboratories, USA

Xavier Paris Francia
Jacksonville State University, USA

ABSTRACT

The proliferation of the Internet has intensified the privacy protection and identity theft crises. A December 2013 report by the U.S. Department of Justice indicates that 16.6 million persons were victims of identity theft with direct and indirect losses amounting to almost $24.7 billion in 2012 (Harrell & Langton, 2013). These startling and apparently persistent statistics have prompted the United States and other foreign governments to initiate strategic plans and to enact several regulations in order to curb the crisis. This chapter surveys recently enacted national and international laws pertaining to identity theft and privacy issues. Further, it discusses the interplay between privacy and security, the various incentives and deterrence for privacy protection, and the prospects for the simulation of the social and behavioral aspects of privacy using the agent-based modeling.

INTRODUCTION

As an extension of an earlier work (Francia & Hutchinson, 2012) on regulations and compliance pertaining to identity theft prevention, detection, and response policies, we describe recently enacted national and international laws pertaining to identity theft. We also expound on the relationship between privacy and security, the various incentives and deterrence for privacy protection, and possible research extensions that include the social and behavioral study on privacy protection through agent-based modeling and simulation.

DOI: 10.4018/978-1-5225-0808-3.ch001

BACKGROUND

Identity theft is a threat that has confounded society since the biblical times. The ubiquity of the Internet and the convenience of electronic transactions have exacerbated the threat and made it even much easier to execute. A most recent report by the Department of Justice indicates staggering losses amounting to almost $25 billion incurred due to almost 17 million cases of identity theft losses (Harrell & Langton, 2013). Snapshots of several alarming statistics, which are gathered from the same source and are pertinent to identity theft, are shown in Figure 1 and Table 1. Figure 1 depicts the allocation of ID thefts by type. The inner chart further breaks the existing account slice into three categories: credit card, bank account, and other account.

Table 1 shows the actions taken by individuals to reduce their risk of identity theft. Note the alarming percentage of people using an ID theft protection service.

Figure 1. Types of identity theft

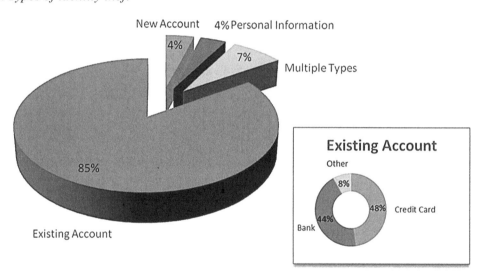

Table 1. Actions taken to reduce the risk of ID theft

Action Taken	Percentage
Checked credit report	37.9
Changed passwords on financial accounts	28.6
Purchased identity theft insurance/credit monitoring service	5.3
Shredded/destroyed documents with personal information	67.4
Checked bank or credit statements	74.8
Used identity theft security program on computer	16.6
Purchased identity theft protection	3.5

(Harrell & Langton, 2013).

These alarming statistics and their perceived persistent nature should motivate everyone, most importantly private and public institutions, to adhere and remain in compliance with policies and regulations that promote privacy and security protections. We begin with the definition of important concepts pertaining to regulatory compliance and identity theft.

REGULATORY LAWS AND COMPLIANCE

ID Theft protection is a subject of a variety of additional security-focused legislation. For example, health care providers and their affiliates are subject to the Health Insurance Portability and Accountability Act of 1996 (HIPAA), which specifically protects the rights and information of patients and health care plan participants (Salomon, Cassat, & Thibeau, 2003). Educators must contend with the Family Education Rights and Privacy Act, or FERPA, which strives to protect the information of students (Salomon et al., 2003). In fact, some educational institutions may find themselves covered by both FERPA and HIPAA if that institution is affiliated with a health care provider.

An update to an earlier work (Francia & Hutchinson, 2012) which describes several laws and regulations that pertain to information security and identity theft prevention or response is presented in the following.

HITECH Act

The Health Information Technology for Economic and Clinical Health (HITECH) Act is part of the American Recovery and Reinvestment Act (ARRA) of 2009 (U.S. Government Printing Office Public Law 111-5, 2009). Among its many purposes is the promotion of health information technology which ensures that the patient's health information is secure and protected. The security provisions closely related to the protection of health information includes:

- Notification of affected patients in cases of security breaches;
- Restrictions on the sale and marketing of health information;
- The provision of patient access to electronic health information;
- Accounting of disclosures of health information to patients; and
- Additional HIPAA regulations covering business partners such as vendors and exchanges.

COPPA

The Children's Online Privacy Protection Act (COPPA), which was enacted in 1998 and became effective in April, 2000, applies to the online collection of personal information of children under the age of 13. It includes provisions to protect the children's privacy rights, to restrict marketing to those children, and to seek verifiable consent from the parent or guardian (Legal Information Institute, 2014). The authority to issue regulations and enforce COPPA is with the Federal Trade Commission (FTC). In December 2012, the FTC issued revisions to the rules which include four new categories to the definition of personal information: geolocation information; photo, videos or audio files; user names; and persistent identifiers that can be used to identify a user over time and across multiple websites. Enforcement actions of the FTC include a deterrent civil penalty of up to $16,000 per violation (Bureau of Consumer Protection, 2014).

U.S.-EU Safe Harbor Framework

The U.S. Safe Harbor Framework is a process with which U.S. companies can transfer personal data from the European Union (EU) to the United States. This process is consistent with the requirements of the EU Data Protection Directive (Bureau of Consumer Protection, 2014B). It would take a U.S. company's self-certification of compliance with the seven principles and other requirements by the Commerce Department to be able to join the U.S.-EU Safe Harbor. The seven principles are:

- **Notice:** Organizations must notify an individual about the purpose of privacy-related data collection.
- **Choice:** Organizations must provide an individual the option to choose whether personal data collection can or cannot be continued and/or disclosed to a third party.
- **Onward Transfer:** Organizations must apply the notice and choice principles when disclosing to a third party.
- **Access:** Individuals must be provided access to their own personal data and must be able to correct, amend, or delete any of that information.
- **Security:** Organizations must provide adequate protection of personal data.
- **Data Integrity:** Organization must ensure that the personal information remain accurate, complete, and current for its intended purpose.
- **Enforcement:** To ensure compliance, effective means of enforcement of these rules must be in place.

Other International Privacy Laws

During the last decade other countries have vigorously pursued and enacted legislation on privacy rights protection. Among these countries are Malta (*Personal Data and Protection of Privacy Regulation (SL 399.25)*), Romania (*Processing of Personal Data and the Protection of Privacy in the Electronic Communications Sector; Law no. 506 (2004)*), and Singapore (*Banking Act, the Statistics Act, the Official Secrets Act, and the Statutory Bodies and Government Companies (Protection of Secrecy) Act*). (Francia and Ciganek, 2010).

Recently enacted laws related to privacy rights protection include Australia's *Personally Controlled Electronic Health Records Act 2012 (ALRC, 2014)*, Mexico's *Protection of Personal Data Held by Private Parties Law 2010* (IAPP, 2014), and Belgium's *Royal Decree on Data Retention 2013* (Data Guidance, 2014).

PRIVACY AND SECURITY

The Difference between Privacy and Security

The words "privacy" and "security" can invoke similar imagery, such as a picture of a closed door or thoughts of one's home; however, the two are separate concepts that must both be taken into account whenever someone's information or safety is at risk. Privacy may be defined as "the quality or state of being apart from company or observation", "freedom from unauthorized intrusion", or simply "the state of being alone" (Merriam-Webster, Incorporated, 2014).

One of the key issues when attempting to protect privacy or security is a difference in expectations. United States law on the subject remains ambiguous, stating that citizens have a "reasonable" expectation of privacy and should be protected from "unreasonable" searches and seizures, but what is and is not reasonable is ill-defined and must often be revisited with the emergence of new technologies (Verrecchia & Weiss, 2013). The now-famous case of *Olmstead v. United States* first brought this issue to light as the country struggled to determine how private a telephone conversation really is, and who would be allowed to listen in (and to what extent, and under what circumstances) without penalty. This same issue has been revisited recently in light of even more advanced technology that allows for the collection of massive amounts of data, which has been used by the National Security Agency (NSA) to amass a bulk collection of citizens' phone record metadata in the name of preventing potential terrorist attacks and other threats (Savage, 2013). In the Olmstead case, it was ruled that citizens had a right to an expectation of privacy when speaking on the telephone; in a later case (*Smith v. Maryland*), the ruling stated that while the content of a phone conversation was expected to be private, records of the call itself (such as the parties involved, the time of the call, and its length) were considered to be public information kept by the phone companies and could be used in police investigations (Verrecchia & Weiss, 2013). The more recent question seems to be, given the newfound ease with which such large amounts of metadata can be collected and analyzed to infer additional information, can the collection of such data on this scale still be considered a "reasonable" breach of the average citizen's privacy? While firm action has not been taken one way or the other as of this writing, the ruling of at least one District Court judge Richard J. Leon indicates that such behavior is unconstitutional, opposing the fifteen Foreign Intelligence Surveillance Court judges who have previously examined this issue (Savage, 2013).

Privacy vs. Security

Several recent political debates have chosen to frame issues in this context: would you rather be private or secure? While this "either-or" mentality has always had some presence in courtrooms due to concerns over unconstitutional searches and seizures in the name of preventing future crimes, it has become far more prevalent following the United States' long anti-terrorism campaign and its attempts to justify ever more invasive security measures. This approach of gathering data on everyone in an attempt to locate a few potential criminals is called a dragnet approach (Noble, 2013).

Some security experts argue that the privacy versus security standpoint is in itself a "false choice" and that traditional security measures have always been designed to reinforce security without compromising privacy, such as door locks, fences, and firewalls (Sullivan, 2013). One oft-quoted argument of those willing to give up their privacy is "nothing to hide", which is used to insinuate that anyone who wants to protect their privacy must have something to hide and is therefore to be treated with suspicion. The fallacy of this argument lies in the fact that everyone does, in fact, have something to hide – personal information in the wrong hands can be used to directly harm an individual financially, emotionally, or even physically, and it is not always apparent who will abuse that information until they have already done so.

The legal decisions currently being made about massive data collection and dragnet techniques are important because they will play a part in defining what personal data can be collected by government entities, corporations, and individuals and how that data may be handled by those who collect it.

INCENTIVES AND DETERRENCE FOR PRIVACY PROTECTION

Incentives for Individuals

The primary incentive for an individual to protect his or her private information is a strong one; aside from the general feeling of security that accompanies control over one's personal information, maintaining privacy greatly reduces the risk of identity theft, which can have lasting fiscal and social repercussions for the victim. While everyone can benefit from basic security measures like using strong passwords or shredding sensitive documents, particular circumstances or statistics can further incentivize individuals to invest in their privacy and the privacy of those around them.

Another area of privacy protection that is easily overlooked is the protection of one's personal information from friends, family, neighbors, and coworkers. Sadly, not all cases of identity theft are the work of major data breaches or faceless hackers in far-away locations. In a 2007 FTC report, sixteen percent of surveyed identity theft victims reported that they knew the perpetrator personally with an alarming six percent reporting a family member (Federal Trade Commission, 2007). Keeping sensitive documents out of sight, not lending credit and debit cards for others to use, and keeping passwords or lock combinations private are all simple precautions that can help to reduce the temptation of someone close to home in committing identity theft.

In spite of all preventative measures, the truth is that no amount of precaution, monitoring, or paid services can guarantee identity theft protection. Major data breaches are becoming more commonplace, and sensitive data has become cheap. According to a set of statistics reported by Robert Siciliano, a compromised U.S. bank account with a balance of $70,000 - $150,000 can be purchased online for as little as $300, while as little as $8 will buy a stolen U.S. credit card (CVV number included) and a mere $40 will purchase a stolen U.S. identity (Siciliano, 2014). Persons and businesses whose information has not yet been compromised cannot feel entirely safe, either; $25 to $100 will buy a dedicated criminal to extract substantial information on a given person or business through means such as Trojan infiltration or social engineering (Siciliano, 2014).

Incentives for Corporations

Various organizations gather immense amounts of personal data about their customers, ranging from consumer shopping habits to names, credit card numbers, passwords, email addresses, and other information. Some of this information is required in order to conduct business. Medical facilities must keep their patients' medical histories on hand for the purpose of informed diagnosis and treatment. All of this personal data could be abused should the company suffer from a data breach.

Particular attention has been paid to large corporation data breaches of late as they appear to be growing in both frequency and scale. The potential for a data breach to occur should give any corporation reason to invest in the security of its collected information since the compromised data can result in millions of dollars' worth in damage control. Target in particular has suffered staggering losses from its 2013 holiday data breach, including $61 million expenses in 2013 alone as well as more than 80 as of yet unresolved lawsuits against the company (Lobosco, 2014). In an infographic posted by security researchers, the financial costs of another major data breach – Sony in 2011 – are listed as $171 million as of the time the research was conducted with an estimated potential for up to $24 billion total in damages before the lingering effects of the data breach would subside (Veracode, 2014). Both breaches could have been prevented, or at least mitigated, by stronger security precautions such as more careful system monitoring or code checks.

Major credit card companies also suffer from each data breach because they may be responsible for partially or fully absorbing the cost of an identity theft, depending on how much protection the company offers its card holders and whether the thief is ever proven or apprehended. For this reason, several U.S. credit companies are pressuring other corporations to adopt the Europay, Mastercard and Visa (EMV) technology currently used in Europe (Harris, Perlroth, & Popper, 2014). This technology embeds small chips into credit and debit cards which produce a new code for each transaction, making them much more difficult to counterfeit than a card which only uses traditional CVV information and protecting users from having their card information easily stolen by point-of-sale attacks at a cash register. The United States has been slow to adopt this technology even though this country accounts for roughly 47% of all credit card fraud (though, interestingly, only 27% of all credit transactions) (Harris, Perlroth, & Popper, 2014).

Deterrence for Individuals

Despite the enormous damages that can be incurred from having one's personal information used in a malicious way, there is a great deal of deterrence in the modern world against keeping such information private. The mere existence of social media sites such as Facebook and Twitter encourage users to share large amounts of personal information such as likes and dislikes, phone numbers, marital status, current location, schools and universities attended, and anything else that a person might be convinced to share with friends online. For users, sharing this information may allow them to locate long-lost contacts or connect with people who claim to share similar interests. The value of this data for the social media sites is that it can be collected and used to provide marketers with targeted advertisements for users of the site to generate more revenue by tailoring ads to those whom are most likely to follow through and make purchases from them. However, widely available personal data can also be used maliciously in social engineering, fraud, or harassment.

Social media aside, many individuals may be convinced to part with a little bit of privacy here and there in order to receive some other benefit; for instance, whenever a consumer signs up for a loyalty card at a local retail outlet, the outlet is likely to collect data about that user such as an identifying name, phone number, or email address as well as more particular data about how often the user shops at that location and what items he or she tends to purchase (Privacy and Data Security: Protecting Consumers in the Modern World, 2011). In return for this personal information, the consumer may receive a discount on goods purchased, though perhaps without knowledge of the precise quantity of information that has just been traded or what will be done with it.

A less obvious but far more common means of deterrence against privacy can be found in the average terms of service or privacy policy itself. In 2008, it was estimated that it would take the average American over 200 hours every year to read the privacy policies of every site they were likely to use – and that is assuming that the reader is able to understand the policy the first time it is read, if at all (Misener, 2014). It is likely that this number has increased over the years as more companies use the Internet to provide additional services and reach new audiences. Additionally, companies are not always required to notify their users when the terms of service or privacy policies change, and can reserve the right to alter them at any time and any number of times within a given year (Misener, 2014). It should come as no surprise, then, that the average user "accepts" these terms and policies without having the slightest idea about what he or she is agreeing to.

Deterrence for Corporations

Just as the potential loss of profit and trust can incentivize large companies or organizations to protect the personal data they collect, so too can the potential for greater profit deter them from sharing this data.

Marketing is a common driving force behind data sharing. A 2003 study highlighted some of the benefits for marketers when choosing targeted advertising as a medium; in particular, fewer wasted dollars are spent advertising to users who were unlikely to ever follow through with a purchase and greater spending occurs in the advertising industry overall since targeted ads tend to generate more revenue than other, more traditional mediums (Iyer, Soberman, & Villas-Boas, 2003). By knowing the age, location, and personal preferences of many individuals, advertising companies can further refine their marketing strategies by choosing whether to target specific advertisements and offers toward those who are mostly likely to buy the product or toward consumers who are thought to have weak branding preferences and therefore may be swayed to try a product for the first time or to leave competing brands (Iyer, Soberman, & Villas-Boas, 2003).

Facebook in particular is known for collecting large amounts of data on its users over time and then offering to target advertisements based on that data. It has been a successful business strategy, generating over $2.34 billion in advertisement revenue alone as of the end of quarter on December 31, 2013 (Goel, 2014).

Aside from its use in generating advertising revenue and allowing retailers to adjust their stock and marketing campaigns to suit the interests of the consumers who are most likely to spend money, there is pure profit to be made by simply selling collected information. Entities that deal primarily in the buying and selling of personal information are called data brokers, and the information they trade could include anything from one's religious views and political affiliations to user names, income, medical history, web browsing history, known contacts and psychiatric profile (Kroft, 2014). This information may appear useful not only to those in the marketing or sales industries, but also to researchers or even prospective employers conducting a background check.

FURTHER RESEARCH DIRECTIONS

In theory, personal data protection appears simple; just perform the risk assessment, create the policy and procedures, then audit and revise as necessary. Unfortunately, it is often much more complex in practice.

Privacy laws can significantly differ across physical and cultural boundaries. Although humans are bound by core ethical standards, societal and business laws may be greatly influenced by culture. The need for an in-depth study of privacy laws that transcends physical and cultural boundaries provides a challenging extension to this research project.

The weakest link in the enforcement of privacy protection policies is always the people involved. Some individuals are especially prone to social engineering no matter how many information security awareness training they have undergone. Discovering the actual thoughts and actions of those that handle confidential information can be a tricky process, and changing a person's nature, beliefs or daily habits can prove nearly impossible. Thus, a study on the social behavior towards privacy protection and trust is a logical extension to this research.

In economics, utility functions have been used to describe and explain the behavior of consumers (users) within a system of constraint. Traditional, normative economic theory posits that human behavior is rational whereas behavioral economists have come to the conclusion that human behavior is best described as irrational. By incorporating psychological factors and processes into utility functions, behavioral economists have been able to describe human behavior with much more accuracy, and this increased precision has led to improvements in altering human behavior for the benefit of society (Kahneman & Tversky, 2000). Although this research has substantial implications for decision making involving privacy, there has been little attempt to evaluate the predictions of prospect theory as it relates to risky decisions in cyberspace, particularly in privacy protection. Thus, another natural extension to this work is the design and implementation of an agent-based model that can be used to simulate cyber risks and decision making processes in light of privacy protection.

CONCLUSION

Our discussions on the recently enacted national and international laws pertaining to privacy protection and identity theft prevention reveal a common thread: a continuous enhancement of the existing laws and regulations. It is easy to recognize that this phenomenon is brought about by technological advancements that are rapidly obliterating several restrictions to information access. As such, there is a constant need to improve various incentives and deterrence for privacy protection. Further, as we become more intimately bound by technology, a solid comprehension and understanding of our social and behavioral attitude on privacy and risky decisions in cyber space must be fully developed.

REFERENCES

Australian Law Reform Commission (ALRC). (2014). *Health information privacy*. Retrieved May 1, 2014 from http://www.alrc.gov.au/publications/3-overview-current-law/health- information-privacy#_ftnref20

Bureau of Consumer Protection. (2014). *Complying with COPPA: Frequently asked questions*. Retrieved April 30, 2013 from http://www.business.ftc.gov/documents/0493-Complying-with-COPPA-Frequently-Asked-Questions

Bureau of Consumer Protection. (2014B). *Federal trade commission enforcement of the U.S.- EU and U.S.-Swiss safe harbor frameworks*. Retrieved April 30, 2013 from http://www.business.ftc.gov/documents/0494-federal-trade-commission-enforcement-us-eu-and-us-swiss-safe-harbor-frameworks

Federal Trade Commission. (2007, November 27). *FTC releases survey of identity theft in the U.S. study shows 8.3 million victims in 2005*. Retrieved March 12, 2014, from Federal Trade Commission: http://www.ftc.gov/news-events/press-releases/2007/11/ftc-releases-survey-identity-theft-usstudy-shows-83-million

Federal Trade Commission. (2010, March 9). *LifeLock will pay $12 million to settle charges by the FTC and 35 states that identify theft prevention and data security claims were false*. Retrieved March 7, 2014, from Federal Trade Commission: http://www.ftc.gov/news-events/press-releases/2010/03/lifelock-will-pay-12-million-settle-charges-ftc-35-states

Federal Trade Commission. (2012, July). *How to keep your personal information secure*. Retrieved March 12, 2014, from Federal Trade Commission: http://www.consumer.ftc.gov/articles/0272-how-keep-your-personal-information-secure

Francia, G. A., & Ciganek, A. (2010). Global information security regulations, case studies and cultural issues. In M. E. Whitman & H. J. Mattord (Eds.), Readings and cases in the management of information security, volume II: Legal and ethical issues in information security management. Course Technology.

Francia, G. A., & Hutchinson, F. (2012). Regulatory and policy compliance with regard to identity theft prevention,detection, and response. In T.-S. Chou (Ed.), *Information assurance and security technologies for risk assessment and threat management: Advances* (pp. 292–322). IGI Global Pub. doi:10.4018/978-1-61350-507-6.ch012

Goel, V. (2014, January 29). *Big profit at Facebook as it tilts to mobile*. Retrieved March 15, 2014, from The New York Times Company: http://www.nytimes.com/2014/01/30/technology/rise-in-mobile-ads-pushes-up-revenue- and-profit-at-facebook.html

Guidance, D. (2014). *Belgium: Decree fully transposes data retention directive*. Retrieved May 1, 2014 from http://www.dataguidance.com/dataguidance_privacy_this_week.asp?id=2128

Harrell, E., & Langton, L. (2013). *Victims of identity theft, 2012*. U.S. Department of Justice, Bureau of Justice Statistics, December, 2013, NCJ 243779. Retrieved April 30, 2014, from http://www.bjs.gov/content/pub/pdf/vit12.pdf

Harris, E. A., Perlroth, N., & Popper, N. (2014, January 24). *Neiman Marcus data breach worse than first said*. Retrieved March 15, 2014, from The New York Times Company: http://www.nytimes.com/2014/01/24/business/neiman-marcus-breach-affected-1-1- million-cards.html?_r=1

Identity Theft Assistance Center. (2013). Retrieved March 7, 2014, from http://www.identitytheftassistance.org/pageview.php?cateid=47#childIDfraudReport

International Association of Privacy Professionals (IAPP). (2014). *Mexico federal data protection act*. Retrieved May 01, 2014 from https://www.privacyassociation.org/media/pdf/knowledge_center/Mexico_Federal_Data_ Protection_Act_July2010.pdf

Iyer, G., Soberman, D., & Villas-Boas, J. M. (2003, May). *The targeting of advertising*. Retrieved March 15, 2014, from http://groups.haas.berkeley.edu/marketing/PAPERS/VILLAS/tgtadv1_apr03.pdf

Kahneman, D., & Tversky, A. (2000). *Choices, values, and frames*. Cambridge University Press.

Kroft, S. (2014, March 9). *The data brokers: Selling your personal information*. Retrieved March 15, 2014, from http://www.cbsnews.com/news/the-data-brokers- selling-your-personal-information/

Legal Information Institute (LII). (2014). *TOPN: Children's online privacy protection act of 1998*. Retrieved April 30, 2014, from http://www.law.cornell.edu/topn/childrens_online_privacy_protection_act_of_1998

Lobosco, K. (2014, March 14). *Target details risks from giant data breach*. Retrieved March 15, 2014, from Cable News Network: http://money.cnn.com/2014/03/14/news/companies/target-breach/

Merriam-Webster, Incorporated. (2014). Retrieved February 28, 2014, from Merriam- Webster.com: www.merriam-webster.com

Misener, D. (2014, January 21). *Google's Nest deal highlights privacy-policy issues: Dan Misener.* Retrieved March 15, 2014, from http://www.cbc.ca/news/technology/google-s-nest-deal-highlights-privacy-policy-issues-dan-misener-1.2504839

Noble, J. (2013, September 11). *U.S. debates security vs privacy 12 years after 9/11.* Retrieved March 10, 2014, from USA Today: http://www.usatoday.com/story/news/nation/2013/09/10/us-debates-security-vs-privacy- 12-years-after-911/2796399/

Russer, M. (2010, June). *Maximize profits through hyper-targeted Facebook ads.* Retrieved March 15, 2014, from http://realtormag.realtor.org/technology/mr-internet/article/2010/06/maximize-profits-through-hyper-targeted-facebook-ads

Salomon, K. D., Cassat, P. C., & Thibeau, B. E. (2003, March 20). *IT security for higher education: A legal perspective.* Retrieved September 22, 2010, from http://net.educause.edu/ir/library/pdf/CSD2746.pdf

Savage, C. (2013, December 16). Judge questions legality of N.S.A. phone records. *The New York Times.* Retrieved March 2, 2014, from http://www.nytimes.com/2013/12/17/us/politics/federal-judge-rules-against-nsa-phone-data-program.html?pagewanted=1&_r=2

Siciliano, R. (2014, January 27). *Stolen identities are cheap on the darknet.* Retrieved March 10, 2014, from http://bestidtheftcompanys.com/2014/stolen-identities-are-cheap-on-the-darknet

Sullivan, B. (2013, July 6). *Privacy vs. security: 'False choice' poisons debate on NSA leaks.* Retrieved March 7, 2014, from http://www.nbcnews.com/business/consumer/privacy-vs-security-false-choice-poisons-debate-nsa-leaks-f6C10536226

Talbot, D. (2013, September 16). *Encrypted heartbeats keep hackers from medical implants.* Retrieved March 12, 2014, from MIT Technology Review: http://www.technologyreview.com/news/519266/encrypted-heartbeats-keep-hackers- from-medical-implants/

U.S. Government Printing Office Public Law 111-5. (2009). *American Recovery and reinvestment act of 2009.* Retrieved April 24, 2014 from http://www.gpo.gov/fdsys/pkg/PLAW-111publ5/pdf/PLAW-111publ5.pdf

Veracode. (2014). *Sony PSN breach infographic.* Retrieved March 15, 2014, from http://www.veracode.com/sony-psn-breach-infographic

Verrecchia, P., & Weiss, D. M. (2013). *Privacy vs. security.* Retrieved March 2, 2014, from York College of Pennsylvania: http://www.ycp.edu/offices-and- services/advancement/communications/york-college-magazine/fall-2013/privacy-vs.- security/

ADDITIONAL READING

Birrell, E., & Schneider, F. (2013, September-October). B. "Federated Identity Management Systems: A Privacy- Based Characterization. *IEEE Security and Privacy*, *11*(5), 36–48.

De Cristofaro, E. (2014, March-April). Genomic Privacy and the Rise of a New Research Community. *IEEE Security and Privacy*, *12*(2), 80–83.

Ellyatt, H. (2013, December 9). *How business can shed light on the 'dark net'*. Retrieved March 7, 2014, from CNBC.com: http://www.cnbc.com/id/101234129

Greene, S. S. (2006). *Security Policies and Procedures: Principles and Practices*. Upper Saddle River: Pearson Education, Inc.

Kahneman, D., & Tversky, A. (1979). Prospect theory: An analysis of decision under risk. *Econometrica*, *47*, 263–291.

Singla, A., & Krause, A. (n.d.). *Truthful Incentives for Privacy Tradeoff: Mechanisms for Data Gathering in Community Sensing*. Retrieved March 10, 2014, from http://www.ics.uci.edu/~qliu1/MLcrowd_ICML_workshop/Papers/ActivePaper3.pdf

Tormo, G., Marmol, F., Girao, J., & Perez, G. (2013, November-December). Identity Management--In Privacy We Trust: Bridging the Trust Gap in eHealth Environments. *IEEE Security and Privacy*, *11*(6), 34–41.

KEY TERMS AND DEFINITIONS

Compliance: The act of being in conformity with official regulations.

Identity Theft: The fraudulent use of another person's personal information.

Personally Identifiable Information: Any personal information by which an individual may be identified (SSN, bank account number, username/password combination, etc.).

Policy Compliance: A goal set by an organization in its attempt to encourage and achieve compliance by its members/employees with regard to the organization's policies.

Privacy: The state of being free of infringement.

Regulatory Compliance: A goal set by an organization in its attempt to comply with all laws or regulations relevant to that organization.

Security: The state being of being safe from danger.

This work was previously published in the Handbook of Research on Emerging Developments in Data Privacy edited by Manish Gupta, pages 133-143, copyright 2015 by Information Science Reference (an imprint of IGI Global).

Chapter 2
Overview of the U.S. Criminal Justice System and Safety Tips for International Students

Thomas C. Johnson
Western Carolina University, USA

ABSTRACT

While most international students have a rewarding educational experience in the United States, a small percentage are arrested for criminal behavior or victimized by criminals. The author discusses safety from crime and provides safety tips to help reduce crime victimization potential. Further, since the American criminal justice system can be overwhelming, confusing, and intimidating for anyone who does not work within the system on a regular basis, this chapter provides international students and higher education officials with an overview of this system. The author also briefly discusses constitutional rights and the arrest and trial process. Finally, the author addresses some behaviors that international students should avoid to not place themselves at risk for receiving a criminal summons, citation, or arrest.

INTRODUCTION

While studying in the United States, international students will experience many differences from their home countries including differences in laws and safety issues related to crime. United States laws can differ substantially from an international student's home country's laws. For example, the Netherlands has completely decriminalized the use of marijuana while marijuana use is still criminalized in many U.S. states (DrugAbuse.net, 2015). Each country's laws are based upon their needs, cultures, and traditions. Law differences in the United States are exacerbated due to the decentralized nature of government. Laws exist at the federal, state, and local levels and are not always congruent. Further, there are different types of laws in the U.S. such as criminal and civil laws.

This chapter is designed to provide an overview of the U.S. criminal justice system and information about American laws and legal issues. While every international student hopes that his or her educational experience in the United States will be rewarding, an understanding of the U.S. criminal justice system,

DOI: 10.4018/978-1-5225-0808-3.ch002

legal issues, safety and protective behaviors, hate crimes, and some behaviors that result in the offender receiving a citation or being arrested can help the international student avoid problems. The following sections are designed to encourage international students and university administrators to think about these issues and identify behaviors that avoid problems that could adversely affect the educational experience.

OVERVIEW OF THE U.S. CRIMINAL JUSTICE SYSTEM

The U.S. criminal justice system is designed to identify, apprehend, and punish people who commit crimes. Inherent in this system is the desire to protect society from these criminals. Crimes are behaviors or actions that violate laws that define which socially harmful behaviors are subject to the government's power to impose punishment (Cole, Smith, & DeJong, 2014, p. 44). There are two crime categories: *mala in se* and *mala prohibita*. *Mala in se* crimes are those behaviors that are wrong by their very nature (Cole & Smith, 2006, p. 40). For example, most people would agree that it is wrong to steal from another person. *Mala prohibita* crimes are those behaviors that are prohibited by law but are not necessarily viewed by everyone as being wrong (Cole & Smith, 2006, p. 41). For example, not everyone believes that gambling or prostitution is inherently wrong. These law types form the basis for the U.S. criminal justice system's purpose; that is, doing justice, controlling crime, and preventing crime (Cole, Smith, & DeJong, 2014, p. 45).

The U.S. Constitution forms the framework for all U.S. laws, but also provides safeguards to protect individuals from the unequitable enforcement of laws and administration of justice. Without these safeguards, there would be little difference between the U.S. criminal justice system and those of authoritarian countries without legal protections for its citizens (Cole, Smith, & DeJong, 2014, p. 340). These safeguards help establish a justice system that holds offenders accountable, protect the rights of persons who have contact with the U.S. criminal justice system, and ensures like offenses will be treated similarly (Ward & Langlands, 2008).

Crime is controlled through the arresting, prosecuting, convicting, and punishing of offenders (Cole, Smith, & DeJong, 2014, p. 6). However, unlike other countries where law enforcement is conducted with societal interests paramount to individual interests, the U.S. criminal justice system places high priority on the individual interests. While U.S. laws are designed to protect society, they must be enforced with attention to individual rights. Therefore, enforcement and prosecution techniques and efforts must pass constitutional muster; that is, they must be acceptable to a court that is presided over by a judge who is sworn to uphold the U.S. Constitution.

Criminal Justice Agencies

Government in the U.S. is decentralized and exists at the federal, state, and local levels. Since criminal justice is a function of governments, criminal justice systems exist at each level. There are more than 60,000 separate public and private agencies employing more than 2.5 million people at these different levels (Kyckelhahn & Martin, 2013). Each government level is based upon an ideology that serves a different purpose. These different purposes result in criminal justice agencies with different missions and functions.

Most police agencies in the U.S. exist at the local government level with responsibility for enforcing local ordinances and state laws (Hess, Orthmann, & Cho, 2015). The most prevalent of the local police agencies are the city police and county sheriff's departments (Reaves, 2015b). However, there are many specialized police agencies at the local level such as municipal park, airport, and port police departments (Parfaniuc, 2011). Further, there are police agencies that exist at other government levels that are modeled after city police departments. For example, most public colleges and universities are state government units; yet, their campus police departments are modeled after municipal police departments.

Forty-nine of the 50 U.S. states have a primary state law enforcement agency that operates either as a state police or highway patrol agency (Dempsey & Forst, 2012, p. 53) and enforce state laws. State police organizations provide law enforcement services to unincorporated areas and small towns without police departments in states where the sheriff's department focuses more on duties, such as jails and courts, than law enforcement (Dempsey & Forst, 2012, p.53). Highway patrols exist in states where the sheriff's departments are the principal providers of law enforcement services in the unincorporated areas. Highway patrols provide statewide enforcement of traffic laws on interstate, U.S., and state highways in a particular state (Dempsey & Forst, 2012, p. 53). In most states, highway patrols have full authority to enforce all laws anywhere in the state. While state police and highway patrols are the primary state law enforcement agencies, there are other state law enforcement agencies such as wildlife, alcohol and drug, park, marine, and state investigative agencies.

Federal law enforcement agencies are responsible for enforcing federal laws. Federal law enforcement agencies generally exist by function and are not centralized. For example, there is no U.S. Police Department. Rather, there are 65 federal law enforcement agencies usually assigned a specific law responsibility area and allocated to one of the 15 federal departments (IACP, 2015). The most recognized federal law enforcement agency is the Federal Bureau of Investigation (FBI) (Dempsey & Forst, 2012, p. 41). Other major federal law enforcement agencies include the U.S. Marshals, the Drug Enforcement Administration, the Bureau of Alcohol, Tobacco, and Firearms, and the U.S. Secret Service.

Campus Security, Public Safety, and Police

U.S. higher education institutions are generally classified as public or private (Reaves, 2015a). Since public institutions are created by state governments, these governments have the authority to create police departments. Approximately 93% of public higher education institutions have their own police department (Dempsey & Forst, 2012, p. 51). Further, many states have enacted laws that allow private institutions to create their own police departments. In states where no such laws exist, private institutions have created police departments whose officers are sworn through a local police or sheriff's department. For example, University of Miami (FL) police officers are sworn through the City of Coral Gables Police Department (University of Miami, 2015). Approximately 42% of private institutions have their own police department (Dempsey & Forst, 2012, p. 51). These police departments operate similar to city police departments. Campus police officers have the authority to enforce states laws and campus rules.

Higher education institutions without a sworn police department frequently use a public safety or security department (Reaves, 2015a). These departments are comprised of non-sworn officers who do not enforce laws but do enforce campus rules. Their focus is on providing a safe and secure campus and their duties include patrolling campus, responding to calls for service, and providing crime prevention training and information. These agencies usually have close working relationships with local law enforcement agencies upon whom they can call for crime issues and problems. The principal disadvantage to a non-sworn security force is that their response protocol to a violent crime (Gray, 2012). Since most non-sworn officers do not carry a firearm (Reaves, 2015a), they cannot confront an armed offender, a task that is better served by sworn, armed, trained police officers. The evolution of most colleges and universities from an education to a business model have resulted in many campus security, public safety, or police departments adopting a more customer-oriented approach to working with students, faculty, and staff.

While the U.S. criminal justice is similar in many respects to other Western countries' criminal justice systems, the U.S. government's decentralized nature creates multiple layers of criminal justice agencies with different responsibilities and functions. However, all criminal justice system aspects are responsible for doing justice, controlling crime, and preventing crime (The Criminal Justice System, 2009). The most prevalent criminal justice aspects exist at the local government level. City police departments and county sheriff departments are the most common police agency types and most likely to be encountered by international students who live and transact business off-campus. While most international students have rewarding experiences in the U.S., the potential for violating the law or being victimized by a crime suggest that international students and higher education administrators should be familiar with the U.S. criminal justice system. Many higher education institutions have their own police department for enforcing laws and campus rules, and providing for safety and security on campus. Because of the business model that many colleges and universities follow, campus police departments tend to be more aware of and sensitive to the issues and problems of students.

INTERNATIONAL STUDENTS AND LEGAL ISSUES IN THE U.S.

While few international students violate U.S. law, any violation can be a major problem. There are a few reasons why an international student may commit a crime. First, cultural influences affect what behaviors an international student considers are crimes (Forbes-Mewett, McCulloch, & Nyland, 2015). For example, simple possession of child pornography is illegal in the U.S. but permissible in many other countries (ChartsBin Statistics Collector Team, 2010). Second, the natural tendency of international students to associate with their own national group may bring them into contact with unscrupulous members that solicit their participation in crimes (Forbes-Mewett, McCulloch, & Nyland, 2015). For example, several years ago, the author had the occasion to investigate an international student group that perpetrated insurance fraud by staging phony car crashes and filing claims with different insurance companies. This group only solicited international students from their home country's region to participate in this group. After the author identified the perpetrators, they were deported from the U.S. Finally, the opportunity to commit a crime may present too great of a temptation for anyone including an international student (Forbes-Mewett, McCulloch, & Nyland, 2015).

Even the commission of minor offenses may result in international students being removed from the higher education institution and facing possible deportation or denial of entry into the U.S. For example, if an international student is arrested for an impaired driving offense and fingerprinted, the fingerprints are entered into the National Crime Information Center's (NCIC) computer database (Dempsey & Forst, 2012, p. 56). If the international student leaves the U.S. and returns home, the international student will generally need to reapply for a student visa. When the international student's fingerprints are discovered in NCIC, there will probably be a delay in issuing the visa until an investigation and decision are made on issuing the visa. Even if the visa is issued, it may be done after the semester starts causing the international student to fall behind in his or her studies. Further, there is the possibility that the international student's visa may be denied.

International students need to be concerned with their student status when committing even a minor offense. Most higher education institutions have a student code of conduct that includes sanctions for law violations (Smith, 2011). While the student code of conduct is frequently used as for educating students and changing their behavior rather than meting out punishment (Office of the Dean of Student Life, 2008), any disciplinary action becomes part of the international student's permanent record that may be examined by immigration and other officials, and future employers. Further, for offenses where the international student is deemed to be a threat to another person, the institution may suspend or even expel the international student (Sandhills Community College, n.d.), a move that will affect the student's ability to remain in the U.S.

While a crime conviction poses serious consequences, it is important to realize there is a difference between being charged with a crime and being convicted of a crime. There can be different outcomes to an arrest besides conviction that include the charges being dropped or reduced, or the arrestee being directed to a pre-trial diversion program (Cole, Smith, & DeJong, 2014, p. 234). However, if the international student understands how the U.S. criminal justice works, he or she is better able to understand options and determine the best course of action for resolving a case.

At the arrest stage, the arrestee is taken into custody (Fuller, 2013, p. 204). The arrest may occur pursuant to a warrant obtained by the police officer or the officer witnessing or discovering evidence of the offense. Arrest entails the arrestee being physically seized by a police officer who searches and usually handcuffs the arrestee for transport to a local jail. Handcuffs are used even for minor offenses (Dempsey & Forst, 2012). Police officers are extremely cautious and want to ensure that the arrestee is not in a position to harm him- or herself or the police officer. At the jail, the arrestee's personally identifying information is obtained so that the police officer can process the arrestee. Depending upon the offense, the arrestee may be fingerprinted and photographed.

Some states, such as North Carolina (North Carolina General Statutes, 2014), require that a police officer take an arrestee immediately before a magistrate. A magistrate is a court official who has the authority to issue warrants, call witnesses, and examine prisoner's charges (Dempsey & Forst, 2012, p. 400). The police officer presents his or her probable cause for arrest to the magistrate who makes a finding for whether the arrest is warranted and what charges may be filed. The appearance before the magistrate is not a trial, but is done to establish the charges and set bail. Bail is a monetary or property value that is posted by the arrestee to guarantee his or her appearance in court (Cole, Smith, & DeJong, 2014, p. 257). An arrestee is generally provided the opportunity to bail out of jail in all criminal cases except homicide or other serious crimes (Cole, Smith, & DeJong, 2014, p. 257). Once bail has been set and the arrestee processed, the arrestee may post the bail. However, in cases where the arrestee does not have the cash or real property to make bail, the arrestee may secure the services of a professional bailsman whose fee is usually 10% of the bail (Fuller, 2013, p. 314). The bailsman is an employee of an insurance company that actually guarantees the bail. If the arrestee uses a bailsman, the fee paid to the bailsman is the cost for the insurance company guaranteeing the bail and is not returned to the arrestee even if he or she appears at all court hearings. When posting bail, the arrestee is provided with a court date. If the arrestee posts cash or real property for bail and appears for all court appearances, the cash or real property is returned upon the disposition of the case (Fuller, 2013, p. 314).

For minor offenses, an arrestee may be allowed to be released on his or her recognizance, sometime referred to as ROR (Fuller, 2013, p. 314). An arrestee who is permitted to be released on recognizance generally signs a form promising to appear in court to answer to the charge(s). Generally, ROR is available to individuals who have ties to the community and are not considered a flight risk. Given that international students are not permanent members of the community and, depending upon their court date, may leave the country at the end of the semester, a court may be reluctant to award ROR to an international student. A court considering allowing an arrested international student to be released on recognizance may rely upon the higher education institution to provide evidence of the student's good standing with the university and intent to remain in the community. Further, the court may impose special conditions such as requiring the international student to surrender his or her passport until the case is disposed of.

Although international students are not U.S. citizens, they are still entitled to the protections of the U.S. Constitution (Dempsey & Forst, 2012, p. 185). Constitutional protections that relate to interrogations are referred to as Miranda warnings and include the international student not having to answer any incriminating questions and having an access to an attorney even if the international student cannot afford an attorney (Cole, 2003; Dempsey & Forst, 2012, p. 411). If the arrestee cannot afford an attorney, he or she may be entitled to the services of a public defender attorney (Cole, Smith, & DeJong, 2014, p. 240). The appointment of a public defender attorney usually requires an indigency hearing before a judge where the arrestee has to prove that he or she does not have the means to hire a private attorney (Cole, Smith, & DeJong, 2014, p. 241). Once the court determines that the international student is indigent, the court will appoint a public defender. In rural areas where there may be limited resources, the court may appoint a private attorney at taxpayer expense if no public defender exists.

While having a free or reduced-fee public defender sounds like a bargain, it is important to understand that there are disadvantages to having a public defender in a criminal case (Cole, Smith, & DeJong, 2014, p. 240). First, public defenders usually work for the government on behalf of their clients. This means that public defender offices tend to be understaffed and lack the resources of a well-paid private law firm. Further, public defenders have extremely large caseloads that result in their only being able to give minimal attention to each case. It is not uncommon, in some cases, for the public defender to first meet the clients on the first day of the trial (Williams, 2013). Second, because public defenders are not well-paid when compared to private attorneys, many public defenders are inexperienced individuals who have recently completed law school and use the public defender's office as a starting point for their careers before moving into private practice. Finally, public defenders typically only handle criminal cases. If there is an associated civil case with the criminal case, such as driver's license revocation hearing as part of an impaired driving offense, the public defender will usually not represent the arrestee in the revocation hearing.

After the arrestee is processed at the jail, the arrest documents are forwarded to a prosecuting attorney who represents the state. The prosecuting attorney reviews the case and charges and determines whether to file the case with the court as charged, amend the charges, or dismiss the case, a process known as prosecutorial discretion (Cole, Smith, & DeJong, 2014, p. 230). If the prosecuting attorney decides to prosecute the case, he or she then files the charges with the court in a document known as an information (Cole, Smith, & DeJong, 2014, p. 23). At this point, the arrestee is considered the defendant in the case. From this point forward until the trial stage, the defendant's attorney and the prosecuting attorney may meet or call to discuss the case. During this time, a number of things may happen including filing pre-trial motions, taking depositions, and holding pre-trial hearings. During this time, the attorneys may work on a plea agreement that allows for a resolution to the case without the case going to trial. If the defendant is a first-offender, meaning he or she has not previously been arrested for and convicted of an offense, and the current offense is not that serious, the likelihood of a plea bargain is great. Further, as part of the plea bargain, the defendant may ask that he or she not be adjudicated guilty to not have a conviction on the record.

For serious offenses where a plea bargain is not reached, the case will proceed to trial. In the U.S., defendants have the right to have their case heard by a judge or jury. Usually, for lesser offenses, a judge trial is held while a jury trial is held for more serious offenses. The defendant's attorney will usually advise the defendant on which trial type to select. The prosecuting attorney must first present the case that typically consists of witnesses and evidence that the state feels is most favorable to its case and will help prove the guilt of the defendant. The evidence must support a conviction above and to the exclusion of every reasonable doubt as determined by the judge or jury. At the conclusion of the state's presentation, the defense attorney may present a defense to the state's case. The defense is under no obligation to provide a defense as the burden of proof is upon the state. After all evidence is presented, the attorneys will make arguments for and against the guilt of the defendant based upon the evidence presented in court. At the arguments' conclusions, the judge or jury will render a verdict based upon their interpretation of the evidence. If the defendant is found guilty, the court will determine an appropriate sentence that may include a fine, probation, incarceration in a county or state prison, or a combination of these sentences.

International students need to be concerned with engaging in behaviors that may lead to their arrest while they are in the U.S. Arrests not only pose consequences in terms of possible fines, probation, or jail sentences, but may also affect whether the international student is suspended or expelled from the higher education institution and deported. Arrests may occur pursuant to a warrant or based upon a police officer's observations. Arrestees are booked into a jail and may appear before a magistrate who sets bond. Arrestees have the right to have access to an attorney; indigent arrestees may have a public defender appointed to represent them. The prosecuting attorney files the formal charges with the court. In many cases, a plea bargain is reached before a case goes to court that avoids a trial. Cases that go to trial may be heard by a judge or jury. After the state presents its case, the defendant may present a defense but is under no obligation to do so. Based upon their interpretation of the evidence, a judge or jury decides if the defendant is guilty. If the defendant is found guilty, the court will sentence the defendant to a fine, probation, and/or jail.

SAFETY FROM CRIME

One aspect of American culture that may differ from other countries is responsibility for safety and security. In the United States, emphasis is placed on individuals being responsible and accountable for their own safety and security (Patar & Remo, 2012). Conversely, Bénabou and Tirole (2006) suggest that western European culture places greater emphasis on the community as the primary source of safety and security. This diversity regarding safety responsibility beliefs indicates that international students in the U.S. may need to shift their focus about personal safety and learn more about self-protecting behaviors.

Key to protecting one's self from crime is awareness of surroundings and personal vulnerability to crime (McMullen, 2013). However, many international students do not view their victimization potential as high and this may affect whether they engage in self-protective behaviors. According to Coston (1996), generally, many international students have low concern for crime victimization. Coston (1996, 2004) found that international students at urban colleges and universities, female international students, international students who had been previous victimized in their home country, international students who had heard about crime directly from other international students who had been victimized, and students who had poor mastery of English had any appreciable fear of being a crime victim. International students from countries with high crime rates also tended to be more cognizant of crime victimization (Forbes-Mewett, McCulloch, & Nyland, 2015).

Forbes-Mewett, McCulloch, & Nyland (2015) also found that international students' naivety about local customs and crimes issues influenced their potential for crime victimization. Knowledge of crime and safety factors help international students understand the risks they may assume. Similarly, colleges and universities must ensure they make timely and accurate crime and safety information available for review by perspective international students. Since safety factors are an important consideration in aiding international students in their decision about which host country they will attend (Cohen, 2003; Mazzarol & Soutar, 2002), colleges and universities have a stake in ensuring that the information is readily available.

Another reason for ensuring that international students have access to timely and accurate crime and safety information is to avoid misperceptions about crime in the U.S. that affect their concerns for safety. One reason that misperceptions may occur is due to the media's coverage of crime. Media coverage trends that impact crime perceptions include the media focusing primarily on violent crime, covering crime as individual and isolated events, establishing a nexus between crime and race, and only focusing on certain groups, such as youth, in the context of violence (Dorfman & Schiraldi, 2001; The Sentencing Project, 2014). Despite how the media portrays crime, most areas in the U.S. are reasonably safe. Many higher education institutions have proactive crime prevention and safety programs and campuses tend to be safer than their surrounding communities (Henson & Stone, 1999). However, international students cannot rely entirely upon higher education administrators to provide for their safety; international students must educate themselves about local crime and be proactive in protecting their property and themselves.

An overview of U.S. crime may help international students better prepare to protect themselves and their property. There are many ways to classify crimes in the U.S.; however, police agencies generally classify crimes by three types: crimes against persons, crimes against property, and crimes against society (FBI, 2011). Crimes against persons tend to be physical, violent, and often high profile. Crimes against persons' examples include murder, assault, armed robbery, rape, and threats. The key characteristic of this classification is that the target of the crime is always a person. Crimes against property examples include burglary, theft, motor vehicle theft, arson, fraud, and embezzlement. The focus of a crime against property is to obtain something of value by illegal means. Finally, crimes against society, sometimes referred to as victimless crimes (Cole, Smith, & DeJong, 2014, p. 48), represent society's prohibition on activities considered immoral or harmful such as gambling, prostitution, underage consumption of an alcoholic beverage, or drug use, possession, or sale.

Crimes against persons do not occur as frequently as other crimes (Dempsey & Forst, 2012, p. 380). However, because of the violence level and the sometimes use of a weapon, these crimes receive much media attention and are treated by the criminal justice system as the most serious offenses. Similarly, these offenses tend to have more serious penalties than other crimes (Cole, Smith, & DeJong, 2014, p.45). However, despite the perception that most violent crimes are perpetrated by strangers, statistics indicate that most victims knew their assailants (Cole, Smith, & DeJong, 2014, p.45). This suggests that, in many cases, the key to preventing a crime against a person involves ensuring that the international student learn much about the people he or she interacts with before trusting or investing too much in the relationship. Further, the potential for these crimes to result in great bodily harm or death requires that everyone take proper precautions to avoid victimization (see Table 1).

Table 1. Crime prevention tips

Crimes Against Persons
Plan the safest route to your destination; choose well-lighted, busy pathways and streets.
Share your class schedule with parents and trusted friends and give them your telephone number(s).
Travel in groups and avoid going out alone at night.
Use the campus escort or shuttle services at night.
Tell friends or roommates where you are going and when you expect to return.
Do not become so intoxicated that you cannot control or protect yourself.
Stay alert to your surroundings and the people around you.
Check out a first date or blind date with friends first. Better yet, go with other friends on your first date. Always trust your instincts.
Crimes Against Property
Always lock your room or apartment when you leave, even if it is "just for a moment."
Never leave pursues, computer and book bags, or other valuables unattended such as in bookstores, the classroom, or the library.
Record the date of purchase, price, brand and model names, and serial number for all major items, such as bicycles and computers. Give this information to police if an item is stolen.
Never allow anyone to borrow your credit/ATM card or give them your PIN.
Cybercrime/Identity Theft
Keep your computer password protected. Change passwords frequently and do not share them.
Have a virus/spam protector on your computer. Do not open e-mails from unknown sources that have an attachment or a link.
Purchase a shredder and shred any documents with personal information including account numbers after the documents are no longer of value.
Keep your social security number confidential. If you have a card, do not carry it but keep it locked.
Regularly pick up your mail and do not throw away credit card or similar offers into public trash receptacles. Rather, shred these offers.
If you receive a telephone call or e-mail from someone alleging to be a bank, public safety, or other official requesting personal or account information, do not give them this information over the telephone or through the e-mail. Instead, offer to meet the person at their place of business to discuss their inquiry.
Review bank and credit card statements frequently. Immediately report any suspicious transactions to the financial institution.

Crimes against property are the most common crime type (Dempsey & Forst, 2012, p. 380). These crimes may be categorized further into crimes where property is stolen and property is destroyed (Arbetman & McMahon, 2009). There are steps that international students can take to protect their property (see Table 1). A relatively new property crime category is identity theft. The concept of stealing someone's personal identity actually refers to the theft of a person's legal identity consisting of document identifiers such as driver's licenses, birth certificates, passports, and credit reports and then using these identifiers in fraudulent activity (Vieraitis, Copes, Powell, & Pike, 2015). The prolific use of computer technology by international students for academic and personal use may make them vulnerable to this type of crime. International students need to take proper precautions to reduce the potential for someone accessing their computer records and obtaining personally identifying information (see Table 1).

One crime that is frequently perpetrated via the computer is fraud. This crime manifests itself in a variety of methods (see Table 2). Many such frauds begin through e-mails advertising that the recipient has been selected for or awarded some benefit (FBI, n.d.). One such example is an e-mail from a sender

Table 2. Common scams

Craigslist and similar online scams	The Internet has given rise to online auctions and personal sales of property. Many auctions and sales are legitimate; however, the potential buyer should communicate with the seller and ask for documentation of the seller's identity and property. Thieves may attempt to dispose of stolen property through a means like craigslist. A similar scam may occur when a person tries to sell an item. Let's say that you want to sell your iPhone online for $200. You receive a response saying, "I hope I can trust you. All I have right now is a check for $1,000. I will send it to you and you can cash the check and keep $200 for the iPhone and send me back the remaining $800. I need it for food this week." However, after you deposited their check and sent them $800, the bank notifies you that their check is a fake. You end up losing the $800 and possibly your iPhone. Keep online transactions simple, public, and in cash. If you need help ask an U.S. friend or someone from the international student's office.
Visa or citizenship assistance scam	If you receive an offer of assistance for help with visa or citizenship issues that require you to provide money up front, it is probably a fraud. Contact the international students' office for help with visa and citizenship issues.
Taxis/Transport services	Some taxi or transport drivers try to take advantage of those unfamiliar with the area by overcharging or driving a long route to increase the fare. Always get fare information first. Explore other transportation options such as public transportation or shuttles.
Advertising	Be wary of advertised products that sound too good to be true. Sometimes, unscrupulous sales people use a tactic called bait-and-switch. In this tactic, they advertise a produce for a very low price. Then, when the buyer comes to the store, they find that the product is no longer available but has been replaced with a higher priced one or the sales person attempts to pressure the buyer to purchase a more expensive item.
Sales items	Unscrupulous retailers will sometimes advertise items as being on sale when there is no difference between the sale price and regular price or the sale price may even be higher than the regular price. Always comparison shop and look at other merchant's prices.
Landlord issues	While institutions' residential living offices work to have good relationships with students, off-campus landlords may not be so scrupulous. When living off-campus, international students may have to pay a damage deposit with their rent application along with the first month's rent. The damage deposit is to cover any damage the international student and his or her guests may cause to the apartment or house. Generally, if there is no damage beyond normal wear-and-tear, the international student should have the damage deposit refunded when the lease expires. Unfortunately, unscrupulous landlords may refuse to refund the damage deposit and claim that there was damage to the apartment or house. When inspecting the apartment or house before moving in, the international student should insist that the landlord is present and that notations are made of any existing damage. Further, if there is any damage, it should be documented, preferably through photos or video. These photos or video can dispel claims that the international student caused any damage.
Used car purchases	Because of the many regulations that an international student must follow if he or she chooses to drive, it is recommended that international students use public transportation. However, if an international student chooses to drive and looks to purchase a used car, there are two choices: purchase the vehicle from an individual or from a used car dealer. In either case, there is the potential for the buyer to spend a lot of good money on a bad car. In order to avoid being scammed when buying a used car, the buyer should: • determine how much car he or she can afford; • identify the car type that he or she wants; • understand the true value of the car by researching Kelly's Blue Book (www.kbb.com) or a similar source • locate used cars that fit the criteria; • check the vehicle's history through Carfax® or AutoCheck®; • contact the seller and establish a relationship – ask questions about the vehicle including why it is being sold; • test drive the vehicle (ensure you have obtained your driver's license first); • have the vehicle inspected by a reputable mechanic; • negotiate your best deal; and • close the deal – ensure the seller has a clear title to the vehicle with no liens against the title.

who is in another country claiming to have received a large sum of money from an inheritance. However, since the sender is another country, they need someone in the U.S. to represent them. In exchange for this representation, the sender will share the inheritance. However, the recipient must first put up earnest money to show their good faith. After the recipient puts up the earnest money, he or she never hears from the sender again and finds their money gone.

HATE CRIMES

The terms *hate crimes* or *bias-based crimes* are used to describe crimes that are committed against an individual based upon a specific characteristic of that individual such as his or her race, sex, sexual orientation, religion, disability, or ethnicity (Cole & Smith, 2006, p. 50). The term is misleading in that it implies that there is a separate crime for the offense of hate. Indeed, early attempts to enforce laws based upon hate were largely considered unconstitutional. For example, in the case of *R.A.V v. City of St. Paul* (1992), the U.S. Supreme Court ruled unconstitutional a law that made it an offense to use "race-baiting" words. The court has held that even language that is hateful can be protected free speech that is permissible under the First Amendment to the U.S. Constitution. However, the court has held that providing enhanced penalties that are based on ordinary crimes when the perpetrator intentionally selects the person whom the crime is committed against because of the race, religion, color, disability, sexual orientation, national origin or ancestry of that person (Wisconsin v. Mitchell, 1993) is constitutional and acceptable. Therefore, hate crimes generally refer to enhanced penalties for these crimes.

First Amendment issues confound hate speech. Hate speech is considered any comments, gesture, conduct, writing, or display that disparages any person or group and may incite violence or prejudicial action (American Bar Association, n.d.). However, as harmful as hate speech may be, in many cases, it is legally allowed. When examining speech issues, the U.S. Supreme Court has consistently held that "debate on public issues should be uninhibited, robust, and wide-open" (Stone, 1994, p. 79). This comment does not mean that all hate speech is protected. For example, the U.S. Supreme Court has held that *fighting words*, that is, words that are uttered in a face-to-face confrontation and are likely by their very utterance to inflict injury or tend to incite an immediate breach of the peace enjoy a very low level of protection from the First Amendment (Chaplinsky v. New Hampshire, 1942). Indeed, hate speech that accompanies an offensive act may be evidence of a crime. For example, if during an assault, the assailant utters hateful words directed at the victim's race, sex, sexual orientation, religion, ethnicity, or some other characteristic, this utterance may be used in court as evidence that the crime was motivated by hate.The U.S. population is becoming increasingly diversified (U.S. Census Bureau, 2010).

Unfortunately, this diversification has led to racial, religious, and cultural conflicts in some communities (Dempsey & Forst, 2012, p. 320). Further, the September 11th terrorist attacks have transformed the rights of immigrants visiting, studying, and working in the U.S. In particular, students from Middle Eastern countries may face heightened scrutiny and even racial hostility and violence from campus and community members. Higher education institutions that receive federal funds are subject to the Title VI of the Civil Rights Act of 1964. This law requires these institutions to make a reasonable effort to provide educational environments that are free from racial hostility and harassment. Generally, higher education institutions have policies and processes in place to protect campus members from harassment. Unfortunately, these policies and processes usually only cover the campus and do not extend into the surrounding community.

Individuals who utter hate speech at international students may be a threat to their safety. International students should ensure they do not escalate the situation. It may even be that, when these incidents occur, the best course of action is for the international student to walk away rather than remain in the confrontation. In all harassment cases, international students must advocate for themselves. International students can do this by immediately reporting incidents. Although there may be reasons why international students may be reluctant to report crimes, such as language issues or concerns that they may be sent back to their home country (Cobler, 2014), international students will find that most law enforcement agencies are willing to work with them when they have been victimized. There are also compelling reasons to report hate crimes. First, colleges and universities have an affirmative obligation to have environments that are free from any form of harassment or discrimination (Title VI, 2000). Second, hate crimes are a serious societal problem (National Crime Prevention Council, 2015) and colleges and universities want them investigated to identify and punish offenders and prevent future victimization of others.

If the hate crime occurs on campus, the incident should be reported to campus police/safety/security officials, the international students' office, and/or a student affairs administrator. If the incident occurs off-campus, it should be reported to the local police and campus officials. Similarly, the international student should document the incident by writing or recording an account of the event including date, time, and location of the incident, the name(s) or description(s) of the offender(s), exactly what was said or done, and the name(s) and telephone number(s) of any witness(es). Finally, if the higher education institution or local police have a victim advocate or other support person or group, the international student should contact them for support in pursuing the complaint and protecting him- or herself. If the police arrest someone for committing the offense, the international student needs to be prepared to testify in court against the arrestee. Usually, the police or the prosecuting attorney's office will contact the international student before the court appearance to help familiarize the international student with court proceedings and/or victim services.

SELF-PROTECTION

A long-standing concept in the U.S. is that a person has a right to protect him- or herself and his or her property from criminal activity. Most state have codified this concept into state law. Some states have even gone further by codifying in law that a person has no obligation to retreat from any place that he or she has a right to be and, when his or her personal safety is threatened, may use any level of force, including deadly force, to preserve that right (McClellan & Tekin, 2012).

Many international students are aware of their right to defend themselves and even carry weapons. A study by Coston (1996) found that 64% of international student surveyed admitted to carrying some type of weapon including mace, knife, stun gun, and handgun. International students must be careful about carrying weapons particularly on campus. The proliferation of active shooter events on campuses have resulted in much concern with weapons on campus and approximately 20 states have laws prohibiting the carrying of weapons on campus (National Conference on State Legislatures, 2015) while most college and university campuses prohibit weapons by rule (Armed Campuses, 2013).

While an international student has the right to protect him- or herself from an aggressive individual, the international student must ensure that he or she is not the original aggressor. Further, the best protection is to avoid incidents to begin with. Therefore, if an international student finds him- or herself in a situation where another person is provoking or challenging the international student, it may be best to walk away from the situation and report it to authorities.

ALCOHOL AND DRUGS

Alcohol

A concerning issue for international students is illegal behaviors associated with alcohol and drug use. However, many young people do not view these behaviors as inherently wrong (Pennay, 2012). Generally, in the U.S., young people must be 21 years of age to lawfully consume alcoholic beverages (ICAP, 1998). Underage drinking, particularly drinking to excess, can result in behaviors that are dangerous and harmful (see Table 3). These behaviors not only place international students in jeopardy for arrest, suspension or expulsion from their higher education institution, and deportation, but minimizes their chances for success academically, and threatens their personal safety (Cleveland, Harris, & Wiebe, 2010, p. 1). Underage alcoholic beverage consumption among college students is generally attributed to two factors. First, there are stresses in adjusting to a new environment while subjected to the demands of a college or university education (Ham & Hope, 2003). Second, there is a belief that the college culture includes student consumption of copious amounts of alcoholic beverages (Baer, Davenport, Molna, & Wechsler, 1999).

U.S. college students represent that largest group for consuming alcoholic beverages, even more than their non-college peers (Blanco, Okuda, Wright, Hasin, Grant, Liu, & Olfson, 2008; NIAAA, 2002). Although studies (Johnston, O'Malley, Bachman, & Schulenberg, 2009; Meilman, Presley, & Cashin, 1997) have indicated that the excessive consumption of alcoholic beverages as part of the college culture is largely untrue, this belief persists among students who sometimes face peer pressure to buy into it. This peer pressure is exacerbated through acculturation where new students, such as freshmen and international students, are trying to fit in to a new community and environment. This acculturation process places international students at high risk for underage alcoholic beverage consumption (Frey & Roysircar, 2006; Yoon & Portman, 2004). Even international students who come from social and religious cultures where alcoholic beverage consumption is not so prolific demonstrate an increase in alcoholic beverage consumption as part of the acculturation process in the U.S. (Hendershot, MacPherson, Myers, Carr, & Wall, 2005).

Table 3. Underage drinking problems (Center for Disease Control Fact Sheet – Underage Drinking, 2014)

Youth who Drink Alcoholic Beverages are More Likely to Experience
• School problems such as higher absences and poor grades.
• Social problems such as arguing and fighting.
• Legal problems such as arrest for driving or physically hurting someone while drunk.
• Physical problems such as hangovers or illnesses.
• Unwanted, unplanned, and unprotected sexual activity.
• Disruption of normal growth and sexual development.
• Physical and sexual assault.
• Higher risk for suicide and homicide.
• Alcohol-related car crashes and other unintentional injuries.
• Memory problems.
• Drug abuse.
• Changes in brain development that may have life-long effects
• Death from alcohol poisoning.

Research suggests a number of steps that higher education administrators may take to reduce the incidents of underage consumption (NIAAA, 2005). First, higher education administrators can form or join a joint college-community coalition that brings together health care professionals to address physical and mental health issues that contribute to self-medicating through alcoholic beverage use. Second, higher education administrators can form a joint college-community task force or coalition that includes all interested stakeholders on campus, including students, and in the community, including businesses that sell alcoholic beverages, that can develop and monitor drinking initiatives designed to reduce underage drinking. Finally, higher education administrators can plan activities strategically that are designed to reduce underage drinking and have measureable objectives within targeted timelines for which an assigned person or group is accountable. Further, there should be a means to collect and assess data on these activities.

Drugs

Most of the research on college student drug use focuses on domestic students (e.g., Burnett, Sabato, Wagner, & Smith, 2014; Coleman & Trunzo, 2015; Reid, Graziano, Balkhi, McNamara, Cottler, Meneses, & Geffken, 2015). Research on international students drug use in the U.S. is sparse. However, it is assumed that the same inherent problems with domestic students illegal drug use will apply to international students. Many problems are similar to those associated with illegal alcohol consumption. Next to alcoholic beverage consumption, marijuana use is the second most commonly used illicit drug on campus (SAMHSA, 2010). Reasons that college students use marijuana is believed to mirror the same reasons for underage alcoholic beverage consumption; that is, to cope with stress and be acculturated to the new student environment. However, research suggests that marijuana use to cope with stress actually increases anxiety (Johnson, Bonn-Miler, Leyro, & Zvolensky, 2009). Therefore, marijuana use may exacerbate anxiety and other disorders in international students creating difficulties to becoming acculturated and successful in college. The use of other drugs by international student may be rare. According to a study by Vivancos, Abubakar, and Hunter (2009) of international students alcohol and drug use in Great Britain, approximately 31% of international students used marijuana, while only about 2% of international students reported using other drugs. More research is necessary to determine if this finding is consistent with international students' drug use in the U.S.

However, a larger drug issue is pharmaceutical drug use. Over half the students in higher education institutions use at least one pharmaceutical drug for conditions that include pain, stimulation, sedation or anti-anxiety, and sleep (McCabe, Teter, & Boyd, 2006). There are many reasons as to why pharmaceutical drugs are widely abused. First, because they are prescribed drugs, they are viewed as being safer and less addicting than street drugs (Bardhi, Sifaneck, Johnson, & Dunlap, 2007). Second, unlike other drugs that a student may consume alone or with a friend, pharmaceutical drugs are usually taken in social settings among students from similar socioeconomic backgrounds (McCabe, Teter, & Boyd, 2006; Quintero, 2009) and appear to be part of the acculturation process. Finally, some students believe the use of pharmaceutical drugs will improve their academic performance (Rozenbroek & Rothstein, 2011). For example, some students believe that stimulant use will allow them to stay away long hours studying while anti-anxiety drug use will reduce test anxiety.

International students should be aware that pharmaceutical drugs are as hazardous as street drugs (Khosla, Juon, Kirk, Astemborski, & Mehta, 2011). Further, simply because a drug is obtained with a valid prescription does not make it legal for the sharing or using of the drug by a person not named in the prescription (Garnier, Arria, Caldeira, Vincent, O'Grady, & Wish, 2010). There are several steps that individuals, including international students, may take to reduce pharmaceutical drug abuse. First, individuals who obtain pharmaceutical drugs through a valid prescription should keep the drugs secure (Mayo Clinic, 2015). Leaving the drugs sitting on a dresser in a residence hall room or in a cabinet in a common bathroom leaves the drug vulnerable to theft. Second, everyone should avoid ordering pharmaceutical drugs online (Mayo Clinic, 2015). Even with a valid prescription, there are many drugs sold online that are counterfeit or something other than what is represented. With a valid prescription, international students should always deal with a pharmacy. This step allows the international student to talk to the pharmacist about dependency and abuse issues with the drug. Third, everyone should dispose of outdated pharmaceutical drugs (Mayo Clinic, 2015). A local pharmacist can help with this. Finally, no one should give or accept pharmaceutical drugs to or from another person (Seminole Prevention Coalition, n.d.). In many states, the law makes no distinction between selling drugs and giving drugs – both actions constitute dealing in drugs. For example, the Florida law indicates

Except as provided in this chapter, it is unlawful to sell or deliver in excess of 10 grams of any substance named or described in s. 893.03(1)(a) or (1)(b), or any combination thereof, or any mixture containing any such substance. Any person who violates this paragraph commits a felony of the first degree. (Drug Abuse Prevention and Control, 2008, para. 5)

In many states, there are enhanced penalties that may include mandatory prison sentences for dealing in drugs on an educational campus. For example, in Connecticut, individuals who deal drugs on or near educational property may be sentenced to between three months and one year in jail (Reinhart, 2010). Additionally, international students who are convicted of felony drug offenses may face deportation (Oakland Community College, 2010).

DOMESTIC VIOLENCE

Domestic violence is defined as physical, sexual, or psychological abuse, and control by an intimate partner (Kalokhe, Potdar, Stephenson, Dunkle, Paranjape, del Rio, & Sahay, 2015). Domestic violence is recognized as a global social, health, and human rights issue (Dempsey & Forst, 2012, p. 332). International students may be at increased risk for arrest and/or other sanctions for domestic violence as research suggests that immigration intensifies domestic violence and increases vulnerability for the spouses or significant others of immigrants (Davis & Erez, 1998; see also Erez, 2000, 2002; Raj & Silverman, 2002). These studies assess domestic violence among immigrants. What is unknown is how these studies' results specifically apply to international students.

Nevertheless, international students must be concerned about domestic violence. For international students, being arrested and convicted of domestic violence can have serious consequences that can affect their good academic standing that is necessary for remaining in the U.S. (Raj & Silverman, 2002). For example, in 2014, an international student enrolled at Santa Barbara City College was arrested for felony domestic violence and animal abuse stemming from a domestic violence incident (edhat Santa Barbara, 2015). If convicted of the offense, the international student faces a sentence of up to six years in a California prison (edhat Santa Barbara, 2015).

One problem for international students is that some may not be aware that domestic violence is a crime in the U.S. (Bauer, Rodriguez, Quiroga, & Flores-Ortiz, 2000). Similarly, not every international student understands that domestic violence involves more than physical assault and can include sexual, economic, psychological, and emotional abuse (Bekmuratova, 2012). Further, cultural and situational factors may exacerbate issues among international students regarding domestic violence. Domestic violence in some cultures may not be prohibited and is even allowed (Bauer, Rodriguez, Quiroga, & Flores-Ortiz, 2000; Prince, 2011; WHO, 2005). For example, Islamic scholars argue over whether the Quran allows a man to hit a woman (Hajjar, 2004). Similarly, there are at least 20 countries that have no laws preventing domestic violence including Russia and many countries in the Middle East and Africa (Alfred, 2014). Individuals from these cultures may fear that their culture will be criticized if they disclose that domestic violence is permitted (Haile-Mariam & Smith, 1999). Spouses or domestic partners of international students may accompany the student to the U.S. on a dependent visa that does not allow them to work. This makes them rely upon the international student for support, a factor that increases their dependency and makes them more vulnerable to domestic violence (Raj & Silverman, 2002). For example, the Asian Family Support Services at the University of Texas receives about 250 calls a years from spouses and domestic partners of Asian students inquiring about domestic violence services (Cobler, 2014). Officials believe the number of domestic violence incidents may be higher but, due to cultural stigma in Asian countries, victims are too embarrassed to report domestic abuse and sexual assault (Cobler, 2014).

Spouses and domestic partners of international students may be disadvantaged because of their status. As most are on an F-2 dependent visa, they cannot enroll in classes or obtain employment (Teshome & Osei-Kofi, 2012). This limits the resources available to them for addressing domestic violence. Further, many spouses or domestic partners of international students view themselves as guests of the international student who can remove them from his or her apartment or house or have their visa cancelled (Cobler, 2014). These spouses or domestic partners have a limited support network in the U.S. and this increases their isolation and victimization potential. Many cases of domestic violence never come to the attention of the police or higher education administrators because of these factors (Urias, 2006).

All states have laws against domestic violence. Further, there are 21 states that have requirements in their laws that if a police officer sees evidence of domestic violence, he or she *must* arrest the offender (ABA Commission on Domestic Violence, 2010). Domestic violence is a crime against a person and considered a crime of violence. Higher education institutions' codes of student conduct may require the suspension of the student from the institution if he or she is deemed a threat to another person. These consequences may result in the international student's visa being revoked and the student deported. Even if the student is not immediately deported, a domestic violence charge on his or her record will require investigation for future applications for a student visa.

International students need to understand that U.S. society has taken a stand against domestic violence and that it is not tolerated regardless of cultural traditions. For international students choosing to break their cycle of abuse against a spouse or domestic partner, many higher education institutions have counseling services that can assist with addressing emotional and other underlying abuse causes. Victims of domestic violence should seek assistance and protection through local resources and authorities. All states have laws that provide for domestic violence injunctions or protective orders (FindLaw, 2014). These injunctions or orders can require that the abuser vacate the apartment or home, but continue to support the victim and any children (FindLaw, 2014). Further, these injunctions or orders generally require that the abuser have no contact with the victim (FindLaw, 2014). Many campuses and communities have women centers or shelters that assist victims with obtaining protection and legal services.

Higher education institutions play a role in protecting spouses and domestic partners of international students from abuse. While these victims may not be students, campus resources should be available to them given their limited support network in the U.S. For example, the University of Iowa provides the spouses and significant others of international students with information about domestic violence and the resources that are available to them (The University of Iowa International Programs, 2015). Indeed, spouses and significant others may turn to the institution's international students' office for assistance. However, many of these offices do not have programs specifically designed to address domestic violence (Joshi, Thomas, & Sorenson, 2013). Nevertheless, as the primary point of contact for international students and their families, these offices are positioned to help victims report domestic violence incidents as required by law and obtain assistance from other resources.

CONCLUSION

Most international students have rewarding educational experiences in the U.S. Unfortunately, some international students may experience legal issues resulting from either being a crime victim or committing an offense that violates a law. This chapter's purpose has been to provide an overview of the U.S. criminal justice system and crime-related issues to help international students and student affairs/international students' officials aware of these issues and suggestions to avoid potential problems. Generally, international students are aware of crimes that are wrong in and of themselves, that is *mala in se* crimes; however, international students need to understand that the U.S. has many regulations that are codified into law and of which they may not be aware. It can be easy to violate one of these *mala prohibita* laws without realizing it. By having a close relationship with higher education officials and asking questions about situations, international students can limit the possibility of violating a *mala prohibita* law.

The U.S. criminal justice system differs from that of many other countries. All laws and processes are based upon the U.S. Constitution, which guarantees certain rights to all individuals. When any person, including an international student, is arrested for violating the law, law enforcement officers, prosecuting attorneys, and judges must ensure that the actions they take protect the arrested person's constitutional rights. U.S. laws are enforced by a multitude of law enforcement agencies that exist at the local, state, and federal government levels. Most law enforcement agencies exist at the local level. Most international students' interactions with law enforcement agencies will occur with local agencies including campus police agencies. Although campus law enforcement agencies at public colleges and universities may be considered state agencies, they operate similar to local police departments.

There are many crimes to which an international students can become a victim. Crime against property include the theft and vandalism of property and fraud including identity theft. Crimes against a person include assault, rape, and even murder. Of particular concern to international students are hate crimes. International students should ensure they report all crimes to the appropriate law enforcement agency. By reporting these crimes, they not only assist in apprehending and punishing the offenders, but may help to prevent future crimes. Further, the reporting of hate crimes allows international students easier access to victim services.

While many young people at higher education institutions, including international students, consume alcoholic beverages, this consumption may result in health and legal problems. International students generally consume alcoholic beverages due to the stresses of being a student and acculturation issues. Further, the myth that college life includes the consumption of copious amounts of alcoholic beverages may cause students to consumer more alcoholic beverages than intended. This excessive consumption of alcoholic beverages can cause students to become uncontrollable and increase their chance for victimization. The use of illegal drugs has similar consequences for international students. Of particular concern is the use of pharmaceutical drugs. Despite pharmaceutical drugs being obtained with a prescription and from a pharmacy, they can be just as dangerous and addicting as street drugs. Further, the sharing and/or selling of pharmaceutical drugs is a crime. Domestic violence is a serious social problem; it is also unlawful. International students who engage in domestic violence are subject to arrest and suspension or expulsion from their institution since this is a crime of violence. Higher education institutions should provide resources to help international students and their spouses or domestic partners combat domestic violence.

REFERENCES

Alfred, C. (2014, March 8). These 20 countries have no law against domestic violence. *The World Post*. Retrieved from http://www.huffingtonpost.com/2014/03/08/countries-no-domestic-violence-law_n_4918784.html

American Bar Association. (n. d.). Debating the "mighty constitutional opposites": Debating hate speech. Retrieved from http://www.americanbar.org/groups/public_education/initiatives_awards/students_in_action/debate_hate.html

American Bar Association (ABA) Commission on Domestic Violence. (2010). Domestic violence arrest policies by state. Retrieved from http://www.americanbar.org/content/dam/aba /migrated/domviol/docs /Domestic_Violence_Arrest_Policies_by_State_11_07.pdf

Arbetman, L., & McMahon, E. (2009). *Street law: A course in practical law* (8th ed.). New York: McGraw-Hill.

Armed Campuses. (2013). *Guns on campus' laws for public colleges and universities: A guide for students and parents*. Retrieved from http://www.armedcampuses.org/

Bardhi, F., Sifaneck, S., Johnson, B., & Dunlap, E. (2007). Pills, thrills and bellyaches; Case studies of prescription pill use and misuse among marijuana/blunt smoking middle class young women. *Contemporary Drug Problems, 34*(1), 53–101. PMID:19081798

Bauer, H., Rodriguez, M., Quiroga, S., & Flores-Ortiz, Y. (2000). Barriers to health care for abused Latina and Asian immigrant women. *Journal of Health Care for the Poor and Underserved, 11*(1), 33–44. doi:10.1353/hpu.2010.0590 PMID:10778041

Bekmuratova, S. (2012). *Study of international students' definations of and perceptions about domestic violence against women*. Theses, Dissertations, and Other Capstone Projects Paper 55. Retrieved from http://cornerstone.lib.mnsu.edu/cgi/viewcontent.cgi?article=1054&context=etds&seiredir=1&referrer=http%3A%2F%2F

Bénabou, R., & Tirole, J. (2006). Belief in a just world and redistributive politics. *The Quarterly Journal of Economics*, *121*(2), 699–746. doi:10.1162/qjec.2006.121.2.699

Blanco, C., Okuda, M., Wright, C., Hasin, D., Grant, B., Liu, S., & Olfson, M. (2008). Mental health of college students and their non-college-attending peers: Results from the National Epidemiologic Study on Alcohol and Related Conditions. *Archives of General Psychiatry*, *65*(12), 1429–1437. doi:10.1001/archpsyc.65.12.1429 PMID:19047530

Burnett, A., Sabato, T., Wagner, L., & Smith, A. (2014). The influence of attributional style on substance use and risky sexual behavior among college students. *College Student Journal*, *48*(2), 325–336.

Center for Disease Control (CDC). (2014). *Facts sheet – Underage drinking*. Retrieved from http://www.cdc.gov/alcohol/fact-sheets/underage-drinking.htm

Chaplinsky v. New Hampshire. 315 U.S. 568. (1942).

ChartsBin Statistics Collector Team. (2010). *Legal status of child pornography by country*. Retrieved from http://chartsbin.com/view/q4y

Cobler, N. (2014, April 3). International students and their partners face additional barriers when dealing with domestic violence. *The Daily Texan*. Retrieved from http://www.dailytexanonline.com/news/2014/04/01/international-students-and-their-partners-face-additional-barriers-when-dealing-with

Cohen, D. (2003). Australia has become the academic destination for much of Asia. Can it handle the influx? *The Chronicle of Higher Education*, *49*(21), 1–40. doi:10.1023/A:1024448212746

Cole, D. (2003). Are foreign nationals entitled to the same constitutional rights as citizens? *Georgetown Law Faculty Publications and Other Works*. Paper 297. Retrieved from http://scholarship.law.georgetown.edu/facpub/297

Cole, G., & Smith, C. (2006). *The American system of criminal justice* (11th ed.). Belmont, CA: Wadsworth.

Cole, G., Smith, C., & DeJong, C. (2014). *Criminal justice in America* (8th ed.). Boston, MA: Cengage.

Coleman, J., & Trunzo, J. (2015). Personality, social stress, and drug use among college students. *Psi Chi Journal of Psychological Research*, *20*(1), 52–56.

Coston, C. (1996). Fear of crime among foreign students in the United States. In A. Sulton (Ed.), *African-American perspectives on crime causation, criminal justice administration, and crime prevention* (pp. 83–101). Newton, MA: Butterworth-Heinemann.

Coston, C. (2004). Worries about crime among foreign students studying in the United States. In C. Coston (Ed.), *Victimizing vulnerable groups: Images of uniquely high-risk crime targets* (pp. 173–193). Westport, CT: Praeger.

Davis, R., & Erez, E. (1998). *Immigrant population as victims: Toward a multicultural criminal justice system* [Research in brief]. Washington, DC: National Institute of Justice.

Dempsey, J., & Forst, L. (2012). An introduction to policing (6th Ed.). Clifton, Park, NY: Delmar.

Dorfman, L., & Schiraldi, V. (2001). *Off balance: Youth, race, & crime in the news*. Washington, DC: Building Blocks for Youth.

Drug Abuse Prevention and Control. F.S.S. 893.13(1)(b). (2008).

DrugAbuse.net. (2015). *Laws around the world*. Retrieved from http://www.drugabuse.net/drug-policy/drug-laws-around-the-world/

edhat Santa Barbara. (2015, March 27). *Alleged domestic and animal abuser in court*. Retrieved from http://www.edhat.com/site/tidbit.cfm?nid=150313

Erez, E. (2000). Immigration, culture conflict and domestic violence/woman battering. *Crime Prevention and Community Safety: An International Journal*, 2(1), 27–36. doi:10.1057/palgrave.cpcs.8140043

Erez, E. (2002). Migration/immigration, domestic violence and the justice system. *International Journal of Comparative and Applied Criminal Justice*, 26(2), 277–299. doi:10.1080/01924036.2002.9678692

Erez, E., Adelman, M., & Gregory, C. (2009). Intersection of immigration and domestic violence: Voices of battered immigrant women. *Feminist Criminology*, 4(1), 32–56. doi:10.1177/1557085108325413

Federal Bureau of Investigation (FBI). (2011). *Crimes against persons, property, and society*. Retrieved from http://www.fbi.gov/about-us/cjis/ucr/nibrs/2011/resources/crimes-against-persons-property-and-society

Federal Bureau of Investigation (FBI). (n. d.). *Common fraud schemes*. Retrieved from http://www.fbi.gov/scams-safety/fraud

FindLaw. (2014). *Domestic violence: Orders of protection and restraining orders*. Retrieved from http://family.findlaw.com/domestic-violence/domestic-violence-orders-of-protection-and-restraining-orders.html

Forbes-Newett, H., McCulloch, J., & Nyland, C. (2015). *International students and crime*. New York: Palgrave MacMillan.

Frey, L., & Roysircar, G. (2006). South Asian and east Asian international students' perceived prejudice, acculturation, and frequency of help resource utilization. *Journal of Multicultural Counseling and Development*, 34(4), 208–222. doi:10.1002/j.2161-1912.2006.tb00040.x

Fuller, J. (2013). *Criminal justice: Mainstream and crosscurrents* (3rd ed.). Upper Saddle River, NJ: Pearson.

Garnier, L., Arria, A., Caldeira, K., Vincent, K., O'Grady, K., & Wish, E. (2010). Sharing and selling of prescription medications in a college student sample. *Journal of Clinical Psychiatry, 71*(3), 262–269. Retrieved from http://0-dx.doi.org.wncln.wncln.org/10.4088/JCP.09m05189ecr

Gray, R. (2012). 1 in 3 campus public safety officers need more less-lethal training. *Campus Safety*. Retrieved from http://www.campussafetymagazine.com/article/CS-Survey-Part-2-42-of-Campus-Public-Safety-Departments

Haile-Mariam, T., & Smith, J. (1999). Domestic violence against women in the international community. *Emergency Medicine Clinics of North America, 17*(3), 617–630. doi:10.1016/S0733-8627(05)70086-9 PMID:10516842

Hajjar, L. (2004). Religion, state power, and domestic violence in Muslim societies: A framework for comparative analysis. *Law & Social Inquiry, 29*(1), 1–38. doi:10.1111/j.1747-4469.2004.tb00329.x

Ham, L., & Hope, D. (2003). College students and problematic drinking: A review of the literature. *Clinical Psychology Review, 23*(5), 719–759. doi:10.1016/S0272-7358(03)00071-0 PMID:12971907

Hendershot, C., MacPherson, L., Myers, M., Carr, L., & Wall, T. (2005). Psychosocial, cultural and genetic influences on alcohol use in Asian-American youth. *Journal of Studies on Alcohol and Drugs, 66*(2), 185–195. doi:10.15288/jsa.2005.66.185 PMID:15957669

Henson, V., & Stone, W. (1999). Campus crime: A victimization study. *Journal of Criminal Justice, 27*(4), 295–307. doi:10.1016/S0047-2352(99)00003-3

Hess, K., Orthmann, C., & Cho, H. (2015). *Introduction to law enforcement and criminal justice* (11th ed.). Boston, MA: Cengage.

International Association of Chiefs of Police (IACP). (2015). *Types of law enforcement agencies*. Retrieved from http://discoverpolicing.org/whats_like/?fa=types_jobs

International Center for Alcohol Policies (IACP). (1998). *Drinking age limits*. Retrieved from http://www. icap.org/portals/0/download/all_pdfs/icap_reports_english/report4.pdf

Johnson, K., Bonn-Miler, M., Leyro, T., & Zvolensky, M. (2009). Anxious arousal and anhedonic depression symptoms and the frequency of current marijuana use: Testing the mediating role of marijuana-use coping motives among active users. *Journal of Studies on Alcohol and Drugs, 70*(4), 543–550. doi:10.15288/jsad.2009.70.543 PMID:19515294

Johnston, L., O'Malley, P., Bachman, J., & Schulenberg, J. (2009). Monitoring the future national survey results on drug use, 1975–2008: Volume II, college students and adults ages 19–50 (NIH Publication No. 09-7403). Bethesda, MD: National Institute on Drug Abuse.

Joshi, M., Thomas, K., & Sorenson, S. (2013). Domestic violence and international students: An exploratory study of the practices and role of US university international offices. *Journal of College Student Development, 54*(4), 527–533. doi:10.1353/csd.2013.0080

Kalokhe, A., Potdar, R., Stephenson, R., Dunkle, K., Paranjape, A., del Rio, C., & Sahay, S. (2015). How well does the World Health Organization definition of domestic violence work for India? *PLoS ONE, 10*(3), 1–16. doi:10.1371/journal.pone.0120909 PMID:25811374

Khosla, N., Juon, H., Kirk, G., Astemborski, J., & Mehta, S. (2011). Correlates of non-medical prescription drug use among a cohort of injection drug users in Baltimore City. *Addictive Behaviors, 36*(12), 1282–1287. doi:10.1016/j.addbeh.2011.07.046 PMID:21868170

Kyckelhahn, T., & Martin, T. (2013, July). Justice expenditure and employment extracts, 2010 – preliminary. *Bureau of Justice Statistics Bulletin*. NCJ. Retrieved from http://www.bjs.gov/index.cfm?ty=pbdetail&iid=4679

Mayo Clinic. (2015). *Prescription drug abuse*. Retrieved from http://www.mayoclinic.org/diseases-conditions/prescription-drug-abuse/basics/prevention/CON-20032471

Mazzarol, T., & Soutar, G. (2002). "Push-pull" factors influencing foreign students' destination choice. *International Journal of Education Management, 16*(2/3). 82–91. doi:021041840310.1108/0951354

McCabe, S., Teter, C., & Boyd, C. (2006). Medical use, illicit use, and diversion of abusable prescription drugs. *Journal of American College Health, 54*(5), 269–278. doi:10.3200/JACH.54.5.269-278 PMID:16539219

McClellan, C., & Tekin, E. (2012). *Stand your ground laws, homicides, and injuries* (NBER Working Paper No. 18187). Retrieved from http://www.nber.org/papers/w18187

McMullen, L. (2013). How to practice self-defense through awareness. *U.S. News*. Retrieved from http://health.usnews.com/health-news/health-wellness/articles/2013/10/16/how-to-practice-self-defense-through-awareness

Meilman, P., Presley, C., & Cashin, J. (1997). Average weekly alcohol consumption: Drinking percentiles for American college students. *Journal of American College Health, 45*(5), 201–204. doi:10.1080/07448481.1997.9936885 PMID:9069677

National Conference on State Legislatures. (2015). *Guns on campus: Overview*. Retrieved from http://www.ncsl.org/research/education/guns-on-campus-overview.aspx

National Crime Prevention Council. (2015). *Hate crimes*. Retrieved from http://www.ncpc.org/topics/hate-crime

National Institute on Alcohol Abuse and Alcoholism (NIAAA). (2002). *High risk drinking in college: What we know and what we need to learn*. Washington, DC: U.S. Department of Health and Human Services. Retrieved from http://www.collegedrinkingprevention.gov/media/FINAL Panel1.pdf

National Institute on Alcohol Abuse and Alcoholism (NIAAA). (2005). *How to reduce high-risk college drinking: Use proven strategies, fill research gaps*. Retrieved from http://www. collegedrinkingprevention.gov/NIAAACollegeMaterials/Panel02 /KeyResearch_04.aspx

North Carolina General Statute (NCGS). Powers of magistrates in infractions or criminal actions. G.S. §7A-273. (2014).

Oakland Community College. (2010). *Legal information for F-1 visa students*. Retrieved from https://www.oaklandcc.edu/International/Documents/F1LegalInfo.pdf

Office of the Dean of Student Life. (2007). *Rights and responsibilities of community: A code of student behavior*. Fargo, ND: NDSU.

Parfaniuc, N. (2011). Historical development of police agencies and their jurisdiction. Retrieved from http://www.scribd.com/doc/49065966/Historical-Development-of-Police-Agencies-and-their-jurisdiction

Patar, R., & Remmo, C. (2012). Personal responsibility for safety. *Professional Safety, 57*(9), 26–29.

Pennay, A. (2012). Carnal pleasures and grotesque bodies: Regulating the body during a "big night out" of alcohol and party drug use. *Contemporary Drug Problems, 39*(3), 397–428. doi:10.1177/009145091203900304

Prince, D. (2011, Oct 27). *Violence against women and culture: A symbiotic relationship.* Retrieved from http: //www.genderacrossborders.com/2011/10/27/violence-against-women-and-culture-a-symbiotic-relationship/

Quintero, G. (2009). Rx for a party: A qualitative analysis of recreational pharmaceutical use in a collegiate setting. *Journal of American College Health, 58*(1), 64 – 70. doi:10.3200/JACH.58.1.64-72

Raj, A., & Silverman, J. (2002). Violence against immigrant women: The roles of culture, context, and legal immigrant status on intimate partner violence. *Violence Against Women, 8*(3), 367–398. doi:10.1177/10778010222183107

R.A.V. vs. City of St. Paul. 112 S.Ct. 2538. (1992).

Reaves, B. (2015a). *Campus law enforcement, 2011–12.* Washington, DC: US Department of Justice.

Reaves, B. (2015b). *Local police departments, 2013: Personnel, policies, and practices.* Washington, DC: US Department of Justice.

Reid, A., Graziano, P., Balkhi, A., McNamara, J., Cottler, L., Meneses, E., & Geffken, G. (2015). Frequent nonprescription stimulant use and risky behaviors in college students: The role of effortful control. *Journal of American College Health, 63*(1), 23–30. doi:10.1080/07448481.2014.960422 PMID:25222628

Reinhart, C. (2010). *People incarcerated for non-violent crimes.* Retrieved from http://cga.ct.gov/2010/rpt/2010-R-0157.htm

Rozenbroek, K., & Rothstein, W. (2011). Medical and nonmedical users of prescription drugs among college students. *Journal of American College Health, 59*(5), 358–363. doi:10.1080/07448481.2010.5 12044 PMID:21500053

Sandhills Community College. (n.d.). *Campus violence prevention policy.* Retrieved from http://www.sandhills.edu/security/violence-prevention.php

Seminole Prevention Coalition. (n.d.) *How to prevent prescription drug abuse.* Retrieved on February 23, 2015 from http://www.seminolepreventioncoalition.org/pitchyourpills /prescription -drug-abuse-prevention.html#.VOwHGi5y5GY

Smith, W. (2011). *All about the college code of conduct.* Retrieved from http://www.brighthub.com/education/college/articles/114106.aspx

Stone, G. (1994). Hate speech and the U.S. Constitution. *3 East European Constitutional Rev*iew, 78–82.

Substance Abuse and Mental Health Services Administration (SAMHSA). (2010). Results from the 2009 national survey on drug use and health: Volume I. Summary of national findings.

Teshome, Y., & Osei-Kofi, N. (2012). Critical issues in international education: Narratives of spouses of international students. *Journal of Studies in International Education, 16*(1), 62–74. doi:10.1177/1028315311403486

The Criminal Justice System. [Powerpoint slides]. (2009, June 2). Retrieved from http://www.powershow. com/view/7971-M2E4Z/The_Criminal_Justice_System_powerpoint_ppt _presentation

The Sentencing Project. (2014). *Race and punishment: Racial perceptions of crime and support for punitive policies.* Washington, DC: The Sentencing Project.

The University of Iowa International Programs. (2015). *Spouses.* Retrieved from http://international. uiowa.edu/isss/community/guide/spouses

Title VI Statute. 42 U.S.C §§ 2000d - 2000d-7.

University of Miami. (2015). *UM police (umpd).* Retrieved from http://www.miami.edu/ref/index.php/ umpd/

Urias, D. (2006). Empowering the disenfranchised: Supporting spouses of international students and scholars. *International Educator, 15*(2), 42–47.

U.S. Census Bureau. (2010). *2010 census.* Retrieved from http://www.census.gov/2010census/

Vieraitis, L., Copes, H., Powell, Z., & Pike, A. (2015). A little information goes a long way: Expertise and identity theft. *Aggression and Violent Behavior, 20,* 10–18. doi:10.1016/j.avb.2014.12.008

Vivancos, R., Abubakar, I., & Hunter, P. (2009). Sexual behaviour, drugs and alcohol use of international students at a British university: A cross-sectional survey. *International Journal of STD & AIDS, 20*(9), 619–622. doi:10.1258/ijsa.2008.008421 PMID:19710334

Ward, T., & Langlands, R. (2008). Restorative justice and the human rights of offenders: Convergences and divergences. *Aggression and Violent Behavior, 13*(5), 355–372. doi:10.1016/j.avb.2008.06.001

Wechsler, H., Molnar, B. E., Davenport, A. E., & Baer, J. S. (1999). College alcohol use: A full or empty glass? *Journal of American College Health, 47*(6), 247–252. doi:10.1080/07448489909595655 PMID:10368558

Wiebe, R., Cleveland, H., & Harris, K. (2010). *The need for college recovery services.* doi:10.1007/978-1-4419-1767-6_1

Williams, M. (2013). The effectiveness of public defenders in four Florida counties. *Journal of Criminal Justice, 41*(4), 205–212. doi:10.1016/j.jcrimjus.2013.05.004

Wisconsin v. Mitchell. (92-515) 508 U.S. 47. (1993).

World Health Organization (WHO). (2005). *WHO multi-country study on women's health and domestic violence against women. Summary report.* Retrieved from http://www.who.int/gender /violence/ who_multicountry_study/summary_report/summary_report_English2.pdf

Yoon, E., & Portman, T. (2004). Critical issue of literature on counseling international students. *Journal of Multicultural Counseling and Development, 32*(1), 33–44. doi:10.1002/j.2161-1912.2004.tb00359.x

KEY TERMS AND DEFINITIONS

Alcohol Abuse: The recurring use of alcoholic beverages despite their harmful effects and consequences.

Criminal Justice System: The term used to refer to a system for investigating, apprehending, trying, convicting, and punishing people who commit crimes.

Domestic Violence: The term commonly used to refer to intimate partner violence or violent victimization between spouses, boyfriends, and girlfriends or those formerly in intimate relationships.

Drug Abuse: The recurring use of drugs, whether street, over-the-counter, or pharmaceutical drugs, despite their harmful effects and consequences.

International Students: An individual who is enrolled for credit at an accredited higher education institution in the U.S. on a temporary visa, and who is not an immigrant, or an undocumented immigrant, or a refugee.

Law Enforcement: The police function of controlling crime by intervening in situations in which the law has clearly been violated and the police need to apprehend the guilty person.

Prosecuting Attorney: A legal representative of the state with sole responsibility for bringing criminal charges. In some states, this person is referred to as the district attorney, solicitor, state attorney, commonwealth attorney, or county attorney.

Public Defender: An attorney employed either part-time or full-time, on a salaried basis by a public or private nonprofit organization to represent indigents.

U.S. Constitution: A document written in 1789 that established the governing principles of the United States. It is frequently called the *law of the land*. Of particular interest to criminal justice practitioners is the first 10 amendments to the Constitutions, commonly referred to as the *Bill of Rights*. This Bill of Rights established rights for individuals in America to protect them from government abuses. For individuals who have been arrested, these rights include the right to not be compelled to be a witness against one's self, the right to legal counsel, the right to reasonable bail, and the right to be free from cruel and unusual punishment.

This work was previously published in Campus Support Services, Programs, and Policies for International Students edited by Krishna Bista and Charlotte Foster, pages 264-288, copyright 2016 by Information Science Reference (an imprint of IGI Global).

Chapter 3
Identity and Access Management in the Cloud Computing Environments

Manoj V. Thomas
National Institute of Technology Karnataka, India

K. Chandrasekaran
National Institute of Technology Karnataka, India

ABSTRACT

Nowadays, the issue of identity and access management (IAM) has become an important research topic in cloud computing. In the distributed computing environments like cloud computing, effective authentication and authorization are essential to make sure that unauthorized users do not access the resources, thereby ensuring the confidentiality, integrity, and availability of information hosted in the cloud environment. In this chapter, the authors discuss the issue of identity and access management in cloud computing, analyzing the work carried out by others in the area. Also, various issues in the current IAM scenario in cloud computing, such as authentication, authorization, access control models, identity life cycle management, cloud identity-as-a-service, federated identity management and also, the identity and access management in the inter-cloud environment are discussed. The authors conclude this chapter discussing a few research issues in the area of identity and access management in the cloud and inter-cloud environments.

INTRODUCTION

Even though cloud computing has become one of the most promising paradigms in the IT domain, many organizations and the enterprises are still reluctant to adopt the cloud for critical workloads or services because of the concern about the security of their personal data (King & Raja, 2012). Hence, managing user identities and their access in the cloud system is a critical problem to be solved effectively so that the cloud computing is safe and secure. Digital identity of a user represents who he is, and it is used to decide his access rights or privileges when he interacts with other users or accesses resources or services

DOI: 10.4018/978-1-5225-0808-3.ch003

online. The identity of a cloud user authorizes him to access data or resources from the cloud environment. When the users make requests to access the cloud resources and services, it is highly important that the identity and the access rights of the users are verified before granting the requested services.

An effective Identity and Access Management (IAM) mechanism is required to make the cloud computing platform trusted, secure, reliable and scalable. Normally, on-premise applications can rely on various on-premise identity infrastructure services such as Active Directory (Microsoft, 2009) and Lightweight Directory Access Protocol (Wahl et al., 1997) for verifying the user identity information. Similarly, an effective identity service in the cloud should solve this issue in the cloud environment. Identity and Access Management deals with the process of identifying entities in a computing system, and also managing access to the available resources in the system based on access rules or policies. In the cloud computing domain, the private data of the cloud customers are stored in the servers or the data centers of the CSPs; rather than keeping it on-premise on the user's computer. Hence, the CSPs need to address the privacy concerns of the cloud users through proper IAM mechanisms so that the trust level of the cloud users in the Cloud Computing domain is increased. Proper identity management is the first step to be enforced in the cloud environment, in order to avoid unauthorized access of cloud resources.

In this chapter, the authors discuss the issue of identity and access management in the cloud and inter-cloud environments. The analysis of the work done by the researchers in this area shows the merits and demerits of various approaches. The various issues in the identity and access management in cloud computing, such as authentication, authorization, access control models, identity life cycle management are discussed. The authors explain the emerging concepts in identity management, such as the federated identity management, Single Sign-On (SSO) and cloud identity-as-a-service. Also, the various issues in the identity and access management in the inter-cloud (cloud federation) environment are discussed in this chapter. Finally, the authors conclude the chapter discussing a few research issues in the area of identity and access management in the cloud and inter-cloud environments.

BACKGROUND

In the Cloud Computing domain, an efficient IAM is essential for maintaining the confidentiality, integrity and availability of the data stored in the cloud. Generally, in the cloud environment, access control mechanism is required at each of the following layers (Alliance, 2011):

1. **Network Layer:** An access control mechanism at the network layer should not allow a user to see any system or a specified portion of a network (Ping, Route commands) in the cloud unless the access policies allow him to do so.
2. **System Layer:** A user should not be allowed to access any particular host or system in the cloud unless the access policies allow him to do so.
3. **Application Layer:** Access to the cloud applications or any functionality of the applications should be governed by the access control rules, and the access should be permitted after verifying the identities and attributes of a cloud user.
4. **Process Layer:** Access control policies and rules should be effectively used to define the processes or functions that a user is allowed to run within an application.

5. **Data Layer:** In the cloud domain, access policies or rules could be used to control the user's access to the data area and file system. Also, the individual files and the various fields (as in a database system) should be controlled from illegal access.

When an organization adopts cloud services, its trust boundary is more dynamic since the resources used by the organization extends into the domain of the CSP. Hence, there should be a proper IAM mechanism implemented in the cloud computing domain for its widespread adoption among the service consumers.

Literature Review

This section throws light on the research activities in the area of IAM in the cloud and inter-cloud environments, analyzing the works carried out by the researchers. The work carried out in (Wei et al., 2010) presents an attribute and role based access control (ARBAC) model. Before invoking services, requestors of various services provide their attribute information to the service providers. When the service providers receive the requests, they determine whether to permit or deny these requests according to their access control policies. In this work, access negotiation mechanism is not added into the ARBAC model. How to enforce access control, on the numerous users who are not defined in the system in the distributed computing environment is discussed in the work carried out in (Lang et al., 2007). The access control method based on trust makes decisions based on the trust evaluation of the requestor. In (Wang et al., 2007), the proposed scheme cryptographically provides role-based access control and delegation, based on Hierarchical Identity-Based Signature (IBS).

In (Feng et al., 2008), a Trust and Context based Access Control (TCAC) model, extending the RBAC model is proposed for open and distributed systems. A trust evaluation mechanism based on the local and global reputation, to compute the trust value of users in a distributed system is provided. When the trust value of the requester is not less than the trust threshold defined by the system policies, the user will be assigned to some roles. In (Gunjan et al., 2012), the authors discuss the issue of identity management in the cloud computing scenario. They also show the privacy issues associated with cloud computing. The paper gives a review of the existing approaches in identity management in cloud computing. In this work, loss of control, lack of trust and multitenancy issues are identified as major problems in the present cloud computing model.

The research in the field of IAM in the Inter-Cloud environment is still in its nascent stage, and some of the relevant approaches proposed by the researchers in that area follow. In (Stihler et al., 2012), the authors propose the architecture for Federated Identity Management in a scenario similar to the Inter-Cloud environment. The main objective of the proposed architecture is to provide a platform for the sharing of various resources and services among the Inter-cloud consumers. The work focuses on sharing of information or resources across all the three cloud service models such as SaaS, PaaS and IaaS. The works carried out in (Celesti et al., 2010a; Tusa et al., 2011) present a heterogeneous horizontal cloud federation model, for CLoud-Enabled Virtual EnviRonment (CLEVER). These works use the concept of a middleware component called the Cross-Cloud Federation Manager (CCFM) that could be integrated into the Cloud Manager component of the CSP. This helps the participating clouds to be a part of the cloud federation. The CCFM consists of three sub-components, called the Discovery Agent, Match-Making Agent and Authentication Agent, and they are responsible for performing the required functions for the cloud federation.

The work in (Bernstein & Vij, 2010a) discusses the inter-cloud security considerations. In (Bernstein & Vij, 2010b), the authors propose an authentication mechanism for inter-cloud environments using SAML profile over XMPP. The architecture discussed in this work is based on the internet scale. The work shown in (Yan et al., 2009) discusses a Federated Identity Management approach using Hierarchical Identity-Based Cryptography. This mechanism makes collaboration possible within a Hybrid Cloud, which is a combination of private and public clouds. The work focuses on the Private Key Generator (PKG) hierarchical model. This model assumes a root PKG for managing the entire Hybrid Cloud. Before applying this model to the inter-cloud scenario, issues regarding the control of the root PKG should be solved.

Many works related to the identity management and the Single Sign-On in the cloud computing domain have been published, and the relevant papers are discussed in this section. (Fugkeaw et al., 2007) have presented an SSO model based on Multi-Agent System (MAS) and strong authentication based on PKI. User authorization is not considered as part of this work. (Wang et al., 2013) present a security analysis of various Single Sign-On mechanisms in the distributed networks. They have identified various flaws such as impersonation of a user, impersonation of a service provider etc. during the authentication process. They have also proposed a secure scheme by using RSA-based signatures.

(Celesti et al., 2010b) have implemented a three-phase mechanism for cross-cloud Single Sign-On authentication. The three phases discussed in this paper are Discovery, Match-Making and Authentication. They have focused mainly on authentication in their work and tried to solve the issue by defining their own Security Assertions Markup Language (SAML) profile. They also extended their work in (Celesti et al., 2011) by developing a CLoud Enabled Virtual EnviRonment (CLEVER). Also, in this work, they have only focused on a single Identity Provider rather than having multiple Identity Providers. (Kumar & Cohen, 2000) have proposed the MAS based network security for authentication and authorization. They have implemented an Adaptive Agent Architecture based on MAS. (Chan & Cheng, 2000) present various security flaws in the authentication scheme using smart cards such as the off-line password guessing attacks, impersonation attacks, the intruder-in-the-middle attacks and the denial-of-service attacks.

In order to overcome the problems of guessing attacks in the authentication schemes, (Lee et al., 2002) have proposed an authentication scheme which uses one-way hash functions. (Ren & Wu, 2012) also proposed a dynamic approach for PAS. It uses One-Time Passwords (OTP) unlike traditional static passwords. This OTP is used for authentication along with the user's private identity information and also considering the current authenticating time. Major benefits of this work are its resistance to various real time attacks in the network such as the MITM, replay attacks etc. At the same time, the method is still vulnerable to types of phishing attacks.

Selected Case Studies

1. Amazon Web Services (AWS) - IAM
    AWS Identity Management (AWS-IAM, 2015) provides the following security options for the cloud customers to secure their AWS account and control the access to it. AWS-IAM helps the cloud customers create multiple users and deal with the access permissions for each of these users within the AWS account. The customer AWS account considers a user as an identity having unique security attributes or credentials that could be used for accessing the AWS services. Using AWS-IAM, the customers can implement security features such as 'principle of least privilege' by providing unique identity credentials to each cloud user within their AWS account, and thereby

allowing a user to access the AWS services and resources that are required for the users to perform the designated job. AWS-IAM is considered secure by default, since new users are not allowed to access the AWS services until access permissions are granted explicitly.

2. AWS-Multi-Factor Authentication (AWS-MFA)

    AWS-MFA (AWS-MFA, 2015) offers additional control over AWS account settings, and also helps in the management of AWS services and resources. In order to use this security feature, the AWS users have to provide a six-digit single-use code, in addition to their standard username and password credentials while accessing their AWS account settings, services or resources. The AWS customers get this single-use code from the authentication device they keep with them. Since this authentication mechanism requires two factors, it is called two-factor authentication and it is considered to be more secure than the single factor authentication which normally requires user names and passwords.

3. Eucalyptus - Identity and Access Management

    Eucalyptus is an open source cloud software for building private or hybrid clouds that are compatible with Amazon Web Service (AWS) APIs (Kumar et al., 2014). Identity and Access Management (IAM) in the Eucalyptus private cloud offers authentication, authorization, and accounting features along with the management of user identities and the enforcement of access controls over cloud resources. Access control policies and the user identities are stored in the local Cloud Controller (CLC) database of the Eucalyptus. Identity data of the cloud users can also be accessed from LDAP or Active Directory. Eucalyptus IAM offers various services such as secure credential management and also policy based resource access management.

4. OpenStack Identity Service - Keystone

    OpenStack is an open source cloud computing software (Kumar et al., 2014). The default identity management service for OpenStack is the OpenStack Identity Service, Keystone. Keystone integrates the OpenStack functions for authentication, policy management, and catalog services (Rhoton, 2013). The implementation of Keystone uses a centralized architecture wherein all users are to be enrolled in its database before accessing any of the cloud services in the OpenStack. The enrolling of user identity details can be done either manually by the OpenStack administrator using the command line interface, or by using the bulk loading from an external corporate database such as LDAP.

5. OpenNebula - Users and Group Management

    OpenNebula is an open source cloud computing platform used for the management of heterogeneous cloud infrastructures (Kumar et al., 2014). For the Identity and Access Management, OpenNebula provides a comprehensive user and group management system. In OpenNebula, the cloud resources are accessed by the users, and a permissions system similar to UNIX system is used to manage the access requests made by the users. By default, various resources such as VM images can be used and managed by the owner of the resources. Even though OpenNebula provides an internal username/password authentication system; an external authentication system may also be integrated if required. OpenNebula also supports three customizable authentication configurations such as Command Line Interface, Sunstone and Servers Authentication Mechanisms.

6. Google IAM

    Google Cloud Identity and Access Management (IAM) mechanism helps the cloud users to manage access permissions for Google Cloud resources (Google Cloud IAM, 2015). This IAM mechanism unifies access control for the various Cloud Platform products into a single system and provides a consistent set of operations to the users. The IAM provides a simple and consistent access control interface for all Cloud Platform products. Also, it provides resource-level access control such that cloud users can be assigned with suitable roles to access resources at a finer granularity level. It also helps to assign flexible roles to the cloud users. The Google Cloud IAM provides Google Cloud Console UI and REST-based IAM APIs that can be used by the cloud users to create and manage the IAM policies in the cloud environment. Using the Google Cloud IAM, access to different types of identities can be managed. A Google account used by a developer, an administrator, or any other person who interacts with Cloud Platform can be managed using the email address associated with the corresponding Google account. It can also be used to manage the service account that belongs to a cloud application other than the individual end user. Service account can be used to run the code that is hosted on Cloud Platform. Also, Google Group that is a named collection of Google accounts and service accounts can be managed using the unique email address associated with the group. In Groups, access is granted to a group, instead of granting access to individual users or service accounts. Also, a Google Apps domain that represents a virtual group of all the members in an organization can be managed. After the identity of the user making the access request is authenticated, IAM takes an authorization decision as to whether that identity is allowed to perform the requested operation in the system. IAM policies are used for deciding the access rights of a cloud user.

7. Microsoft IAM

    Microsoft's Identity and Access Management (IAM) system (Microsoft Identity Manager, 2015) provides the identity management services to the cloud and on-premises environments. This system provides various services such as federation, identity management, user provisioning, application access control, and data protection. It offers the IAM services by combining Windows Server Active Directory, Microsoft Identity Manager, and Microsoft Azure Active Directory that can be used by various organizations to secure their hybrid cloud infrastructure. Microsoft Identity Manager combines Microsoft's IAM solutions together (Microsoft Identity Manager, 2015). It combines the various on-premises authentication stores such as Active Directory, LDAP and Oracle Azure Active Directory. Microsoft Identity Manager supports hybrid infrastructure by offering the features such as cloud-ready identities, powerful user self-service, and enhanced security.

Azure Active Directory (Microsoft Azure, 2015) can be used to provide Single Sign-On to various cloud (SaaS) apps and other on-premise web apps. It offers security features such as Multi-Factor Authentication (MFA), access control based on user location, and identity and holistic security reports, audits, and alerts. It can be used to connect Active Directory and other on-premises directories to Azure Active Directory easily. It employs unique machine learning-based mechanisms to identify potential security threats. It can be used to access the on-premises web applications of cloud users from everywhere.

FUNCTIONAL REQUIREMENTS AND CHALLENGES OF THE IAM

In this section, the functional requirements and the implementation challenges of the IAM mechanism in the cloud environment are discussed.

Functional Requirements

An efficient IAM should be implemented in the cloud environment in order to enforce mutual authentication, authorization and auditing in the cloud computing environment. Based on the digital identity of the user, the cloud recognizes who this user is and what he is allowed to do. The overview of the access control module of a CSP is shown in the Figure 1. Whenever an access request is received by a CSP, the IAM module deals with the authentication and authorization processes of the cloud customers. In order to avoid unauthorized or illegal access of the cloud resources, the implementation of the authentication and the authorization processes should be efficient. As shown in the figure, the major components in the access control module are:

1. **Policy Enforcement Point (PEP):** This component is a part of the authorization process in the cloud environment. PEP interacts with the Policy Decision Point (PDP) for validating the access requests of clients, and implements the authorization decisions taken by the PDP. Policy Enforcement Point is the access management layer that enforces the PDP's decisions.
2. **Policy Decision Point (PDP):** This component of the authorization process takes the authorization decision when an access request is received by a CSP. PDP interacts with policy storage database stored locally with the CSP. In cloud systems, PDP is the authorization layer where the access control policies are evaluated and authorization decisions are taken.

Thus, the major functional requirements of IAM in the cloud environment are Dynamic Provisioning and De-provisioning (Identification), Authentication, Authorization, Accounting and Auditing, Support for compliance, identity life cycle management (Hovav & Berger, 2009). Identity life cycle management manages the entire life cycle of user identities. These components are explained in later sections in this chapter.

Identity Management Challenges in the Cloud

The present day business requirements of the organizations using cloud services are diverse. In order to have an effective access control system, the identity management in the cloud should consider the following issues or challenges.

Figure 1. Overview of the access control module

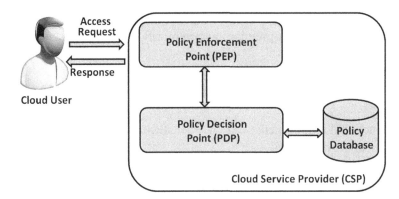

1. It has to effectively deal with the authentication and authorization of various heterogeneous users who are accessing the cloud services from any place, any time and through any supported devices.
2. Due to various business reasons, the roles and responsibilities of users in an organization who use cloud services might change. How to rapidly and dynamically provision users in such cases is another issue.
3. How to manage the staff turnover as far as the identities of the users are concerned.
4. How to handle the user identities when there are merger or de-merger between companies or service providers is another issue which requires proper solutions. And also, the identity management in the cloud should take enough care to avoid duplication of identities, attributes or credentials of users in the system.
5. The IAM techniques also need to be user-friendly for its easier adoption among the business users.

Responsibilities of CSPs and CSCs

The CSPs and the Cloud Service Consumers (CSCs) have to understand their roles and responsibilities in the identity management, in order to have a secure access control in the cloud environment.

CSP Responsibilities

1. The CSPs should support the authentication of the cloud users through identity federation and SSO. Since the users will be accessing the cloud services from anywhere, any time round the clock, and also using any device, the authentication and authorization mechanisms adopted by the CSPs should support them.
2. CSPs need to communicate to the CSCs regarding any changes being made in the account management policies of the CSP.
3. The CSPs should have the required support for identity management when various services are integrated in scenarios such as hybrid clouds.
4. Also, the CSPs should support the regulatory and policy requirements of the cloud users such as Separation of Duty (SoD), least-privilege-based access control etc.
5. Provisioning and de-provisioning to the cloud instances should be done in time, as and when required.

CSC Responsibilities

1. When using the cloud services, the cloud customers need to understand the user provisioning, authentication and authorization methods unique to a CSP, as the CSPs may vary in terms of the lag time for activating the users, and also the attributes of the users supported.
2. Customers have to evaluate and utilize the support extended by the CSPs in identity federation features such as Single Sign-On (SSO).
3. Customers have to verify that whether the log files maintained by the CSPs would be made available to the user for security auditing purposes, if needed.
4. The cloud customers should also monitor the CSP's compliance with government regulations from time to time.

AUTHENTICATION

The cloud users have serious concerns about the confidentiality, integrity and availability of their data stored in the cloud (Sood, 2012). The users worry about the leakage of their sensitive data or their loss of privacy while using cloud services. All these points stress on the need for an effective authentication mechanism in the cloud environment. Authentication in the cloud is the process by which the identity of a user or an entity requesting some resources or service is verified by the CSP. The entity could be a person, process, program or software agent requesting access to cloud resources.

Authentication Requirements of the Cloud Environment

In open service-oriented systems such as the cloud computing systems, in many cases, the service providers and the service consumers are strangers. Since they do not have a pre-established trust value between them, the service provider must be able to authenticate the unfamiliar users and then determine whether the requestors have enough privileges to access the requested services. In the cloud, both the cloud users and the cloud service providers want the information to be secure and well protected in the cloud, irrespective of the service delivery models and the deployment models in the cloud computing paradigm.

Authentication Challenges

The cloud service consumers may use any type of device to connect to the cloud services, and also they may use the cloud service from any location, any time. Hence, a continuously available authentication mechanism is required in the cloud to verify that unauthorized users do not access the cloud resources.

Multi-Factor Authentication

The authentication mechanism in the cloud environment could be based on the four main approaches (Suhendra, 2011). 1. Authentication by something the user knows such as the username or password or PIN (Personal Identification Number) 2. Authentication by something the user has, such as the smart card. 3. Authentication by something the user is such as the bio-metric features of the user, such as fingerprint, retina or iris details. 4. Multi-factor authentication that could use a combination of any two or more of the above mentioned authentication approaches. In a cloud computing environment, the process of authentication needs to be implemented in such a way that the unauthorized users do not access the networks, hosts or the applications to use the data or resources in the cloud.

Authentication Solutions and Recommendations

Strong authentication mechanisms such as multi-factor authentication are required to protect the private information of cloud users. The enterprises can establish VPN tunneling (Padhy et al., 2012) from the CSP to the enterprise network and authenticate the cloud users using the enterprise user directory such as AD or LDAP. Risk-based authentication approaches considering various parameters such as device identifier, geo-location, heuristic information etc. could be employed in the cloud. In the cloud environment, high-risk transactions should be allowed only after strong authentication procedures.

The CSPs should have the capability to consume authentication tokens from authoritative sources using protocols such as SAML. It should be ensured that the authentication service is OAuth-compliant so that the organizations can avoid getting locked into one vendor's authentication credentials. The Cloud Security Alliance (CSA) (Kumaraswamy et al., 2010) suggests the use of user-centric authentication approaches such as OpenID so that the same user identity credentials could be used for availing services from multiple CSPs.

AUTHORIZATION

Authorization in cloud environment is the process by which the access rights or privileges of a user or entity are verified by the cloud system against predefined security policies. In order to avoid unauthorized access my malicious users, the authorization process should verify the access rights of a user who is requesting some service from a CSP.

Authorization Requirements of the Cloud Environment

The CSPs need to ensure that the user requesting some service has the necessary privileges to perform the requested operation in the system. Normally, the authorization process follows the authentication step. In the cloud computing, the business requirements and security requirements of the CSP are turned into access control policies or rules which are used to evaluate the access requests of cloud users. In the cloud environment, XML-based access control policy language, XACML (eXtensible Access Control Markup Language) could be used for managing the access control policies.

Access Control Models

Access control models come in between access control policies and access control mechanisms and, they bridge the gap between an access control policy and the corresponding mechanism. Security models describe what security properties are associated with an access control system. Security models help to formally present the security policy applicable to a computing system, and also to discuss and analyze any theoretical limitations of a particular system in ensuring the proper access control. An access control mechanism is designed according to the properties of the corresponding access control model. From a user's point of view, an access control model represents a clear and precise expression of the security requirements. From the vendor's point of view, access control models act as security design and implementation requirements.

Types of Access Control Models

An access control model should make sure that there is no leakage of access permissions to an unauthorized principal. In another way, the access control system should be 'safe'. Some of the access control models used in cloud computing paradigm are given as follows.

1. Role-Based Access Control (RBAC)

    This model is suitable for organizations where static hierarchy is maintained, and the members have defined roles such as Manager, Accountant or Clerk, and specific access rights are associated with each role. Here, the access rights of users are decided by the roles which they are members of (Ferraiolo et al., 2001). Users are mapped to roles and roles are mapped to privileges. The basic RBAC model is shown in the Figure 2. Apart from the basic or core RBAC model, there are extended models of RBAC (Hu et al., 2006) such as hierarchical RBAC, which supports the role hierarchy and inheritance of privileges; statically constrained RBAC, which supports static constraints; and dynamically constrained RBAC, which supports time-variant constraints.

2. Attribute-Based Access Control

    In this model, access to the resources are allowed or rejected depending on the attributes of the subject, context, resource and action (Wei et al., 2010). Subject attributes include user id, group membership etc. Context attributes include time and location of access request made. Resource attributes include the resource id, and the action represents the type of operation requested by the user such as read or write. As shown in the Figure 3, whenever an access request is initiated, the attributes pertaining to the access request are compared with the stored access control policies, and then the Policy Evaluation module either accepts or rejects the access request.

Figure 2. Role-based access control

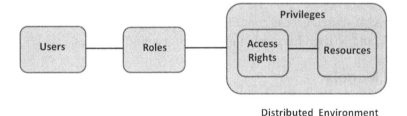

Figure 3. Attribute-based access control

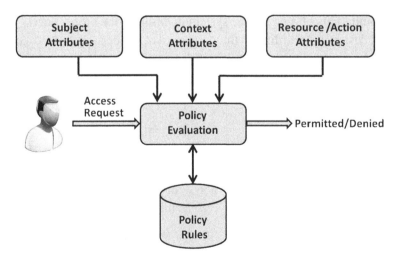

3. Risk-Based Access Control

In a highly dynamic environment like the cloud, the prediction of resources to be accessed by users is not always possible, and risk-based access control models could be used in such environments (health care or military domain). If strict access control is enforced over the usage of resources in such environments, it might result in poor response during an emergency or crisis, and subsequent losses or damages. In the risk-based model, real time decisions are taken to allow or reject a user request, by calculating the risk involved in allowing the access. Figure 4 shows the Risk-Based Access Control model in which the access requests are given to the Policy Enforcement Point (PEP). The PEP contacts the Policy Decision Point (PDP) for the access decision and the PDP takes the access decision by calculating the risk involved in the access request made. In this case, the calculation of the risk considers various parameters such as the attributes of the user, his trustworthiness, context information of the access request such as time, location and also, the sensitivity level of the resource requested and the previous access history. Risk threshold levels are specified by the security policy from time to time, and the decision to grant or deny the request is taken based on that threshold value.

Logging and Auditing in Identity Management

The logging process collects the identification details of a user, such as the time of access, resource accessed, etc. and they are entered in a log file which could be stored for future security auditing purposes (Wang et al., 2010). The log files should be updated to record all the events in the system. The process of auditing in the cloud environment involves monitoring the recorded actions performed by users in the cloud system which could later be used for security purposes. This process involves analyzing the log files to collect information about user behavior, resource usage, access requests for a particular resource etc. Hence, the process of logging and auditing involves the verification of the authentication and authorization records to ensure the compliance of the IAM procedures with security policies and procedures so that any violation of the security policies is detected. Auditing thus helps to improve the security of the cloud system by recommending the required changes in the IAM implementation strategy adopted in the organization. Hence, auditing requires proper and effective identity management for verifying the entities in the log file.

Figure 4. Risk-based access control

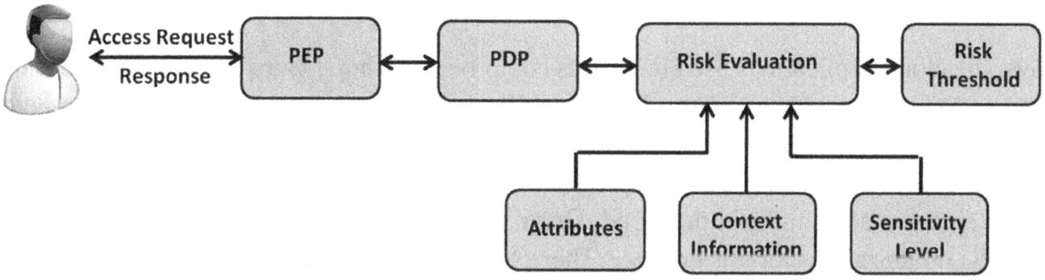

Recommended Practices

1. In the cloud computing domain, the CSPs should use access control languages such as XACML that provides a standardized method of access control and policy enforcement across various applications.
2. Open standards such as SAML could be used for authenticating the cloud users.
3. Wherever required, risk-based authorization to the cloud applications should be implemented in the cloud.
4. Temporal attributes of cloud users, such as the geo-location should undergo real-time attribute checking throughout the transaction, in order to provide effective authorization functions.
5. Logging of authorization decisions or access granted should be performed in a common format for later security analysis. The cloud service providers are requested to keep the log of the details of users' access to various resources in the cloud, and they should produce it for auditing, whenever required.

IDENTITY PROVISIONING AND DE-PROVISIONING

The process of identity provisioning associates digital identities to various users, and the process of identity de-provisioning removes the identities from a user so that the specified identity is no longer valid with that user.

Identity Provisioning and De-provisioning in the Cloud

In the case of Identity Provisioning in the cloud, it associates the user's identity to the applications or the systems, and provides the users with the required access rights to the data or resources maintained in the system. After the identity provisioning, various users can access the resources or services stored in the cloud using the unique user identity. That is, provisioning means in-time or on-demand provisioning of users to the cloud services so that the users can access the required services. In the case of Identity De-provisioning, it deletes or deactivates the identity of a user, or the access rights or privileges assigned to the user identity. Hence, de-provisioning is the real-time de-activation of the user accounts for the cloud services so that the users are no longer able to access them.

Requirements and Challenges in the Cloud

Nowadays, the cloud applications used by clients could be a mashup (Marston et al., 2011) of multiple cloud applications hosted on the same or different CSPs. In this case, how can the users be authenticated for accessing all these cloud applications seamlessly, and also, how can the user's attributes such as group association, access rights, roles are shared across these cloud applications are issues to be solved in the identity and access management in the cloud. Open standards such as SAML, OAuth, XACML could be used by the organizations for this purpose. There should be timely revocation of the user accounts or access rights in the cloud, when the user leaves or moves to another role in an organization with different access rights. The provisioning of user entities in a cloud system requires the understanding of the complete life cycle management of the user account, including its creation, management and the deletion. In cloud computing, user accesses various services from different cloud service providers, and the consumers are really sensitive to the delay involved in service provisioning. Hence dynamic provisioning and de-provisioning of user identities is required. The CSPs should use SPML for user provisioning. CSPs should follow the 'principle of least privilege' when provisioning an account.

Identity Life Cycle Management

Identity Life Cycle Management shows the various stages through which a user identity goes (Mather et al., 2009). That is, it shows how the identity is managed when it is created, used or terminated. The cloud Identity Life Cycle Management is shown in the Figure 5. As shown in the figure, the five stages in the Identity Life Cycle Management include Identity Provisioning, Authentication, Authorization, Self-Service, Password Management, Compliance and Audit, and the identity de-provisioning. The Identity Provisioning and de-provisioning, Authentication and Authorization have been explained in the previous sections.

Self-service

This phase shows how the user can maintain, update or reset his identity credentials. Ensuring self-service in the IAM in the cloud environment helps the users reset their account passwords, maintain and update the user information, and thereby accessing the services without the service provider's interaction.

Credentials Management

This phase of the identity life cycle shows how the user password is stored in the cloud servers. This focuses on various factors such as how the passwords of various cloud users are stored in the cloud database, which is the encryption algorithms used by the CSPs (such as MD5 or SHA1). It also supports the features to facilitate SSO to access the cloud services.

Figure 5. Identity life cycle management

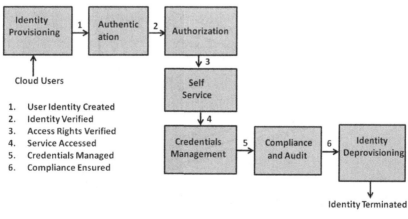

Compliance and Audit

In this phase, users' access to cloud resources will be monitored to ensure that the security requirements of the cloud system are not violated. Periodic auditing and the analysis of the log files maintained by the CSPs will help enforce the required access control policies from time to time.

FEDERATED IDENTITY MANAGEMENT IN THE CLOUD

Federation is an association between multiple entities or organizations that have predefined goals, and standards for operation (Ghazizadeh et al., 2012). Nowadays, a user or an organization may subscribe to services from multiple CSPs. The organization can also integrate the individual services from various cloud service providers and provide the final combined service to its customers. This scenario shows that effective identity management is essential in the cloud computing domain. The current cloud computing paradigm can make use of federated identity management approaches such as Single Sign-On, for authentication of the cloud users. That is, in the cloud, user-centric identity management is preferred over the application-centric approach. The overview of the Identity Federation is shown in the Figure 6.

In the application-centric identity management, each application keeps track of the users using its own specific identity. In this case, if a user uses multiple services offered by more than one service provider, or by the same service provider itself, he has to create multiple accounts to use each application or service with the CSP. In the user-centric identity management (El Maliki & Seigneur, 2007), a user is uniquely identified by the user identifier which could be recognized by more than one CSP. Hence, in the federated identity management, identity of a cloud user is provided by the Identity Provider (IdP), and the same identity could be utilized by the CSPs who trust that IdP. CSP-specific identity credentials are eliminated in this case.

Figure 6. Overview of identity federation

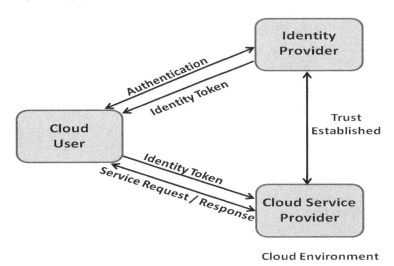

Single Sign-On (SSO)

Single Sign-On (SSO) is a mechanism used for authentication in which a service consumer is required to be authenticated only once while accessing various services from multiple service providers, or when accessing multiple services from the same service provider (Almulla & Yeun, 2010). The process of SSO involves the association between the following entities: Cloud Service Consumer (CSC), Relying Party or Cloud Service Provider (CSP) and the Identity Provider (IdP). The CSP and the IdP have mutual trust established between them. That is, IdP offers Identity Management functions to the CSP. Before accessing the services from the CSP, a Cloud Service Consumer has to get authenticated as a valid user from the IdP. Since the CSP and IdP are part of the association, and they have mutual trust with each other, the user is allowed to access the services from the CSP after successful authentication. Hence, in SSO, the users are able to access multiple services from the same or different CSPs using the identity token issued by the Identity Provider. Because of this association, the service providers can concentrate more on their core services, since the identity management operations are taken care of by the Identity Providers.

Identity Providers (IdPs)

The Identity Providers are trusted entities in the cloud computing environment that provide the identity tokens to the cloud users (Smith, 2008). These tokens could be used by cloud users for availing services from the CSPs. Examples of IdP are Ping Identity, Symplified etc. In the Cloud Computing domain, the IdP accepts the cloud user's credentials such as user ID, password, certificate etc. and returns a signed security token identifying the user. The CSP that has trust established with the IdP uses the identity token in order to allow services or resources to the user. In this case, the service provider has no direct information of the cloud user, but relies on the IdP. Thus, IdPs allow the CSPs to offload the task of identity management to the third parties and help the CSPs concentrate more on their core services.

Identity providers such as Symplified (Symplified, 2015) offers SSO systems which can synchronize and communicate with the Active Directory (AD) maintained in an organization to verify the identity credentials of users who want to log into a cloud application. The cloud customers are to be authenticated by the SSO provider, and it is synchronized with the AD maintained in the organization. This gives the organization the required flexibility to decide which of their accounts are used to access the cloud applications. When the user accounts in the AD are deactivated, no users will be able to utilize that account to access the cloud application. Federated Identity Management thus reduces the complexity of the authentication process for the cloud users by employing SSO. Similarly, Sun Microsystems' Open SSO (Oracle, 2015) externalizes the authentication and the authorization components from the applications. Various CSPs such as Salesforce.com, Google, Microsoft etc. support standards such as SAML that facilitates SSO using identity federation.

Types of Identity Federation

There are two types of identity federation possible for an organization in a cloud environment, depending on the implementation of the IdP in the domain (Radha & Reddy, 2012).

1. Enterprise IdP within the Security Perimeter of the Organization
   In this case, the IdP is maintained in the organization that subscribes to the cloud services. The various CSPs establish trust relationships with this IdP in delivering services to the cloud consumers. In this case, more control in the authentication, authorization and the policy management is achieved as it is managed internally to the organization.
2. Trusted Cloud-Based Identity Management Services
   In this case, for identity management purposes, cloud-based identity service providers are used. They are also known as Cloud Identity-as-a-service (IDaaS) providers. This concept is explained in the next section.

The Impact of Trust in the Federated Identity Management

Trust of an entity shows the level of confidence or reliance such that the entity would behave exactly as promised (Khan & Malluhi, 2010). In a multi-domain environment like cloud computing, the trust needs to be established between the cloud service provider and service consumers, and also between the providers of various services and the identity providers. Trust in the cloud computing domain is dynamic, and the trust value of the entities such as cloud users, CSPs or Identity Providers need to be calculated by considering various parameters such as the past behavior of the entities and also recommendations from other Trusted Third Parties (TTPs) in the system. Effective trust management in the cloud environment is still an issue which requires further research.

Identity Management Standards and Protocols

There are several standards and protocols which can be used for the identity management in the cloud environments. The various identity management protocols differ in their features such as the data format supported, protocols to exchange credentials between the entities involved etc. Some of the well-known identity management protocols which help in establishing a federation among the individual partners are given below. An organization can use the following IAM standards or specifications to implement efficient IAM mechanisms in the cloud environment. Since the different identity management protocols have non-similar features, the selection of a particular protocol depends on the requirements of the applications and also their architectural features.

1. Security Assertion Markup Language (SAML)
   The SAML (Cantor et al., 2005) includes a set of specifications for exchanging the authentication, authorization and attribute assertions across the federation. SAML uses XML-based data format and this protocol is managed under the Organization for the Advancement of Structured Information Standards (OASIS). The various use cases of SAML include SSO in the federation, identity/account linkage, session management and secure web services. Three releases of SAML namely SAML 1.0, SAML 1.1 and SAML 2.0 are available.
2. Service Provisioning Markup Language (SPML)
   This is an XML-based security framework developed by OASIS, and it could be used to exchange information related to the users, resources and service provisioning within a group of cooperating organizations (Standard, 2003). This helps in automating the provisioning and de-provisioning of user accounts with the CSP.

3. eXtensible Access Control Markup Language (XACML)

    In order to implement an access control mechanism, this XML-based access control language developed by OASIS could be used (Godik et al., 2002). This language provides the XML-schema which could be used to protect the resources by making access decisions over these resources.

4. Shibboleth

    Shibboleth (Cantor & SCAVO, 2005) is an open source Identity Management project and is based upon SAML. This protocol helps to establish SSO solutions in the federation. Shibboleth uses the SAML specifications to achieve the authentication and authorization in the federated environment. Shibboleth provides federated identity management, and it involves the two main components such as the Service Provider (SP) and the IdP. In line with their privacy policies, IdP can decide the SPs that are allowed to access the users' authentication data.

5. OpenID

    OpenID (Recordon & Reed, 2006) provides a user-centric identity framework for the authentication purposes. OpenID 2.0 supports the identification of users through URL or XRI addresses. OpenID uses the concept of Relying Party (RP) and OpenID providers. Users' authentication data are stored by the OpenID provider, and the user has the flexibility to decide who have access to his authentication data maintained by the OpenID provider. In the OpenID mechanism, a user is associated with one primary user-id which could be used to authenticate the user against various CSPs.

6. OAuth

    OAuth (Hardt, 2012) is an open source Identity Management protocol that could be used to provide the authorization of users across different applications without disclosing the user's identity credentials. Identity tokens, issued by the identity provider, are used by the third party applications to gain access to the user's protected data.

7. OpenID Connect

    OpenID Connect (Sakimura et al., 2011) is an open source Identity Management protocol, which could be used to provide standardized authentication and authorization functions across federated applications. OpenID Connect combines the authentication and authorization processes of OpenID and OAuth. OpenID Connect protocol uses OpenID 2.0 and OAuth 2.0, and provides APIs to be used by the third party applications.

8. WS-Federation

    WS-Federation (Goodner & Nadalin, 2009) is a part of the web services security specifications, and is meant for the federation of applications or web services. WS-Federation specifications are extensions to WS-Trust protocol. This protocol can be used to share the identity information of various users across multiple security domains and organizations. WS-* suite of protocols are developed in a collaborative effort by Microsoft, IBM, VeriSign, RSA Security and Ping Identity. It includes WS-Trust, WS-Security, WS-Federation and WS-Policy, and used for authentication, authorization and policy management in multiple security domains. In order to manage and exchange the security or identity tokens across various applications, WS-Federation uses the Security Token Service (STS), as used by the WS-Trust protocol specifications.

Recommended Practices

1. In the cloud computing paradigm, the implementers of the federation are required to understand the trust relationship between the various entities such as CSPs, Cloud users and Identity Providers

involved in the federation, as bidirectional trust relationship is needed in the cloud federation for its successful implementation.

2. The cloud customers have the responsibility to check and verify the support extended by a CSP for IAM features such as SSO using identity federation. The cloud customers should select those CSPs who incorporate the latest security mechanisms, for availing the required services.

3. In the cloud computing domain, the customers should understand the federation protocols supported by the CSPs and the integration requirements for using multiple cloud services.

4. The CSPs should offer standard APIs such as OAuth for the management of authentication and authorization to various applications deployed on the cloud platform.

5. Organizations can rely on the identity federation products such as Sun's Open SSO, Oracle's Federation Manager (Oracle, 2015) and CA's federation Manager (CA, 2015) which could integrate with the directory services maintained in the organization such as LDAP or AD to enable the SSO feature for using various cloud services.

6. The CSPs implementing federation should use open standards such as SAML and OAuth.

7. The identity standards and the protocols used by a CSP and an IdP should be compatible in such a way that the CSP is interoperable with the third party IdP.

8. The usage of SAML and XACML protocols are recommended by the NIST (National Institute of Standards and Technology) (Linstrom & Mallard, 2003) for authentication and authorization purposes between any two cooperating environments such as cloud domains.

CLOUD IDENTITY-AS-A-SERVICE

Cloud Identity-as-a-Service (IDaaS) is an emerging cloud service delivery model where the management of user identities is performed outside the applications of the cloud service providers (Kumaraswamy et al., 2010; Mather et al., 2009). This is another type of service offered by the cloud domain wherein various identity and access management functions such as identity life cycle management and single sign-on etc. are provided by the specialized CSPs. Also, this SaaS model for identity management offers services such as user account provisioning and de-provisioning, account auditing, password management and user self services. By using this service model, an organization can automate the user account provisioning and auditing by offloading the activities to the third party CSP. The SaaS IdP stores the user identities in a trusted identity store, and acts as a proxy for the user's access to the cloud services. Various CSPs will find it attractive to use the services offered by the IDaaS provider, as it would help the CSPs offer quality services without being worried about the identity management functionalities.

The overview of the Cloud IDaaS model is shown in the Figure 7. As shown in the figure, in this service delivery model, the identity management functions offered by the Cloud Identity Service providers (IDaaS) are used by various clients such as cloud users and organizations. When these clients interact with heterogeneous CSPs, the IDaaS provider acts as a Multi-Protocol Federation Gateway offering the interoperability between various CSPs. In the case of IDaaS, an organization can also follow the hybrid approach where the user identities are managed internally within the organization, and other functionalities such as authentication are implemented using a Service Oriented Architecture (SOA) offered by the IDaaS service provider. Thus, using this model, an organization can outsource the identity management requirements of various cloud users to a third-party service provider, such as Ping Identity, TriCipher (TriCipher, 2015), or Symplified. IDaaS offers easier management of user identities

Figure 7. Cloud identity-as-a-service (IDaaS)

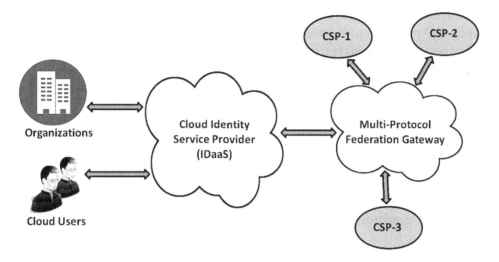

with a wide range of integration options. (Rimal et al., 2009; Subashini & Kavitha, 2011). Even though this service model offers various advantages to the cloud users, this identity and access management model has several challenges also associated with its implementation. Outsourcing any part of identity management functions to third-party IDaaS provider introduces several security and privacy challenges related to the user's Personally Identifiable Information (PII).

Advantages of IDaaS

In case an organization does not have strong IAM practices, or if it doesn't have a federated architecture, it can make use of Identity management-as-a-service (IDaaS) for cooperating with different partners and cloud service federation schemes. In this case, the CSPs can delegate the authentication of the cloud users to an IDaaS provider. Hence, the CSPs can concentrate more on their core services rather than identity management functions, thereby improving the efficiency and productivity of the CSPs. It also supports federation gateways for the integration of multiple IAM protocols. That means, this model helps an organization to use the services from different CSPs supporting different identity federation standards, by utilizing the federation gateways offered by the cloud identity providers. Thus, a federation gateway reduces the complexity of integrating with multiple CSPs supporting different federation standards. If an organization outsources the identity management functionalities to a third party CSP, it would help the organization in using multiple services from different CSPs, each using different protocols such as SAML, OAuth for the identity management. Another benefit of using this service model is that the architectural changes required for an organization to use this model are comparatively less, as the users can sign on to the cloud services using their corporate identities, after the identity synchronization between the organization directory and the identity service directory in the cloud.

Federation Gateways

Federation Gateways (Kumaraswamy et al., 2010) are used in the federated identity management scenario to translate the identity tokens of cloud users from one format to another. Using this approach, organizations using different cloud services can achieve the required identity translation while accessing services from different cloud providers. If an organization has to interfere with more than one CSP each supporting different federation standards and procedures, it can benefit from the multi-protocol federation gateways. Organizations can set up the federation gateway either in their internal network, or it can be the part of various cloud identity-as-a-service providers. There are different IAM standards with different maturity levels, and their adoption rates by the CSPs in the cloud computing domain are also different. Assume that an organization accesses service-1 from CSP-1 and service-2 from CSP-2. Also, assume that CSP-1 supports, say SAML 1.1 for identity management functions, and CSP-2 supports, say SAML 2.0 for identity management functions. In this case, the organization can use the multi-protocol federation gateways hosted by the identity providers such as Symplified or TriCipher. Multi-protocol federation gateways support both the standards, and hide the integration complexity from a cloud user adopting multiple services. Thus, these gateways provide federation among various cloud services supporting different IAM standards or protocols.

Challenges for Deployment

In this model, since an organization depends on a third party cloud service for identity management functionalities, it has little knowledge in the implementation and architecture details adopted by the identity service provider. Hence the organization has to rely on the SLA agreed by the identity service provider as far as the identity management functionalities of the users are considered. Hence, the performance and availability aspects of the IDaaS provider depend on the SLA, and also on the trust level shared between the CSP and the IdP. Thus, trust between the IdP and the cloud users and also between the IdP and the CSP is an important factor for the successful deployment of this service.

INTER-CLOUD IDENTITY MANAGEMENT

Inter-cloud is the federation of Cloud Providers (Celesti et al., 2010a). In the standard Cloud Computing model, a client gets the required service from a single Cloud Service Provider or data centre, and this approach introduces several challenges. Due to some reasons, if the CSP cannot handle the service requests initiated from the cloud customers, it can leave thousands of customers who depend solely on that Service Provider, without access to the required resources. Also, this approach of depending on a single cloud data centre makes it difficult to ensure adequate responsiveness and Quality of Service (QoS) to the clients. Thus, the motivating factors for the adoption of Inter-Cloud computing paradigm are the enhanced collaboration between the various Cloud Service Providers and the improved QoS delivered to the cloud consumers. Practically, the resources of a CSP are finite, and hence a CSP form the federation or inter-cloud environment with other CSPs where they cooperate with each other in delivering better QoS and achieve economy of scale. Inter-cloud is formed with the purpose of enlarging the computing and storage capacities of individual CSPs. Identity and Access Management of cloud users is an important activity in the inter-cloud environment.

Need for IAM in the Inter-Cloud

In the inter-cloud model, a CSP in the federation can use resources from another CSP in the federation. This collaboration ensures the support in terms of information and resource sharing among the partners in the inter-cloud environment ensuring better QoS. The QoS includes factors such as availability, reliability and response time of the services delivered by various cloud service providers. In the inter-cloud environment, the identity management systems should uniquely identify the inter-cloud users, and also various resources associated with different partner clouds of the cloud federation should be uniquely named and identified. In the cloud computing, the cloud deployments are dynamic with servers launched or terminated run-time. Hence, in the cloud domain, whenever a service or a machine is decommissioned, the information regarding this should be communicated to the IAM module so that future access to it are revoked or managed properly. Another issue in the cloud federation is how the authentication of cloud users could be performed among the heterogeneous inter-cloud partners in the cloud federation. Generally, the authentication and the identity management mechanisms adopted by each CSP may be different from that of the other clouds. Hence, the identity management technology and protocols should be interoperable in the inter-cloud environment. The inter-cloud environment is required to have proper Identity and Access Management mechanism to deal with the access requests of various cloud customers.

Federated Identity Management in the Inter-Cloud

One of the significant reasons for the widespread adoption and popularity of Cloud Computing paradigm is its ability to provide rapid elasticity and on-demand provisioning of computing, storage and network resources. Even though the cloud computing paradigm promises to offer infinite resources, in reality, the resources with each and every Cloud Service Provider are finite. When a CSP runs out of resources, it can get the required services from partners in the cloud federation or the inter-cloud. This scenario indicates that proper identity and access management is essential in the cloud federation. The current inter-cloud computing domain can make use of federated identity management approaches such as Single Sign-On, for authentication of the cloud users in the federation. The overall view of the SSO in Cloud Federation is shown in the Figure 8. The users in a cloud federation don't need to use separate credentials for each cloud service provider or service they subscribe to; instead, they can have the identity issued by the Identity Provider (Ping Identity, Symplified etc.). They can submit the security tokens (normally SAML assertions) issued by the identity provider, to the Service Providers in the cloud federation. This approach is both efficient and secure, and relieves the users of the multiple credentials problem when accessing services from multiple cloud service providers in the federation.

Thus, in the SSO mechanism in Cloud Federation, a user needs to verify his credentials and get authenticated himself only once during an active session of accessing the cloud services. The cloud users are benefitted in such a way that they will be able to access all the related services that are offered by a single CSP or multiple CSPs in the federation seamlessly, without the need to provide the identity credentials again and again for accessing different services. It also helps in increasing the productivity of the users as well as the developers by reducing the number of times a user must login, also reducing the number of credentials one has to remember.

Figure 8. Single Sign-On (SSO) in cloud federation

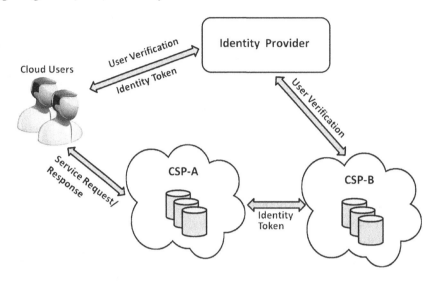

Workflow Model of the Single Sign-On Approach

The sequence of steps involved in the workflow of the implementation of SSO in the Cloud Federation is shown in the Figure 9.

In this figure, the authors have shown only two CSPs in the Cloud Federation. As shown in the figure, the various steps involved are:

Step 1: The Cloud User wants to access the service hosted by the CSP-1, and submits the identity credentials to the CSP-1.
Step 2: The CSP-1 contacts the associated Identity Provider (IdP) for the authentication of the user.

Figure 9. Workflow model of the Single Sign-On approach

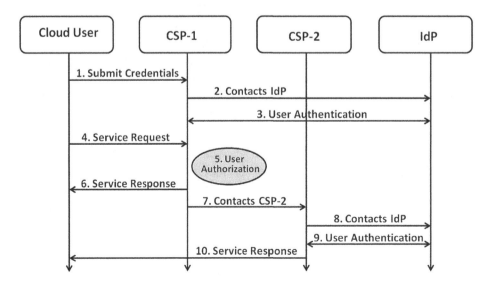

Step 3: The CSP-1 gets the result of user verification from the IdP.

Step 4: The user submits the service request for accessing the resources from the CSP-1.

Step 5: User authorization is performed by the CSP-1 to decide whether to accept or reject the request.

Step 6: The local resources (if available at the CSP-1) are allocated to the user.

Step 7: The CSP-1 contacts the other CSP(s) in the federation (CSP-2), if the local resources are not sufficient to satisfy the user's request.

Challenges for the Identity Management in the Inter-Cloud

The challenges for developing an effective Identity and Access Management mechanism in the inter-cloud environment can be broadly categorized as follows (Núñez et al., 2011; Dreo et al., 2013)

1. Naming and Identification of the Inter-Cloud Resources
    All the resources (servers, storage systems, processors, virtual machines, applications) present in the inter-cloud environment could be considered as potential resources. Hence, the identity of each of these resources should be properly established in the inter-cloud so that the resources could be distinguished one from the other in a particular context.

2. Interoperability of Identity Information in the Inter-Cloud
    The standards, protocols, formats and attributes used by the inter-cloud partners in the identity management should be such that they are interoperable with each other. Also, the identity management system used in the inter-cloud should be interoperable with the identity management systems in the organization or the individual CSP, in order to enable the CSP to join the inter-cloud or cloud federation, and deliver the services effectively.

3. Identity Life Cycle Management in the Inter-Cloud
    In the life cycle of the identity of a cloud user, some changes could happen in its attribute values, authorization decisions or access rights from time to time depending on the policy of the CSP. Hence, whenever there is a change in the identity information of a cloud user, there should be proper synchronization among the inter-cloud partners so that the inter-cloud resources are protected from malicious access. The synchronization should be done in-time as any delay would cause security vulnerabilities.

4. Single Sign-On for interactions in the Inter-Cloud
    The federated identity management in the inter-cloud should support SSO in such a way that the users are allowed to access the resources and services offered by the inter-cloud partners, after the verification of their identities by the IdPs in the inter-cloud. That means, users are not required to be authenticated at individual CSPs if they are authenticated by a CSP where they make the initial access request.

5. Exchange of Identity Information
    In the Inter-Cloud environments, multiple Identity Providers and Service Providers can be present. Hence, the extent of information about users, apps/devices etc. that need to be exchanged among the different service domain, is an issue to be solved as far as protecting the privacy of the cloud users is concerned. Also, the development of an interoperable data format and the protocols used for exchanging the information is another concern in the inter-cloud environment.

6. Dynamic Extensibility

   In the Inter-Cloud environment, new Cloud services may be added from time to time. How can the existing IAM systems be dynamically extended with the new cloud services is an issue to be solved. Also, how the trustworthiness of such services will be verified by the existing users is also a concern to be addressed.

An efficient IAM system in the Inter-Cloud environments should support the various identity standards such as X.509 certificates, SAML, and WS-Federation (Bernstein & Vij, 2010b). Inter-Cloud environment should support XACML-compliant access management mechanisms (Bernstein & Vij, 2010b) as it offers a standardized language for access control and policy enforcement. Scalability is another issue to be considered for Identity management in the inter-cloud environments.

FUTURE RESEARCH DIRECTIONS

Based on the discussion carried out, it is seen that IAM is an important issue and surely there are many aspects which require further research and proper solution. Effective trust management in the cloud environment is still an issue which requires further research. It is necessary to have further research in the establishment of a dynamic trust relationship between user domains and cloud domains, and between various cloud domains and the identity providers to have a proper solution for the identity management. Single Sign-On mechanism implemented in the cloud environment should address the security issues such as impersonation of a user, impersonation of a Service Provider etc. during the authentication process. Also, it should be resistant against various attacks such as Man-in-the-Middle attacks, replay attacks, phishing attacks etc. The identity federation mechanism adopted in the cloud environment should support multiple identity providers, and hence the interoperability between various entities in the identity federation is an issue which requires effective solutions. In the case of cloud mashups, how can the users be authenticated for accessing all the cloud applications integrated in the mashups seamlessly, and also, how can the user's attributes such as group association, access rights, roles are shared effectively across these cloud applications are issues to be solved in the identity and access management in the cloud.

In the inter-cloud environment, the identity management systems should uniquely identify the inter-cloud users, and also various resources associated with different partner clouds of the cloud federation should be uniquely named and identified. Another issue in the cloud federation is how the authentication of cloud users could be performed among the heterogeneous inter-cloud partners in the cloud federation. Generally, the authentication and the identity management mechanisms adopted by each CSP could be different from that of the other clouds. Hence, the identity management technology and protocols adopted by the partner clouds should be interoperable in the inter-cloud environment. Hence, it is clear that the issue of identity and access management in the cloud computing domain has enormous potential for further active research, in order to make the cloud computing paradigm secure, reliable and scalable.

CONCLUSION

In this chapter, the authors have discussed the issue of Identity and Access Management (IAM) in the cloud and inter-cloud environments. The analysis of the work done by the researchers in this area is carried out. The important features and functionalities of IAM are discussed. The various issues in the identity and access management in cloud computing, such as access control models, identity life cycle management, federated identity management, Single Sign-On (SSO) and cloud identity-as-a-service are discussed. The emerging area of inter-cloud domain is discussed and the importance of an effective identity management in that domain is highlighted. Also, some of the future research directions in IAM in the cloud and inter-cloud domains are also highlighted.

REFERENCES

Almulla, S. A., & Yeun, C. Y. (2010, March). Cloud computing security management. *Proceedings of the 2010 Second International Conference on Engineering Systems Management and Its Applications (ICESMA)* (pp. 1-7). IEEE.

Amazon Web Services-Identity and Access Management. (2015). Retrieved from http://aws.amazon.com/iam

Amazon Web Services-Multi Factor Authentication. (2015). Retrieved from http://aws.amazon.com/mfa

Microsoft Azure. (2015). Retrieved from http://azure.microsoft.com/en- in/documentation/infographics/cloud-identity-and-access/

Bernstein, D., & Vij, D. (2010a, July). Intercloud directory and exchange protocol detail using XMPP and RDF. *Proceedings of the 2010 6th World Congress on Services (SERVICES-1)* (pp. 431-438). IEEE.

Bernstein, D., & Vij, D. (2010b, November). Intercloud security considerations. *Proceedings of the 2010 IEEE Second International Conference onCloud Computing Technology and Science (CloudCom)* (pp. 537-544). IEEE. doi:10.1109/CloudCom.2010.82

CA's Federation Manager. (2015). Retrieved from http://www.ca.com/in/securecenter/ca-federation.aspx

Cantor, S., & SCAVO, T. (2005). Shibboleth architecture. *Protocols and Profiles*, 10.

Cantor, S., Kemp, I. J., Philpott, N. R., & Maler, E. (2005, March). Assertions and protocols for the oasis security assertion markup language. *OASIS Standard*.

Celesti, A., Tusa, F., Villari, M., & Puliafito, A. (2010a, July). How to enhance cloud architectures to enable cross-federation. *Proceedings of the 2010 IEEE 3rd International Conference on Cloud Computing (CLOUD)* (pp. 337-345). IEEE. doi:10.1109/CLOUD.2010.46

Celesti, A., Tusa, F., Villari, M., & Puliafito, A. (2010b, July). Three-phase cross-cloud federation model: The cloud sso authentication. *Proceedings of the 2010 Second International Conference on Advances in Future Internet (AFIN)* (pp. 94-101). IEEE.

Celesti, A., Tusa, F., Villari, M., & Puliafito, A. (2011). Federation establishment between clever clouds through a saml sso authentication profile. *International Journal on Advances in Internet Technology*, 4(1 & 2), 14-27.

Chan, C. K., & Cheng, L. M. (2000). Cryptanalysis of a remote user authentication scheme using smart cards. *IEEE Transactions on* Consumer Electronics, *46*(4), 992–993.

Dreo, G., Golling, M., Hommel, W., & Tietze, F. (2013, May). ICEMAN: An architecture for secure federated inter-cloud identity management. *Proceedings of the 2013 IFIP/IEEE International Symposium onIntegrated Network Management (IM 2013)* (pp. 1207-1210). IEEE.

El Maliki, T., & Seigneur, J. M. (2007, October). A survey of user-centric identity management technologies. *Proceedings of the International Conference on Emerging Security Information, Systems, and Technologies SecureWare '07* (pp. 12-17). IEEE. doi:10.1109/SECUREWARE.2007.4385303

Feng, F., Lin, C., Peng, D., & Li, J. (2008, September). A trust and context based access control model for distributed systems. *Proceedings of the 10th IEEE International Conference on High Performance Computing and Communications HPCC '08* (pp. 629-634). IEEE. doi:10.1109/HPCC.2008.37

Ferraiolo, D. F., Sandhu, R., Gavrila, S., Kuhn, D. R., & Chandramouli, R. (2001). Proposed NIST standard for role-based access control. *ACM Transactions on Information and System Security, 4*(3), 224–274. doi:10.1145/501978.501980

Fugkeaw, S., Manpanpanich, P., & Juntapremjitt, S. (2007, April). A robust single sign-on model based on multi-agent system and PKI. *Proceedings of the Sixth International Conference on Networking ICN '07.* (pp. 101-101). IEEE. doi:10.1109/ICN.2007.10

Ghazizadeh, E., & Zamani, M. Jamalul-lail Ab Manan, & Pashang, A. (2012, December). A survey on security issues of federated identity in the cloud computing. In CloudCom (pp. 532-565).

Godik, S., Anderson, A., Parducci, B., Humenn, P., & Vajjhala, S. (2002). *OASIS eXtensible access control 2 markup language (XACML) 3. Tech. rep.* OASIS.

Goodner, M., & Nadalin, T. (2009). Web Services Federation Language (WS-Federation) Version 1.2. OASIS Web Services Federation (WSFED) TC.

I am Google Cloud. (2015). Retrieved from https://cloud.google.com/iam/

Gunjan, K., Sahoo, G., & Tiwari, R. K. (2012, June). Identity management in cloud computing–a review. International Journal of Engineering Research and Technology, 1(4).

Hardt, D. (2012). *The OAuth 2.0 Authorization Framework.*

Hovav, A., & Berger, R. (2009). Tutorial: Identity management systems and secured access control. *Communications of the Association for Information Systems, 25*(1), 42.

Hu, V. C., Ferraiolo, D., & Kuhn, D. R. (2006). *Assessment of access control systems.* US Department of Commerce, National Institute of Standards and Technology.

Khan, K. M., & Malluhi, Q. (2010). Establishing trust in cloud computing. *IT Professional, 12*(5), 20–27. doi:10.1109/MITP.2010.128

King, N. J., & Raja, V. T. (2012). Protecting the privacy and security of sensitive customer data in the cloud. *Computer Law & Security Report, 28*(3), 308–319. doi:10.1016/j.clsr.2012.03.003

Kumar, R., Gupta, N., Charu, S., Jain, K., & Jangir, S. K. (2014). Open Source Solution for Cloud Computing Platform Using OpenStack. *International Journal of Computer Science and Mobile Computing, 3*(5), 89–98.

Kumar, S., & Cohen, P. R. (2000, June). Towards a fault-tolerant multi-agent system architecture. *Proceedings of the fourth international conference on Autonomous agents* (pp. 459-466). ACM. doi:10.1145/336595.337570

Kumaraswamy, S., Lakshminarayanan, S., Stein, M. R. J., & Wilson, Y. (2010). Domain 12: Guidance for identity & access management v2. 1. Cloud Security Alliance. Retrieved from http://www.cloudsecurityalliance.org/guidance/csaguide-dom12-v2,10

Lang, B., Wang, Z., & Wang, Q. (2007, July). Trust representation and reasoning for access control in large scale distributed systems. *Proceedings of the 2nd International Conference on Pervasive Computing and Applications ICPCA '07* (pp. 436-441). IEEE. doi:10.1109/ICPCA.2007.4365483

Lee, C. C., Li, L. H., & Hwang, M. S. (2002). A remote user authentication scheme using hash functions. *Operating Systems Review, 36*(4), 23–29. doi:10.1145/583800.583803

Linstrom, P. J., & Mallard, W. G. (2003, March). National Institute of Standards and Technology: Gaithersburg. MD, USA.

Marston, S., Li, Z., Bandyopadhyay, S., Zhang, J., & Ghalsasi, A. (2011). Cloud computing—The business perspective. *Decision Support Systems, 51*(1), 176–189. doi:10.1016/j.dss.2010.12.006

Mather, T., Kumaraswamy, S., & Latif, S. (2009). *Cloud security and privacy: an enterprise perspective on risks and compliance.* O'Reilly.

Microsoft Active Directory. (2009). Retrieved from http://www.microsoft.com/windowsserver2003/technologies/directory/activedirectory/default.mspx

Microsoft Identity Manager. (2015). Retrieved from http://www.microsoft.com/en-in/server-cloud/products/microsoft-identity-manager/

Núñez, D., Agudo, I., Drogkaris, P., & Gritzalis, S. (2011). Identity management challenges for intercloud applications. In Secure and Trust Computing, Data Management, and Applications (pp. 198-204). Springer Berlin Heidelberg.

Oracle: SunOpenSSO Enterprise 8.0 TechnicalOverview. (2015). Retrieved from http://docs.sun.com/doc/820-3740

Oracle's Federation Manager. (2015). Retrieved from http://www.oracle.com/identity

Padhy, R. P., Patra, M. R., & Satapathy, S. C. (2012). Design and implementation of a cloud based rural healthcare information system model.[VPN tunneling]. *Univers J Appl Comput Sci Technol, 2*(1), 149–157.

Radha, V., & Reddy, D. H. (2012). A Survey on single sign-on techniques. *Procedia Technology, 4*, 134–139. doi:10.1016/j.protcy.2012.05.019

Recordon, D., & Reed, D. (2006, November). OpenID 2.0: a platform for user-centric identity management. *Proceedings of the second ACM workshop on Digital identity management* (pp. 11-16). ACM.

Ren, X., & Wu, X. W. (2012, October). A novel dynamic user authentication scheme. *Proceedings of the 2012 International Symposium on Communications and Information Technologies (ISCIT)* (pp. 713-717). IEEE.

Rhoton, J. Discover OpenStack: the identity component keystone. Retrieved from http://www.ibm.com/developerworks/cloud/library/cl-openstack-keystone/

Rimal, B. P., Choi, E., & Lumb, I. (2009, August). A taxonomy and survey of cloud computing systems. Proceedings of the Fifth International Joint Conference on INC, IMS and IDC, NCM '09 (pp. 44-51). IEEE. (2013). doi:10.1109/NCM.2009.218

Sakimura, D. N., Bradley, J., Jones, M., de Medeiros, B., & Jay, E. (2011). OpenID Connect Standard 1.0-draft 20.

Security guidance for critical areas of focus in cloud computing v3. 0. (2011). Cloud Security Alliance.

Smith, D. (2008). The challenge of federated identity management. *Network Security, 2008*(4), 7–9. doi:10.1016/S1353-4858(08)70051-5

Sood, S. K. (2012). A combined approach to ensure data security in cloud computing. *Journal of Network and Computer Applications, 35*(6), 1831–1838. doi:10.1016/j.jnca.2012.07.007

OASIS Standard. (2003). Service Provisioning Markup Language (SPML) Version 1

Stihler, M., Santin, A. O., Marcon, A. L., & Fraga, J. S. (2012, May). Integral federated identity management for cloud computing. *Proceedings of the 2012 5th International Conference on New Technologies, Mobility and Security (NTMS)* (pp. 1-5). IEEE. doi:10.1109/NTMS.2012.6208751

Subashini, S., & Kavitha, V. (2011). A survey on security issues in service delivery models of cloud computing. *Journal of Network and Computer Applications, 34*(1), 1–11. doi:10.1016/j.jnca.2010.07.006

Suhendra, V. (2011). A survey on access control deployment. In *Security Technology* (pp. 11–20). Springer Berlin Heidelberg. doi:10.1007/978-3-642-27189-2_2

Symplified. (2015). Retrieved from http://www.symplified.com-Symplified

TriCipher. (2015). Retrieved from http://www.tricipher.com

Tusa, F., Celesti, A., Paone, M., Villari, M., & Puliafito, A. (2011, June). How clever-based clouds conceive horizontal and vertical federations. *Proceedings of the 2011 IEEE Symposium on Computers and Communications (ISCC)* (pp. 167-172). IEEE. doi:10.1109/ISCC.2011.5984011

Wahl, M., Howes, T., & Kille, S. (1997). Lightweight directory access protocol (v3).

Wang, C., Wang, Q., Ren, K., & Lou, W. (2010, March). Privacy-preserving public auditing for data storage security in cloud computing. Proceedings of the '10 INFOCOM '10 (pp. 1-9). IEEE. doi:10.1109/INFCOM.2010.5462173

Wang, G., Yu, J., & Xie, Q. (2013). Security analysis of a single sign-on mechanism for distributed computer networks.. *IEEE Transactions on* Industrial Informatics, *9*(1), 294–302.

Wang, J., Li, D., Li, Q., & Xi, B. (2007, September). Constructing Role-Based Access Control and Delegation Based on Hierarchical IBS. *Proceedings of the NPC Workshops IFIP International Conference on Network and Parallel Computing Workshops*. (pp. 112-118). IEEE. doi:10.1109/NPC.2007.106

Wei, Y., Shi, C., & Shao, W. (2010, May). An attribute and role based access control model for service-oriented environment. *Proceedings of the 2010 Chinese Control and Decision Conference* (CCDC) (pp. 4451-4455). IEEE.

Yan, L., Rong, C., & Zhao, G. (2009). Strengthen cloud computing security with federal identity management using hierarchical identity-based cryptography. In *Cloud Computing* (pp. 167–177). Springer Berlin Heidelberg. doi:10.1007/978-3-642-10665-1_15

KEY TERMS AND DEFINITIONS

Access Control Model: Access control models describe what security properties are associated with an access control system. They bridge the gap between an access control policy and the corresponding mechanism, and help to discuss and analyze any theoretical limitations of a particular system in ensuring the required access control.

Authentication: Authentication is the process of verifying the identity of an entity in a system. It verifies that the entity is really who it claims to be.

Authorization: Authorization is the process by which the access rights or privileges of an entity are verified by the system against predefined security policies. Normally, authorization process follows the authentication step and it is required to avoid unauthorized access of resources by malicious users.

Federation Gateway: Federation Gateways are used in the federated identity management scenario to translate the identity tokens of cloud users from one format to another. Using this approach, organizations using different cloud services can achieve the required identity translation while accessing services from different cloud providers.

Identity Federation: In the Identity Federation scenario, there is an association between CSPs and IdPs in such a way that the identity tokes issued by the IdP are used by the CSPs to deliver the requested services to the cloud users.

Identity Life Cycle Management: Identity Life Cycle Management shows the various stages through which a user identity goes through. That is, it shows how the identity is managed when it is created, used or terminated.

Identity Provider: The Identity Providers (IdPs) are trusted entities in the cloud computing environment that provides the identity tokens to the cloud users. These tokens could be used by the CSPs for delivering the requested services to cloud users.

Single Sign-On: Single Sign-On (SSO) is a mechanism used for authentication in which a service consumer is required to be authenticated only once while accessing various services from multiple service providers, or when accessing multiple services from the same service provider. The process of SSO involves Identity Federation, and it helps the users to access multiple services from the same or different CSPs using the identity tokens issued by the Identity Provider.

This work was previously published in Developing Interoperable and Federated Cloud Architecture edited by Gabor Kecskemeti, Attila Kertesz, and Zsolt Nemeth, pages 61-90, copyright 2016 by Information Science Reference (an imprint of IGI Global).

Chapter 4
A Routine Activity Theory–Based Framework for Combating Cybercrime

Dillon Glasser
The Richard Stockton College of New Jersey, USA

Aakash Taneja
The Richard Stockton College of New Jersey, USA

ABSTRACT

Since the government began tackling the problems of cybercrime, many laws have been enacted. A lack of a comprehensive definition and taxonomy of cybercrime makes it difficult to accurately identify report and monitor cybercrime trends. There is not just a lack of international agreement on what cybercrime is; there are different laws in every state within the United States, reflecting the inconsistency of dealing with cybercrime. There is also concern that many times lawyers and information technology professions are unable to understand each other well. The deficiency of cyber laws is an obvious problem and development of effective laws is emerging as an important issue to deal with cybercrime. This research uses the routine activity theory to develop a unified framework by including the motivation of the offender to use a computer as a tool/target, suitability of the target, and the presence (or absence) of guardian. It could help states that want to update their existing laws and cover areas that were previously uncovered.

INTRODUCTION

Originally the Internet was considered the Wild West, but legislators and law enforcement have made significant strides in tackling cybercrime. However, cybercrime has changed in recent years due to the growth of new phenomena in internet environments, such as peer to peer networks, social networks, organized cybercrime groups, and powerful new "smart" viruses (Berg, 2007). Cybercrime has "historically referred to crimes happening specifically over networks, especially the Internet, but that term has gradually become a general synonym for computer crime." (Alkaabi, 2011). Cybercrime is different from other crimes because of the way it changes rapidly along with the technology that it uses or abuses.

DOI: 10.4018/978-1-5225-0808-3.ch004

Cybercriminals today are becoming more sophisticated and organized. They are now using botnets to accomplish crimes such as spamming and denial of service attacks. Technology and cybercrime are moving targets and there should be concern that the slow nature of our government may not be keeping pace. It is therefore not a surprise that old laws are being applied to new age crime. For example, Indiana has no laws pertaining to fraud or theft using a computer. Unfortunately, Indiana is not the only state that is lacking in cyber laws. It has been hard in the past to come to an agreement on what exactly constitutes cybercrime. As lack of a comprehensive definition and taxonomy of cybercrime makes it difficult to accurately identify report and monitor cybercrime trends. The deficiency of cyber laws is an obvious problem and development of effective laws is emerging as an important issue to deal with and combat cybercrime.

According to the routine activity theory, three specific criteria must exist for a crime to take place. There must be a motivated offender, a suitable target, and the absence of a capable guardian. The objective of this research is to use routine activity theory by including the suitability of target and motivation behind cybercrime for creating a unified framework which can be used to develop capable guardians (appropriate laws and policies) to effectively coordinate cybercrime regulation and legislation.

The rest of the paper is organized as follows. Section 2 of the paper describes the background in the areas of cybercrime, federal and state laws related to cybercrime. Section 3 discusses the routine activity theory followed by the unified framework in section 4. Lastly, we present our conclusions and the work ahead.

BACKGROUND

Cybercrime

Cybercrime is a very broad term that has "historically referred to crimes happening specifically over networks, especially the Internet, but that term has gradually become a general synonym for computer crime. Cybercrime is different from other crimes because of the way it changes rapidly along with the technology that it uses or abuses. There is a lack of international agreement on what cybercrime is, which the UN has stated as one of the reasons for the lack of international cooperation on tackling cybercrime (Alkaabi, 2011). That is not to say that there is a complete lack of cooperation. When it comes to spam, there has been a significant amount of international cooperation on creating laws to combat it. The Tripartite Memorandum of Understanding on Spam Enforcement cooperation is one example of this. This is a law internationally agreed upon between the United States, Australia, Canada, and the European Union for the purposes of fighting spam (Kigerl, 2012). However, many other areas of cybercrime legislation do not have the same level of cooperation that spam receives, including such things as intellectual property, identity theft, and fraud. This lack of cooperation is a serious problem when considering the international nature of the internet. It is quickly becoming our most important tool, responsible for many different aspects of our everyday life. Technology is always expanding into more parts of our lives.

Not just internationally, there are different laws in every state within the US, reflecting the inconsistency of dealing with cybercrime. For example, New Jersey, the United States 7th largest state by GDP, does not have laws for Content Violations, Unauthorized alteration of data or software for personal or organization gain, or improper use of communications; Alaska, 46th, lacks laws pertaining to interruption of Services such as the infamous Denial of Service attacks that plague the internet. "By far the greatest number of state cybercrime statutes are concerned with computer intrusions and damage caused by intrusions" (Brenner, 2001). This is an epidemic of cybercrime that cannot simply be solved with an expansion of previous non-cybercrime related laws. Given the nature of the cybercrime, these gaps and legal contradictions can cause many issues.

Federal Laws Related to Cybercrime

Brenner (2001) suggests it is odd that one of the most advanced countries doesn't have uniform federal laws for cybercrime; instead it has many different state laws. These state laws create a complex web with many gaps in the areas of law that should be covered. It states that if federal jurisdiction to legislate exists, federal legislation is appropriate only when federal intervention is required. That will be very difficult with cybercrime due to the fact that the majority of the crimes will take place out of the state's jurisdiction. The federal government's intervention might be necessary in almost all cases. In addition, although federal legislative authority can pre-empt the states' ability to legislate in a given area, it rarely does, so it is unusual for federal criminal law to overlap with state prohibitions that address essentially the same issues.

There are federal laws in the United States that pertain to internet fraud, online child pornography, child luring and related activities, internet sale of prescription drugs and controlled substances, internet sale of firearms, internet gambling, internet sale of alcohol, online securities fraud, and software piracy and intellectual property theft. It is interesting to note that the majority of federal legislation pertaining to cybercrime has to do with internet gambling.

Online gambling can be considered effectively illegal since November 2002 when the United States Court of Appeals for the Fifth Circuit ruled that the Federal Wire Act prohibits electronic transmission of information for sports betting across telecommunications lines. The ruling was not intended to outlaw all forms of gambling. However, the federal department of justice continues publically to take the position that the wire act covers all forms of gambling. Since then legislation has been passed to directly outlaw online gambling within the United States, for example 18 U.S.C. § 1955 (prohibition of illegal gambling businesses). When it became illegal, online gambling companies based in the United States either closed down or went overseas. Gambling continues to flourish online despite it being illegal. As observed by Grossman (2010), "In many cases, we're trying to apply US federal and state statues that were written at a time when there were still rotary phones". This casts doubt into whether or not the current cyber laws are effective.

State Laws Related to Cybercrime

The framework of our government is that "There is no formal mechanism—at either the state or federal level—which requires or even prods states to adopt uniform, consistent laws" (Brenner, 2001). This is apparent given the many different legal landscapes of each state, and in many cases this is a good thing. It allows our states to provide a more personalized form of government for each region and experiment with new ideas in government on a state level. In regards to cybercrime this may not be the best way to handle things.

In 2001, "Only sixteen states outlawed online stalking or harassment, and several of them required that an offender transmit a 'credible threat' to injure the victim, the victim's family, or 'any other person'" (Brenner, 2001). This lack of legislation on the part of the rest of the states has been filled in to some extent since then, but in different ways. Some states expanded their "obscene phone call" statutes to encompass using a telephone or an "electronic communication device" to contact someone and threaten to injure that person or his/her family, to use obscene language, or to make repeated contacts in an effort to annoy the person (Brenner, 2001 "By far the greatest number of state cybercrime statutes are concerned with computer intrusions and damage caused by intrusions" (Brenner, 2001). This is an epidemic of cybercrime that cannot simply be solved with an expansion of previous non-cybercrime related laws. For something like stalking or harassment, which existed even before the internet in some form, it is not a huge issue to expand previous laws in this manner, but for newer threats that were never before experienced, simply repurposing old laws is not an option.

LexisNexis 50 State Comparative Legislation/Regulations

LexisNexis, a corporation that provides computer-assisted legal research, has compiled a list of all 50 states comparative legislation/regulations. This list provides a different set of categories for splitting up cybercrime. They have Intellectual Property (**I**), Theft using a computer (**T**), Destruction of a computer (**D**), trespass on a network (**N**), and the destruction of data with a Harmful Program (**H**). These are comparable to the old categories as shown table 1 below.

Alkaabi's Cybercrime Classification

Alkaabi (2011) has developed a cybercrime classification to help organizations fight such crimes by primarily dividing (and subsequently subdividing) computer crime into two categories: Type I crime where the computer, computer network, or electronic device is the target of the criminal activity; and Type II crime where the computer, computer network, or electronic device is the tool used to commit or facilitate the crime. Alkaabi's research led to refined cybercrime classifications in an attempt to create

Table 1. LexisNexis categorization and cybercrime categories: a comparison

Serial Number	Crime	Description	LexisNexis Classification
1	Unauthorized Access	Hacking: Unauthorized copying, modifying, deleting or destroying computer data or programs	N
2	Malicious Code	Virus, Worm, Trojan Horse, Software bomb	H
3	Interruption of Services	A successful DoS attack or partially successful attack	D
4	Theft of services or Misuse of services	Theft or Misuse	T, N
5	Content violations	Child pornography, Harmful Contents, Copyright crimes, Hate crimes, Military Secrets, Intellectual property, Forgery/counterfeit documents	I
6	Unauthorized Alteration of data or software for personal or organizational gain	Identity theft, Online Fraud, Privacy, Sabotage, Telemarketing/Internet Fraud, Electronic, manipulation of share markets	T
7	Improper use of communications	Harassment, Online Money laundering, Cyber stalking, Spamming, Conspiracy, Extortion, Drug trafficking, Social engineering fraud.	T

a comprehensive taxonomy of cybercrime. According to Alkaabi (2011), Type 1 crimes include crimes where the computer hardware is the target of the criminal activity. This was split into four sub-categories which include unauthorized access, malicious code, interruption of services, and theft or misuse of services. Type 2 crimes occur when the hardware is used as a tool and is split into three sub-categories: content violation offences, unauthorized alteration of data, and improper use of telecommunications. So, the motivation of a cybercriminal is to either use computer as a tool to commit crime, or as a target of crime. While the motivation of the offender to use computer as a tool / target is included in Alkaabi's classification, it is also important to consider the characteristics of the target which are being breached to get a complete view of the crime for developing appropriate laws pertaining to the crime.

ROUTINE ACTIVITY THEORY

Routine Activity Theory is a widely used criminology theory to predict and aggregate street crime rates but has been applied to cybercrime recently (Kigerl, 2012). According to the routine activity theory, three elements are required for a crime to take place: i) a motivated offender; ii) a suitable target, and iii) the absence of a capable guardian. The presence of these components increases the chance that a crime will take place. For example, the availability of suitable targets such as homes containing easily sellable goods in the absence of capable guardians such as police, homeowners, or friends and the presence of motivated offenders such as large number of unemployed teenagers increases the likelihood that a predatory crime will take place. The routine activity perspective has been a staple of the criminal victimization literature in general for nearly three decades now (Pratt et al. 2010).

In the field of cybercrime, Pratt and colleagues (2010) draw on routine activity theory to understand how online routines increase individuals' chances of being targeted for fraud online. According to Reyns (2013), Online banking, shopping, e-mail, instant messaging and downloading behaviors are risky online routines that increase victimization and expose users to the threat of identity theft. Reyns (2013) conclude that the routine activity approach is effective in explaining online crimes.

Figure 1. Routine activity theory

A UNIFIED FRAMEWORK

For the current research, we are focusing on five states: Alabama, Alaska, California, Louisiana, and New Jersey to show the lack of, and difference in laws related to cybercrime in different states These states were chosen with consideration for geography, economics, population, politics, and to some extent their laws. California has the highest GDP of any state. Alaska is one of two Non-contiguous states. New Jersey is the most densely populated of the states. Louisiana, Alabama, and Alaska were Republican states in the recent 2012 election, while California and New Jersey were Democratic. Louisiana was specially picked due to the fact that it is missing no cyber law classifications and was the first state to outlaw online gambling. Table 2 shows states with their LexisNexis classifications compared with their Alkaabi classifications.

From just this comparison it is apparent that Louisiana has laws that cover more areas of cybercrime than the other four states. Alabama needs laws that touch on malicious code, but has laws in the other areas. California interestingly seems to be lacking laws regarding content violations. Considering the fact that Hollywood, which is located in Los Angeles, California, is a nexus of film (a heavily pirated product) the lack of content violations seems incredibly strange. New Jersey is lacking laws in many areas as there are laws that insufficiently cover content violations, unauthorized alteration of data or software, and improper use of communications.

The variations among the state cybercrime statutes may be confusing to victims, lawyers alike. It is therefore important to offer a simpler understanding in the form of a framework that may serve as a guideline for states to consider in developing or amending their statutes and applying them. This study uses routine activity theory to develop such a framework.

Motivated Offender

It is important to consider the motivation of an offender behind a crime while developing any law pertaining to the crime. For example, a crime where the computer is the target of a criminal activity is different than the crimes where the computer is the tool to commit a crime (Alkaabi, 2011). According to Alkaabi (2001), type 1 crimes included crimes where the computer hardware was the target of the criminal activity. This was split into four sub-categories which include unauthorized access, malicious code, interruption of services, and theft or misuse of services. Type 2 crimes are when the hardware is

Table 2. State laws: LexisNexis classifications and Alkaabi classifications

States	LexisNexis Classifications	Alkaabi Classification	
		Laws Present	**Laws Absent**
Alabama	I, T, D, N	1, 2, 3, 4, 5, 6, 7,	None (since August 1, 2012)
Alaska	T, N, H	1, 2, 3, 4, 6,	5,7 (Content violations, Improper use of communications)
California	T, D, N, H	1, 2, 3, 4, 6, 7	5 (Content Violations)
Louisiana	I, T, D, N, H	1, 2, 3, 4, 5, 6, 7	None
New Jersey	D, N, H	1, 4, 6	2, 3, 5, 7 (Malicious Code, Interruption of Services, Interruption of Services, Content violations, Improper use of communications)

used as a tool and was split into three sub-categories. These three sub categories are content violation offences, unauthorized alteration of data, and improper use of telecommunications. Of course some of these can overlap; therefore some of these may have multiple types. We use Alkaabi's taxonomy to include various cybercrimes.

Target Characteristic/Suitability

It is important to protect the devices that store, manipulate, and transmit the information, and finally protecting information that provides value to people and organizations that is stored on those devices. To help accomplish these responsibilities there are protections such as CIA and AAA. CIA is Confidentiality, Integrity, and Availability while AAA is Authentication, Authorization, and Accounting. AAA a set of concepts used to protect property, data, and systems from intentional or even unintentional damage. AAA is used to support the Confidentiality, Integrity, and Availability (CIA) security concept. In addition, there is also a need to protect against Nonrepudiation (Table 3 provides definitions for all these terms). Suitability of the target depends on the characteristics of the target in terms of presence, absence, or chances of breaching these protection mechanisms. A target lacking any of these protection mechanisms is prone to cybercrime Cyber-criminals look for targets without adequate protections or try to breach these protections for achieving their objective of using computer as a target or tool to perform the attack.

We propose a two dimensional unified framework (Table 4) by incorporating the motivation behind a cybercrime (y-axis), suitability of the target (x-axis) and appropriate cyber-laws (each cell value). The existing states and federal laws can be mapped on the framework to determine their scope. This framework can also be used to develop cyber-laws that respond to motivation behind the crime and the target characteristic impacted due to the crime.

FUTURE RESEARCH DIRECTIONS

Future studies can use this framework to study various existing laws in the states and compare them with each other.

Table 3. Protection mechanism

Protection	Definition
Confidentiality	Ensures that only authorized parties can view the information.
Integrity	Ensures that the information is correct and no unauthorized person or malicious software has altered the data.
Availability	Ensures that data is accessible to authorized users.
Authentication	Ensures that the individual is who they claim to be and not an imposter.
Authorization	The ability to access.
Accounting	Tracking of events such as time, date, or location of access.
Authenticity	Provides proof of the genuineness of the user.
Non Repudiation	Proves that a user performed an action.

Table 4. Combating cybercrime: a unified framework

				Target Characteristic (Suitability)							
				Confidentiality	Integrity	Availability	Authentication	Authorization	Accounting	Non repudiation	Other
Motivation	Type I Crime	Unauthorized Access	Hacking	Law/Statute	Law/Statute						
			Other	Law/Statute	Law/Statute						
		Malicious Code	Virus								
			Worm								
			Trojan Horse								
			Software Bomb								
			Other								
		Interruption of Services	Disrupting services								
			Denying services								
			Other								
		Theft or misuse of services	Theft of services								
			Misuse of services				Law/Statute	Law/Statute			
			Other				Law/Statute	Law/Statute			
	Type II Crime	Content Violation	Child Pornography								:
			Hate crime	:							
			Harmful Content								
			Military services								
			Copyright crimes								
			Intellectual property								
			Forgery								
			Other								
		Unauthorized alteration of data / software	Identity Theft				:				
			Online Fraud								
			Privacy								
			Sabotage								
			Internet Fraud								
			Electronic manipulation of share marketers								
			Other								
		Improper use of communication	Harassment								
			Online money laundering								
			Cyber stalking								
			Spamming								
			Conspiracy						Law/Statute	Law/Statute	Law/Statute
			Extortion						Law/Statute	Law/Statute	Law/Statute
			Drug Trafficking						Law/Statute	Law/Statute	Law/Statute
			Social engineering / phishing						Law/Statute	Law/Statute	Law/Statute
			Other						Law/Statute	Law/Statute	Law/Statute

CONCLUSION

We expect the results of this study to make significant contribution to researchers and legislators who want to shape the future of cybercrime law. We expect that our proposed framework will help to better comprehend the motivation behind a cybercrime, suitability of the target and the presence (or absence) of adequate laws. Such a snapshot will help to develop capable guardians (for example: laws, policies) for effectively coordinating cybercrime regulation and legislation. It could help states that want to update their existing laws and cover areas that were previously uncovered. Eventually it could help consolidate laws internationally.

REFERENCES

Alkaabi, A., Mohay, G., McCullagh, A., & Chantler, N. (2011). Dealing with the problem of cybercrime. In *Proceedings of 2ⁿᵈ International ICST Conference on Digital Forensics & Cyber Crime*, (vol. 53, pp. 1867-8211). ICST. doi:10.1007/978-3-642-19513-6_1

Berg, T. (2007). The Changing Face of Cybercrime New Internet Threats Create Challenges to Law Enforcement. *Michigan Bar Journal*, *86*(6), 18.

Brenner, S. W. (2001). State Cybercrime Legislation in the United States of America: A Survey. *Richmond Journal of Law & Technology*, *7*, 28–34.

Grabosky, P. N. (2001). Virtual criminality: old wine in new bottles? *Social & Legal Studies*, *10*(2), 243–249.

Grossman, W. M. (2010). The charmed life of cybercrime. *Infosecurity*, *7*(1), 19–21. doi:10.1016/S1754-4548(10)70014-0

Guinchard, A. (2007). *Criminal Law in the 21st Century: The Demise of Territoriality?* http://dx.doi.org/10.2139/ssrn.1290049

IC3. (2012). Retrieved from Federal Bureau of Investigation website: http://www.ic3.gov/media/annualreport/2011_IC3Report.pdf

Jewkes, Y., & Yar, M. (2010). *Handbook of Internet Crime*. London: Taylor & Francis.

Kigerl, A. (2012). Routine activity theory and the determinants of high cybercrime countries. *Social Science Computer Review*, *30*(4), 470–486. doi:10.1177/0894439311422689

Koops, B. (2010). *The Internet and its Opportunities for Cybercrime* (Vol. 1, pp. 735–754). Transnational Criminology Manual.

Legal Information Institute. (2012). Retrieved from http://www.law.cornell.edu/uscode/text

LexisNexis. (2011). Retrieved from http://www.lexisnexis.com/en-us/home.page

Pratt, T. C., Holtfreter, K., & Reisig, M. D. (2010). Routine online activity and internet fraud targeting: Extending the generality of routine activity theory. *Journal of Research in Crime and Delinquency*, *47*(3), 267–296. doi:10.1177/0022427810365903

Reyns, B. W. (2013). Online Routines and Identity Theft Victimization Further Expanding Routine Activity Theory beyond Direct-Contact Offenses. *Journal of Research in Crime and Delinquency*, *50*(2), 216–238. doi:10.1177/0022427811425539

KEY TERMS AND DEFINITIONS

Cyber-Laws: Laws as applicable to the use of computers, and activities performed and transactions conducted over internet and other networks.

Cyber Stalking: The use of the Internet or other electronic means to stalk or harass an individual, a group of individuals, or an organization.

Hacking: Seeking and exploiting vulnerabilities in a computer system or computer network.

Identity Theft: A form of stealing someone's identity in order to access resources or other benefits in that person's name.

Phishing: An attempt to acquire personal information by impersonating as a trustworthy entity in an electronic communication.

Privacy: The ability of an individual or group to seclude information about themselves or selectively reveal their information.

Social Engineering: Psychological manipulation of people into performing actions or divulging confidential information.

Spam: Use of electronic messaging systems to send unsolicited bulk messages.

Statutes: Formal written enactment of a legislative authority that governs a state, city, or country.

Trojan Horses: A malware which gains privileged access to the operating system while appearing to perform a desirable function but instead drops a malicious payload.

This work was previously published in the Handbook of Research on Digital Crime, Cyberspace Security, and Information Assurance edited by Maria Manuela Cruz-Cunha and Irene Maria Portela, pages 398-406, copyright 2015 by Information Science Reference (an imprint of IGI Global).

Chapter 5
Security and Privacy Issues, Solutions, and Tools for MCC

Darshan M. Tank
Gujarat Technological University, India

ABSTRACT

With the development of cloud computing and mobility, mobile cloud computing has emerged and become a focus of research. Mobile Cloud Computing (MCC) integrates mobile computing and cloud computing aiming to extend mobile devices capabilities. By the means of on-demand self-service and extendibility, it can offer the infrastructure, platform, and software services in a cloud to mobile users through the mobile network. There is huge market for mobile based e-Commerce applications across the globe. Security and privacy are the key issues for mobile cloud computing applications. The limited processing power and memory of a mobile device dependent on inherently unreliable wireless channel for communication and battery for power leaves little scope for a reliable security layer. Thus there is a need for a lightweight secure framework that provides security with minimum communication and processing overhead on mobile devices. The security and privacy protection services can be achieved with the help of secure mobile-cloud application services.

INTRODUCTION

Mobile Cloud Computing (MCC) integrates mobile computing and cloud computing aiming to extend mobile devices capabilities. By the means of on-demand self-service and extendibility, it can offer the infrastructure, platform, and software services in a cloud to mobile users through the mobile network.

There is huge market for mobile based e-Commerce applications across the globe. Security and privacy are the key issues for mobile cloud computing applications. The limited processing power and memory of a mobile device dependent on inherently unreliable wireless channel for communication and battery for power leaves little scope for a reliable security layer. Thus there is a need for a lightweight secure framework that provides security with minimum communication and processing overhead on mobile devices. The security and privacy protection services can be achieved with the help of secure mobile-cloud application services. There are many frameworks and models suggested by different researcher

DOI: 10.4018/978-1-5225-0808-3.ch005

in concern with privacy and security. However, there is still plenty of scope for improvement. Taking support from a proximate cloud a security service could be devised for a mobile device which works as an interface and adaptively provides optimum security solutions based on communication channel capacity, available system resources both hardware and software and user-defined parameters (Dinh 2011).

Mobile Cloud Computing (MCC) is the combination of cloud computing, mobile computing and wireless networks to bring rich computational resources to mobile users, network operators, as well as cloud computing providers. The ultimate goal of MCC is to enable execution of rich mobile applications on a plethora of mobile devices, with a rich user experience. MCC provides business opportunities for mobile network operators as well as cloud providers.

MCC can be defined as a rich mobile computing technology that leverages unified elastic resources of varied clouds and network technologies toward unrestricted functionality, storage, and mobility to serve a multitude of mobile devices anywhere, anytime through the channel of Ethernet or Internet regardless of heterogeneous environments and platforms based on the pay as you use principle. Mobile Cloud Computing refers to an infrastructure where both the data storage and the data processing occur outside of the mobile device. Mobile cloud applications move the computing power and data storage away from mobile phones and into the cloud, bringing applications and mobile computing not only to smart phone users but also to a much broader range of mobile subscribers (Zissis and Lekkas 2012).

Mobile devices are increasingly becoming an essential part of human life as the most effective and convenient communication tools not bounded by time and place. Mobile users accumulate rich experience of various services from mobile applications, which run on the devices and/or on remote servers via wireless networks. The rapid progress of mobile computing becomes a powerful trend in the development of IT technology as well as commerce and industry fields. However, the mobile devices are facing many challenges in their resources and communications. The limited resources significantly impede the improvement of service qualities (Fernando 2013).

There are so many cloud storage service providers around e.g. One Drive (Microsoft Corporation), Dropbox (Dropbox Inc), Google Drive (Google Inc), Box, Amazon Cloud Drive and Apple icloud. Cloud computing applications are the cloud-based services e.g. Mobile Email, Google Maps, Google Cloud Print (Google Inc), Other Apps (Real Estate, Insurance, Surveying, Navigation app) (Ranbijay Kumar and Rajalakshmi 2013). Recently, the mobile cloud computing is becoming a new hot technology. And the security solution for it has become a research focus. With the development of the mobile cloud computing, new security issues will happen, which needs more security approaches.

ARCHITECTURE OF MOBILE CLOUD COMPUTING

MCC uses computational augmentation approaches by which resource constraint mobile devices can utilize computational resources of varied cloud based resources. In MCC, there are four types of cloud based resources, namely distant immobile clouds, proximate immobile computing entities, proximate mobile computing entities, and hybrid. Giant clouds such as Amazon EC2 are in the distant immobile groups whereas cloudlet or surrogates are member of proximate immobile computing entities. Smart phones, tablets, handheld devices, and wearable computing devices are part of the third group of cloud based resources which is proximate mobile computing entities.

Mobile devices are connected to the mobile networks via base stations that establish and control the connections and functional interfaces between the networks and mobile devices. Mobile users' requests and information are transmitted to the central processors that are connected to servers providing mobile network services. The subscribers' requests are delivered to a cloud through the Internet. In the cloud, cloud controllers process the requests to provide mobile users with the corresponding cloud services.

Advantages of MCC (Mobile Cloud Computing)

1. Extending battery lifetime.
2. Improving data storage capacity and processing power.
3. Improving reliability.
4. Dynamic provisioning.
5. Scalability.
6. Multi-tenancy.
7. Ease of integration.

Applications of MCC (Mobile Cloud Computing)

Mobile applications gain increasing share in a global mobile market. Various mobile applications have taken the advantages of MCC.

1. Mobile commerce.
2. Mobile learning.
3. Mobile healthcare.
4. Mobile gaming.
5. Other practical applications.
   a. Keyword-based searching.
   b. Voice-based searching.
   c. Tag-based searching.

MCC Issues

1. Mobile communication issues:
   a. Low bandwidth: One of the biggest issues, because the radio resource for wireless networks is much more scarce than wired networks.
   b. Service availability: Mobile users may not be able to connect to the cloud to obtain a service due to traffic congestion, network failures, mobile signal strength problems.
   c. Heterogeneity: Handling wireless connectivity with highly heterogeneous networks to satisfy MCC requirements (always-on connectivity, on-demand scalability, energy efficiency) is a difficult problem (Dev & Baishnab 2014).
2. Computing issues:
   a. Computation offloading:
      i. One of the main features of MCC.
      ii. Offloading is not always effective in saving energy.

iii. It is critical to determine whether to offload and which portions of the service codes to offload (Wang 2014).

iv. Two types: Offloading in a static environment and Offloading in a dynamic environment.

MCC Security Issues

1. Protecting user privacy and data/application secrecy from adversaries is a key to establish and maintain consumers' trust in the mobile platform, especially in MCC.

2. MCC security issues have two main categories.
   a. Security for mobile users:
      i. Mobile devices are exposed to numerous security threats like malicious codes and their vulnerability.
      ii. GPS can cause privacy issues for subscribers.
      iii. Security for mobile applications: Installing and running security software are the simplest ways to detect security threats. Mobile devices are resource constrained, protecting them from the threats is more difficult than that for resourceful devices.
   b. Securing data on clouds.

Privacy Issues in MCC

1. Location based services (LBS) faces a privacy issue on mobile users' provide private information such as their current location. This problem becomes even worse if an adversary knows user's important information.

2. Zhangwei and Mingjun propose the Location Trusted Server (LTS) approach. After receiving mobile users' requests, LTS gathers their location information and cloaks the information called "cloaked region" to conceal user's information. The "cloaked region" is sent to LBS, so LBS know only general information about the users but cannot identify them.

SECURITY-RELATED ISSUES IN MCC

Protecting user privacy and data/application secrecy from adversary is a key to establish and maintain consumers' trust in the mobile platform, especially in MCC. The security related issues in MCC are introduced in two categories: the security for mobile users and the security for data.

1. Security for Mobile Users

Mobile devices such as cellular phone, personal digital assistant (PDA), and smart phone are exposed to numerous security threats like malicious codes (e.g., virus, worm, and Trojan horses) and their vulnerability. In addition, with mobile phones integrated global positioning system (GPS) device, they can cause privacy issues for subscribers (Suo 2013).

2. Securing Data on Clouds

Although both mobile users and application developers benefit from storing a large amount of data/applications on a cloud, they should be careful of dealing with the data/applications in terms of their integrity, authentication, and digital rights.

3. Security for Mobile Applications

Presently Mobile devices run security checks on devices itself, which costs in terms of computation and power. MCC sows the seeds of a new model where detection services are carried out on cloud, saving the device CPU and memory requirements, but demanding the increase of bandwidth. One such approach has been proposed in, but it has its own privacy issues to battle up (Suo 2013).

4. Privacy

Providing sensitive or private information such as providing user's current location creates scenarios for privacy issues. The best example is global positioning system (GPS), which provides the use of location based services (LBS) (Sanaei 2014).

SECURITY THREATS AND COUNTER MEASURES

There are numerous challenges existing in the field of MCC, including data replication, consistency, and limited scalability, and unreliability, unreliable availability of cloud resources, portability, trust, security, and privacy. The above-mentioned challenges have become a barrier in the rapid growth of MCC's subscriber. According to survey, 74% of IT Executives and Chief Information Officers are not willing to adopt cloud services due to the risks associated with security and privacy. To attract potential consumers, the cloud service provider has to target all the security issues to provide a completely secure environment. Research organizations and academia have undertaken a massive amount of work to secure a cloud computing environment. There are still some grey areas that need to be addressed, such as the security and privacy of user's data stored on cloud servers, security threats caused by multiple virtual machines, and intrusion detection. As MCC is based on cloud computing, all the security issues are inherited in MCC with the extra limitation of resource constraint mobile devices. Due to resource limitation, the security algorithms proposed for the cloud computing environment cannot be directly run on a mobile device. There is a need for a lightweight secure framework that provides security with minimum communication and processing overhead on mobile devices (Huang 2010).

The security and privacy protection services can be achieved with the help of secure cloud application services. In addition to security and privacy, the secure cloud application services provide the user management, key management, encryption on demand, intrusion detection, authentication, and authorization services to mobile users. There is a need for a secure communication channel between cloud and the mobile device. The secure routing protocols can be used to protect the communication channel between the mobile device and cloud.

Virtualization improves the utilization of cloud resources but introduces new security issues due to the lack of perfect isolation of virtual machines hosted on a single server. The security issues imposed by virtualization can be tackled to some extent with the help of virtual machine secure monitoring, mirror, and migration. To provide the transparent cloud environment, mobile users must have the facility to audit the security level of the hosted services. The audit can be done with the help of a cloud service monitor. The cloud service monitor examines the security level and flows of the running environment. The security level should meet the user security requirements and the flow of the running environment should be normal. The security verification of uploaded data on cloud can be done using a storage security verification service. The physical security of the datacenter plays a very important role to achieve security and privacy. Physical security deals with the measures taken to avoid unauthorized personnel physically accessing the resources of the cloud service provider. Physical security can be achieved with the help of security guards, video surveillance, security lighting, sensors, and alarms (Jia 2011).

The researchers have done a massive amount of work to provide an energy-aware high performance computing environment. However, there is also a need for energy-efficient security frameworks for mobile devices to provide security and privacy services in an MCC environment. For the last few years, MCC has been an active research area. As MCC is in the preliminary stages, limited surveys are available in various domains of MCC. The mobile communication issues are associated with low bandwidth, service availability, and heterogeneity. The computing issues are linked with computing offloading, security, data access, and context-aware mobile cloud services.

TRUST MANAGEMENT IN MOBILE CLOUD COMPUTING ENVIRONMENT

The concept of trust, adjusted to the case of two parties involved in a transaction, can be described as follows: "An entity A is considered to trust another entity B when entity A believes that entity B will behave exactly as expected and required". Thereinafter, an entity can be considered trustworthy, if the parties or people involved in transactions with that entity rely on its credibility. In general, the concept described above can be verbally represented by the term reliability, which refers to the quality of a person or entity that is worthy of trust. Trust in the information society is built on various different grounds, based on calculus, on knowledge or on social reasons. The notion of trust in an organization could be defined as the customer's certainty that the organization is capable of providing the required services accurately and infallibly. A certainty which also expresses the customer's faith in its moral integrity, in the soundness of its operation, in the effectiveness of its security mechanisms, in its expertise and in its abidance by all regulations and laws, while at the same time, it also contains the acknowledgement of a minimum risk factor, by the relying party. The notion of security refers to a given situation where all possible risks are either eliminated or brought to an absolute minimum.

Trust in a cloud environment depends heavily on the selected deployment model, as governance of data and applications is outsourced and delegated out of the owner's strict control. In traditional architectures, trust was enforced by an efficient security policy, which addressed constraints on functions and flow among them, constraints on access by external systems and adversaries including programs and access to data by people. In a cloud deployment, this perception is totally obscured. In the case of public or community clouds, control is delegated to the organization owning the infrastructure. When deploying on a public cloud, control is mitigated to the infrastructure owner to enforce a sufficient security policy that guarantees that appropriate security activities are being performed to ensure that risk is reduced. This introduces a number of risks and threats, as essentially security is related to trusting the processes and computing base implemented by the cloud owner. It is crucial to differentiate between deployment models, as a private cloud, where the infrastructure is operated and managed on premise by a private organization, does not introduce additional unique security challenges, as trust remains within the organization. In such a situation the infrastructures owner remains the data and process owner (Dev and Baishnab 2014).

The trust management model of mobile cloud includes identity management, key management, and security policy enforcement. An ESSI owner has the full control over the data possessed in the ESSI, and thus a user-centric identity management framework is a natural choice. The user-centric identity management allows an individual has full control of his/her identities, in which third party authenticates them. It also implies that a user has control over the data his/her sharing over the Internet, and can transfer and delete the data when required.

AUTHENTICATION AND AUTHORIZATION PROCESS

Authentication is the process of determining whether someone or something is, in fact, who or what it is declared to be. Logically, authentication precedes *authorization*. The two terms are often used synonymously but they are two different processes (Yan 2015).

Authentication is a process in which the credentials provided are compared to those on file in a database of authorized users' information on a local *operating system* or within an *authentication server*. If the credentials match, the process is completed and the user is granted authorization for access. The permissions and folders returned define both the environment the user sees and the way he can interact with it, including hours of access and other rights such as the amount of *allocated* storage space.

Authentication Factors

1. **Knowledge Factors:** A category of authentication credentials consisting of information that the user possesses, such as a personal identification number (PIN), a user name, a password or the answer to a secret question.
2. **Possession Factors:** A category of credentials based on items that the user has with them, typically a hardware device such as a security token or a mobile phone used in conjunction with software token.
3. **Inherence Factors:** A category of user authentication credentials consisting of elements that are integral to the individual in question, in the form of biometric data.

User location and current time are sometimes considered the fourth factor and fifth factor for authentication. The ubiquity of smart phones can help ease the burdens of multifactor authentication for users. Most smart phones are equipped with *GPS*, enabling reasonable surety confirmation of the login location. Lower surety measures include the *MAC* address of the login point or physical presence verifications through cards and other possession factor elements.

Authorization is the process of giving someone permission to do or have something. In multi-user computer systems, a system administrator defines for the system which users are allowed *access* to the system and what privileges of use (such as access to which file directories, hours of access, amount of allocated storage space, and so forth). Assuming that someone has logged in to a computer *operating-system* or *application*, the system or application may want to identify what resources the user can be given during this session. Thus, authorization is sometimes seen as both the preliminary setting up of permissions by a system administrator and the actual checking of the permission values that have been set up when a user is getting access. Logically, authorization is preceded by *authentication*.

The process of an administrator granting rights and the process of checking user account permissions for access to resources are both referred to as authorization. The privileges and preferences granted for the authorized account depend on the user's permissions, which are either stored locally or on the authentication server. The settings defined for all these environment variables are set by an administrator.

ACCESS CONTROL

Access control is a security technique that can be used to regulate who or what can view or use resources in a computing environment. There are two main types of access control: physical and logical. Physical access control limits access to campuses, buildings, rooms and physical IT assets. Logical access limits connections to computer networks, system files and data. The four main categories of access control are:

1. Mandatory access control.
2. Discretionary access control.
3. Role-based access control.
4. Rule-based access control.

Access control systems perform *authorization* identification, *authentication*, access approval, and accountability of entities through login credentials including *passwords*, personal identification numbers (PINs), *biometric* scans, and physical or electronic keys.

An access control list (ACL) is a table that tells a computer *operating system* which access rights each user has to a particular system object, such as a file *directory* or individual *file*. Each object has a security attribute that identifies its access control list. The list has an entry for each system user with access privileges. The most common privileges include the ability to read a file, to write to the file or files, and to execute the file. Microsoft Windows NT/2000, Novell's *NetWare*, Digital's *OpenVMS*, and *UNIX*-based systems are among the operating systems that use access control lists. The list is implemented differently by each operating system (Oberheide 2008).

In Windows NT/2000, an access control list (ACL) is associated with each system object. Each ACL has one or more access control entries (ACEs) consisting of the name of a user or group of users. The user can also be a role name, such as "programmer," or "tester." For each of these users, groups, or roles, the access privileges are stated in a string of bits called an access mask. Generally, the system administrator or the object owner creates the access control list for an object.

RSA ALGORITHM

RSA is a cryptosystem for public-key *encryption*, and is widely used for securing sensitive data, particularly when being sent over an insecure network such as the *Internet*. RSA was first described in 1977 by Ron Rivest, Adi Shamir and Leonard Adleman of the Massachusetts Institute of Technology. Public-key *cryptography*, also known as *asymmetric cryptography*, uses two different but mathematically linked *keys*, one public and one private. The *public key* can be shared with everyone, whereas the *private key* must be kept secret. In RSA cryptography, both the public and the private keys can encrypt a message; the opposite key from the one used to encrypt a message is used to decrypt it. This attribute is one reason why RSA has become the most widely used asymmetric *algorithm*: It provides a method of assuring the confidentiality, integrity, authenticity and non-reputability of electronic communications and data storage.

Many protocols like *SSH*, OpenPGP, *S/MIME*, and *SSL/TLS* rely on RSA for encryption and *digital signature* functions. It is also used in software programs - *browsers* are an obvious example, which need to establish a secure connection over an insecure network like the Internet or validate a digital signature. RSA signature verification is one of the most commonly performed operations in IT.

RSA derives its security from the difficulty of factoring large integers that are the product of two large *prime numbers*. Multiplying these two numbers is easy, but determining the original prime numbers from the total - factoring - is considered infeasible due to the time it would take even using today's super computers.

DATA ENCRYPTION STANDARD (DES) ALGORITHM

The Data Encryption Standard (DES) is a symmetric-key method of data *encryption*. DES works by using the same *key* to encrypt and decrypt a message, so both the sender and the receiver must know and use the same *private key*. Once the go-to, symmetric-key algorithm for the encryption of electronic data, DES has been superseded by the more secure *Advanced Encryption Standard* (AES) algorithm.

Originally designed by researchers at *IBM* in the early 1970s, DES was adopted by the U.S. government as an official Federal Information Processing Standard (*FIPS*) in 1977 for the encryption of commercial and sensitive yet unclassified government computer data. It was the first encryption *algorithm* approved by the U.S. government for public disclosure. This ensured that DES was quickly adopted by industries such as financial services, where the need for strong encryption is high. The simplicity of DES also saw it used in a wide variety of embedded systems, *smart cards*, *SIM cards* and network devices requiring encryption like *modems*, *set-top boxes* and *routers*.

ADVANCED ENCRYPTION STANDARD (AES) ALGORITHM

The Advanced Encryption Standard or AES is a symmetric *block cipher* used by the U.S. government to protect classified information and is implemented in software and hardware throughout the world to encrypt sensitive data.

The origins of AES date back to 1997 when the *National Institute of Standards and Technology (NIST)* announced that it needed a successor to the aging *Data Encryption Standard (DES)* which was becoming vulnerable to *brute-force attacks*.

This new *encryption algorithm* would be unclassified and had to be "capable of protecting sensitive government information well into the next century." It was to be easy to implement in hardware and software, as well as in restricted environments (for example, in a *smart card*) and offer good defenses against various attack techniques.

TWO-FACTOR AUTHENTICATION (2FA) SYSTEM

A password is inherently weak. It can easily be lost or forgotten; many people write their passwords down where they can be seen by others; some use the same password over and over or use weak passwords that can be easily guessed.

The use of two-factor Web authentication ensures that this won't happen. A password is one of two necessary authentication factors that must be provided before access is granted. All 2FA systems are based on two of three possible factors: a knowledge factor (something the user knows, like a password), a possession factor (something the user has, like a token; more on that below), and an inherence factor (something the user is, such as a fingerprint). In this scenario, even if a malicious party obtains a person's password, he or she would not be able to provide the relevant second element needed to complete the authentication process. This lowers risk and the potential for unscrupulous behavior, as a compromised password alone is not enough to compromise the authentication system.

In the enterprise, *two-factor Web authentication* systems rely on hardware-based security tokens that generate pass codes; these pass codes or PINs are valid for about 60 seconds and must be entered along with a password. In a consumer-oriented Web-based environment, it's cost-prohibitive for a service provider to distribute physical tokens to each and every individual user.

Instead, most websites ask users to undergo a one-time registration process during which users register one or more of their mobile devices with the website provider. This is a trusted device under the users' control that can receive a verification code via SMS or another means to verify the user's identity.

Any time a user signs into the website, a pass code is sent to the registered device. The user must enter the password and verification code to fully sign in and use the services. Two-factor Web authentication systems rely on hardware-based security tokens that generate pass codes that are valid for about 60 seconds and must be entered along with a password.

Recently Apple joined a growing number of major consumer brands like Facebook, Google, Microsoft and PayPal in offering two-factor authentication (2FA) to help customers better secure their user accounts against hacking. Apple has expanded its use of two-factor authentication to its iCloud backup service.

CLOUD COMPUTING SECURITY ATTACKS

Cloud security is an evolving sub-domain of *computer security*, *network security*, and, more broadly, *information security*. It refers to a broad set of policies, technologies, and controls deployed to protect data, applications, and the associated infrastructure of *cloud computing*.

1. Denial-of-Service Attack (DoS)

Cloud is more penetrable to DoS attacks, because so many users are involved in the usage of cloud services and resources, therefore DoS attacks can be more damaging. When workload start increasing on Cloud, Cloud Computing operating system start to provide more computational power in the form of more virtual machines, more service instances to cope with the additional workload. Thus, the server hardware boundaries for more workload start restricting. In that sense, the Cloud system is trying to work against the attacker, but actually to some extent even supports the attacker by enabling the attacker to do most possible damage on services availability, starting from a single flooding attack entry point.

Thus, the attacker does not have to flood all n servers that provide a certain service in target, but merely can flood a single, Cloud-based address in order to perform a full loss of availability on the intended service. Some security concerning professionals proposed solution aims to detect and analyze Distributed Denial of Service (DDoS) attacks in cloud computing environments, using Dempster- Shafer Theory (DST) operations in 3-valued logic and Fault-Tree Analysis (FTA) for each VMbased Intrusion Detection System (IDS) (Yan 2015).

2. Cloud Malware-Injection Attack

It is the first considerable attack attempt that inject implementation of a malicious service or virtual machine into the Cloud. The purpose of malware cloud is anything that the adversary is interested in, it may include data modifications, full functionality changes/reverse or blockings. In this attack adversary creates its own malicious service implementation module (SaaS or PaaS) or virtual machine instance (IaaS), and add it to the Cloud system. Then, the adversary has to pretend to the Cloud system that it is some the new service implementation instance and among the valid instances for some particular service attacked by the adversary. If this action succeeds, the Cloud automatically redirects the requests of valid user to the malicious service implementation, and the adversary code is executed. The main scenario behind the Cloud Malware Injection attack is that an attacker transfers a manipulated/wrong copy of a victim's service instance so that malicious instance can achieve access to the service requests of the victim's service. To achieve this, the attacker has to derive control over the victim's data in the cloud. According to classification, this attack is the major representative of exploiting the service-to-cloud attack surface (Zonouz et al. 2013).

3. Side Channel Attack

An attacker attempts to compromise the cloud system by placing a malicious virtual machine in close propinquity to a target cloud server system and then debut a side channel attack. Side-channel attacks have egressed as a kind of effective security threat targeting system implementation of cryptographic algorithms. Evaluating cryptographic systems resilience to side-channel attacks is therefore important for secure system design. Side channel attacks use two steps to attack- VM CO-Residence and Placement i.e., an attacker can often place his or her instance on the same physical machine as a target instance and VM Extraction i.e., the ability of a malicious instance to utilize side channels to learn information about co-resident instances.

4. Authentication Attack

Authentication is a weak issue in the hosted and virtual services and is very frequently targeted. There are so many ways to authenticate users which can be based upon what a user knows, has, or is. The mechanisms and the methods that are used to secure the authentication process are mostly targeted by the attackers. Recently, regarding the architecture of cloud computing, SaaS, IaaS and Paas, there is only IaaS which is able to offer this kind of information protection and data encryption. If the transmitted data confidentiality is under the category high for any enterprise, the cloud computing service based on IaaS architecture will be the most suitable and possible solution for secured data communication.

5. Man-in-the-Middle Cryptographic Attacks

This attack is carried out when an attacker places himself between two users. Anytime attackers can place themselves in the communications path, there is the possibility that they can intercept and modify communications.

DENIAL OF SERVICE (DOS) ATTACK

A denial of service (DoS) attack is an incident in which a user or organization is deprived of the services of a resource they would normally expect to have. In a distributed denial-of-service, large numbers of compromised systems attack a single target.

Although a DoS attack does not usually result in the theft of information or other security loss, it can cost the target person or company a great deal of time and money. Typically, the loss of service is the inability of a particular network service, such as e-mail, to be available or the temporary loss of all network connectivity and services. A denial of service attack can also destroy programming and files in affected computer systems. In some cases, DoS attacks have forced Web sites accessed by millions of people to temporarily cease operation. Common forms of denial of service attacks are:

1. Buffer Overflow Attacks.
2. SYN Attack.
3. Teardrop Attack.
4. Smurf Attack.
5. Viruses.
6. Physical Infrastructure Attacks.

DISTRIBUTED DENIAL OF SERVICE (DDOS) ATTACK

A distributed denial-of-service (DDoS) attack is one in which a multitude of compromised systems attack a single target, thereby causing *denial of service* for users of the targeted system. The flood of incoming messages to the target system essentially forces it to shut down, thereby denying service to the system to legitimate users. In a typical DDoS attack, the assailant begins by exploiting vulnerability in one computer system and making it the DDoS *master*. The attack master, also known as the botmaster, identifies and identifies and infects other vulnerable systems with *malware*. Eventually, the assailant instructs the controlled machines to launch an attack against a specified target (Yan 2015).

There are two types of DDoS attacks: a network-centric attack which overloads a service by using up bandwidth and an application-layer attack which overloads a service or database with application calls. The inundation of *packets* to the target causes a denial of service. While the media tends to focus on the target of a DDoS attack as the victim, in reality there are many victims in a DDoS attack - the final target and as well the systems controlled by the intruder. Although the owners of co-opted computers are typically unaware that their computers have been compromised, they are nevertheless likely to suffer a degradation of service and not work well. A computer under the control of an intruder is known as a *zombie* or *bot*. A group of co-opted computers is known as a *botnet* or a zombie army. Both Kaspersky Labs and Symantec have identified botnets - not spam, viruses, or worms - as the biggest threat to Internet security.

HOW TO PREVENT A DENIAL-OF-SERVICE (DOS) ATTACK?

A *distributed denial-of-service attack* is an Internet assault in which a number of systems attack a single target, causing a denial of service for legitimate users of the targeted system. While many technologies today are designed to prevent various types of attacks, *preventing a distributed denial-of-service (DDoS) attack* is impossible, and stopping one once it has started can be quite a challenge.

As a top priority, make sure enough bandwidth is available to handle not only the surge in legitimate traffic, but also possible small-scale denial-of-service (DoS) attacks. I would also recommend initiating a Web infrastructure vulnerability assessment and a penetration test, including DoS testing, before the new campaign goes live. It should be noted that these attacks can last hours, days or even weeks. Any time you believe you are under a DoS attack, you should contact your ISP representative immediately.

There's no way to completely protect your network from denial-of-service attacks, especially with the prevalence of distributed denial-of-service (DDoS) attacks on the Internet today. It's extremely difficult to differentiate an attack request from a legitimate request because they often use the same protocols/ports and may resemble each other in content. However, there are some things we can do to reduce your risk:

1. Purchase a lot of bandwidth. This is not only the easiest solution, but also the most expensive. If you simply have tons of bandwidth, it makes perpetrating a DoS attack much more difficult because it's more bandwidth that an attacker has to clog.
2. Use DoS attack detection technology. Intrusion prevention system and firewall manufacturers now offer DoS protection technologies that include signature detection and connection verification techniques to limit the success of DoS attacks.
3. Prepare for DoS response. The use of throttling and rate-limiting technologies can reduce the effects of a DoS attack. One such response mode stops all new inbound connections in the event of a DoS attack, allowing established connections and new outbound connections to continue.

PHISHING ATTACK AND SPOOFING

Phishing is the attempt to acquire *sensitive information* such as usernames, passwords, and *credit card* details, often for malicious reasons, by masquerading as a trustworthy entity in an *electronic communication*. The word is a *neologism* created as a *homophone* of *fishing* due to the similarity of using fake *bait* in an attempt to catch a victim. Communications purporting to be from popular social web sites, auction sites, banks, online payment processors or IT administrators are commonly used to lure unsuspecting victims. Phishing emails may contain links to websites that are infected with *malware*. Phishing is typically carried out by *email spoofing* or *instant messaging*, and it often directs users to enter details at a fake website whose *look and feel* are almost identical to the legitimate one. Phishing is an example of *social engineering* techniques used to deceive users, and exploits the poor usability of current web security technologies. Attempts to deal with the growing number of reported phishing incidents include *legislation*, user training, public awareness, and technical security measures. Many websites have now created secondary tools for applications, like maps for games, but they should be clearly marked as to who wrote them, and users should not use the same passwords anywhere on the internet.

Phishing is a continual threat, and the risk is even larger in social media such as *Facebook*, *Twitter*, and *Google+*. Hackers could create a clone of a website and tell you to enter personal information, which is then emailed to them. Hackers commonly take advantage of these sites to attack people using them at their workplace, homes, or in public in order to take personal and security information that can affect the user or company. Phishing takes advantage of the trust that the user may have since the user may not be able to tell that the site being visited, or program being used, is not real; therefore, when this occurs, the hacker has the chance to gain the personal information of the targeted user, such as passwords, usernames, security codes, and credit card numbers, among other things.

Spoofing is the creation of TCP/IP packets using somebody else's IP address. Routers use the "destination IP" address in order to forward packets through the Internet, but ignore the "source IP" address. That address is only used by the destination machine when it responds back to the source. A common misconception is that "IP spoofing" can be used to hide your IP address while surfing the Internet, chatting on-line, sending e-mail, and so forth. This is generally not true. Forging the source IP address causes the responses to be misdirected, meaning you cannot create a normal network connection. However, IP spoofing is an integral part of many network attacks that do not need to see responses. In *computer networking*, IP address spoofing or IP spoofing is the creation of *Internet Protocol* (IP) *packets* with a forged source *IP address*, with the purpose of concealing the identity of the sender or impersonating another computing system.

SSL AND TLS

SSL is short for Secure Sockets Layer. Secure Sockets Layer (SSL) is a *protocol* developed by *Netscape* for transmitting private documents via the *Internet*. SSL uses a *cryptographic* system that uses two *keys* to *encrypt* data – a public key known to everyone and a private or secret key known only to the recipient of the message. Most *Web browsers* support SSL, and many *websites* use the protocol to obtain confidential user information, including credit card numbers. By convention, *URLs* that require an SSL connection start with https: instead of http:

When a *Web browser* tries to connect to a website using SSL, the browser will first request the web server identify itself. This prompts the web server to send the browser a copy of the *SSL Certificate*. The browser checks to see if the SSL Certificate is trusted - if the SSL Certificate is trusted, then the browser sends a message to the Web server. The server then responds to the browser with a digitally signed acknowledgement to start an SSL *encrypted* session. This allows encrypted data to be shared between the browser and the server. You may notice that your browsing session now starts with https (and not http).

Transport Layer Security (TLS) and its predecessor, Secure Sockets Layer (SSL), both of which are frequently referred to as 'SSL', are *cryptographic protocols* designed to provide *communications security* over a *computer network*. Several versions of the protocols are in widespread use in applications such as *web browsing*, *email*, *Internet faxing*, *instant messaging*, and *voice-over-IP* (VoIP). Major web sites use TLS to secure all communications between their servers and *web browsers*. The primary goal of the TLS protocol is to provide privacy and data integrity between two communicating computer applications.

TYPES OF CYBER ATTACK OR THREATS

A cyber attack, in simple terms, is an attack on your digital systems originating from malicious acts of an anonymous source. Cyber attack allows for an illegal access to your digital device, while gaining access or control of your digital device. A different types of cyber attacks can be defined as an offensive tactic to gain an illegal control or access to your digital device, called the target system, initiated by a person or a computer against a website, computer system or a single digital device as well as a whole, which poses a serious threat to computer systems, information stored, financial structures and the entire network itself. Cyber attacks work towards compromising the integrity of the digital device and the information stored in it.

Types of Cyber Attack or Threats

1. **Backdoors:** Backdoor is a type of cyber threat in which the attacker uses a back door to install a key logging software, thereby allowing an illegal access to your system. This threat can turn out to be potentially serious as it allows for modification of the files, stealing information, installing unwanted software or even taking control of the entire computer.
2. **Denial-of-Service Attack:** A denial-of-service or a DOS attack generally means attacking the network to bring it down completely with useless traffic by affecting the host device which is connected to the internet. A DOS attack targets websites or services which are hosted on the servers of banks and credit card payment gateways.
3. **Direct-Access Attack:** A direct-access attack simply means gaining physical access to the computer or its part and performing various functions or installing various types of devices to compromise security. The attacker can install software loaded with worms or download important data, using portable devices.
4. **Eavesdropping:** As the name suggests, eavesdropping means secretly listening to a conversation between the hosts on a network. There are various programs such as Carnivore and NarusInsight that can be used to eavesdrop.
5. **Spoofing:** Spoofing is a cyber attack where a person or a program impersonates another by creating false data in order to gain illegal access to a system. Such threats are commonly found in emails where the sender's address is spoofed.
6. **Tampering:** Tampering is a web based attack where certain parameters in the URL are changed without the customer's knowledge; and when the customer keys in that URL, it looks and appears exactly the same. Tampering is basically done by hackers and criminals to steal the identity and obtain illegal access to information.
7. **Repudiation Attack:** A repudiation attack occurs when the user denies the fact that he or she has performed a certain action or has initiated a transaction. A user can simply deny having knowledge of the transaction or communication and later claim that such transaction or communication never took place.
8. **Information Disclosure:** Information disclosure breach means that the information which is thought to be secured is released to unscrupulous elements that are not trustworthy.
9. **Privilege Escalation Attack:** A privilege escalation attack is a type of network intrusion which allows the user to have an elevated access to the network which was primarily not allowed. The attacker takes the advantage of the programming errors and permits an elevated access to the network.

10. **Exploits:** An exploit attack is basically software designed to take advantage of a flaw in the system. The attacker plans to gain easy access to a computer system and gain control, allows privilege escalation or creates a DOS attack.

11. **Social Engineering:** An attack by a known or a malicious person is known as social engineering. They have knowledge about the programs used and the firewall security and thus it becomes easier to take advantage of trusted people and deceive them to gain passwords or other necessary information for a large social engineering attack.

12. **Indirect Attack:** Indirect attack means an attack launched from a third party computer as it becomes more difficult to track the origin of the attack.

13. **Computer Crime:** A crime undertaken with the use of a computer and a network is called as a computer crime.

14. **Malware:** Malware refers to malicious software that are being designed to damage or perform unwanted actions into the system. Malware is of many types like viruses, worms, Trojan horses, etc., which can cause havoc on a computer's hard drive. They can either delete some files or a directory or simply gather data without the actual knowledge of the user.

15. **Adware:** Adware is software that supports advertisements which renders ads to its author. It has advertisements embedded in the application. So when the program is running, it shows the advertisement. Basically, adware is similar to malware as it uses ads to inflict computers with deadly viruses.

16. **Bots:** Bots is a software application that runs automated tasks which are simple and repetitive in nature. Bots may or may not be malicious, but they are usually found to initiate a DoS attack or a click fraud while using the internet.

17. **Ransomware:** Ransomware is a type of cyber security threat which will restrict access to your computer system at first and will ask for a ransom in order for the restriction to be removed. This ransom is to be paid through online payment methods only which the user can be granted an access to their system.

18. **Rootkits:** A rootkit is malicious software designed in such a way that hides certain process or programs from normal antivirus scan detection and continues to enjoy a privilege access to your system. It is that software which runs and gets activated each time you boot your system and are difficult to detect and can install various files and processes in the system.

19. **Spyware:** Spyware, as the name suggests, is software which typically spies and gathers information from the system through a user's internet connection without the user's knowledge. Spyware software is majorly a hidden component of a freeware program which can be downloaded from the internet.

20. **Scareware:** Scareware is a type of threat which acts as a genuine system message and guides you to download and purchase useless and potentially dangerous software. Such scareware pop-ups seem to be similar to any system messages, but actually aren't. The main purpose of the scareware is to create anxiety among the users and use that anxiety to coax them to download irrelevant softwares.

21. **Trojan Horses:** Trojan Horses are a form of threat that are malicious or harmful codes hidden behind genuine programs or data which can allow complete access to the system and can cause damage to the system or data corruption or loss/theft of data. It acts as a backdoor and hence it is not easily detectable.

22. **Virus:** A computer virus is a self replicating program which, when executed, replicates or even modifies by inserting copies of it into another computer file and infects the affected areas once the virus succeeds in replicating. This virus can be harmful as it spreads like wildfire and can infect majority of the system in no time.

23. **Worm:** Just like a virus, worm is a self replicating program which relies on computer network and performs malicious actions and spreads itself onto other computer networks. Worms primarily rely on security failures to access the infected system.

24. **Phishing:** Phishing is a cyber threat which makes an attempt to gain sensitive information like passwords, usernames and other details for malicious reasons. It is basically an email fraud where the perpetrator sends a legitimate looking email and attempts to gain personal information.

25. **Identity Theft:** Identity theft is a crime wherein your personal details are stolen and these details are used to commit a fraud. An identity theft is committed when a criminal impersonates individuals and use the information for some financial gain.

26. **Intellectual Property Theft:** Intellectual Property theft is a theft of copyrighted material where it violates the copyrights and the patents. It is a cybercrime to get hands onto some trade secrets and patented documents and research. It is basically a theft of an idea, plan and the methodology being used.

27. **Password Attacks:** Password attack is a form of a threat to your system security where attackers usually try ways to gain access to your system password. They either simply guess the password or use an automated program to find the correct password and gain an entry into the system.

28. **Bluesnarfing:** Bluesnarfing is a threat of information through unauthorized means. The hackers can gain access to the information and data on a Bluetooth enabled phone using the wireless technology of the Bluetooth without alerting the user of the phone.

29. **Bluejacking:** Bluejacking is simply sending of texts, images or sounds, to another Bluetooth enabled device and is a harmless way of marketing. However, there is a thin line between bluejacking and bluesnarfing and if crossed it results into an act of threat.

30. **DDoS:** DDoS basically means a Distributed Denial of Service. It is an attempt to make any online service temporarily unavailable by generating overwhelming traffic from multiple sources or suspend services of a host connected to the internet.

31. **Key Logger:** A key logger is a spyware that has the capability to spy on the happenings on the computer system. It has the capability to record every stroke on the keyboard, web sites visited and every information available on the system. This recorded log is then sent to a specified receiver.

FEATURES OF CLOUDSIM (A FRAMEWORK FOR MODELING AND SIMULATION OF CLOUD COMPUTING INFRASTRUCTURES AND SERVICES)

Cloud computing is the leading technology for delivery of reliable, secure, fault-tolerant, sustainable, and scalable computational services. For assurance of such characteristics in cloud systems under development, it is required timely, repeatable, and controllable methodologies for evaluation of new cloud applications and policies before actual development of cloud products. Because utilization of real testbeds limits the experiments to the scale of the testbed and makes the reproduction of results an extremely difficult undertaking, simulation may be used.

CloudSim goal is to provide a generalized and extensible simulation framework that enables modeling, simulation, and experimentation of emerging Cloud computing infrastructures and application services, allowing its users to focus on specific system design issues that they want to investigate, without getting concerned about the low level details related to Cloud-based infrastructures and services.

CloudSim is developed in the Cloud Computing and Distributed Systems (CLOUDS) Laboratory, at the Computer Science and Software Engineering Department of the University of Melbourne. CloudSim is powered by *jProfiler*.

Main Features

1. Support for modeling and simulation of large scale Cloud computing data centers.
2. Support for modeling and simulation of virtualized server hosts, with customizable policies for provisioning host resources to virtual machines.
3. Support for modeling and simulation of energy-aware computational resources.
4. Support for modeling and simulation of data center network topologies and message-passing applications.
5. Support for modeling and simulation of federated clouds.
6. Support for dynamic insertion of simulation elements, stop and resume of simulation.
7. Support for user-defined policies for allocation of hosts to virtual machines and policies for allocation of host resources to virtual machines.

FUTURE RESEARCH DIRECTIONS

Mobile cloud computing is becoming a new hot technology. And the security solution for it has become a research focus. With the development of the mobile cloud computing, new security issues will happen, which needs more security approaches.

There is huge market for mobile based e-Commerce applications across the globe. Security and privacy are the key issues for mobile cloud computing applications. The limited processing power and memory of a mobile device dependent on inherently unreliable wireless channel for communication and battery for power leaves little scope for a reliable security layer. Thus there is a need for a lightweight secure framework that provides security with minimum communication and processing overhead on mobile devices. The security and privacy protection services can be achieved with the help of secure mobile-cloud application services. There are many frameworks and models suggested by different researcher in concern with privacy and security. However, there is still plenty of scope for improvement.

CONCLUSION

Mobile cloud computing is one of mobile technology trends in the future since it combines the advantages of both mobile computing and cloud computing, thereby providing optimal services for mobile users.

This article has provided an overview of mobile cloud computing in which its definitions, architecture, advantages and challenges have been presented. The applications supported by mobile cloud computing including mobile commerce, mobile learning, and mobile healthcare have been discussed which clearly show the applicability of the mobile cloud computing to a wide range of mobile services. Then, the issues and related approaches for mobile cloud computing have been discussed. Finally, the future research directions have been outlined.

REFERENCES

Abdul Nasir Khana, M. L. (2012, August). Towards secure mobile cloud computing: A survey. *Future Generation Computer Systems*.

Al-Ahmad, A. S., & Aljunid, S. A. (2013). Mobile Cloud Computing Testing Review. *IEEE International Conference on Advanced Computer Science Applications and Technologies*.

Buyya, R. (2014). Introduction to the IEEE Transactions on Cloud Computing. *IEEE Transactions on Cloud Computing*, *1*(1), 3–9. doi:10.1109/TCC.2013.13

Chow, R., Jakobsson, M., Masuoka, R., Molina, J., Niu, Y., Shi, E., & Song, Z. (2010). Authentication in the clouds: a framework and its application to mobile users. In *Proceeding ACM Cloud Computing Security Workshop, CCSW '10*. doi:10.1145/1866835.1866837

Dev, D., & Baishnab, K. L. (2014). A Review and Research towards Mobile Cloud Computing. *2nd IEEE International Conference on Mobile Cloud Computing, Services, and Engineering*. doi:10.1109/MobileCloud.2014.41

Dinh, H. T., Lee, C., Niyato, D., & Wang, P. (2013). *A survey of mobile cloud computing: Architecture, applications, and approaches*. Wireless Communications and Mobile Computing.

Fernando, Loke, & Rahayu. (2013). Mobile cloud computing: A survey. *Future Generation Computer Systems, 29*(1), 84–106.

Hoang, T. (2011). *A survey of Mobile Cloud Computing: Architecture, Applications, and Approaches*. Wireless Communications and Mobile Computing.

Hsueh, S. C., Lin, & Lin. (2011). Secure cloud storage for conventional data archive of smart phones. In *Proc. 15th IEEE Int. Symposium on Consumer Electronics*.

Hu, H., Wen, Y., Chua, T. S., & Li, X. (2014). Toward Scalable Systems for Big Data Analytics: A Technology Tutorial. *IEEE Access, 2*, 652–687. doi:10.1109/ACCESS.2014.2332453

Huang, X., Zhang, M., Kang, & Luo. (2010). MobiCloud: building secure cloud framework for mobile computing and communication. In *Proceeding 5th IEEE International Symposium on Service Oriented System Engineering, SOSE '10*. doi:10.1109/SOSE.2010.20

Jia, W., Zhu, H., Cao, Z., Wei, L., & Lin, X. (2011). SDSM: a secure data service mechanism in mobile cloud computing. In *Proceeding IEEE Conference on Computer Communications Workshops, INFOCOM WKSHPS*.

Jla, W., Zhu, H., Cao, Z., Wei, L., & Lin, X. (2011). SDSM: A secure data service mechanism in mobile cloud computing. In *Proc. IEEE Conference on Computer Communications Workshops, INFOCOM WKSHPS.*

Khalid, O., Khan, M., Khan, S., & Zomaya, A. (2014). *Omni Suggest: A Ubiquitous Cloud based Context Aware Recommendation System for Mobile Social Networks. IEEE Transactions on Services Computing.*

Khanai, & Kulkarni. (2014). Crypto-Coding as DES-Convolution for Land Mobile Satellite Channel. *International Journal of Computer Applications, 86*(18).

Khanai, R., Kulkarni, G.H., & Torse, D.A. (2014). Neural Crypto-Coding as DES: Turbo over Land Mobile Satellite (LMS) channel. In *Communications and Signal Processing (ICCSP), 2014 International Conference.*

Kulkarni & Khannai. (n.d.). Addressing Mobile Cloud Computing Security Issues: A Survey. *IEEE ICCSP 2015 Conference.*

Kumar, R., & Rajalakshmi. (2013). Mobile Cloud Computing Standard approach to protecting and securing of mobile cloud ecosystems. *IEEE International Conference on Computer Sciences and Applications.*

Oberheide, J., Veeraraghavan, K., Cooke, E., & Jahanian, F. (2008). Virtualized in-cloud security services for mobile devices. In *Proceedings of the 1st Workshop on Virtualization in Mobile Computing (MobiVirt).* doi:10.1145/1622103.1629656

Portokalidis, G., Homburg, P., Anagnostakis, K., & Bos, H. (2010). Paranoid Android: versatile protection for smartphones. In *Proceedings of the 26th Annual Computer Security Application Conference (ACSAC).*

Qiao Yan, Yu, Gong, & Li. (n.d.). Software-Defined Networking (SDN) and Distributed Denial of Service (DDoS) Attacks in Cloud Computing Environments: A Survey, Some Research Issues, and Challenges. *IEEE Communications Surveys & Tutorials.*

Rassan, & AlShaher. (2014). Securing Mobile Cloud Computing using Biometric Authentication (SMCBA). *IEEE International Conference on Computational Science and Computational Intelligence.*

Sanaei, Z., Abolfazli, S., Gani, A., & Buyya, R. (2014). Heterogeneity in Mobile Cloud Computing: Taxonomy and Open Challenges. *IEEE Communications Surveys and Tutorials, 16*(1), 369–392. doi:10.1109/SURV.2013.050113.00090

Shanna, & Garg. (2014). *An Efficient and Secure Data Storage in Mobile Cloud Computing through RSA and Hash Function.* IEEE.

Suo, H. (2013). *Security and Privacy in Mobile Cloud Computing.* IEEE.

Varadharajan, V. (2014). *Security as a Service Model for Cloud Environment. IEEE Transactions on Network and Service Management, 11(1).*

Wang, H., Wu, S., Chen, M., & Huazhong, W. W. (2014, March). Secunty ProtectIOn between Users and the Mobile Media Cloud. *IEEE Communications Magazine, 52*(3), 73–79. doi:10.1109/MCOM.2014.6766088

Wang, S. & Wang, X. (2010). In-device spatial cloaking for mobile user privacy assisted by the cloud. In *Proceeding 11th International Conference on Mobile Data Management, MDM '10.*

Xiao, S., & Gong, W. (2010). Mobility can help: protect user identity with dynamic credential. In *Proceeding 11th International Conference on Mobile Data Management, MDM '10*. doi:10.1109/MDM.2010.73

Yang, Wang, Wang, Tan & Yu. (2011). Provable data possession of resource constrained mobile devices in cloud computing. *Journal of Networks*, 1033–1040.

Zhang, X., Schiffman, J., Gibbs, S., Kunjithapatham, A., & Jeong, S. (2009). Securing elastic applications on mobile devices for cloud computing. In *Proceeding ACM workshop on Cloud computing security, CCSW '09*. doi:10.1145/1655008.1655026

Zissis, D., & Lekkas, D. (2012, March). Addressing cloud computing security issues. *Future Generation Computer Systems*, 28(3), 583–592. doi:10.1016/j.future.2010.12.006

Zonouz, Houmansadr, Barthier, Borisov, & Sanders. (2013). Secloud: A cloud based comprehensive and lightweight security solution for smartphones. *Science Direct Journal of Computers and Security, 37*, 215-227.

Chapter 6
National Security Policy and Strategy and Cyber Security Risks

Olivera Injac
University of Donja Gorica, Montenegro

Ramo Šendelj
University of Donja Gorica, Montenegro

ABSTRACT

This chapter gives explanation on theoretical framework of the national security policy and strategy. Moreover, it analyzes selected countries approaches to cyber security in national policy and how countries build their capacities to face with risks, and address objectives in some cyber security policies. Also, in this chapter are described different sorts and sources of cyber threats, techniques of cyber attacks and frequently used tools (software and hardware) by cyber attackers. In addition, according with Symantec's and Kaspersky's annual report about Internet security threats for 2014, were analyzed the most important cyber threats and attacks during 2013. Furthermore, the chapter shows organization structure of cyber security system of Montenegro, statistical analysis of users activities in cyber space and cyber incidents that happened in Montenegro during 2014.

INTRODUCTION

In informatics age, where online communication has become the norm, internet users are facing increased number of threats and becoming the targets of cyber-attacks. We are witnesses of the global phenomenon of the rise of threats based on the main aspects of globalization (e.g. ICT) and security threats in the age of globalization are in connection with different dimensions of globalization (economic, political, cultural, ICT, ecological).

Cyber security threats are one of the biggest challenges for national security systems, because they tend to destroy economic and national security in the 21st century.

DOI: 10.4018/978-1-5225-0808-3.ch006

There are many reasons which contribute to the rise of cyber security threats, such as growing dependence of information technologies, interconnections of critical infrastructures and different weaknesses in some sectors (government, industry, financial system, etc.).

While cyber criminals continue to develop and make their techniques more advanced, they are also shifting targets focusing, for example, on theft of financial information, business espionage and accessing government information.

As it was stated by Stevens (2012), in contemporary time we have huge prevalence of information communications technologies, and what is paradoxically it became a symbol of the "uncertainty and irreversibility of the patterns of global emergence" (Stevens, 2012, p.1).

Importance of cyberspace for national security, has expressed US President Barack Obama in his speech in May 2009, saying that it is ironic to have technologies which at the same time could support world development and being misused for the world destruction.

Cyber security has strategic and tactical dimensions in national security, because it affects all levels of society. The cyber threats and their performance techniques are continuously evolving, and it represents threats to data security, electronic systems and personal privacy, what makes challenging tasks for states to response on them.

Some of the past occurred cyber-attacks (Estonia and Georgia), were directed on different organizations including parliaments, banks, ministries, newspapers, and broadcasters and even the effects were localized to those countries, they do show what a cyber-attack can produce (Miklaucic, M. & Brewer, 2013).

There could be expectations that danger will grow in a future and cyber-attacks will be able to destroy state infrastructure, what could directly threaten citizens and significantly block state system under attack.

Expectations from the states are to be prepared and to work on their own capacities for cyber protection and for response on cyber threats, and in addition to that, it is necessary to adapt comprehensive national security policy and strategy.

The term cyberspace covers enormous field of the technology and networks, including Internet, telecommunications networks, computer systems and processors in critical industries. The usage of the term cyberspace also refers to the virtual environment of information and interactions between people. The globally interconnected and interdependent cyberspace is main sphere which provide support for modern society, the world economy, civil infrastructure, public safety and national security.

As some experts stressed, cyberspace protection requires strong vision and leadership, as well as changes in priorities, policies, technologies, education, laws and international agreements (Branon, 2014). Confronting to cyber threats require strong commitment of all actors to be innovative and adopt efficient technologies that can be adequate to contribute on enhancing national security, the global economy and individual freedoms.

Cyber threats and challenges can causes significant effects for the states, and it force them to find new solutions, to develop tools and mechanisms for prevention and response, and also to adapt adequate security policy for cyber threats.

The thesis of chapter is that states have different approaches towards cyber security policy, and if it is guided by security sector reform and national security policy development, than states are mainly concentrated on institutional building and resources improvement. That is shown on the case study of Montenegro.

NATIONAL SECURITY POLICY AND CYBER THREATS

National security policy represents institutional and legislative framework on which country take activities for providing security for the state and its citizens. National security policy framework hat shapes functioning of the national security system is defined in the laws, strategies and other official national documents, but also it could be presented as an integrated document. Some authors indicate that national security strategy is guideline which directs development of security policy towards different threats (Svete, 2012).

All sorts of national policy documents can be classified by two main criteria:

1. **The Aim and Purpose of Document:** Due to the typology, national security policy documents are classified in four categories:
   a. **Constitutional Document:** It contains basis and structural elements of the national security policy;
   b. **Presentation Document:** It presents security capacities intended for internal and external use (e.g. White Papers),
   c. **Operational Leading Document:** For operational and tactical usage of the security forces,
   d. **Developing Document:** It gives vision and direction for development of the national security policy (Tatalović, Grizold & Cvrtila, 2008, p.27).
2. **The Field of Engagement:** Depending on the field, used as guidance there can be military, defense, civil-military documents.

Depending on the level of country development and the aim of security policy as well as different level of the prioritization, states normally use any of this categorized security policy documents for the presentation of the national capabilities. For example, states which are in transition or in the process of establishing national security system, they give priority to constitutional documents which consist of framework that serves later on for shaping of developing and operational documents aimed for the security capacity building. On the other side, developed states which have stabile and clear national system, give priority to developing documents as a starting point from which goes further improvement of the national security policy.

In formulation of the security policy and strategy in the specific areas, states make an announcement in some sort of the national policy documents (security or defense strategy) and then make elaboration in other documents, such as it is case with cyber security policy.

Because of the increased impact of "soft" security threats, national security policies and strategies, besides traditional security challenges, include contemporary ones, such as cyber security threats, in addition to improve capacities to face with contemporary challenges.

Basic approaches, norms, standards and guidelines are drafted in different national security policy and strategy documents which are systematically formulated to include majority of security threats and problems and provide adequate measures for addressing those problems.

When it comes to cyber security, two the most important approaches in addressing national security policy and strategy is how to response on security threats and how to protect critical infrastructure. National security policy and strategy should determine priorities as the most relevant condition for countering wide range of cyber threats and to give recommendations for engagement of the necessary national security resources. In some cases, it includes all national security institutions and others from public sphere, but also partnership with the private sector.

National security policy and strategies should be relevant both on national and international level and they need to consider and involve international standards and practices. In the case of the United States, central focus in security policy and strategy is on norms not only with the aim to improve national but also to improve global standards for cyber security (Stevens, 2012).

Many countries have developed cyber security strategy as a separate document, with the concrete measures and efforts, and that is often document which consolidate national capacities, while others are drafted cyber security in general national policy documents which provides a strategic framework for a state's approach to cyber security.

As it is stated in the ENISA Report (2012), national cyber security strategy (NCSS) is a tool to improve security and protect national infrastructures, and depending on the approach, strategy should give guidelines for achievement of the national objectives and priorities in cyber security. The European Union member states, started with adoption of the national cyber security strategies from 2008 after the Estonian cyber-attack but still not many of them don't have formal strategy and prior to that only Germany and Sweden had semi-formal documents on cyber security (ENISA, May 2012).

Some of the necessary measures that national security policy and strategy documents should consist towards cyber security threats are:

1.   Discover needs what have to be protected from cyber security threats and identify critical infrastructure;
2.   Determine capabilities and resources that could be used for cyber security protection;
3.   Applying best practices for protection;
4.   Follow achievements in this field based on national policy and strategy perspectives;
5.   Developing norms and standards for countering cyber security threats.

National policy for cyber threats is driven by many elements (economic, political, cultural, techno-logical, and scientific) and also depends on the national interests, international position and obligations, foreign policy, economic growth, etc. For example, NATO and EU members, try to reconcile policy and strategy regarding common framework towards cyber security.

Both organizations have clear attitude towards cyber security challenges, expressed in EU and NATO official Documents:

- **Report on Implementation EU Security Strategy (2008)** : Cyber-crime is identified as a new threat, explained with the following statement: "Modern economies depend on critical infrastructure - transportation, information flow and supply. All of them are vulnerable and become targets of crimes committed using the Internet. *Strategy for Development of the Information Society* is not enough. Comprehensive approach on Cyber Crime has to be developed within the EU" (Report on the Implementation of the European Security Strategy - Providing Security in a Changing World, 2008).
- **NATO's New Strategic Concept (2010)** : Cyber security threats are emphasized as a priority which requires planning approach in preparation for defense against cyber-attacks and in improving awareness on cyberthreats.

Development of the national security policy and strategy towards cyber threats was unfolded progressively and with raising awareness, what could be followed across two main aspects:

Identifying Cyber in National Security Strategy and Policy Documents

National security policy framework is developed upon the security strategy documents and legislation, which in some cases identify cyber security. In that sense, we used as example for building security policy towards cyber security experience as of the United States, Russia and United Kingdom.

- United States started to build national security policy framework from early 2000's, but the first big step was adoption of the strategic document National Strategy to Secure Cyberspace in 2003, which was integral part of the National Strategy for Homeland Security.

United States have a serious national security policy and strategy approach towards cyber space based on different aspects of protection and safety, but cyber is first identified in National Security Strategy in 2002 and later was adopted in other strategic security and defense documents.

In the book edited by Seymour, E. G. &Herbert, S.L. (2007) Toward a Safer and More Secure Cyberspace, policy makers are invited "to create a sense of urgency about the cybersecurity problem commensurate with the risks" (Seymour, E. G. &Herbert, S. L, 2007, p.229).

- Russia stressed awareness on cyber threats impact on national security in the document National Security Strategy till 2020(2009), but also cyber identified in other national security policy documents, such as in National Security Concept (2000) and Concept of the Foreign Policy (2013).
- United Kingdom security policy is drafted in National Security Strategy: *A Strong Britain in an Age of Uncertainty* (2010), where is addressed that cyber threats are one of the most dangerous threats for the national security. Shortly after, United Kingdom adopted national cyber policy guidebook *Cyber Security Strategy: Protecting and Promoting the UK in a Digital World* (2011).

Development and Maintaining National Cyber Security Strategy

It seems that development of the national cyber security strategies, was taking place gradually or after emergence of new threats and circumstances, what indicates that is necessary to have more dynamic and focused systems for cyber security protection and prevention.

The first national cyber security strategic documents in European states and elsewhere have started to adopt during the first years of the previous decade and one of the first countries which recognised cyber security as a national strategic matter was the United States, when in 2003 published cyber security concept.

But, we can speak about the big bang in adoption of the cyber security strategies started from 2008 to 2011, and prior to that, cyber threats were recognized in national security policy and strategy just occasionally and in other types of national documents.

In 2008 three the EU members (Finland, Estonia and Slovakia) have adopted formal NCSS and main focus in this documents was on information system and data protection, as well as on the prevention (ENISA, May 2012). Then in 2011 seven EU countries adopted NCSS (Czech Republic, France,

Germany, Lithuania, Luxembourg, Netherlands and United Kingdom), with wider perspectives and comprehensive approach.

This trend was followed by other developed countries (US, Japan, and Canada), which have adopted NCSS in 2010 and 2011, and they had a numerous key areas of action, such as institutions and capacity building, law enforcement, proactive approach, etc.

It is obvious that countries give efforts and use knowledge, skills and experiences to improve cyber security policy and strategy, but this threats request to work on it more effectively and more widely, because of the constant development of new threats, risks and emergences.

One of the main obstacles in ensuring cyber security is related with gap between national cybersecurity posture and the cyber threats appearance, as well as on short-term strategies. National cyber security policy goals and objectives are addressed due to the national interests, and they are very different, what depends on threats they are facing, assessments, capacities, principles, etc. By definition of the Cyberspace Policy Review of the United States(2009), cyber security policy „includes strategy, policy and standards regarding the security and operations in cyberspace and encompasses the full range of threat reduction, vulnerability reduction, deterrence, international engagement, incident response, resiliency and recovery policies and activities, including computer network operations, information assurance, law enforcement, diplomacy, military, and intelligence missions as they relate to the security and stability of the global information and communications infrastructure. (Cyberspace Policy Review, 2009)

In addition to show specifies of the national policies, we will present cyber policy objectives of the few countries:

- *United Kingdom has four main strategic objectives*: To repress cyber-crime and ensure cyber space for free and safe business, provide resistance from cyber-attacks in all areas of the national interest, enable open and stable cyberspace for citizens based on the open society principles and to improve knowledge, skills and capabilities for establishment of each of this four principles (*Cyber Security Strategy: Protecting and Promoting the UK in a Digital World, 2011*).
- *United States started with three defined strategic objectives in 2003:* Prevent and protect critical infrastructure, reduce vulnerability from cyber-attacks and take measures to solve damage and establishing system after the attack (The National Strategy to Secure Cyberspace, 2003). Than in National Security Presidential Directive (2008) was adopted thirteen objectives, such as: to establish National Cyber Security Centre in DHS, to develop detection, prevention and intervention system, to connect present cyber security operation centres, to improve intelligence capabilities, to expand cyber education, provide security for classified networks, to identify priorities for cyber security in private sector, to establish risk management system, etc.
- *Germany established strategic objectives and measures in ten specific areas:* Critical infrastructure protection, secure IT public system and in public administration, establishing new institutions, confront cyber-crime, wide activities across the Europe, provide safe communication systems, improve skills, tools and capabilities to respond to cyber-attack, etc. (Cyber Security Strategy for Germany, 2011).
- *France gives four strategic objectives of the national cyber policy:* To become world power in cyber defense, to provide cyberspace security, to protect information important for state sovereignty,

to protect critical infrastructure (Information Systems Defense and Security: France's Strategy, 2011).

- *Netherlands have more paradigmatic strategic objectives, based on security and trust in digital age:* To strengthen security in digital age and safe individuals, business and public sector, to ensure safety of the free digital society with aim to support economy and business, to provide legal protection and perform adequate action in case of cyber-attacks (National Cyber Security Strategy: Strength Through Cooperation, 2011).

CYBER-ATTACKS AND THREAT SOURCES

All sorts of cyber vandalism, protest, crime, terrorism, war and other forms are included in cyber-attacks. These attacks have two specific priorities that are particular to their virtual medium. First, most of cyber-attacks are asymmetric in the sense that a high-value target can be crashed with limited resources. Second, property is at the advantageous position for offense in cyberspace.

There are both intentional and unintentional, and targeted or non-targeted cyber threats. The sources of cyber threats are also numerous: they may be launched by opponent nations during cyber warfare or by malicious users such as criminals, hackers, and virus writers. They may even come from discontent employees or parties within an organization. Unintentional threats can occur due to system upgrades, maintenance operations, equipment break downs or careless and unqualified users that may cause the accidental disruption of the information system.

Intentional threats can be targeted or non-targeted. Targeted threats are the ones where malicious users direct their attack particularly to a specific pat of the system. Non-targeted attacks, on the other hand, are the one without a specific target. For example, release of malicious software like virus or worm to the general network, without a specific target, is not a targeted attack.

Attacks launched by a user who has legitimate permissions to access a system are presumably the most dangerous ones. These users may also be used other malevolent actors. For example, a crime or terrorist organization may make a deal with a discontent employee, or may take advantage of an ignorant user.

Cyber-attacks are usually considered as asymmetric, sneaky, and ever-evolving. A single user, for example, can target critical information systems and cause a devastating damage with a limited amount of money and equipment. Some other examples of cyber threats include unauthorized access to an information system that may result in compromise of the confidential information, or intrusion to telecommunication networks to disable or disorganize the critical infrastructure operations.

Cyber Threats

The United Kingdom's Strategy for cyber security describes ICT threats as one that deserve the greatest possible attention (Government of UK, 2011). Therefore, the protection of cyberspace is one of its top national security priorities (Klimburg, 2011). There is addressed a whole range of cyberspace threats, ranging from hostile attacks from other countries to people using it for terrorist purposes and, what may be the most evident one, cyber criminals. However, Internet still enables many possibilities for all users. Such Internet-related dangers and possibilities will probably undergo a significant increase over the next five to ten years and thus will depend on web communications and transactions. Hence, security of the use of ICT is now more important than ever before.

By official data, this is the list of the most important threats in cyber space (ENISA.2014):

- **Drive-By Downloads:** Web pages, web servers and web services have become the most important attack surface: attackers target web sites with the aim to infect them with malicious code, usually exploit kits. Infected web sites are referred to as malicious URLs and are "door openers" for other threats such as exploit kits and malicious code infections (i.e. Worms/Trojans). Visitors of these web sites are automatically scanned through the maliciously installed exploit kits for weaknesses/ vulnerabilities. Once vulnerabilities have been found in the device of the visitor, exploit kits automatically install the appropriate malware on the device.
- **Malicious Code – Worms/Trojans:** Worm is an autonomous piece of code that can reproduce and infect by copying itself through network system without requiring any user action. Virus is s computer code that damages computer systems by infecting usually executable files in the system. It typically propagates through execution of infected files by an ignorant user. Unlike worms viruses need human performance to infect and spread through computer system. Trojan horse is a computer program that apparently seen as useful software but actually masking some malicious code.
- **Code Injection:** Nowadays there are a lot of tools available to perform code injection attacks remained unchanged: Cross-Site Scripting (XSS), Directory Traversal, SQL injection (SQLi) and Cross-Site Request Forgery (CSRF). The proliferation of automated attack tools impacted the frequency of this threat in the reporting period: hackers are in the position to launch large vulnerability scans in short time.
- **Exploit Kits:** Exploit kits are the main tools in the hands of threat agents. These are ready-to-use software tools offering a large variety of functions, configuration options and automated means to launch attacks. Exploit kits search for vulnerabilities in order to abuse them and launch any applicable attack to take over an asset. The ability for updating, customization and the degree of automation provided is considered to be one of the main parameters for increase in all kinds of threats supported, such as malware, code injections, exploitation of vulnerabilities, etc.
- **Botnets:** A network that is under the control of malicious user without the knowledge of actual users of the computers is called botnet. The malicious user can launch coordinated attacks through this network, or can use it to spread infected software.
- **Physical Damage/Theft/Loss of Media:** This threat has increased in last two years due to the increasing number of mobile devices used and consequently stolen, lost or damaged. Taking ENISA's reported (ENISA.2014) percentages as a basis, we can conclude that some 70-80 million devices have been broken, stolen or lost. Meanwhile, it is considered that hacking is not the main cause of data loss: ca. 36% of data breaches are attributed to theft/loss of devices.
- **Identity Theft/Fraud:** Identity theft and identity fraud are threats that have led to some of the most impressive successful attacks. Identity theft is one of the core activities of many threat agent groups, as it gives access to a lot of data that bear potential for numerous malicious activities. Malware and Trojans belong to the main tools to perform identity theft.
- **Denial of Service (DoS)/Distributed Denial of Service (DDoS):** A kind of the denial of service attacks is the one is launched from not a single source but by a distributed system of computers in a coordinated manner. Commonly worms are used to infect the participant computers to form the distributed attack system. The distributed nature of this attack ensures the obscurity of the source and diversity of the attacks.

- **Phishing:** Using cyberspace tools such as pup-up messages and spam to deceive users to reveal their confidential personal information.
- **Spam:** Advertise products, Web pages, or services via sending unsolicited commercial emails. They can also be used to spread malware infection or any other kind of cyber threats through internet.
- **Rogueware/Ransomware/Scareware:** This threat is used to obtain profits from terrified end users. Rogue security software, ransomware and scareware are malicious pieces of software - distributed by threat agents - to terrify/blackmail users, thus demanding ransom payments.
- **Information Leakage:** With information leakage we cover a set of threats related to the unintentional or maliciously triggered revelation of information of security related information to an unauthorised party. This threat is differentiated from data breaches, as it merely concerns technical or organisational information that might be interesting for threat agents in order to perform reconnaissance and delivery of their attacks; as opposed to data breach which is a result of a successful attack targeting customers' data.
- **Targeted Attacks:** Targeted attacks are characterized with their long endurance and specificity of the victim. Targeted attacks are further characterised by the capability level and dedication of the threat agent deploying the attack. Important observation in the ENISA's report (ENISA.2014) is on a shift of targets from financial institutions to politically motivated targets such as NGOs, governmental organisations, politically active groups.
- **Watering Hole Attacks:** Watering hole attacks consist of the attempt to attack a certain target group by manipulating web sites visited and trusted by members of this target group. When visiting a manipulated web site, devices of members of the target group get eventually infected.

Cyber Threats Agent

Verizon (Verizon. 2013) specifies three primary categories of threat actors—external, internal, and partner.

- **External:** External actors originate outside the victim organization and its network of partners. Typically, no trust or privilege is implied for external entities.
- **Internal:** Internal actors come from within the victim organization. Insiders are trusted and privileged (some more than others).
- **Partners:** Partners include any third party sharing a business relationship with the victim organization. Some level of trust and privilege is usually implied between business partners.

A threat agent is someone or something with decent capabilities, a clear intention to manifest a threat and a record of past activities in this regard. Figure 1 shows major threat agents.

The major threat agents are identified as follows:

- **Corporations:** One of the main objectives of corporations is creation of competitive advantages. Hence, corporations may act as hostile threat agents when involved in activities to: collect business intelligence, to breach intellectual property rights, to gather confidential information on competitors, to be engaged in intelligence gathering connected to bids, etc. Depending on their size, corporations may possess significant cyber capabilities to perform malicious activities to-

Figure 1. The major threat agent
(Verizon.2013).

wards achieving their objectives or may engage threat agents from other groups to achieve their objectives.

- **Nation States:** If we analyze reports (Corporation, 2014), (Cisco, 2014), (Kaspersky, 2014), (Verizon.2013), about cyber incident during 2014 we can conclude that cyber activities are not connecting only two nation states. In many cases, multiple nation states have developed join capabilities that can be used to perform cyber-attack to some governmental or/and private organization in order to achieve their objectives. Main targets of this threat agent group are state secrets, military secrets, data on intelligence, and critical infrastructures.

- **Hacktivists:** Hacktivists is a threat agent group that has enjoyed great media attention. Hacktivists are ideologically motivated individuals that can dynamically form groups/subgroups, usually lacking a central organisation structure. Their main motivation is usually the defense of ideas that are sometime manifested. The hacktivists are usually selected targets in order to create great media attention in case of successful cyber-attacks.

- **Cyber Terrorists:** This threat agent group is mainly used to attribute potential threats to cyber-targets that will harm national security and society. Characteristic of this threat agent group is the indiscriminate use of violence in order to influence decisions/actions of states towards their politically or relationally motivated objectives. Activities of this threat group are mostly impact oriented and may affect or harm large parts of society, just to generate necessary pressure.

- **Cybercriminals:** This threat agent group is the most widely known as its objective is to obtain profit from illegal/criminal activities in the cyberspace. Cybercriminals act mainly in the cyberspace and so do their victims. Hence, cybercriminals are involved in fraud regarding all kinds of e-finance, e-commerce, e-payment, ransom ware, cybercrime-as-a-service, delivery and development of malicious tools and infrastructures.

- **Cyber Fighters:** Cyber fighters are groups of nationally motivated citizens. This is an emerging phenomenon where patriotic motivated groups of citizens bear the potential to launch cyber-attacks in a coordinated manner. Such groups might have strong feelings when their political, national or religious values seem to be threatened by another group and are capable of launching cyber-attacks.

- **Script Kiddies:** On Internet it can be found many sites where young people learn to write malicious code and learn how to hack. Despite being in a self-discovery phase and technically novice, due to their large number, script kiddies are susceptive to external influences from other threat agent groups, in particular cyber criminals and hacktivists. Typically this threat agent group is engaged in DDoS and code injection attacks. Script kiddies may also form ad-hoc groups with common targets and develop to a considerable striking power.

- **Online Social Hackers:** Over the last two years it can be seen an increasing significance of social engineering as element of cyber-attack pattern. Therefore this threat agent group plays a key role when deploying cyber threats. These online social hackers are skilled with social engineering knowledge, are in the position to analyse and understand behaviour and psychology of social targets and to generate false trust relationships.
- **Employees:** This threat agent group can be staff, contractors, operational staff, former employees, etc. The reasons for acting within threat agent group may vary significantly, i.e. lax handling of security procedures, user error or even malicious intent. This threat group is usually equipped with low to medium-tech methods and tools.

Figure 2 present an overview of existing agents/actors acting in cyber space. It can be seen that the mentioned threat are depicted in the figure through the right hand branch, annotated as *Hostile Cyber Agent*, whereas the left hand branch of it stays for other agents who serve friendly tasks in cyber space. The purpose of this figure is to deliver information on agents/actors acting in cyber space such as motive, capability or areas of engagement.

In order to identify required levels of cyber security in Montenegro it is common to perform a threat assessment. Process of analysing threats and threats agent are important elements in risk assessment.

Figure 2. Overview of threats agents in cyber space
(Source: ENISA Threat Lendscape 2013).

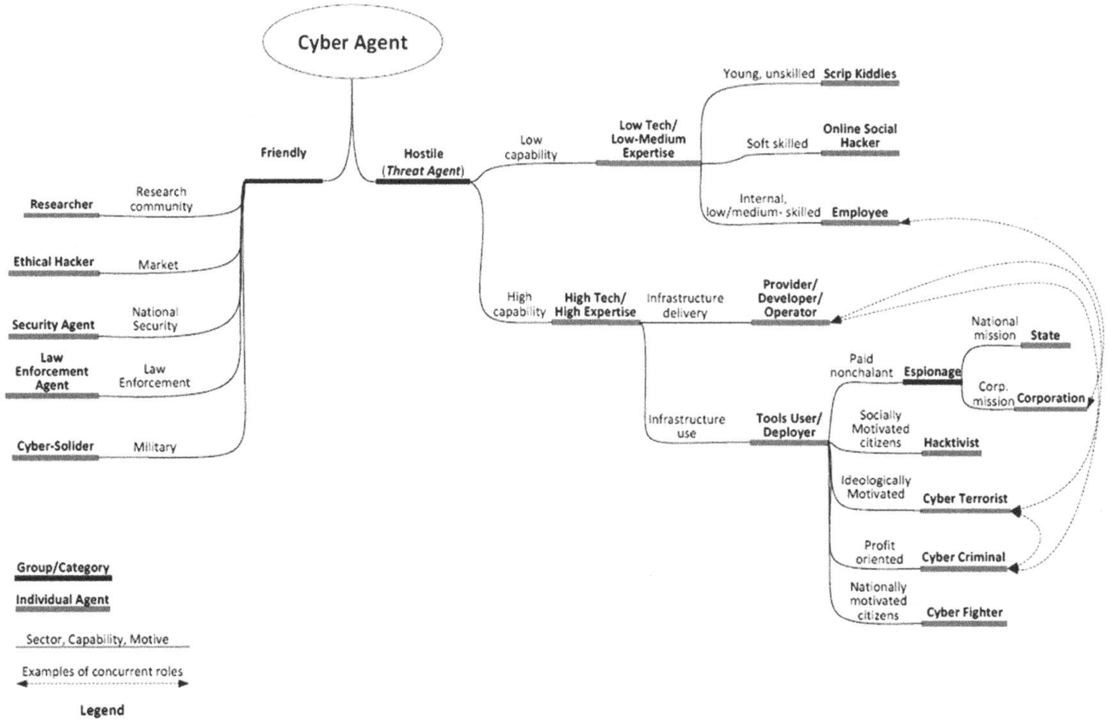

The role of threats in the risk assessment can be described by the widely accepted ISO 27005 definition risks emerge: *"Threats abuse vulnerabilities of assets to generate harm for the organization"*. In accordance with the definitions, we need to recognize number of threats to which IT and their related assets are exposed.

The Figure 3 is adopted from ISO 13335-4, showing threats agent (TA), their aims to exploit asset vulnerabilities (V) by deploying threats (T), in order to harm/take over the asset. In order to protect the asset and eliminate negative effects of threat exposure, the asset owner should implement adequate security measures (M).

The involvement of the above threat agents in the deployment of the identified top threats is presented in the Table 1. The purpose of this table is to visualize which threat agent groups use which threats. The target group of this information are individuals who wish to assess possible threat agent involvement in the deployment of threats. This information might be useful when assessing which capability level can be assumed behind the top threats and thus supported in decisions concerning the strength of the implemented security measures.

Figure 3. Threats targeting an asset by trying to exploit its vulnerabilities
(Source: ISO 13335-4).

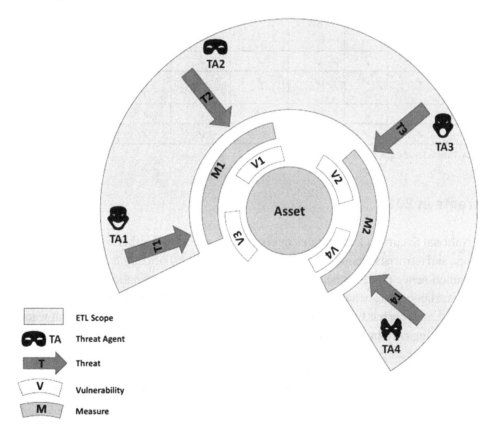

Table 1. Involvement of threat agents in the top threats

Threats	Threats Agent								
	Corporation	Nation State	Hactivists	Cyber Terrorists	Cyber Criminal	Cyber Fighters	Script Kiddies	Online Social Hackers	Employs
Drive-by download		✓			✓				
Worms/Trojans		✓		✓	✓	✓		✓	✓
Code injection	✓	✓	✓	✓	✓	✓	✓		
Exploit kits			✓	✓	✓	✓	✓		
Botnet	✓	✓	✓	✓	✓	✓			
Physical Damage/ Theft/ Loss	✓	✓	✓	✓	✓	✓	✓	✓	✓
Identity Theft/. Fraud	✓	✓	✓	✓	✓	✓	✓	✓	✓
DoS, DdoS		✓	✓	✓	✓	✓	✓		✓
Phishing	✓	✓			✓			✓	
Spam	✓				✓			✓	
Rogueware/ Ransomware/ Scareware					✓				
Data Breach	✓	✓	✓	✓	✓	✓	✓		✓
Information leakage	✓	✓	✓	✓	✓	✓	✓	✓	✓
Targeted Attacks	✓	✓	✓	✓	✓	✓		✓	
"Watering hole"	✓	✓			✓	✓			

(Source: ENISA Threats Landscape, 2013).

Cyber Threats in 2014

The British National Security Council rates cyber-attacks performed either by other states or organised criminal groups and terrorists among the four threats of the highest priority for the next five years (Svete. 2012).The Council hence places cyber threats side-by-side to the international terrorism, international military crises and large-scale or natural disasters. The newest British National Security Strategy explains that United Kingdom is currently not facing military threats but that there are states that want to improve their position by using certain methods such as cyber-attacks and espionage (Svete. 2012).

For analyzing cyber threats we are used annually reports: "Internet Security Threat Report 2014", done by Corporation, and "Global IT Risks Report 2014" done by Kaspersky. According with these reports "Symantec and Kaspersky have established the most comprehensive source of Internet threat data in the world through the Global Intelligence Network, which is made up of more than 80 million attack sensors and records thousands of events per second". This two networks monitor threat activity in over 160 countries and territories.

One of the most interesting suggestions that were highlighted in survey for 2014 is so called 'the perception gap'. It explains the difference between our perception of what is happening and the reality on the ground. We truly believe that "the perception gap" in Montenegro is much higher than it is a global average.

In the Table 2 is shown influence of the external threats in some of the world regions.

Taking into consideration these data presented in the reports, we can conclude that 94% of companies have experienced some form of external security threat, and yet only 68% have fully implemented anti-malware on their workstations, and only 44% employ security solutions for their mobile devices. We need to recalibrate our perceptions of the industry to better understand the threats. And not just the visible security breaches, but the daily and ongoing security threats, too. A big concern is the control and integration of mobile devices into normal working practices, and security relating to virtualization. However, only 34% of IT decision makers have a clear understanding of the virtual security solutions available, and 46% of businesses think that their conventional security solutions provide adequate protection Table 3 shows influence of internal threats in some of the world regions.

Cyber Security and National Security Policy of Montenegro

Every country is obliged to protect own national information infrastructure, as well as cyberspace that is covered with a national domain (Klimburg, 2012). Montenegro's strategic objective is to build an integrated, functional and efficient cyberspace, in accordance with international standards and principles.

This chapter analyse national security policy of Montenegro, as well as cyber policy, capabilities and readiness to response on cyber security threats. Montenegro has started to develop national security policy after getting independence on 21 May 2006, when was launched and construct strategic and institutional framework, as well as legislation for security system with aim to implement reforms in all areas. Priorities for implementation of the national security policy of Montenegro were institutional reforms and establishment of an efficient system for countering contemporary security challenges.

Table 2. External cyber threats by region

External Cyber Threats	Global	Europe	Russia	Chine	America	Asia	M. East
Spam	64%	63%	75%	63%	72%	63%	62%
Viruses, worms, spyware	61%	54%	78%	59%	66%	62%	51%
Phishing attacks	38%	41%	25%	41%	57%	33%	24%
Network intrusion / hacking	25%	22%	21%	40%	21%	23%	24%
Theft of mobile devices	22%	25%	15%	25%	19%	23%	8%
DoS, DdoS	18%	17%	17%	34%	15%	17%	22%
Theft of larger hardware	16%	16%	11%	20%	12%	18%	9%
Corporate espionage	16%	12%	24%	26%	6%	16%	10%
Targeted Attacks	12%	10%	9%	20%	10%	12%	13%
Criminal damage	6%	5%	5%	6%	5%	8%	3%
None	6%	7%	3%	1%	7%	6%	11%

(Source: Global IT Risk Survey 2013 by Kaspersky).

Table 3. Internal cyber threats by region

Internal Cyber Threats	Global	Europe	Russia	Chine	America	Asia	M. East
Customer/client information	36%	32%	50%	38%	33%	37%	23%
Internal operational information	29%	26%	34%	42%	26%	25%	25%
Financial information about the organisation	26%	29%	19%	27%	22%	24%	25%
Intellectual property	21%	18%	22%	32%	12%	21%	18%
Market intelligence/competitive intelligence	20%	18%	18%	30%	16%	22%	13%
Payment information	16%	15%	10%	25%	14%	17%	11%
HR/Personnel information	16%	15%	10%	25%	14%	17%	11%
Other	17%	19%	14%	9%	26%	14%	30%

(Source: Global IT Risk Survey 2013 by Kaspersky).

The reform started with adoption of the first National Security Strategy of Montenegro in July 2006 as a constitutional document of the national security system. Then in 2007 have been adopted three key documents on national defense - the Defense Strategy, the Law on Defense and Law on Army. Also, for the first time in 2007 were formed a particular national institutions, that is the Ministry of Defense and the Army of Montenegro.

In the document of National Security Strategy that is currently in power, cyber security and critical infrastructure protection are highlighted as some of the national goals and interests, and in Article 2 is stated "ensuring the protection of information resources of Montenegro from unauthorized access or modification of information storage, processing or transmission, including measures of detection, documentation and removal of threats" (National Security Strategy of Montenegro, 2008).Also, in other national security policy documents is identified cyber security, such as in the document Defense Strategic Review from 2013.

In order to respond to cyber threats, which are constantly changing, Montenegro goal is to have flexible and dynamic cyber security organization. The cross border nature of threats makes it necessary for the countries to focus on strong international cooperation. Comprehensive national cyber security strategies are the first step in this direction. In 2013 Government of Montenegro adopted *National Cyber Security Strategy* for a period of five years. The Strategy presents a national vision against the concept of cyber security and express guaranty, and in the corresponding annual action plans are also clearly defined objectives and priorities (Government of Montenegro, 2013).

Over the last couple of years, Montenegro has begun, through the criminal law reforms, to build a corresponding legal and regulatory framework that legally prevents any kind of accidental or deliberate distortion and prevention of the computer system functioning. An appropriate legal framework represents a link between legal and IT areas, which will, by joint cooperation, contribute to successful clarification of the case in the field of computer crime and punishing the perpetrators.

The Convention on Cybercrime or known in the international community as the *Budapest Convention,* was adopted on 21st November 2001 by the Council of Europe, and is effective from July 2004. The Convention was signed by 51 countries. This Convention is one of framework conventions, which means that its provisions are not directly applicable, but it is necessary that states implement these provisions in their own national legislation.

Criminal offenses indicated under this Convention as cybercrime include a wide range of spreading viruses, unauthorized access to a computer network through piracy to pornography and intrusion into the banking systems, abuse of credit cards and all other criminal offences in which computers are used. Montenegrin criminal legislation complies with the provisions of *Budapest Convention*.

The Convention on Cybercrime also involves procedural provisions for the field of cybercrime. The Convention recommends to States parties to adopt all appropriate legislative and other measures in their national legislatures in order to establish certain powers and procedures for the punishment of criminal offenses related to cybercrime.

Montenegro adopted a new *Criminal Procedure Code*, which is in accordance with international legal standards and fully or partially complied national procedural norms with certain procedural provisions stipulated by *Budapest Convention*. Equally, Convention Articles relating to evidentiary actions, secret surveillance measures and temporary seizure of objects and confiscation measures have been implemented in our criminal *Procedure Code*.

Legal documents that form the basis of the functioning and further development of modern concept of information security in Montenegro are:

- Law on Ratification of the Convention on Cybercrime.
- Criminal Code (Parliament of Montenegro. 2008).
- Criminal Procedure Code (Parliament of Montenegro. 2006).
- Law on Information Security (Parliament of Montenegro. 2010).
- Law on the National Security Agency (Parliament of Montenegro. 2010/8).
- Law on Classified Information (Parliament of Montenegro. 2008/4).
- Electronic Signature Law (Parliament of Montenegro. 2005).
- Law on Electronic Communications (Parliament of Montenegro. 2013).
- Electronic Commerce Law (Parliament of Montenegro. 2004).

The following institutions have been identified as crucial in the field of cyber security in Montenegro (Government of Montenegro, 2013):

- Ministry for Information Society and Telecommunications (National CIRT).
- Ministry of Defence.
- Ministry of the Interior.
- Ministry of Justice.
- National Security Agency.
- Police Administration.
- Military of Montenegro.
- Directorate for the Protection of Classified Information.
- Universities of Montenegro.

The Strategy recognises the National CIRT as a central point for coordination and exchange of information, cyber defence and elimination of the consequences of cyber security incidents for the area of Montenegro (Government of Montenegro, 2013).

Cyber Security Strategy for Montenegro contains seven key areas (Government of Montenegro, 2013):

1. Defining institutional and organisational structure in the field of cyber security in the country.
2. Protection of critical information structures in Montenegro.
3. Strengthening capacities of state law enforcement authorities.
4. Incident Response.
5. The role of Ministry of Defence and Military of Montenegro in cyberspace.
6. Public-private partnership.
7. Raising public awareness and protection on the Internet.

In accordance with *the Law on Information Security of Montenegro* (Parliament of Montenegro. 2010), Government of Montenegro established the National Montenegrin Computer Incident Response Team (CIRT) in 2012. CIRT functions as governmental and national CIRT. Primary constituency for CIRT is defined as:

- All government institutions in Montenegro
- Critical national infrastructure in Montenegro

As a part of its operations CIRT is implementing proactive and reactive measures. Proactive measures act before the incident and other events that could endanger the security of information systems occurs, in order to prevent or mitigate potential damage. Reactive measures present assistance in identifying the perpetrators and restore system in the working condition.

The main CIRT activities are (Klimburg, 2012):

- Coordination and communication;
- Prevention, treatment and elimination of consequences of computer security incidents on the Internet and other information systems security threats;
- User education in the field of information security includes:
  ○ CIRT is a member of *ENISA* (European Union Agency for Network and Information Security) and
  ○ *FIRST* (Forum for Incident Response and Security Team) since 2012.

In 2013 Government of Montenegro established *National Cyber Security Council*. The responsibilities of the Council are activities from the domain of cyber security and INFOSEC. Council members are representatives of institutions that are identified as key in the field of cyber security.

In addition, the Strategy defines that all state authorities and administration bodies who maintain a database of national importance or manage critical part of IT infrastructure need to form local CIRT teams shown in Figure 4. During 2014, local CIRT teams in key institutions have been established to fight against cyber-crime with a view to establish National CIRT infrastructure.

In last six years, Montenegro was concentrated on security sector reform, which consisted of institutional changes and finding solutions to overcome problems with limited resources for implementation of the security policy. Cyber security policy of Montenegro became part of that concept and it is determined by institutional reforms and limited resources for policy implementation.

Figure 4. Organization scheme of cyber security of Montenegro
(Source: Government of Montenegro, 2013, pp. 19).

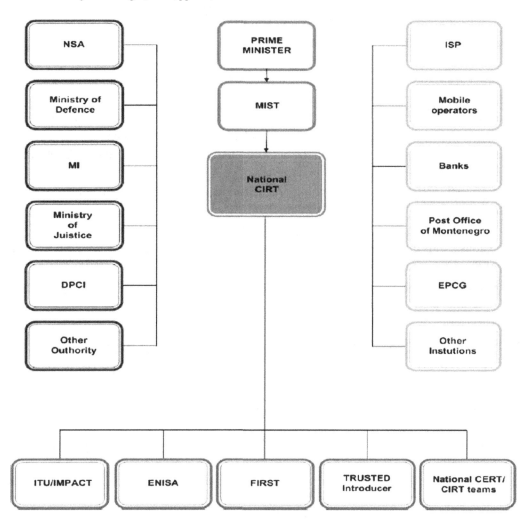

Description of Montenegrin Cyber Space

In order to understand the complexity of Montenegro's cyberspace, it is important to look at the statistical data of using information and communication technologies in Montenegro. The Statistical Office of Montenegro, conducted a survey on ICT usage in the period from 1st to 15th April 2014 (MONTSAT. 2014). The survey refers to the ICT usage in households, by individuals, and in enterprises. The ICT usage survey which was conducted in households, according to the Eurostat methodology, includes households with at least one member aged between 16 and 74 years old, and individuals of the same age. 1 200 households, with 1200 individuals, were interviewed face-to-face. The ICT usage survey which is conducted in enterprises covers 578 enterprises with 10 or more employees from 10 business sectors according to NACE Rev. 2; who were interviewed by telephone.

Summarized data shows that (MONTSAT. 2014):

- Percentage of households that have access to computers is 53.7%.
- Percentage of households with Internet access at home is 63.6%.
- Percentage of households with TV set access (in house) is 99.2%.
- Percentage of households with mobile phone is 93.6%.

Furthermore, access to cyber space is characterized with the following data:

- Access to the Internet via a PC achieves 75.1% of households that have Internet access.
- Access to the Internet via a laptop achieves 57.6% of households that have Internet access.
- Access to the Internet via a mobile phone achieves 38.5% of households that have Internet access.

Figure 5 presents participation of technology in the total number of broadband connections. It shows that (MONTSAT. 2014):

- Of the households that have access to the Internet, 79% answered that they use DSL or some other type of fixed broadband connection to the Internet.
- Of the households that have access to the Internet, 29.6% answered that they use 3G or some other type of mobile broadband connection to the Internet.

It is interesting to consider the reasons for having no access to the Internet, since 33.2% said that they have a lack of ICT literacy in using it (see Table 4).

Figure 5. Participation of technology in the total number of broadband connections in Montenegro (MONTSAT, 2014).

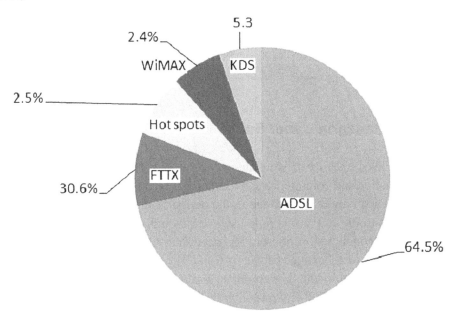

Table 4. Reasons for having to access to the Internet

Reasons	Percentage (%)	Reasons	Percentage (%)
I do not want to have Internet access	36.8	Physical disability	9.5
I have lack of ICT literacy	33.2	I access to Internet at some another place	7.5
Internet access is too expensive	29.9	Broadband connections are disabled	5.8
Equipment is too expensive	27.8	Other reasons	19.6

(MONTSAT. 2014).

Furthermore, use of Internet by individuals is represented with (see Figure 6):

- The percentage of persons who used a computer in the last 3 months is 64.5%.
- The percentage of persons who never used a computer is 30.6%.
- As for the use of the Internet, 63.9% of them reported that they had used the Internet in the last 3 months.

Also, we have deeper analyses of Internet users (based on age category), presented in Table 5.

Figure 6. Use of computer, Internet, and smart phones in last 3 months (MONTSAT, 2014).

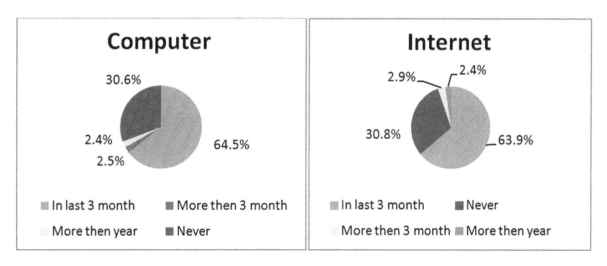

Table 5. Use of Internet based on age category and gender

Use of Internet	Age Category						Gender	
	16-24	25-34	35-44	45-54	55-64	65-74	Male	Female
Every day or almost every day	89.9	85.7	83.0	72.3	68.7	39.0	80.5	80,7
At least once a week	8.1	13.2	15.7	18.3	19.8	56.0	14.5	15.1
Less than once a week	2.1	1.1	1.3	9.5	11.5	5.0	3.1	4.1

(MONTSAT, 2014).

Furthermore, kinds of activities that users of Internet in last 3 months have used are presented in Table 6, while Table 7 gives more information regarding for which kind of activities users are aware and capable to use.

The following indicators show the use of e-government services by individuals and provide information on the perceived quality of public authorities' websites and satisfaction with e-government services. They cover contacts or interactions with websites concerning citizen's obligations, rights, official documents, public educational services and public health services.

Methodology that was used for estimation is developed by EU and company Campegini (source: www.euprava.me).

Level 1: On-line information;
Level 2: One directional interaction (information and forms download),
Level 3: Both directional (on-line submission of forms, authentication),
Level 4: Transaction (complete processing of subject, on-line payment services),
Level 5: Personalization.

Overall, there seems to be considerable scope for improving e-government services and increasing take-up by individuals in the future (Table 8).

Table 6. Activities on Internet

Type of Activities	Percentage (%)
Telephone calls via Internet/video calls	80.5%
Sending/Receiving e-mails	75.2%
Use of social networks	73.4%
Read or download on-line newsletters and newspapers	64.7%

(MONTSAT, 2014).

Table 7. Kinds of activities that users performed via Internet in last 3 months

Type of Activities	Percentage (%)
Copy and move file/folder	78.7%
Copy and paste tools for managing information inside a document	72.6%
Transfer of data from computer to other devices	51.9%
Installation and connection of other devices (e.g. printer, modem, etc.)	42.7%
File compressing (ZIP, RAR)	32.6%
Use of basic arithmetic formulas in spreadsheets	22.9%
Creation of.ppt presentation	18.9%
Installation of new or upgrading existing operating system	14.6%
Creation of a program by using programming languages	11.4%
Changes of configuration parameters of software applications	6.9%

(MONTSAT, 2014).

Table 8. Basic Services of e-government

Name of Service	Max Level	MNE Level	Name of Service	Max Level	MNE Level
Services for Individuals			**Services for Legal Entity**		
Submitting taxes	5	4	Social Insurance for Employees	4	2
Searching for job	4	3	Calculation, registration and payment of taxes	4	4
Social Help	5	1	VAT	4	2
Personal Documents	5	1	Firm Registration	4	3
Car Registration	4	1	Sending Data to the Statistic Department	5	4
Building Permits	4	2	Customs Declaration	4	4
Police Reporting	3	2	Ecological Permits	5	2
Public Libraries	5	3	Public Procurement	4	2
The documents (list of births, deaths, marriages...)	4	4			
Application and Enrolment to High School	4	2			
Changing Permanent Address	5	1			
Health Services	4	2			

(MONTSAT, 2014).

To summarize presented data, type of activities that are performed by individuals in Montenegro is characterized with the following numbers (MONTSAT. 2014):

- Number of persons that in the last 3 months bought or ordered goods or services over the Internet is 7%, while the percentage of those who have never bought or ordered goods or services is 81%.
- Percentage of Internet use every day or almost every day is marginally higher in men and is 82.5%, while 80.7% of women.
- 93.9% of surveyed enterprises use computers in their business.
- The survey showed that 98.1% of enterprises that use a computer have Internet access.
- Of the enterprises that have access to the Internet, 73.3% answered that they have a Web Site.
- Of the companies that have access to the Internet, 96.5% said they use DSL or some other type of fixed broadband connection to the Internet.

On the other side, use of Internet in business sector is characterized with data presented on the following figures: 98.1% Companies in Montenegro used computers; 93.9% use Internet; 68% company has own web site; 57% use company's e-mail; 47.8 use some service on cloud.

In Table 9 is shown progress of e-commerce activities at enterprises in Montenegro in period 2012-2014.

All these data presented in Table 9 were collected by Montenegrin bodies, and to the best of our knowledge this is the most comprehensive analysis about use of ICTs in Montenegro.

Table 9. Activity of e-commerce

Activity	2012	2013	2014
Orders placed via the Internet	11,7	17,2	24,3
Orders received via the Internet	8,1	11	14,7

Cyber Incidents in Montenegrin Cyber Space during 2014

From January 2014 to August 2014 CIRT of Montenegro is *registered* 55 different kinds of cyber-attacks. We emphasize the period of registered incidents, since we would like to point out that realistically number of cyber incidents is significantly higher.

During 2014, the attackers were tried or taken control on web site of several Montenegrin governmental institutions, finance institutions, and Internet service providers. Also there were several cases where attackers took control on user profiles on social networks. The attackers left inappropriate content with the aim to compromise owner or some political message. In several cases Montenegrin computer systems were compromised by international cyber attackers and used for attacking computer system in other countries (bootnet). Finally, there is a significant number of banking fraud and phishing attacks. This type of crime is currently the most popular in Montenegro and throughout the Balkans. The last examples of cyber incidents show that there are a large number of fake websites of foreign banks which used and hosted Montenegrin national domain (ME). Cyber criminals were using these fake web sites to perform many international finance transactions. Some of the biggest and the most famous incidents that happened in the world's cyber space had an effect on the territory of Montenegro. Among the incidents highlights the appearance of a Trojan horse, "MiniDuke" targeting a state institutions at the international level. Furthermore, CIRT team noticed one case of cyber espionage called "Red October" where one of the affected IP address was from Montenegro. By following the urgent notification of international partner organizations (FIRST and other national CERT), CIRT of Montenegro recognized a worms "Conficker" and "isolated" IP addresses contained in cyberspace Montenegro.

The Table 10 shows a number and types of cyber-attacks that took place in cyberspace of Montenegro. If we compare this number with cyber incident in some developed countries shown in Symantec 2013 and Kaspersky 2013 annual reports we can make a wrong conclusion about no alarming figure. However, direct and indirect damage caused by these attacks are not negligible.

Table 10. Recognized cyber threats

Cyber Attack Techniques	Percentage (%)
Distributed Denial of Service Attack (DDoS)	32%
Phishing attacks	25%
Network intrusion / hacking	19%
Theft of larger hardware	15%
Corporate espionage	9%
SUMA	55 (100%)

The targets of cyber-attacks were state institutions, domestic and international financial institutions, domestic and international private companies and a large number of citizens.

Analyzing the techniques of attacks in Table 10 and Table 11 we can see that the attackers used well-known techniques and tools in the execution of attacks on information systems in Montenegro. CIRT recognized almost 90% of threat action and they are categorised as: Malware (Spyware, Backdoor, Export data, Capture stored data, Downloader, Password dumper), Hacking (Use of stolen creds, Use of backdoor, Brute force, SQLi), Social (Phishing), Misuse (Privilege abuse, Unapproved hardware, Embezzlement), Physical (Tampering).

The national CIRT managed in a relatively short period of time to detect an isolated incident and thus diminish their influence (Table 12). However, if we analyse cyber-attacks on institutions which will be recognize as holder critical information infrastructure (government institutions, finance institutions, etc.) we can notice that this period is not adequate.

The main activity for cyber security system in Montenegro in the next year is to define and protect of critical information infrastructure. It is necessary first to define critical information infrastructure in Montenegro and develop procedures for protection to ensure its smooth operation. Next step will be to define methodology to be used for the purpose of identifying critical information infrastructure. All institutions that are recognized as cyber security stakeholders have to be included in this activity.

Table 11. Attacked institutions

Institutions	Percentage (%)
Government institutions	25%
Financial institutions in MNE	25%
International partners	12%
Private company	15%
Individuals	23%
SUMA	55 (100%)

Table 12. The time period required for the detection of fraud

Time Period for the Detection of Fraud	Percentage (%)
Below 1 minute	0%
1 min – 1 hour	2%
1 hour – 6 hour	4%
6 hour – 24 hour	11%
1 day – 7 days	56%
7 day – 1 month	21%
1 month – 3 month	4%
3 month – 12 month	1%
More then 1 year	1%
SUMA	55 (100%)

CONCLUSION

Cyber incidents do not stop at borders in the interconnected digital economy and society. All actors, from national competent authorities, CERT's and law enforcement to industry, must take responsibility both nationally and internationally, and work together to strengthen cyber security (European Commission, 2013).

Supervision approach is not the answer on the complexity of the cyber issues and the diverse range of actors that are involved and centralised. Cyber security policy needs to have comprehensive and holistic approach, not only in collecting national capacities for prevention, detection, response and prosecution of cyber threats, but as well as to the prior identification of sources and early warning detection.

It is obvious that states adopt and develop national security policy and strategy after certain incidents, whether they on national or international level, or initiatives that comes aftermath, and could be concluded that so far states had an pro-reactive approach, but this sort of security threats, require pro-active and more dynamic approach.

National capacities for cyber prevention and detection are in a constant process of improvement, but there is delay in the field of critical infrastructure protection in some countries, because it is necessary to identify what is national critical infrastructure, what is more relevant for the countries whose systems depend on information technologies. But, in digital age which bring dependency on ICT, is requested to bring huge efforts of all actors (states, companies and individuals) to identify "Achilles heels" in cyberspace and implement protection systems. Still it is not guarantee that actors will be safe from cyber threats, and it is always hot issue how to be protected and how much security do we need, from threats that are invisible and unpredictable?

National interest of Montenegro is to fully implement cyber policy and to improve national security capacities, but also to raise awareness, education and research in the field of cyber security. In last period, cyber security policy of Montenegro was created parallel with the national security sector reforms based on institutional and normative changes as well as resources improvement.

In a future, we can expect very dynamic approach, because even if it is small state, Montenegro try to develop well placed system for cyber security policy implementation and, comparing to other cyber security policy which were analysed, that process is initiated in a timely manner.

Government of Montenegro is able to organise prevention and response to cyber incidents and attacks on critical information infrastructure and to establish contacts and networks with the private sector and the general public across their established policy streams and legal frameworks. At the same time, due to the potential or actual borderless nature of the threats, an effective national response would often require international level involvement.

REFERENCES

Baykal, N. (2013). *Hands-on cyber defence training course for system/network administrators. Lecture Notes*. Ankara, Turkey: Institute of Informatics.

Brannon, R. (2014). Cyber security studies. *Per Concordiam, 5*(2), 48–51.

Brussels, Belgium European Council. (2008). *Report on the implementation of the European security strategy - providing security in a changing world.*

Cloud Security Alliance. (2011). *Security guidance for critical areas of focusing in cloud computing* V.3.0.

ENISA. (2014). Threats Landscape 2013. Brussels, Belgium European Commission. (2013). Cybersecurity strategy of the European Union.

European Union for Network and Information Security. (2012, May). *Report on national cyber security strategies: setting the course for national efforts to strengthen security in cyberspace*. Heraklion, Greece.

Goodman, S., & Lin, H. (2007). *Toward a safer and more secure cyberspace*. Washington, DC: National Academies Press.

Government of France. (2011). *Information systems defence and security: France's strategy.*

Government of Germany. (2011). *Cyber security strategy.*

Government of Montenegro. (2008). *National security strategy of Montenegro.*

Government of Montenegro. (2013). *National cyber security strategy of Montenegro.*

Government of Netherlands (2011).*National cyber security strategy: strength through cooperation*

Government of the Russian Federation. (2000). *National security concept.*

Government of the Russian Federation. (2009). *National security strategy of Russia till 2020.*

Government of the Russian Federation. (2013). *Concept of the foreign policy.*

Government of the United Kingdom. (2010). *National security strategy of the United Kingdom 2010.*

Government of the United States. (2009). *Cyberspace policy review.*

Government of the United States. (2010).*National security strategy of the United States 2010.*

Government of Turkey. (2012). *National military strategy for cyberspace operations*. Ankara, Turkey.

Grizold. A.& Injac. O. (2012). *Bezbjednosna paradigma u globalizovanom svijetu*. Podgorica, Crna Gora: Crnogorska akademija nauka i umjetnosti

Kaspersky Lab. (2013). *Global corporate IT security risks.*

Kaspersky Lab. (2014). *IT security threats and data breaches.*

Klimburg, A. (2011). *Mobilising cyber power*. London, UK: Routledge.

Klimburg, A. (2012). *National cyber security framework manual*. Tallinn, Estonia: NATO CCD COE.

Miklaucic, M., & Brewer, J. (Eds.). (2013). *Convergence – illicit networks and national security in the age of globalization*. Washington, DC: NDU Press.

North Atlantic Treaty Organization. (2010). *New strategic concept*. Brussels, Belgium.

Phahlamohlaka, J. (2008). Globalization and national security issues for the state: implications for national ICT policies. In C. Avgerou, M. L.Smith, & P. Van den Besselaar (Eds.), Social dimensions of information and communication technology policy, 282, 95-107. IFIP International Federation for Information Processing.

Seymour, E. G., & Herbert, S. L. (Eds.). (2007). *Toward a safer and more secure cyberspace*. Washington, DC: NDU Press.

Stevens, T. (2012). A cyberwar of ideas: Deterrence and Norms in Cyberspace. *Contemporary Security Policy, 33*(1), 1–2. doi:10.1080/13523260.2012.659597

Svete, U. (2012). European e-readiness? Cyber dimension of national security policies. *The Journal of comparative politics*. Volume 5 (1). 38-59

Symantec Corporation. (2014). *Internet security treat report 2014* (Vol. 19).

Tatalović, S., Grizold, A., & Cvrtila, V. (2008). *Suvremene sigurnosne politike*. Zagreb, Hrvatska: Golden Marketing

The U.S. Army. (2013). *Concept capability plan for cyberspace operations 2016-2028*.

KEY TERMS AND DEFINITIONS[1]

Antivirus Software: A program that monitors a computer or network to detect or identify major types of malicious code and to prevent or contain malware incidents. Sometimes by removing or neutralizing the malicious code.

Asset: A person, structure, facility, information, and records, information technology systems and resources, material, process, relationships, or reputation that has value.

Attack: An attempt to gain unauthorized access to system services, resources, or information, or an attempt to compromise system integrity.

Availability: The property of being accessible and usable upon demand.

Bot: A computer connected to the Internet that has been surreptitiously / secretly compromised with malicious logic to perform activities under remote the command and control of a remote administrator.

Botnet: A collection of computers compromised by malicious code and controlled across a network.

Confidentiality: A property that information is not disclosed to users, processes, or devices unless they have been authorized to access the information.

Critical Infrastructure: The systems and assets, whether physical or virtual, so vital to society that the incapacity or destruction of such may have a debilitating impact on the security, economy, public health or safety, environment, or any combination of these matters.

Cyber Infrastructure: The information and communications systems and services composed of all hardware and software that process, store, and communicate information, or any combination of all of these elements: Processing includes the creation, access, modification, and destruction of information. Storage includes paper, magnetic, electronic, and all other media types. Communications include sharing and distribution of information.

Cybersecurity: The activity or process, ability or capability, or state whereby information and communications systems and the information contained therein are protected from and/or defended against damage, unauthorized use or modification, or exploitation.

Cyberspace: The interdependent network of information technology infrastructures, which includes the Internet, telecommunications networks, computer systems, and embedded processors and controllers.

Data Breach: The unauthorized movement or disclosure of sensitive information to a party, usually outside the organization, that is not authorized to have or see the information.

Denial of Service: An attack that prevents or impairs the authorized use of information system resources or services.

Globalization: Process of expansion, deepening and accelerating global interdependence in all aspects of modern life (economy, politic, ICT, etc.).

Incident: An occurrence that actually or potentially results in adverse consequences to (adverse effects on) (poses a threat to) an information system or the information that the system processes, stores, or transmits and that may require a response action to mitigate the consequences.

Integrity: The property whereby information, an information system, or a component of a system has not been modified or destroyed in an unauthorized manner.

Malicious Code: Program code intended to perform an unauthorized function or process that will have adverse impact on the confidentiality, integrity, or availability of an information system.

National Security: Protection and safety of the political, economic and other interests and values of the state.

Passive Attack: An actual assault perpetrated by an intentional threat source that attempts to learn or make use of information from a system, but does not attempt to alter the system, its resources, its data, or its operations.

Risk Assessment: The product or process which collects information and assigns values to risks for the purpose of informing priorities, developing or comparing courses of action, and informing decision making.

Risk Management: The process of identifying, analysing, assessing, and communicating risk and accepting, avoiding, transferring or controlling it to an acceptable level considering associated costs and benefits of any actions taken.

Risk: The potential for an unwanted or adverse outcome resulting from an incident, event, or occurrence, as determined by the likelihood that a particular threat will exploit a particular vulnerability, with the associated consequences.

Security Policy: Set of rules, guidelines and procedures represented in official security documents that define way in which state will protect its own national security interests.

Security Sector Reform: Concept which promote reform or building of the state security institutions, legislation and system for democratic control.

Security Strategy: Strategic, overall and systematic approach for developing, applying, and coordinating the instruments of national power to achieve objectives that contribute to national security.

Security: Condition of absence of danger and threat or functions and activities on protection.

Threat Agent: An individual, group, organization, or government that conducts or has the intent to conduct detrimental activities.

Threat Assessment: The product or process of identifying or evaluating entities, actions, or occurrences, whether natural or man-made, that have or indicate the potential to harm life, information, operations, and/or property.

Threat: A circumstance or event that has or indicates the potential to exploit vulnerabilities and to adversely impact (create adverse consequences for) organizational operations, organizational assets (including information and information systems), individuals, other organizations, or society.

Vulnerability Assessment and Management: Conducts assessments of threats and vulnerabilities, determines deviations from acceptable configurations, enterprise or local policy, assesses the level of risk, and develops and/or recommends appropriate mitigation countermeasures in operational and non-operational situations.

Vulnerability: A characteristic or specific weakness that renders an organization or asset (such as information or an information system) open to exploitation by a given threat or susceptible to a given hazard.

ENDNOTE

[1] We used The NICCS Portal's cybersecurity lexicon in order to enable clearer communication and common understanding of cybersecurity terms and Thesaurus of Security Culture and thematic lexicons for other explanations.

This work was previously published in the Handbook of Research on Civil Society and National Security in the Era of Cyber Warfare edited by Metodi Hadji-Janev and Mitko Bogdanoski, pages 22-48, copyright 2016 by Information Science Reference (an imprint of IGI Global).

Chapter 7
Identity Management Systems:
Models, Standards, and COTS Offerings

Reema Bhatt
State University of New York – Buffalo, USA

Manish Gupta
State University of New York – Buffalo, USA

Raj Sharman
State University of New York – Buffalo, USA

ABSTRACT

Identity management is the administration of an individual's access rights and privileges in the form of authentication and authorization within or across systems and organizations. An Identity Management system (IdM) helps manage an individual's credentials through the establishment, maintenance, and eventual destruction of their digital identity. Numerous products, applications, and platforms exist to address the privacy requirements of individuals and organizations. This chapter highlights the importance of IdM systems in the highly vulnerable security scenario that we live in. It defines and elaborates on the attributes and requirements of an effective identity management system. The chapter helps in establishing an understanding of frameworks that IdM systems follow while helping the reader contrast between different IdM architecture models. The latter part of this chapter elaborates on some of today's most popular IdM solutions.

1. INTRODUCTION

We live in an age where information systems dominate our world. For everything, from paying bills to ordering food or from buying apparel to managing bank accounts; we make use of the vulnerable and susceptible medium-the internet. Organizations-whether commercial or governmental, rely heavily on their intranet and internal information systems for efficient operations, management and day to day functioning. When making services available via computer networks, there is often a need to know who the users of the system are and what information they are authorized to view or access (Jøsang & Pope).

DOI: 10.4018/978-1-5225-0808-3.ch007

Almost all websites and web services require users to present their identities in order to be authenticated and granted access. Users are identified by their digital identities that comprise of usernames passwords, date of birth, search history, purchasing behavior, passphrases etc. This calls for user privacy management and related issues. Researchers argue that information exchanged online is susceptible to numerous threats which arise from two main factors. Firstly, users have no control over who views their information for e.g. a user knows that their passwords are stored in a database but they have no control over people who access the database. Secondary to this threat is the fact that the user's information is stored indefinitely which means that the identity thief can lie in the future as well (Alkhalifah & D'Ambra, 2012). According to a recent Forrester Research (Kark, 2010) identity and access management was identified as a top security issue for 2011 that needed to be considered as a critical component of corporate security strategies (Cser, 2008).

Two parts of identity management are identified by:

1. Providing users with credentials that can uniquely identify them; and
2. Using these credentials to authenticate users and grant them access and privileges based on these credentials (Jøsang & Pope). The dominance of digital identities, however, also raises concerns about protecting user privacy. Privacy is one of the most challenging issues related to identity management. Privacy related requirements impose several restrictions on identity management systems and therefore are extremely critical (Glasser & Vajihollahi). Users seldom have control over their own digital identity. Information that they provide as a part of mandatory disclosure is stored indefinitely in systems and databases that the users themselves have no control over. This has made it possible for hackers and criminals to rob people off money and information from the comfort of their own homes. Identity theft is thus increasingly becoming one of the prominent cyber-crimes; hackers that can manage to steal an individual's digital identity get access to confidential information such as credit card numbers, bank passwords, SSN etc. Identity management systems, IdM, were therefore created to address these security concerns.

The contributions of this chapter are manifold. First it provides an overview of different architectures and applications of IdM systems. It provides an insightful discourse on the components and attributes of IdM systems so as to be able to decide what kind of systems will best fit the reader's organizational needs and requirements. It will serve as an excellent primer for IT and security professionals in understanding what options are available to them, which can immensely help them in decision making. It also presents a rich discussion of the background of IdM systems and the challenges that today's organizations can face in management of IdM systems. The last section presents some of the most popular and effective commercial off the shelf IdM systems that are available for purchase. This section will benefit organizations that do not wish to build customized IdM solutions but instead purchase one from commercial software vendors; which is not only the most widely used but also considered to be the most cost effective approach. Discussions and presentations in this chapter can act as an aid for security managers and professionals in understanding the current identity management solutions and technologies while facilitating their decision making and risk management. The goal of this chapter is to provide a broad view of IdM systems and help professionals make decisions that would benefit their company.

The organization of this chapter is as follows. Section 2 throws light on why IdM systems should be used, how they help a business and how they work. Section 3 highlights the key components of identity management systems while section 4 outlines the most common architectures of IdM systems. Section

5 details the attributes of a good IdM system. Section 6 describes some commercial software solutions available off the shelf from the market. Section 7 describes some challenges that can be anticipated while implementing IdM systems. Section 8 describes the applications of identity management. Sections 9 describes some industry standards used for identity management while section 10 outlines some of the risks associated with IdM implementation.

2. BACKGROUND

An identity management system is a framework of processes including the technology that facilitates management of digital identities in systems and organizations. The technology initiates, records and manages a user's identity and administers access rights and privileges based on the user's identity. IdM systems are a tool for IT managers to control access and protect critical systems and information from unauthorized use. Numerous technologies such as password management, monitoring software, digital certificates etc. fall under this category. After going through years of evolution and enhancements, today these technologies are available as software suits that provide sophisticated capabilities such as federated identity management, credential administration and management.

2.1 Functional Attributes of Identity Management Systems

IdM systems typically consist of the following functional attributes (Balasubramaniam, A.Lewis, Morris, Simanta, & B.Smith, 2009):

- **Identity Provisioning:** Provisioning is the process of creating and maintaining a user's identity. An example of this would be creating a user account on your bank's web portal.
- **Storage Management and Retrieval of ID Information:** User created digital identities are stored in databases and repositories, and consulted when a user seeks access to information assets.
- **Authentication and Authorization:** Often implemented using ID repositories, databases and directory services; these attributes identify, authorize and authenticate users seeking access to systems by verifying their credentials against their established identities.
- **Single Sign-On:** This allows users the flexibility to use the same identity and credentials across various systems, making them user friendy. This can be implemented using technologies such as Security Assertion Markup Language (SAML).
- **Auditing and Reporting:** An auditing system that periodically stores all activities taking place across the organization.

2.2 Identity Management Terminology

Identity management has two principal components – management of identity and management by identity. Management of identity is the process of issuing and using digital identities and credentials (such as usernames and passwords). Management by identity combines the proven identity of the user with their authorization, in order to grant access to resources (Wood, 2005). Listed below are some commonly used terms in the identity management domain

- **Provisioning:** As mentioned earlier, the process of creating user identities, defining their access privileges and saving them in the ID repository.
- **De-Provisioning:** The process of deleting a user's identity from the repository and revoking all access rights.
- **Federated Identity Management:** Also known as single sign-on, federated identity management is a mechanism that allows users to share the same credentials across multiple systems among trusted partners.
- **Identity Synchronization:** The process of keeping all identity repositories consistent.
- **Identity Lifecycle Management:** This is the set of all processes such as provisioning, de-provisioning, synchronizing etc. for maintaining digital identities.

2.3 Why Should One Invest in Identity Management?

In order for organizations to enhance business productivity by protecting their digital assets and information, IdM needs to be an integral part of their systems for numerous reasons.

- **Security:** Managing the humongous information systems and interconnected computer systems, especially for large enterprises, becomes a little less complex and cost effective by making ID management a centralized process.
- **Controlled Access:** Considering the increase in commercial use of hand held devices such as cell phones, PDAs, laptops; ID management helps an organization keep track of the devices that are connected to its network—a must to ensure security.
- **Government:** Laws and government regulations such as Sarbanes-Oxley, Gramm-Leach-Bliley, HIPAA etc. require organizations to ensure confidentiality of client and employee information.
- **Competitive Advantage:** Implementing IdM is a best practice; it can give an organization a competitive edge over rivals. It provides a way for providing better customer service, by providing them access to your information systems, without having to compromise on security.
- **Cost Savings:** A study has revealed that most of the help desk calls received are for password resets, thus making automated password reset one of the biggest cost saving techniques for organizations. IdM systems automate password resetting and various other time intensive tasks.

3. COMPONENTS OF IDM SYSTEMS

According to Mark Berman and Joel Cooper, an identity management infrastructure is a collection of technology, business processes, and underlying network systems that determines access and authorization parameters (Tracy, 2008). This definition highlights the following basic components of IdM systems:

- A repository that defines and stores the digital identities of all users,
- A set of tools that can be used for adding, modifying or deleting that user data,
- A system for enforcing security policies and access control mechanisms, and
- An auditing system that records all the activities that take place on the system.

These components can be architected by an IdM system based on the requirements of enterprise such as security and privacy concerns, sensitivity of data that is protected, number of users, ease of use and so on. To aid such technical specifications, there are several approaches that have been suggested.

4. ARCHITECTURE

A general design is usually followed while designing and developing IdM systems. First and foremost, the system must have a source of information that verifies which users should and should not exist, as well as what their access permissions should be. If every random user can create a user account on an organization's intranet; the purpose of using identity management is lost. This is usually controlled through the use of an enterprise resource planner (ERP) such as SAP. The basic functions of the IdM server are to assign resources, remove resources, and disable resources. The IdM server creates user accounts and allocates resources based upon the information provided by the ERP system. With IdM in place a user may log in to an e-mail system and as a result of the credentials being checked, may also be granted access to their active directory without having to do anything else (Tracy, 2008). However, this is just a general architecture, there is lots of room for variation. IdM systems can be broadly classified into three main models i.e. isolated, centralized and federated identity systems (Miyata, Koga, Madsen, & Adachi, 2006):

4.1 Isolated Model

This identity model is one where the service provider also acts as the identity provider, and both identity and user operations are provided by the same server (Cao & Yang, 2010). The service provider manages both the name space and authentication for all of its users, making it the identity provider as well. Unique users create their own identifiers and set their own authentication passwords within the system. The biggest advantages of this model are its simplicity and the fact that personal information being exposed solely to the service provider.

However, a disadvantage of this model is that it used solely for access to one system, and thus a user must create their own identifier and authentication criteria for every service provider they encounter. It is not uncommon for users to forget the details to service providers they use infrequently, preventing the services from being used to their full potential (Jøsang et al., 2007). Resultantly, user account and password management have long been major expenses for organizations (Gupta and Sharman, 2008a).

4.2 Common Identity Domain Model

In the Common Identity Domain Model, there is only one common identity provider that encompasses multiple service providers. In this method a user could use the same identity information over multiple services. A common authentication token in this model is to use a public-key certificate. Such a solution would be good for an organization that is able to assign a single, non-changing identifier to a user. Advantage of this model is that it is simple to manage for both the service provider and user. Only one set of identifiers and authentication information is needed by users, and thus it is easier to maintain.

Figure 1. Silo model

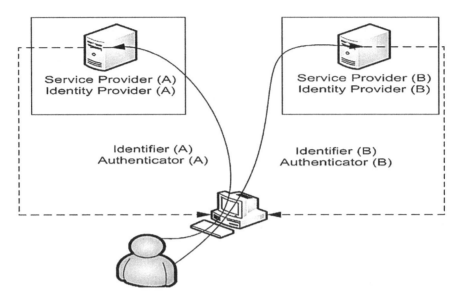

On the other side, this can also turn into a disadvantage. It is difficult to manage a set of unique name spaces and identifiers for a huge number of users that are considered to be both stable and without privacy implications. For e.g., users are likely to have numerous e-mail addresses and as a result e-mail would not be a good identifier.

4.3 Centralized Single Sign-on Identity Model

This model allows for the use of a centralized identity provider that manages the name space, authentication tokens, and authentication of users. In sequence, a user sends their identifier and authentication

Figure 2. Common identity domain model

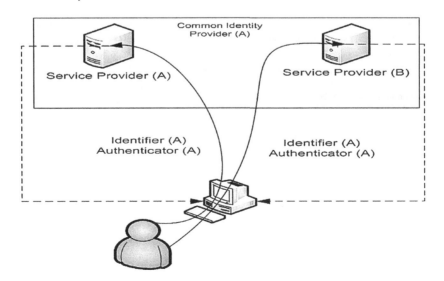

information to the identity provider, the provider then sends a security assertion to the service provider(s); the service provider then grants the requested access. This model fits well into closed networks where multiple service providers are managed by a single organization. In such closed networks it is assumed that the identity and service providers are governed by the same authority with the same policies in place, making implementation a simpler process. A disadvantage of this model could be that it is considered to be unsuitable for environments where the service providers are not governed by a common authority. It is not that the model itself does not allow for easy implementation, but that it is unlikely that different service providers would accept an outside identity provider to manage and authenticate identities on their behalf. It would violate certain privacy protection principles regarding exposure of personal information (Jøsang et al., 2007). Recent research has proposed some improvements to commonly adopted SSO architectures (Cahill et al., 2011; Chadwick et al., 2011; Sun et al., 2010; Takeda et al., 2006).

However, in spite of the disadvantages; increased security and compliance, improved user productivity and convenience and real cost savings are few motivations that drive SSO implementation (Impravata, n.d, 2009). At the same time, there has been good amount of research done in the SSO domain to recommend improvements and to address some of the identified concerns. For example, Mustafic et al. (2011) and Suoranta et al. (2012) proposed solution to single point of failure issue by suggesting improving strength of authentication. Alsaleh and Adams (2006) also suggest privacy enhancements, while Linden and Vapula (2005) propose improvements around usability. According to a Gartner report Single Sign-On system can save up to $300 per user per year which can account to huge amounts (Connolly, 2000). Single Sign-On (SSO) systems provide users the convenience of accessing multiple applications and systems while having to provide credentials only once (Gupta and Sharman, 2010). Most of the cross-enterprise SSO implementations are done using standards such as SAML or OAuth (Cantor and Kemp, 2005; Hirsch et al., 2005; Hardt, 2012), which also used by many commercially available products.

Figure 3. Centralized single sign-on model

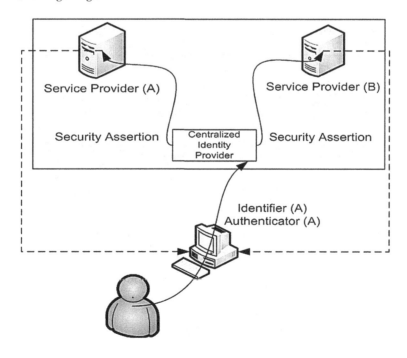

4.4 Centralized Model with Browser Support

It essentially takes the centralized single sign on method that Microsoft attempted to implement through the Passport service, but with multiple identity providers would be involved. The idea is that a user may want to use different identities for different situations. In such a system, a user has multiple 'InfoCards' stored on a computer contained in a 'CardSpace,' which do not contain any sensitive information. Each of these InfoCards points to a centralized identity provider where the sensitive information is stored. In this method a security assertion is first sent from an identity provider to the CardSpace module, and further forwarded to the service provider. The advantage of this model is that it improves upon centralized single sign on where service providers are not governed by a common authority. By allowing for support of multiple identity providers and centralized domains, the problem of leaving personal information in the hands of one giant identity provider is no longer a problem.

When it comes to disadvantages it can be said that they are amplified over the previous centralized model. The same problem exists with a third party identity provider holding personal information, albeit it is multiple providers instead of just one. This model also brings back a problem seen in the silo model. A user will be responsible for remembering multiple sets of identifier and authentication information due to the likeliness that they will be interacting with multiple identity providers for the different services they are using. Finally, if someone with ill intentions finds a way to exploit the CardSpace system, they could use the InfoCards and pointers that they have to identity providers to utilize a person's identity without having to actually steal it (Jøsang et al., 2007).

4.5 Federated Single Sign-on Identity Model

This model builds on single sign-on, with the idea that groups of service providers enter into a mutual security and authentication agreement. This agreement enables service providers to recognize user

Figure 4. Centralized model with browser support

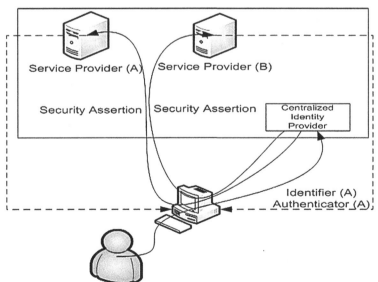

identities from other service providers (Rochet and Tirole, 2003). Like in the silo model, each identity provider is also its own service provider. The difference, however, is that the providers are linked. As an example, when logging in Provider A, a user will be identified as Identifier A. Provider A can send a security assertion to Provider B verifying the authenticity of the user that has Identifier A. The user will then be authenticated in the other providers system with its own unique Identifier B. The biggest advantage to this model is that it allows for single sign-on in environments where multiple entities are involved. It can also be retrofitted to an existing silo model, allowing for service providers to keep existing name space and authentication systems without the worry of conflict.

Federated identity management has its own drawbacks such as high investment costs, trust issues between partners, data synchronization and consistency and interoperability (Jensen, 2012). The main disadvantage here is that it relies heavily on trust between multiple organizations. Service providers must be able to trust security assertions from each other and have confidence that another providers will not try to exploit this in any way. This demands enterprises to enable convenient and secure business interactions with internal and external stakeholders, and create relationships to trust the electronic identities to access critical information resources. Federated identity management (FIM) is a system that enables individuals to use the same credentials or identification data to obtain access to the networks of multiple enterprises to conduct business transactions. FIM has demonstrated huge potential in providing reliable and scalable solutions to problems in systems security and access management. SAML (Security Assertion Markup Language) is the dominant web services standard for FIM (Gupta and Sharman, 2008b).

5. ATTRIBUTES OF A GOOD IDM SYSTEM

Listed below are some attributes to look out for, when selecting an identity management system (Alotaibi & Wald, 2012):

Figure 5. Federated single sign-on model

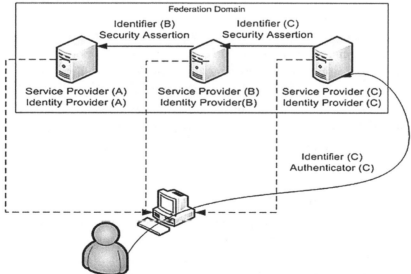

- **Multifactor Authentication:** Use of multiple authentication mechanisms for e.g. a combination of passwords and biometrics strengthens security of the system. However, this also depends on the criticality of the resource being protected.

- **Compliance with Standards:** Complying with international IdM standards facilitates an organization to implement hassle free updates, extensions and integration with other systems; if the need may arise in future.

- **Effectiveness and Efficiency:** The system should ensure that users are able to perform their tasks effectively with minimum time delay and should require users to perform minimum number of steps for authentication.

- **Usability and Memorability:** The system should implement uncomplicated account setup, recovery management and access management procedures that do not require lengthy interactions from the user's end. It should provide users with clear and concise instructions and error messages, where required. Functions and operations must be set in a logical order that are not very difficult for users to memorize.

- **Consistency:** Consistent procedures and operations across the system make it easy for users to grasp and comprehend information.

- **Security:** The most important attribute of an IdM system, strong and reliable authentication and authorization mechanisms that enforce access control. For e.g. a system that uses nonce based authentication makes replay attacks almost impossible, as opposed to one that uses timestamp based authentication. A nonce is a random value that is generated every time encryption is done, and therefore has a new random value every time a user attempts authentication. This leads to a stronger notion of not only privacy but also authenticity (Rogaway, 2004).

6. MOST POPULAR SOFTWARE SOLUTIONS

In this section, we discuss some of the most popular IdM solutions available in the market today. These discussions are based completely off of information found on the websites of said solutions. The software systems are listed by company name in a random fashion order without any bias through the order.

1. **NetIQ Identity Manager 4:** NetIQ Identity Manager 4 was awarded the Readers Trust Award for "Best Identity Management Solution" at the 2014 SC Awards ceremony on February 25, 2014. It is a comprehensive identity management suite that provides an intelligent identity framework to leverage new as well as existing IT assets by reducing costs and ensuring compliance across various environments. NetIQ Identity Manager includes integration modules for several commonly used systems such as MS Active Directory, LDAP, eDirec-tory, Lotus Notes etc. in order to cater to the diver user base, Identity Management solution is available in two different editions—the standard as well as advanced version. Their motto is to provide "simple, secure access for the right people at the right time." (NetIQ, 2014)

2. **CyberArk Application Identity Manager:** This is one of the numerous software solution offered by CyberArk in the domains of threat protection, security, secured access etc. It helps businesses protect the valuable information that lies in their internal information systems by implementing secure and robust authentication mechanisms. It eliminates all hard coded passwords from scripts, application code and configuration files thus making them inaccessible to developers and support

staff. It aims to deliver high availability, redundancy and business continuity through secured caching capabilities. The Identity Manager provides accountability through maintaining logs of each transaction, password synchronization and encryption, and simple integration with third party applications (CyberArk, 2014).

3. **Enterprise Random Password Manager by Lieberman Software:** The Enterprise Random Password Generator (ERPG) is a privileged identity management product that can discover, track, secure and audit privileged accounts across an enterprise. Some of the features ERPG provides are super-user login accounts for that are used for configuration settings and other administrative tasks, service accounts that require privileged login ID and password, and application to application passwords that are used to connect databases, middleware and more. ERPM also has a feature called as True Discovery™ that on addition of new hardware or software, continuously discovers and secures new privileged identities. With the help of real time visualization ERPM provides dashboards that help organizations identify security and productivity issues (Lieberman Software, 2014).

4. **Identity and Access Management Suite by Evidian:** Awarded the best IAM Solution by SC Magazine in 2013, the Identity and access management system by Evidian helps organizations deploy a step by step a coherent access policy. It helps organizations unify digital identities from multiple sources such as HR, payroll etc. It automates the implementation of the access policy by creating roles directly at the IT system and constantly monitors its application. It implements a clean and simple system that facilitates quick and thorough audits. Evidian I&A Manager can efficiently integrate with existing systems to accommodate existing users without having to replace them. Its interoperability with other user access services, multilingual support and scalability make it a comprehensive solution (Evidian, 2014).

5. **CloudMinder™ Identity Management by CA Technologies:** A robust cloud-based service, the CloudMiner IAM solution helps organizations realize the benefits of cloud computing while at the same time miminizing security risks. Some of the features of CA CloudMiner are advanced authentication via multifactor credentials and device identification with SaaS model, federated single sign-on to cloud as well as on premise applications, automated user provisioning and de-provisioning along with synchronization with LDAP/Active directory. Some of the benefits that CloudMiner aims to provide organizations with are; reduction in deployment time, minimal operational and administration costs, better user productivity and reduced costs (CA Technologies, 2014).

6. **Centrify Server Suite by Centrify:** The Centrify Server Suite aims to protect mission critical servers from identity related risks and threats by leveraging existing Active Directory infrastructures to centrally manage authentication, access control, policy enforcement and compliance. They have a patented 'Zone' technology that provides unique access control. The Centrify Server Suite 2014 provides full activity audit trails and videos that can trace back every activity to individuals. The latest version supports over 450 platforms including various versions of Windows, Linux and Unix operating systems. By combining privilege management, Active Directory bridging and user activity monitoring in one comprehensive solution, Centrify provides organizations with a unique solution (Centrify, 2014).

7. **Universal Key Manager by SSH Communications Security:** The Universal SSH Key Manager (UKM) is a multiplatform, scalable solution that reduces the risks of unauthorized access from internal as well as external entities. It claims to implement identity management using a non-

disruptive approach that allows enterprises to gain control of SSH infrastructure without having to replace any existing systems. This approach is based on three principles: discover trust relationships and policy violations, remediate invalid keys and incorrect policy compliance and manage by eliminating manual processes, enforcing compliance and maintaining proper audit trails. This highly scalable solution guarantees high availability, simpler compliance, stronger security while leveraging existing IAM infrastructures (SSH Communications Security, 2014).

8. **OneLogin, Identity Management in the Cloud:** OneLogin is one of the fastest IdM systems available for use with the cloud infrastructure that simplifies identity management among various users and across various devices and applications. It provides on demand solutions and services such as single sign-on, user provisioning, directory integration by connecting users Active Directory or LDAP servers with OneLogin, real time cloud search, strong authentication using PKI certificates, mobile access, password vaulting and reporting and analytics. OneLogin makes use of multiple data centers, redundant DNS app and database servers to guarantee a 99.99% system uptime. It is simple to use- has a clean interface and fast setup process. One of the best features of OneLogin is that they offer clients numerous subscription plans to choose from (OneLogin, 2014).

9. **HID Global's 4TRESS Authentication Appliance for Enterprises:** The 4TRESS authentication appliance is an identity assurance solution for enterprises that provides strong authentication for all employees seeking access various applications such as cloud, VPN, workstations etc. it makes uses of multiple authentication technologies such as OTP tokens, smart cards, temporary activation codes, LDAP passwords, PKI, third party tokens among others to strengthen security at client systems. 4TRESS has a robust and resilient architecture that can accommodate from a 100 to a million users. It is compliant with OATH industry standards, thus preventing vendor lock-in; and provides easy integration with existing systems. 4TRESS aims to improve organizational productivity by allowing employees to connect to internal information systems through a variety of devices and at the same time decreasing risks by implementing robust, multifactor authentication that inhibits breaches (4TRESS, 2014).

10. **Access Sentinel by ViewDS Identity Solutions:** ViewDS is a developer of innovative Identity and access management software products that are deployed in a variety of industries. The ViewDS suite comprises of three products; ViewDS Directory Server-an XML enabled search server that offers search capability, Access Sentinel-an authorization server and Identity Bridge- a synchronization and integration tool. Access Sentinel Authorization Policy Server for Attribute Based Access Control built on ViewDS solutions, thus enabling storage of roles, policies and identity information on a single repository. It is an XACML (Extensible Access Control Markup Language) V3 standard based solution that manages authorization for clients making their systems faster and safer to use. It provides added security and flexibility via attribute based access control (ABAC) and role-based access control (RBAC). Access Sentinel is a scalable, secure and efficient solution with a unique architecture that provides indexed search on any attribute (ViewDS Solutions, 2014).

11. **Access: One by Pirean Software:** Access: One is a leading, award winning access management platform that provides authentication, federated identity management and single sign n functionality. One of the striking features of this software is that it gives the organization full flexibility over interactions that users have in its digital presence. It provides services such as: Webtop- a central, cross platform launchpad that allows secure access from multiple devices, Access Store-enable users to manage access to numerous applications; and QRyptoLogin- a multifactor authentication mechanism that allows users to scan QR codes based on one time passwords. Access: One provides

support for Automated User Management, LDAP Integration, Contextual Step-Up authentication, integration with Google and other applications, audit reporting, identity intelligence among various other services (Access: One, 2014).

12. **Shibboleth® by Internet2®:** Shibboleth, one of the world's most popularly deployed federated identity solutions, is a standards based open source software that allows single sign-on across and within organizational boundaries. It implements the OASIS Security Assertion Markup Language (SAML) to provide an attribute exchange framework. It provides extended privacy by allowing users to control attributes released to applications. Developed as an open source software, Shibboleth is released under the Apache License (Shibboleth, 2014).

13. **TridentHE by Aegis Identity Software:** Aegis Identity offers identity management solutions for the educational market. The TridentHE Identity Manager from Aegis is the education market's first open standards identity management solution specifically built for higher education. It provides features like provisioning-managing user roles and resources, password management-password synchronization, maintaining password policy, reconciliation and fine grained audit policies. Based on open standards such as SPML, SCIM, Eclipse among others, its SOA facilitates integration between systems. It aims to reduce the total cost of ownership by implementing a system that is simple, easy to install and maintain (Aegis Identity, 2014).

14. **ForeFront Identity Manager 2010 R2 by Microsoft:** Microsoft's ForeFront Identity Manager aims to reduce complexity of identity management by offering self-service identity management for e.g. by automation of remediation like password reset, automated lifecycle and role management, and a strong framework for corporate security policies and audit. The four feature areas provided by this solution are policy management, credential management, user management, and group management. It uses a SharePoint based console for policy enforcement and authoring. ForeFront supports heterogeneous identity synchronization and cross platform support. Easy extensibility and easy to use interface makes it a user friendly portal where users can manage their own identities (Microsoft, 2014).

15. **Oracle Identity Management:** Oracle Identity Management facilitates organizations to manage the user identity lifecycle within or beyond organizational boundaries via identity governance, access management, and directory services. Oracle has numerous different identity management suites which can be licensed separately or bundled together. These are Oracle Identity Manager, Oracle Identity Analytics, Oracle Access manager, Oracle Web Services Manager, Oracle Identity Federation, Security Token Service, Oracle Enterprise Single Sign-On, Oracle Entitlements Server, Oracle Adaptive Access manager, Oracle Directory Services, and Oracle Platform Security Services. Separately they do such things as manage privileges, deal with regulatory compliance, implement single-sign on, protection of web services access and dealing with security token issuance, validation, and exchange amongst other things. (Oracle-IDM, 2014).

16. **Tivoli® Identity Manager by IBM®:** IBM Tivoli is a policy based Identity Manager that provides a secure, automated user man agement system that helps legacy and e-business systems. Some of the striking features of Tivoli are a role based administration model, web administrative interface and automated submission and approval of user requests. Highlights of this system include centralized web administration to reduce complexity, scalability, user identity lifecycle management support, and easy updates via the application management toolkit (Tivoli, 2014).

17. **PingFederate® by Ping Identity:** PingFederate is a lightweight identity management system that provides federated access management over the client's existing architecture or over the cloud. It

uses token based security for authenticating users. Using adaptive federation, it encourages user customization of access scenarios. One of the striking features of PingFederate is that it can be deployed in any environment in less than a day. Some of the features of PingFederate include secured mobile access, integration with social media and automated user provisioning.

7. EVALUATION FACTORS FOR COMPARING VARIOUS SOLUTIONS

With the innumerable options for off the shelf software solutions available in the market, how does one decide which solution will maximize profits for their implementation effort? How do we compare various IdM solutions so as to pick the best one for our organization's needs? Given below are some evaluation criteria that help professionals distinguish between features of various commercial IdM solutions and make a decision on the best suited product for their business needs as well as technological environment.

- **Effort Required for Integrating with Current Applications, User Base, and Business Processes:** The solution that seamlessly integrates with the technological and organizational infrastructure should be the best bet, since it minimizes effort as well as cost.
- **Simplified Account Provisioning:** Comparing user account management functions i.e. creating, deleting, updating user profiles can help provide a good estimate of the effectiveness of the chosen system. These functions should be automated and available via a remotely accessible interface, so as to limit dependency on administrators for non-critical tasks. Critical tasks such as revoking access rights, recognizing illegitimate accounts, terminating users should be executed with minimum time delay. Select the system that can be altered to suit your specific business requirements, such as specific formats for auto generated user IDs.
- **Role Based Access:** In the best solution, different kinds of users should be able to access different, specific sets of information depending on their role/account type.
- **Compatibility with Servers:** Since every IdM needs to interface with various databases and application servers, evaluate solutions based on their compatibility with the leading names in the industry.
- **Speed of Access:** Does the solution create its own identity repository on implantation? Or can it integrate with the existing repository? Does it use indexing or any other such fast retrieval methods for? Organizations generate a humongous amount of user traffic on a daily basis and undoubtedly, the best solution is one that best manages the ever increasing user traffic with negligible down time.
- **Flexibility and Long Term Support:** In order to ensure easy maintenance, support and future enhancements, it is very important for the selected solution to adhere to industry standards. Using tools and technologies that are on the verge of extinction is not just monetarily but also technologically a bad decision; no matter how simple, cost effective or advantageous they may seem.
- **Scalability:** How many users and applications can the system support? Does it allow to extend these numbers in the future? How time/effort consuming would this be? Non scalable systems are usually a bad choice.
- **Accountability:** A good solution is one that supports full accountability by maintaining exhaustive object, user and application level audit trails. Flexibility in generating audit reports such as

predefined v/s on demand reports, access control, compatibility with other reporting tools are desirable features.

- **Performance Tracking:** Does the system allow tracking details on system performance metrics such as user provisioning time, response time, number of users online, disabled accounts, locked-out accounts etc.? This makes evaluating performance of the IdM system a simple and comprehensible task. Availability of visualization of these metrics via a graphical user interface is a huge advantage.
- **Strength of Security:** Needless to say, this is the most important factor while evaluating different IdM systems. The best solution will be one that enforces multifactor authentication, strong passwords and identities, simple yet secure password recovery, secure communication over networks etc. among others.
- **Synchronization:** Although identity synchronization is a choice of the organization, a solution that supports federated identity management and single is almost always desirable over one that supports a silo model so as to ease the process of future enhancements and extensions.
- **Usability:** Even the most secure, most profitable and easily deployable systems can be unsuccessful if the end users fail to use it with ease. Over complicated account setup, extremely stringent password rules, lengthy authentication process are features that you should avoid in a solution.

Although trying to find a single software that matches all these factors will be like looking for a droplet in the rain, the best way to go is prioritize on a set of factors necessary for your business and use them for evaluating options.

8. CHALLENGES

Implementing an identity management system for an organization requires thorough knowledge of not only the organization's internal information systems but also its functional/non-functional requirements; along with a good understanding of what solutions are available and which best fits the organization's specifications. Although it may seem to be a straight forward task, implementation of identity management is faced with numerous challenges. The most common ones are explained below.

- **User Access Control via Definition of Roles:** Companies are increasingly moving towards allowing external users to access their internal information systems. In order to provide access rights to internal users such as employees and contractors as well as to external users such as customers, vendors etc.; companies need to be able to distinguish between these users and accordingly provide access rights. This gives rise to the challenge of defining various user roles and assigning specific privileges to those roles. For e.g. a user may be able to view their utility bill on the web portal using their own credentials, but only an authenticated employee can make amendments to the bill.
- **User Administration/Account Setup:** Each kind of user requires their own account setup process. In order to enforce strict security, only legitimate members of the organization should be able to create user accounts with the system. When a user initiates account setup, the system should be able to recognize whether the user is authorized to hold an account. A generic example of this

is when customers need to verify their email address and phone numbers in order to complete the account setup process. Employees can be identified by their employee ID's, names, date of birth or a combination of these factors.

- **User Provisioning/Account Maintenance:** Account maintenance can cost a company millions of dollars, if the optimal account setup processes are not in place. Managing the hundreds of users and maintaining their accounts can become a nightmare if accounts are incorrectly setup or worse if user roles are incorrectly defined. When a system has a large number of users, even a small task like resetting password becomes resource and time intensive. A study says that 45% of calls to IT help desks are from users who face issues in account setup, password resetting etc (Lee, 2003). The key here is to automate as many processes as possible.

- **Configuration for Account/Access Termination:** In the absence of accurate documentation that details all the rights and privileges that a user has been granted, account termination can be tricky. The identity management system should be configured for a simple and easy account termination process. Delay in revoking access rights of terminated users can prove to be a major security hazard.

- **Integrated Identity:** There are numerous applications and resources in organizations that users seek to access. Employees require credentials to access payroll, network systems, databases, email etc. Enforcing different credentials for use with every system complicates it not only for the user but also is an unnecessary overhead for the system. This calls for integrated or federated identity that allows users to use the same identity (credentials) across various systems.

- **Ensuring Regulatory Compliance:** Compliance to regulations and government laws that state what user information can be stored, storage restrictions; performing periodic audits and maintaining audit trails. This can be challenging when different national and state laws, organizational regulations and work domain specifications exist.

- **User Privacy:** Identity management systems store sensitive user information such as date of birth, passwords etc. This information is protected by user privacy laws. Adherence to these laws and strict compliance is of utmost importance.

- **User Acceptance:** Often the most neglected attribute, user acceptance often determines the success or failure of an implementation. A system that is too complicated for users has a high chance of failure. A simplified end user interface, quick and concise processes, procedures and access to resources, integrated identities, appropriate error messages and quick recovery management are some usability attributes that make a good system.

- **Performance:** In order to obtain ROI on implementing identity management, the system should be quick in activation and deactivation of user accounts; require minimal manual intervention; be flexible i.e. changing and updating user profiles and roles should be simple; robust i.e. should be able to handle increasing volume of users efficiently, and consistent i.e. user identities and information about users should be maintained consistent across the different data stores (Hitachi ID Systems Inc, 2014).

9. APPLICATIONS

We make use of computer networks and the internet for almost every activity from our lives- from maintaining a balanced diet and keeping count of calories to maintaining bank accounts and keeping track of our finances. This exhibits the omnipresence of user accounts and thus identity management. Identity management is used in various areas that include but are not limited to an individual's personal documents, work connectivity, and attachment to social media networks etc.

9.1 Consumer

Consumer IdM systems aim to enable smooth interactions between the customers and user services by eliminating the need for users to maintain various identities and credentials and allowing them to use the same credentials across multiple systems. Various consumer domains that can benefit from identity management are Ecommerce, healthcare, education, banking, finance, cloud storage among others. In this area there is typically a trusted third party who acts as the identity service provider and also as a point of authentication to the consumer to access their services. We can see this at play in various systems. Numerous websites allow new users to register with their existing Facebook, Twitter or Google credentials. Microsoft also now allows users to access their Windows 8 account, MS Office, Skype, and other services through a single account. An example of where this is currently in wide use is with Microsoft's Windows Live platform. Windows Live is a freely available service which allows a user to integrate their e-mail, Windows Live Messenger, online storage, Xbox gaming experience, and other Microsoft provided services. When a user logs in to one of these services and continues on to use another of the services included in Windows Live, they are automatically logged in and are able to continue on without any further proof of identification. When registering to create a Windows Live ID, it is marketed as something that "gets you in to all Windows Live services," and that is exactly what it does (MS Live, 2010)

9.2 Commercial

In the commercial workspace, the administration of user accounts has, and will most likely continue to be a task that that consumes a large amount of an IT department's time and resources. In most organizations that have the ability and means to do so, IdM solutions have been implemented which allow for easier modification of user roles across the entire organization as opposed to an individual basis. This does not eliminate the administration of individual users on a case by case basis, but does greatly simplify the task of performing updates to groups of user accounts.

An important aspect of commercial based IdM which utilizes the technology to its fullest is when inter-organization shared space is involved. When two organizations collaborate, it brings about a situation where both security and quick access are required; and both organizations are likely to need access to certain parts of the others system. Having an appropriate IdM solution in place, allows for the needs of both organizations to be met without much overhead. When collaboration ends, the organizations are also able to easily cut access ties with little to no hassle.

9.3 Government

In the government realm there is a never ending list of forms of identities issued with the most common ones including a driver's license, passport, and social security number. The management of identities within this realm is considered to be fragmented as citizens are identified by different government institutions through different credentials.

Implementation of IdM in the government sector involves exposing government services on the Internet and integrating mechanisms that allow for the proper identification of citizens. In government usage, citizens would essentially have IdM forced upon them whereas in consumer uses it is by choice; in commercial uses it is as a result of employment. The government must weigh social and legislative aspects of implementation across a nation. Privacy and freedom that the government would both need to guarantee to the public, and follow through with law establishing all aspects of the system (Casassa et al., 2002).

9.4 Mobile

The Pew Internet Project's research related to mobile technology revealed that 90% of American adults own a cell phone out of which 58% own smartphones (Pewinternet.org). It also revealed that more than making phone calls, people use their smart phones to connect to social media, share pictures, share their location, access the internet, pay bills, send/receive email, share/store work related documents, coordinate meetings etc. Not only are people shifting from desktop computers to laptops, tablets and netbooks for everyday chores, but the usage of smartphones is at an all-time high.

With every operating system on a phone comes a different type of IdM that will connect the user to different services. A few of the more popular operating systems are Microsoft's Windows Mobile, Apple's iPhone OS, and Google's Android. As an example, on phones running the Android operating system, the screen a user encounters upon first boot of the phone asks for their Google Mail login information. Once a user does this, their phone syncs with their Google account and pulls mail, contacts, calendar events, and anything else they may use through Google. When the user updates or changes anything either through their phone or personal computer, the other is instantly updated.

10. STANDARDS RELATED TO IDM SYSTEMS

In order to establish definitive and widely accepted definitions of identity management methods, processes and terminology, various groups are working towards developing and establishing standards and frameworks that promote best practices in identity management solutions, and enable simple integration between different disparate systems. Some of the most widely used standards are discussed below:

- **INCITS/CS1:** Established in 2005, the InterNational Committee for Information Technology Standards- Cyber Security 1 includes standardization in the area of identity management in the form of an identity management framework, role based access control, single-sign on, privacy framework, role-based access control, anonymity and credentials among others. It also includes the areas of entity-authentication, non-repudiation and key management (INCITIS, 2014).
- **ISO/IEC JTC 1/SC 27:** The ISO/IEC JTC 1/SC 27 is a sub-committee of the ISO/IEC JTC 1 of the International Standards Organization (ISO). This group works towards general methods, standards and techniques for protecting information and privacy. Some of the published standards under this area are ISO/IEC 9798-3:1998/Cor 2:2012, ISO/IEC 9798-1:2010 and ISO/IEC 9798-2:2008 for entity authentication, ISO/IEC 13888-3:2009, ISO/IEC 13888-2:2010 for non-repudiation. It also has published a framework for identity management ISO/IEC 24760-1:2011- that defines identity management terminology and core concepts (ISO, 2014).

- **SAML by OASIS:** The Security Assertion Markup Language by the Security Services Technical Committee of OASIS is an XML based framework for exchanging security information. There are four main components of SAML. Packets of information known as assertions-, protocols, mappings from SAML messages to standard message protocols called as bindings and profiles that define the usage of SAML specific to the applications (Cantor et al., 2005; Hirsch et al., 2005). The latest version of SAML i.e. V2.0 is used in a number of applications such as single sign-on, attribute based authentication and securing web services (OASIS, 2014).
- **WS Security by OASIS:** Web Service Security, WSS is a set of security policy assertions for use with the WS Policy framework. It defines use of token types and defines cryptographic algorithms, transport level security among other parameters, in an attempt to promote interoperability and compatibility among different web service participants. WS Security mainly describes three components: signing SOAP messages to ascertain integrity, encryption of SOAP messages to guarantee integrity maintain security tokens to confirm message sender's identity (OASIS, 2014).
- **XACML by OASIS:** Extensible Access Control Markup Language, XACML, is a standard for representing and evaluating access control policies. XACML is primarily an Attribute Based Access Control (ABAC) system, however, Role Based Access Control (RBAC) can also be implemented in XACML. Applications of XACML include defining access control policies for web servers and services, gateways, firewalls, applications etc. (OASIS, 2014).
- **XCBF by OASIS:** The OASIS XML Common Biometric Format that provides a standard way to describe biometric information such as DNA, fingerprint, iris scan etc. The standard can widely help in various applications in areas of law enforcement, government, and corporate privacy (OASIS, 2014).

11. RISK ASSESSMENT

The primary goal of implementing identity management is to ensure that access to an organization's private and confidential information is granted only after execution of appropriate security processes and controls. It is a convoluted process with a simple goal- to protect organizational assets from unauthorized access. Although successful implementation reduces the security risks in an organization by a huge factor, it also brings business, usability and other risks that should be managed and mitigated. The implementation of identity and access management systems entails risks and challenges. A successful implementation will require changes to the processes and security operations, which introduces business risks (Aldhizer et al., 2008; Reymann, 2008). At the same time, they also introduce new risks in the technical and operational environments of any company while helping mitigate security risks through strong access management enforcement (Rai,et al., 2007; Engelbert, 2009; Links, 2008). Some of these are presented next.

- **Identity Chaos:** In the absence of federated identity or single sign-on systems, decentralized management of identities can result in a situation known as identity or password chaos where individuals seek access to numerous systems and have different credentials or each of these systems. To add to the confusion, different systems have different rules and constraints, expiration dates etc. on passwords. This leads to two things, increased support and maintenance costs because users will frequently forget their passwords and reduced learnability, and usability.

- **Extremely Stringent Constraints Can Reduce Productivity:** Stringent password rules such as use of alphanumeric characters, frequent update policy, lengthy passwords, account lock out after failed attempts etc.; that aim to strengthen security; can result in reduced user productivity when they fail to remember their complex passwords and frequently need to reset their password.
- **Insider Threat:** When the IdM system carries a huge amount of personal data from users, employee negligence as well as employees with malicious intent pose a great threat to data confidentiality. The people who are in control of the IdM system often have root access and all privileges to access all systems. Such people should be closely monitored, there should be thorough accountability and auditability in order to ensure non repudiation.
- **Securing Data Centers:** The databases, data stores and data centers where user's private information is store should also be highly protected via information security as well as physical security measures. Communication networks that are used for exchanging messages containing user identity attributes are common entry points for hackers and identity thieves. Securing these channels is of utmost importance to maintain user privacy
- **Business Risk:** One of the greatest risks, while implementing IdM systems is that of gaining a return on investment, ROI. The implemented security policies should not only help the organization move towards its goals and objectives, but the implementation project also should be able to fetch appropriate returns. Assessment to identify the level of security appropriate for the organization can help in minimizing business risk.

Numerous risk metrics for identity management systems facilitate reporting, interpreting audit logs and quantifying the risks related to and effectiveness of the IdM system. Some of these metrics are listed below:

- **Identity Count:** The number of user profiles that the identity repository holds.
- **Authentication Claims Count:** The number of successful and unsuccessful attempts made by users for authentication/authorization purposes.
- **Provisioning/De-Provisioning Efficiency:** The amount of time/resources expended in account setup and termination processes.
- **Password Strength:** The amount of time required to crack passwords.
- **Audit System Usage:** The percentage of successful/failed authentication or authorization activities logged, change tracking.
- **Compliance Scores:** A measure of how closely the system matches industry best practices and regulations.
- **Security Systems Coverage:** A measure of how well the organization is protected from the most common threats. In other words, the percentage of potential threats covered by antivirus, firewalls, antispyware systems, etc.

12. CONCLUSION

Identity Management covers the spectrum of tools and processes that are used to represent and administer digital identities and manage access for those identities (Allan et al., 2008). Usually people use different digital identities in different contexts depending on association of different information with each identity (Gupta and Sharman, 2008c). The three main business drivers for identity management solutions are security efficiency (lower costs and improved service), security effectiveness (including regulatory compliance) and business agility and performance (including workforce effectiveness and customer convenience) (Allan et al., 2008). Identity Management is a means to reduce such risks, representing a vital part of a company's security and auditing infrastructure (Buell and Sandhu, 2003). The secure and efficient administration of numerous personal attributes that make up digital identities is one of the key requirements in open and closed networks. Especially in respect to confidentiality and integrity, the users themselves, rather than popular external threads like viruses, phishing, or pharming attacks represent the main risk (Stanton et al, 2005). As a result of incorrect account management and inadequately enforced security policies users accumulate a number of excessive rights within the organizations' IT systems over time, violating the principle of the least privilege (Ferraiolo et al., 2003). Moreover, people have a hectic life and cannot spend their time administering their digital identities (El Maliki and Seigneur, 2007). Identity Management in open networks like the Internet has received tremendous attention throughout the last years with researchers. Although considered important, Identity Management in closed networks, however, has not gained comparable significance within the research community.

Identity management has shown to enhance employee efficiency and also bolster security posture while containing costs (Penn, 2002). Enterprises, including commercial corporations and government agencies, are increasingly relying on identities of customers and citizens to provide services and consummate transactions over Internet (Mont et al., 2000). While recent laws and legislations (S.761, 2006)(1999/93/EC, 1999) aim at speeding up the process of adoption of digital identities by recognizing the legal validity of digital signatures both on electronic documents and electronic transactions, Internet identity thefts, and related frauds (Arnold, 2000; Coates et al., 2000) are fast growing crimes that take advantage of poor security and privacy practices and the underestimation of the involved risks. The maintenance of security of IdM systems has become challenging due to the diversity of today's specifications concerning, for example, privacy, system integrity and distribution on the Web (Gaedke, Meinecke, & Nussbaumer, 2005).

IdM software and solutions are used in practically all digital interactions where a person must identify themselves whether people realize it or not. The current status of IdM is one where users have learned to jump from one method to the other in their everyday lives with little thought of the inefficiencies that still exist, purely because each advancement in this area is still one step in the direction of becoming more efficient. A user that at one point was required to have twenty sets of identifier and authentication information will certainly be happy with being able to lower it to ten; no complaints will be made about wanting to have only one. In the scheme of things IdM is fairly matured, at least in the product offerings and architectures given the current state of technologies. At the same time, with new threats emerging all the time, there are enough growth opportunities in this field for further improvement and innovation.

Through taking a quick outside look at all of the aforementioned companies, it can be said that many provide similar services. However, it would be impossible to recommend any of these software solutions because just like every lock has a different key; every organization has different needs that an IdM system fulfills. And how well a solution fits into the organizational structure is determined by the organizational goals and requirements. A risk assessment against company's IDM requirements is very vital in ensuring right selection of tools for best risk management. There are many security risk management methods and tools available that can be leveraged for this purpose (Matulevicius et al., 2008) and they do offer flexibility in terms of analyzing certain aspects such as processes or issues in more details (Smojver, 2011; Taubenberger, 2011). Even more growing in importance in last few years is the emphasis on data privacy concerns which should be included in these assessments (Lund et al., 2011).

REFERENCES

1999/93/EC – Directive. (1999). *1999/93/EC of the European Parliament and of the Council of 13, December 1999 on a Community Framework for Electronic Signature – 1999.* Author.

Access: One. (2014). Retrieved online on 4/12/2014 from http://pirean.com/access-one/

Aegis Identity Software. (2014). Retrieved online on 4/12/2014 from http://aegisidentity.com/identity-software/products/tridenthe/

Aldhizer, G. III, Juras, P., & Martin, D. (2008). Using automated identity and access management controls. *The CPA Journal, 78*(9), 66–71.

Alkhalifah, A., & D'Ambra, J. (2012). The role of identity management systems in enhancing protection of user privacy, cyber security, cyber warfare and digital forensic. In *Proceedings of 2012 International Conference.* SyberSec.

Allan, A., Perkins, E., Carpenter, P., & Wagner, R. (2008). What is identity 2.0? Key issues for identity and access management, 2008. *Gartner Research Report,* ID Number: G00157012.

Alotaibi, S. J., & Mike, W. (2012). Security, user experience, acceptability attributes for the integration of physical and virtual identity access management systems. In *Proceedings of International Conference on Information Society (i-Society 2012).* Academic Press.

Alsaleh, M., & Adams, C. (2006). Enhancing consumer privacy in the liberty alliance identity federation and web servies frameworks. In *Proceedings of the 6th International conference on Privacy Enhancing Technologies (PET'06).* Springer-Verlag. doi:10.1007/11957454_4

Arnold, T. (2000). *Internet identity theft: A tragedy for victims* (White Paper). SIIA.

Balasubramaniam, S., Lewis, G. A., Morris, E., Simanta, S., & Smith, D. B. (2009). Identity management and its impact on federation in a system-of-systems context. In *Proceedings of 3rd Annual IEEE International Systems Conference.* IEEE.

Buell, A. D., & Sandhu, R. (2003). Identity management. *IEEE Internet Computing, 7*(6), 26–28. doi:10.1109/MIC.2003.1250580

Cahill, C. P., Martin, J., Phegade, V., Rajan, A., & Pagano, M. W. (2011). Client-based authentication technology: User-centric authentication using secure containers. In *Proceedings of the 7th ACM Workshop on Digital Identity Management.* Chicago: ACM. doi:10.1145/2046642.2046659

Cantor, S., & Kemp, J. (2005). *Liberty ID-FF protocols and schema specification.* Technical Report for Liberty Alliance Project, version: 1.2- errata-v3.0; 2004-2005.

Cao, Y., & Yang, L. (2010). A survey of identity management technology. In *Proceedings of 2010 IEEE International Conference on Information Theory and Information Security (ICITIS)*. IEEE.

CA Technologies. (2014). Retrieved online on 4/12/2014 from http://www.ca.com/us/products/detail/ca-cloudminder-identity-management/details.aspx

Casassa, M., Bramhall, P., Gittler, M., Pato, J., & Rees, O. (2002). Identity management: A key e-business enabler. Paper presented at SSGR2002s, L'Aquila, Italy.

Centrify Corporation. (n.d.). Retrieved from http://www.centrify.com/blogs/tomkemp/privilege_management_made_easy.asp

Chadwick, D. W., Inman, G. L., Siu, K. W., & Ferdous, M. S. (2011). Leveraging social networks to gain access to organizational resources. In *Proceedings of the 7th ACM Workshop on Digital Identity Management*. ACM. doi:10.1145/2046642.2046653

Chappell, D. (2006, April). *Introducing Windows CardSpace*. Retrieved from http://msdn.microsoft.com/en-us/library/Aa480189

Coates, D., Adams, J., Dattilo, G., & Turner, M. (2000). *Identity theft and the Internet*. Colorado University.

Connolly, P. (2000, September 29). *Single signon dangles prospect of lower help desk costs*. Retrieved march 21, 2009, from infoworld: http://www.infoworld.com/articles/es/xml/00/10/02/001002esnsso.html

Cser, A., & Penn, J. (2008). *Identity management market forecast: 2007 to 2014*. Forrester Research Report. Retrieved on 4/18/2014 from http://www.securelyyoursllc.com/files/Identity%20Management%20Market%20Forecast%202007%20To%202014.pdf

CyberArk Software Inc. (2014). Retrieved online on 4/12/2014 from http://www.cyberark.com/product-etail/application-identity-manager-features

El Maliki, T., & Seigneur, J.-M. (2007). A survey of user-centric identity management technol ogies. In *Proceedings of Emerging Security Information, Systems, and Technologies, 2007*. Academic Press.

Engelbert, P. (2009). *5 keys to a successful identity and access management implementation*. A CA white paper. Retrieved on 4/18/2014 from http://www.ca.com/files/whitepapers/iam_services_implementation_whitepaper.pdf

Evidian. (2014). Retrieved online on 4/12/2014 from Retrieved from http://www.evidian.com/pdf/fl-iamanager-en.pdf

Ferraiolo, D. F., Kuhn, R. D., & Chandramouli, R. (2003). Role-based access control. Artech House Computer Security Series.

Gaedke, M., Meinecke, J., & Nussbaumer, M. (2005). A modeling approach to federated identity and access management. In *Proceedings of International World Wide Web Conference*. Academic Press. doi:10.1145/1062745.1062916

Glasser, U., & Mona, V. (2008). Identity management architecture. In *Proceedings of IEEE International Conference on Intelligence and Security Informatics*. IEEE.

Gupta, M., & Sharman, R. (2008a). Security-efficient identity management using service provisioning (markup language). In Handbook of research on information security and assurance (pp. 83-90). Hershey, PA: IGI Global.

Gupta, M., & Sharman, R. (2008b, December). Dimensions of identity federation: A case study in financial services. *Journal of Information Assurance and Security, 3*(4), 244–256.

Gupta, M., & Sharman, R. (2008c). Emerging frameworks in user-focused identity management. In Handbook of research on enterprise systems (pp 362-377). Hershey, PA: IGI Global.

Gupta, M., & Sharman, R. (2010). Activity governance for managing risks in role design for SSO systems. *Journal of Information Assurance and Security, 5*(6).

Hardt, D. (2012). *The OAuth 2.0 authorization framework*. RFC 6749, IETF; October 2012.

HID Global's 4TRESS Authentication Appliance. (n.d.). Retrieved from http://www.hidglobal.com/sites/ hidglobal.com/files/resource_files/identity-assurance-4tress-authentication-appliance-ds-en.pdf

Hirsch, F., Philpott, R., & Maler, E. (2005). *Security and privacy considerations for the OASIS security assertion markup language (SAML) v2.0.* Technical report, OASIS; March 2005.

Hitachi ID Systems Inc. (2014). Retrieved online on 4/12/2014 from User Provisioning Best Practices.

Imprivata. (n.d.). *Benefits of single sign on*. Retrieved March 22, 2009, from Imprivata: http://www. imprivata.com/contentmgr/showdetails.php ?id=1170

INCITS. (2014). Retrieved online on 4/12/2014 from https://standards.incits.org/a/public/group/cs1

ISO. (n.d.). Retrieved from http://www.iso.org/iso/iso_catalogue/catalogue_tc/catalogue_tc_browse. htm?commid=45306

Jensen, J. (2012). Federated identity management challenges. In *Proceedings of 2012 Seventh International Conference on Availability, Reliability and Security (ARES)*. Academic Press. doi:10.1109/ARES.2012.68

Jøsang, A., Al Zomai, M., & Suriadi, S. (2007). Usability and privacy in identity management architectures. In *Proceedings of the Australasian Information Security Workshop 2007*. Ballarat, Australia: Academic Press.

Jøsang, A., & Pope, S. (n.d.). User centric identity management. *CRC for Enterprise Distributed Systems Technology* (DSTC Pty Ltd). The University of Queensland.

Kark, K. (2010). *Twelve recommendations for your 2011 security strategy*. Forrester Research Report. Retrieved on 4/18/2014 from http://www.forrester.com/Twelve+Recommendations+For+Your+2011 +Security+Strategy/fulltext/-/E-RES57684

Lee, S. (2003). An introduction to identity management systems. *SANS Institute InfoSec Reading Room*. Retrieved online on 4/12/2014 http://sans.org/reading_room/whitepapers/authentication/introduction-identity-management_852

Lieberman Software. (2014). Retrieved online on 4/12/2014 from http://www.liebsoft.com/Enterprise_ Random_Password_Manager/

Linden, M., & Vilpola, I. (2005). An empirical study on the usability of logout in a single sign-on system. In *Proceedings of the 1st International Conference in Information Security Practice and Experience* (LNCS), (vol. 3439, pp. 243-254). Springer-Verlag. doi:10.1007/978-3-540-31979-5_21

Links, C. H. (2008). *IAM success tips: Identity and access management success strategies*. CreateSpace Independent Publishing Platform.

Lund, M. S., Solhaug, B., & Stølen, K. (2011). *Model-driven risk analysis: The CORAS approach*. Springer.

Matulevicius, R., Mayer, N., Mouratidis, H., Dubois, E., Heymans, P., & Genon, N. (2008). Adapting secure tropos for security risk management in the early phases of information systems development. In *Proceedings of CAiSE* (pp. 541–555). CAiSE. doi:10.1007/978-3-540-69534-9_40

Microsoft. (2014). Retrieved online on 4/12/2014 from file:///C:/Users/Reema/Dropbox/Sem%202/ IDM%20Chapter/FIM_datasheet_MSForeFront.pdf

Miyata, T., Koga, Y., Madsen, P., & Adachi, S. (2006, January). A survey on identity management protocols and standards. *IEICE Transactions on Information and Systems, E89-D*(1), 112–123. doi:10.1093/ ietisy/e89-d.1.112

Mont, M. C., Bramhall, P., Gittler, M., Pato, J., & Rees, O. (2000). *Identity management: A key e-business enabler*. Retrieved from hpl.hp.com

MS-Live. (2010). *Home - Windows Live*. Retrieved online from http://home.live.com

Mustafic, T., Messerman, A., Camtepe, S. A., Schmidt, A. D., & Albayrak, S. (2011). Behavioral biometrics for persistent single sign-on. In *Proceedings of the 7th ACM Workshop on Digital Identity Management*. ACM. doi:10.1145/2046642.2046658

NetIQ Identity Management. (2014). Retrieved online on 4/12/2014 from https://www.netiq.com/solutions/identity-access- management/

OASIS. (2014a). Retrieved online on 4/12/2014 from http://docs.oasis-open.org/ws-sx/ws-securitypolicy/ v1.3/errata01/os/ws-securitypolicy-1.3-errata01-os-complete.pdf

OASIS. (2014b). Retrieved online on 4/12/2014 from http://docs.oasis-open.org/xacml/3.0/xacml-3.0-core-spec-os-en.pdf

OASIS. (2014c). Retrieved online on 4/12/2014 from https://www.oasis-open.org/committees/tc_home. php?wg_abbrev=security

OASIS. (2014d). Retrieved online on 4/12/2014 from https://www.oasis-open.org/committees/xcbf/ipr.php

OneLogin. (2014). Retrieved online on 4/12/2014 from http://www.onelogin.com/product/

Oracle-IDM. (n.d.). Retrieved from http://www.oracle.com/technetwork/middleware/id-mgmt/overview/ index.html?ssSourceSiteId=opn

Penn, J. (2002). *IT trends 2002: Directories and directory-enabled applications*. GIGA Report.

Rai, S., Bresz, F., Renshaw, T., Rozek, J., & White, T. (2007). *Global Technology Audit Guide: Identity and Access Management*. The Institute of Internal Auditors.

Reymann, P. (2008). *Aligning people, processes, and technology for effective risk management*. Retrieved on 4/18/2014 from: http://www.theiia.org/intAuditor/itaudit/archives/2008/january/aligning-people-processes-andtechnology-for-effective-risk-management

Rochet, J—C., & Tirole, J. (2003). Platform competition in two–sided markets. *Journal of the European Economic Association, 1*(4), 990–1029.

Rogaway, P. (2004). *Nonce-based symmetric encryption*. International Association for Cryptologic Research. Retrieved from: http://www.pewinternet.org/fact-sheets/mobile- technology-fact-sheet/

Shibboleth. (2014). Retrieved online on 4/12/2014 from https://shibboleth.net/about/

Smojver, S. (2011). Selection of information security risk management method using analytic hierarchy process (ahp). In *Proceedings of Central European Conference on Information and Intelligent Systems*. Academic Press.

SSH Communications Security. (2014). Retrieved on 04/17/2014 from http://www.ssh.com/resources/datasheets/3-universal-ssh-key-manager

Stanton, J. M., Stam, K. R., Mastrangelo, P., & Jolton, J. (2005). Analysis of end user security behaviors. *Computers & Security, 24*(2), 124–133. doi:10.1016/j.cose.2004.07.001

Sun, S.-T., Boshmaf, Y., Hawkey, K., & Beznosov, K. (2010). A billion keys, but few locks: The crisis of web single sign-on. In Proceedings of the 2010 Workshop on New Security Paradigms. Academic Press. doi:10.1145/1900546.1900556

Suoranta, S., Tontti, A., Ruuskanen, J., & Aura, T. (2013). Logout in single sign on systems. In Policies and research in identity management: Third IFIP WG 11.6 working conference. London: Springer.

Takeda, Y., Kondo, S., Kitayama, Y., Torato, M., & Motegi, T. (2006). Avoidance of performance bottlenecks caused by HTTP redirect in identity management protocols. In *Proceedings of the Second ACM Workshop on Digital Identity Management*. ACM. doi:10.1145/1179529.1179535

Taubenberger, S., Jürjens, J., Yu, Y., & Nuseibeh, B. (2011). Problem analysis of traditional IT-security risk assessment methods – An experience report from the insurance and auditing domain. In *Proceedings of SEC* (pp. 259–270). SEC.

IBM Tivoli. (n.d.). Retrieved on 2/2/2011 from http://www.rv-nrw.de/content/koop/tim/identity-mgr_43.pdf

Tracy, K. (2008). Identity management systems. *IEEE Potentials*, (November/December), 2008.

ViewDS Identity Solutions. (2014). Retrieved online on 4/12/2014 from http://www.viewds.com/images/pdf/AccessSentinel.pdf

Wood, P. (2005, September). Implementing identity management security - An ethical hacker's view. *Network Security, 2005*(9), 12–15. doi:10.1016/S1353-4858(05)70282-8

KEY TERMS AND DEFINITIONS

Authentication: Verifying user's assertion of its identification through credentials.

Authorization: Verifying user's privileges to a system.

Identity Management Architecture: Design of identity system for managing credentials and entitlements for users of covered system(s).

Identity Management System: A system for managing user identities.

Multiple Factor Authentication: An authentication system that is based on more than one factor of authentication such as something user knows (knowledge), something that user possesses (possession) and something user is (behavioral or physical trait).

Password Management: Managing users' passwords for purpose of authenticating users.

Role Management: Managing users' entitlements and rights to application(s).

Single Sign On: Use of single set of credentials to provide access to multiple applications and systems.

This work was previously published in the Handbook of Research on Emerging Developments in Data Privacy edited by Manish Gupta, pages 144-169, copyright 2015 by Information Science Reference (an imprint of IGI Global).

Section 2
Technologies and Applications

This section presents an extensive coverage of various tools and technologies available in the field of Identity Theft and discusses a variety of applications and opportunities available that can be considered by practitioners in developing viable and effective Identity Theft programs and processes. With 7 chapters, this section offers a broad treatment of some of the many tools and technologies within the Identity Theft field. These chapters enlighten readers about fundamental research on the many tools facilitating the burgeoning field of Identity Theft and review topics from case studies to best practices and ongoing research. Further chapters discuss Identity Theft in a variety of settings. Contributions included in this section provide excellent coverage of today's IT community and how research into Identity Theft is impacting the social fabric of our present-day global village. It is through these rigorously researched chapters that the reader is provided with countless examples of the up-and-coming tools and technologies emerging from the field of Identity Theft.

Chapter 8
The German Electronic Identity Card:
Lessons Learned

Christoph Sorge
CISPA and Institute of Legal Informatics, Saarland University, Germany

ABSTRACT

Authentication is an important aspect of e-government applications, as in many cases the identity of a citizen has to be established before provision of a service. Germany is among the countries that have established an electronic identification and authentication infrastructure, based on an electronic identity card. The card enables both local and remote authentication to service providers and authorities. While privacy-enhancing technologies have been used to a large extent in its design and there are no known attacks on its security protocols, the eID card has been harshly criticized. Less than a third of the citizens requesting an identity card choose to activate the eID function. Using the example of Germany, this chapter discusses whether the establishment of an electronic authentication infrastructure makes sense and presents possible reasons for the German eID card's lack of success. In addition, the author considers electronic signatures and their integration in an electronic authentication infrastructure.

INTRODUCTION

In many countries, the provision of identity cards, enabling citizens to prove their identities to authorities or private companies (like banks), is considered as a task of the state. Smartcard technology allows integrating additional features, like storage of biometric data, in such identity cards. Given the growing importance of e-business and e-government transactions, some countries have also decided to support remote authentication to the respective service providers. Both developments can be combined (i.e., remote authentication can be performed by a chip on an identity card), but this is not strictly a necessity. For example, Malaysia's MyKad (Loo, Yeow, & Chong, 2009) uses a multi-application smartcard that can, in principle, be used locally and remotely. The Austrian Bürgerkarte for remote authentication, on the other hand, is not bound to a national identity card scheme. There is a multitude of design options for

DOI: 10.4018/978-1-5225-0808-3.ch008

identity card schemes and electronic authentication; for an (incomplete) overview of existing schemes in Europe, see (Zefferer, 2010).

In this chapter, we focus on Germany, where a new identity card was introduced in November, 2010. Besides changing the dimensions of the identity card and improving the protection against forgery, the main innovation lies in the addition of a contactless smartcard. Like existing electronic passports, the smartcard can be used at border controls and during other inspections of the identity card by authorities; this way, the authenticity of the data contained on the card can be confirmed, and (optionally) stored fingerprints can be used for biometric verification of the card holder's identity. Like in case of the (older) electronic passport, data stored on the smartcard can be digitally signed, thus making it very difficult (if not impossible) to forge any information.

In addition, the smartcard can also be used for (remote) authentication to service providers, e.g. online retailers, banks or e-government services (so-called eID function). This feature requires the user to purchase a smartcard reader; the service provider needs a certificate confirming his authorization to use specific information from the identity card, and server software implementing the protocols used by the card. For each service provider, a different identifier is used; the creation of user profiles across service providers is therefore not possible based on those identifiers.

Finally, the electronic identity card is a secure signature creation device, as specified by the European Signature Directive; thus, it can potentially be used to sign documents in a legally binding manner. However, the certificates used in the signature creation process are issued by private companies.

The remainder of this chapter is structured as follows: First, we give a short overview on smartcards, and describe the technology and the infrastructure used for the German eID card. We then comment on the current adoption of the electronic authentication infrastructure based on the eID card. Next, based on the example of Germany, we discuss whether the introduction of such an infrastructure makes sense, and describe related benefits. The chapter concludes with an outlook on possible future research directions.

BACKGROUND

In this section, we first provide some general background about smartcards, before looking at the Geman eID card in more detail.

Smartcards

Though the idea of smartcards has been around since 1968, the first major successful rollout was not until the 1990s (Shelfer & Procaccino, 2002). Among the earliest applications was the replacement of banking cards with magnetic stripes: smartcards have the advantage of a greater memory capacity. In this chapter, we focus on smartcards that come with a processor, instead of pure storage cards; in fact, some authors consider only such processor cards as smartcards.

Such a processor can enforce access control restrictions, and in addition, it can perform (cryptographic) computations. For example, cryptographic keys can be stored on the card, and the processor makes sure that these keys are only used after the card holder has been authenticated using a secret PIN. The keys never have to leave the card. As a consequence, some operations that have to be performed by a trustworthy component (e.g. the computation of an electronic wallet's current balance) can be performed on the card, while previously (using magnetic stripes), a trusted server had to be contacted.

Among the most common smart cars are bank cards and subscriber identity modules (SIM cards) used for the authentication of mobile phones to GSM, UMTS or LTE networks. In addition, Shelfer & Procaccino (2002) point out that "just about anything found in a person's wallet has the potential to be stored on a smart card".

The ISO 7816 standard, consisting of 15 parts, specifies the most relevant aspects of smartcards, including physical dimensions, electrical and electronic aspects, and communication protocols. For a more detailed introduction, refer to Shelfer & Procaccino, 2002.

Identity Cards in Germany

All Germans who are at least 16 years old, and who spend most of their time in Germany, are required to possess an identity card.[1] The identity card can be replaced by a passport; however, as the identity card is smaller, cheaper, and also valid as a travel document in most European countries, most citizens request one instead of, or in addition to, a passport.

Until October, 2010, the identity card was designed for visual/optical inspection (including by electronic readers) only, and used the ID-2 format. The newly introduced identity card uses the ID-1 format (credit card format), and contains a smartcard with a wireless interface.

In the remainder of this chapter, we will focus on the features of this smartcard and ignore the features of the identity card designed for visual inspection.

Security Protocols

The German electronic identity card implements a number of security protocols, specified by the German Federal Office for Information Security (Bundesamt für Sicherheit in der Informationstechnik, 2012):

- **The PACE Protocol (Password-Authenticated Connection Establishment):** Establishes a secure connection between the smartcard reader and the identity card, authenticated by a password. In case of local inspection by police or other authorities entitled to verify citizens' identities, a number printed on the eID card, the Card Access Number (CAN), is used as the password for this protocol. However, this authentication requires the subsequent terminal authentication to be performed with a certificate specifically issued for that purpose. If the user intends to authenticate towards a service provider, a secret six-digit PIN is used instead. The PACE protocol has been proven secure against offline password-guessing, so eavesdropping is not an issue despite the wireless communication channel. Brute-force attacks on the PIN are prevented as the card is locked after three unsuccessful authentication attempts. It can be unlocked using the CAN or, if the new attempt also fails, using a long PIN Unblocking Key (PUK). During the PACE protocol, the communication partners also agree on key material, which is used for authentication and encryption of the subsequent communication.
- **The Extended Access Control (EAC) Protocol, Version 2:** It consists of terminal authentication and chip authentication. The terminal authentication protocol is executed between the eID card and the terminal, i.e. the actual intended communication partner to which the user would like to authenticate. For example, the terminal can be run by an e-government service or a company to which service provision is outsourced. Terminal authentication is based on a certificate, which contains information about the service provider and attributes that provider has access to.

- **Chip Authentication:** Executed between the same two parties, is based on Diffie-Hellman, where the eID card's key pair is static, and the public Diffie-Hellman value is signed by the eID card's issuer ("passive authentication").

- **The Restricted Identification Protocol:** Once an eID card has been recognized as authentic, the Restricted Identification protocol is used to generate an identifier which is unique for the tuple (eID card, service provider), with the service provider's identity taken from the certificate used during terminal authentication. Tracking the usage of one eID card across several service providers is not possible, as the respective identifiers cannot be linked to each other. In essence, the Restricted Identification protocol can be thought of as generating a hash value of (secret stored by eID card ‖ service provider identity). The actual protocol is based on the Diffie-Hellman principle, thereby achieving additional functionality: The identifier used by a specific eID card for a specific service provider can be reconstructed by two cooperating authorities to enable revocation. To prevent abuse of the revocation feature, a single authority cannot do the same.

Figure 1 illustrates the relation between the PACE, terminal authentication, and chip authentication protocols. Restricted identification is performed over the secure channel established after the aforementioned protocols have been executed.

In addition to the security protocols in a narrower sense, two more features are worth mentioning: The eID card can do more than just transmit previously stored, authenticated data. For the age verification feature, the terminal transmits a date to the eID card. The card answers whether or not its owner was born before that date. This way, transmission of the precise date of birth is avoided when it is not required. Note that age verification can only be performed once per execution of the terminal authentica-

Figure 1. Relation between PACE, terminal, and chip authentication performed during use of the eID card. PACE requires the user to enter his PIN code; in addition, the user may select (restrict) the data fields to be transmitted to a service provider. This user interaction is omitted in the figure.

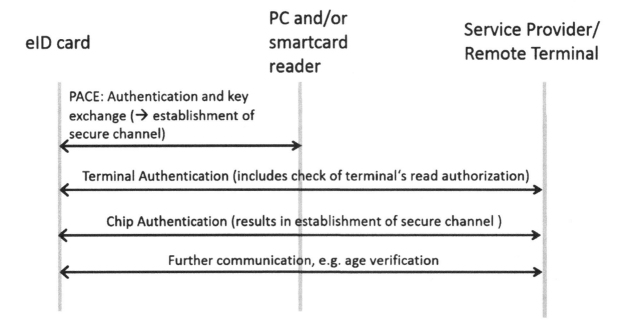

tion and PACE protocols (thus, once per PIN entry). As a result, the service provider cannot determine the date of birth more precisely by querying the eID card several times (Bundesamt für Sicherheit in der Informationstechnik, 2013).

Community ID verification was also designed with the goal to transmit as coarse-grained information as possible. Each German municipality has a unique identifier, the municipality key. It consists of identifiers for the country, state, administrative region, county and municipality. The municipality key for the eID card holder's place of residence is stored on the card. Depending on the required granularity, a service provider can read parts of the municipality key (e.g., only the state, or the state and the administrative region within that state). Use of this feature makes sense if services are supposed to be available only for inhabitants of a certain region, e.g. all citizens residing in a certain state (Bundesamt für Sicherheit in der Informationstechnik, 2011).

Public-Key Infrastructure

The eID card heavily relies on public-key cryptography. Therefore, a public key infrastructure (PKI) must be in place to ensure authenticity of public keys. More specifically, there are two separate infrastructures. One PKI has been established for signing data stored on eID cards: The root certification authority, called the Country Signer Certificate Authority (CSCA) signs the Document Signer (DS) certificates of identity card manufacturers, which sign the data on the cards.

The second PKI is defined for granting access to the cards. The certificates of this PKI are used during the terminal authentication protocol. There are three separate certification trees: One is for official inspection of the identity card, e.g. by police and other authorities that are entitled to verify citizens' identities. If a terminal has such a certificate, the Card Access Number is used instead of the user's PIN during the PACE protocol. As the CAN is only printed on, but not stored outside the card, this is supposed to make sure that such an inspection is only performed locally.

The second certification tree is for the eID function, i.e. for electronic authentication both to private companies and to e-government services. Service providers can request certificates authorizing access to eID cards. Access can be restricted, e.g. to age verification only; when requesting a certificate, a service provider must state reasons why it needs the specific data it requests access to. There is a fee for certificate issuing, but it is negligible in comparison to the operating cost of an eID server.

Finally, the last certification tree is required for the electronic signature function. Owners of an eID card who want to use it to electronically sign documents need access to the card in the first place, i.e. their smartcard readers require a certificate, just like a service provider.

Security Assessment

There are no known attacks on the security protocols used, and the eID card appears to be a well-engineered system reaching the goals it was designed for. The PACE protocol has been proven secure (Bender, Fischlin, & Kügler, 2009); other protocols used rely on widely accepted principles and assumptions. There have, however, been claims of security breaches, which were discussed in the general press. This is not a contradiction to the stated security of the system, but illustrates mismatches between:

- The expectations of the general public and the actual design goals of the eID card and its environment, and

- The security achieved by cryptographic protocols on the one hand and the security achieved by actual implementations and by embedding the eID card system in an insecure environment on the other hand.

Remaining security issues with the eID card are as follows:

- The eID card does not know the current date or time, so it may accept an expired certificate during the terminal authentication protocol. However, during terminal authentication, the eID card stores the date when the presented terminal certificate was issued. During future executions of the terminal authentication protocol, certificates that have expired before that date will no longer be accepted.
- Security of the authentication depends on a secure PIN entry method. The eID card can be used with secure smartcard readers, which have their own PIN pad and their own display. While it is not completely impossible to compromise these smartcard readers, they achieve a much higher security level than the users' PCs: Due to their specialization, their smaller code base, and their limited interface, there are fewer possibilities of attack. However, the eID card can also be used in conjunction with simple smartcard readers, in which case the PIN is entered on the user's PC. In that case, malware on the PC can read the PIN. Afterwards, the eID card can thus be used by the malware to authenticate to arbitrary service providers, as long as the card is in proximity to the reader.
- The software written to support the eID card could also introduce security issues, as the security of complex software cannot be guaranteed given the current state of the art. This concerns both the server-side and the client-side software. However, the client-side software has been particularly criticized. It uses plug-ins for communication with web browsers. At the time of this writing, the application supports (only) Internet Explorer, Firefox, and iceweasel. In case of Firefox, only the so-called "Extended Support Release" of version 24 is supported, while version 29 is current. Versions of the application for different operating systems have download sizes between about 60 and about 90 megabytes, despite limited functionality and a simplistic user interface. The first major vulnerability of the application was discovered less than a day after its initial publication (Kossel, 2010).
- The eID card provides secure authentication, electronic signatures, and age and address verification. It does not go beyond that; in particular, after an authentication has taken place, communication sessions between the user and the service provider could, for example, be taken over by an attacker who has installed malware on the user's PC. This is obvious to computer scientists, but not necessarily to the general public.

There is another aspect of the electronic identity card that may be considered as a less-than-elegant design decision: Chip authentication is based on a traditional public-key cryptographic scheme. If applied in a straightforward manner, this would render the Restricted Identification protocol useless: Service providers could track their customers (and exchange information about them with other service providers) based on the public key[2] presented during chip authentication. There are cryptographic protocols with which an entity can prove that it belongs to a certain group (in case of the eID card, the group would be the entirety of all valid eID cards), without revealing any additional information (like a specific public key). Both anonymous credential schemes and the related group signature schemes (Bellare, Micciancio, & Warinschi, 2003)would be suited for that purpose. However, implementation of these schemes on (contactless) smartcards is still a challenge, so it was not an option for eID cards introduced in 2010. Instead, all eID cards of one batch share a common key pair for chip authentication to private sector terminals. If an attacker manages to extract the private key from one eID card, this implies that the corresponding public key for more than a million eID cards must be revoked. However, chances for a successful attack on a state-of-the-art smartcard are considered slim.

The privacy features of the German eID card, such as the Restricted Identification protocol and the age verification scheme, are unique, at least for such a large-scale and general-purpose electronic authentication infrastructure. There are currently no known attacks on these features.

Adoption

To become useful, an electronic authentication must be accepted by service providers and used by the respective users. At the time of this writing, the German Ministry of the Interior's website (Federal Ministry of the Interior, 2013) lists:

- Eight insurance companies,
- Six finance-related service providers, and
- Seven other service providers

accepting the eID card (in addition to e-government services, which we will discuss separately). While most of these service providers allow the eID card to be used for the login to each session, a few of them only use the card for a one-off registration – relying on traditional means of authentication for later application sessions. In particular, there is no bank among the finance-related service providers that allows the eID card to be used for frequent tasks in online banking (like checking the account balance or performing money transfers). There is, however, a bank running an automated teller machine that accepts the eID card.

Due to the low number of services, and due to their nature, it is unlikely that any citizens frequently use the eID card for private sector services.

The adoption of the eID card for e-government services is more difficult to judge. There are a few federal agencies supporting the eID card for specific applications. In addition, all federal states allow (one-off) registration for an electronic filing of tax declarations with authentication based on the eID card. 9 out of 16 states offer additional services, sometimes limited to a few cities per state (Federal Ministry of the Interior, 2013).

The limited number of services corresponds to a lack of user acceptance. According to a report from November, 2013 (three years after introduction of the eID card), 21 million eID cards, plus 2.2 million eID cards for foreigners (electronic resident permit), having the same electronic functionality, had been issued by that time (Borchers, 2013). However, only 28% of the users decided to activate the eID function (which is free if chosen when the card is first issued).

GOVERNMENT-OPERATED ELECTRONIC AUTHENTICATION INFRASTRUCTURES: HELPFUL OR USELESS?

In this section, we discuss if the establishment of electronic identification and authentication infrastructures (we will omit the identification aspect for brevity) makes sense. We deal with the question whether such infrastructures should be run by governments, and try to identify reasons for their lack of acceptance. The section concludes with remarks on electronic signatures, which may also benefit from the availability of an electronic authentication infrastructure.

Costs and Benefits of Electronic Authentication Infrastructures

From an economic perspective, answering the question whether the establishment of an electronic authentication infrastructure makes sense seems simple only at first glance: If – and only if – the benefit (for the economy of the whole) outweighs the costs, then such an infrastructure should be introduced.

Determining the costs to be borne by the operator is relatively simple, though a lot of factors (like the establishment of new business processes, training measures, and cost of hardware including guarantees for long-term availability) have to be taken into account. Moreover, the question is which part of the costs is to be considered: in the German example, one motivation for the introduction of the new eID card was to improve the identity card's protection against forgery, as the chip stores data which can be electronically signed. In other words, one has to consider only the additional costs of establishing an electronic authentication infrastructure (beyond the components needed for border controls and inspection by the police).

For various reasons, the benefit is almost impossible to be measured beforehand.

Firstly, the benefit of the infrastructure depends on its acceptance by service providers and end users. In case of Germany, despite all theoretic advantages, the eID card and its infrastructure have little benefit because they are hardly used. Alternative means of authentication must still be available to be able to serve all users. In addition to the many German citizens who do not want to use the eID card, and the citizens who wait for the expiration of their old ID card until requesting the eID card, there is a huge group who is not entitled to get one: Foreigners cannot get the normal eID card (which is reserved for Germans). While there is a specific eID card for foreigners, it is only available to non-EU foreigners. Citizens of European Union member states cannot get either of the cards.

Secondly, the main benefit of an authentication infrastructure is to reduce the damage (and/or costs) caused by the drawbacks of existing authentication mechanisms. The costs of existing authentication mechanisms could be:

- *Caused by a lower reliability of these alternative mechanisms.* The problem of identity theft, for example, can be attributed to the use of weak authentication schemes. Unfortunately, getting reliable numbers concerning the magnitude of identity theft is difficult. The U.S. Department of Justice reports that 7% of all U.S. citizens aged 16 or above were victims of identity theft in 2012, resulting in direct and indirect losses of 24.7 billion US$ (Harrell & Langton, 2013). Yet, this number is not an indication for the severity of the problem in other countries, as the susceptibility to identity theft is influenced by a lot of factors. Consumers' attitudes, the prevalence of electronic payment schemes, and the availability of a (non-electronic) identification/authentication infrastructure may play a role.

- *Even if the total damage caused by identity theft is known, a closer investigation is required to find out how much of the damage was related to electronic authentication,* and was caused by usage of a weak authentication scheme (i.e. could have been avoided by a better one).
- *Direct costs related to the alternative mechanisms.* For example, the identity of a person may be verified by sending a letter to the person's address, and verifying that this letter actually arrives. Besides the postage, direct costs include expenses for paper, printing, and processing of replies. To achieve a higher security level, additional services are available. For example, Deutsche Post offers a service called "Postident", which involves checking the consumer's identity card or passport. Prices are dependent on the number of identity checks performed, but Deutsche Post's website states a maximum price of EUR 6.61, plus VAT and return postage (Deutsche Post, 2014); obviously, variable costs for an electronic authentication infrastructure can be lower. Whether this outweighs the fixed costs of establishing an electronic authentication scheme is unclear; among others, this depends on the number of authentications actually required.
- *Caused by a lower user acceptance for the alternative mechanisms.* This seems plausible in case of media discontinuities (if use of an electronic service requires the user to authenticate using non-electronic means, and possibly to wait to the next business day for this authentication to take place). Given the current adoption of the German eID card, however, it seems the user acceptance of alternative mechanisms is not lower at all.

To summarize, there is no general answer to the question whether an electronic authentication infrastructure makes sense, as the answer depends on country-specific circumstances. The current lack of user acceptance for the German solution does not mean that electronic authentication infrastructures are a bad idea in general, but could also be attributed to specific mistakes made by German authorities.

OPERATION BY THE GOVERNMENT?

Assuming it does make sense to introduce such an infrastructure, the next question is by whom it can – and should – be operated, and whether the state is the appropriate entity.

Independent of the technology used, a major cost factor of electronic authentication is the verification of the users' identities. A number of industries have access to data that can be used for identity verification (or at least address verification), e.g. utilities, banks, or postal services. The Austrian electronic authentication concept, the Bürgerkarte, allows eID cards to be issued by banks or other service providers. The same concept could have been applied in Germany. However, the use of state-issued identity cards enables a higher coverage, and is also very reliable: Banks and other companies that require secure authentication use the government-issued identity card for that purpose, so they cannot achieve a higher reliability than provided by that card itself.

In addition to being reliable, a requirement for an electronic authentication infrastructure is for it to be trusted. There has been little research to assess whether involvement of the government is helpful to achieve this trust. A qualitative assessment has been provided by researchers investigating the acceptance of the German eID card using the focus group method (Harbach, Fahl, Rieger, & Smith, 2013): Apparently, there are users for whom government involvement is a deterrent, and others who trust the government more than private companies. The authors get to the result that on the whole, the government was considered more trustworthy with respect to the gathering of personal data than companies.

Due to the limited number of persons involved in the study, this result cannot simply be transferred to the German population as a whole, let alone other countries.

Even if we assume that a government should run an electronic authentication infrastructure, and is best-suited to establish the identity of citizens, the question remains whether the infrastructure should be directly coupled with existing identification schemes. More precisely, is the German solution of combining the eID card with the national identity card reasonable?

Once again, there is the cost argument. As becomes visible when looking at the electronic passport – which was introduced long before the eID card – the addition of a smartcard to identity documents has been considered advantageous even without the benefits of a generally available electronic authentication infrastructure. On the long run, adding some functionality – part of which uses cryptographic algorithms anyway implemented – seems to be the more efficient option in comparison to the roll-out of separate cards. In addition, a single card is easier to store, and more convenient to handle, than if several separate cards were used.

Interestingly, Harbach et al. (2013) point out that the official nature of the identity card may even deter people from using it for internet-based services; one of their participants pointed out that the identity card was a "very personal document" and might therefore not be suited for "playing around on the Internet". In addition, they observe that the use of an identity card with a photo can be perceived to contradict the pseudonymous authentication feature provided by the card. Both aspects are related to the fact that the eID card is government-issued, but are reinforced by the combination with the mandatory national identity card.

Usefulness for E-Government Services

A lot of electronic government services are currently offered that do not use strong authentication, or even do not use any authentication at all. To judge the usefulness of an electronic authentication infrastructure, the question is whether existing e-government services would still benefit from a more secure authentication, and whether additional services could be offered with such an infrastructure.

A benefit can only be expected from an electronic authentication infrastructure for services which do not require the physical presence of the citizen.

According to American literature (Cook, 2000), citizens commonly wish for services like renewal of driver's licenses, voter registration and the filing of (state) taxes. These services can benefit from an electronic authentication infrastructure, as they require secure authentication. In contrast to the U.S., however, voters do not need to register in Germany; moreover, the need for renewing driver's licenses was only introduced so recently that no German driver's license has expired yet. On the other hand, German residents have to report their place of residence when moving – this service, too, could be offered electronically and requires authentication of the citizen.

Cook (2000) also lists voting on the Internet – which is currently out of the question, as even the use of computers as voting machines within a polling station is not legal in Germany due to the requirement for verifiability of the election process (Bundesverfassungsgericht/Federal Constitutional Court, 2009). Requesting hunting and fishing licenses, and ordering birth, death, and marriage certificates (as also listed by Cook), on the other hand, would make sense in Germany as well. The latter is already possible in some municipalities, even without using eID-based authentication;[3] introducing an authentication requirement would further reduce the risk of abuse, but given the limited information available on these certificates, it seems that authentication is not currently considered necessary.

Further services listed by Cook (2000) are state park information and reservations (which do not require strong authentication), access to "one-stop shopping" (with authentication only required for transactional services, which we have already listed separately), and accessing medical information from the National Institute of Health (which is a research institute, so this service is not about individuals' medical records and does not require strong authentication either).

To summarize, while the services that can benefit from an electronic authentication infrastructure may differ between countries, there are services for which such an infrastructure (as offered in Germany on the basis of the eID card) makes sense. Whether the number of such services justifies the effort invested into that infrastructure is a different issue – therefore, allowing private-sector service providers to benefit from the infrastructure appears to be a good move of German authorities.

Beyond Authentication: Electronic Signatures

Closely related to electronic authentication infrastructures are electronic and digital signatures.

Digital signature schemes are public-key cryptographic schemes that ensure integrity and authenticity of the document, and which also achieve non-repudiation: Only the owner of a private cryptographic key can generate a signature, which can be verified by anyone with access to the corresponding public key.

Digital signatures are a common technique to achieve authentication. A simple authentication protocol may consist of a random number sent as challenge, and a digital signature of that random number sent in response as a proof of identity. Still, an infrastructure for electronic authentication is not equivalent to an infrastructure for signatures. There is an important difference concerning regulation: For so-called electronic signatures, a legal framework has been established by the European Union (European Signature Directive, 1999). It defines electronic signatures as "data in electronic form which are attached to or logically associated with other electronic data and which serve as a method of authentication". There are different categories of electronic signatures: (Simple) electronic signatures as defined above, advanced electronic signatures (which require the use of cryptographic digital signature scheme), and qualified electronic signatures (a term not used in the directive itself, which calls them "advanced electronic signatures which are based on a qualified certificate and which are created by a secure-signature-creation device")[4]. The latter are of particular interest, as there are legal consequences attached to them. For example, qualified electronic signatures are considered as equivalent to handwritten signatures for most purposes. In some cases, they are already used for e-government services – in Germany, one example is the electronic request for a court order for payment (*Mahnbescheid*).

Unfortunately, while purely software-based solutions (which can even be obtained for free) are sufficient for the generation of advanced electronic signatures, the two additional requirements for qualified electronic signature are not as easy to fulfill. A qualified certificate requires the involvement of a certification authority, which must adhere to certain regulations, and can be held liable for mistakes made during the certification process. Operation of such certification authorities is not limited to governments. Instead, the legislator has chosen to allow competition between private companies, as long as the companies fulfill the requirement set forth in the directive and national laws.

A secure signature creation device must guarantee security of the private key; typically, secure signature creation devices are implemented as smartcards.

Both requirements are not necessarily met in an electronic authentication infrastructure. However, if that infrastructure is sufficiently reliable, it can enable a simpler and cheaper authentication of customers towards the certification authority, so a certificate can be issued purely based on the electronic authentication. The German eID card supports both; given that secure key storage and implementation of cryptographic algorithms were anyway required, the main functionality of a secure signature creation device was already available. When the eID card was introduced, it was decided not to ship the card with a pre-installed certificate, but to keep the concept of private-sector certification authorities. Once authentication to a certification authority (using the eID card) is successful, a qualified certificate can be loaded onto the card, and it can be used to sign documents. However, it took more than two years after introduction of the eID card for the first certification authority to support this process.

Lessons Learned

While a quantification of individual influence factors seems difficult, a number of possible reasons for the limited adoption of the German eID card solution have been identified, and could be addressed by the government:

- **Usability Could be Improved:** In particular, the necessity for users to install an application that supports only a limited set of browser versions is problematic.
- **Security of the Overall System Could be Improved:** This includes an audit of the above-mentioned client application, but also the promotion of secure smartcard readers (with their own display and PIN pad). Unfortunately, this contradicts the cost efficiency of the system. On the other hand, authentication based on the eID card is more secure than purely password-based authentication, even if insecure readers are used (a fact that has not been communicated very well).
- **Trust in the System Requires Information:** For example, the study by Harbach et al. (2013) considers insufficient information as a major obstacle for the system's adoption. Official information about the eID card is available on the Internet and from the Federal Ministry of the Interior, but Harbach et al. report difficulties in getting that information on a local level.
- **The Number of Services Could be Increased:** Partly, this can be achieved by the (federal and state) governments themselves by providing additional e-government services. In addition, the costs for private sector service providers can be influenced, for example by providing the required server software for free.

The German example does not provide clear insights for other countries, as the local circumstances may have a major influence on eID solutions. However, in addition to the issues listed above, an important consideration for the introduction of an eID scheme is the desired security level: Which services are to be supported, and do they allow making a tradeoff between security and usability – both on the service provider and on the user side? For example, alternative solutions to the German one could enable some limited features without authorization certificates, or could omit PIN entry in case of low security requirements. Obviously, such a decision requires a detailed analysis of the individual services, and the security and privacy implications of the chosen tradeoff.

FUTURE RESEARCH DIRECTIONS

There are still lots of open research issues in the field of electronic authentication infrastructures. Some of them are technological questions. Looking at the German eID card, an obvious issue is the chip authentication towards service providers with a key pair shared by a large number of cards: Replacing that concept with an anonymous credential or group signature scheme would be more elegant, but additional research is required to achieve a practical implementation for contactless smartcards – though major steps in this direction have already been taken; for example, there is an implementation for java cards that takes a few seconds for the execution of an anonymous credential protocol (Bichsel, Camenisch, Groß, & Shoup, 2009).

To achieve a breakthrough for the usage of an eID infrastructure, however, more relevant issues concern the integration into a larger context: Business processes of companies and government agencies have to be adapted, the legal framework has to be in place, and people have to perceive a benefit before using the eID card. To better understand the impediments of eID adoption, an interdisciplinary effort is required, involving not just computer scientists, but also taking social sciences' perspective into account.

CONCLUSION

This chapter has introduced the core concepts of the German electronic identity card. The electronic authentication infrastructure built around the card is well-designed, and there are no known attacks on the security protocols employed, or affecting the privacy of users of the eID card. Mistakes have still been made – including the provision of a client application for the eID card whose first major vulnerability was discovered within a day of its publication. Less than a third of the citizens requesting a new identity card also opt for the eID feature, though its activation is free. The number of private sector services taking advantage of the card is still very low, and not all states offer e-government services (beyond tax filing) which support eID-based authentication.

The combination of a national identity card, an electronic authentication infrastructure and an infrastructure for electronic signatures could still prove useful, but requires more investments, and in particular the provision of services that actually benefit from its use.

REFERENCES

Bellare, M., Micciancio, D., & Warinschi, B. (2003). Foundations of Group Signatures: Formal Definitions, Simplified Requirements, and a Construction Based on General Assumptions. In E. Biham (Ed.), *Advances in Cryptology—EUROCRYPT 2003: International Conference on the Theory and Applications of Cryptographic Techniques* (LNCS), (*vol. 2656*, pp. 614-629). Berlin: Springer. doi:10.1007/3-540-39200-9_38

Bender, J., Fischlin, M., & Kügler, D. (2009). Security Analysis of the PACE Key-Agreement Protocol. In P. Samarati, M. Yung, F. Martinelli, & C. Ardagna (Eds.), *Information Security: 12th International Conference, ISC 2009,* (LNCS), (vol. 5735, pp. 33-48). Berlin: Springer. doi:10.1007/978-3-642-04474-8_3

Bichsel, P., Camenisch, J., Groß, T., & Shoup, V. (2009). Anonymous credentials on a standard java card. In *Proceedings of the 16th ACM Conference on Computer and Communications Security (CCS '09)* (pp. 600-610). New York: ACM. doi:10.1145/1653662.1653734

Borchers, D. (2013, November 1). *Der ePerso hat Geburtstag: Drei Jahre neuer Personalausweis*. Retrieved from Heise Online: http://heise.de/-2037387

Bundesamt für Sicherheit in der Informationstechnik. (2011, March 10). *Technical Guideline TR-03127: Architecture electronic Identity Card and electronic Resident Permit*. Retrieved January 20, 2014, from https://www.bsi.bund.de/SharedDocs/Downloads/DE/BSI/Publikationen/TechnischeRichtlinien/TR03127/BSI-TR-03127_en_pdf.pdf?__blob=publicationFile

Bundesamt für Sicherheit in der Informationstechnik. (2012, March). *Technical Guideline TR-03110-1, Version 2.10: Advanced Security Mechanisms for Machine Readable Travel Documents Part 1*. Retrieved from https://www.bsi.bund.de/SharedDocs/Downloads/EN/BSI/Publications/TechGuidelines/TR03110/TR-03110_v2.1_P1pdf.pdf?__blob=publicationFile

Bundesamt für Sicherheit in der Informationstechnik. (2012, March). *Technical Guideline TR-03110-2, Version 2.10: Advanced Security Mechanisms for Machine Readable Travel Documents Part 2*. Retrieved from https://www.bsi.bund.de/SharedDocs/Downloads/EN/BSI/Publications/TechGuidelines/TR03110/TR-03110_v2.1_P2pdf.pdf?__blob=publicationFile

Bundesamt für Sicherheit in der Informationstechnik. (2013, July). *Technical Guideline TR-03110-3, Version 2.11: Advanced Security Mechanisms for Machine Readable Travel Documents Part 3*. Retrieved from https://www.bsi.bund.de/SharedDocs/Downloads/EN/BSI/Publications/TechGuidelines/TR03110/TR-03110_v2_11_P3pdf.pdf?__blob=publicationFile Bundesverfassungsgericht/Federal

Constitutional Court. (2009, March 3). *Judgment of the Second Senate of 3 March 2009 on the basis of the oral hearing of 28 October 2008*. Retrieved January 20, 2014, from https://www.bundesverfassungsgericht.de/entscheidungen/rs20090303_2bvc000307en.html

Cook, M. E. (2000, October). *What Citizens Want From E-Government: Current Practce Research*. Retrieved January 20, 2014, from http://www.netcaucus.info/books/egov2001/pdf/citizen.pdf

Deutsche Post. (2014). *Postident*. Retrieved January 20, 2014, from https://www.deutschepost.de/dpag?tab=1&skin=hi&check=yes&lang=de_EN&xmlFile=link1017202_1009859 Directive 1999/93/EC

Federal Ministry of the Interior. (2013). *German National Identity Card*. Retrieved January 20, 2014, from http://www.personalausweisportal.de/EN/Citizens/Applications/applications_node.html

Harbach, M., Fahl, S., Rieger, M., & Smith, M. (2013). On the Acceptance of Privacy-Preserving Authentication Technology: The Curious Case of National Identity Cards. In E. De Cristofaro & M. Wright (Eds.), *Privacy Enhancing Technologies:13th International Symposium, PETS 2013* (LNCS), (*vol. 7981*, pp. 245-264). Berlin: Springer. doi:10.1007/978-3-642-39077-7_13

Harrell, E., & Langton, L. (2013, December). *Victims of Identity Theft, 2012*. Retrieved January 20, 2014, from U.S. Department of Justice, Bureau of Justice Statistics: http://www.bjs.gov/content/pub/pdf/vit12.pdf

Kossel, A. (2010, November 9). *Neuer Personalausweis: AusweisApp mit Lücken*. Retrieved January 20, 2014, from Heise Online: http://heise.de/-1133376

Loo, W., Yeow, P., & Chong, S. (2009, April). User acceptance of Malaysian government multipurpose smartcard applications. *Government Information Quarterly, 26*(2), 358–367. doi:10.1016/j.giq.2008.07.004

Shelfer, K., & Procaccino, J. (2002, July). Smart Card Evolution. *Communications of the ACM, 45*(7), 83–88. doi:10.1145/514236.514239

Yeow, P., & Loo, W. (2011). Acceptability of ATM and Transit Applications Embedded in Multipurpose Smart Identity Card: An Exploratory Study in Malaysia. In *Applied Technology Integration in Governmental Organizations* (pp. 118–137). New E-Government Research.

Zefferer, T. (2010). *STORK Work Item 3.3.5: Smartcard eID comparison.* Retrieved from STORK Project: https://www.eid-stork.eu/index.php?option=com_processes&Itemid=&act=streamDocument&did=1384

ADDITIONAL READING

Aichholzer, G., & Strauss, S. (2009). The Citizen's Role in National Electronic Identity Management - A Case-study on Austria. In *The Second International Conference on Advances in Human-oriented and Personalized Mechanisms, Technologies, and Services, 2009. CENTRIC '09* (pp. 45-50). Washington, D.C.: IEEE Computer Society. doi:10.1109/CENTRIC.2009.13

Arcieri, F., Ciclosi, M., Fioravanti, F., Nardelli, E., & Talamo, M. (2004). The Italian electronic identity card: a short introduction. In *Proceedings of the 2004 annual national conference on Digital government research* (Vol. 262 of the ACM International Conference Proceeding Series). Digital Government Society of North America.

Arora, S. (2008, May). National e-ID card schemes: A European overview. *Information Security Technical Report, 13*(2), 46–53. doi:10.1016/j.istr.2008.08.002

Bramhall, P., Hansen, M., Rannenberg, K., & Roessler, T. (2007, July-August). User-Centric Identity Management: New Trends in Standardization and Regulation. *IEEE Security and Privacy, 5*(4), 84–87. doi:10.1109/MSP.2007.99

El Maliki, T., & Seigneur, J.-M. (2007). A Survey of User-centric Identity Management Technologies. In L. Peñalver, O. Dini, J. Mulholland, & O. Nieto-Taladriz (Eds.), *The International Conference on Emerging Security Information, Systems, and Technologies, 2007. SecureWare 2007.* (pp. 12-17). Washington, D.C.: IEEE Computer Society. doi:10.1109/SECUREWARE.2007.4385303

Grönlund, Å. (2010, July). Electronic identity management in Sweden: Governance of a market approach. *Identity in the Information Society, 3*(1), 195–211. doi:10.1007/s12394-010-0043-1

Hammershøj, A., Sapuppo, A., Iqbal, Z., Elahi, N., Chowdhury, M., Heikkinen, S., et al. (2009, May). *User Profiles, Personalization and Privacy: WWRF Outlook Jointly Prepared by WG1, WG2 and WG7.* Retrieved January 20, 2014, from Wireless World Research Forum: http://wwrf.ch/files/wwrf/content/filcs/publications/outlook/Outlook3.pdf

Hansen, M., Schwartz, A., & Cooper, A. (2008, March-April). Privacy and Identity Management. *IEEE Security and Privacy, 6*(2), 38–45. doi:10.1109/MSP.2008.41

Martens, T. (2010, July). Electronic identity management in Estonia between market and state governance. *Identity in the Information Society*, *3*(1), 213–233. doi:10.1007/s12394-010-0044-0

Mason, S. (2012). *Electronic Signatures in Law* (3rd ed.). Cambridge, UK: Cambridge University Press. doi:10.1017/CBO9780511998058

McKenzie, R., Crompton, M., & Wallis, C. (2008, March-April). Use cases for identity management in e-government. *IEEE Security and Privacy*, *6*(2), 51–57. doi:10.1109/MSP.2008.51

Naumann, I., & Hogben, G. (2008, August). Privacy features of European eID card specifications. *Network Security*, *2008*(8), 9–13. doi:10.1016/S1353-4858(08)70097-7

Noack, T., & Kubicek, H. (2010, July). The introduction of online authentication as part of the new electronic national identity card in Germany. *Identity in the Information Society*, *3*(1), 87–110. doi:10.1007/s12394-010-0051-1

Rissanen, T. (2010, July). Electronic identity in Finland: ID cards vs. bank IDs. *Identity in the Information Society*, *3*(1), 175–194. doi:10.1007/s12394-010-0049-8

Sorge, C., & Westhoff, D. (2008). eIDs und Identitätsmanagement. *Datenschutz und Datensicherheit*, *32*(5), 337–341. doi:10.1007/s11623-008-0080-1

Stallings, W. (2013). *Cryptography and Network Security: Principles and Practice* (6th ed.). Harlow, England: Pearson Education.

Wolf, C., Preneel, B., & De Cock, D. (2006). The Belgian Electronic Identity Card (Overview). In J. Dittmann (Ed.), Sicherheit 2006: Sicherheit - Schutz und Zuverlässigkeit, Beiträge der 3. Jahrestagung des Fachbereichs Sicherheit der Gesellschaft für Informatik e.v. (GI), 20.-22. Februar 2006 in Magdeburg (Vol. 77 of the series Lecture Notes in Informatics (LNI), pp. 298-301). Bonn: Bonner Köllen Verlag.

Zwingelberg, H. (2011). Necessary Processing of Personal Data: The Need-to-Know Principle and Processing Data from the New German Identity Card. In S. Fischer-Hübner, P. Duquenoy, M. Hansen, R. Leenes, & G. Zhang (Eds.), *Privacy and Identity Management for Life: 6th IFIP WG 9.2, 9.6/11.7, 11.4, 11.6/PrimeLife International Summer School, Helsingborg, Sweden, August 2-6, 2010, Revised Selected Papers* (Vol. 352 of the series IFIP Advances in Information and Communication Technology, pp. 151-163). Berlin/Heidelberg: Springer.

KEY TERMS AND DEFINITIONS

Digital Signature: Public-key cryptographic scheme that ensures authenticity and integrity of a document, and which also reaches the goal of non-repudiation (i.e. the holder of a private key cannot deny having signed a document if verification with the corresponding public key is successful).

eID Card: Smartcard that implements protocols used for the authentication of a user towards a service provider over an electronic communication channel.

Electronic Signature: Legal term, describing data attached to other data (e.g., a document) and that serve the purpose of authentication.

Extended Access Control (EAC): Protocol, consisting of terminal authentication and chip authentication, that enables mutual authentication and establishment of a secure communication channel between a smartcard (eID card) and a terminal.

Password Authenticated Connection Establishment (PACE): Protocol used for authentication of a smartcard reader towards the German eID card, and for establishment of a secure channel between the card and the reader.

Public Key Infrastructure (PKI): Infrastructure for the authentication of public keys used in digital signature schemes and/or for the encryption of data. Public keys are usually authenticated by trusted certification authorities, which use digital signature schemes to confirm the mapping between a public key and the identity of its owner.

Restricted Identification (RI): Protocol that allows generation of an identifier which is specific for one combination of an eID card and a service provider.

ENDNOTES

[1]   Identity Card Act (Personalausweisgesetz) of 2009, section 1, subsection 1. There are exceptions to the general rule, which are omitted in this chapter for clarity.

[2]   More precisely: The public Diffie-Hellman value.

[3]   The author encountered this as an electronic service in the e-government portal of one state, and was given the choice to either use eID-based authentication, or to just supply his address with no authentication at all.

[4]   The presentation of electronic signature legislation in this chapter is simplified. For a more detailed discussion of the different categories of electronic signatures, see the specialized literature.

This work was previously published in the Handbook of Research on Democratic Strategies and Citizen-Centered E-Government Services edited by Ćemal Dolićanin, Ejub Kajan, Dragan Randjelović, and Boban Stojanović, pages 214-230, copyright 2015 by Information Science Reference (an imprint of IGI Global).

Chapter 9
The Role of Radio Frequency Identification in Modern Libraries

Kijpokin Kasemsap
Suan Sunandha Rajabhat University, Thailand

ABSTRACT

This chapter reveals the role of radio frequency identification (RFID) in modern libraries, thus demonstrating the theoretical and practical concept of RFID; the utilization of RFID in global operations; RFID perspectives in modern libraries (i.e., operating cost, information technology infrastructure cost, skilled RFID workers, access rate, patron policy, data security, barcode factor, and patron issues); the applications of RFID in modern libraries (i.e., data management, circulation, inventory, assistance in searching and orientation, data accuracy and reliability, theft prevention, utilization statistics for serials, and personal service); and the significance of RFID in modern libraries. RFID solutions can be utilized to reduce the operating costs through decreasing labor costs, enhancing automation, improving tracking and tracing, and preventing the loss of materials. Applying the RFID will significantly improve educational performance and gain sustainable competitive advantage in modern libraries.

INTRODUCTION

As a technology solution, RFID has proven increased efficiency and accuracy within traditional production and inventory control environments (Ryan, Lewis, Doster, Daily, & Glass, 2013). RFID becomes an increasing interest in several application areas (Wu, Wang, Sheng, & Siror, 2010). RFID technology has gained considerable attention from business executives because of its potential to change the way commerce is conducted (Park, Koh, & Nam, 2010). The developments of information and communication technology (ICT) systems are rapidly becoming the vital and core component for conducting and transacting business in organizations (Makori, 2013). University libraries are increasingly adopting RFID technology in order to improve the efficiency of information services and increase quality service (Makori, 2013).

DOI: 10.4018/978-1-5225-0808-3.ch009

RFID technology is broadly utilized in many university libraries (Hossain & Prybutok, 2008). RFID technology has potential for both cost savings and revenue enhancement (Zelbst, Green, Baker, & Sower, 2010). RFID technology is emerging as the innovative solution for managing information operations and services in university libraries (Makori, 2013). The use of RFID can significantly transform the current practice of conducting business, improve efficiency of operation and management, and support decision-making process (Barjis & Fosso Wamba, 2010). The application of RFID makes the technology the next big thing as the total RFID market (including RFID tags, RFID readers, software, and services) has been forecast to exponentially grow (Wyld, 2006).

The strength of this chapter is on the thorough literature consolidation of RFID in modern libraries. The extant literature of RFID in modern libraries provides a contribution to practitioners and researchers by describing a comprehensive view of the functional applications of RFID in modern libraries to appeal to different segments of RFID in modern libraries in order to maximize the business impact of RFID in modern libraries.

BACKGROUND

RFID system began during the Second World War in the 1940s, when the system was used to locate and distinguish friendly aircraft from enemy ones. With time the system spread to other business industries such as manufacturing firms and livestock (Waddenkeri, 2006). Adopting a technological innovation for the right business need at the right time is one of most important strategic decisions that a firm has to make to gain and retain a competitive advantage (Park et al., 2010).

There are various reasons that motivate university libraries increasingly to go for RFID solutions. A number of authors (Biswas & Paul, 2010; Howard & Anderson, 2007; Madhusudhan, 2010; Waddenkeri, 2006) have advanced numerous reasons that make RFID systems practically attractive in library and information establishments. The development and evaluation of the library application has demonstrated that RFID can be successfully integrated into library systems (Mehrjerdi, 2011). The success of RFID application depends on many factors such as the size of enterprise as data should travel along the movement path of tracked objects, hardware components (tag readers) should be installed, signal collision among RFID tags at different levels (i.e., item, box, and pallet) need to be dealt with (Barjis & Fosso Wamba, 2010).

RFID in modern libraries is recognized as a productive tool for flow management rather than barcodes and other identification technologies (Koneru, 2004). RFID technology is the rising interest in the library community because of its applications, which promise to increase efficiency and productivity and enhance user satisfaction (Biswas & Paul, 2010). Technical challenges of RFID implementation include tag cost, standards, tag and reader selection, data management, systems integration and security (Li, Visich, Khumawala, & Zhang, 2006).

ROLE OF RADIO FREQUENCY IDENTIFICATION IN MODERN LIBRARIES

This section demonstrates the theoretical and practical concept of RFID; the utilization of RFID in global operations; RFID perspectives in modern libraries (i.e., operating cost, information technology infrastructure cost, skilled RFID workers, access rate, patron policy, data security, barcode factor, and patron issues); the applications of RFID in modern libraries (i.e., data management, circulation, inventory, assistance in searching and orientation, data accuracy and reliability, theft prevention, utilization statistics for serials, and personal service); and the significance of RFID in modern libraries.

Concept of Radio Frequency Identification

RFID system has received increased attentions from academicians and practitioners. The origins of RFID technology can be traced way back to laboratory research in the 1940s that focused on reflected power communication. RFID is used for technologies utilizing radio waves for automatically identifying individual items (Mehrjerdi, 2011). RFID is a data acquisition and storage method, providing accurate, real-time data without human intervention (Li et al., 2006). A basic RFID system includes RFID tags (i.e., active, passive, or semi-passive tags), which are called RFID chips or transponders, serving as a digital data store that can be embedded or attached to a physical item to be identified and tracked (Fosso Wamba, Anand, & Carter, 2013).

RFID is a subset of the larger radio frequency (RF) market, with the wider market encompassing an array of RF technologies, including: cellular phones, digital radio, global positioning system (GPS), high-definition television, and wireless networks (Malone, 2004). Waddenkeri (2006) indicated that RFID is a form of identification that involves the use of small electronic devices that consist of a small chip and an antenna. The system consists of various technologies including RF based and microchip technology. A polarized slot-array antenna consists of a slot series-fed by a microstrip line for RFID shelf applications in the ultra-high frequency (UHF) band (Choi, Bae, Chae, Park, & Pyo, 2013).

RFID is a powerful technology that enables wireless information storage and control in an economical way (Barrero, Hernández-Castro, Peris-Lopez, Camacho, & R-Moreno, 2014). The matching and forward patterns of tag antenna in each band are desirable (Aliakbari, Mallahzadeh, & Nezhad, 2012). The tag antenna can operate effectively with different UHF RFID chips (Tang, Wu, Zhan, & Hu, 2014). The hardware used in the design and implementation of the prototypes are a laptop to host the server, a router to create the wireless network, a personal digital assistant (PDA) to host the applications, RFID tags, and RFID readers in order to organize RFID communication (Mehrjerdi, 2011).

RFID readers are RF transmitters and receivers controlled by a microprocessor or digital signal processor that communicates with RFID tags (Attaran, 2007). RFID readers can be configured to control the timing communication with RFID tags (Asif & Mandviwalla, 2005). RFID tags are the chips that are embedded in the product, pallet, or case that store and transmit information about the specific unit (Attaran, 2007). RFID tags can be active, passive or semi-passive (Li et al., 2006). RFID tags are cheap, simple devices that can store unique identification information and perform simple computation to keep better inventory of packages (Liu, Bailey, & Krishnamurthy, 2010). RFID tags are usually attached to entities (objects or persons), and the entities can be identified by accessing the tags (Qian, Chen, You, & Lu, 2012).

Active RFID tags contain a battery that provides power so the RFID tag can transmit a signal to a reader. Passive RFID tags can be classified in terms of reading range (Catarinucci, Colella, & Tarricone, 2012). Short-range tags communicate with the reader up to a few centimeters. Medium-range tags reach almost 5 meters. Long-range tags work properly up to almost 12 meters (Catarinucci et al., 2012). Passive RFID tags do not contain a battery and are much cheaper than active tags. Passive RFID tags are read when they pass through the electromagnetic field of a reader (Dinning & Schuster, 2003). A third type of tag is a semi-passive tag that is powered by both an internal battery and the electromagnetic waves submitted by RFID reader (Angeles, 2005).

Finkenzeller (2003) stated that RFID can be divided into three categories (i.e., 30-300 kHz (low frequency: LF); 3-30 MHz (high frequency: HF and RF); and 300 MHz-3 GHz (UHF) or over 3 GHz (micro wave). RFID tags can hold more information than data carrier systems such as bar code system. RFID systems work at a number of different frequencies including 125 KHz, 13.56 MHz, 2.45 GHz and 5.8 GHz and for UHF 860-950 MHz range. LF tags work along 120 KHz-140 KHz frequencies while HF tags work along the 13.56 MHz radio frequencies. UHF tags work along the 850-900 MHz range. LF tags are less expensive and use less power compared to other kinds of tags, though HF tags and UHF tags have better ranges and transfer data faster. However, these two types of tags use more power and are more expensive (Mehrjerdi, 2011).

RFID technologies encompass a myriad of technological components such as RFID tags, RFID readers, middleware, enterprise systems and collaborative networks that both channel partners must adopt (Fries, Turri, Bello, & Smith, 2010). The middleware is an intermediate layer between the RFID readers and the enterprise application systems (Wang, Wang, & Yang, 2010). Collaborative RFID programs require investments by both parties involved in the channel relationship before the benefits of the technology can be fully optimized (Hausman & Stock, 2003). RFID is a method for sending and receiving data between the interrogators and tags using electromagnetic waves (Card Technology Today, 2004). RFID is a fast-growing technology for increasing efficiency and improving profitability, and is an important area of study in information environment (Madhusudhan, 2010).

RFID is an imperative technology for Internet of Things (Zhang, Lu, Chen, Yan, & Zheng, 2012). The wireless channels between RFID tags and RFID readers are not secure in Internet of Things (Li, Wang, & Zheng, 2014). The utilization of RFID technology leads to improved manufacturing efficiency and manufacturing effectiveness (Zelbst, Green, Sower, & Reyes, 2012). The commercial use of RFID began in the 1980s, primarily in railroad and trucking industries (Landt, 2001). RFID applications that provide batch access, storage mass data and reprogramming are better than barcodes (Yu, 2007). RFID applications use battery powered active RFID tags and proprietary systems to track and manage capital assets, such as rail cars and cargo containers (Dinning & Schuster, 2003).

RFID is a type of auto-identification technology that uses radio waves to identify physical objects (Davis & Luehlfing, 2004). There are examples in the literature of the assessment of the impact of RFID implementation on business performance through simulation (Ustundag & Tanyas, 2009) and case study (Tzeng, Chen, & Pai, 2008). Whitaker et al. (2007) empirically assessed the relationship between RFID adoption and expectation of early return on RFID investment. The fulfillment of RFID technology can result in improved downstream partner (customer) satisfaction by, for example, assuring accurate logistics and reducing physical receiving requirements (efficiency outcomes) as well as facilitating just-in-time (JIT) ordering, and reducing material flow uncertainty (effectiveness outcomes) (Cannon, Reyes, Frazier, & Prater, 2008).

RFID systems rely on the significant technology of remote, automatic identification with small, low-cost RF elements to fulfill RF communications securely among all entities (Cheng, Liu, Chang, & Chang, 2013). RFID technology is widely recognized as a new wave of supporting technologies and business process enablers (Barjis & Wamba, 2010). Kern (2004) described the components and technical features of a modern RFID library system in order to provide a guideline for the evaluation of different systems. RFID is considered as a major innovation with the potential to offer many new opportunities for construction companies to improve communication, facilitate teamwork, improve information management skills, and encourage greater cross-fertilization between business processes (El Ghazali, Lefebvre, & Lefebvre, 2012).

El Ghazali et al. (2012) stated that RFID is considered as an enabler of knowledge management (KM). KM, organizational learning, and knowledge-sharing behavior are definitely correlated with organizational performance (Kasemsap, 2013a). Organizational learning, organizational innovation, and organizational performance help organizations acquire sustainable competitive advantage in global business (Kasemsap, 2013b). KM, organizational culture, and organizational climate lead to increased job performance in modern organizations (Kasemsap, 2014a). KM, strategic orientation, and organizational innovation are practically related to improved organizational performance (Kasemsap, 2014b).

KM, organizational learning, and organizational culture are effectively correlated with job satisfaction (Kasemsap, 2014c). KM capability, organizational learning, and human resource management lead to improved organizational performance in global business (Kasemsap, 2015a). Using data mining methods for business intelligence makes it easier for the users to promote its overall contribution to the KM process (Kasemsap, 2015b).

In order to ensure adequate security of information resources, RFID tags are affixed in materials with a property sticker (Makori, 2013). The RFID antenna is used to read the RFID tags and manage the various library functions. RFID technology can be used to track documents such as library books and legal files (Collins, 2004a). The various components of RFID system include automatic self-return, self checkout, security, conversion, staff service station, inventory and docking or server. RFID reader will fail to identify tags if a collision occurs (Tian, Chen, & Li, 2013). RFID yoking proof scheme can generate proofs of simultaneous presence of two tags in the range of a specified reader (Chien, Yeh, Wu, & Lee, 2011).

The expansion of RFID into a wide variety of business applications has been due to the reduction in the cost of RFID technology through the use of non-battery powered passive tags that can replace bar codes as a means of gathering information (Li et al., 2006). Bar codes are used from the container level to the individual item level and though are currently in widespread use, they have limitations. Bar codes are the same for all items of a unique stock-keeping unit (SKU) and do not differentiate between items. The same bar code for all SKUs makes it difficult to track and trace items that may need to be recalled, for example, due to quality or safety concerns.

RFID is used to identify products at the item level, can be read with no requirement for direct line of sight to the reader or scanner and can operate in harsh environments, where dirt, dust and moisture conditions can affect other types of automatic data capture systems, such as bar codes and anti-theft devices (Li et al., 2006). Multiple tags can be read simultaneously. RFID tags are capable of carrying more than 64 bits of information compared with only 19 bits in bar-code technology, thus enabling RFID to store additional information such as location, move history, destination, expiration date and environmental conditions (i.e., temperature and moisture).

Kakkainen (2003) described the potential of RFID implementation for increasing supply chain efficiency of short shelf life products through RFID trial. Smaros and Holmstrom (2000) considered RFID as a data capture method in consumers' refrigerators to develop a new type of electronic grocery-related service. Lapide (2004) suggested the benefits of RFID for forecasting, such as improved forecast accuracy, more accurate point of sale data from retailers, and better tracking of products sold with or without promotion.

Utilization of Radio Frequency Identification in Global Operations

RFID becomes increasingly widespread in various applications (Sun, Zhang, & Mo, 2011), such as supply chain management (Ramanathan, Ramanathan, & Ko, 2014), fashion (Moon & Ngai, 2008), and services (Lee, Fiedler, & Smith, 2008). RFID is an enabling technology for a variety of applications in next-generation network (Cho, Pack, Kwon, & Choi, 2010). The adoption of RFID technology has both efficiency and effectiveness implications (Green, Whitten, & Inman, 2009). RFID creates business value by improving in-stock position and improved inventory accuracy (Hardgrave, Aloysius, & Goyal, 2009). Organizations with RFID implementation can expect business processes to satisfy customers toward better organizational performance (Lim & Koh, 2009).

RFID enables visibility into the movement of inventories in supply chain (Hardgrave, Aloysius, & Goyal, 2013). RFID technology promises numerous benefits in supply chain management: improved speed, accuracy, efficiency and security of information sharing across the supply chain (Jones, Clarke-Hill, Hillier, Shears, & Comfort, 2004), reduced storage, handling and distribution expenses; increased sales through reduced stock outs; and improved cash flow through increased inventory turns (Kakkainen, 2003).

RFID technology has the potential to positively impact the efficiency and effectiveness of both manufacturing organization and supply chain in which the organization is a partner (Angeles, 2007; Green et al., 2009; Zhou, 2009). RFID technology can help a wide range of organizations and individuals such as hospitals and patients, retailers, and customers, and manufacturers and distributors throughout supply chain to realize significant productivity gains and efficiencies (Sabbaghi & Vaidyanathan, 2008). Li and Visich (2006) reviewed the relevant literature and discussed the advantages, supply chain impacts, and the implementation challenges and the corresponding strategies of RFID in supply chain.

RFID industries have taken a great interest in utilizing the benefits of RFID for supply chain management, inventory control and various other applications (Chae, Park, Cui, & Lee, 2010). RFID is an important technology for many aspects of business including supply chain management (Park et al., 2010). Srivastava (2004) demonstrated the benefits, current applications and impediments to implementation of RFID in supply chain management. RFID allows real-time data communication and narrows information gaps in supply chain management, especially in retailing and logistics (Kim, Ko, Kim, & Koh, 2008; Moon & Ngai, 2008).

RFID technology plays an important role in promoting logistics and supply chain processes because of their ability to identify, trace and track information throughout the supply chain (Zhu, Mukhopadhyay, & Kurata, 2012). RFID technology can be used to track production operations (Lee, Choy, Ho, & Law, 2013). Brewer et al. (1999) recognized RFID as an intelligent tracking technology in manufacturing to support logistics planning and execution. Jansen and Krabs (1999) stated that RFID is utilized to control returnable containers in supply chain. Karkkainen and Holmstrom (2002) defined RFID as a wireless product identification technology to enable material handling efficiency, customization and information sharing in supply chain.

McFarlane and Sheffi (2003) used a ship/receive (S/R) pair structure to examine four basic logistics processes (i.e., shipping, transportation, receiving and in-facility operations) and discussed how low cost RFID can be used to improve each process. Effective information sharing and real-time data communication allow better control of supply chain management (Angeles, 2005; Prater, Frazier, & Reyes, 2005). RFID programs enhance information visibility across supply chain, thus increasing the efficiency of both demand management and order fulfillment activities (Tajima, 2007). Demand management includes the approaches to forecasting and managing demand in production and distribution (Lambert & Cooper, 2000).

RFID technology utilization can result in improved efficiency and a reduction in costs (Zelbst et al., 2012). RFID technology enables the identification and tracking of objects by means of the wireless signals emitted by a tag attached to the objects of interest (Li & Liu, 2011). Employing RFID in Lean manufacturing initiatives can reduce some wastes but not all types of waste (Chongwatpol & Sharda, 2013). Raw material, work in process, and finished goods inventories can be more efficiently managed to eliminate waste and shortfall/over supply within the manufacturing organization while contributing to the outcomes through improved production planning and capacity utilization (Stambaugh & Carpenter, 2009; Zhou, 2009).

The highly constrained features of common RFID tags and their passive role in the network highlights the requirement of an adequate secure communication model with personal tags, which enables their participation as a member of the personal network (Najera, Roman, & Lopez, 2013). RFID technology can be linked with other instruments, such as automated weighing devices, video cameras, infrared beams to detect the direction of movement, and temperature loggers, to collect additional data (Bonter & Bridge, 2011).

Dinning and Schuster (2004) provide an RFID scorecard and payback table that Dell Computer uses to make RFID investment decisions. The scorecard is used to identify high potential RFID projects that become candidates for more detailed financial analysis using the payback table. The payback table considers benefits, one-time costs, and recurring costs. According to Roberti (2004a), companies should not wait for the price of tags to drop to 5 cents before deploying an RFID system. Companies need to explore opportunities in using RFID so they can develop a business case for deploying RFID. Wal-Mart has mandated that tags be read 100 percent of the time as pallets move through loading dock doors and as cases move at up to 540 feet per minute on conveyors (Roberti, 2004b).

RFID reader transmits an electromagnetic field that wakes-up the tag and provides the power required for the tag to operate. RFID readers usually cost around $1,000-2,000. The RFID tag cost can be broken down into the following components: chip; inlay/substance with antenna; assembly; and licensing (Mehrjerdi, 2011). Many of Wal-Mart's suppliers take a low cost approach to RFID implementation with little or no information technology systems integration (O'Connor, 2005). Organizations are worried about the payoff of RFID implementation due to unresolved issues such as cost, standards, tag performance, and security in RFID implementation (Kakkainen, 2003).

The benefits of RFID include automatic non-line-of-sight scanning, labor reduction due to increased automation, enhanced visibility of supply chains, improved asset tracking and inventory management, item level tracking, traceable warranties and targeted product recalls, improved reliability, quality control and regulation, improved utilization of resources, security against product shrinkage, durability, and capacity to hold more information (Bhattacharya, Chu, Hayya, & Mullen, 2010; Mehrjerdi, 2009; Visich, Li, Khumawala, & Reyes, 2009). RFID can improve business processes and enhance organizational performance (Wu, Nystrom, Lin, & Yu, 2006).

Concerning health care industry, RFID has been recognized as the next wave of information technology innovation that will widen healthcare transformation (Oztekin, Pajouh, Delen, & Swim, 2010). RFID technology can be applied in health care management in respect to patient flow management and patient basic medical information implant (Barjis & Fosso Wamba, 2010). RFID is used to track and manage hospital equipment and surgical instruments (McGee, 2004). Hosaka (2004) simulated hospital bedside and nursing station conditions to automatically authenticate the matching of patients and their medical articles in order to reduce medical errors.

RFID technology can facilitate patient identification, tracking, and tracing within the health care value chain (Fisher & Monahan, 2008). RFID technology offers an improved means of reducing errors in patient care, including adverse drug effects, allergies, patient–medication mismatches and medication dosage errors (Thuemmler, Buchanan, & Kumar, 2007; Tu, Zhou, & Piramuthu, 2009). RFID practically promotes better management of critical health care assets (i.e., infusion pumps and wheelchairs) by enabling real-time identification, tracking and tracing (Bendavid, Boeck, & Philippe, 2010; Symonds, Parry, & Briggs, 2007).

RFID Perspectives in Modern Libraries

There are many challenges and impediments to successful implementations of RFID that yet to be identified and discussed (Kapoor, Zhou, & Piramuthu, 2009). The challenges hindering the large-scale implementation of RFID in industry and business vary from privacy concerns to technical challenges, economics, and operational impacts. Although from economic point of view, RFID is at a price point that can enable its large-scale adoption (Want, 2006), but it is still about the ethical, organizational, and managerial challenges that are more dominant then the cost of technology alone.

Libraries are facing the challenge of managing the growing size of collection and keeping operating budget low (Zhu et al., 2012). RFID seems a very promising technology here where books can have an embedded RFID chip with all relevant information. RFID can be successfully implemented and integrated into business processes (Fosso Wamba & Chatfield, 2009). The major concerns related to the modern libraries having RFID system with the identified capabilities are explained.

Operating Cost

RFID has a role to play in creating a system that allocates recovery costs to individual producers (O'Connell, Hickey, Besiou, Fitzpatrick, & Van Wassenhove, 2013). Cost and privacy concerns have been recognized as the major factors influencing the success of RFID applications (Juels, 2006; Rieback, Crispo, & Tanenbaum, 2006; Zhang, Ouyang, & He, 2008). The cost is one of the major factors influencing acceptance of RFID, although the production costs of RFID have reduced (Collins, 2004b). The costs for RFID reader, peripheral equipment and application software will be even more of a burden. Lowered operational costs, increased product availability and cleaner product data enabled by RFID systems not only benefit adopting organizations but also translate into benefits for the end consumer (Osyk, Vijayaraman, Srinivasan, & Dey, 2012).

Information Technology Infrastructure Cost

A library with over 200,000 collections must have sufficient funds to invest in the purchase of tags alone although, the costs for the reader, peripheral equipment and application software will be even more of the problem (Mehrjerdi, 2011). Costs for RFID adoption may be significant, including the purchase of initial hardware/software, integrating RF-enabled technology into distribution and warehousing activities and existing management systems, and additional maintenance costs for application upgrades, readers and software, and employee training (Smith, 2005).

Regarding the investment in infrastructure for RFID, organizations integrating the technology into their processes enhance the accuracy and availability of information, thus allowing for quicker reaction to the potential changes (Vijayaraman, Osyk, & Chavada, 2008). The high implementation costs of the technology remains a major inhibitor for its widespread adoption and use, as well as the substantial gap between the technology implementation costs and the RFID-enabled benefits (Bensel et al., 2008).

Skilled RFID Workers

About two-thirds of respondents pointed out that training their employees to become proficient in RFID is the biggest challenge they faced in order to succeed in RFID market (Mehrjerdi, 2011). RFID has the capability of sharing information across organizational boundaries (Park et al., 2010). The existence of cross-functional teams is likely to enable the successful implementation of RFID programs (Fries et al., 2010).

Access Rate

RFID technology is used in a range of applications, including access control to buildings, document tracking, livestock tracking and identification, vehicle security, pay-at-the-pump gasoline sales, product authentication, retail, sports timing, supply chain, ticketing, and wireless payment (Attaran, 2007). Libraries that emphasize patron services might not be able to sustain such check in/out errors. Even with extremely strict requirements for baggage identification in airports, the identification rate is still not at 100 per cent (Gilbert, 2004).

Patron Privacy

The universality of RFID systems with inherent weaknesses has been a cause of concern about their privacy and security (Alagheband & Aref, 2013). A major concern is the invasion of privacy due to the use of RFID that has been a major issue fueling the opposition from consumer protection organizations (Jones et al., 2004). Privacy advocates are concerned about tracking customers (Ferguson, 2006). In addition, Butters (2007) discussed about the RFID standards and privacy. The privacy issue is a subject of debate in the application of RFID technology.

All patron activities such as reading, browsing, and action behavior will be detected by RFID readers which are installed in libraries. These operations are similar to surveillance and may be a privacy problem for the patron. Such issues and concerns about privacy may prevent the application of active services in libraries. Cost, standards, and privacy concerns have generally been recognized as some of the most important major factors influencing the success of RFID applications (Kwang, Koh, & Nam, 2010).

Data Security

The biggest issue that must be taken into consideration when a new technology is addressed and employed is the level of security that it may provide in order to keep organizational data at the safe level (Mehrjerdi, 2011). Methods of cracking smart cards apply to RFID chips. The character of RFID wireless communication can catch transmitted data through intercepted wireless signals. RFID must encode information to prevent eavesdropping, replacement, and misuse.

The interference from wireless equipment, stability, international standards, size, and material of RFID tags still present various problems that need to be solved. The key factor for application in libraries is system integration, and this issue relies on coordination with libraries and system factors to accumulate more experience and know-how. Managers are facing difficult decisions about whether to adopt RFID or wait until the technology matures further (Osyk et al., 2012). Uncertainties around future RFID developments can span strategy, technology, system implementation, data security, investment payback horizon, and human acceptance (Lee & Ozer, 2007).

Barcode Factor

The attractiveness of RFID technology as a replacement for the traditional barcode system has necessitated the need for securing RFID systems (Doss, Zhou, Sundaresan, Yu, & Gao, 2012). Barcode technology has been globally institutionalized (Wyld, 2006). Barcodes are employed by both library systems and book publishers. The popularity of barcodes is an issue since almost all book retailers are set up with the bar coding system (Mehrjerdi, 2011).

The major utilizations of RFID implementation in libraries are limited to information management, circulation, and inventory (Yu, 2007). For a successful deployment of RFID, it is important to have a set of widely accepted standards and regulations, similar to the growing path of barcode standards. Their movement, from proprietary standards to globally open standards, has played a pivotal role in modern business (Michael & McCathie, 2005).

Patron Issues

Some patrons refuse to accept the new RFID system at first. Some patrons might be unwilling to use any new technology for not putting their own or family security and privacy at risk (Mehrjerdi, 2011). Security based on obscurity, and proprietary protocols, are not enough (Molnar & Wagner, 2004). This may become an even greater problem if there is convergence in the protocols and technology that will allow all these systems to readily talk to one another (Tien, 2005). Faced with uncertainty regarding whether RFID is ready to support their needs, managers may put off adoption, hindering broad adoption and scale economies that decrease costs (Heim, Wentworth, & Peng, 2009).

Applications of RFID in Modern Libraries

RFID was invented in 1948, although a crude version was used during the Second World War by the British to identify friendly aircraft (Yu, 2007). Radar pulses drove the transponder, which was installed in aircraft to respond to coded messages (Ollivier, 1995). The major applications of RFID include farm produce tracing, vehicle identification, entrance guards, and trade control (Kern, 1999). Employing RFID systems to supply inventory, entrance guard, and to gather reading statistics is possible (Yu, 2007). The functionality and benefits offered by the RFID systems match the needs of library systems and the improvements to be made in other situations. The development and evaluation of the library applications demonstrated that RFID can be successfully integrated into library systems.

RFID is used to do one or more of the following important tasks: read tags instead of bar codes; determine the location of materials in the library; trace of the materials; finding whether journals and newspapers are at their place or in use; identify the patron in the library and serve them if it is necessary; check in/out materials; manage the inventory of books and materials; quick identification of lost materials on a hourly/daily basis; online data collection and utilization; prevent from losing its materials through theft or other forms of possible loss; use robots to take books off the shelf for patron or librarian; and use conveyor belt to send book down the line from the shelf to patron or circulation desk.

Curran and Porter (2007) have proposed and outlined a library prototype that utilizes RFID to enhance and speed up the current customer book search and identification processes. RFID has various benefits (i.e., speed up the search of books; improve the stock control of the library; increase the security; bring convenience to library system; support disabled students in searching the books; facilitate library workflow; increase staff productivity; enhance customer service; and improve process efficiency) in modern libraries.

Data Management

The large-scale RFID application often requires a highly efficient database system in data processing (Suei, Lu, Liao, & Lo, 2012). The large-scale utilization of RFID technology results in a more complex data management system (Barjis & Fosso Wamba, 2010). RFID tags can store a digital representation of the physical object and transmit it wirelessly to pervasive, context-aware applications running on mobile devices (Carreton, Pinte, & Meuter, 2013). RFID tag provides memory to record information and to supply the system (Yu, 2007).

RFID has been widely deployed for its high capabilities in simple computation, storage, long scan distance, and simultaneous reading (Yang & Hu, 2012). The memory not only stores bibliographic records and circulation status, but the system also traces the location of the specific collection material. RFID system can offer assistance in tracing service when looking for particular material in modern libraries. RFID can provide accurate information on the inventory of finished goods, work-in-progress, and in-transit stages with reliable due dates (Bose & Pal, 2005).

Circulation

RFID systems provide efficient operation processing (Yu, 2007). Librarians do not need to scan barcodes one by one. Patrons can simultaneously process check in/out, verification, and entrance guard control with RFID reader equipment. Because RFID tags do not use demagnetization to modify data, they can use tags to manage magnetic materials the same as the books. Library cards will include RFID tags. Readers will detect and fetch information from library cards when patrons enter the library, and the system will be transmitted to a backend system process. Later, the front desk shows loan, overdue, reserve, and other circulation status on the exploration about this patron. Librarians depend on these circulation messages to provide the service.

Inventory

RFID is recognized as an enabling technology with products such as smart-shelving and smart dump-bins (Butters, 2007). Batch processing can apply to libraries to perform inventory or shelf-reading (Yu, 2007). Readers can immediately detect all of the collection within this range, including abnormal situations such as books put on the wrong shelf. Libraries can utilize RFID to replace barcodes and obtain several advantages (Kern, 2004). Libraries can reduce queues at the front desk; decrease repeatable tasks; decrease repeatable tasks; extend internal security; lower the cost of manipulating and managing collections; procure collections, checking and accepting automation; and raise the efficiency of inventory and arrangement (Yu, 2007).

RFID integrates with RFID quick response (Yu, 2007). Durable characters promote operational efficiency and precision, while the cost is one of the major factors influencing acceptance of novel technology in libraries. This will stretch the budget and the schedule for implementation of RFID solutions difficult because some libraries hold enormous collections. Although RFID can improve efficiency, the essence of service will not change. Therefore, innovating services is an essential factor for libraries.

Assistance in Searching and Orientation

RFID tags continually gather information as products move from shelves to the checkout counter (Attaran, 2007). The application of RFID in industrial circles (Bhuptani & Moradpour, 2005), provides material flow management similar to library circulation. It develops services such as assistance in searching and orientation based on detectable characters of RFID (Yu, 2007). The disadvantage of open-shelf libraries is that materials are easy to put on the wrong shelf or to be unaccounted for. Library automation systems can only query once about check in/out situations, but not where material is if it is not on the correct shelf. If a reader is installed on each gate in the library, as soon as a patron takes one material and enters another room, the system will detect who took it and where it is. This information will pass to the automation system to record the position of this material.

Data Accuracy and Reliability

The effective deployment of RFID has a potential to provide accurate and reliable data that exceeds the bar coding or manual capabilities (Mehrjerdi, 2011). RFID data improves the accuracy of the data collection as the products move from the production line to the consumer (Delen, Hardgrave, & Sharda, 2007). More accurate point-of-sale data results in reduced uncertainty and more efficient flows of goods through supply chain (Lambert & Cooper, 2000). Brintrup et al. (2010) stated that RFID is a tool to achieve visibility of inventory through automated data collection. Effectiveness outcomes of RFID such accuracy and availability of information, level of customer service, delivery performance, fill rate, and order fulfillment should lead to improved organizational performance (Zelbst et al., 2012).

Theft Prevention

For those public and university libraries that are in search of technology to keep the theft away from the library by not allowing them to take materials without check in them, RFID is the answer (Mehrjerdi, 2011). Replacing barcodes and magnetic strips with RFID has the advantages of self check-in/out, theft detection, rapid inventory, and finding incorrectly shelved materials (Yu, 2007). RFID technology allows for tracking of products as they move through supply chain and has been shown to reduce shrinkage due to theft, spoilage or damage (Lee & Ozer, 2007).

Utilization Statistics for Serials

There is no proper and accurate method to calculate the reading rate of magazines and that which are on the periodical rack (Yu, 2007). Systems do not record when they are used in open shelves and read in libraries. Patron response is uncertain if questionnaires are pasted onto magazines. Utilizing the detection scope of RFID, it is possible to collect materials from the periodical rack and readers.

Personal Service

Utilizing frequencies of about 900 MHz UHF provides more detection scope to embed library cards and locations into RFID tags (Yu, 2007). Combined with patron data, environment position data, and collection data, process time and service mode completely record and manage information about people, events, times, places, and objects. When someone enters the library, the system identifies the patron's status, depending on RFID tag in the library card. The library immediately acquires information about this patron and supplies appropriate personal service. The problems of RFID implementation are cost and operation in coordination with suppliers. When constructing a complete solution, planning the necessary accessories must be done with the supplier

The library can be supplied with hand-held guiding equipment (i.e., RFID reader and display device) for patrons to recognize the library environment. The system can automatically verify patron categories to decide the guiding scope, and is always detecting tags and obtaining information to show on screen at each position, such as at copy machines. Audio-visual materials can depend on being detected and recorded onto the tag in the library card. Combining charges and fines to a single payment mode can also be implemented.

Significance of RFID in Modern Libraries

Although RFID has improved the efficiency of libraries, the essence of the library service has not changed (Yu, 2007). Librarians should keep in mind that since the integrated library systems. Many RFID vendors are responding to the security criticisms and are offering a next generation of RFID labels that have improved security features than those labels previously available. Performance metrics should be aligned with the firm's objectives and reflect such topics as improved cash-to-cash cycles, leaner inventories, reduced stock outs, and more accurate data (Spekman & Sweeny, 2006).

RFID-based systems move beyond security to become tracking systems that combine security with more efficient tracking of materials throughout the library, including easier and faster charge and discharge, inventory and materials handling (Waddenkeri, 2006). Kern (2004) stated that RFID systems had been in use in libraries for five years for book identification, for self-checkout, for anti-theft control, for inventory control, and for sorting and conveying of library books. RFID applications can lead to significant savings in labor costs, enhance customer service, reduce book theft and provide a constant record update of media collections (Kern, 2004).

RFID is a rising technology in library processes (Madhusudhan, 2010). RFID technology is used in libraries to automate library operations and services, including check-in, check-out, inventory control and self-management (Biswas & Paul, 2010; Koneru, 2004). RFID system interacts with an integrated library management system to enhance and support efficient library operations and services (Yu, 2007). Butters (2007) provided an overview of the perceived threats of RFID systems in modern libraries, probed their technical feasibility and presented a perspective of what may and may not be done by libraries to mitigate the risk that actually exists.

FUTURE RESEARCH DIRECTIONS

The strength of this chapter is on the thorough literature consolidation of RFID in modern libraries. The extant literature of RFID in modern libraries provides a contribution to practitioners and researchers by describing a comprehensive view of the functional applications of RFID in modern libraries to appeal to different segments of RFID in modern libraries in order to maximize the business impact of RFID in modern libraries. The classification of the prevailing literature in the domains of RFID in modern libraries will provide the potential opportunities for future research. Future research direction should broaden the perspectives in the implementation of RFID to be utilized in the knowledge-based libraries.

Practitioners and researchers should recognize the applicability of a more multidisciplinary approach toward research activities in implementing RFID in terms of KM-related variables (i.e., knowledge-sharing behavior, knowledge creation, organizational learning, learning orientation, and motivation to learn). It will be useful to bring additional disciplines together (i.e., strategic management, marketing, finance, and human resources) to support a more holistic examination of RFID in order to combine or transfer existing theories and approaches to inquiry in this area.

CONCLUSION

This chapter revealed the role of RFID in modern libraries, thus demonstrating the theoretical and practical concept of RFID; the utilization of RFID in global operations; RFID perspectives in modern libraries (i.e., operating cost, information technology infrastructure cost, skilled RFID workers, access rate, patron policy, data security, barcode factor, and patron issues); the applications of RFID in modern libraries (i.e., data management, circulation, inventory, assistance in searching and orientation, data accuracy and reliability, theft prevention, utilization statistics for serials, and personal service); and the significance of RFID in modern libraries. The types of operations that can be done by RFID technology and the benefits offered by that match the requirements of libraries and the perspectives of improvement in the field of library and information science that management have in mind.

Successful implementation of RFID system will require a long-term strategic plan, careful planning at the tactical level to roll out deployment throughout organization, and a change in operational business processes. Since RFID will cut across organizational business functions, cross-functional teams will also be needed as well. The practice of RFID is crucial for in modern libraries that seek to serve academicians and researchers, increase academic performance, strengthen competitiveness, and achieve continuous success in global education. Therefore, it is necessary for modern libraries to examine their RFID applications, create a strategic plan to regularly monitor their functional advancements, and rapidly respond to RFID needs of academicians and researchers in global education.

RFID tags can help libraries accurately manage collections and extend their services. RFID technology supports library processes such as stocktaking and book searches. Library employees and patrons share the same convenience and ease of operations utilizing RFID system. RFID solutions can be utilized to reduce operating costs through decreasing the labor costs, enhancing automation, improving tracking and tracing, and preventing the loss of materials under any circumstances. Applying the RFID in modern libraries will effectively enhance educational performance and achieve educational goals in global education.

REFERENCES

Alagheband, M. R., & Aref, M. R. (2013). Unified privacy analysis of new-found RFID authentication protocols. *Security and Communication Networks*, *6*(8), 999–1009. doi:10.1002/sec.650

Aliakbari, H., Mallahzadeh, A., & Nezhad, S. M. A. (2012). A tri-band, small size radio frequency identification tag antenna with U-shaped slots. *Microwave and Optical Technology Letters*, *54*(8), 1975–1978. doi:10.1002/mop.26949

Angeles, R. (2005). RFID technologies: Supply-chain applications and implementation issues. *Information Systems Management*, *22*(1), 51–65. doi:10.1201/1078/44912.22.1.20051201/85739.7

Angeles, R. (2007). An empirical study of the anticipated consumer response to RFID product item tagging. *Industrial Management & Data Systems*, *107*(4), 461–483. doi:10.1108/02635570710740643

Asif, A., & Mandviwalla, M. (2005). Integrating the supply chain with RFID: A technical and business analysis. *Communications of the Association for Information Systems*, *15*(24), 393–427.

Attaran, M. (2007). RFID: An enabler of supply chain operations. *Supply Chain Management: An International Journal*, *12*(4), 249–257. doi:10.1108/13598540710759763

Barjis, J., & Fosso Wamba, S. (2010). Organizational and business impacts of RFID technology. *Business Process Management Journal*, *16*(6), 897–903. doi:10.1108/14637151011092973

Barrero, D. F., Hernández-Castro, J. C., Peris-Lopez, P., Camacho, D., & R-Moreno, M. D. (2014). A genetic tango attack against the David–Prasad RFID ultra-lightweight authentication protocol. *Expert Systems: International Journal of Knowledge Engineering and Neural Networks*, *31*(1), 9–19. doi:10.1111/j.1468-0394.2012.00652.x

Bendavid, Y., Boeck, H., & Philippe, R. (2010). Redesigning the replenishment process of medical supplies in hospitals with RFID. *Business Process Management Journal*, *16*(6), 991–1013. doi:10.1108/14637151011093035

Bhattacharya, M., Chu, C., Hayya, J., & Mullen, T. (2010). An exploratory study of RFID adoption in the retail sector. *Operations Management Research*, *3*(1-2), 80–89. doi:10.1007/s12063-010-0029-z

Bhuptani, M., & Moradpour, S. (2005). *RFID field guide: Deploying radio frequency identification systems*. Upper Saddle River, NJ: Prentice–Hall.

Biswas, G., & Paul, D. (2010). *RFID technology is the revolution in library automation system: Implicated at National Institute of Technology, Silchar, Assam*. Paper presented at the *11th Annual National Convention of Malibnet*, Siva Sivani Institute of Management, Secendarbad, India.

Bonter, D. N., & Bridge, E. S. (2011). Applications of radio frequency identification (RFID) in ornithological research: A review. *Journal of Field Ornithology*, *82*(1), 1–10. doi:10.1111/j.1557-9263.2010.00302.x

Bose, I., & Pal, R. (2005). Auto–ID: Managing anything, anywhere, anytime in the supply chain. *Communications of the ACM*, *48*(8), 100–106. doi:10.1145/1076211.1076212

Brewer, A., Sloan, N., & Landers, T. L. (1999). Intelligent tracking in manufacturing. *Journal of Intelligent Manufacturing*, *10*(3–4), 245–250. doi:10.1023/A:1008995707211

Brintrup, A., Ranasinghe, D., & McFarlane, D. (2010). RFID opportunity for leaner manufacturing. *International Journal of Production Research*, *48*(9), 2745–2764. doi:10.1080/00207540903156517

Butters, A. (2007). RFID systems, standards and privacy within libraries. *The Electronic Library*, *25*(4), 430–439. doi:10.1108/02640470710779844

Cannon, A., Reyes, P. M., Frazier, G. V., & Prater, E. (2008). RFID in contemporary supply chains: Multiple perspectives on its benefits and risks. *International Journal of Operations & Production Management*, *28*(5), 433–454. doi:10.1108/01443570810867196

Today, C. T. (2004). Another link in the chain. *Card Technology Today*, *16*(4), 11–12. doi:10.1016/S0965-2590(04)00083-0

Carreton, A. L., Pinte, K., & Meuter, W. D. (2013). Software abstractions for mobile RFID-enabled applications. *Software, Practice & Experience*, *43*(10), 1219–1239. doi:10.1002/spe.1114

Catarinucci, L., Colella, R., & Tarricone, L. (2012). Design, development, and performance evaluation of a compact and long-range passive UHF RFID tag. *Microwave and Optical Technology Letters*, *54*(5), 1335–1339. doi:10.1002/mop.26777

Chae, H. S., Park, J. G., Cui, J. F., & Lee, J. S. (2010). An adaptive load balancing management technique for RFID middleware systems. *Software, Practice & Experience*, *40*(6), 485–506. doi:10.1002/spe.967

Cheng, Z. Y., Liu, Y., Chang, C. C., & Chang, S. C. (2013). Authenticated RFID security mechanism based on chaotic maps. *Security and Communication Networks*, *6*(2), 247–256. doi:10.1002/sec.709

Chien, H. Y., Yeh, M. K., Wu, T. C., & Lee, C. I. (2011). Comments on enhanced yoking proof protocols for radio frequency identification tags and tag groups. *Journal of Shanghai Jiaotong University (Science)*, *16*(5), 604–609. doi:10.1007/s12204-011-1196-2

Cho, K., Pack, S., Kwon, T., & Choi, Y. (2010). An extensible and ubiquitous RFID management framework over next-generation network. *International Journal of Communication Systems*, *23*(9–10), 1093–1110. doi:10.1002/dac.1073

Choi, W., Bae, J. H., Chae, J. S., Park, C. W., & Pyo, C. (2013). Slot-array antenna for UHF RFID shelf applications. *Microwave and Optical Technology Letters*, *55*(7), 1511–1515. doi:10.1002/mop.27653

Chongwatpol, J., & Sharda, R. (2013). Achieving Lean objectives through RFID: A simulation-based assessment. *Decision Sciences*, *44*(2), 239–266. doi:10.1111/deci.12007

Collins, J. (2004a). RFID brings order to the law. *RFID Journal*. Retrieved from www.rfidjournal.com/article/articleview/977/1/4/

Collins, J. (2004b). Alien cuts tag price. *RFID Journal*. Retrieved from www.rfidjournal.com/article/articleview/857/1/1/

Curran, K., & Porter, M. (2007). A primer on radio frequency identification for libraries. *Library Hi Tech, 25*(4), 595–611. doi:10.1108/07378830710840536

Davis, H. E., & Luehlfing, M. S. (2004). Radio frequency identification: The wave of the future. *Journal of Accountancy, 198*(5), 43–49.

Delen, D., Hardgrave, B., & Sharda, R. (2007). RFiD for better supply–chain management through enhanced information visibility. *Production and Operations Management, 16*(5), 613–624. doi:10.1111/j.1937-5956.2007.tb00284.x

Dinning, M., & Schuster, E. (2003). Fighting friction. APICS – The Performance Advantage, February, pp. 26–31.

Dinning, M., & Schuster, E. (2004, October). Getting on board: Building a business case for auto–ID at Dell. APICS – The Performance Advantage, 34–37.

Doss, R., Zhou, W., Sundaresan, S., Yu, S., & Gao, L. (2012). A minimum disclosure approach to authentication and privacy in RFID systems. *Computer Networks, 56*(15), 3401–3416. doi:10.1016/j.comnet.2012.06.018

El Ghazali, Y., Lefebvre, E., & Lefebvre, L. A. (2012). The potential of RFID as an enabler of knowledge management and collaboration for the procurement cycle in the construction industry. *Journal of Technology Management & Innovation, 7*(4), 81–102. doi:10.4067/S0718-27242012000400007

Ferguson, R. B. (2006). RFID loses reception: High tag costs are still putting the kibosh on returns on investment. *e-Week, 23*(10), 11–12.

Finkenzeller, K. (2003). *RFID handbook: Fundamentals and applications in contactless smart cards and identification.* Chichester, UK: John Wiley & Sons. doi:10.1002/0470868023

Fisher, J. A., & Monahan, T. (2008). Tracking the social dimensions of RFID systems in hospitals. *International Journal of Medical Informatics, 77*(3), 176–183. doi:10.1016/j.ijmedinf.2007.04.010 PMID:17544841

Fosso Wamba, S., Anand, A., & Carter, L. (2013). A literature review of RFID-enabled healthcare applications and issues. *International Journal of Information Management, 33*(5), 875–891. doi:10.1016/j.ijinfomgt.2013.07.005

Fosso Wamba, S., & Chatfield, A. T. (2009). A contingency model for creating value from RFID supply chain network projects in logistics and manufacturing environments. *European Journal of Information Systems, 18*(6), 615–636. doi:10.1057/ejis.2009.44

Fries, J. L., Turri, A. M., Bello, D. C., & Smith, R. J. (2010). Factors that influence the implementation of collaborative RFiD programs. *Journal of Business and Industrial Marketing, 25*(8), 590–595. doi:10.1108/08858621011088329

Gilbert, A. (2004). *Patent problems plague RFID*. Retrieved from www.zdnet.com.au/insight/hardware/0,39023759,39159309,00.htm

Green, K. W., Whitten, D., & Inman, R. A. (2009). The impact of RFID technology utilization on supply chain productivity and organizational performance. *International Journal of Innovation and Learning*, *6*(2), 147–162. doi:10.1504/IJIL.2009.022810

Hardgrave, B. C., Aloysius, J. A., & Goyal, S. (2009). Does RFID improve inventory accuracy? A preliminary analysis. *International Journal of RF Technologies: Research and Applications*, *1*(1), 44–56. doi:10.1080/17545730802338333

Hardgrave, B. C., Aloysius, J. A., & Goyal, S. (2013). RFID-enabled visibility and retail inventory record inaccuracy: Experiments in the field. *Production and Operations Management*, *22*(4), 843–856. doi:10.1111/poms.12010

Hausman, A., & Stock, J. (2003). Adoption and implementation of technological innovations within long-term relationships. *Journal of Business Research*, *56*(8), 681–686. doi:10.1016/S0148-2963(01)00313-7

Heim, G. R., Wentworth, W. R. Jr, & Peng, X. (2009). The value to the customer of RFID in service applications. *Decision Sciences*, *40*(3), 477–512. doi:10.1111/j.1540-5915.2009.00237.x

Hosaka, R. (2004). Feasibility study of convenient automatic identification system of medical articles using LF-band RFID in hospital. *Systems and Computers in Japan*, *35*(10), 571–578. doi:10.1002/scj.10581

Hossain, M. M., & Prybutok, V. R. (2008). Consumer acceptance of RFID technology: An exploratory study. *IEEE Transactions on Engineering Management*, *55*(2), 316–328. doi:10.1109/TEM.2008.919728

Howard, L., & Anderson, M. (2007). RFID technology in the library environment. *Georgia Library Quarterly*, *44*(1), 16–20.

Jansen, R., & Krabs, A. (1999). Automatic identification in packing – radio frequency identification in multi-way system. *Packaging Technology and Science*, *12*(5), 229–234. doi:10.1002/(SICI)1099-1522(199909/10)12:5<229::AID-PTS479>3.0.CO;2-6

Jones, P., Clarke-Hill, C., Hillier, D., Shears, P., & Comfort, D. (2004). Radio frequency identification in retailing and privacy and public policy issues. *Management Research News*, *27*(8-9), 46–56. doi:10.1108/01409170410784563

Juels, A. (2006). RFID security and privacy: A research survey. *IEEE Journal on Selected Areas in Communications*, *24*(3), 381–394. doi:10.1109/JSAC.2005.861395

Kakkainen, M. (2003). Increasing efficiency in the supply chain for short shelf life goods using RFID tagging. *International Journal of Retail & Distribution Management*, *31*(10), 529–536. doi:10.1108/09590550310497058

Kapoor, G., Zhou, W., & Piramuthu, S. (2009). Challenges associated with RFID tag implementations in supply chains. *European Journal of Information Systems*, *18*(6), 526–533. doi:10.1057/ejis.2009.41

Karkkainen, M., & Holmstrom, J. (2002). Wireless product identification: Enabler for handling efficiency, customization and information sharing. *Supply Chain Management: An International Journal, 7*(4), 242–252. doi:10.1108/13598540210438971

Kasemsap, K. (2013a). Synthesized framework: Establishing a causal model of organizational learning, knowledge management, knowledge-sharing behavior, and organizational performance. *International Journal of the Computer, the Internet and Management, 21*(2), 29–34.

Kasemsap, K. (2013b). Unified framework: Constructing a causal model of Six Sigma, organizational learning, organizational innovation, and organizational performance. *The Journal of Interdisciplinary Networks, 2*(1), 268–273.

Kasemsap, K. (2014a). Unifying a framework of organizational culture, organizational climate, knowledge management, and job performance. In R. Perez-Castillo & M. Piattini (Eds.), *Uncovering essential software artifacts through business process archeology,* (pp. 336–362). Hershey, PA: IGI Global. doi:10.4018/978-1-4666-4667-4.ch013

Kasemsap, K. (2014b). Strategic innovation management: An integrative framework and causal model of knowledge management, strategic orientation, organizational innovation, and organizational performance. In P. Ordóñez de Pablos & R. Tennyson (Eds.), *Strategic approaches for human capital management and development in a turbulent economy,* (pp. 102–116). Hershey, PA: IGI Global. doi:10.4018/978-1-4666-4530-1.ch007

Kasemsap, K. (2014c). The role of knowledge management on job satisfaction: A systematic framework. In B. Tripathy & D. Acharjya (Eds.), *Advances in secure computing, Internet services, and applications,* (pp. 104–127). Hershey, PA: IGI Global. doi:10.4018/978-1-4666-4940-8.ch006

Kasemsap, K. (2015a). Developing a framework of human resource management, organizational learning, knowledge management capability, and organizational performance. In P. Ordoñez de Pablos, L. Turró, R. Tennyson, & J. Zhao (Eds.), *Knowledge management for competitive advantage during economic crisis,* (pp. 164–193). Hershey, PA: IGI Global. doi:10.4018/978-1-4666-6457-9.ch010

Kasemsap, K. (2015b). The role of data mining for business intelligence in knowledge management. In A. Azevedo & M. Santos (Eds.), *Integration of data mining in business intelligence systems,* (pp. 12–33). Hershey, PA: IGI Global. doi:10.4018/978-1-4666-6477-7.ch002

Kern, C. (1999). RFID technology – recent development and future requirements. Paper presented at the *European Conference on Circuit Theory and Design, ECCTD'99*, Stresa, Italy.

Kern, C. (2004). Radio-frequency-identification in libraries. *The Electronic Library, 22*(4), 317–324. doi:10.1108/02640470410552947

Kim, E. Y., Ko, E., Kim, H., & Koh, C. E. (2008). Comparison of benefits of radio frequency identification: Implications for business strategic performance in the US and Korean retailers. *Industrial Marketing Management, 37*(7), 797–806. doi:10.1016/j.indmarman.2008.01.007

Koneru, I. (2004). RFID technology: A revolution in Library Management. Paper presented at the *Second International Convention CALIBER-2004*, New Delhi, India.

Kwang, S. P., Koh, C. E., & Nam, K. (2010). Perceptions of RFID technology: A cross-national study. *Industrial Management & Data Systems, 110*(5), 682–700. doi:10.1108/02635571011044722

Lambert, D., & Cooper, M. (2000). Issues in supply chain management. *Industrial Marketing Management, 29*(1), 65–83. doi:10.1016/S0019-8501(99)00113-3

Landt, J. (2001). *Shrouds of time: The history of RFID*. Pittsburgh, PA: AIM.

Lapide, L. (2004). RFID: What's in it for the forecaster? *Journal of Business Forecasting, 23*(2), 16–19.

Lee, C. K. H., Choy, K. L., Ho, G. T. S., & Law, K. M. Y. (2013). A RFID-based resource allocation system for garment manufacturing. *Expert Systems with Applications, 40*(2), 784–799. doi:10.1016/j.eswa.2012.08.033

Lee, L. S., Fiedler, K. D., & Smith, J. S. (2008). Radio frequency identification (RFID) implementation in the service sector: A customer-facing diffusion model. *International Journal of Production Economics, 112*(2), 587–600. doi:10.1016/j.ijpe.2007.05.008

Lee, H., & Ozer, O. (2007). Unlocking the value of RFiD. *Production and Operations Management, 16*(1), 40–64. doi:10.1111/j.1937-5956.2007.tb00165.x

Li, J. S., & Liu, K. H. (2011). A hidden mutual authentication protocol for low-cost RFID tags. *International Journal of Communication Systems, 24*(9), 1196–1211.

Li, S., & Visich, J. K. (2006). Radio frequency identification: Supply chain impact and implementation challenges. *International Journal of Integrated Supply Management, 2*(4), 407–424. doi:10.1504/IJISM.2006.009643

Li, S., Visich, J. K., Khumawala, B. M., & Zhang, C. (2006). Radio frequency identification technology: Applications, technical challenges and strategies. *Sensor Review, 26*(3), 193–202. doi:10.1108/02602280610675474

Li, C., Wang, G., & Zheng, J. (2014). An aggregated signature-based fast RFID batch detection protocol. *Security and Communication Networks, 7*(9), 1364–1371. doi:10.1002/sec.838

Lim, S. H., & Koh, C. E. (2009). RFID implementation strategy: Perceived risks and organizational fits. *Industrial Management & Data Systems, 109*(8), 1017–1036. doi:10.1108/02635570910991274

Liu, A. X., Bailey, L. A., & Krishnamurthy, A. H. (2010). RFIDGuard: A lightweight privacy and authentication protocol for passive RFID tags. *Security and Communication Networks, 3*(5), 384–393. doi:10.1002/sec.138

Madhusudhan, M. (2010). RFID technology implementation in two university libraries in New Delhi. *Program: Electronic library and information systems, 43*(2), 202–214

Makori, E. O. (2013). Adoption of radio frequency identification technology in university libraries: A Kenyan perspective. *The Electronic Library, 31*(2), 208–216. doi:10.1108/02640471311312384

Malone, R. (2004). Reconsidering the role of RFID. *Inbound Logistics*. Retrieved November 9, 2014, from www.inboundlogistics.com/articles/supplychain/sct0804.shtml

McFarlane, D., & Sheffi, Y. (2003). The impact of automatic identification on supply chain operations. *International Journal of Logistics Management*, *14*(1), 1–17. doi:10.1108/09574090310806503

McGee, M. (2004, May 10). Health-care I.T. has a new face. *InformationWeek*, 16.

Mehrjerdi, Y. Z. (2009). RFID–enabled supply chain systems with computer simulation. *Assembly Automation*, *29*(2), 174–183. doi:10.1108/01445150910945624

Mehrjerdi, Y. Z. (2011). RFID: The big player in libraries of the future. *The Electronic Library*, *29*(1), 36–51. doi:10.1108/02640471111111424

Michael, K., & McCathie, L. (2005). *The pros and cons of RFID in supply chain management*. Paper presented at the International Conference on Mobile Business. Sydney, Australia

Molnar, D., & Wagner, D. (2004). *Privacy and security in library RFID issues, practices, and architectures*. Paper presented at the 11th ACM Conference on Computer and Communications Security (CCS' 04). New York, NY.

Moon, K. L., & Ngai, E. W. T. (2008). The adoption of RFID in fashion retailing: A business value-added framework. *Industrial Management & Data Systems*, *108*(5), 596–612. doi:10.1108/02635570810876732

Najera, P., Roman, R., & Lopez, J. (2013). User-centric secure integration of personal RFID tags and sensor networks. *Security and Communication Networks*, *6*(10), 1177–1197.

O'Connell, M., Hickey, S., Besiou, M., Fitzpatrick, C., & Van Wassenhove, L. N. (2013). Feasibility of using radio frequency identification to facilitate individual producer responsibility for waste electrical and electronic equipment. *Journal of Industrial Ecology*, *17*(2), 213–223. doi:10.1111/j.1530-9290.2012.00573.x

O'Connor, M. C. (2005). Suppliers meet mandate frugally. *RFID Journal*. Retrieved from www.rfid-journal.com/article/articleview/1308/1/1/

Ollivier, M. (1995). RFID enhances materials handling. *Sensor Review*, *15*(1), 36–39. doi:10.1108/EUM0000000004267

Osyk, B. A., Vijayaraman, B. S., Srinivasan, M., & Dey, A. (2012). RFID adoption and implementation in warehousing. *Management Research Review*, *35*(10), 904–926. doi:10.1108/01409171211272651

Oztekin, A., Pajouh, F. M., Delen, D., & Swim, L. K. (2010). An RFID network design methodology for asset tracking in healthcare. *Decision Support Systems*, *49*(1), 100–109. doi:10.1016/j.dss.2010.01.007

Park, K. S., Koh, C. E., & Nam, K. (2010). Perceptions of RFID technology: A cross–national study. *Industrial Management & Data Systems*, *110*(5), 682–700. doi:10.1108/02635571011044722

Prater, E., Frazier, G. V., & Reyes, P. M. (2005). Future impacts of RFID on e–supply chains in grocery retailing. *Supply Chain Management: An International Journal*, *10*(2), 134–142. doi:10.1108/13598540510589205

Qian, Z., Chen, C., You, I., & Lu, S. (2012). ACSP: A novel security protocol against counting attack for UHF RFID systems. *Computers & Mathematics with Applications (Oxford, England)*, *63*(2), 492–500. doi:10.1016/j.camwa.2011.08.030

Ramanathan, R., Ramanathan, U., & Ko, L. W. L. (2014). Adoption of RFID technologies in UK logistics: Moderating roles of size, barcode experience and government support. *Expert Systems with Applications*, *41*(1), 230–236. doi:10.1016/j.eswa.2013.07.024

Rieback, M. R., Crispo, B., & Tanenbaum, A. S. (2006). The evolution of RFID security. *IEEE Pervasive Computing / IEEE Computer Society [and] IEEE Communications Society*, *5*(1), 62–69. doi:10.1109/MPRV.2006.17

Roberti, M. (2004a). Tag cost and ROI. *RFID Journal*. Retrieved from www.rfidjournal.com/article/articleview/796/1/2/

Roberti, M. (2004b). Wal-Mart suppliers discuss RFID. *RFID Journal*. Retrieved from www.rfidjournal.com/ article/articleprint/956/-1/1/

Ryan, J., Lewis, C., Doster, B., Daily, S., & Glass, R. (2013). A phased approach to implementing radio frequency identification technologies within the perioperative process. *Health Technology*, *3*(1), 73–84. doi:10.1007/s12553-013-0054-7

Sabbaghi, A., & Vaidyanathan, G. (2008). Effectiveness and efficiency of RFID technology in supply chain management: Strategic values and challenges. *Journal of Theoretical and Applied Electronic Commerce Research*, *3*(2), 71–80. doi:10.4067/S0718-18762008000100007

Smaros, J., & Holmstrom, J. (2000). Viewpoint: Reaching the consumer through e-grocery VMI. *International Journal of Retail & Distribution Management*, *28*(2), 55–61. doi:10.1108/09590550010315098

Smith, A. (2005). Exploring radio frequency identification technology and its impact on business. *Information Management & Computer Security*, *13*(1), 16–28. doi:10.1108/09685220510582647

Spekman, R., & Sweeny, P. (2006). RFID: From concept to implementation. *International Journal of Physical Distribution & Logistics Management*, *36*(10), 736–754. doi:10.1108/09600030610714571

Srivastava, B. (2004). Radio frequency ID technology: The next revolution in SCM. *Business Horizons*, *47*(6), 60–68. doi:10.1016/j.bushor.2004.09.009

Stambaugh, C. T., & Carpenter, F. W. (2009). RFID. *Strategic Finance*, *91*(6), 35–40.

Suei, P. L., Lu, Y. F., Liao, R. J., & Lo, S. W. (2012). A signature-based Grid index design for main memory RFID database applications. *Journal of Systems and Software*, *85*(5), 1205–1212. doi:10.1016/j.jss.2012.01.026

Sun, Q., Zhang, H., & Mo, L. (2011). Dual-reader wireless protocols for dense active RFID identification. *International Journal of Communication Systems*, *24*(11), 1431–1444. doi:10.1002/dac.1225

Symonds, J., Parry, D., & Briggs, J. (2007). An RFID-based system for assisted living: Challenges and solutions. *The Journal on Information Technology in Healthcare*, *5*(6), 387–398. PMID:17901606

Tajima, M. (2007). Strategic value of RFiD in supply chain management. *Journal of Purchasing and Supply Management*, *13*(4), 261–273. doi:10.1016/j.pursup.2007.11.001

Tang, Z. J., Wu, X. F., Zhan, J., & Hu, S. G. (2014). Broadband UHF RFID tag antenna design matched with different RFID chips. *Microwave and Optical Technology Letters*, *56*(1), 55–57. doi:10.1002/mop.28046

Thuemmler, C., Buchanan, W., & Kumar, V. (2007). Setting safety standards by designing a low-budget and compatible patient identification system based on passive RFID technology. *International Journal of Healthcare Technology and Management*, *8*(5), 571–583. doi:10.1504/IJHTM.2007.013524

Tian, Y., Chen, G. L., & Li, J. H. (2013). Bi-slotted binary tree algorithm with stack for radio frequency identification tag anti-collision. *Journal of Shanghai Jiaotong University (Science)*, *18*(2), 173–179. doi:10.1007/s12204-013-1380-7

Tien, L. (2005). *T08... RFID and privacy: Potential and perils*. Paper presented at the Michigan Library Association Annual Conference, Grand Rapids, MI.

Tu, Y. J., Zhou, W., & Piramuthu, S. (2009). Identifying RFID-embedded objects in pervasive healthcare applications. *Decision Support Systems*, *46*(2), 586–593. doi:10.1016/j.dss.2008.10.001

Tzeng, S. F., Chen, W. H., & Pai, F. Y. (2008). Evaluating the business value of RFID: Evidence from five case studies. *International Journal of Production Economics*, *112*(2), 601–613. doi:10.1016/j.ijpe.2007.05.009

Ustundag, A., & Tanyas, M. (2009). The impacts of radio frequency identification (RFID) technology on supply chain costs. *Transportation Research*, *45*(1), 29–38. doi:10.1016/j.tre.2008.09.001

Vijayaraman, B. S., Osyk, B. A., & Chavada, D. (2008). An exploratory study of RFID adoption in the paperboard packaging industry. *Journal of Technology Management and Innovation*, *3*(4), 95–110. doi:10.4067/S0718-27242008000200008

Visich, J., Li, S., Khumawala, B., & Reyes, P. (2009). Empirical evidence of RFID impacts on supply chain performance. *International Journal of Operations & Production Management*, *29*(12), 1290–1315. doi:10.1108/01443570911006009

Waddenkeri, M. (2006). *RFID technology in library and information centers: Relevance and Prospects*. Paper presented at the 4th International Convention CALIBER–2006, Gulbarga, India.

Wang, Y. M., Wang, Y. S., & Yang, Y. F. (2010). Understanding the determinants of RFID adoption in the manufacturing industry. *Technological Forecasting and Social Change*, *77*(5), 803–815. doi:10.1016/j.techfore.2010.03.006

Want, R. (2006). An introduction to RFID technology. *IEEE Pervasive Computing / IEEE Computer Society [and] IEEE Communications Society*, *5*(1), 25–33. doi:10.1109/MPRV.2006.2

Whitaker, J., Mithas, S., & Krishnan, M. S. (2007). A field study of RFID deployment and return expectations. *Production and Operations Management*, *16*(5), 599–612. doi:10.1111/j.1937-5956.2007.tb00283.x

Wu, N., Nystrom, M., Lin, T., & Yu, H. (2006). Challenges to global RFID adoption. *Technovation*, *26*(12), 1317–1323. doi:10.1016/j.technovation.2005.08.012

Wu, J., Wang, D., Sheng, H. Y., & Siror, J. (2010). Toward an SCA–OSGi based middleware for radio frequency identification applications. *Journal of Shanghai Jiaotong University (Science)*, *15*(2), 199–206. doi:10.1007/s12204-010-9557-9

Wyld, D. (2006). RFID 101: The next big thing for management. *Management Research News*, *29*(4), 154–173. doi:10.1108/01409170610665022

Yang, M. H., & Hu, H. Y. (2012). Protocol for ownership transfer across authorities: With the ability to assign transfer target. *Security and Communication Networks*, *5*(2), 164–177. doi:10.1002/sec.300

Yu, S. C. (2007). RFID implementation and benefits in libraries. *The Electronic Library*, *25*(1), 54–64. doi:10.1108/02640470710729119

Zelbst, P. J., Green, K. W., Baker, G., & Sower, V. E. (2010). RFID utilization and information sharing impact supply chain performance. *Journal of Business and Industrial Marketing*, *25*(8), 582–589. doi:10.1108/08858621011088310

Zelbst, P. J., Green, K. W., Sower, V. E., & Reyes, P. M. (2012). Impact of RFID on manufacturing effectiveness and efficiency. *International Journal of Operations & Production Management*, *32*(3), 329–350. doi:10.1108/01443571211212600

Zhang, Z., Lu, Z., Chen, Q., Yan, X., & Zheng, L. R. (2012). Code division multiple access/pulse position modulation ultra-wideband radio frequency identification for Internet of Things: Concept and analysis. *International Journal of Communication Systems*, *25*(9), 1103–1121. doi:10.1002/dac.2312

Zhang, T., Ouyang, Y., & He, Y. (2008). Traceable air baggage handling system based on RFID tags in the airport. *Journal of Theoretical and Applied Electronic Commerce Research*, *3*(1), 106–115.

Zhou, W. (2009). RFID and item–level information visibility. *European Journal of Operational Research*, *198*(1), 252–258. doi:10.1016/j.ejor.2008.09.017

Zhu, X., Mukhopadhyay, S. K., & Kurata, H. (2012). A review of RFID technology and its managerial applications in different industries. *Journal of Engineering and Technology Management*, *29*(1), 152–167. doi:10.1016/j.jengtecman.2011.09.011

ADDITIONAL READING

Angeles, R. (2009). Perceptions of the importance of absorptive capacity attributes as they relate to radio frequency identification implementation by firms anticipating radio frequency identification use. *International Journal of Management and Enterprise Development*, *6*(1), 88–117. doi:10.1504/IJMED.2009.021738

Azadeganm, A., Porobic, L., Ghazinoory, S., Samouei, P., & Kheirkhah, A. S. (2011). Fuzzy logic in manufacturing: A review of literature and a specialized application. *International Journal of Production Economics*, *132*(2), 258–270. doi:10.1016/j.ijpe.2011.04.018

Bunduchi, R., Weisshaar, C., & Smart, A. U. (2011). Mapping the benefits and costs associated with process innovation: The case of RFID adoption. *Technovation*, *31*(9), 505–521. doi:10.1016/j.technovation.2011.04.001

Camdereli, A. Z., & Swaminathan, J. M. (2010). Misplaced inventory and radio-frequency identification (RFID) technology: Information and coordination. *Production and Operations Management*, *19*(1), 1–18. doi:10.1111/j.1937-5956.2009.01057.x

Cardiel, I. A., Gil, R. H., Somolinos, C. C., & Somolinos, J. C. (2012). A SCADA oriented middleware for RFID technology. *Expert Systems with Applications*, *39*(12), 11115–11124. doi:10.1016/j.eswa.2012.03.045

Chang, Y. B. (2011). Does RFID improve firms' financial performance? An empirical analysis. *Information Technology Management*, *12*(3), 273–285. doi:10.1007/s10799-011-0088-3

Chen, J. C., Cheng, C. H., & Huang, P. B. (2013). Supply chain management with lean production and RFID application: A case study. *Expert Systems with Applications*, *40*(9), 3389–3397. doi:10.1016/j.eswa.2012.12.047

Chen, R., & Tu, M. (2009). Development of an agent-based system for manufacturing control and coordination with ontology and RFID technology. *Expert Systems with Applications*, *36*(4), 7581–7593. doi:10.1016/j.eswa.2008.09.068

Chong, A. Y. L., & Chan, F. T. S. (2012). Structural equation modeling for multi-stage analysis on radio frequency identification (RFID) diffusion in the health care industry. *Expert Systems with Applications*, *39*(10), 8645–8654. doi:10.1016/j.eswa.2012.01.201

Collins, J. D., Worthington, W. J., Reyes, P. M., & Romero, M. (2010). Knowledge management, supply chain technologies, and firm performance. *Management Research Review*, *33*(10), 947–960. doi:10.1108/01409171011083969

Erguler, I., & Anarim, E. (2012). Practical attacks and improvements to an efficient radio frequency identification authentication protocol. *Concurrency and Computation*, *24*(17), 2069–2080. doi:10.1002/cpe.1838

Fu, L., Shen, X., Zhu, L., & Wang, J. (2014). A low-cost UHF RFID tag chip with AES cryptography engine. *Security and Communication Networks*, *7*(2), 365–375. doi:10.1002/sec.723

Gruninger, M., Shapiro, S., Fox, M. S., & Weppner, H. (2010). Combining RFID with ontologies to create smart objects. *International Journal of Production Research*, *48*(9), 2633–2654. doi:10.1080/00207540903564975

Katz, J., & Rice, R. (2009). Public views of mobile medical devices and services: A US national survey of consumer sentiments towards RFID healthcare technology. *International Journal of Medical Informatics*, *78*(2), 104–114. doi:10.1016/j.ijmedinf.2008.06.001 PMID:18619897

Kumar, S., Anselmo, M. J., & Berndt, K. J. (2009). Transforming the retail industry: Potential and challenges with RFID technology. *Transportation Journal*, *48*(4), 61–71.

Lee, C., & Chan, T. (2009). Development of RFID-based reverse logistics system. *Expert Systems with Applications, 36*(5), 9299–9307. doi:10.1016/j.eswa.2008.12.002

Li, S., Godon, D., & Visich, J. K. (2010). An exploratory study of RFID implementation in the supply chain. *Management Research Review, 33*(10), 1005–1015. doi:10.1108/01409171011084003

Lin, C. Y. (2009). An empirical study on organizational determinants of RFID adoption in the logistics industry. *Journal of Technology Management & Innovation, 4*(1), 1–7. doi:10.4067/S0718-27242009000100001

Mukherjee, S. (2013). Detection and identification of objects based on radio-frequency signatures. *Annals of telecommunications - Annales des télécommunications, 68*(7–8), 459–466.

Muller-Seitz, G., Dautzenberg, K., Creusen, U., & Stromereder, C. (2009). Customer acceptance of RFID technology: Evidence from the German electronic retail sector. *Journal of Retailing and Consumer Services, 16*(1), 31–39. doi:10.1016/j.jretconser.2008.08.002

Neganov, V. A., Plotkinov, A. M., & Tabakov, D. P. (2013). Electrodynamic analysis of resonance tags for radio-frequency identification of objects based on the method of singular integral equations. *Journal of Communications Technology and Electronics, 57*(7), 674–681. doi:10.1134/S1064226912060071

Ngai, E. W. T., Chau, D. C. K., Poon, J. K. L., Chan, A. Y. M., Chan, B. C. M., & Wu, W. W. S. (2012). Implementing an RFID-based manufacturing process management system: Lessons learned and success factors. *Journal of Engineering and Technology Management, 29*(1), 112–130. doi:10.1016/j.jengtecman.2011.09.009

Norwood, J., & Skinner, B. (2012). Implementing RFID in a hospital library: A scoping study. *Health Information and Libraries Journal, 29*(2), 162–165. doi:10.1111/j.1471-1842.2012.00987.x PMID:22630364

Pedroso, M. C., Zwicker, R., & de Souza, C. A. (2009). RFID adoption: Framework and survey in large Brazilian companies. *Industrial Management & Data Systems, 109*(7), 877–897. doi:10.1108/02635570910982256

Poon, T., Choy, K., Chow, H., Lau, H., Chan, F., & Ho, K. (2009). A RFID case-based logistics resource management system for managing order-picking operations in warehouses. *Expert Systems with Applications, 36*(4), 8277–8301. doi:10.1016/j.eswa.2008.10.011

Pramatari, K., & Theotokis, A. (2009). Consumer acceptance of RFID-enabled services: A model of multiple attitudes, perceived system characteristics and individual traits. *European Journal of Information Systems, 18*(6), 541–552. doi:10.1057/ejis.2009.40

Rekik, Y., Sahin, E., & Dallery, Y. (2009). Inventory inaccuracy in retail stores due to theft: An analysis of the benefits of RFID. *International Journal of Production Economics, 118*(1), 189–198. doi:10.1016/j.ijpe.2008.08.048

Tsai, M. C., Lee, W., & Wu, H. C. (2010). Determinants of RFID adoption intention: Evidence from Taiwanese retail chains. *Information & Management, 47*(5-6), 255–261. doi:10.1016/j.im.2010.05.001

Upfold, C., & Liu, H. (2010). Radio frequency identification (RFID) adoption in the South African retail sector: An investigation of perceptions held by members of the retail sector regarding the adoption constraints. *Electronic Journal Information Systems Evaluation*, *13*(1), 87–96.

Veronneau, S., & Roy, J. (2009). RFID benefits, costs, and possibilities: The economical analysis of RFID deployment in a cruise corporation global service supply chain. *International Journal of Production Economics*, *122*(2), 692–702. doi:10.1016/j.ijpe.2009.06.038

Wei, Z. (2009). RFID and item-level information visibility. *European Journal of Operational Research*, *198*(1), 252–258. doi:10.1016/j.ejor.2008.09.017

Zelbst, P. J., Green, K. W. Jr, & Sower, V. E. (2010). Impact of RFID technology utilization on operational performance. *Management Research Review*, *33*(10), 994–1004. doi:10.1108/01409171011083996

Zhou, W., Kapoor, G., & Piramuthu, S. (2009). RFID–enabled item-level product information revelation. *European Journal of Information Systems*, *18*(6), 570–577. doi:10.1057/ejis.2009.45

KEY TERMS AND DEFINITIONS

Business: An organization or economic system where goods and services are exchanged for one another or for money.

Collection: A process of recovering amounts owed to a firm by its customers.

Data Communications: The high speed data exchange between computers and/or other electronic devices through cable or wireless.

Digital Library: A collection of digitized documents, images, and sounds that can be accessed and read by the use of computers.

Electronic Library: A Physical site and/or website that provides 24-hour online access to digitized audio, video, and written material.

Information Science: The body of knowledge that provides theoretical basis for information technology and includes subjects such as computer science, library science, artificial intelligence, mathematics of programming, and theory of problem solving.

Information Technology: A set of tools, processes, and methodologies and associated equipment employed to collect, process, and present information.

Knowledge Management: The strategies and processes designed to identify, capture, structure, value, leverage, and share an organization's intellectual assets to enhance its performance and competitiveness.

Radio Frequency Identification (RFID): An automatic identification of packages, products, and machinery through attached transponders.

Chapter 10
A Novel Technique for Securing E-Commerce Transaction

Arnab K. Maji
North Eastern Hill University, India

ABSTRACT

The emergence of online businesses along with the use of the Internet as its basic network has brought new concerns and risks to the e-commerce environment. It is essential for the online companies to gain customers' trust to retain their existing e-commerce market share and provide for growth, because e-commerce transactions take place in an open environment that cannot be trusted since the network is highly vulnerable to outside security threats. The main problem of e-commerce transaction is anonymity. One may steal another's identity and get access of his confidential information such as banking password, credit card details, etc. very easily. The most convenient way to prevent such kind of identity theft is digital certificate. But that is very expensive. In this chapter, a novel attempt is made to prevent identity theft using Visual Cryptography and Steganography during e-commerce transaction, in a very cost-effective manner.

1. INTRODUCTION

Electronic Commerce is a commercial transactions conducted electronically using computers over a large network like Internet. It involves exchange of business information using EDI (Electronic Data Interchange), email, electronic bulletin boards, online transactions etc. During Online transactions of E-commerce, Identity Theft is identified as a major security threat, as the major problem of internet is anonymity. If we briefly classify the different security issues of E-Commerce they can be classified as:

- **Network Security:** This is probably the most obvious issue for e-commerce applications, since the amount and severity of hack attacks are increasing. Fortunately, significant progress has been made in this area through firewall security products that protect against basic network-level attacks. A proper security strategy should not end here, though.

DOI: 10.4018/978-1-5225-0808-3.ch010

- **Identity:** Since e-commerce implies trading with potentially unknown and untrusted partners, identification of trading partners can be crucial. Once again, work has been done to provide standardized methods to identify users by using certificates based on the X.509 standard. Unfortunately the deployment of these certificates for general e-commerce applications has been slow.

- **Authorization:** In order to automate trading processes, it is often required to verify more than identity. Various emerging standards such as certificates, authorization servers and the use of a database with registered users and privileges inside the application, all contribute to address the authorization issue of who may do what.

- **Host and Application Security:** The protection offered by most operating systems falls short in a global networked environment. Efforts such as signed applets and signed executables are commendable, but will most probably not solve the problem of virus and Trojan attacks. In addition to these obvious flaws, more subtle problems such as buffer overflow attacks on certain networked applications can also lead to security compromises.

- **Transaction Security:** The protocols used for electronic transactions range from the primitive to the very sophisticated. Older secure protocols, for example those used in Point of Sale terminals, rely on the DES algorithm, and typically require some form of secure storage for the cryptographic keys. Many newer protocols (e.g. SET) are based on public key mechanisms, but have not yet achieved widespread adoption.

Today, most applications are only as secure as their underlying system. Since the design and technology of middleware has improved steadily, their detection is a difficult problem. As a result, it is nearly impossible to be sure whether a computer that is connected to the internet can be considered trustworthy and secure or not. The virtual market is facing a continuously growing threat in terms of identity theft (Vasistha, 2005) that is causing short-term losses and long-term economic damage. Among several identity thefts, phishing and its various variants are most common and deterrant to e-commerce. The scams and frauds on internet like identity theft leads to the problem of computer theft and massive penetration and espionage. Phishing is an outcome of unsolicited bulk email and unsolicited commercial e-mail also referred to as spam. Unfortunately some companies realized that not only could they communicate by e-mail with staff and existing business partners, but also they could also reach out to millions of potential new customers on web, introducing themselves and their services for minimum cost and required only a tiny response and service uptake to make it all worthwhile. Email spam has become a fact of life. A variety of new message threats now combine to attack individuals, organizations and businesses and thus prove to be a great threat of e-commerce, they include email born viruses, spyware, adware, Trojan horses, directory harvesting attacks(DHA), denial of services (DOS) attacks and more importantly phishing attacks(Banday, 2007).

So here introduces a new method which can be used as a safe way against online identity theft. In this approach website cross verifies its own identity and proves that it is a genuine website, during E-commerce Transaction before the end users and make the both the sides of the system secure as well as an authenticated one.

The concept of image processing and an improved Visual Cryptography and Steganography is used. Image processing is a technique of processing an input image and to get the output as either improved form of the same image and/or characteristics of the input image. In Visual Cryptography (VC) an image is decomposed into shares and in order to reveal the original image appropriate number of shares should be combined. Steganography is the art and science of writing hidden messages in such a way that no one apart from the intended recipient knows the existence of the message.

This chapter is organized into seven sections Section 2 deals with the back ground, Section 3 describes about Visual Cryptography, Section 4 describes Steganography, Section 5 deals with proposed Methodologies, Section 6 presents the implementation and analysis and Section 7 contains the conclusions.

2. BACKGROUND

The major drawback of the internet is anonymity. Anybody can steal others identity very easily as there is no face-to-face interaction between the two communicating parties. There are several ways to steal others identity as described. Most of these kinds of web pages have high visual similarities to scam their victims. Some of these kinds of web pages look exactly like the real ones.. Phishing approaches used for identity thefts are constantly growing and new variants are tried and used to attack business organizations, financial institutions and customers Victims of phishing web pages may expose their bank account, password, credit card number, or other important information to the phishing web page owners. It includes techniques such as tricking customers through email and spam messages, man in the middle attacks, installation of key loggers and screen captures. Some of the most prevalent types of phishing attacks are presented hereunder.

1. **Deceptive Phishing:** It involves sending message about the need to verify account information, system failure require user to re-enter the information, fictitious account charges, undesirable account charges information are broadcasted to a wide group of recipients with a hope that the unwary will respond by clicking a link to or signing onto a bogus site where their confidential information can be collected.
2. **Malware-Based Phishing:** It refers to scams that involve users to unknowingly running malicious software on their pc. That software can easily collect the information and send the attacker the confidential information.
3. **Keyloggers and Screenloggers:** They are particular varieties of software that track keyboard input in the backdoor and send relevant information to the hacker via web.
4. **Session Hijacking:** In this type of attack user's activities are monitored until they sign in to a target account or transaction and establish their bona fide credentials. At that point the malicious software takes over and undertakes unauthorized actions, such as transferring funds, without the user's knowledge.
5. **Web Trojans:** are a type of pop up running invisibly on user machines. When users are attempting to log in, they collect the user's credentials locally and transmit them to the phisher.
6. **Hosts File Poisoning:** involves changing the host files of the operating system that contain the IP addresses corresponding to the web addresses. When a user types a URL to visit a website it must first be translated into an IP address before it's transmitted over the Internet. The majority of SM B users' PCs running a Microsoft Windows operating system first look up for these "host names" in their "hosts" file before undertaking a Domain Name System (DNS) lookup. By "poisoning" the hosts file, hackers have a bogus address transmitted, taking the user unwittingly to a fake "look alike" website where their information can be stolen.

7. **System Reconfiguration Attacks:** It modifies settings on a user's PC for malicious purposes. For example: URLs in a favorites file might be modified to direct users to look alike websites. For example: a bank website URL may be changed from "statebank.com" to "statebanc.com".

8. **Data Theft:** It refers to stealing subset of sensitive information stored locally on unsecured PCs which actually is stored elsewhere on secured servers. Certainly PCs are used to access such servers and can be more easily compromised. Data theft is a widely used approach to business espionage. By stealing confidential communications, design documents, legal opinions, and employee related records, etc., thieves profit from selling to those who may want to embarrass or cause economic damage or to competitors.

9. **DNS-Based Phishing (Pharming):** It is a term given to hosts file modification or Domain Name System (DNS) based phishing. With a pharming scheme, hackers tamper with a company's host files or domain name system so that requests for URLs or name service return a bogus address and subsequent communications are directed to a fake site. This results in users falling unwarily victims by working on the websites controlled by hackers where they enter confidential information.

10. **Content-Injection Phishing:** It is used to describe the situation where hackers replace part of the content of a legitimate site with false content designed to mislead or misdirect the user into giving up their confidential information to the hacker. For example, hackers may insert malicious code to log user's credentials or an overlay which can secretly collect information and deliver it to the hacker's phishing server.

11. **Man-in-the-Middle Phishing:** It is harder to detect than many other forms of phishing. In these attacks hackers position themselves between the user and the legitimate website or system. They record the information being entered but continue to pass it on so that users' transactions are not affected. Later they can sell or use the information or credentials collected when the user is not active on the system.

2.1. Growth of Identity Theft

An estimated one million computers are under the control of hackers worldwide. German security analysts at Aachen University reported more than 100 botnets in three months, which ranged in size from a few hundred compromised computers to 50,000 machines (Holz, 2005). The effects caused by phishing on business and customers are far reaching and include substantial financial loss, brand reputation damage, lost customer data files, possible legal implications, significant decrease in employee productivity, improper IT resource utilization, and other administrators impacts. Besides direct financial loss, erosion of public trust in the Internet is a direct impact of fishing on electronic trading. Over the past several years, law enforcing officials have successfully apprehended, prosecuted, and convicted phishers. However, apprehending these criminals is becoming increasingly difficult as they become more professional and sophisticated in their operations. Organizations such as the Anti-Phishing Working Group (APWG), the Federal Trade Commission, Digital Phishnet, Korean Internet Security Center, and others have initiated collaborative enforcement programs to combat phishing and identity theft. These industry groups - many of which are global and pan-industrial in scope - focus on numerous areas, including identifying phishing Web sites, sharing best practice information, aiding criminal law enforcement, and assisting in apprehending and prosecuting those responsible for phishing and identity theft crimes. Eight of the top 10 U.S. banks belong to the APWG; its network of global research partners includes some of the world's top e - commerce associations and watchdogs.

According to Korea Phishing Activity Trends Report, published by Korean Internet Security Center (KrCERT/CC-2006), in the year 2006 the total number of phishing sites reported is 1,266, and the average number per month is 105.5. Compared with the average number of phishing sites in 2005, it can be inferred that the recent average number of phishing sites is little bit increased, and that the hacking attempts with the financial objectives are increasing. The second half of year 2006 has many cases so-called "ROCK Phish", in which one IP system hosts many different domain names. This means the number of targeted financial institutions is far more than the number of IP of the phishing hosts. As per the same report most of the phishing attacks used port 80. Further, the most hijacked brands reported are online marketplace company (e-commerce) and online payment gateway company (financial service) in November 2006. These two brands take 46% of all phishing. The report also indicated the most targeted industry sector for phishing attacks is financial service with e - commerce remaining the second (Figure 1).

2.2. Existing Methods for Preventing Identity Theft

Researchers propose user-based mechanisms to authenticate the server. Automated Challenge Response Method (Bin, 2010) is one such authentication mechanisms, includes challenge generation module from server which in turn interacts with Challenge-Response interface in client and request for response from user. Challenge-Response module in turn will call the get response application which is installed in the client machine. Once the challenge-response is validated user credentials are demanded from client and it is validated by server to proceed the transaction. Automated Challenge-Response Method ensures two way authentication and simplicity. The proposed method also prevents man-in-the middle attacks since the response is obtained from the executable which is called by the browser and third man interruption

Figure 1. Countries to which Hijacked brands belongSource: K orean Phishing Activity Report

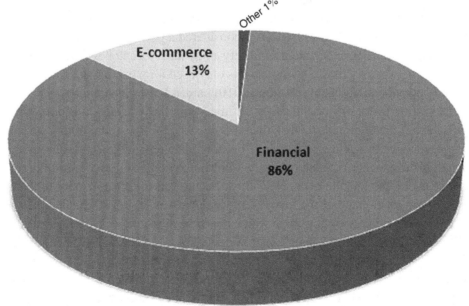

is impossible. Here instead of getting response from get-response executable it is better to update the get-response executable automatically from bank server when the responses are about to nullify.

Now there are DNS-based anti-phishing approach (Nourian, 2009), technique which mainly includes blacklists, heuristic detection, the page similarity assessment. But they do have some shortcomings.

Blacklist is a DNS based anti-phishing approach technique now most commonly used by the browser. Anti-Phishing Work Group, Google and other organizations have provided an open blacklist query interface. Internet Explorer7, Netscape Browser8. 1, Google Safe Browsing (a feature of the Google Toolbar for Firefox) are important browsers which use blacklists to protect users when they are navigating through phishing sites. Because every URL in the blacklist has been verified by the administrator, the false alarm probability is very low. However, there are a lot of technical disadvantages. Firstly, the phishing websites we found is a very small proportion, so the failed alarm probability is very high. Secondly, generally to say, the life cycle of a phishing website is only a few days. A website might be shut down before we found and verified it is a phishing website.

Heuristic-based anti-phishing technique is to estimate whether a page has some phishing heuristics characteristics. For example, some heuristics characteristics used by the Spoof Guard (Stamm, 2007) toolbar include checking the host name, checking the URL for common spoofing techniques, and checking against previously seen images. If you only use the Heuristic-based technique, the accuracy is not enough. Besides, phishers can use some strategies to avoid such detection rules. The user may be deceived by the phishing website because the phishing website imitates a legitimate website. Its pages are often similar with the legitimate sites. Therefore, some researchers proposed a similarity assessment method to detect phishing sites. For example, CANTINA (Anthony, 2008) is a content similarity based approach to detect phishing websites. First, it calculates the suspicious page's lexical signature using TF-IDF and then feed this lexical signature to a search engine. According to the suspicious page's sort order in the search results we can determine whether it is a phishing site. Wenyin, L proposed a page visual similarity assessment method to detect phishing websites (Wenyin, 2006). If a web page is similar to a financial organization's page, but it is not the organization's web page itself, it is considered a phishing site's page. JungMin & Lee (2007) proposed the URL similarity assessment method, if an URL is similar to a bank's URL, but it is not the bank's URL, it is considered a phishing website's URL. There is low assess accuracy rate for the URL and content similarity assessment techniques. The speed of calculating the visual similarity between pages is too slow, so it is only used for phishing-spam detection generally.

A three factor authentication scheme (Nirmal, 2010) named Phish-Secure focuses to counter attack phishing. Here as a first factor of authentication, an image similarity detection is done which helps in finding out which page the user tends to visit, then it is checked for Phishing.For this purpose a system captures the image of a webpage in a particular resolution in the required format. This image is termed as Visual image. If the attacker is going to create a Phishing site he is going to use the replica of the original webpage in order to fool the users. Now Phish-Secure gets the Visual image of the visited page and collects the mean RGB value of the image. This is termed as V_RGB. The database with Phish-Secure uses consists of details about the page which has to be authenticated. The actual mean RGB of various WebPages is stored in the database which is denoted as A_RGB. Phish-Secure will utilize this information and make a comparison to find out the similarity between the visited page and the page in the database. The similarity is obtained in means of percentage, if the percentage of similarity (PS) is greater than 99% then Phish-Secure concludes which website the user is tending to visit. This is carried out by taking the corresponding URL in the database and checking is done in order to find whether the site is Phishing or not.

As a second factor of authentication Phish-Secure grabs the destination IP in Layer 3 which gives information about to which IP address the user is getting connected, this is referred as V_IP. If an attacker's web server IP address has already been found guilty the particular IP is blacklisted. Phish-Secure check this Blacklist with the V_IP and will warn the user. On the other hand if the V_IP is not found in Blacklist, further verification is done in the following step.

Here in this step Phish-Secure grabs the actual list of IP address of the provider which he tends to connect. This is because any provider may have multiple servers for the purpose of load balancing and the user may be connected to his location accordingly. In order to avoid any confusion Phish-Secure gets the list of IP address which is referred to as actual IP and is checked with the V_IP (i.e.) the IP address to which the user is getting connected. If these two IP address are same Phish-Secure identifies the particular site as genuine and returns a message as authenticated. On the other hand if there is a mismatch in the above verification Phish-Secure identifies the site as Phishing and warns the user. In addition to this the V_IP is added to the black list so that in future if the attacker uses the same web server and tries to attack, Phish-Secure detects the site as Phishing in the second step.

These popular technologies have several drawbacks:

1. Blacklist-based technique with low false alarm probability, but it cannot detect the websites that are not in the blacklist database. Because the life cycle of phishing websites is too short and the establishment of blacklist has a long lag time, the accuracy of blacklist is not too high.
2. Heuristic-based anti-phishing technique, with a high probability of false and failed alarm, and it is easy for the attacker to use technical means to avoid the heuristic characteristics detection.
3. Similarity assessment based technique is time-consuming. It needs too long time to calculate a pair of pages, so using the method to detect phishing websites on the client terminal is not suitable. And there is low accuracy rate for this method depends on many factors, such as the text, images, and similarity measurement technique. However, this technique (in particular, image similarity identification technique) is not perfect enough yet.

An offline phishing detection system named LARX, acronym for Large-scale Anti-phishing by Retrospective data-eXploration (Tianyang, 2011) to counter phishing attacks has been proposed. First, it uses traffic archiving in a vantage point to collect network trace data. Secondly, LARX leverage cloud computing technology to analyze the experimental data in a way similar to the "divide and conquer" scheme. It used two existing cloud platforms, Amazon Web Services and Eucalyptus. A physical server is also used for comparison. All of LARX's phishing filtering operations are based on a cloud computing platform and work in parallel. Finally, as an offline solution, LARX can be effectively scaled up to analyze a large volume of network trace data for phishing attack detection.

To meet the need that user effectively manage more and more accounts and passwords, OpenID was born. OpenID is a convenient, simple, user-centric ID management system. OpenID provides single sign-on (SSO) service, that is, we login only once and can enjoy the service of multiple sites. But OpenID is vulnerable to phishing attacks. To avoid phishing attacks, many methods have been proposed, but there is no satisfactory method. "New Anti-phishing Method with Two Types of Passwords in OpenID System" (Qingxiang, 2011), proposes a model of two types of passwords for anti-phishing which is convenient and safe for OpenID users. An OpenID account has a fixed password and several temporary passwords. The fixed password can only be used in bound PCs, that is, we must bind the fixed password on several known PC. Users can login on any PC with a temporary password. However, we need to access the mailbox or mobile phone for getting the temporary password, and we only use it in a period of time. Through analysis, this method can effectively avoid phishing.

Detecting and identifying any phishing website in real-time, particularly for e-banking, is really a complex and dynamic problem involving many factors and criteria. Because of the subjective considerations and the ambiguities involved in the detection, Fuzzy Data Mining (DM) Techniques can be an effective tool in assessing and identifying phishing websites for e-banking.

Since it offers a more natural way of dealing with quality factors rather than exact values. "Modeling Intelligent Phishing Detection System for e-Banking using Fuzzy Data Mining (Maher, 2009), a novel approach to overcome the 'fuzziness' in the e-banking phishing website assessment propose an intelligent resilient and effective model for detecting e-banking phishing websites. The proposed model is based on Fuzzy logic (FL) combined with Data Mining algorithms to characterize the e-banking phishing website factors and to investigate its techniques by classifying there phishing types and defining six e-banking phishing website attack criteria's with a layer structure. The proposed e-banking phishing website model showed the significant importance of the phishing website two criteria's (URL & Domain Identity) and (Security & Encryption) in the final phishing detection rate result, taking into consideration its characteristic association and relationship with each other as showed from the fuzzy data mining classification and association rule algorithms.

Haijun et al. (2011) proposed a textual and visual content based anti-phishing mechanism using Bayesian approach. This framework synthesizes multiple cues, i.e., textual content and visual content, from the given web page and automatically reports a phishing web page by using a text classifier, an image classifier, and a data fusion process of the classifiers. A Bayesian model is proposed to estimate the threshold, which is required in classifiers to determine the class of web page. It also develop a Bayesian approach to integrate the classification results from the textual and visual contents. The main contributions of this paper are threefold. First, it propose a text classifier using the naive Bayes rule for phishing detection. Second, it propose a Bayesian approach to estimate the threshold for either the text classifier or the image classifier such that classifiers enable to label a given web page as "phishing" or "normal." Third, a novel Bayesian approach to fuse the classification results from the text classifier and the image classifier is proposed.

There are various mutual authentication methods using cell phones such as browsing using phones, password generation etc. There are various problems regarding these methods such as hijacking account setup, theft of the trusted device and attacks on the network.

Thus there are various methods present in online manipulations for making the systems safe from these types of attacks. But we can see that they have its own problems which make it again unsafe. So a system based on visual cryptography and steganography which can perform as a new method can overcome these problems effectively.

3. VISUAL CRYPTOGRAPHY

One of the best known techniques to protect data is cryptography. It is the art of sending and receiving encrypted messages that can be decrypted only by the sender or the receiver. Encryption and decryption are accomplished by using mathematical algorithms in such a way that no one but the intended recipient can decrypt and read the message. Naor & Shamir (1994) introduced the visual cryptography scheme

(VCS) as a simple and secure way to allow the secret sharing of images without any cryptographic computations.

Visual cryptography schemes were independently introduced by Shamir and Blakley, and their original motivation was to safeguard cryptographic keys from loss. These schemes also have been widely employed in the construction of several types of cryptographic protocols and consequently, they have many applications in different areas such as access control, opening a bank vault, opening a safety deposit box, or even launching of missiles. A segment-based visual cryptography suggested by Borchert (2007) can be used only to encrypt the messages containing symbols, especially numbers like bank account number, amount etc. The VCS proposed by Yan et al. (2004)] can be applied only for printed text or image.

A recursive VC method proposed by Monoth et al., (2011) is computationally complex as the encoded shares are further encoded into number of sub-shares recursively. Most of the previous research work on VC focused on improving two parameters: pixel expansion and contrast. In these cases all participants who hold shares are assumed to be honest, that is, they will not present false or fake shares during the phase of recovering the secret image. Thus, the image shown on the stacking of shares is considered as the real secrete image. But, this may not be true always. So cheating prevention methodologies are introduced by Horng et al. (2006) and Hu et al. (2007). But, it is observed in all these methodologies, there is no facility of authentication testing.

VCS is a cryptographic technique that allows for the encryption of visual information such that decryption can be performed using the human visual system. We can achieve this by one of the following access structure schemes:

1. **(2, 2)-Threshold VCS scheme:** This is a simplest threshold scheme that takes a secret message and encrypts it in two different shares that reveal the secret image when they are overlaid.
2. **(n, n)-Threshold VCS scheme:** This scheme encrypts the secret image to n shares such that when all n of the shares are combined will the secret image be revealed.
3. **(k, n) Threshold VCS scheme:** This scheme encrypts the secret image to n shares such that when any group of at least k shares are overlaid the secret image will be revealed.

In the case of (2, 2) VCS, each pixel P in the original image is encrypted into two sub pixels called shares. Figure. 1 denotes the shares of a white pixel and a black pixel. Note that the choice of shares for a white and black pixel is randomly determined (there are two choices available for each pixel). Neither share provides any clue about the original pixel since different pixels in the secret image will be encrypted using independent random choices. When the two shares are superimposed, the value of the original pixel P can be determined. If P is a black pixel, we get two black sub pixels; if it is a white pixel, we get one black sub pixel and one white sub pixel.

4. STEGANOGRAPHY

STEGANOGRAPHY is an ancient technology that has applications even in today's modern society. It is derived from Greek words *"stegos"* meaning cover and *"graphia"* meaning writing. Steganography conceptually implies that the message to be transmitted is not visible to the normal eye. It is an art of hiding information inside information. The main objective of Steganography is mainly concerned with

Figure 2. Illustration of a 2-out-of-2 VCS scheme with 2 sub pixel construction.

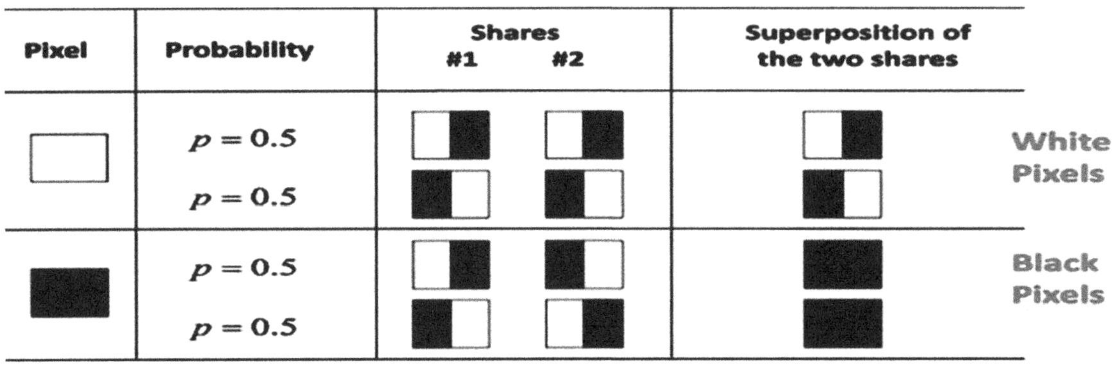

Pixel	Probability	Shares #1 #2	Superposition of the two shares	
	$p = 0.5$			White Pixels
	$p = 0.5$			
	$p = 0.5$			Black Pixels
	$p = 0.5$			

the protection of contents of the hidden information. Some historical and modern-day examples of steganography are as follows:

- Tattoo a message on a shaved head.
- Invisible Ink: milk, lemon juice, vinegar.
- Microdot: a photograph the size of a printed period having the clarity of a type-written page.
- Null Ciphers: take the nth letter of each word in a passage in a book, magazine, etc.

4.1. Steganographic Methods

The following formula provides a very generic description of the pieces of the Steganographic process:

cover_medium + hidden_data + stego_key = stego_medium

In this context, the *cover_medium* is the file in which we will hide the *hidden_data*, which may also be encrypted using the *stego_key*. The resultant file is the *stego_medium* (which will, of course be the same type of file as the cover_medium). The cover_medium (and, thus, the stego_medium) are typically image or audio files. In this paper, we will focus on image files and will, therefore, refer to the cover_image and stego_image.

Before discussing how information is hidden in an image file, it is worth a fast review of how images are stored in the first place. An image file is merely a binary file containing a binary representation of the color or light intensity of each picture element (pixel) comprising the image.

The size of an image file, then, is directly related to the number of pixels and the granularity of the color definition. A typical 640x480 pixel image using a palette of 256 colours would require a file about 307 KB in size (640 • 480 bytes), whereas a 1024x768 pixel high-resolution 24-bit color image would result in a 2.36 MB file (1024 • 768 • 3 bytes).

To avoid sending files of this enormous size, a number of compression schemes have been developed over time, notably Bitmap (BMP), Graphic Interchange Format (GIF), and Joint Photographic Experts Group (JPEG) file types. Not all are equally suited to steganography, however.

GIF and 8-bit BMP files employ what is known as lossless compression, a scheme that allows the software to exactly reconstruct the original image. JPEG, on the other hand, uses lossy compression, which means that the expanded image is very nearly the same as the original but not an exact duplicate. While both methods allow computers to save storage space, lossless compression is much better suited to applications where the integrity of the original information must be maintained, such as steganography. While JPEG can be used for stego applications, it is more common to embed data in GIF or BMP files.

The simplest approach to hiding data within an image file is called least significant bit (LSB) insertion. In this method, we can take the binary representation of the hidden_data and overwrite the LSB of each byte within the cover_image. If we are using 24-bit color, the amount of change will be minimal and indiscernible to the human eye. As an example, suppose that we have three adjacent pixels (nine bytes) with the following RGB encoding:

```
10010101 00001101 11001001
10010110 00001111 11001010
10011111 00010000 11001011
```

Now suppose we want to "hide" the following 9 bits of data (the hidden data is usually compressed prior to being hidden): 101101101. If we overlay these 9 bits over the LSB of the 9 bytes above, we get the following (where bits in bold have been changed):

```
10010101 0000110**0** 11001001
1001011**1** 0000111**0** 1100101**1**
10011111 00010000 11001011
```

Note that we have successfully hidden 9 bits but at a cost of only changing 4, or roughly 50%, of the LSBs.

This description is meant only as a high-level overview. Similar methods can be applied to 8-bit color but the changes, as we might imagine, are more dramatic. Gray-scale images, too, are very useful for Steganographic purposes. One potential problem with any of these methods is that they can be found by an adversary who is looking. In addition, there are other methods besides LSB insertion with which to insert hidden information.

Without going into any detail, it is worth mentioning steganalysis, the art of detecting and breaking steganography. One form of this analysis is to examine the color palette of a graphical image. In most images, there will be a unique binary encoding of each individual color. If the image contains hidden data, however, many colours in the palette will have duplicate binary encodings since, for all practical purposes, we can't count the LSB. If the analysis of the colour palette of a given file yields many duplicates, we might safely conclude that the file has hidden information.

5. PROPOSED METHODOLOGY

We introduce a new method which can be used as a safe way against online identity theft during e-commerce transactions. It is an image based authentication using Visual Cryptography (VC) and Steganography is used. The use of visual cryptography is explored to preserve the privacy of image captcha by decomposing the original image captcha into two shares that are stored in separate database servers such that the original image captcha can be revealed only when both are simultaneously available; the individual sheet images do not reveal the identity of the original image captcha. Once the original image captcha is revealed to the user it can be used as the password. Steganographic techniques are also used to provide better security to the shares, where we hide the share within a cover image to prevent the suspicion, when the share is transmitted through network.

Our proposed methodology has divided the e-commerce transaction into two phases which are described as follows:

5.1. Registration Phase

The following steps are carried out during Registration Phase:

1. A key String and a cover image along with the User name will be asked from the user. The key string can be a combination of alphabets and numbers to provide more secure Environment. These information will be sent to the server.
2. The Server will concatenate the randomly generated string along with the original key String. An image Captcha will be generated from it.
3. Using Visual Cryptographic Technique divide the Image Captcha into two shares (i.e. Share -1 and Share-2).
4. One (i.e. Share-2) will be kept at the server side.
5. Another one (i.e. Share-1) Share -1 and the original captcha image will be put inside a Cover Image using Steganography techniques and sent to the User. User will be having the COVER IMAGE+ SHARE-1 + CAPTCHA IMAGE Server will be having the COVER IMAGE+ SHARE-2 + CAPTCHA IMAGE

The process is depicted in Figure 3.

Figure 3. Flow of data during registration phase

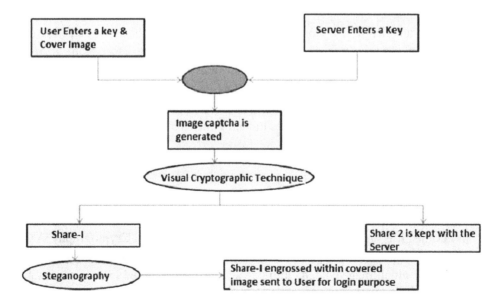

5.2 Login Phase

The following steps are carried out during Log in phase:

1. User send the username and his share (i.e.) concealed within the cover image
2. Server receives it and then extracts the share from the cover image.
3. Server's share (Share-2) and User's share (Share-1) stacked Together to get the original captcha. The captcha is again concealed inside the covered image and sent to the user.
4. User Extract the Captcha from the Cover image and if it matches with original captcha provided earlier by the system then the user enter his password along with the captcha key to log on into the system.
5. Otherwise log on process is aborted.

    The process is depicted in Figure 4.

6. IMPLEMENTATION AND ANALYSIS

The proposed methodology is implemented in Java. The following section describes briefly about the algorithm used for this purpose:

In the registration phase the most important part is the creation of shares from the image captcha where one share is kept with the user and other share can be kept with the server. The steganographic algorithm steps (see Box 1) are used for Image Captcha Generation from key string.

Figure 4. Flow of data during Log in phase

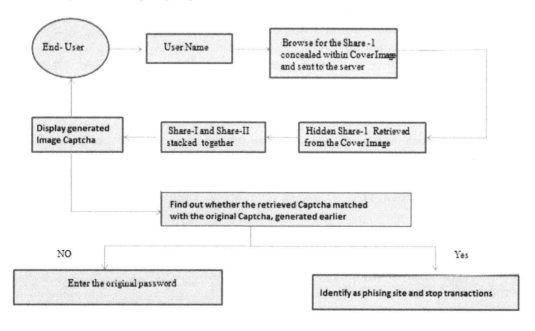

Box 1. Steganographic algorithm

```
The text to be Hidden and the Cover Image is selected.
For each pixel of the Cover Image.
    If all the characters of the Hidden Text are not stego then
        Take a character from the Hidden Text.
        Find the ASCII value of the Character (ASCII value lies between 0 -
255).
        Convert this value from Decimal to Binary (8-bit).
        Break this 8-bit into three parts: First 3 MSB bits, Next 3 bits, Last 2
LSB bits.
        Find the Red, Green and Blue Components values of the pixel.
        Convert the values of Red, Green and Blue Components from Decimal to Bi-
nary.
        For Red Component
            Break this 8-bit into two parts: First 5 MSB bits, Last 3 LSB bits.
            Replace the 2nd part (Last 3 LSB bits) with the 1st part (First 3 MSB
bits) of binary representation of the ASCII value of the character of the Hid-
den Text.
            Convert the value of this new 8-bit from Binary to Decimal, which is
the value of the resultant Red Component.
        For Green Component
            Break this 8-bit into two parts: First 5 MSB bits, Last 3 LSB bits.
            Replace the 2nd part (Last 3 LSB bits) with the 2nd part (Next 3 bits)
of binary representation of the ASCII value of the character of the Hidden
Text.
            Convert the value of this new 8-bit from Binary to Decimal, which is
the value of the resultant Green Component.
        For Blue Component
            Break this 8-bit into two parts: First 6 MSB bits, Last 2 LSB bits.
            Replace the 2nd part (Last 2 LSB bits) with the 3rd part (Last 2 LSB
bits) of binary representation of the ASCII value of the character of the Hid-
den Text.
            Convert the value of this new 8-bit from Binary to Decimal, which is
the value of the resultant Blue Component.
            Compute the new pixel from the newly computed resultant Red, Green
and Blue Component. This is a pixel of the Stego Image.
        Else
        Copy the pixel from the Cover Image to Stego Image.
        End of If
End of For.
End.
```

Another important steps during Registration and Login phase is keeping the share within a cover image. The algorithmic steps shown in Box 2 are used to do the same.

For dividing the captcha image into shares the visual cryptographic encryption and decryption technique are used, which are described as follows:

Box 2.

```
The Image to be Hidden and Cover Image is selected.
For each pixel of the Hidden Image.
        Take two consecutive pixels (in a row/column) from the Cover Image.
        Find the Red, Green and Blue Component values for all these three pixels.
        Convert the values of Red, Green and Blue Components of all three pixels
from Decimal to Binary (8-bit).
        For all the Component (Red, Green and Blue) of all these three pixels,
break the 8-bit into two parts: First 4 MSB bits, Last 4 LSB bits.
        For Red Component of the Hidden Image
                Replace the 2ⁿᵈ part (Last 4 LSB bits) of 1ˢᵗ pixel of the Cover
Image with the 1ˢᵗ part (First 4 MSB bits) of the pixel of the Hidden Image.
                Replace the 2ⁿᵈ part (Last 4 LSB bits) of 2ⁿᵈ pixel of the Cover
Image with the 2ⁿᵈ part (Last 4 LSB bits) of the pixel of the Hidden Image.
                Convert the two new 8-bit values from Binary to Decimal, which
are the values of the Red Component of the 1ˢᵗ and 2ⁿᵈ pixel of the Stego Image.
        For Green Component of the Hidden Image
                Replace the 2ⁿᵈ part (Last 4 LSB bits) of 1ˢᵗ pixel of the Cover
Image with the 1ˢᵗ part (First 4 MSB bits) of the pixel of the Hidden Image.
                Replace the 2ⁿᵈ part (Last 4 LSB bits) of 2ⁿᵈ pixel of the Cover
Image with the 2ⁿᵈ part (Last 4 LSB bits) of the pixel of the Hidden Image.
                Convert the two new 8-bit values from Binary to Decimal, which
are the values of the Green Component of the 1ˢᵗ and 2ⁿᵈ pixel of the Stego Im-
age.
        For Blue Component of the Hidden Image
                Replace the 2ⁿᵈ part (Last 4 LSB bits) of 1ˢᵗ pixel of the Cover
Image with the 1ˢᵗ part (First 4 MSB bits) of the pixel of the Hidden Image.
                Replace the 2ⁿᵈ part (Last 4 LSB bits) of 2ⁿᵈ pixel of the Cover
Image with the 2ⁿᵈ part (Last 4 LSB bits) of the pixel of the Hidden Image.
                Convert the two new 8-bit values from Binary to Decimal, which
are the values of the Blue Component of the 1ˢᵗ and 2ⁿᵈ pixel of the Stego Im-
age.
        Compute the two pixels of the Stego Image from the newly computed Red,
Green and Blue Components.
        Place these two pixels in the same consecutive way in which two pixels
were taken from the Cover Image.
End of For.
End
```

Steps for Encryption:

1. First, we generate all combinations of n - bits 0's and 1's.
2. Then we select only those combination in which there are only k-1 0's.
3. A matrix is form, transpose this matrix.
4. Each row gives the pattern in which a share is to be formed.

Example: Suppose n=5 and k=3, i.e., an image is to be broken into 5 shares, of which, stacking any 3 of them can recover the image, but any 2 of them gain no information about the image.

1. First, we generate all combinations of 5 - bits 0's and 1's.
   00000, 00001, 00010, 00011, 00100, 00101, 00110, 00111, 01000, 01001, 01010, 01011, 01100, 01101, 01110, 01111, 10000, 10001, 10010, 10011, 10100, 10101, 10110, 10111, 11000, 11001, 11010, 11011, 11100, 11101, 11110, 11111.
2. Select only those combination in which there are only 2 (3-1) 0's.
   00111, 01011, 01101, 01110, 10011, 10101, 10110, 11001, 11010, 11100.
3. A matrix is formed, transpose this matrix.
   00111
   01011
   01101
   01110
   10011
   10101
   10110
   11001
   11010
   11100
   The transpose of the matrix:
   0000111111
   0111000111
   1011011001
   1101101010
   1110110100
4. Each row gives the pattern in which a share is to be formed.
5. Here, 0's denote the corresponding pixels, from the image not to be included in that share, and 1's denote the corresponding pixels to be included in that share.

The process for creating shares are shown in Figure 5.

Steps for Decryption: Performing OR operation on any k rows of the matrix, will result in all bits as 1's, but performing OR operation on less than k rows, won't give the all bits as 1's i.e., full information.

Example: In our example we took n=5 and k=3, since we have generated the rows of the matrix for the shares. Let's perform OR operation on any three rows (see Figure 6)

All bits '1', i.e., all the pixels are retrieved. Hence image is retrieved losslessly.

Figure 5. Process for Creating Shares

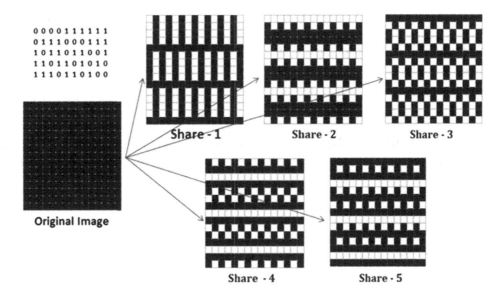

Figure 6. Steps for Decryption

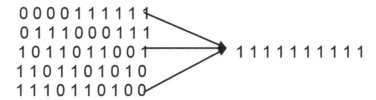

7. CONCLUSION

Our proposed model is an effective tool for preventing the online identity theft, which is very common during e-commerce transaction. Digital Certificate is a similar tool which also provides the authenticity for the parties involved during e-commerce transaction that can be also used for preventing the identity theft. But it is very costly for procuring by the individuals as third party is involved. But using our methodology, as no third party is involved cost is very less and it also provides three layers of security. 1st layer verifies whether the website is a genuine/secure website or a phishing website. If the website is a phishing website (website that is a fake one just similar to secure website but not the secure website), then in that situation, the phishing website can't display the image captcha for that specific user (who wants to log in into the website) due to the fact that the image captcha is generated by the stacking of two shares, one with the user and the other with the actual database of the website. Second layer cross validates image captcha corresponding to the user. The image captcha is readable by human users alone and not by machine users. Only human users accessing the website can read the image captcha and ensure that the site as well as the user is permitted one or not. So, using image captcha technique, no machine based user can crack the password or other confidential information of the users. As a third layer of security it prevents intruders' attacks on the user's account. This method provides additional security in terms of not letting the intruder log in into the account even when the user knows the username of a particular user.

REFERENCES

Anthony, Y. F., & Wenyin, L. (2008). Detecting phishing web pages with visual similarity assessment based on earth mover's distance (EMD). *IEEE Transactions on Dependable and Secure Computing*, *3*(4), 301–311.

Banday, M. T., & Qadri, J. A. (2007). Phishing -A growing threat to e-commerce. *Business Review (Federal Reserve Bank of Philadelphia)*, *12*(2), 76–83.

Bin, S., & Qiaoyan, W. (2010). A DNS based anti-phishing approach. In *Proceedings of IEEE- Second International Conference on Networks Security, Wireless Communications and Trusted Computing* (pp. 210-225). IEEE.

Borchert, B. (2007). *Segment based visual cryptography*. WSI Press.

Haijun, Z., Gang, L., Tommy, W., & Chow, S. (2011). Textual and visual content-based anti-phishing: A Bayesian approach. *IEEE Transactions on Neural Networks*, *22*(10), 1532–1546.

Holz, T. (2005). *On the economics of botnets*. Retrieved March 15, 2013, from http://honeyblog.org/archives/54-On-the-Economi cs-of-Botnets-Part-2.html

Horng, G. B., Chen, T. G., & Tsai, D. S. (2006). Cheating in visual cryptography, designs, codes. *Cryptography*, *38*(2), 219–236. doi:10.1007/s10623-005-6342-0

Hu, C. M., & Tzeng, W. G. (2007). Cheating prevention in visual cryptography. *IEEE Transactions on Image Processing*, *16*(1), 36–45. doi:10.1109/TIP.2006.884916 PMID:17283763

JungMin., K., & Lee, K.(2007). Advanced white list approach for preventing access to phishing sites. In *Proceedings of International Conference on Convergence Information Technology, ICCIT 2007* (pp. 491-496). Bangladesh: Academic Press.

Maher, A., Hossain, M. A., & Dahal, K. (2009). Modelling intelligent phishing detection system for e-banking using fuzzy data mining. In *Proceedings of IEEE Conference on CyberWorlds* (pp. 47-52). Academic Press.

Monoth, T., & Babu, A. P. (2011). Recursive visual cryptography using random basis column pixel expansion, In *Proceedings of IEEE International Conference on Information Technology* (pp. 41-47). IEEE.

Naor, M., & Shamir, A. (1994). Visual cryptography. In *Proc. EUROCRYPT*. Academic Press.

Nirmal, K., Ewards, S. E. V., & Geetha, K. (2010). Maximizing online security by providing a 3 factor authentication system to counter-attack 'Phishing'. In *Proceedings of IEEE International Conference on Emerging Trends in Robotics and Communication Technologies* (pp. 365-377). London: IEEE.

Nourian, A., Ishtiaq, S., & Maheswaran, M. (2009). CASTLE: A social framework for collaborative antiphishing databases. In *Proceedings of IEEE 5th International Conference on Collaborative Computing: Networking, Applications and Worksharing* (pp. 237-248). IEEE.

Qingxiang, F., Kuo-Kun, T., & Jeng-Shyang, P. (2011). New antiphishing method with two types of passwords in OpenID system. In *Proceedings of IEEE Fifth International Conference on Genetic and Evolutionary Computing* (pp. 39-45). IEEE.

Stamm, S., & Zulfikar, R. (2007). Drive-by pharming. In *Proceeding 9th International Conference on Information and Communications Security (ICICS)* (pp. 495-506). New York: Academic Press.

Tianyang, L., Fuye, H., Shuai, D., & Zhen, C. (2011). LARX: Large-scale anti-phishing by etrospective data-exploring based on a cloud computing platform. In *Proceedings of IEEE 20th International Conference on Computer Communications and Networks* (pp. 35-67). Berlin: IEEE.

Vasistha, S. D. (2005). E-commerce in Indian perspective. *Business Review (Federal Reserve Bank of Philadelphia)*, *11*(7), 69–82.

Wenyin, L., Xiaotie, D., & Guanglin, H. (2006). An antiphishing strategy based on visual similarity assessment. *IEEE Internet Computing*, *10*(2), 58–65. doi:10.1109/MIC.2006.23

Yan, W.-Q., Jin, D., & Kanakanahalli, M. S. (2004). Visual cryptography for print and scan applications. *IEEE Transactions on Image Processing*, *32*(10), 572–575.

ADDITIONAL READING

Blakley, G. R. (1970). Safeguarding Cryptographic Keys, Proceedings of *AFIPS Conference*, (310-317), Germany.

Blundo, C., & De Santis, A. (1999). On the contrast in Visual Cryptography Schemes. *International Journal of Cryptography and Network Security*, *12*(5), 261–289.

Borchert, B. (2007). *Segment Based Visual Cryptography, PA*. Germany: WSI Press.

Eisen, P. A., & Stinson, D. R. (2002). Threshold Visual Cryptography with specified Whiteness Levels of Reconstructed Pixels. *Journal of Cryptography*, *25*(1), 15–61.

Kim, H. J., Sachnev, V., Choi, S. J., & Xiang, S. (2007). An Innocuous Visual Cryptography Scheme, in Proceedings of *IEEE-8th International Workshop on Image Analysis for Multimedia Interactive Services*, 123-132, France.

Menezes, A., Van Oorschot, P., & Vanstone, S. (1997). *Handbook of Applied Cryptography*. Boca Raton, FL: CRC Press.

Monoth, T., & Babu, A. P. (2007). Recursive Visual Cryptography Using Random Basis Column Pixel Expansion, in Proceedings of *IEEE International Conference on Information Technology*, pp. 41-43, India.

Ollmann, G. (2011). *The Phishing Guide Understanding & Preventing Phishing Attacks*. PA: NGS Software Insight Security Research.

Shamir, A. (1979). How to Share a Secret. *Communications of the ACM*, *22*(4), 612–613. doi:10.1145/359168.359176

Verheul, E. R., & Van Tilborg, H. C. A. (1997). Constructions and Properties of k out of n Visual Secret Sharing Schemes. *Designs, Codes and Cryptography*, *11*(2), 179–196.

Yan, W.-Q., Jin, D., & Kanakanahalli, M. S. (2004). Visual Cryptography for Print and Scan Applications. *IEEE Transactions on Network Security*, *14*(2), 572–575.

KEY TERMS AND DEFINITIONS

Captcha: It is an acronym for "Completely Automated Public Turing test to tell Computers and Humans Apart). It is a type of challenge-response test used in computing to determine whether or not the user is human.

E-Commerce: Electronic commerce or e-commerce refers to a wide range of online business activities for products and services. It also pertains to "any form of business transaction in which the parties interact electronically rather than by physical exchanges or direct physical contact.

Least Significant Bit (LSB): In the case of Big-endian, LSB is usually the farthest to the right most (Last) bits. In the case of little endian it follows the reverse sequence.

Phishing: Trying to obtain financial or other confidential information from the internet users by typically sending an e-mail that looks as if it is from a legitimate organization, usually a financial institution, but contains a link to fake website that replicates the real one.

Steganography: Hiding a secret message within a digital medium (i.e. text/audio/video) in such a way that other than the authentic users nobody can identify the presence of secret message.

Visual Cryptography: Visual Cryptography is a special encryption technique to hide information in images in such way that it can be decrypted by the human vision if the correct key image is used.

Chapter 11
Analysis of Various Security Issues and Challenges in Cloud Computing Environment:
A Survey

Zhaolong Gou
Yamaguchi University, Japan

Shingo Yamaguchi
Yamaguchi University, Japan

B. B. Gupta
National Institute of Technology Kurukshetra, India

ABSTRACT

Cloud computing is a system, where the resources of a data center are shared using virtualization technology, such that it provides elastic, on demand and instant services to its customers and charges them based on the resources they use. In this chapter, we will discuss recent developments in cloud computing, various security issues and challenges associated with Cloud computing environment, various existing solutions provided for dealing with these security threats and will provide a comparative analysis these approaches. This will provide better understanding of the various security problems associated with the cloud, current solution space, and future research scope to deal with such attacks in better way.

1. INTRODUCTION

Along with the increase of various internet-related services, the concept of cloud computing (Mather, 2009) is becoming more well-known. Cloud computing is a terminology that involves resource through the internet to provide dynamic and scalable system virtualization. Cloud computing involves deploying groups of remote servers and software networks, and allows centralized data storage and online access to computer services or resources. The definition of cloud computing is mainly based on five

DOI: 10.4018/978-1-5225-0808-3.ch011

characteristics: multi-tenancy (shared resources), massive scalability, elasticity, pay as you go, and self-provisioning of resources. Cloud computing is a system, where the shared resource is used by the data center virtualization technology (Hassan, 2011), such that it provides elastic, on demand and instant services to its customers and charges them based on the resources they use.

Cloud computing applications are already present on the market, trying to help companies and individuals to stretch resources and work smarter by moving everything to the cloud. Nowadays the business operations (Marston, 2011) are more and more dependent on cloud computing (Mather, 2009), the situations are more focused on business growth and product enhancements, rather than worrying about storage or maintaining 24-hour server to ensure maximum throughput.

For example the first approaches belongs to the Amazon and it is called AWS (Amazon Web Services), launched in 2002. (Surcel, 2008) AWS is a collection of remote services intended for client applications or web sites. According to the Amazon news, there are almost 500,000 developers that are subscribed to the AWS.

However, there are various security issues and challenges being related to cloud security. There are many security issues and challenges which we are faced in, so we should analyses for cloud computing situations.

Therefore, in this chapter, we will discuss recent developments in cloud computing, various security issues and challenges associated with Cloud computing environment, various existing solutions provided for dealing with these security threats and will provide a comparative analysis these approaches. This will provide better understanding of the various security problems associated with the cloud, current solution space, and future research scope to deal with such attacks in better way.

In Sect.2 we will discuss about the background of Cloud computing, including its history and models. In Sect.3 we discuss mainly about issues in cloud computing, and Sect.4 we reveal challenges in Cloud computing. Finally we discuss current situations about Cloud computing.

2. PRELIMINARY

2.1 History

Firstly, the word "Cloud Computing" is new, but this idea can go back from several decades. It was pioneered by John McCarthy, a well-known computer scientist who initiated timesharing in late 1957 on modified IBM 704 and IBM 7090 computers (Mell, 2011).

In 1983, Sun Microsystems proposed the idea about "The Network is the Computer". In 2006, Amazon released a service named "Elastic Compute Cloud" (EC2), and this year Google CEO Eric Schmidt at SES first proposed the "cloud computing" concept. In 2007, Google and IBM began at the American University campus, including Carnegie Mellon University, MIT, Stanford University, University of California at Berkeley, University of Maryland, and so on, had a plan to promote cloud computing. The program hopes to reduce the cost of distributed computing technology in academic research, and to provide relevant software and hardware equipment and technical support for these universities. In 2008, Yahoo, HP and Intel announced a joint research program, which covers the United States, Germany and Singapore, to improve cloud computing. In July 2010, NASA and Rackspace, AMD, Intel, Dell and other vendors announced they will support "OpenStack" open-source project, and Microsoft said to support OpenStack which integrated with Windows Server 2008 R2 in October 2010; and Ubuntu has already added OpenStack to the 11.04 version. In 2011, Cisco Systems officially joined OpenStack, focus on developing OpenStack network services.

2.2 Models

Cloud computing can be classified as deployment models and service delivery models. Deployment models of the cloud including private, community, public and hybrid cloud, and each model has its own issues. According to the service aspects, cloud computing can be considered to consist of three layers associated with each deployment model (Bhadauria, 2011), namely SaaS, IaaS and PaaS, with specific issues related to each.

2.2.1 Service Delivery Models

We can see there are different kinds of services offered in Cloud computing, and in general it can be considered to consist of three layers. Usually these three different service delivery models are delivered to the end user. The three delivery models are the SaaS, PaaS and IaaS. (Subashini, 2011)These models can provide software, application platform and infrastructure resources, as services to the user. These service models also set a different level of security requirement at the cloud computing environment.

SaaS (Software as a Server), it is a model over the Internet; a software deployment thus a provider licenses application to customers for use as on-demand services. From a technical point of view SaaS is simple to deploy, and don't need to buy any hardware, at the beginning just simply registered is available. Enterprises no longer equipped with IT aspects of expertise and technical personnel, while to get the latest technology to meet the business needs for information management. SaaS can largely relieve pressure on enterprises in human and financial resources, funds to enable it to focus on core business operations effectively. SaaS as a completely separate system enables users in the world, if users are connected to a network, they can access the system.

IaaS (Infrastructure as a Server): Consumers can obtain service from a good computer infrastructure over the Internet, and this method completely changed the developers to deploy their applications. (Subashini, 2011) Instead of spending big own data center or colocation or managed services company, then hire an operator to get it to go, they can go to IaaS providers, virtual servers running in minutes and pay only for the resources they use. With cloud brokers they can easily expand without having to worry about things like scaling and extra security. In conclusion, IaaS and other related services have enabled start-ups and other businesses to focus on their core competencies, without having to worry much about the configuration and management of infrastructure. IaaS completely abstract the hardware underneath and allows users to consume infrastructure as a service, regardless of the complexity of the underlying matter.

PaaS (Platform as a Server): This is the business model of the server platform as a service. (Subashini, 2011)This kind of server provides a set of integrated development environment that developers can use to build their applications without having to know anything about what is happening in the service following clues. The most fundamental difference PaaS services and other services provided are: PaaS provides a foundation platform, rather than some kind of application.

A Cloud services delivery model can referred into three accepted services: SaaS, PaaS and IaaS. The relationship (Mather, 2009) between three delivery models is shown in Figure 1.

Figure 1. Cloud service delivery models

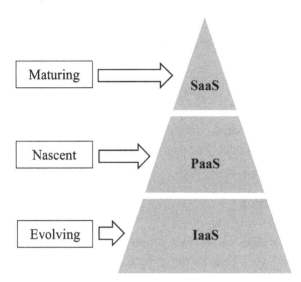

However, most enterprises, especially large enterprises are still reluctant to use SaaS; because of security issues, such as lack of visibility about the way their data is stored and secured. Therefore, to solve enterprise security issue has become the biggest challenge to the adoption of cloud SaaS applications. However, to overcome the data and application security about customer focus, vendors must address these issues. There is a strong concern about insider violation, as well as the availability of applications and systems that may lead to the loss of sensitive data and money loophole. These challenges can be from the use of cloud SaaS applications dissuade businesses.

There also have some problems about IaaS. Security vulnerabilities exist, such as service provider is a shared infrastructure, that some of the components or features for the users of the system in terms of not completely isolated. This will produce a result that, when an attacker to succeed, all the servers to the attacker opened the door, even with a hypervisor, some guest operating system can also gain access to the underlying platform uncontrolled.

2.2.2 Deployment Models

Each service delivery model can be through four ways to deploy depending on requirements of customers: (Bhadauria, 2011)

- **Public Cloud:** The cloud infrastructure available to many customers and by third-party management. For example, several companies provide the infrastructure work at the same time. Users can provide the resources from a network of dynamic remote service providers.
- **Private Cloud:** The cloud infrastructure is only available to specific customers, either by the organization itself or a third-party service provider to manage. This model uses the concept of a virtual machine, and requires a proprietary network.
- **Community Cloud:** The cloud infrastructure is shared by several organizations composed of a variety of factors, and can be managed by them or a third-party service provider.

- **Hybrid Cloud:** The cloud infrastructure is a combination of two or more of the cloud deployment models, linked in a way that data transmission occurs between them will not affect each other.

2.2.3 Relationships

Service delivery models are associated with each deployment models (Khalil, 2014), the relationship between service delivery models and deployment models can be illustrated in Figure 2.

3. BARRIERS, SECURITY ISSUES, AND THREATS

3.1 Barriers

There is a circumstance that many related organizations do not have enough confident towards certain aspects of cloud computing behind it. So there are many barriers appeared and we will have a discussion about it in this part (Jensen, 2009).

Privacy and Security: Privacy almost not have relationship with the public interest, the group don't want to inconvenience others to know of others' personal information, the group don't want others to intrude with or inconvenience to others intrude private matter, and the parties do not want others to invade or invasion of personal inconvenience to others in the field. (Mather, 2009)

Privacy issues all the characteristics of cloud computing environments faced with network privacy issues, and increased as a result of cloud computing environment brought about new features. (Modi, 2013)

The problem is whether the data resides in Cloud at a safe level to keep away from any form of security vulnerabilities or more secure cloud data stored away in our own personal computer or hard drive.

Figure 2. Cloud deployment models and service deployment models

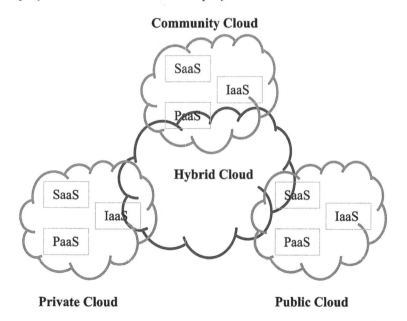

We can always use our hard drive and system whenever we want to use, but Cloud servers may reside any place in the world and any form of network failure may refuse to lie us into the data in Cloud computing. Cloud service providers adhere to their servers and storage in which the data is fully protected from any kind of intrusion and theft. These companies believe that the data on their server itself is more secure than a number of data resides in personal computers and laptops. However, it is also part of cloud architecture; no matter where the data on the basis of the final repository on the data stored in the client will be distributed among the individual computers (Subashini, 2011).

Performance, Latency, and Reliability: Performance, latency, and reliability are important in Cloud and expected to flow around different cloud data (Bhadauria, 2011). The delay is to encrypt and decrypt data, around it unreliable and public networks, other factors congestion, packet loss, and window movement. (Hassan, 2011) When the network traffic congestion by increasing the delay is high, and there are many requests (which may be the same priority) needs to be performed simultaneously. Another technique is the window in which the receiver has to send a message that it has received to the earlier transmitted, thereby increasing the network delay sending the message. In addition, the performance of the system should also be a factor to consider. Sometimes short-term cloud service provider can run or access by allowing too many virtual machines or because of high demand from customers arising from part of their Internet connection throughput threshold limit is reached. This hurts system performance and increased system latency. (Bhadauria, 2011)

Portability and Interoperability: It must advance to the next cloud provider may think the situation needs to be replaced occurs, so portability and interoperability must be seen as part of a cloud project risk management and safety assurance of progress. The organization may need to change the cloud service provider, and there have been when the company cannot become their data and applications, if they find another cloud platform, they want more than they use. In addition, the cloud service provider is different applications and different cloud services on the basis of some enterprises use the platform to provide their requirements (Khalil, 2014). In some cases, different cloud platforms are used for specific application or different cloud platforms must interact with each other in order to accomplish a specific task. The organization's internal infrastructure needs maintenance processing different cloud platform interoperability balances between operations.

Data Storage over IP Networks: Online data storage is becoming very popular; it has been observed that most enterprise storage networking in the next few years, because it allows companies to maintain large chunks of data does not provide the necessary framework. Although there are many advantages of online data storage, there is a security threat could lead to data leakage, at a critical time or data is not available. In the case of such problems continued in the cloud compared to the static data flow with dynamic data observed more frequently. Depending on the level of processing and storage provided by these network devices to the SAN (storage area network) and NAS (network attached storage), and because they reside in different storage network server, there are multiple threats or attached to them risk.

Data-Breach through Fiber Optic Networks: It has noticed for security risks during transmission of data have increased in the past few years. Data changes are normal nowadays; it can contain multiple data centers and other kinds of cloud deployment model. Such as transform data from a public or private cloud data center to another data center, it has many times in violation of the recent major concerns. There are indications that can be used, even it does not interfere with, access fiber, and the device data is being transmitted through the data stream. They are generally laid in the ground, so it should not be a difficult task to access the cables. Thus it becomes a very important factor to ensure security of the data in the transition network.

3.2 Security Issues

There are many security issues in the cloud computing, so here should have a method to classify there issues. According Ref. (Khalil, 2014) and other surveys we classified cloud computing security issues which are important. We classified them by four aspects: Cyber Security Standards, Computer Network, Access Control and Cloud Infrastructure.

The *Cyber Security Standards* class in order to prevent or alleviate network security attacks. It mainly concentrates on governing bodies and regulatory authorities. These have been defined cloud security policies can ensure the security of the working environment about Cloud computing. Service level agreements, audit and other agreements are usually mentioned, among users, service providers and other stakeholders.

The *Computer Network* class is a usually category which we often used. The network just a connection, the computer or other hardware components interconnected through a communication channel, allowing shared resources and information. It is about the medium which the users connect to cloud infrastructure to perform the required computations. It includes browsers, network connections and information exchange through registration.

The *Access Control* class is mentioned about physical security and referred to user-oriented category. In this field, access control is about getting an access of selective constraints. This class includes identification, authentication and authorization issues.

The *Cloud Infrastructure* class includes some security issues within SaaS, PaaS and IaaS and is particularly related with virtualization environment.

3.2.1 Cyber Security Standards

This class described the required criterions to take preventive measures in cloud computing security for the purpose to prevent malicious behavior. It dominated cloud security strategy without affecting the reliability and performance (Table 1).

- **Scarcity:** While almost every cloud service providers have a deployment, the deployment of the security measures in this way to protect the data stored on their servers, but the cloud is still not recognized safety standards.
- **Compliance Risks:** Many security and compliance risks remain, due to the lack of assessment of regulatory audit and corporate standards. And cloud customer does not flow, processes and supplier practices sufficient knowledge, especially in terms of identity management and the division of responsibilities in the field.

Table 1. Cyber security standards

Cyber Security Standards	Scarcity
	Compliance risks
	Lack of auditing
	Lack of legal aspects
	Trust

- **Lack of Auditing:** Organizations that seek to obtain certifications may be put on risk by denying an audit by cloud customers. One of the most important aspects of cloud computing security is auditability; however, we do not have an audit net for cloud service providers. If a service provider outsources a service to a third party where functionality is not transparent, users must be able to inspect the whole process.
- **Lack of Legal Aspects (Service Level Agreement):** A safety standard mainly involves administration service level agreements (SLA) and legal aspects were also not taken into account a portion of the cloud computing practice. SLA defines the relationship between the parties, such as the relationship between the suppliers and recipient, which is both extremely important points. It includes the identification and definition of customer needs, simplifies complex problems, in case of disputes is triggered to encourage dialogue, and provides a framework to identify, reduce and eliminate the conflict areas, the elimination of unrealistic expectations.
- **Trust:** Users may feel pain in preventing data loss on the side, if these factors are not considered under the premise, cannot meet the service provider claims. When faced with users and different stakeholders interact to form a cloud of these data in the cloud infrastructure required for the transfer of the trust relationship. We need to have good reason to get this aspect of customer trust.

3.2.2 Computer Network

This class is mainly concerned with some of the serious network attacks. For example, connection availability attack, DoS (Denial of service) attack, DDoS (Distributed denial of service) attack, flood attack, and internet protocol vulnerabilities, and so on. In this part we will talk about issues in computer network about cloud computing security (Table 2).

- **Proper Installation of Network Firewalls:** To allow users to system security promoted, it is now in many free software firewalls installed on the system, and set up a hardware-based firewall backup. (Scott, Internet Tips: Ultimate Network Security-How to Install a Firewall) But the main problem now is that it is difficult to understand and configure the firewall, even experienced computer users will feel confused.
- **Network Security Configurations:** In the cloud and on the Web, there are many neglected security configuration, these so-called security configuration easier for hackers to identity of legitimate users access the cloud. Hackers can generate false data and consume resources (hardware or application), you can run malicious code on a hijacked resources.
- **Internet Protocol Vulnerabilities:** For example, DOS attacks can be the first to identify vulnerabilities in Internet protocol, such as SIP (Session Initiation Protocol), which can cause the system to think that the Internet is not credible.

Table 2. Computer network

Computer Network	Proper installation of network firewalls
	Network security configurations
	Internet Protocol vulnerabilities
	Internet Dependence

- **Internet Dependence:** As a major media cloud access, migrate to the cloud systems will increase reliance on the Internet. So, if for some attacks that crashed the Internet and making cloud services become unavailable, which may result in productivity is badly weakened. Thus, there are many problems regarding the Internet dependence.

3.2.3 Access Control

Here we are not only talking about Access Control, but also including authentication about access. It grabbed influence of users' information privacy and their data storage situation (Table 3).

- **Account and Service Hijacking:** Accounts and their services may involve the hijacking phishing, fraud and loopholes in the software to steal credentials and unauthorized access to the server (Mather, 2009) and other issues. These unauthorized accesses are to the integrity, confidentiality, and data services threaten availability. Unauthorized access can be launched from inside or outside the organization, and this is where we should be vigilant.
- **Malicious Insiders:** Malicious insiders, such as dishonesty administrator will seriously affect the security of an organization. Given their level of access to enterprise penetration attacks they carried out resulting in brand damage, and the loss of financial and productivity. Therefore, we must clearly Cloud Client judge, so cloud providers to detect and combat insider threats is essential defense guarantees.
- **Authentication Mechanism:** The current authentication mechanism may not apply to customers of a cloud environment because it no longer belongs to or be able to access a tightly controlled system (Bhadauria, 2011). A client can access the data, services and the use of mobile applications or browser component multiple cloud service providers.
- **Privileged User Access:** As mentioned above, a single client can access the data, and the use of mobile applications or browsers consisting of multiple cloud service providers. This type of access is called privileged user access (Modi, 2013) has brought the level of risk inherent in; unauthorized access could be through browser vulnerabilities.
- **Brower Security:** Browser could allow unauthorized access possible. Thus, the web browser is here to be regarded as browser vulnerability in many subsequent opening of the first stage attacks security measures.

Table 3. Access Control

Access Control	Account and service hijacking
	Malicious insiders
	Authentication mechanism
	Privileged user access
	Brower Security

3.2.4 Cloud Infrastructure

Attack in cloud infrastructure covering specific cloud infrastructure (IaaS is, PaaS and SaaS) such tampering binaries and privileged insiders (Table 4).

- **Insecure Interface of Application Programming Interface (API):** Application Programming Interface (API) issued Unsafe Interfaces coverage holes in the cloud portal set API, customers using these API to connect to the cloud; it can be tissue is exposed to multiple threats, such as unauthorized access, content delivery, reusable tokens, and logging and so on.
- **Quality of Service (QoS):** Quality of Service (QoS) is an unattended problem, because many cloud service providers focus only on fast performance and low cost. In this work, we consider the function or activity is directly or indirectly affects the security domain QoS.
- **Sharing Technical Flaws:** In a simple mistake a cloud or more components of the structure may result in serious consequences, because the cloud configuration may be many services share. Technical flaws cause each virtual machine errors from the damaged server to the server created and transferred to other servers infected by corruption moving virtual machines. Therefore, the best practices to identify and fix the fate shared event and implementation is very important to prevent them from happening again.
- **Reliability of Suppliers:** Reliability of the supplier is required background checks for employees and hardware to control data access (Bhadauria, 2011) is an important factor. Here we strongly recommend that companies should protect their assets and data, and provides this information to the public, in order to win the trust of valued customers and staff.
- **Security Misconfiguration:** Cloud servers are the backbone of the infrastructure, can provide a variety of services, such as directory services, data storage and e-mail, and so on. Intruder system can access when the security attributes of the server is incorrect configuration (security configuration errors). This configuration error may occur in the application stack framework, web server, client code and the platform itself.

3.3 Vulnerabilities, Threats, and Attacks

Inside cloud computing security, there exist some security questions vulnerabilities, threats, and related attacks (Modi, 2013) which we should in-depth discuss. Vulnerabilities in the cloud computing are more prefer to infrastructure problems, which can be utilized by an opponent to get on the network and other infrastructure resources through a complex technology. Threats in cloud computing environment are latent or actual malice event that may be malicious or accidental, such as a storage device failure, the

Table 4. Cloud infrastructure

Cloud Infrastructure	Insecure interface of API
	Quality of service
	Sharing technical flaws
	Reliability of Suppliers
	Security Misconfiguration

impact of cloud resources. Attacks are actions which can do harm to cloud resources. Exploitation of these could involve the availability and economic benefit of Cloud Computing.

Here is a table about Cloud computing Security's vulnerabilities, threats and attacks. (Jensen, 2009)

3.3.1 Vulnerabilities

In this part, we will discuss major Cloud computing security's particular vulnerabilities, which would be a serious threat to the Cloud computing security (Table 5).

- **Internet Protocols:** Vulnerabilities in Internet protocols can be proved to be aggressive manner of attacking the Cloud computing system, including common types of attacks. For example, ARP spoofing, IP spoofing, man-in-the-middle attack, RIP attacks, DNS poisoning, and flooding attacks (Jensen, 2009). In particular, ARP poisoning is known in Internet protocol vulnerability. Exploiting this vulnerability, a malicious virtual machines can be co-located redirect malicious VM virtual machine all inbound and outbound traffic, because ARP is not required to prove the source. On the other hand, there exist loopholes in the HTTP protocol; it's a Web application protocol that requires session state. But they are susceptible to session-riding and session hijacking; these loopholes are necessarily related to the cloud. TCP / IP have some irremediable flaws, such as the status of reliable machinery is always in contact with each machine and default assumptions in the routing table can't be maliciously modified (Modi, 2013). In this case, the attack has become a major key in public cloud, as always provided the backbone of the Internet cloud (Jensen, 2009).
- **Virtualization and Multi-Tenancy:** Virtualization and multi-tenancy play a part in the basis for Cloud computing architecture (Modi, 2013). There are three ways on virtualization: Operating system-level virtualization, application-based virtualization, and hypervisor. In the operating system-level, multiple guest operating systems is the host operating system, has run on each client operating system on the visibility and control. In this type of configuration, the attacker can reduce the host operating system got the whole guest operating system controls. About application-based virtualization, it's enabled at the top of the host operating system. About this kind of configuration, each virtual machine has a guest operating system and related applications. It also suffers from the same flaw in the OS-based vulnerabilities. Hypervisor, which also called virtual machine monitor (VMM) as embedded into the host operating system code. This code may contain errors locally and can be in the host operating system to control multiple guest operating system startup time. If the hypervisor is compromised, then the operating system to control the entire customer could be destroyed (Jensen, 2009). Cloud providers flourish to maintain a maximum level of isolation between VM instances including inter-user processes. Via attacks in VM, hackers can modify the hypervisor which were installed and gain control of the host.

Table 5. Vulnerabilities

Vulnerabilities	Internet protocols
	Virtualization/ and multi-tenancy
	Unauthorized access to the management interface
	Injection vulnerabilities
	Vulnerabilities in browsers and APIs

- **Unauthorized Access to Administration Interface:** In cloud computing, users have no choice but manage their own subscription includes Cloud instance (Bhadauria, 2011). Unauthorized access to this administration interface can become a cloud system is critical. Unlike traditional network system, the larger the number of cloud system administrators and users to increase the possibility of unauthorized access (Jensen, 2009). Advances in cryptanalysis coverage by the encryption algorithm; it can become a powerful encryption into a weak encryption to provide security. Unsafe or outdated encryption vulnerabilities with the cloud, because it is not recommended to use the cloud does not use encryption to protect the privacy of data security and cloud. For example, the discovery by performing signature packaging and cross-site scripting (XSS) attacks, that interface is used to manage cloud resources, password holes Amazon EC2 management interface is hijacked. This attack allows an attacker to modify, create, and delete machine images, and change the admin password and set. Recent studies (Subashini, 2011) showed that the successful attack on a cloud control interface allows the attacker to take complete control of your account, including all stored data.

- **Injection Vulnerabilities:** Vulnerabilities such as SQL, OS, and LightweightDirectory Access Protocol (LDAP) injection flaws are used to disclose application components. These vulnerabilities are the result of the application in the design and structural defects in the system. These data can apply for the organization or private data residing in other organizations the same cloud applications.

- **Vulnerabilities in Browsers and APIs:** Cloud service providers released a set of software interfaces that customers can use it to manage and interact with cloud services. Availability, security and cloud services rely on the safety of these API. Browser-based attacks (HTML-based service) example is SSL certificate spoofing, network attacks and mail client browser cache phishing attacks (Modi, 2013). All key agreement method API should support the WS-Security family of standards specified because the resulting key must be stored directly in the browser.

3.3.2 Threats

In this part, we will discuss about related instructions to alleviate some of the potential threat in Cloud computing security. (Bhadauria, 2011) (Table 6).

Table 6. Cloud security threats

Threats	Changes to business model
	Abuse of cloud computing
	Malicious insiders
	Technical problems about shared / multi-tenant properties
	Insecure interfaces and API
	Risk profiling
	Identity theft
	Service hijacking

- **To Change the Business Model:** Cloud computing is changing IT service delivery. As a server, external storage and application service provider, organizations need to assess and control the risk of loss associated infrastructure. Data traversing over geographical boundaries are subjected to different federal laws. This is one of the main menaces to discourage the use of Cloud Services. A reliable end-to-encryption scheme and the corresponding trust management terminal can be simplified to some extent this threat.

- **Abuse of Cloud Computing:** Cloud computing offers a variety of useful tools, including storage capacity and bandwidth. Some suppliers also give predefined probationary period to use their services. However, attackers don't have sufficient controls about malicious users or spammers; they can take advantage of the test. These can often allow intruders kinds of malicious attacks, proved to be a serious attack platform. These threats can affect IaaS and PaaS. In order to protect, initial registration should be, and verified by a stronger identity through appropriate validation or certification. In addition to this, in the communication network of the user should be fully monitored.

- **Malicious Insiders:** Most organizations hide their level of access to employees and their hiring plans, as a policy for employees. However, using a higher level of access, employees can access confidential data and services. Due to the lack of cloud providers and the transparency of the process, the industries often have privileges. Insider activity is usually caused by a firewall or intrusion detection system (IDS), assuming it is around a legitimate activity. However, there has the possibility of a trusted insider may become rivals. In this case, the industry could lead to a cloud service offerings have a considerable impact, for example, malicious insiders can gain access to confidential data and control risks in cloud services and testing. This type of threat may be relevant to SaaS, PaaS and IaaS. To avoid this risk and increase transparency, we need safety and management processes, including compliance report and notice of default.

- **Technical Problems about Shared / Multi-Tenant Properties:** In a multi-tenant architecture, virtualization for providing shared on-demand services. Shared between virtual machines can access the different users of the same application. Yet, as previously mentioned, the hypervisor vulnerabilities allow legitimate users of a malicious user can access a virtual machine and control. IaaS service is about the use of shared resources, which may not be designed for multi-tenant architecture provides a strong isolation delivery. This can affect the overall structure of the cloud, allows a tenant in other interference, and thus interfere with its proper operation. This type of threat can affect IaaS.

- **Unsafe Interfaces and API:** Cloud service vendors often release a set of API, to allow their customers to design an interface to interact with the cloud service. These interfaces often in the frame, this in turn will increase the complexity of adding layer on top of the cloud. Such an interface allows the holes (in the conventional API) to move to the cloud. Improper use of these interfaces often results in such plain text authentication, content delivery, authorization, improper threats. Such type of threat may affect the service models, such as IaaS, PaaS, and SaaS. This situation can be avoided by using an appropriate interface cloud provider's security model, and then ensure a strong and encrypted transmission of authentication and access control mechanisms.

- **Risk Profiling:** Cloud services allow small businesses involved in the construction and maintenance of software and hardware and it can provides important advantages. However, this also makes them do not realize that internal security procedures and compliance, hardening, patching, auditing and logging of process, and a greater risk of public institutions. To avoid these cloud providers should disclose detailed information about parts of the infrastructure and data logging. In addition to this, it should have a monitoring and alarm systems.

- **Identity Theft:** In the form of identity theft fraud, one of them pretend to be someone else, access resources or obtain credit and other benefits. Victims of identity theft may suffer adverse effects and loss, and held responsible for the behavior of human behavior. Related security risks contain weak password recovery workflows, phishing attacks and key loggers like. This issue would affect the SaaS, PaaS and IaaS. The available solution is using a strong authentication mechanism. (Subashini, 2011)

- **Service Hijacking:** Services hijacking can redirect the client to an illegal website. For example, attacker can use other users' accounts and service through this method. Phishing attacks, fraud, exploitation of software vulnerabilities, reuse certificate and password may result in service or account hijacking. Such type of threat may affect the service models, such as IaaS, PaaS, and SaaS. Some mitigation strategies point to address this threat, including security policy, strong authentication, and activity monitoring.

3.3.3 Attacks

In an information security aspect, attacks are most common and serious problems. So toward analyze the harm in Cloud computing security, we should take it to an important place. By cloud exploit, attackers can fire the following attacks (Table 7).

- **Zombie Attacks:** Via the Internet, the attacker tries to send an innocent victim into a host in the network requests. These types of hosts are known as zombies. In cloud computing, virtual machine requirements (virtual machine) are accessed through the Internet for each user. An attacker could flood with requests by zombies. This attack interrupts the expected behavior of cloud services as well as affects its availability. Cloud computing may be overloaded to serve multiple requests, so exhausted, which could lead to DoS (Denial of Service) or DDoS attack (Distributed Denial of Service) server. Clouds in the attacker's request can't be an effective presence flooded the user's request. However, provide better authentication and authorization, and IDS or IPS can provide protection against such attacks.

Table 7. Cloud security attacks

Attacks	Zombie attacks	
	Service injection attacks	
	Attacks on virtualization	
	Backdoor channel attacks	DoS attacks
		DDoS attacks
	Other attacks	DNS attacks
		SNIFFER attacks
		Man-in-the Middle attacks
		Metadata spoofing attacks
		Phishing attacks

- **Service Injection Attacks:** Cloud system is responsible for determining the requested service and final instance for free. The address used to access the new instance to be transferred back to the requesting user. The opponent is trying to inject malicious service or a new virtual machine to a cloud system that provides services to a malicious user. Cloud malicious software can change or block the cloud capabilities to influence cloud services. Consider a case in which an opponent to create his / her malicious services, such as the SaaS, PaaS or IaaS and add them to the cloud. If the opponents successfully do that, then the valid request will be automatically redirected to a malicious service. To combat this type of attack defense, integrity checking module should be implemented. Strong isolation between virtual machines may inject malicious code to disable attacks from neighbors VM.

- **Attacks on Virtualization:** There are two main types of virtualization over the attack: VM Escape and Rootkit in hypervisor.
  - **VM Escape:** In VM Escape, attacker in a virtual machine program violates the separation layer in order to run with root privileges management program, rather than the VM privilege. So an attacker can interact either directly with the hypervisor. Thus, VM exits from the virtual layer isolated from the offer. Escape through a virtual machine, the attacker access to other virtual machines running on the host operating system and physical access to the machine.
  - **Rootkit in Hypervisor:** It would undermine existing host-based virtual machine rootkit boot manager operating system to a virtual machine. New client operating system assumes it is running and the corresponding control of the host operating system resources, however, in reality this host does not exist.

- **Backdoor Channel Attacks:** This is a kind of passive aggression; it allows hackers to gain remote access to the infected system. Using backdoor channel attacks, hackers are able to control the resources of victims; you can try zombies DDoS attacks. This mode can also be used to expose confidential data of the victims. Between virtual machines better validation and isolation can provide protection against such attacks (Jensen, 2009). Especially, DoS and DDoS attacks are very important:
  - **DoS (Denial of Service) Attacks:** DoS attacks are attempted to make use of them assigned to the authorized user can't provide the service. In this attack, the service provided by the server is overwhelmed by the large number of requests, so the service is not available to authorized users. Sometimes, when we see that we are trying to access a website, due to overloading of the server request to visit the site, we can't access the site and observe the error. When this occurs, the numbers of requests that can be processed by a server exceed its capacity. The occurrence of a DoS attack increases bandwidth consumption besides causing congestion, making certain parts of the clouds inaccessible to the users. The use of intrusion detection systems (IDS) are against this type of attack. (Mirkovic, 2004)
  - **DDoS (Distributed Denial of Service) Attacks:** DDoS attack may be called an advanced version of DOS attack. Important services were denied on the destination server running flood Number of packets so numerous severs target server can't handle it. In a DDoS attack is unlike DOS has been compromised from different dynamic network relay. An attacker with the ability to allow can be controlled by the flow of information in a number of time-specific information. Therefore, under the attacker's information number and type of control for public use is apparently (Mirkovic, 2004). The DDoS attack is basically operating in two stages: The first phase of the invasion, in which the master attempts to compromise less important

machine supports full of more important one, next is the installation DDoS attack tools and attack victims servers or machines. Therefore, the results of a distributed denial of service attacks in making the service unavailable, it was started in a similar way, it is a way of DoS attacks, but different authorized users (Modi, 2013).

- **Other Attacks:** Besides these important attacks, there also have other attacks that might be hazardous to the Cloud computing security.

  ○ **DNS Attacks:** Domain Name Server (DNS) translates domain names to IP addresses. Because of domain names are easy to remember, the DNS server is needed. But in Cloud there also exist cases when the server's name has been invoked, the users have to be routed to some other abnormal cloud, rather than one of his requirements, so using the IP address is not always feasible. When the DNSSEC (Domain Name System Security Extensions) to reduce the impact of DNS threats, but there are some cases, prove to be inadequate, as was rerouted transmitter and receiver paths through some bad connection between these security measures. It may happen that even if all DNS security measures, causing security problems between the sender and the receiver selected still routing (Modi, 2013).

  ○ **SNIFFER Attacks:** This type of attack is based on the application; we can capture data packets flowing through the network launch. If these packets are transmitted through the data is not encrypted, it can be read and have a chance, important information flows on the network can be traced back or captured. Sniffer program through the network interface card (NIC) can ensure that the data and communication with other systems on the network are also recorded. It can be prepared by the NIC in promiscuous mode and it can keep track of all the data streams implemented on the same network. A malicious sniffing detection platform based on address resolution protocol (ARP) and round trip time (RTT) can be used to detect a network sniffer running on the system (Modi, 2013).

  ○ **Man-in-the Middle Attacks:** If the Secure Sockets Layer (SSL) is not configured correctly, the attacker can access any data exchange between the two sides. In cloud computing, an attacker can access data communication between data centers. Between licensees and datacom test appropriate SSL configuration may be useful to reduce the risk of middle attack.

  ○ **Metadata Spoofing Attacks:** About metadata spoofing attacks, in this type of attack, the opponent to modify or change the service's WSDL (Web Services Description Language) file, which is stored examples related services. (Web Services Description Language)If the opponent successfully interrupts delivery time service call code from a WSDL file, then this attack at here has a possibility. In order to overcome this attack, on the services and applications should save the information in an encrypted form. Strong authentication and authorization, and other key information access should be executed.

  ○ **Phishing Attacks:** Phishing attacks are known to manipulate network links and redirect users to a fake link to access sensitive data. In the cloud, it is possible to use a cloud service hosting phishing sites hijack user accounts and other cloud service attacks.

4. SECURITY CHALLENGES

Though there are many issues about Cloud computing security, but we should also think about the goodness about Cloud computing. So in this part, we will declare the challenges about Cloud computing in three aspects: Defense Mechanisms, Technology, and Existing Systems.

4.1 Defense Mechanisms

As there are many attacks in Cloud computing security, so we should analyze the Defense Mechanisms in Cloud computing environment. But in a fact, not every type of these attacks has very effective mechanisms toward defensing them. So in this section we will only show some of the defense mechanisms.

4.1.1 Virtualization Defense

In computing, virtualization refers to the act of creating a virtual (rather than actual) version of something, including virtual computer hardware platform, operating system, a storage device, or computer network resources (but not limited to).Though virtualization can enhance cloud security level, however, an additional layer of software in virtual machines (VMs) added, which could be a single-point of failure. Virtualization technology elaborated open cloud security enhancements.

Security through Virtualization

With virtualization, one physical machine or can be divided into multiple virtual machines (such as server consolidation).This provides better security isolation for each virtual machine and each partition is a possibility of protection from Denial of Service (DoS) attacks isolated from other districts as well as security attacks in a virtual machine and virtual machine from affecting other controls.

In any software failure of a virtual machine does not affect the other virtual machines failed operation will not spread to other virtual machines. Virtualization provides extended computing stack that the hypervisor, which provides visibility of the client operating system, complete with guest isolation.

Virtual Machines as a Sandbox

Sandbox is a virtual system that allows users to run a browser or other programs in the sandbox environment, so run the resulting changes can then be deleted. Sandbox security mechanism can be defined as providing a secure platform to run the program execution. Furthermore, Sandbox can provide tight control of the client operating system of the collection, which allows determining the safety test program running from untrusted code and third-party vendors untested.

Using virtualization, we can find the VM is separated from the physical hardware. Entire virtual machines can be represented as a software component, and can be seen as a binary or digital data. This means that, in the VM can be saved, cloning, encryption, or move easily restored. Virtual machines achieve higher availability and faster disaster recovery.

Virtualization Defense against Intrusions and DDoS Attacks

Intrusion detection and prevention DDoS attacks virtual machine can be designed to support distributed security enforcement. We recommend virtual machine migration life dedicated to building the Distributed Intrusion Detection System (DIDS) design. Multiple ID virtual machines can be in different resource site, including data center deployment.

Distributed Intrusion Detection System design requirements, we believe that among the negative PKI domain. Security policy conflicts must be addressed in the design and updated regularly. Defense program is necessary in order to protect the user's data from the server attacks. The user's personal data shall not be disclosed to other users do not have permission. Google's platform is basically suitable for internal software to protect resources.

4.1.2 DDoS (Distributed Denial of Service) Defense

In general, the method used to fight DDoS attacks involves extensive changes to the underlying network. These modifications often become costly user. Use intrusion detection system in a virtual machine is proposed in order to protect the cloud DDoS attacks. Like intrusion detection mechanism snorted loaded into the virtual machine all sniffing traffic, whether calls or outgoing calls. Commonly used to prevent DDoS another approach is to have the entire physical machine that contains the user's virtual machine on intrusion detection system. This program has been proven in the Eucalyptus cloud to perform quite well. (Bhuyan, 2013)

DDoS defense solution is based on its deployment of three types: the source, the victim ends and intermediate routers defense mechanisms. Of the three, most researchers tend to use the victim's high-end approach. However, a common drawback of the program is a huge consumption of resources, to provide rapid response detection. After the latest DDoS attack scenario, if the attacker gains, they can instantly increase the attack power and access to resources most available, you cannot attack IP spoofing and their activities can be extended to complex database queries affairs also. Typically, such transaction from legitimate inquiry segregation is a difficult task.

Current tools can launch DDoS attacks in different ways (Wang, 2012) such as raising interest rates, at a constant rate, pulse (oscillation between the maximum incidence is 0), and gradually pulses (such as attack rate of maximum 20 seconds, and reduce the 0 of attacks in 10 seconds). These various forms of attack may involve single and multiple attack, that was single and multiple source addresses. Defenders interested in providing and implementation with minimal resource consumption reduction of false alarms a purpose semiautomatic solution. We propose high-level solution is to use an appropriate decision fusion technology to work distributed framework based on an integrated method. Protocol-specific feature extraction in a distributed environment, on the basis of the characteristics of the base layer in a plurality of sensors and detectors DDoS attacks a particular type of individual level will provide a subset of the proposed solution involves. Finally, the individual decisions may be used at any level in the final infer an appropriate combination of rules on participating nodes of a distributed framework combined. Once confirmed the attack occurred, the next task is to selectively limit the instant attack speed without affecting legitimate users of the service, so that the subsequent loss can be minimized immediately. However, for a significant reduction in FAR, the participation of human experts is very useful. Under particular, in DDoS attacks, with the help of false alarms and human analysts and provide adequate diagnostic feedback to the sensor's case, it is very necessary. Three advantages of our solutions are: (1) It can help to achieve a just and a high DR reducing false positives, (2) and minimizing its consumption of resources (3) calculate the costs by sharing it achieve scalability real-time detection performance.

4.2 Technology

Although the development of cloud computing will take years or even decades to fully expanded [10], we should analyze the technology about the Cloud computing security. Security is the most important issue in cloud computing. Because cloud computing is stored in our data through a third party, we do not know the details of specific operations and data. This would be a serious security risk, but we need to be strengthened to improve security.

The greatest advantage of cloud computing is achieving a centralized data. (Velte, 2009) The organization has a major problem in the protection of assets, largely the data being stored in numerous places such as laptops and the desktop. Large clients often download a lot of files, and stored on the hard disk, and there are large number of devices without encryption. Simplified client can provide a better opportunity for the creation of centralized data storage. This method can enhance the security of the system.

Another security advantage is to the cloud provider to provide adequate security. Obviously, no organization has the ability to hire IT security personnel around the clock, the reality is that cloud providers may offer more security features than ever before. Under a lot of customers to pay the premise of this fact allows cloud providers owned relatively robust security, just because the economies of scale covered. In other words there are so many customers pay to providers so providers can do more, because there is more money in the pot. Coupled with its suppliers benefit, they want to get a good reputation.

Besides, the level of logging is also ameliorated; suppliers can add as much memory as they need to expand logging. If there is a violation, cloud providers can react to events, that cost less downtime with local investigates violation. It is easy to establish a forensic server online, before it is put into use until it is almost no cost. If there is a problem in systems, the virtual machine can be cloned in order to off-line analysis. Furthermore, many companies do not have dedicated internal incident response team. If there is a problem, IT staff must quickly closed the investigation to find out why they take the new server, then using the Internet to get it back to work with minimal downtime.

Security vendors are actively developing can be applied to virtual machines and cloud computing products. Security vendors have also been a special opportunity in the cloud. Because this is a new field, vendors have many new opportunities to develop one of the areas.

Above all we discussed about the Cloud computing security in a theory aspects. Now we will show some example about these. Here are some of comparative evaluations of well-known general Cloud computing security mechanisms. (Voron, 2010)

Intrusion Detection Systems (IDS)

An intrusion detection system (IDS) is a device or software application that monitors network or system activities for malicious activities or policy violations and produces reports to a management station. Under normal circumstances the intruder posing as legitimate users can access the cloud infrastructure to become a legitimate user, and lead to real legitimate users cannot use cloud services. This study has shown that an attacker could easily get component information about the victim's computer IaaS cloud computing. These attacks include DoS and DDoS attacks that mainly for data integrity, confidentiality, and availability. Such attacks can be avoided, IDS provides additional security measures through surveys of network traffic, log files, and user behavior.

Type of intrusion detection can be divided into two categories: Misuse Detection (MD) and Anomaly detection (AD). MD handling user input characters, use the database to compare the results of the information, especially in light of previously performed by the same user input to determine. From another aspect, anomaly detection stock piles user behavior in signature database, which can be compared with current behavior, if there is a difference between relatively high rates, then we can say that the invasion took place. IDS have two types: Host based IDS (HIDS) and Network based IDS (NIDS). HIDS monitors the behavior on a single host. NIDS analyses traffic flowing through a network.

Figure 3 represents the basic model of IDS structure. Basically an IDS model mainly consisted in 3 parts: Firstly we put events into models which we want, second we define the model rules, and then detecting the model. If an event is not an attack, this turn IDS's work is done; if the event is an attack, IDS will defend it, and then search it is a new attack or not, if the answer is "Yes", IDS will update this new event to IDS's database. (Voron, 2010) (Figure 3).

Autonomous Systems

An autonomous system is under the control of a regulatory agency, the router and network groups. All routers in an autonomous system must be connected to each other, running with an autonomous system number is assigned the same routing protocol, it is an IDS with a previously specified the basic rules of work. (Khalil, 2014)

These rules can be configuring, optimizing, self-healing and automatic protect themselves, thereby reducing manpower effort and participation. These rules can be managed by artificial intelligence can also be specified. Manage next-generation distributed systems in the absence of autonomic computing is impossible. Event detection intelligent autonomous agent named Security audits as a Service (SaaS). This agent has a prerequisite; it is assumed to know the deployment of cloud instances basic traffic flow. The direct source of SaaS data collection and analysis and summary information, and then distributed. The heart of the system is based on service-level agreements through security (SSLA) for data analysis. SaaS cloud computing security is mainly used to solve three major problems: (1) the abuse of cloud resources; (2) the lack of cloud infrastructure and shared resources; (3) the isolation of a defective safety monitoring. SaaS will use a large number of sensors, which can capture many events. The sensor receives from SSLA security policy. Even the nature of SaaS-based independent agency, its security policy is still based on predefined rules, so this limits the detection capabilities are limited to those already known attacks. In addition, SaaS involves the use of a large number of agents and functionality, which will create a high communication between agents, increased overhead calculation.

Figure 3. Intrusion detection systems

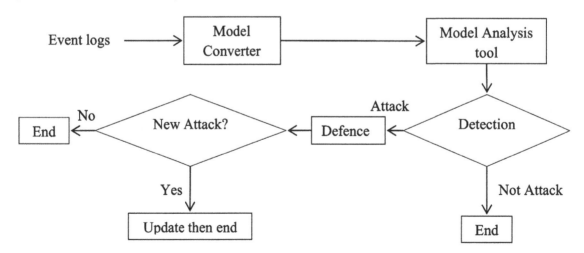

Federated Identity Management System

Cloud computing security is closely linked to the core of identity to access the cloud computing infrastructure. Identity (IDM) management is to maintain the integrity of identity throughout its life cycle, and its associated data (for example, authentication and authorization results) to provide different services in the way of security and privacy protection. The concept of federated identity management (FIM) is about the identity of the subject by allowing one to establish his / her identity, each of which may be used for different services, contact management status across geographical and organizational boundaries. Establishes a logical link between the identities called identity federation. A group of the establishment of the alliance trusts to business cooperation in security organizations. This process is repeated users (single sign-on) to verify the identity of the examples can be combined. The main problem is that the single sign-on, in a more extensive damage, which leads to compromise the case. If the user's identity is compromised, unauthorized users will not be verified again, this may result in a higher level of information leakage. Another problem is the federal system and flexible mechanism FIM lack dynamic. It is a concern and the need for further investigation of the building.

Figure 4 shows basic functions IDM representation, which consists of 8 steps: login, requesting application or data, requesting token for ID verification, generating token, verifying it and sending or accessing the data or application. Through user's login ID and requirements IDM user logs on to the cloud simultaneously access applications or data. Then the cloud Requirements to further verify the IDM to generate the appropriate token users. User requests token from IDM. IDM generate tokens and share it with users and cloud. Users send tokens to the cloud, to complete the final verification steps. Cloud by the user and send the token sent by IDM compare. Finally, if the validation is successful, clouds grant access to users. In the real world, a person usually has a set of cards such as ID cards and driver's license to indicate that she and all of these cards are used for different purposes. The same mechanism has been applied in the information card standard. (Khalil, 2014)

4.3 Existing Systems

Nowadays, such as Amazon and Google, more and more systems are used in Cloud computing.

4.3.1 Amazon

Amazon.com, Inc. is a US e-commerce company, headquartered in Seattle, Washington. (Jopson, 2011) This is the nation's largest Internet-based retailers. Amazon.com began as an online bookstore, but soon developed into a diversified, started selling DVD, MP3 download, streaming media, software, video games, electronics, apparel, furniture, food, toys and jewelry, and so on. The company also manufactures consumer electronics products, it is worth noting that the Amazon Kindle e-book reader, tablet PCs, TVs and fire calls fire - and is a major provider of cloud computing services. Amazon also sells some low-end products, such as USB cable in its interior brand Amazon Basics.

Amazon is one of the pioneers of cloud computing, and the first to provide virtual servers and data storage space for users to pay for access. Over the years it was one of the most cloud computing technology strength of the company. Amazon manages one of the largest online businesses, before giving it an ideal platform to sell to the client organization to test its own technological progress.

Figure 4. Federated identity management system

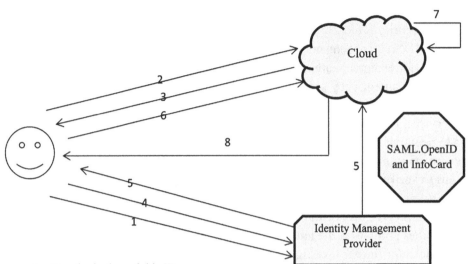

1. User login through his ID
2. Request to access application or see data
3. Ask for token, generated by IM provider
4. Request for token
5. Share token with user/cloud
6. Send token to cloud
7. Verify the token sent by user and IM
8. Send data or allow users to access the application

4.3.2 Google

We all know that Google is a US multinational focus on Internet-related services and products. These include online advertising technology, search, cloud computing and software. Most of its profits come from Ad Words ads, online advertising service, placed near search results list advertising. Rapid growth since its establishment has led to a series of products, acquisitions and partnerships beyond Google's core search engine. It provides include email (Gmail) is the online office software, cloud storage services (Google Drive), office suite (Google Docs) and social networking services (Google+) is. Desktop products, including web browsing, organizing and editing photos and instant messaging applications. Company-led Android mobile operating system and browser, only Chrome operating system development is called chrome book Internet. Google has moved to more and more communications hardware: its main electronics manufacturers (Ricker, 2014) of its production of "low quality" of the Nexus equipment and acquisition of Motorola's mobile in May 2012, to install fiber infrastructure cooperation Partners in Kansas City, to promote Google Fiber broadband service.

The company assessed the data centers around the world are running more than one million servers (as of 2007), and each of the world deal with more than one billion search requests, and user-generated data, about 24 gigabytes (2009). In December 2013 Alexa listed as google.com in the world's most visited sites. Many of the Google website ranking figure in the first one hundred other languages, as do some other Google-owned sites, such as YouTube and Blogger. Because of its monopoly position in the market, leading to prominent media coverage, which include criticism of the company, such as search neutrality, copyright, review and confidentiality and other aspects.

As we all know, Google also used Cloud computing, the mainly application are as below: (Ricker, 2014)

- **Google App Engine:** This is Google's platform-as-a-service (PaaS) basis, provide informa-tion on Google infrastructure building and hosting Web applications. Currently this engine sup-ports mainly including Python programming language and Java. App Engine is free to use the most resources, extra storage fee after that, bandwidth, or CPU cycles required a certain level of applications.
- **Google Apps:** This is Google's software-as-service corporate e-mail and collaboration (SaaS) product. Google's App Engine provides a client organization to enter Google's cloud comput-ing platform, the platform provides tools to build and host Web applications. Its primary product is a SaaS Google Apps, a set of online office productivity tools including email, calendar, word processing and a simple Web site creation tool. Its recent acquisition of Postini provides a set of e-mail and Web security services, making it a reliable player in the field of electronic busi-ness communications. It has a variety of applications similar to traditional office suites, including Gmail, Google Calendar, Talk, files and websites. In addition, Google Apps has many security and compliance products, providing e-mail security and compliance of existing e-mail infrastructure. Standard Edition is free, and provides the same amount of storage as regular Gmail accounts; Premiership version is based on per-user licensing model and associated storage level.

Command-line presence and successful business model allows Google Inc. is automatic begins in the online world. (Marston, 2011) Just by its sheer existence, Google Apps is a suite of software from the industry's move to accelerate, Web hosting services, and App Engine provides a platform as a service market, a reliable choice. Google's financial clout in the long run, be a member to explore the potential of cloud computing has.

4.3.3 Others

Besides Amazon and Google, there are many business applications about the Cloud computing: (Chen, 2010)

Microsoft Azure Services Platform (PaaS)

Azure Services Platform is Microsoft's PaaS offerings is its emphasis on mitigation and desktop divert more resources, part of the web-based products in the company's strategy. It provides an operating system called Windows Azure as a running application, and provides a set of services that allow development, management, hosting and managed applications in Microsoft data centers.

Cisco

Cisco cloud computing relatively late entrants, and actively committed to a set of standards will allow providing portability. An important aspect of this work is to ensure that the workload portability from one autonomous system to another, including (i.e., the workload related to the implementation of complete IT strategies) the consistent implementation of the new system workload.

As the network infrastructure supplier monster, it makes sense to work in the cloud Cisco standard, because they have the ability to completely unrelated cloud provider. They recently into the $ 55 billion server market to their reputation are intact infrastructure providers' sides in SaaS and IaaS market.

AT&T

AT&T offers two cloud services: Synaptic Hosting, by the client company will be able to store the Windows service, Linux client-server applications, and AT&T's cloud Web applications; and Synaptic storage, enabling customers to store their cloud in AT&T's data.

AT&T provides an important part of the necessary infrastructure - the network backbone, and its necessary experience in accounting (i.e. they have an established revenue model). Adding Data Services is to help strengthen their competitive position. One possible competitor is Verizon, which are increasing their cloud offerings.

5. CURRENT ISSUES AND DISCUSSION

Cloud computing environment still has many security issues and challenges and some are discussed below: (Chen, 2010)

Selection of Features and Classifiers: Selection of features or parameters between the victim and other party is a challenging task. By using these features, defense system must be able to identify the class to which that packet belongs to. Moreover, selection of fair classifiers from a group of classifiers is a challenging job.

Quality of Datasets: Creating the dataset with unbiased instances is a difficult and challenging task. Moreover, there are few less datasets available which are free and have enough information on attack traffic.

Location to Place the Defense Mechanism: There has always been a trade-off between safety of the system and correctness for finding the attack possibility based on the location of defense mechanism deployment.

Dynamism of the Defense System: There are always limitations regarding runtime efficiency of the defense system. While detecting and filtering, system always should be able to capture and filter all the attack packets successfully without losing anything.

Environment of Defense Mechanism: The environment, where the systems are working and where the defense mechanisms are deployed, may have critical effect on the result of defense mechanisms. Therefore, it is challenging for the researchers to find out solution which works on every type of environment.

Adaptability to novel Attacks: It is difficult to design a system that can adapt with new type of attacks and give satisfactory solution to defend against them.

6. CONCLUSION

In this chapter, we discussed recent developments in cloud computing, various security issues and challenges associated with Cloud computing environment, various existing solutions provided for dealing with these security threats and will provide a comparative analysis these approaches. This will provide better understanding of the various security problems associated with the cloud, current solution space, and future research scope to deal with such attacks in better way. As we have noted through this chapter, Cloud Computing has the potential to be a disruptive force by affecting the deployment and use of technology. The cloud could be the next evolution in the history of computing, following in the footsteps of mainframes, minicomputers, PCs, servers, smart phones, and so on, and radically changing the way enterprises manage IT.

REFERENCES

Bhadauria, R., Chaki, R., Chaki, N., & Sanyal, S. (2011). *A survey on security issues in cloud computing*. Academic Press.

Bhuyan, M. H., Kashyap, H. J., Bhattacharyya, D. K., & Kalita, J. K. (2013). Detecting distributed denial of service attacks: Methods, tools and future directions. *The Computer Journal*, bxt031.

Brodkin, J. (2008). Gartner: Seven cloud-computing security risks. *InfoWorld, 2008*, 1–3.

Chen, Y., Paxson, V., & Katz, R. H. (2010). *What's new about cloud computing security*. University of California, Berkeley Report No. UCB/EECS-2010-5 January, 20(2010), 2010-5.

Chonka, A., Xiang, Y., Zhou, W., & Bonti, A. (2011). Cloud security defence to protect cloud computing against HTTP-DoS and XML-DoS attacks. *Journal of Network and Computer Applications*, *34*(4), 1097–1107. doi:10.1016/j.jnca.2010.06.004

Chuvakin, A., & Peterson, G. (2009). Logging in the age of web services. *IEEE Security and Privacy*, *7*(3), 82–85. doi:10.1109/MSP.2009.70

Computing, C. (2011). Cloud computing privacy concerns on our doorstep. *Communications of the ACM, 54*(1).

Fernandes, D. A., Soares, L. F., Gomes, J. V., Freire, M. M., & Inácio, P. R. (2014). Security issues in cloud environments: A survey. *International Journal of Information Security*, *13*(2), 113–170. doi:10.1007/s10207-013-0208-7

Hassan, Q. (2011). Demystifying Cloud Computing. *The Journal of Defense Software Engineering*, 16-21.

Hwang, K., Kulkareni, S., & Hu, Y. (2009, December). Cloud security with virtualized defense and reputation-based trust mangement. In *Dependable, Autonomic and Secure Computing, 2009. DASC'09. Eighth IEEE International Conference on* (pp. 717-722). IEEE. doi:10.1109/DASC.2009.149

Jensen, M., Schwenk, J., Gruschka, N., & Iacono, L. L. (2009, September). On technical security issues in cloud computing. In *Cloud Computing, 2009. CLOUD'09. IEEE International Conference on* (pp. 109-116). IEEE. doi:10.1109/CLOUD.2009.60

Jopson, B. (2011). Amazon urges California referendum on online tax. *The Financial Times*.

Khalil, I. M., Khreishah, A., & Azeem, M. (2014). Cloud computing security: A survey. *Computers*, *3*(1), 1–35. doi:10.3390/computers3010001

Kumar, S., Ali, J., Bhagat, A., & Jinendran, P. K. (2013). An Approach of Creating a Private Cloud for Universities and Security Issues in Private Cloud. *International Journal of Advanced Computing, 36*(1), 1134–1137.

Li, J., Li, B., Wo, T., Hu, C., Huai, J., Liu, L., & Lam, K. P. (2012). CyberGuarder: A virtualization security assurance architecture for green cloud computing. *Future Generation Computer Systems, 28*(2), 379–390. doi:10.1016/j.future.2011.04.012

Mahmood, Z. (2011). Data location and security issues in cloud computing. *Emerging Intelligent Data and Web Technologies (EIDWT),2011International Conference on.* IEEE. doi:10.1109/EIDWT.2011.16

Marston, S., Li, Z., Bandyopadhyay, S., Zhang, J., & Ghalsasi, A. (2011). Cloud computing—The business perspective. *Decision Support Systems, 51*(1), 176–189. doi:10.1016/j.dss.2010.12.006

Mather, T., Kumaraswamy, S., & Latif, S. (2009). *Cloud security and privacy: an enterprise perspective on risks and compliance.* O'Reilly Media, Inc.

Mell, P., & Grance, T. (2011). *The NIST definition of cloud computing.* NIST. doi:10.6028/NIST.SP.800-145

Mirkovic, J., & Reiher, P. (2004). A taxonomy of DDoS attack and DDoS defense mechanisms. *Computer Communication Review, 34*(2), 39–53. doi:10.1145/997150.997156

Modi, C., Patel, D., Borisaniya, B., Patel, A., & Rajarajan, M. (2013). A survey on security issues and solutions at different layers of Cloud computing. *The Journal of Supercomputing, 63*(2), 561–592. doi:10.1007/s11227-012-0831-5

Paquette, S., Jaeger, P. T., & Wilson, S. C. (2010). Identifying the security risks associated with governmental use of cloud computing. *Government Information Quarterly, 27*(3), 245–253. doi:10.1016/j.giq.2010.01.002

Ricker, T. (2014). *Google: Nexus program explained, unfazed by Motorola acquisition.* Retrieved from http://www.theverge.com/2011/08/15/motorola-google-nexus-program-explained

Ristenpart, T., Tromer, E., Shacham, H., & Savage, S. (2009, November). Hey, you, get off of my cloud: exploring information leakage in third-party compute clouds. In *Proceedings of the 16th ACM conference on Computer and communications security* (pp. 199-212). ACM. doi:10.1145/1653662.1653687

Rouse, M. (n.d.). *Data availability definition.* Retrieved from http://searchstorage.techtarget.com/definition/data-availability

Spanbauer, S. (n.d.). *Internet Tips: Ultimate Network Security--How to Install a Firewall.* Retrieved from http://www.pcworld.com/article/112920/article.html

Subashini, S., & Kavitha, V. (2011). A survey on security issues in service delivery models of cloud computing. *Journal of Network and Computer Applications, 34*(1), 1–11. doi:10.1016/j.jnca.2010.07.006

Surcel, T., & Alecu, F. (2008). Applications of cloud computing. In *Proc. the International Conference of Science and Technology in the Context of the Sustainable Development* (pp. 177-180).

Velte, T., Velte, A., & Elsenpeter, R. (2009). *Cloud computing, a practical approach.* McGraw-Hill, Inc.

Voron, J. B., Démoulins, C., & Kordon, F. (2010, June). Adaptable Intrusion Detection Systems Dedicated to Concurrent Programs: a Petri Net-Based Approach. In *Application of Concurrency to System Design (ACSD), 2010 10th International Conference on* (pp. 57-66). IEEE. doi:10.1109/ACSD.2010.32

Wang, C., Wang, Q., Ren, K., Cao, N., & Lou, W. (2012). Toward secure and dependable storage services in cloud computing. *IEEE Transactions on Service Computing*, *5*(2), 220–232. doi:10.1109/TSC.2011.24

This work was previously published in the Handbook of Research on Modern Cryptographic Solutions for Computer and Cyber Security edited by Brij Gupta, Dharma P. Agrawal, and Shingo Yamaguchi, pages 393-419, copyright 2016 by Information Science Reference (an imprint of IGI Global).

Chapter 12
Cybercrimes Technologies and Approaches

WeSam Musa
University of Maryland – University College, USA

ABSTRACT

The growth of the Internet has changed our lives significantly. Not so long ago, computers used to be viewed as luxury items to have at home. People used to rely mainly on televisions and newspapers as the primary sources of news. Today, the Internet has become an essential service to depend on for many industries, such as news agencies, airports, and even utility companies. This was the beginning of a new-trillion-dollar industry: the Internet industry. However, the Internet was designed to be an open, academic tool, never to be secure. As a result, cybercrimes, cyber warfare, and other cyber illegal activities have spread to become a significant portion of Internet traffic. Cybercrimes often challenge law enforcement. It is difficult to know the exact location where an attack originated, and there are no cyber borders between nations. As a result, fighting cybercrimes requires international cooperation. The purpose of this chapter is to shed some light on motives of cybercrimes, technologies used by hackers, and solutions that can be adopted by individuals, organizations, and governments. This chapter also presents the United States (USA) and international perspectives on cybercrimes and privacy laws. In summary, individuals, organizations, and nations have roles to play in achieving security and reducing cyber risks.

INTRODUCTION

In the early 1980s, when the Advanced Research Projects Agency Network (ARPANET) developed the Transport Control Protocol/Internet Protocol (TCP/IP), the world became connected through the Internet. Nowadays, the Internet has a profound impact on society. Social interactions, economies, and fundamental life simply depend on cyberspace. The Internet, and more broadly cyberspace, has allowed social interaction worldwide. It has allowed sharing of information and freedom of expression – such as what occurred during the Arab Spring. Social media services, such as Twitter and Facebook played an instrumental role in the Arab Spring movements. While the cyber world brings economical and social

DOI: 10.4018/978-1-5225-0808-3.ch012

benefits, it is also vulnerable. The Internet was never designed to be secure. Identity theft, cybercrimes, cyber warfare, and others cyber illegal activities started surfacing due to lack of appropriate security controls. According to Symantec's annual security report, the numbers of cyber-targeted-attacks are increasing. Cyber attacks target everyone including small companies, large companies, government agencies, executives, and even sales people (Symantec, 2012). The global economy is being affected by cybercrime activities.

Cybercriminals are using sophisticated methods to gain unauthorized access to information systems to steal sensitive data, Personality Identifiable Information (PII), or even classified materials. Some of the creative methods that attackers use to gain unauthorized access are backdoor programs, spear phishing attacks, and social engineering. Tini, Netcat, Wrappers, EXE maker, Pretator, Restorator, and Tetris are well-known backdoor tools that can be used by attackers to setup a backdoor that allows them to connect into the computer systems. Phishing is a technique that attackers use by sending email messages with false links claiming to be a legitimate site in an attempt to acquire users' personal information. Social engineering is a powerful human-based technique that bypasses all network countermeasures by relying on human weakness to gain unauthorized access to the network. The technique targets certain personal, such as helpdesk, or executives by creating an artificial situation by exerting pressure to release the needed information.

Countries may misuse cyberspace for spying on other nations. For example, U.S. National Security Agency (NSA) is being accused for spying on world leaders and listening to 100s of millions of phone conversations worldwide. Additionally, cybersecurity incidents could disrupt water resources, power plants, healthcare, or financial institutions. A study conducted by McGraw (2013) concluded that the U.S IT infrastructure is highly vulnerable to deliberate attacks with possibly disastrous effects. The current cybersecurity technical approaches for many nations do not provide adequate computer or network security. With no surprise, President Obama has declared that, "cyber threat is one of the most serious economic and national security challenges we face as a nation" (Obama, 2012). Similarly, in 2013, in order to fight cybercrimes, the European Commission established the European Cybercrime Centre (EC3) at the European police headquarters in the Netherlands.

For the above stated reasons, governments across the world have started to collaborate by developing cybersecurity strategies. The European Union (EU) has created a cybersecurity strategy that consists of seven pillars. These pillars focus on using cyberspace to befit economically, socially, and even politically. Furthermore, the EU has put forward a framework to set the actions required to build a strong and effective countermeasures against cyber threats. In May 2013, the European Union Agency for Network and Information Security received a new authority, granting it the power to make bigger difference in protecting Europe's cyberspace. Furthermore, the U.S. has passed an executive order in 2013 to develop cybersecurity performance standards to reduce cyber risks to critical infrastructure. In addition, the United Nations Economic and Social Council (ECOSOC) has initiated an international treaty seeking to bring into line national criminal laws of cybercrimes, such as fraud, child pornography, and hate crimes.

The objective of this chapter is to provide an overview of the historical background, and trend of cybercrimes technologies and approaches. This chapter will also discuss relationship between the U.S. and global Internet operations in terms of international collaboration efforts to fight cybercrime activities. The chapter will also cover broader implications for relationships between civil liberties, innovation, and security.

MOTIVES OF CYBERCRIMINALS

Cybercrime by definition is committing an illegal act using a computer or network device (Musa, 2013). Cyber warfare, cybercrime, cyber espionage, and cyber terrorism are all similar activities, and they do overlap. They all share and use telecommunications networks to conduct all sorts of activities with different motives of course. Motives vary from revenge, jokes, terrorism, political and military espionage, business espionage, hate, to personal gain or fame. Cybercrimes can be committed against a person, an organization, or even a government. Cybercrimes against people may include crimes, such as child pornography, sexual harassment, stealing personal credit cards, and even murder. For example, in 2012, a Facebook dispute ended with a man shot in San Bernadino, California.

Cybercrime is typically driven by money or profit (Hunton, 2012). While the activities are usually aimed to harvest the financial transactions and to perform fraudulent transactions, the potential harm to individuals can be catastrophic, especially children – they are the most vulnerable. According to the Internet World Stats website, there are over 2.5 billion Internet users worldwide. Children and teenagers are among the fastest groups of Internet users; representing about 40% of Internet users (Internet Users, 2012). At present, the Internet provides predators secrecy to target children for criminal activities. Offenders can target children through chat rooms, email, or even gaming websites. The possession of online child pornography is illegal in the EU, the U.S, and many other nations. For example, in Mexico, in May 2012, a resident was sentenced to 29 years in prison for possession and production of child pornography. On the contrary, many other countries still lack adequate cybercrime laws. As a result, child pornography has become a billion dollar industry.

Cyber warfare is one of the most destructive cyber-based activities. The aim of cyber warfare can be summarized in one word, destruction. Cyber warfare simply uses cyber mediums, such as Internet or telecommunication lines, as weapons to brutally destroy enemies' critical infrastructures, such as power plants, transportation system, water plants, etc. Cyber warfare may consist of acts, such as espionage or sabotage. Cyber espionage is performed by exploiting vulnerabilities in computer systems to steal military, political, or industrial information of an adversary's networks. Cyber warfare is usually performed by a State. STUXNET virus represents a cyber-warfare activity, as it was aimed to destroy an infrastructure of an adversary (Clarke, 2010). Many believe that the U.S. helped Israel to initiate the attack, due to its level of sophistication.

Anonymous is a well-known cyber group that conducts cyber attacks with "revenge" motives. According to the Guardian magazine, Anonymous claims that it has over 9000 members and their aim is to cyber-fight for perceived injustices (Arthur, 2011). Recently, Anonymous has attacked visa.com, paypal. com, mastercard.com, and many other financial institutions in support of Wiki Leaks. The attack came after these institutions' decision to stop processing donation transfers to the Wiki Leaks group. In 2012, Time magazine categorized Anonymous as one of the 100 most influential people in the world.

CYBER INCIDENT AND SPENDING TRENDS

In the 1990s, cyber attacks and identity theft started developing. Shortly after, organized attacks started to be performed more often. The low cost of cyber network tools required to engage in cybercriminal activities makes it extremely attractive. Absurdly, it costs neither much to buy a couple of computers nor to learn a few computer programs to get engaged in cybercriminal activities.

The protection of information systems is a constant challenge, and the cost of data breach is expensive and severe. Cybercrimes cost over 100 billion dollars annually worldwide (INSA, 2011). Companies spend millions of dollars to ensure that their information systems are protected from various types of cyber attacks. In Fiscal Year (FY) 2012, The U.S. federal government agencies reported total IT security spending of $14.6 billion (OMB, 2012). Figure 1 shows the spending trend for U.S. federal agencies from 2006 to 2012.

On the contrary, the number of attacks against U.S. federal networks increased nearly 20% in 2011 (OMB, 2011). In fact, a recent ArcSight study that was conducted in 2011 concluded that the median annualized cost of companies, as a result of cyber attacks ranges from $8.9 million in US, $6.0 million in Germany, $5.1 in Japan, to $3.2 million in the United Kingdom (UK) (ArcSight, 2011). Despite all of this spending, security breaches are still on the rise. Consequently, it appears that more spending doesn't necessary imply better security or less breaches. Figure 2 illustrates the total reported incidents from 2006 to 2012. According to the U.S. Computer Emergency Readiness Team (CERT), the number of reported incidents increased from 5144 in 2006 to 46,043 incidents in 2012 (US-CERT, 2013).

TYPES OF CYBERATTACKS

Risk is the probability of a system being exploited by a threat. Threat is any person or a tool that can take advantage of vulnerabilities. Information systems' vulnerabilities continue to rise due to many factors. Automation and sophistication of hacking tools are ones of the leading causes. Not surprising, 96% of

Figure 1. Total U.S. Federal Government spending in billions (data source: FISMA reports)

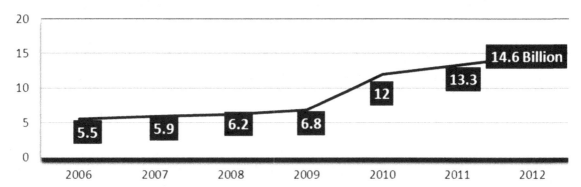

Figure 2. Total incidents per year (data source: US-CERT)

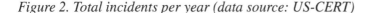
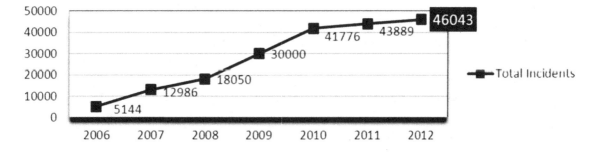

attacks were not highly difficult to launch. In 2011, there were 403 million unique variations of malware verses 286 million in 2010 (Symantec, 2012). Moreover, hackers penetrate systems by using various types of attacks, such as Trojan horse attacks, denial of service, zero-day-attack, fast flux botnet, buffer overflow, spoofing, sniffing, Structured Query Language (SQL) injection, Domain Name Services (DNS) poisoning, and many others.

Trojans are malicious programs that pretend to be something desirable. A Trojan acts as a backdoor that allows an attacker to access a system without users' consent. Trojan horse attack is one of the most critical types of attack, as the Trojan's malicious content appears to be harmless. Trojans are created to steal personal information, credit cards, banking information, and can even use a compromised computer to conduct illegal cyber activities. There are many types of Trojans, such as remote access, proxy, FTP, ICMP backdoor, and reverse connecting Trojans. Trojans use both TCP and User Datagram Protocol (UDP) to transmit information. The transmission works in a client-server relationship, where the infected computer acts as the server and the attacker or command and control machine acts as the client. Many Trojans are known to use common high ports. For example, the GirlFriend Trojan is known to use TCP port 21544, and Online KeyLogger Trojan is known to use UDP port 49301.

Banking Trojans are reaching alarming levels of sophistication. Carberp, Citadel, SpyEye, and Zeus are the most widespread banking Trojans that hit the Internet. Most of banking Trojans are difficult to detect, as they operate in stealth mode. Trojans also act as binary generator, as each Trojan creates a new binary file, which makes it difficult for anti-virus programs to detect. For example, Sdra64.exe program uses process injection to inject code into winlogon.exe or explorer.exe to exit the running processes list. Additionally, Zeus has the ability to can make registry changes to hide its attributes. Zeus allows cybercriminal to search for personal credential, and then sends them to a command and control server in real-time. Zeus Trojan often generates DNS queries to attempt to find the command and control server using DNS fast flux. Zeus can also allow an attacker to combine infected machines into groups to form a high performance botnet. Zeus has many variants. One variant uses encrypted communication. Thus, Zeus Decryptor tool can be used to decrypt the traffic.

SQL injection is a well-known form of code injection that is used to perform a denial of service attack. SQL injection attacks harm database servers by inserting SQL commands into input fields (Walker, 2012). Input validation can be used to mitigate sequel injection and remote file inclusion attacks. Validating input could also be used to reduce the chances of processing unexpected data by denying inclusion of special characters, such as "%" sign. On the other hand, buffer overflow occurs when data copied into the temporary buffers exceed the size of the buffer. Buffers are temporary blocks of memory used to store data. The extra copied data may overflow into enamoring buffers; as a result, it may overwrite existing data. There are several measures that can be taken to reduce or mitigate buffer overflow vulnerabilities. Some of these measures include, but not limited to, code auditing (automated and/or manual), non-executable stack, safe functions, compiler techniques, continuous scanning, and training programmers/software developers to prevent using unsafe functions and group standards.

Advanced Persistent Threat (APT) is a set of stealthy and continuous hacking processes often orchestrated by human targeting a specific entity. APT usually targets organizations and or nations for business or political motives. APT processes require high degree of covertness over a long period of time. As the name implies, APT consists of three major processes, advanced, persistent, and threat. The advanced process signifies sophisticated techniques using malware to exploit vulnerabilities in systems. The persistent process suggests that an external command and control is continuously monitoring and extracting data off a specific target. The threat process indicates human involvement in orchestrating the attack. APTs often breach entities via Internet, infected media, external exploitation, or internal exploitation. Internet breach may take place by sending malicious payload via email attachments, peer-to-peer file sharing, or spear phishing. On the other hand, medial infection may consist of infected Universal Serial Bus (USB) memory sticks, infected memory card, or infected appliance. Furthermore, external exploitation may occur through rogue WiFi penetration, zero day attack, or smart phone bridging. Internal exploitation on the other hand can be encountered by a rogue employee, social engineering, or funded placement. One example of internal exploitation is insider attack. Approximately, 60% of network attacks occur inside the network. An inside attack is easy to initiate and not so easy to detect or prevent. A disgruntled employee who takes revenge of his/her company by compromising its sensitive data is considered an insider attack. Some competitors go even further by sending people to get interviewed for jobs posted by their competitors. Once they get hired, they start stealing sensitive data and eventually bring down the entire organization.

There are 100s of millions of malware variations, which make is extremely challenging to protect organizations from APT. While APT activities are stealthy and hard to detect, the command and control network traffic associated with APT can be detected at the network layer level. Deep log analyses and log correlation from various sources can be useful in detecting APT activities – it's all about the logs. Agents can be used to collect logs (TCP and UDP) directly from assets into a syslog server. Then a Security Information and Event Management (SIEM) tool can correlate and analyze logs. While it is challenging to separate noises from legitimate traffic, a good log correlation tool, such as logRhythm or ArcSight can be used to filter out the legitimate traffic, so security staff can focus on the noises.

As the name implies, in a denial of service attack, a hacker attempts to deny access to a particular service or Internet site by processing so many transactions more than the targeted computers can handle. Denial of service attack can also target a network to a point that nothing can get in or out of the network. Figure 3 explains the most reported attacks by US-CERT. Incident data reveal that malicious code continuous to be the most widely reported incident type across the U.S. federal government. In 2011 malicious code accounted for 26% of total incidents reported by U.S. federal agencies.

Figure 3. Incidents per category 2010-2012 (data source: US-CERT)

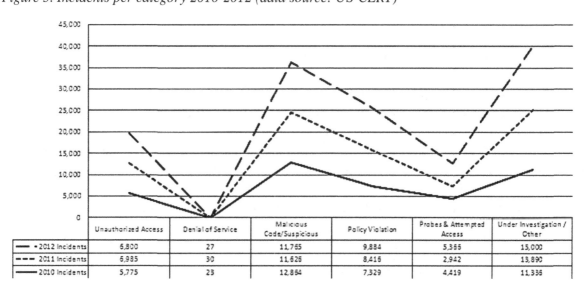

	Unauthorized Access	Denial of Service	Malicious Code/Suspicious	Policy Violation	Probes & Attempted Access	Under Investigation / Other
2012 Incidents	6,800	27	11,765	9,884	5,365	15,000
2011 Incidents	6,985	30	11,625	8,416	2,942	13,890
2010 Incidents	5,775	23	12,864	7,329	4,419	11,335

Another reason for the continuous rise of cyber attacks is the weakness of information systems (Whitman, 2011). Whitman, a Computer Science professor at Kennesaw State University, believes that the recurring events of virus and warm attacks simply illustrate the weakness in current information systems; it suggests the need to provide better security for these systems (Whitman, 2011). Whitman stresses that the purpose of his book, *Principles of Information Security*, is to provide surveys and discipline of information security with a balanced of security management and technical components of security. Whitman argues that people and procedures have always been threats to the system, and they should not be overlooked (Whitman, 2011). Whitman goes further by explaining that a bottom-up approach can be used to the implementation of information security in organizations. He stresses that system administrators who work on a day-to-day basis on these systems, possess the in-depth knowledge that can and must be enhanced to develop and improve information security. Whitman encourages the top-down-approach by strong upper management support and dedicated funding for implementing security.

INTERNATIONAL PRIVACY LAWS

Privacy laws deal with regulation of information and how to collect, store, and use data. Privacy laws can also target specific types of information, such as health, communications, and financial. Many nations, such as Canada, U.S., Brazil, Australia, India, and others, have well-established privacy laws in place.

In 1950, the Council of Europe adopted Article 8 on Human Rights. The purpose of the article is to protect the right to respect for private and family life. Additionally, the United Nations, in 1966, developed Article 17 on Civil and Political Rights. The aim of the article is to prohibit interference with individuals' privacy, family, and home correspondence.

In 1993, the New Zealand Privacy Act was created to establish standards related to collection, storage, and disclosure of personal information. In 1995, China enacted the Computer Processed Personal Information Protection Act. The aim of the act is to protect personal information managed by computers. In 1998, the U.K. enacted the Data Protection Act, which defines U.K. law on data processing. The legislation focuses on the protection of personal data. In India, Information Technology Act of 2000 was enacted to protect individuals' privacy. In 2011 India passed a new privacy law that applies to companies and consumers. In Canada, individuals' privacy is protected by the federal Personal Information Protection and Electronic Documents Act (PIPEDA). Finally, in Brazil, people are protected by the country's constitution. Article 5 of the constitution of Brazil clearly states that "the intimacy, private life, honor and image of the people are inviolable" (Brazil. Const. art. V).

Unfortunately, not all nations follow their privacy laws. Recently, the U.S. intelligence community admitted conducting surveillance on individuals and world leaders. People in Europe and U.S. were not aware of how much data was being collected or how much assistance U.S. companies were providing for the intelligence community. In response to such a privacy breach, in October 2013, the European Parliament voted to fortify Europe's data protection and privacy laws. The parliament is planning to enforce fines of up to 100 million euros on companies that break privacy laws. The parliament is also planning to impose strict rules on how data can be shared or transferred to non-EU countries.

U.S. PRIVACY LAWS

Of the many laws that control data protection in the U.S., there are four major data security acts that promote data privacy and cyber protection. The four acts are the Privacy Act of 1974, the Children's Online Privacy Protection Act the Fair and Accurate Credit Transaction Act (COPPA), the Fair and Accurate Credit Transaction Act (FACTA), and the Health Insurance Portability and Accountability Act (HIPPA).

The Privacy Act was enacted in December 31, 1974. This law governs the collection, storage, use, and dissemination of Personally Identifiable Information (PII). The Privacy Act prohibits the disclosure of information without a written consent of the individual. There are 12 statutory exceptions. Some of these exceptions include disclosure for law enforcement purposes, congressional investigations, and for statistical purposes by the Census Bureau.

The U.S. enacted COPPA in 1998. The aim of the act is to protect the privacy of children under the age of 13. COPPA imposes an obligation on the operations of websites that are directed at children to publish privacy policies specifying whether personal information is being collected. If information is to be collected, the site operators must obtain parental consent. The U.S. Federal Trade Commission (FTC) has brought a number of actions against websites host providers for failure to comply with COPPA. UMG Recording, for example, was fined $400,000 for COPPA violations.

FACTA was passed by the U.S. Congress on November 22, 2003. The aim of the act is to help protect consumers' credit information from the risk of data and identity theft. The law contains seven major titles: identity theft prevention and credit history restoration, improvements in use of and consumer access to credit information, enhancing the accuracy of consumer report information, limiting the use and sharing of medical information in the financial system, financial literacy and education improvement, protecting employee misconduct investigations, and relation to state laws. In response to FACTA, credit cards receipts do not list more than the last four digits of the card number. The act also grants individuals the right to request free credit report from the three credit reporting agencies (Equifax, Experian, and TransUnion).

HIPPA was enacted by President Bill Clinton in 1996. The aim of the act is to protect individuals' health information. The act has two major titles. Title I is health care access, portability, and renewability. The title regulates the group market rules, the availability, and span of group health plans. Title II is the preventing health care fraud and abuse – administrative simplification medical liability reform. The title defines policies and procedures for maintaining the privacy and security of individually identifiable health information.

U.S. CYBERSECURITY STRATEGY

In the U.S., federal cybersecurity regulations are derived from the Congress and the White House. The aim of these regulations is to safeguard the nation as a whole, including infrastructures, and information systems. The purpose of the regulations is to force corporations and government agencies to protect their systems from cyber attacks. Cyber attacks may include code injection, phishing, social engineering, or backdoor Trojans. Cyber attacks are increasing and targeting everyone. Cybersecurity is essential to the economy, as it is vital to the operation of critical systems, such as power plants, hospitals, schools, and even financial institutions. As a result, cybersecurity regulations must exist.

While the U.S. is considered a top-spamming country, it also fosters many cybersecurity related laws – Electronic Communications Privacy Act (ECPA), National Infrastructure Protection Act (NIPA),

Cyberspace Electronic Security Act (CESA), Patriot Act, Cyber Security Enhancement Act (CSEA), and Anti-Phishing Act are just a few. The U.S. has federal and state cybersecurity regulations in place. The Federal Information Security Act (FISMA) regulates federal agencies information systems. FISMA requires federal agencies to undergo security assessment to assure the security of the information systems. On the other hand, a state such as California passed the Notice of Security Breach Act. The act requires companies to disclose details of security incidents. This law, in a way, penalizes companies for not protecting their systems against cyber threats.

The U.S. congress has passed multiple bills that expand cybersecurity regulations. For example, the Consumer Data Security and Notification Act (CDSNA) requires disclosure of security breaches by financial institutions. Additionally, the Security Protect Yourself Against Cyber Trespass Act (SPY-ACT) requires companies to improve cybersecurity; the bill focuses on phishing and spyware. It makes it unlawful to modify settings, or install software without authorization.

In the spirit of enhancing the security and resiliency of the cyber and communications infrastructure of the U.S., the Senate introduced a bill in 2012, which may be cited as the Cybersecurity Act of 2012. Mr. Lieberman, Ms. Collins, Mr. Rockefeller, and Mrs. Feinstein introduced the bill, which consists of nine titles:

Title I: Protecting critical infrastructure;
Title II: Protecting government networks (FISMA Reform);
Title III: Clarifying and strengthening existing roles and authorities;
Title IV: Reduction, recruitment, and workforce development;
Title V: Research and development;
Title VI: Federal acquisition risk management strategy;
Title VII: Information sharing;
Title VIII: Public awareness reports; and
Title IX: International cooperation.

Unfortunately, the bill did not pass. In August 2012, in a 52 to 46 vote, the Senate did not enact the Cybersecurity Act of 2012. The bill failed to gain the 60 required votes, in order to move the bill up for a full vote. In response to the senate's vote on the bill, Senator Lieberman stated "this is one of those days when I fear for our country and I'm not proud of the U.S. Senate. We've got a crisis, and it's one that we all acknowledge. It's not just that there's a theoretical or speculative threat of cyber attack against our country - it's real" (Lieberman, 2012). The blockage of the bill does not necessarily mean the government will stop imposing security measures. The US President, for example, could issue a prudential directive to order federal agencies to establish certain cybersecurity measures. HSPD-23 for example was ordered in 2008. The directive requires government agencies to act as a single network enterprise with Trusted Internet Connection (TIC). It required agencies to deploy Intrusion Prevention Systems (IPS) and Intrusion Detection System (IDS) to detect and prevent malicious traffic within the federal enterprise.

In February 2013, President Obama issued an executive order on Improving Critical Infrastructure Cybersecurity. The Order requires the National Institute of Standards and Technology (NIST) to work with other agencies to develop a voluntary framework for reducing cyber risks to critical infrastructure (White House, 2013). In response, NIST started communicating with other agencies to develop the framework. The framework will consist of standards, guidelines, and best practices to encourage the protection of information systems supporting critical infrastructure operations. The intention of the framework is to create a scalable and cost-effective approach to help agencies to manage cybersecurity related risks, while protecting confidentiality, integrity, and availability of data (NIST, 2013).

EU PRIVACY LAWS

In Europe, privacy laws are a highly mature legal specialty area. The European Convention on Human Rights (ECHR) is an international treaty to protect human rights in Europe. The treaty was drafted in 1950 and then came into force in 1953. Article 8 of this treaty concerns privacy. Article 8 provides the rights to respect for one's private, family life, and home. Furthermore, in 1980, the Organization for Economic Cooperation and Development (OECD), an international economic organization of 34 countries, issued seven principles to help governing personal data. The principles included notice, purpose, consent, security, disclosure, access, and accountability principles pertaining to processing, handling, and storing data. In addition to Article 8 of the ECHR and the seven principles of OECD, directive 1995/46/EC and 2002/58/EC are the two major legislative bodies that govern privacy and electronic communications security in EU.

Directive 95/46/EC is known as the data protection directive. The scope of the directive is to protect individuals with regard to collecting, processing, and storing personal data by automatic means. The directive consists of 34 articles. Article 6 of the directive ensures that the data controller is in compliance with data quality principles. Some of these principles include, but not limited to, fair processing of data, legitimate purpose for processing data, and accuracy of data. In addition, Article 10 and 11 of the directive requires that the data subject must include the identity of the controller, the purpose of processing the data. Article 12 specifically calls for the member States to guarantee that every data subject has the right to know to whom the data was disclosed, and the right to obtain the erasure or blocking of data that do not comply with the directive (European Commission, 1995).

E-privacy directive 2002/58/EC is the second major legal authority that regulates data projection in EU. Directive 2002/58/EC of the European Parliament was enacted on July 12, 2002. The directive is concerning the processing of personal data and the protection of privacy in the electronic communications sector. Electronic communications include, but not limited to, Internet transactions, email, automated calling machines, telefaxes, and SMS messages. The directive consists of 21 articles that discuss the data traffic, unsolicited communications, security, and confidentiality of the data. Article 13 specifically discusses unsolicited communications. The article requires the member States to take proper measures to guarantee that unsolicited communications not to be allowed without a permission of the concerned subscriber, free of charge. The directive makes it clear that equipment on the network is part of the private domain of the users requiring protection under the European Conventional of the protection of Human Rights and Fundamental Freedoms (European Commission, 2002). The directive also prohibits spyware or other unsolicited software to be installed without the users' knowledge. Furthermore, the directive grants users the right to refuse cookies or similar programs stored on computer.

EU CYBERSECURITY STRATEGY

Understanding the increasing threat of cyber crimes and its profound impact on the economy, the European Commission has established a new cybersecurity strategy. According to the European Commission website, the new strategy, also known as Europe 2020 initiative, has a digital agenda that consists of seven pillars (Europe Commission 2020 initiative, 2013).

The first pillar is the digital single market. The aim of the digital single market pillar is to protect EU consumers in cyberspace, and to remove the obstacles that are hindering free flow of online services. The strategy of the pillar is geared toward enhancing the music download business and launching a single area for online payments. Some of the proposed action initiatives that are proposed to achieve the objective of the first pillar, include, but not limited to, simplifying pan-European licensing for online works, revision of the e-Signature directive, and protecting intellectual property rights online.

The second pillar applies to interoperability and standards. The goal of the pillar is to ensure that Europe IT devices, applications, services, and data repositories interact flawlessly (Europe Commission 2020 initiative, 2013). Some of the proposed actions initiatives to achieve this goal include creating a European interoperability framework, promoting standards-setting rules, and identifying and assessing means of requesting significant market to license information about products and services.

The third pillar is pertaining to trust and security. The goal of the pillar is to reduce the risks of malicious software and online fraud. Some of the proposed action solutions, include but not limited to, coordinated European responses to cyber attacks, reinforcing network and information security policy, establish a European cybercrime platform, creating a European Cybercrime Centre, strengthen the fight against cybercrime at the international level, supporting the report of illegal content online, awareness movements on online safety for children, and enforcing rules on personal data protection,

The fourth pillar concerns fast and ultra-fast Internet access. High definition televisions and video-conferences services require high-speed Internet. As a result, currently, Europe needs to have a download speed rate of 30 Mbps for its citizens and 100 Mbps by 2020 (Europe Commission 2020 initiative, 2013). Some of the proposed action solutions include developing national broadband plans, safeguarding the open Internet for consumers, reduction of the cost of deploying high-speed electronic communications network.

The fifth pillar is about enhancing digital literacy, skills and inclusion. 30% of Europeans have never used the Internet at all (Europe Commission 2020 initiative, 2013). The goal of this pillar is to enhance digital skills to people, in order to fully participate in society. Some of the items that the digital agenda is proposing to tackle include prioritizing digital literacy for European social fund, developing a framework to recognize Information and Communication Technology (ICT) skills, and to mainstream e-Learning in national policies.

The sixth pillar focuses on research and innovations. The objective of this pillar is to turn best research ideas into marketable products and services. Such an objective can be achieved by leveraging more private investment for ICT research and innovation, and by reinforcing coordination and merging of resources. Other strategies include developing new generation of web-based applications and services.

The seventh pillar focuses on enabling ICT benefits for EU society. ICT can be used to reduce energy consumption and transform health services. Some of the European Commission's proposed strategies to achieve the objective of the seventh pillar include partnership between the ICT sectors. Other initiatives include launching green paper on solid state lighting, and fostering EU-wide standards interoperability testing and certification of e-Health.

As a collective EU response to the increasing amount of cybercrimes, the European Commission decided to establish a European Cybercrime Centre (EC3) at Europol, which is the European law enforcement agency in The Hague, Netherlands. The objective of the center is to act as a focal point in Europe to fight cybercrime, contribute to the faster reactions in the event of online crimes, and to support international allies. The EC3 officially started its activities on January 1st, 2013. However, it is expected to be fully functional by 2015.

CYBERSPACE CHALLENGES

There is a bridging now from the digital-world to the physical-world. Cyber attacks are capable of taking over industrial systems, such as STUXNET virus that attacked the Iranian nuclear power plant. Cyberspace has a target attribution problem; it is very difficult to know the exact location where the attack originated. For example, an attacker in China could lease a server in Europe to hack into a system in Russia, and then deliver an attack on a financial institution in the U.S. Due to lack of international cybersecurity policies, many governments and businesses are in a very difficult situation in pursuing legal actions against cybercriminals. Consequently, many nations that lack cybersecurity laws are considered cyber-sanctuary to hackers.

The sophistication and relatively cheap cost of hacking tools make cyberspace even more challenging. Cybercriminals constantly evolve their hacking techniques, and even minor changes enable them to escape automated detection. Hackers also share their intelligence as the speed of the Internet. They communicate and collaborate much more freely than law enforcement and security professionals do. Unlike law enforcement or federal agencies, hackers are not regulated. Furthermore, lack of web regulations, lack of skilled security analysts, and poor information security posture are among the leading factors that have led to the flourishing of cybercrimes. The following are some of the causes of poor security posture in many organizations (Musa, 2013):

1. Lack of continuous monitoring.
2. Lack of continuous specialized training.
3. Lack of funding to implement security projects.
4. Lack of cybersecurity awareness training.
5. Lack of knowledgeable assessors.
6. Lack of leadership and leadership support.
7. Lack of strategic planning.
8. Misconfiguration of network devices.
9. Vague security policies and procedures.

Other challenges involved in fighting cybercrime include lack of cybersecurity research and development, and insufficient collaboration between government and private sectors. Governments are encouraged to embrace and effectively fund cybersecurity research and development. Governments must place emphasis on enhancing coordination efforts and fostering cybersecurity initiatives between government and private sectors. Additionally, private sectors need to collaborate in joint initiatives. Some private sectors are hesitant to work collaboratively with other private sectors: they are afraid that their competitors may find a breach to gain competitive advantage. The truth is most competitors are in the same boat of vulnerability; they face the same threats. Working together will most likely enhance their resistance mechanisms against cybercrimes, in both collaborative development and also by peer review. A simple memorandum of agreement or privacy disclosure agreement can protect collaborators.

Jurisdiction is another cyberspace challenge that many nations are facing. Jurisdiction is usually determined based on the location where the offense was committed. In real court systems, judges work on cases that are within their jurisdiction. But in the cyber world, an attacker could be anywhere in the world far from the crime scene. Even if a cybercriminal is brought to trial, law enforcement on an international criminal is very complex in countries which do not have uniform or equivalent cybersecurity laws.

CIVIL LIBERTY AND PRIVACY CONCERNS

Almost all types of communications, including Internet and mobile phones leave trails or digital footprint. Digital footprint provides data on visited web sites, searched links, what was typed, what was said, and even physical location. Some companies use such data in targeted marketing or social influence. Some digital footprint data may be available to the public by performing a simple Internet search, and other material may be inaccessible without access rights. Digital footprint data may deduce personal information, such as race, religion, political views, or intelligence. Therefore, data collected via digital footprint may impact personal privacy and civil liberty.

Digital footprint is controversial in that privacy is in competition. In the U.S., the recent update to the Cyber Intelligence Sharing and Protection Act (CISPA) is a great example. Recently, 34 civil liberties organizations have opposed the new amendments to CISPA. CISPA provides exception to privacy laws. CISPA information sharing allows companies to transfer sensitive data, including Internet data, emails, and others to other companies and government agencies, without prior authorization of the concerned individuals. Unexpectedly, the White House threatens to veto the controversial CISPA unless privacy and civil liberties protections are included to the updated act.

TECHNICAL APPROACHES

Risks can be managed in four ways: they can be accepted, avoided, mitigated, or simply transferred. Risk acceptance indicates accepting the loss from the risk, when it occurs. On the other hand, risk avoidance signifies eliminating the risk by not performing the activity that could carry risk (Poolsappasit, 2010). An example would be not buying a program that handles electronic transactions on an unsecured port, such as port 80. Mitigating the risk would involve reducing the likelihood of the loss from occurring. Additionally, buying insurance on property signifies risk transfer.

There are numerous measures available to mitigate cyber risks. Risks can be mitigated by technical and non-technical approaches. Technical approaches may include access control measures, such as firewall, anti-virus software, content filtering proxy servers, white listing, intrusion detection and prevention systems, vulnerability assessment, disk encryption, and certification and accreditation to ensure that systems have the appropriate security controls in place. Port security and MAC filtering can also be used to prevent rogue devises from connecting to the network. Also, there are several measures that can be taken to reduce or mitigate buffer overflow vulnerabilities, such as code auditing, non-executable stack, safe functions, and compiler techniques.

Layer two security best practices may include using dedicated Virtual Local Area Network (VLAN) identification for trunk ports, avoiding using VLAN1, setting ports to non-trunking, and disabling unused ports. In addition, Dynamic Host Configuration Protocol (DHCP) snooping and VLAN Access List (ACL) can be deployed to stop most DHCP attacks. Furthermore, layer three best practices may include ingress/egress filtering using Unicast Reverse Path Forwarding (RPF) or ACL as necessary. Routers need to be configured with ACL, role based sub-netting, and routing protocol authentication. Other best practices to defeat network attacks may include keeping security patches up to date, shutting down unused services and ports, using passphrases and change them periodically, avoiding unnecessary web page inputs, performing data backup regularly, and enabling full disk encryption. Minimizing administrators' privileges, applying application directory white listing, and implementing digital signature and two-factor authentication solutions are also highly recommended.

NIST suggests that real-time monitoring of security controls using automated tools will provide agencies with a dynamic outlook of the efficiency of security controls and the organization security position. NIST encourages agencies to adopt a hybrid continuous monitoring solution that consists of both manual processes and automated process that consist of vulnerability scanning, penetration testing, log monitoring, log analysis, and log correlation tools.

Some vulnerability assessment methods include network discovery, wireless scanning, password cracking, penetration testing, social engineering, and systems vulnerability scans. There are many vulnerability assessment tools currently available for no change, also known as open source. Some of these tools include, but not limited to, Wireshark, NMAP, OpenVAS, Air Crack, Nikto, WebSecurkity, SQLmap, and Nessus. Nessus is one of the most widely used vulnerability assessment tool. Many security experts consider Nessus as one of the most powerful vulnerability assessment tools (Gascon, Orfila & Blasco, 2011). Nessus is capable of performing verity of network scans, such as discovery, auditing, compliance, patch management, and vulnerability analysis scans.

Penetration testing is a very powerful form of vulnerability assessment that can be used to continuously monitor the network security posture and the network ability to resist attacks. Penetration testing is a security testing that mimics real-world attack. It is used as a method for circumventing the security features of a system (Bechtsoudis & Sklavos, 2012). In addition to the tools referenced above, Core impact pro and Metaspolit framework are considered by many security experts as the best two penetration testing tools.

One of the most powerful automated continuous monitoring tools is IPS. As the name implies, IPS detects and prevents intrusions. There are three major detection methods that most of the IPSs rely on: behavior, signature, and anomaly based detections (Gade & Kumar, 2012). The behavior-based monitoring method depends on the formation of a baseline. Once this baseline is established, the monitoring tool is able to detect activities that vary from that standard of normal. The signature-based monitoring method depends on a database of signatures of known malicious or unwanted activities. An advantage of the signature-based method is that it can rapidly and accurately distinguish any event from its database of signatures (Pao, Or & Cheung, 2013). The anomaly-based monitoring method depends on rules by detecting out of normal operation or invalid form of activity (Stanciu, 2013).

NON-TECHNICAL APPROACHES

Security policies and awareness training are non-technical approaches that can be used as measures to reduce cyber risks. As indicated above, some of the causes of weak security posture include devices misconfiguration, lack of training, and lake of security awareness. Misconfiguration of network devices is a direct result of lack of training (Musa, 2013). A study conducted by Stout (2006) concluded that lack of security training is a factor of the increase of systems' vulnerabilities. Training and motivating employees to work together enables faster problem detection and resolution (Ahmad, Wasay, & Malik, 2012). On the contrary, not providing training is one of the root causes for employees being disgruntled (Raines, 2013). Dissatisfied employees are the greatest threat in an organization when it comes to data leaks. Raines (2013) suggests that employees' satisfaction or dissatisfaction will impact the organization's performance. Therefore, training can be utilized as a tool to mitigate cyber risks.

Developing international agreements between nations is a non-technical solution that can be utilized to minimize cyber risks. The Budapest Convention (also known as the convention of cybercrime) is one of the most powerful international agreements on fighting cybercrimes. The agreement was adopted by committee of Ministers of the Council of Europe (CMCE) in 2001. The agreement targets infringements of copyright, child pornography, hate crimes, and violations of network security. Additionally, EU established EC3, which is cross-border law enforcement against cybercrime. US Vice-President Joe Biden, speaking at the 2011 London Conference on Cyberspace, called EC3 "the best form of international agreement in this area".

In 1997, the Group of Eight (G8), eight great industrialized countries (US, UK, Russia, France, Italy, Japan, Germany, and Canada) released a "Minister's Communique" as a roadmap to fight cybercrime. The agreement mandates that law enforcement must be equipped with the latest technology, in order to properly fight cybercrimes. Furthermore, in 2002, Asia-Pacific Economic Cooperation (APEC) adopted cybersecurity strategy to fight cybercrimes. The strategy consists of six major areas: legal developments, information sharing, security and technical guidelines, public awareness, and training and education. In 2009, the Economic Community of West African States (ECOWAS) adopted a framework on fighting cybercrimes.

National Initiative for Cybersecurity Education (NICE) is a national public awareness program lead by the U.S. NIST to guide the American people to a higher level of Internet safety. The goal of the program is to raise awareness among the American public about the need to strengthen cybersecurity. The objective of the program is to persuade Americans to see Internet safety as a shared responsibility.

FUTURE RESEARCH DIRECTIONS

Cybercriminals continue to target different industries and different users each new year that passes. Cybercriminals are continuously changing the way they target people. Cybercrimes simply gets more sophisticated every year. Many enterprise technologies, such as Bring Your Own Device (BYOD), cloud computing, social media, or mobile devices are transforming the face of information security. Some of the top cybercrime trends that are expected to evolve include, but not limited to, financial industries, human trafficking, and mobile transactions. There are billions of users that are currently using smartphones. People use smartphones to listen to music, conduct banking transactions, purchase clothing, and conduct business transactions. As people depend more on mobile devices, cybercriminals may refine their approaches to exploit mobile transactions.

CONCLUSION

The Internet has become an essential service for support of many industries, such as academic institutes, news agencies, airports, and even utility companies. However, the Internet was designed to be an open, academic tool, never to be secure. As a result, cybercrimes, cyber warfare, and other cyber illegal activities have spread to become a significant portion of Internet traffic. The protection of information systems is a constant challenge, and the cost of each data breach is expensive, but also severe to trust and reputation: cybercrimes cost over $100 billion dollars annually worldwide. Companies spend millions of dollars to protect their assets; despite all of this spending, security breaches are still on the rise. Consequently, it appears that more spending doesn't necessary imply better security or fewer breaches. Factors that contribute to the rise of cybercrime include, but not limited to, lack of international regulations, lack of web security standards, insufficiency of user awareness, lack of collaboration between agencies, and extreme sophistication of hacking tools. While government agencies are regulated, hackers are not. Hackers communicate and collaborate much more freely than law enforcement agencies do.

Today, the Internet offers predators anonymity to target children for criminal activities. While the Internet can be a great knowledge source for children, children can be targeted by offenders through the relative anonymity and insecurity of social media websites, chat rooms, email, and even gaming websites. Many nations have many laws to protect children online; however, children's best online protection is parents. Parents must become computer literate, in order to get involved with their children's online activities. Parents are responsible for mentoring their children about the Internet safety. Parents are also liable for verifying the identity of the individuals interacting with their children. Furthermore, parents should use the parental-control features which are provided by many Internet service providers to control what children can see and browse on the Internet. Parents are highly encouraged to contact local authorities if they suspect that their children have been targeted by sex offenders.

Jurisdiction and target attribution are technical challenges involved in fighting cybercrime. It is difficult to know the exact location where an attack originated, and since cybercriminals can initiate attacks from anywhere in the world, it is challenging to determine who has jurisdiction on a court case. Simply, there are no cyber borders between nations. Making cyberspace reliable and secure is imperative for international economic growth and democracy. Therefore, fighting cybercrimes requires international collaboration; cybersecurity is inherently a global issue, and a global approach is now indispensable.

There are technical and non-technical approaches that can be utilized to mitigate cyber risks. Technical solutions may include white listing, firewall, intrusion prevention systems, and anti-virus services at the host level and gateway level. Trojans and other cyber threats can be detected and prevented by applying layering technologies, such as two-factor authentication, and transaction verification processes. IPS indicators and signatures may also be used to detect and block malware Trojans. Non-technical solutions may include national cybersecurity awareness programs for less-sophisticated users, enforceable policies and procedures on cybersecurity for corporations, and cybersecurity agreements between nations. The United Nations could play a vital role in fighting cybercrimes by fostering and enforcing international cybersecurity frameworks. Governments are encouraged to place primary emphasis on cybersecurity research and development, to harmonize cybersecurity efforts between public and private sectors, and to adopt uniform procedures for enforcement and prosecution. Public and private sectors simply need to collaborate aggressively in joint initiatives. In conclusion, cybercrime impacts public and private sectors together, and it will take society to work collaboratively, in order to make a significant impact against cybercrime. Individuals, organizations, and governments all have roles to play in achieving security and reducing cyber risks.

REFERENCES

Ahmad, M., Wasay, E., & Malik, S. (2012). Impact of employee motivation on customer satisfaction: Study of airline industry in Pakistan. *Interdisciplinary Journal of Contemporary Research in Business*, *4*(6), 531–539.

ArcSight. (2011). *Second annual cost of cybercrime study*. Retrieved from http://www.hpenterprisesecurity.com/collateral/report

Arthur, C. (2011, February 7). Anonymous attacks US security company. *The Guardian Magazine*. Retrieved from http://www.theguardian.com

Bechtsoudis, A., & Sklavos, N. (2012). Aiming at higher network security through extensive penetration tests. *IEEE Latin America Transactions*, *10*(3), 1752–1756. doi:10.1109/TLA.2012.6222581

Brazil Constitution. (n.d.). *Article V*. Retrieved from http://english.tse.jus.br/arquivos/federal-constitution

Clarke, R. (2010). *Cyber war: The next threat to national security and what to do about it*. New York: Ecco.

European Commission. (1995). *Directive 95/46/EC of the European Parliament and of the Council on the protection of individuals with regard to the processing of personal data and on the free movement of such data*. Retrieved from http://ec.europa.eu/justice/policies/privacy/docs/95-46-ce/dir1995-46_part1_en.pdf

European Commission. (2002). *Directive 2002/58/EC of the European Parliament and of the Council of 12 July 2002 concerning the processing of personal data and the protection of privacy in the electronic communications sector*. Retrieved from http://eur-lex.europa.eu/LexUriServ/LexUriServ.do?uri=OJ:L :2002:201:0037:0037:EN:PDF

European Commission. (2013). *Europe 2020 initiative*. Retrieved from http://ec.europa.eu/digital-agenda/en

Gascon, H., Orfila, A., & Blasco, J. (2011). Analysis of update delays in signature-based network intrusion detection systems. *Computers & Security*, *30*(8), 613–624. doi:10.1016/j.cose.2011.08.010

Hunton, P. (2012). Data attack of the cybercriminal: Investigating the digital currency of cybercrime. *Computer Law & Security Report*, *28*(2), 201–207. 10.1016/j.clsr.2012.01.007 doi:10.1016/j.clsr.2012.01.007

Intelligence and National Security Alliance (INSA). (2011). *Cyber Intelligence*. Retrieved from http://issuu.com/insalliance/docs/insa_cyber_intelligence/1

Internet Users. (2012). Retrieved from http://www.internetworldstats.com/stats.htm

Kumar, S., & Gade, R. (2012). Experimental evaluation of Cisco ASA-5510 intrusion prevention system against denial of service attacks. *Journal of Information Security*, *3*(2), 122–137. doi:10.4236/jis.2012.32015

Lieberman, J. (2012). Senator Lieberman's speech on cybersecurity act. *Washington Post.* Retrieved from http://www.washingtonpost.com/blogs/2chambers/post/cybersecurity-bill-fails-in-the-senate/2012/08/02/gJQABofxRX_blog.html

McGraw, G. (2013). Cyber war is inevitable (unless we build security in). *The Journal of Strategic Studies*, *36*(1), 109–119. doi:10.1080/01402390.2012.742013

Musa, W. (2013). *Improving cybersecurity audit processes in the U.S. government.* (Unpublished doctoral dissertation). National Graduate School, Falmouth, MA.

Obama, B. (2012). *President Obama's comments on cyber security.* Retrieved from http://www.whitehouse.gov/cybersecurity

Pao, D., Or, N., & Cheung, R. C. (2013). A memory-based NFA regular expression match engine for signature-based intrusion detection. *Computer Communications*, *36*(10-11), 1255–1267. doi:10.1016/j.comcom.2013.03.002

Poolsappasit, N. (2010). *Towards an efficient vulnerability analysis methodology for better security risk management* (Doctoral dissertation). Retrieved from ProQuest dissertations and theses database. (Document ID 3419113).

Privacy Act of 1974 § 102, 42 U.S.C. § 4332 (1974).

Raines, S. (2013). *Conflict management for managers: resolving workplace, client, and policy disputes.* San Francisco, CA: Jossey-Bass.

Stanciu, N. (2013). Technologies, methodologies and challenges in network intrusion detection and prevention systems. *Informatica Economica*, *17*(1), 144–156. doi:10.12948/issn14531305/17.1.2013.12

Stout, T. (2006). *Improving the decision making process for information security through a pre-implementation impact review of security countermeasures* (Doctoral dissertation). Retrieved from ProQuest dissertations and theses database (Document ID 3215299)

Symantec Corporation. (2012). *2012 Annual Security Report.* Retrieved from http://www.symantec.com/annualreport

United States Computer Emergency Readiness Team (US-CERT). (2013). *Malicious Code.* Retrieved from http://www.us-cert.gov/government-users/reporting-requirements

United States National Institute of Standards and Technology (NIST). (2013). *Cyber Framework.* Retrieved from http://www.nist.gov/itl/cyberframework.cfm

United States Office of Management and Budget (OMB). (2011). *FY2011 Report to congress on implementation the federal information security management act of 2002.* Retrieved from http://www.whitehouse.gov/sites/default/files/omb/assets/egov_docs/fy11_fisma.pdf

United States Office of Management and Budget (OMB). (2012). *FY2011 Report to congress on implementation the federal information security management act of 2002*. Retrieved from http://www. whitehouse.gov/sites/default/files/omb/assets/egov_docs/fy12_fisma.pdf

Walker, M. (2012). *Certified Ethical Hacker: Exam guide: All-in-one*. New York: McGraw-Hill.

White House. (2013). *Executive order on improving critical infrastructure cybersecurity*. Retrieved from http://www.whitehouse.gov/the-press-office/2013/02/12/executive-order-improving-critical-infrastructure-cybersecurity

Whitman, M. (2011). *Principles of information security*. Boston, MA: Course Technology.

KEY TERMS AND DEFINITIONS

APT: Advanced Persistent Threat (APT) is a set of stealthy and continuous hacking processes often orchestrated by human targeting a specific entity.

Cybercrime: Committing an illegal act using a computer or network device.

Cyber Warfare: Utilizes cyber mediums, such as Internet or telecommunication lines, as weapons to brutally destroy enemies' critical infrastructures, such as power plants.

Digital Footprint: A process that provides data on visited web sites, searched links, what was typed, what was said, and even physical location.

IDS/IPS: Intrusion Detection/Prevention System - Software or appliance that detects and prevents malicious traffic.

Risk: The probability of a vulnerability being exploited.

Threat: Entity presenting a danger to an asset.

Trojan: A malicious program that pretends to be something desirable. It hides its true identity.

This work was previously published in the Handbook of Research on Digital Crime, Cyberspace Security, and Information Assurance edited by Maria Manuela Cruz-Cunha and Irene Maria Portela, pages 193-210, copyright 2015 by Information Science Reference (an imprint of IGI Global).

Chapter 13

A Wrapper–Based Classification Approach for Personal Identification through Keystroke Dynamics Using Soft Computing Techniques

Shanmugapriya D.
Avinashilingam Institute for Home Science and Higher Education for Women, India

Padmavathi Ganapathi
Avinashlingam Institute for Home Science and Higher Education for Women, India

ABSTRACT

The password is the most widely used identity verification method in computer security domain. However, due to its simplicity, it is vulnerable to imposters. A way to strengthen the password is to combine Biometric technology with password. Keystroke dynamics is one of the behavioural biometric approaches which is cheaper and does not require any sophisticated hardware other than the keyboard. The chapter uses a new feature called Virtual Key Force along with the commonly extracted timing features. Features are normalized using Z-Score method. For feature subset selection, Particle Swarm Optimization wrapped with Extreme Learning Machine is proposed. Classification is done with wrapper based PSO-ELM approach. The proposed methodology is tested with publically available benchmark dataset and real time dataset. The proposed method yields the average accuracy of 97.92% and takes less training and testing time when compared with the traditional Back Propagation Neural Network.

INTRODUCTION

The confidential information can be secured from unauthorized users by providing authentication. User authentication is defined as the process of verifying the identity claimed by an individual. User Authentication is normally classified into three categories namely, Knowledge based Authentication,

DOI: 10.4018/978-1-5225-0808-3.ch013

Object based Authentication, and Biometric based Authentication (Lawrence O'Gorman, 2003) which is shown in Figure 1.

Knowledge based Authentication is based on "something the user knows". User name and passwords come under this category. However, passwords are vulnerable to password hackers because the users sometimes can't remember the strong passwords and they write them down. Something the user has or possesses is called Object based authentication. Tokens or Personal Identification Numbers (PINs) are the widely used examples of this type of authentication. Tokens are easy to misplace or damage and PINs are vulnerable to shoulder surfing and systematic trial-and-error attacks (Seong-seob Hwang, Cho and Park, 2009). Biometric based authentication provides a very reliable method of authenticating a user and is divided into physiological and behavioral types (Francesco and Picardi, 2002). Physiological biometrics refer to what the person is or they measure physical parameters of certain parts of the body and Behavioral biometrics shows how the person is using the body for authentication. Figure 2. shows an example of different types of biometrics.

Each type of biometrics has its own advantages and limitations. Physiological biometrics are considered to be extremely robust and hence more secure. However, these types of biometrics are not portable and cannot be used for web based applications. Behavioral biometrics such as voice, gait etc., face the problem of high implementation cost as they require special hardware or sensors for capturing the template. An analysis of different types of biometrics is given in the following Table 1.

Keystroke dynamics is a strong behavioral biometric (Ahmed and Traore, 2005) and it is the process of analyzing the way a user types at a terminal by monitoring the keyboard in order to identify the user based on habitual typing rhythm patterns. Unlike other biometric systems, which may be expensive to implement, keystroke dynamics is almost free and it does not require any sophisticated hardware as the only hardware required is the keyboard. Keystroke dynamics has the following advantages.

Figure 1. Authentication types

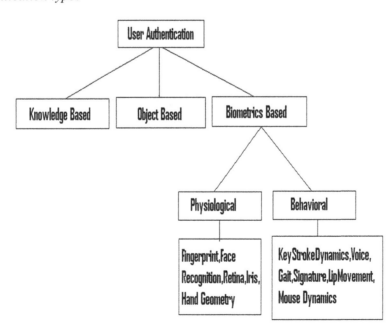

Figure 2. Different types of biometrics

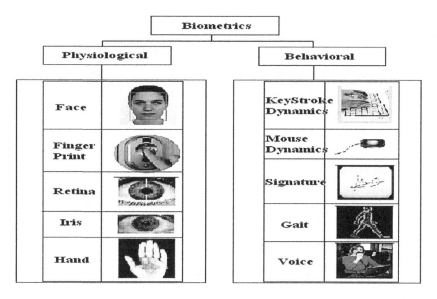

Table 1. Analysis of different types of biometrics

Physiological Biometrics	Behavioral Biometrics
What the person is or measure physical parameters of a certain part of the body	What a person does or how the person uses the body
Examples: Fingerprint, Iris, Face Recognition, etc.,	Examples: Voice, Handwriting, walking gait, Typing rhythm or Keystroke Dynamics
Limitations: • Can be spoofed • Difficulties in implementing • Expensive • Requires special Hardware • More Intrusive	Limitations: • Voice Recognition, the most promising technology but it is difficult to distinguish a live user from a recorded one • Handwriting, gait requires a special device, which can be cost prohibitive and signatures can be forged

- It does not require any special equipment.
- It is user-friendly and noninvasive.
- Flexible enrolment is possible.
- The typing rhythm of the person cannot be lost or forgotten.
- If the template is stolen or guessed, the new one can be easily generated. So it is the only resettable biometric.
- It can be used for remote applications over the Internet.
- Keystroke dynamics can be combined with other authentication technologies.

Keystroke verification contains two approaches Static and Continuous (Gunetti and Picardi, 2005). In Static approach, the system checks the user only at the authentication time and in the Continuous approach, the system checks the user continuously throughout the session and the user's typing behaviour is monitored throughout his/her typing time using the keyboard (Patrick Bours, 2012). The proposed methodology uses Static approach. Timing features are the one most commonly measured from the keystroke. The huge features often lead to degradation of performance of the system. Hence an attempt is made to reduce the dimensionality of features using wrapper approaches. A wrapper based classification approach using Extreme Learning Machine is proposed in this chapter.

The rest of the chapter is organized as follows: the next section discusses the background works done in the area of research followed by methodology and the discussion of the results. Final section concludes the work with future directions.

BACKGROUND

The major steps involved in keystroke authentication are obtaining keystroke data, feature extraction, normalization, feature subset selection and classification. This section discusses the related works done in the features, feature subset selection and neural network based classification areas.

Literature on Feature and Feature Extraction Methods

The raw data that can be obtained from the user when typing via the keyboard are the key press time and release time. After obtaining the raw data, the features such as Duration, which is the amount of time the key is pressed and Flight time or Latency, which is the difference of time between two key actions, can be extracted. This section discusses about the various features and feature extraction techniques available so far in the literature.

Akila and Suresh Kumar (2011) measured Mean, Median and Standard deviation of feature values such as Latency, Duration and Digraph and compared the performance. Digraph with median as the feature gives good result when compared to other features.

Balagani et al. (2011) classified the keystroke feature vectors as Homogeneous if it has either key hold latencies only or key interval latencies only as its features, a heterogeneous vector if it has both key hold and key interval latencies as features, an aggregate vector if its features are derived by aggregating key hold and key interval latencies. They measured all the above mentioned vectors and concluded that a heterogeneous vector has higher discriminability than an aggregate vector, especially when the reference text is short. However, as the length of the text increases, the difference in the discriminability between heterogeneous and aggregate vectors tends to decrease.

Bartlow and Cukic (2006) incorporated shift-key pattern along with keystroke inter-key and hold times. Using the built-in Java event handlers, key hold times and inter-key delays accurate to the millisecond are collected and found that their approach decreases the system penetration rate associated with compromised passwords by 95%-99%.

Typing keystroke duration and isometric force elicited by electrical stimulation are measured by Che-Hsu Chang et al. (2009) after giving isometric exercises to finger. After the finger is exposed to isometric exercises, changes in typing keystroke duration coincided with changes in the physiological state of the finger flexor and extensor muscles.

The applicability of typing pressure instead of using the conventional typing timing characteristics has been investigated by Chen Change Loy et al. (2005). The features such as the arithmetic mean, fundamental frequency, root mean square, energy, peak, kurtosis, signal in noise and distortion, Total harmonic distortion and Skewness are extracted from keystroke pressure. To measure the typing pressure, a normal keyboard is modified into a pressure sensitive keyboard by incorporating pressure resistive force sensors underneath the keyboard matrix. The authors found that combining both latency and pressure patterns can improve the Equal Error Rate (ERR) of the system.

The authors of Cho et al. (2000), Sung and Cho (2006) and Cho and Hwang (2006) measured artificially designed rhythms that include pause, musical rhythm, staccato, legato, and slow tempo. For consistency, timing cues such as auditory, visual, and audiovisual cues are measured. The preliminary experiment showed that there is an improvement in the quality of patterns.

Davoudi and Kabir (2009) used a method to find the distance between a typing sample and a set of samples of a user. For each digraph, histogram-based density estimation is used to find its duration time. This measure has been combined with another measure which is based on the two sample distances. Experimental results showed considerable decrease in False Acceptance Rate (FAR) while False Rejection Rate (FRR) remains constant.

De Ru and Eloff (1997) developed a software methodology that measured the typing difficulty using fuzzy logic.

Eesa Al Solami et al. (2011) suggested four statistical-based feature extraction techniques. The techniques, most frequently typed n-graph selection, quickly-typed n-graph selection, Time-stability typed n-graph selection, and Time-variant typed n-graph selection are tested with k-means clustering algorithm and found that the most-frequent 2-graphs technique can represent user's typing patterns effectively because of their high statistical significance.

Eltahir et al. (2004) developed a pressure sensor based typing biometrics authentication system by implementing the hardware comprising the pressure sensor and the associated data acquisition system. They measured user keystroke pressure along with time between each keystroke latency to create a unique user password typing pattern for authentication. An auto-regressive (AR) classifier is used for the pressure pattern, while a latency classifier is used for the time between keystrokes.

Francesco et al. (2002) measured the duration of trigraph and found that the relative position of a trigraph in a sample depends on the duration of that trigraph. Each user is left free to make typing errors and to decide whether to correct them or not.

Gaines et al. (1980) measured digraph using T-test statistical method and found that a large number of digraphs are represented in ordinary paragraphs and this measurement served as a basis for distinguishing among subjects.

Giovanni Saggio et al. (2011) considered cumulative and ratio timings (sum and ratio of dwell and flight times), which do not change even if the user's typing style evolves with practice.

Giroux et al. (2009a and 2009b) measured key press intervals with the keystroke application software written in Visual C# under the Microsoft® Visual Studio.NET 2003 framework. Results show that authentication with mean key press timings resulted in very good false acceptance rates, while allowing access to appropriate users. Authentication through key press ratios achieves high true acceptance rates and low false acceptance rates in the work of Hu et al. (2008) and authentication with mean key press timings resulted in very good false acceptance rates in the work of Huang et al. (2004).

Gissel Zamonsky Pedernera et al. (2010) measured R-Distance, A- Distance and weighted Distance (Combination of R and A Distance) and evaluated the results using Adapted k-Means (AKM), Adapted Subtractive Clustering (ASC) algorithms. The Best classification results are given by the Weighted A-distance using the median.

Hai-Rong Lv and Wang (2006) used a pressure sensor keyboard to measure five global features of a pressure sequence, such as mean value, standard deviation, the difference between maximum and minimum, Positive Energy Center (PEC) and Negative Energy Center (NEC).

Hu et al. (2008) used the duration of Trigraph as features and normalized the features using distance normalization. The experiment demonstrated the same level of FAR and FRR as that of Gunetti and Picardi (2005) approach. About 66.7% improvement of the authentication speed has been achieved comparatively.

Joyce and Gupta (1990) described a method that used latency as a feature and verified the identity of a user based on such a digital signature, and reports results from the trial usage of the system.

Juan Liu et al. (2014) had investigated feature extraction based on FFT, DCT and Gabor wavelet.

Leberknight et al. (2008) extracted Duration, pressure related characteristics such as amplitude or peak, peak area, and peak sharpness using pressure sensors embedded within the keypad.

A force-sensing keypad is constructed by Liang Tang et al. (2010) by adding the Force Sensitive Resistor (FSR) sensors and extracted applied force and key-press timings. Compared to the traditional dynamics identification methods, the Force time domain information provided more appropriate user input information. Preliminary experimental results show that the force is more difficult to imitate than rhythm.

Margit Antal et al. (2015) examined the effect of touch screen features though their dataset of 42 users. Both time and touch screen features were studied.

Mariusz Rybnik et al. (2008) measured the time between keystrokes, the amount of time specific key is pressed, average keystrokes per minute, overlapping of specific key combinations, the amount of errors, and method of error correcting. The authors developed a methodical approach to select the most interesting features and combined them to obtain a viable indicator of user's identity to prevent unauthorized access.

Monrose and Rubin (2000) measured the duration and latency and examined the non-static biometric technique to identify users based on analyzing habitual rhythm patterns in the way they type. Feature sets are determined through factor analysis. The authors observed that there is significant variability with which typists produce digraphs.

Monrose et al. (1999) measured the duration and latency of the legitimate user's typing patterns and combined them with the user's password to generate a hardened password using mean and standard deviation. This method is proved to be convincingly more secure than conventional passwords against both online and offline attackers.

Obaidat and Sadoun (1997) measured Interkey time, hold time, combined inter key and hold time using Terminate and Stay Resident (TSR) program. It is found that hold times are more effective than inter key times and the best identification performance is achieved using a combination of both.

Pilsung et al. (2009) measured the difference between the distributions of many users with Kolmogorov-Smirnov Test and showed that the authentication performance was not much different from 'R' measure (Relative measure) and 'A' (Absolute) measure.

The authors of (Saevanee and Bhattarakosol, 2009) measured the duration and latency of the legitimate user's typing patterns and combined them with the user's password to generate a hardened password using mean and standard deviation.

Wong et al. (2011) extracted the keystroke latencies using a box plot algorithm to create typing patterns for individuals.

Zhang et al. (2011) analyzed the existing Press Release – Release Press (PR-RP) Model in order to provide a new improved PR-RP model for identity authentication of keystroke rhythm. Press - Press (P-P) and Release – Release (R-R) relay datasets are rebuilt, with the improved PR-RP model. The authors tested the result with four critical datasets and obtained improved recognition rate.

Literature on Feature Subset Selection Methods

Feature subset selection is applied to search for the most optimal features (Singhi and Liu, 2006). It reduces the number of features resulting in speeding up the computation time. There are two feature subset selection approaches (Sung and Cho, 2006): Filter and Wrapper approach. Filter approach filters out the discriminating features and passes only the relevant features to the classifiers. On the other hand, the wrapper approach tries different sets of features using a learning algorithm, and then chooses the best one. This method has the computational overhead of evaluating the feature subset using the learning algorithm. However, if the learning algorithm used to train the classifier is computationally efficient, it yields better results than the filter approach. This section discusses the major feature subset selection methods applied in keystroke dynamics.

Optimization techniques such as Genetic Algorithm (GA) and Particle Swarm Optimization (PSO) are used for feature subset selection and their performance is compared by Akila and Suresh Kumar (2011) and Karnan and Akila (2009a). Particle Swarm Optimization (PSO) gives better performance than Genetic Algorithm with regard to feature reduction rate.

Azevedo et al. (2007a and 2007b) evaluated the feature subset selection based on Support Vector Machine (SVM) with Genetic Algorithm (GA) and a variation in Particle Swam Optimization (PSO). In this study, wrapper based approach with SVM-PSO variation outperformed SVM-GA with regard to classification error and processing time.

Bleha and Obaidat (1991) used a reduction technique based on Fisher analysis. However, the technique considered by keeping m − 1 dimension for each vector, with 'm' number of users in the system.

Boechat et al. (2006) used weighted probability measure to select a subset of 'N' features with the minors of standard deviation. The study eliminates less significant features by keeping 70% of the features. Experiments are done at Zero False Acceptance Rate. False Rejection Rate reduces when the number of selected features increases.

Particle Swarm Optimization (PSO), Genetic Algorithm (GA) and Ant Colony Optimization (ACO) are used by Karnan and Akila (2010) for feature subset selection. Backpropagation Neural Network (BPN) has been used for classification. ACO gives better performance than PSO and GA with regard to feature reduction rate and classification accuracy.

Sung and Cho (2006) adds a uniqueness term in the fitness function of genetic algorithm and used SVM as classifier for classification and Genetic Algorithm (GA) to select the data. The experiments performed better than two phase ensemble selection approach and prediction based diversity term approach.

Yu and Cho (2003, 2004) used wrapper based Support Vector Machines (SVM) and Genetic Algorithms (GA) to reduce the feature size. SVM is applied for training and GA is used for searching. GA-SVM wrapper approach gives good accuracy. Feature Selection (FS) - Ensemble is proposed to deal with the over fitting problems.

Literature on Neural Network Based Classification Approaches

The next step after feature subset selection is classifying the selected features. Classification aims to find the best class that is closest to the classified pattern (Karnan and Akila, 2010). A number of studies have been performed in the area of classification since its inception. Five different classification techniques namely statistical classification, neural network based classification, classification using pattern recognition, hybrid classification techniques and other techniques are being followed in the area of keystroke dynamics.

The proposed research focuses on Neural Network based classification techniques. This section discusses the various Neural Network based classifications followed in the area of keystroke dynamics so far.

Ali et al. (2009) combined Artificial Neural Network (ANN) and Adaptive Neuro-Fuzzy Inference System (ANFIS) and obtained 3.8% FAR.

The Perceptron algorithm is used by Bleha and Obdait (1993) to verify the identity of computer users. Decision functions are derived using part of the training data to compute the weight vectors. The decision functions were applied to the remaining data (testing data) to verify the users. An error of 9% in rejecting valid users, and an error of 8% in accepting invalid users are found.

The effectiveness of ARTMAP-FD in classifying keystroke patterns is analyzed and compared against a number of widely used machine learning systems by Chen Change Loy et al. (2007). The results show that ARTMAP-FD performs well against many of its counterparts in keystroke patterns classification.

Cho et al. (2005) used Multilayer Perceptron (MLP) for classification and compared the performance of MLP with K-Nearest Neighbor algorithm (k-NN). The experimental results involving 21 skilled users showed that the MLP is more effective than the k-NN approach. For 13 owners, the MLP approach achieved perfect authentication. Among the rest, the worst performance is found to be 4% error rate. The overall average error rate is 1%.

Daw-Tung Lin (1997) used three-layered Back Propagation Neural Network with flexible number of input nodes. System verification performance has been improved by setting convergence criteria RMSE to a smaller threshold value during training procedure. The resulting system gives 1.1% FAR (false alarm rate) in rejecting valid users and zero Impostor Pass Rate (IPR) in accepting no impostors.

Eltahir et al. (2004) combined the force and time features and tested with auto-regressive (AR) classifier, Support Vector Machines (SVM), Artificial Neural Network (ANN) and Adaptive Neuro-Fuzzy Inference System (ANFIS). The authors found that complete template is required for the AR classifier, while ANN, ANFIS, and SVM require a vector of highest pressure score for each keystroke.

Fred Kitchens et al. (2003) illustrated the application of the genetic adaptive neural network to the problem of user authentication through the typing characteristics exhibited when typing user passwords. This approach is preceded by Brown and Rogers (1994) who applied the Kohonen Self-Organizing Map and the Back Propagation Neural Network to authenticate person's name. They are able to demonstrate a complete exclusion of imposters and a reasonably low false alarm rate when the sample text is limited to the user's name.

A Multilayer Perceptron (MLP) neural network with a Back Propagation (BP) learning algorithm is used by Harun et al. (2010) Fto train and validate the features. The simulation results revealed that MLP with BP network is suitable to discriminate and classify a nonlinear keystroke database as high as 98% in correct acceptance rate.

Karnan and Akila (2009b and 2010) obtained 92.8% classification accuracy using Back Propagation Neural Network (BPN). The authors applied feature subset selection methods before classification.

Mantyjarvi et al. (2002) implemented a virtual keyboard and conducted keystroke recognition experiments with the keyboard utilizing proximity measurements. An infrared (IR) transceiver array is used for detecting the proximity of a finger. Keystroke recognition accuracy is examined with k-nearest neighbor (k-NN) classifier while a multilayer perceptron (MLP) classifier is designed for online implementation. The recognition accuracy between 78% and 99% is obtained for k-NN classifier and between 69% and 96% for MLP classifier, depends mainly on the location of a specific key on the keyboard area.

Marcus Brown and Samuel Rogers (1994) utilized the ADAptive LINear Element (ADALINE) and Back Propagation Neural Network (BPN) to identify the typing pattern characteristics of a particular user. A simple measure of geometric distance is also used for comparison. The authors found that ADALINE technique has given FAR of 17.4% in the smallest imposter group, and FAR of 18% for the larger imposter group. The partially connected BPN gives FAR of 12% for the smaller group, and FAR of 14% for the larger imposter group and concluded that the larger imposter samples do not have the effect of significantly increasing the FAR of the ADALINE or back propagation discrimination methods.

Margit Antal et al. (2015) used machine learning classification algorithms like Random Forest, Bayseian Nets and SVM. The author concluded with an increase of 10% increase in the accuracy using touch screen features.

Obaidat and Macchairolo (1994) used Multilayer feedforward network trained using the back propagation algorithm, a sum-of-products network trained with a modification of back propagation. A combination of above two neural networks has obtained a classification accuracy of 97.5%.

Orcan Alpar (2014) introduced authentication and discrimination system using artificial neural networks with RGB histograms. Keycodes and interkeytimes for passwords were used as feature. The system has granted 90% of real user attempts and rejected 90% of frauds.

Revett (2007) compared Probabilistic Neural Network (PNN) with back-propagation trained neural network and the result showed that PNN performs superior in terms of reduced training time and classification accuracy when compared with a typical Multi Layered Feedforward Network (MLFN) back-propagation trained neural network.

Shrijit Joshi and Phoha (2007) suggested an architecture that consists of a set of Self Organizing Maps (SOM) where each user has a distinct map. Each map consists of 'n' neurons in the input layer where 'n' is the length of a keystroke pattern. The decision on the authenticity is made using threshold criteria. Evaluation results showed the False Accept Rate of 0.88% when False Reject Rate is 3.55% with authentication accuracy of 97.83%.

Sinthupinyo et al. (2009) employed Back propagation Neural Network to classify the users using keystroke latency times from non-fixed length text. The employed method combines a clustering capability of SOM to help the neural networks to classify a set of digraph latency times entered by a user. The results show that the method can recognize unseen users with a higher accuracy.

Radial Basis Function (RBF) is used for classification by Sulong et al. (2009) and the system generated very low FRR.

Tai-Hoon Cho (2006) performed a comparison experiment for keystroke identification using a k-NN classifier, a back-propagation neural network classifier, and a Bayesian classifier. Performance of k-NN classification performed best with small data samples available per user and with large data samples per user Bayesian classification gives good results. Although the performance of the neural network classifier was relatively good, it requires a time-consuming learning process.

Yong et al. (2004) used a common 64-input node Deterministic RAM Network (DARN) network to authenticate the users through two different validation approaches. DARN performs quite well in distinguishing one user from several others, but the performance generally deteriorates when there are more users to authenticate.

METHODOLOGY

The entire methodology is divided into four phases namely, feature extraction phase, normalization phase, feature subset selection phase and classification phase after obtaining the raw keystroke data (press time and release time). This section explains each step in detail.

Feature Extraction

Keystroke Dynamics is one of the famous and inexpensive behavioral biometric technologies, which will try to identify the authenticity of a user when the user is working with the keyboard. The key function of feature extraction in keystroke dynamics is to extract the fundamental features from the timestamp collected from raw keystroke data for creation of template. There are many features that can be acquired using keystroke of the user. The Figure 3 shows the various features that can be measure from keystrokes.

The following Table 2 gives the definition of the timing features of keystrokes.

Force of key typed is one of the features which can be obtained using a special force sensitive keyboard which is expensive and also may not be available commonly (Liang Tang et al, 2010). In addition to the entire timing features such as duration, latency, digraph and trigraph, a new proposed Feature

Figure 3. Timing features from the keystrokes

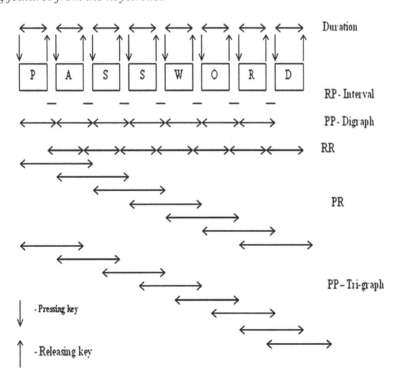

Table 2. Definition of timing features of keystrokes

Features	Definition	Formula
Dwell Time or Duration (DT)	How long a key is pressed until it is released	DT=R1-P1
Flight Time (FT) or latencies	Interval time between key press and release of different keys	
a. Release-Press (RP)	Interval between a key release and next key press time	RP=P2-R1
b. Press-Press (PP) (Digraph)	Interval between a key Press and next key Press	PP=P2-P1
c. Release-Release (RR)	Interval between two successive key Releases	RR=R2-R1
d. Press - Release (PR)	Elapsed time between Pressing of first key and releasing of next key	PR=R2-P1
Trigraph(TRI)	Elapsed time between the first key press and the third key press	TRI=P3-P1

called Virtual Key Force (VKF) has been introduced. The Virtual Key Force is measured without using any special key board which also improves the accuracy when the feature is used for classification. The Virtual Key Force is calculated based on the typing speed and the behavior of the user at the keyboard. It measures the time taken by the user between releasing one key and pressing another key. It is based on the fact that each user has different typing speed and each user takes his/her own time to release and press another key. Virtual Key Force can be determined from the Complexity Label (CL), Average time taken to press the keys and Key Complexity (KC).

The Complexity Label (CL) calculation is fully user dependent and also depends on the hand used by the user.

In the Figure 4, for the keys T, H, E the complexity label is assigned as CL = (0,1). i.e. the distance from T and H is nearer(0) and the distance between H and E is longer(1). In the following Figure 4, key positions in a keyboard and the timing intervals between keys T, H, E are shown.

Figure 4. Timing intervals between keys

After calculating the complexity label, the average time is calculated. It is the total time taken divided by time taken to press a key. If the actual time is less than the average time, then the key complexity is assumed as 0 (i.e Shorter Interval between Keys) otherwise key complexity is assumed as 1 (i.e longer Interval between keys).

Based on the key complexity and the complexity label, the following algorithm which is shown in Table 3 has been formulated.

The three levels of force namely High, Medium and Low are identified. If the key distance is nearer or longer and time interval taken to hit the key is below average then the key is assumed to be hit with low force. If the key distance is nearer and time interval taken to hit the key is above average then the key is assumed to be hit with medium force. If the key distance is longer and time interval taken to hit the key is above average then the key is assumed to be hit with high force. The Virtual Key Force for each character is stored as feature for the passwords. The Table 4 shows the extracted features from the password used for the study.

Normalization

After feature extraction, preprocessing has to be done. This section focuses on the preprocessing using normalization techniques. The typing pattern of the user varies from time to time even for the same user. There will also be a significant difference in the keystroke patterns exhibited from person to person, even when asked to type the same words (Chen and Chang, 2004). Therefore, data normalization is done between 0 and 1 to preprocess the data. Min-Max, Z-Score, Zero Mean and Standard Deviation, Median - MAD, and Tanh normalizations are done and Z-score normalization is found to be effective compared to other normalization methods.

Table 3. Virtual key force algorithm

```
if (key distance is nearer || longer && time interval is below average)
VKF=3 (low)
else if (key distance is nearer && time interval is above the average)
VKF=2(medium)
else if (keys are longer and the average time interval is above the average)
VKF=1 (high)
end
```

Table 4. Features extracted from the password

S.no	Passwords	No. of Characters	DT	RP	PP	RR	PR	TRI	VKF	Total
1	drizzle	7	7	6	6	6	6	5	7	43
2	jeffrey allen	13 (including space)	13	12	12	12	12	11	13	85
3	.tie5Roan1	11 (including shift key to press R)	11	10	10	10	10	9	11	71
4	nopassword	10	10	9	9	9	9	8	10	64
5	pass_tie.R	12 (including shift key to press _ and R)	12	11	11	11	11	10	12	78

Feature Subset Selection

Feature selection techniques are divided into two types namely, feature ranking and feature subset selection. Feature ranking ranks the features by a metric and eliminates all features that do not achieve an adequate score. Subset selection searches for the set of possible features to construct the optimal subset. To carry out this search, a starting point, a strategy to traverse the space of subsets, an evaluation function and a stopping criterion are to be specified. Although there are varieties of subset selection techniques developed, usually two methods namely filter and wrapper approaches are considered. In Filter approach, the feature subset selection is done independently of the learning algorithm. The subset selection procedure in this case can be seen as a preprocessing step.

In the wrapper approach, the feature subset selection is done by induction algorithm. The feature subset selection algorithm conducts a search for a good subset using the induction algorithm as a part of the evaluation function. The purpose of the induction algorithm is to induce from training data a classifier that will be useful in classifying future cases. The accuracy of induced classifiers is estimated by accuracy estimation technique. The classification algorithm itself is used to determine the attribute subset. Since the wrapper approach optimizes the evaluation measure of the classification algorithm while removing features, it mostly leads to greater accuracy than the filter approaches such as X^2Statistic, Information gain, Symmetrical uncertainty, ReliefF and Correlation based feature selection. Wrapper methods generally result in better performance than filter methods because the feature selection process is optimized by the classification algorithm to be used. Hence a wrapper based feature subset selection approach is proposed.

Feature subset selection is fundamentally an optimization problem, which concerns searching the space of possible features to be familiar with one that is optimum or near-optimal in accordance with some performance measure (Robinson, Liang, Chambers and MacKenzie, 1998). The purpose is to obtain any subset that reduces or to improve a particular measure. After preprocessing with Z-Score normalization, feature subset selection is done for reducing the features for further processing. Particle Swam Optimization (PSO) is wrapped with Extreme Learning Machine (ELM) which routinely selects an appropriate subset of features and the rest will not be considered, thus concluding in a more comprehensive model.

Particle Swam Optimization (PSO)

The authors of Sidhartha Panda and Padhy (2007), and Kennedy and Eberhart (1995) defines that Particle Swarm Optimization (PSO) is a stochastic search technique that aims to optimize an objective function, motivated by social activities of birds gathering or fish schooling. PSO is a population dependent search algorithm in which each individual is indicated as a particle and represents a candidate solution. All the particles in PSO moves through the search space with an adjustable velocity that is dynamically transformed based on its individual moving experience and also the moving experience of the other particles. In PSO each particles attempt to enhance themselves by imitating traits from their successful peers. The position in proportion to the best fitness is known as pbest (Particle best) and the overall best out of all the particles in the population is called gbest (Global best) (Sidhartha Panda and Padhy, 2007). The velocity $v_i(t)$ a nd the positions $x_i(t)$ of the particles are updated with the following equations.

$$v_i(t+1) = w * v_i(t) + c_1 r_1 (y_i(t) - x_i(t)) + c_2 r_2 (y'(t) - x_i(t))$$

$$x_i(t+1) = x_i(t) + v_i(t+1)$$

where i=1, 2, …, n

$v_i(t)$: Velocity of agent i at iteration t and must lie in the range $v_{min} \leq v_i(t) \leq v_{max}$
w: inertia weight factor
c_1, c_2: Cognitive and social acceleration factors respectively,
r_1, r_2: Uniformly distributed random number between 0 and 1,
$x_i(t)$: Current position of agent i at iteration t,
$y_i(t)$: Personal best (pbest) and is updated using the following equation.
$y'(t)$: Global best (gbest) and is updated using the following equation.

$$y_i(t+1) = \begin{cases} y_i(t), f(x_i(t+1)) \geq f(y_i(t)) \\ x_i(t+1), f(x_i(t+1)) < f(y_i(t)) \end{cases}$$

$$y'(t+1) = \arg\min \left\{ f(yi(t+1)) \right\}, 1 \leq i \leq s$$

where s = number of particles in the swarm.

Extreme Machine Learning (ELM)

Extreme Learning Machine is used as induction algorithm in PSO for wrapper based feature subset selection. BPN and SVM are the commonly used learning algorithms. BPN and SVM require manual tuning which degrades the performance of the system. ELM on the other hand does not require any manual tuning and avoids the issues such as local minima, improper learning rate and over fitting, etc., faces by other learning algorithms. The Extreme Machine Learning algorithm is narrated below:

If there are N samples/features (x_i, t_i) with $x_i \in R^n$, $t_i \in R^m$, then Single Layer Feedforward Network (SLFN) with N Hidden nodes is designed using the following equation:

$$\sum_{i=1}^{H} \beta_i f(w_i x_j + b_i), j \in [1, N]$$

where f=activation function, w_i=input weights, b_i=bias and β_i=output weights.

The error between the target output and actual output is given by the following equation:

$$\sum_{i=1}^{H} \beta_i f(w_i x_j + b_i) = t_j, j \in [1, N]$$

where t_j is the actual output. The above equation can be simply written as $\beta = H^\dagger Y$ where

$$\beta = (\beta_1^T \cdots \beta_1^T)^T, \quad Y = (y_1^T \cdots y_N^T)^T$$

and H = the Hidden layer output matrix and is calculated using the following equation:

$$H = \begin{pmatrix} f(w_1 x_1 + b_1) & \cdots & f(w_H x_1 + b_H) \\ \vdots & \ddots & \vdots \\ f(w_1 x_N + b_1) & \cdots & f(w_H x_N + b_H) \end{pmatrix}$$

The hidden layer output matrix H is determined by randomly initializing the weights w_i and the bias b_i

The output weights β are calculated from the knowledge of the hidden layer output matrix H and target values Y using a Moore-Penrose generalized inverse of the matrix H, which is denoted as $H^\dagger$. Table 5 summarizes the ELM Algorithm (Huang et al., 2004 and 2006).

Wrapper Based Feature Subset Selection Using PSO-ELM

In the proposed PSO-ELM Wrapper approach, Duration, Latency, Trigraph, Digraph and the proposed Virtual Key Force are given as input features. Feature subset selection is done and the selected features are evaluated by Extreme Learning Machine in order to find the fitness value. The process is repeated until the best solution is obtained. Flow chart for proposed PSO-ELM wrapper approach for feature subset selection is given in the following Figure 5. The fitness function of the PSO is evaluated using ELM.

The algorithm of the proposed PSO-ELM Wrapper approach is given below:

Input: Duration, Latency, Trigraph, Digraph, Virtual Key Force
Output: Subset feature values.
Step 1: Initialize the number of Iterations, Number of particles, Weight,c_1, c_2, r_1,r_2, $v_i(t)$
Step 2: Compute the feature values of $x_i(t)$ (Duration, Latency, Digraph, Trigraph, and Virtual Key Force).
Step 3: Evaluate fitness for each feature value using ELM.
Step 4: The following is repeated for number of iterations:
1. Check if p>=pbest then, pbest=p else pbest= pbest.
2. If pbest >=gbest then, gbest= pbest else gbest=gbest.
3. Update velocity, position, pbest, and gbest position are updated using (34) and (5).

Step 4 is repeated until gbest is optimum value.

Table 5. Extreme Learning Machine Algorithm

Given a training set $N=(x_i, t_i)$, $x_i \in R^n$, $t_i \in R^m$, an activation function $f : R \longmapsto R$ and the number of hidden nodes H.
- *Randomly assign input weights wi and bias $b_i \in [1,H]$*
- *Calculate the hidden layer output matrix H*
- *Calculate the weight matrix $\beta = H^\dagger Y$*

Figure 5. Flowchart of proposed PSO-ELM wrapper feature subset selection

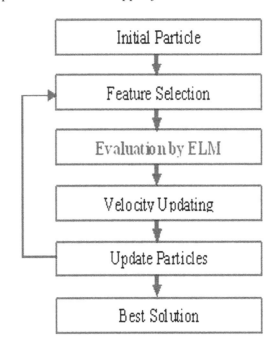

Classification

The purpose of classification is to find the best class that is closest to the classified pattern (Karnan and Akila, 2009a). The selected features by PSO are given as input to Extreme Learning Machine and Back Propagation Neural Network (BPN). The wrapper based classification approach using PSO-ELM yields the average accuracy of 97.92% and takes less training and testing time when compared to BPN.

EXPERIMENTAL RESULTS

The methodology is tested with data from real time users and bench mark datasets. The datasets used are described as follows.

Dataset Description

Three different types of dataset are used to test the methodology. KSP Dataset -Pressure sensitive keystroke dynamics dataset (2010), which represents the typing of 103 individuals on three different words ('drizzle', 'jeffrey allen', 'pr7q1z'). From the dataset, the following passwords are considered for the study. drizzle – Weak password. jeffrey allen– Strong password. DSL Dataset - Keystroke Dynamics - Benchmark Data Set (2009) consists of keystroke-timing information from 51 subjects each typing a password (.tie5Roanl – Medium password) 400 times. Real time dataset with 100 users in the age group of 18-60 each typing the following 3 different passwords for 10 times. 'pass_tie.R' – Strong password, '.tie5Roanl' – Medium password, 'nopassword' – Weak password. Three different strength passwords (weak, medium and strong) have been chosen for study. The reason for choosing different strength passwords is that the weak and medium passwords can be easily guessed and vulnerable to hacker attacks. The strong passwords are complex to remember and the user may store or write it which may lead to Dictionary attacks. For all such types of passwords, security can be more tightened using Keystroke dynamics.

All the above passwords are checked for strength using publicly available strength checker (Microsoft, 2008) and the checker determines the strength of a password depending on the different types of characters that is used, the overall length of the password (it should be 8 or more characters long), and whether the password can be found in a dictionary. The strength of the password also varies from software to software used for checking.

Performance Metrics

The Particle Swarm Optimization Algorithm for wrapper based feature subset selection is implemented with 30 particles, 100 iterations, coefficients of positive acceleration (c_1, c_2) as 1 and random Variables (r_1, r_2) as 0.9. The Extreme Learning Machine is implemented with 5 and 20 input and hidden neurons, Sigmoid as activation function and Levenberg-Marquardt as training algorithm.

The following Table 6 shows the number of features selected by wrapping PSO with ELM and BPN.

It is observed from the above table that PSO-ELM wrapper has reduced the more number of features than BPN. The proposed PSO-ELM wrapper based approach has selected fewer features for classification which is shown in the Table 7.

Table 6. Features Selected

Classifier	Dataset											
	KSP Weak Password		KSP Strong Password		DSL Medium Password		Real Time Weak Password		Real Time Medium Password		Real Time Strong Password	
	F	FS	F	FS	F	FS	F	FS	F	FS	F	FS
BPN	43	31	85	67	71	60	64	56	71	55	78	64
PSO-ELM	43	30	85	59	71	57	64	50	71	53	78	58

F- Number of Features, FS – Features selected.

Table 7. Feature selection percentage with virtual key force

Classifier	Dataset											
	KSP Weak Password		KSP Strong Password		DSL Medium Password		Real Time Weak Password		Real Time Medium Password		Real Time Strong Password	
	FS	S%	FS	S%	FS	S%	FS	S%	FS	S%	FS	S%
BPN	31	72.09	67	78.82	60	84.51	56	87.5	55	77.5	64	82.1
PSO-ELM	30	69.77	59	69.41	57	80.28	50	78.1	53	74.7	58	74.4

F- Number of Features, S%- Selection percentage

After feature subset selection, classification is done. 70% of the selected features are used as training set and the remaining is used as test set. Table 8 shows the average classification accuracy obtained using the wrapper based classification by wrapping PSO with the classifiers BPN and ELM.

It is observed that PSO-ELM wrapper based classification approach gives an average accuracy of 97.92% for real time medium password. The proposed wrapper based classification gives more accuracy for all types of passwords and for all datasets compared to that of BPN.

The training time (in sec) taken by the approaches are given in the Table 9. It is observed that the PSO - ELM wrapper approach takes the least time for training when compared with the other method.

The testing time (in sec) taken by the approaches are given in the Table 10. It is observed that the PSO - ELM wrapper approach takes less time for testing than the other method.

From the above obtained results, it is observed that the proposed PSO-ELM wrapper based classification method outperforms BPN.

Table 8. Percentage of accuracy (%) obtained with wrapper based classification

Classifier	Dataset					
	KSP Weak Password	KSP Strong Password	DSL Medium Password	Real Time Weak Password	Real Time Medium Password	Real Time Strong Password
BPN	90.42	90.04	90.66	92.96	94.31	94.77
PSO-ELM	96.90	96.46	95.21	96.64	97.92	96.3

Table 9. Training time (in sec)

Classifier	Dataset					
	KSP Weak Password	KSP Strong Password	DSL Medium Password	Real Time Weak Password	Real Time Medium Password	Real Time Strong Password
BPN	8.61082	16.76341	17.66666	18.09596	11.67424	19.66666
PSO-ELM	0.11009	0.09615	0.03421	0.20628	0.12500	0.03421

Table 10. Testing time (in sec)

Classifier	Dataset					
	KSP Weak Password	KSP Strong Password	DSL Medium Password	Real Time Weak Password	Real Time Medium Password	Real Time Strong Password
BPN	0.02389	0.01892	0.03381	0.03427	0.03381	0.03381
PSO-ELM	0.02186	0.01241	0.01560	0.02502	0.01561	0.01561

CONCLUSION AND FUTURE DIRECTIONS

Feature extraction, normalization, feature subset selection and classification are done to identify the users using keystroke dynamics. The extraction of features can be done from the press and release time measured from the users. The features such as duration, latency, digraph and trigraph can be extracted from the users' press and release time. This research work proposes a new feature called Virtual Key Force. The proposed Virtual Key Force can be extracted from the press time and release time measured from the users keystroke without using special Force Sensitive keyboard. However, an additional feature Virtual Key Force is added to the feature set. The obtained experimental results show that when the proposed feature is used with wrapper based approaches, the accuracy is improved. Feature subset selection is done using Particle Swarm Optimization wrapped with Extreme Learning Machine. A wrapper based classification technique is proposed using PSO-ELM method and compared with Back Propagation Neural Network. An average accuracy of 97.92% is obtained and proposed method takes less training and testing times. In future, other bio inspired techniques such as Ant Colony Optimization and Genetic Algorithm can be considered.

REFERENCES

Ahmed, A. A. E., & Traore, I.(2005). Anomaly Intrusion Detection based on Biometrics. In *Proceedings of 6th IEEE Information Assurance Workshop*. doi:10.1109/IAW.2005.1495997

Akila, M., & Suresh Kumar, S. (2011). Improving Feature Extraction in Keystroke Dynamics using Optimization Techniques and Neural Network. In *Proceedings of the International Conference on Sustainable Energy and Intelligent Systems (SEISCON 2011)*. doi:10.1049/cp.2011.0493

Al Solami, E., Boyd, C., Clark, A., & Ahmed, I. (2011). User-Representative Feature Selection for Keystroke Dynamics. In *Proceedings on 5th International Conference on Network and System Security (NSS)*.

Alpar, O. (2014). Keystroke recognition in user authentication using ANN based RGB histogram technique. *Engineering Applications of Artificial Intelligence*, *32*, 213–217. doi:10.1016/j.engappai.2013.11.009

Antal, M., Szabó, L. Z., & László, I. (2015). Keystroke Dynamics on Android Platform. In *Procedia Technology* (pp. 820–826). Elsevier.

Azevedo, G. L. F., Cavalcanti, G. D. C., & Carvalho Filho, E. C. B. (2007a). Hybrid Solution for the Feature Selection in Personal Identification Problems through Keystroke Dynamics. In *Proceedings of International Joint Conference on Neural Networks*. doi:10.1109/IJCNN.2007.4371256

Azevedo, G. L. F., Cavalcanti, G. D. C., & Filho, E. C. B. (2007b). An Approach to Feature Selection for Keystroke Dynamics Systems based on PSO and Feature Weighting. In *IEEE Congress on Evolutionary Computation*. doi:10.1109/CEC.2007.4424936

Balagani, K. S., & Vir, V. (2011). On the discriminability of keystroke feature vectors used in fixed text keystroke authentication. *Pattern Recognition Letters*, *32*(7), 1070–1080. doi:10.1016/j.patrec.2011.02.014

Bartlow, N., & Cukic, B. (2006). Evaluating the Reliability of Credential Hardening through Keystroke Dynamics. In *17th International Symposium on Software Reliability Engineering*, 117–126. doi:10.1109/ISSRE.2006.25

Bleha, S., & Obaidat, M. (1991). Dimensionality Reduction and Feature Extraction Applications in Identifying Computer Users. *IEEE Transactions on Systems, Man, and Cybernetics*, *21*(2), 452–456. doi:10.1109/21.87093

Bleha, S. A., & Obaidat, M. S. (1993). Computer Users Verification using the Perceptron Algorithm. *IEEE Transactions on Systems, Man, and Cybernetics*, *23*(3), 900–902. doi:10.1109/21.256563

Boechat, G., Ferreira, J., & Carvalho, E. (2006). Using the Keystrokes Dynamic for Systems of Personal Security. Proceedings of World Academy of Science, Engineering and Technology, 18, 200–205.

Bours, P. (2012). Continuous keystroke dynamics: A different perspective towards biometric evaluation. *Information Security Technical Report*, *17*(1-2), 36–43. doi:10.1016/j.istr.2012.02.001

Brown, M., & Rogers, S. J. (1994). A Practical Approach to User Authentication. In *Proceedings of the Conference on Computer Security Applications*. doi:10.1109/CSAC.1994.367316

Chang, C.-H., Johnson, P. W., Katz, J. N., Eisen, E. A., & Dennerlein, J. T. (2009). Typing Keystroke Duration Changed after Submaximal Isometric Finger Exercises. *European Journal of Applied Physiology*, *105*(1), 93–101. doi:10.1007/s00421-008-0878-4 PMID:18853179

Chen, W., & Chang, W. (2004). Applying Hidden Markov Models to Keystroke Pattern Analysis for Password Verification. In *Proceedings of IEEE International Conference on Information Reuse and Integration*. doi:10.1109/IRI.2004.1431505

Cho, S., & Seongseob Hwang. (2006). Artificial Rhythms and Cues for Keystroke Dynamics based Authentication. In *Proceedings of the International Conference on Biometrics*.

Cho, S., Han, C., Han, D. H., & Kim, H. I. (2000). Web-based Keystroke Dynamics Identity Verification using Neural Network. *Organizational Computing and Electronic Commerce*, *10*(4), 295–308. doi:10.1207/S15327744JOCE1004_07

Cho, T.-H. (2006). Pattern Classification Methods for Keystroke Analysis. In *Proceedings of International Joint Conference SICE-ICASE*.

Davoudi, H., & Kabir, E. (2009). A New Distance Measure for Free Text Keystroke Authentication. In *Proceedings of 14th International CSI Computer Conference*. doi:10.1109/CSICC.2009.5349640

De Ru, W. G., & Eloff, J. H. P. (1997). Enhanced Password Authentication through Fuzzy Logic. *IEEE Expert*, *12*(6), 38–45. doi:10.1109/64.642960

DSL Dataset - Keystroke Dynamics - Benchmark Data Set. (2009). Retrieved July 2010, from http://www.cs.cmu.edu/~keystroke/

Eltahir, W. E., Salami, M. J. E., Ismail, A. F., & Lai, W. K. (2004). Dynamic Keystroke Analysis using AR Model. In *IEEE International Conference on Industrial Technology*.

Francesco, B. D., & Gunetti, C. (2002). User Authentication through Keystroke Dynamics. *ACM Transactions on Information and System Security*, 5(4), 367–397. doi:10.1145/581271.581272

Gaines, R. S., Lisowski, Press, S., & Shapiro, N. (1980). *Authentication by Keystroke Timing: Some Preliminary Results.* RAND Report R-256-NSF, RAND Corporation.

Giroux, S., Wachowiak Smolikova, R., & Wachowiak, M. P. (2009). Keystroke-based Authentication by Key Press Intervals as a Complementary Behavioral Biometric. In *IEEE International Conference on Systems, Man and Cybernetics*. doi:10.1109/ICSMC.2009.5346319

Giroux, S., Wachowiak Smolikova, R., & Wachowiak, M. P. (2009). Keypress Interval Timing Ratios as Behavioral Biometrics for Authentication in Computer Security. In *First International Conference on Networked Digital Technologies*. doi:10.1109/NDT.2009.5272133

Gunetti, D., & Picardi, C. (2005). Keystroke Analysis of Free Text. *ACM Transactions on Information and System Security*, 8(3), 12–34. doi:10.1145/1085126.1085129

Harun, N., Woo, W. L., & Dlay, S. S. (2010). Performance of Keystroke Biometrics Authentication System using Artificial Neural Network (ANN) and Distance Classifier Method. In *International Conference on Computer and Communication Engineering (ICCCE)*. doi:10.1109/ICCCE.2010.5556852

Hu, J., Gingrich, D., & Sentosa, A. (2008). A k-Nearest Neighbor Approach for User Authentication through Biometric Keystroke Dynamics. In *IEEE International Conference on Communications*. doi:10.1109/ICC.2008.301

Huang, G. B., Zhu, Q. Y., & Siew, C. K. (2004). Extreme Learning Machine: A New Learning Scheme of Feedforward Neural Networks. In *Proceedings of 2004 International Joint Conference on Neural Networks*. doi:10.1109/IJCNN.2004.1380068

Huang, G. B., Zhu, Q. Y., & Siew, C. K. (2006). Extreme Learning Machine: Theory and Applications. *Neurocomputing*, 70(1-3), 489–501. doi:10.1016/j.neucom.2005.12.126

Joyce, R., & Gupta, G. (1990). Identity Authentication based on Keystroke Latencies. *Communications of the ACM*, 33(2), 168–176. doi:10.1145/75577.75582

Kang, P., Park, S., Yoon, J.-H., Kim, M., Park, J., & Cho, S. (2009). Keystroke dynamics analysis based on long & free text. In *Korean Data Mining Society Conference*.

Karnan, M., & Akila, M. (2009a). Identity Authentication based on Keystroke Dynamics using Genetic Algorithm and Particle Swarm Optimization. In *Proceedings of 2nd IEEE International Conference on Computer Science and Information Technology*. doi:10.1109/ICCSIT.2009.5234420

Karnan, M., & Akila, M. (2009b). Personal Authentication based on Keystroke Dynamics using Ant Colony Optimization and Back Propagation Neural Network. *International Journal of Computer and Network Security*, 1(2), 8–15.

Karnan, M., & Akila, M. (2010). Personal Authentication based on Keystroke Dynamics using Soft Computing Techniques. In *Second International Conference on Communication Software and Networks*. doi:10.1109/ICCSN.2010.50

Kennedy, J., & Eberhart, R. (1995). Particle Swarm Optimization. In *Proceedings of International Conference on Neural Networks*. doi:10.1109/ICNN.1995.488968

Kitchens, Sharma, & Booker. (2003). Identity Authentication based on Keystroke Latencies using the Genetic Adaptive Neural Network. In *Proceedings of the First Security Conference.*

KSP dataset - Pressure sensitive keystroke dynamics dataset. (2010). Retrieved July 2010, from http://jdadesign.net/2010/04/pressure-sensitive-keystroke-dynamics-dataset/

Leberknight, C. S., Widmeyer, G. R., & Recce, M. L. (2008). An Investigation into the Efficacy of Keystroke Analysis for Perimeter Defense and Facility Access. In *IEEE Conference on Technologies for Homeland Security*. doi:10.1109/THS.2008.4534475

Lin. (1997). Computer-access Authentication with Neural Network based Keystroke Identity Verification. In *Proceedings of International Conference on Neural Networks.*

Liu, J., Zhang, B., Zeng, H., Shen, L., Liu, J., & Zaho, J. (2014). The BeiHang Keystroke Dynamics systems, Databases and baselines. *Neurocomputing, 144*, 271–281. doi:10.1016/j.neucom.2014.04.044

Loy, C. C., Lai, W. K., & Lim, C. P. (2005). *Development of a Pressure-based Typing Biometrics User Authentication System*. ASEAN Virtual Instrumentation Applications Contest Submission.

Loy, C. C., Lai, W. K., & Lim, C. P. (2007). Keystroke Patterns Classification using the ARTMAP-FD Neural Network. In *Proceedings of Third International Conference on Intelligent Information Hiding and Multimedia Signal Processing*. doi:10.1109/IIH-MSP.2007.218

Lv, H.-R., & Wang, W.-Y. (2006). Biologic Verification based on Pressure Sensor Keyboards and Classifier Fusion Techniques. *IEEE Transactions on Consumer Electronics, 52*(3), 1057–1063. doi:10.1109/TCE.2006.1706507

Mantyjarvi, J., Koivumaki, J., & Vuori, P. (2002). Keystroke Recognition for Virtual Keyboard. In *Proceedings of IEEE International Conference on Multimedia and Expo*. doi:10.1109/ICME.2002.1035630

Microsoft Password Checker. (2008). Retrieved July 2010, from http://www.microsoft.com/protect/yourself/password/checker.mspx

Monrose, F., & Reiter, M. K., & Wetzel, S. (1999). Password Hardening based on Keystroke Dynamics. In *Proceedings of the 6th ACM Conference on Computer and Communications Security.*

Monrose, F., & Rubin, A. D. (2000). Keystroke: Dynamics as a Biometric for Authentication. *Future Generation Computer Systems, 16*(4), 351–359. doi:10.1016/S0167-739X(99)00059-X

O'Gorman, L. (2003). Comparing Passwords, Tokens, and Biometrics for User Authentication. *Proceedings of the IEEE, 91*(12), 2021–2040. doi:10.1109/JPROC.2003.819611

Obaidat, M. S., & Macchairolo, D. T. (1994). A Multilayer Neural Network System for Computer Access Security. *IEEE Transactions on Systems, Man, and Cybernetics, 24*(5), 806–813. doi:10.1109/21.293498

Obaidat, M. S., & Sadoun, B. (1997). Verification of Computer Users using Keystroke Dynamics. *IEEE Transactions on Systems, Man, and Cybernetics. Part B, Cybernetics, 27*(2), 261–269. doi:10.1109/3477.558812 PMID:18255865

Panda, , & Padhy, N.P. (2007). Comparison of Particle Swarm Optimization and Genetic Algorithm for TCSC-based Controller Design. *World Academy of Science. Engineering and Technology*, *27*, 497–505.

Pedernera, Sznur, S., Ovando, G., Garcia, S., & Meschino, G. (2010). Revisiting Clustering Methods to their Application on Keystroke Dynamics for Intruder Classification. In *Proceedings of 2010 IEEE Workshop on Biometric Measurements and Systems for Security and Medical Applications (BIOMS)*.

Revett, K., Gorunescu, F., Gorunescu, M., Ene, M., Magalhaes, S. T., & Santos, H. M. D. (2007). A Machine Learning Approach to Keystroke Dynamics based User Authentication. *Int. J. Electronic Security and Digital Forensics*, *1*(1), 55–70. doi:10.1504/IJESDF.2007.013592

Robinson, J. A., Liang, V. W., Chambers, J. A. M., & MacKenzie, C. L. (1998). Computer User Verification using Login String Keystroke Dynamics. *IEEE Transactions on Systems, Man, and Cybernetics. Part A, Systems and Humans*, *28*(2), 236–241. doi:10.1109/3468.661150

Rybnik, M., Tabedzki, M., & Saeed, K. (2008). A Keystroke Dynamics based System for User Identification. In *Proceedings of the 7th Computer Information Systems and Industrial Management Applications*. doi:10.1109/CISIM.2008.8

Saevanee, H., & Bhattarakosol, P. (2009). Authenticating User using Keystroke Dynamics and Finger Pressure. In *Proceedings of 6th IEEE Consumer Communications and Networking Conference*. doi:10.1109/CCNC.2009.4784783

Saggio, G., Costantini, G., & Todisco, M. (2011). Cumulative and Ratio Time Evaluations in Keystroke Dynamics to Improve the Password Security Mechanism. *Journal of Computer and Information Technology*, *1*(2), 2–11.

Seong-seob, H., Cho, S., & Park, S. (2009). Keystroke Dynamics-based Authentication for Mobile Devices. *Computers & Security*, 85–93.

Shrijit, S., & Joshi, V., & Phoha. (2007). Competition between SOM Clusters to Model User Authentication System in Computer Networks. In *Proceedings of 2nd International Conference on In Communication Systems Software and Middleware*.

Singhi, S. K., & Liu, H. (2006). Feature Subset Selection Bias for Classification Learning. In *Proceedings of the 23rd International Conference on Machine Learning*. doi:10.1145/1143844.1143951

Sinthupinyo, S., Roadrung Wasinkul, W., & Chantan, C. (2009). User Recognition via Keystroke Latencies using SOM and Backpropagation Neural Network. In ICCAS-SICE, 3160–3165.

Sung, K. S., & Cho, S. (2006). GA SVM Wrapper Ensemble for Keystroke Dynamics Authentication. In *Proceedings of the International Conference on Biometrics*.

Tang, , & Yang, , & Wu. (2010). User Authentication based on Force-Sensing Keypad by Fuzzy C-Means Clustering Method. *Journal of Computer Information Systems*, *6*(11), 3659–3667.

Wahyudi, & Salami, M.J.E. (2009). Keystroke Pressure based Typing Biometrics Authentication System by Combining ANN and ANFIS-based Classifiers. In *Proceedings of 5th International Colloquium on Signal Processing & its Applications*.

Wahyudi & Siddiqi, M.D. (2009). Intelligent Keystroke Pressure-based Typing Biometrics Authentication System using Radial Basis Function Network. In *Proceedings of 2009 5th International Colloquium on Signal Processing & Its Applications*.

Wong, F., Wong, M.H., Supian, A.S.M., Ismail, A.F., Kin, & Soon. (2011). Enhanced User Authentication through Typing Biometrics with Artificial Neural Networks and k-Nearest Neighbor Algorithm. In *Conference Record of the Thirty-Fifth Asilomar Conference on Signals, Systems and Computers*.

Yong, S., Lai, W.K., & Goghill, G. (2004). Weightless Neural Networks for Typing Biometrics Authentication. *Knowledge-Based Intelligent Information and Engineering Systems*, (pp. 284– 293).

Yu, E., & Cho, S. (2004). Keystroke Dynamics Identity Verification: Its Problems and Practical Solutions. *Computers & Security*, *23*(5), 428–440. doi:10.1016/j.cose.2004.02.004

Yu, E., & Cho, S. (2003). GA-SVM Wrapper Approach for Feature Subset Selection in Keystroke Dynamics Identity Verification. In *Proceedings of the International Joint Conference on Neural Networks*.

Zhi-Yuan, Z., Chuang-bai, X., De-Qun, Z., Hong, S., Kai, X., & Guo-Zhong, T. (2011) Identity Authentication System based on Improved PR-RP Model. In *Proceedings of 2nd International Conference on Advanced Computer Control (ICACC)*.

This work was previously published in Developing Next-Generation Countermeasures for Homeland Security Threat Prevention edited by Maurice Dawson, Dakshina Ranjan Kisku, Phalguni Gupta, Jamuna Kanta Sing, and Weifeng Li, pages 330-353, copyright 2017 by Information Science Reference (an imprint of IGI Global).

Section 3
Social Implications, Critical Issues, and Emerging Trends

This section contains 6 chapters, giving a wide range of research pertaining to the social and behavioral impact of Identity Theft, and a wide variety of perspectives and advancement of the discipline on Identity Theft. The reader is presented with an in-depth analysis of research into the integration of global Identity Theft as well as the most current and relevant issues within this growing field of study in which crucial questions are addressed and theoretical approaches discussed. Chapters in this section discuss the effects of user behavior as well as future research directions and topical suggestions for continued debate.

Chapter 14
Cyber Risk:
A Big Challenge in Developed and Emerging Markets

Maria Cristina Arcuri
University of Modena and Reggio Emilia, Italy

Marina Brogi
University of Roma "La Sapienza", Italy

Gino Gandolfi
University of Parma, Italy

ABSTRACT

The dependence on cyberspace has considerably increased over time, as such, people look at risk associated with cyber technology. This chapter focuses on the cyber risk issue. The authors aim to describe the global state of the art and point out the potential negative consequences of this type of systemic risk. Cyber risk increasingly affects both public and private institutions. Some of the risks that entities face are the following: computer security breaches, cyber theft, cyber terrorism, cyber espionage. Developed nations but also emerging markets suffer from cyber risk. It is therefore important to examine the different security regulation implemented across different markets. Moreover, cyber risk is a concern for all economic sectors. In particular, it is a crucial issue in banking sector because of the negative effects of cyber attacks, among others, the financial losses and the reputational risk. However, the awareness is increasing and cyber insurance is growing.

INTRODUCTION

The growth of the internet has been a big social and technological change. It reduces barriers to trade and allows people across the world to communicate and collaborate. In other words, information technology represents an important driver for the economic development.

The dependence on cyberspace has considerably increased over time, as such, we look at risk associated with cyber technology. Cyber risk could be considered as an emerging risk, a "newly developing or

DOI: 10.4018/978-1-5225-0808-3.ch014

changing risk that is difficult to quantify and could have a major impact on society and industry" (Swiss Re, 2013). Considering its potentially systemic nature, cyber risk is a global risk.

Cyber risk increasingly affects both public and private institutions. Some of the risks that entities face are the following: computer security breaches, cyber theft, privacy theft, cyber terrorism, cyber extortion, cyber espionage, cyber threats to infrastructure. Therefore, an information security breach can have negative economic impacts: lower sales revenues, higher expenses, decrease in future profits and dividends, worse reputation, reduction in the market value. Since the market value represents the confidence that investors have in a firm, measuring the market value allows to calculate the impact of a cyber attack.

In recent years, cyber-crime has become increasingly sophisticated, making it difficult to prevent, detect and mitigate. Developed nations but also emerging markets suffer from cyber risk.

Information security breaches are a concern for all economic sectors, from telecommunications, to media and entertainment, from energy to transportation, from military industries to banking and finance. All rely on increasingly-sophisticated, critical information technology infrastructures which must be protected.

According to a recent estimate, cyber crime costs the global economy about USD445 billion every year and in the last years about 90% of large organisations suffered at least one security breach.

Recent surveys reveal that today approximately 80% of executives are not confident in their company's current level of protection but only about 60% plans to invest on cybersecurity in the future. Nevertheless, the awareness is increasing. The demand for cybersecurity jobs is expanding and cyber insurance is growing.

The objective of the chapter is to describe the global state of the art and point out the potential negative consequences of this type of systemic risk.

INFORMATION SECURITY: A GROWING CHALLENGE

In the last years, digital technology has revolutionised economic and social interaction. Internet has often improved the way to conduct business. Nevertheless, widespread interconnectivity has increased the vulnerability of the critical infrastructures to information security breaches.

A 2013 PwC survey demonstrates that more than 90% of large organisations recently suffered a security breach. Moreover, a 2013 ACE survey conducted of 650 executives across a range of industries and 15 countries all over the world shows that businesses expect cyber risk will have significant financial impact in the next two years. It follows that cyber risk has become a very debated issue.

Some of the risks that entities face in this realm include:

- Legal liability;
- Computer security breaches;
- Privacy breaches;
- Cyber theft;
- Cyber espionage (it is the use of computer networks to gain illicit access to confidential information, held by a government or other organization);
- Cyber spying (it is a form of cybercrime in which hackers target computer networks in order to gain access to profitable information);

- Cyber extortion (it is an attack, or threat of attack, against an enterprise, coupled with a demand for money to avert/stop the attack);
- Cyber terrorism (according to the U.S. Federal Bureau of Investigation, it is a "premeditated, politically motivated attack against information, computer systems, computer programs, and data which results in violence against non-combatant targets by sub-national groups or clandestine agents);
- Loss of revenue;
- Recovery of costs;
- Reputational damage;
- Business continuity/supply chain disruptions;
- Cyber threats to infrastructure.

In general, cyber-crime can be understood as an attack on the confidentiality, integrity and accessibility of an entity's online/computer presence or networks, and information contained within. A more detailed definition is the following: "Cyber-Crime is a harmful activity, executed by one group through computers, IT systems and/or the internet and targeting the computers, IT infrastructure and internet presence of another entity" (Tendulkar, 2013).

Among others, cyber-crime includes the following activities: traditional crimes (e.g. fraud and forgery); publication of harmful, illegal or false information via electronic media; new internet crimes (e.g. denial of service and hacking); 'platform crimes' which use computer and information systems as a platform for performing other crimes (e.g. use of botnets, that are networks consisting of computers connected to the Internet and infected with malware).

The 2013 ACE survey reveals that viruses and deliberate introduction of malware cause companies the greatest concern. Follow the following categories of cyber risks: hacking/Denial of service attacks, data theft by third parties and staff, operational error, business interruption, accidental loss, computer fraud and violation of customer privacy/data security breach.

The playing field is broad and can include large and powerful groups with destructive political, economic or ideological aims. Potential actors could include:

- Criminal groups seeking large-scale financial hauls;
- Terrorist groups seeking to hold a government ransom or destroy it;
- Ideological or political extremists such as anti-capitalists who may wish to destroy the financial system;
- A nation state aiming to undermine a rival state's economy or to strike out as an act of cyber warfare;
- Moreover, in some cases, cyber-attacks may be operated from somebody on 'the inside' (e.g. an employee). A 2013 PwC survey suggests that more than 40 per cent of economic crime was committed by employees within an organisation.

Many authors deal with the topic of cyber risk. Some studies present a list of sets of attacks, defences and effects (Cohen, 1997a; Cohen, 1997b; Cohen et al., 1998). Others (Gupta et al., 2000) demonstrate that the attacker's motivations determine the level of attack intensity.

Cyber risk is a potential threat to public and private institutions. But also small and medium-size enterprises are exposed to cyber risk. Furthermore, they, often, are more at risk than large corporations, partly because they cannot afford the same level of security.

In this regard, Cashell et al. (2004) analyze the resources devoted to information security and state that important answers about this issue come from economic analysis.

Anyway, cyber attacks can reduce market integrity and efficiency. This is especially true of attacks against systemically important institutions, critical financial infrastructures and/or providers of essential services. Moreover, in recent years, cyber-crime has become increasingly sophisticated, making it difficult to combat, detect and mitigate.

Cyber risk could affect all economic sectors. Table 1 shows the sectors identified as critical by both the US government in the US Presidential Policy Directive 21, and by the European Commission, as stated in the proposal, Directive on European Critical Infrastructure.

In particular, the 2013 ACE survey shows that cyber risk is the top concern for two sectors: communications, and media and entertainment. But, information security is a very important issue in financial sector, considering the potential impact of reputation. Reputation of financial intermediaries is, in fact, crucial because of their role (Bhattachrya and Thakor, 1993; Allen and Santomero, 1997, 2001). Furthermore, today the online presence of the banking industry is significant (Pennathur, 2001), consequently cyber risk has to be included among all others banking risks.

The authors argue that it is necessary to examine and assess exposure to cyber risk. In fact, an information security breach can have potential high negative economic impacts. Among others, the negative

Table 1. Critical sectors

American Government	European Commission
Food and Agriculture	Food
Water and Wastewater Systems	Water
Dams	Research Facilities
Healthcare and Public Health	Health
Nuclear Reactors, Materials and Waste	Nuclear Industry
Emergency Services	Space
Information Technology	Information, Communication Technology (ICT)
Energy	Energy
Transportation Systems	Transport
Financial Services	Financial
Chemical	Chemical Industry
Communications	
Defense Industrial Base	
Commercial Facilities	
Critical Manufacturing	
Government Facilities	

Source: US Presidential Policy Directive 21 and Council Directive 2008/114/EC

consequences could be the following: lower sales revenues, higher expenses, decrease in future profits and dividends, worse reputation, reduction in the market value (Power, 2002; Gordon et al, 2003). In light of this, it is important to understand what happens when a company suffers from a cyber attack.

CYBER RISK IN THE SECURITIES MARKETS: A FOCUS ON THE FINANCIAL SYSTEM

The soundness, efficiency and stability of securities markets relies on the quality of information provided; the integrity of people and service provision; the effectiveness of regulation; and increasingly the robustness of supporting technological infrastructure. Since the market value represents the confidence that investors have in a firm, measuring the market value allows to calculate the impact of a cyber attack.

Several researches (Campbell et al., 2003; Cavusoglu et al., 2004; Hovav and D'Arcy, 2003; Kannan et al., 2007) have examined the impact of announcements of cyber attacks on the stock market returns of publicly traded companies. In general, there is a consensus that the announcements have a negative impact. However, the findings from these studies are mixed: the announcements have often, but not always, had a significant negative impact.

Some researches (Campbell et al., 2003; Cavusoglu et al., 2004; Hovav and D'Arcy, 2004) consider the type of breach and use the event study methodology to estimate the cyber attacks consequences on the market value of breached firms. Using the event study methodology, researchers measure the effects of an economic event (e.g. a cyber attack) on the value of firms. And this because the effect of an event will be reflected immediately in security prices (MacKinlay, 1997). The aim of the methodology is to verify the null hypothesis that the event has no impact on the distribution of returns. The analysis is conducted on a specific time period, the so called "event window". The event study is based on the measurement of the abnormal stock returns, that are the actual ex post returns of the security over the event window minus the normal returns of the firm over the same event window.

The authors propose, below, a summary of the main results obtained in the literature.

Campbell et al. (2003) state that the nature of breach influences the Cumulative Abnormal Return (CAR), while Cavusoglu et al. (2004) and Hovav and D'Arcy (2004) find that the nature of attack is not a determinant of CAR.

Acquisti et al. (2006) show that there is a negative and statistically significant impact of data breaches on a company's market value on the announcement day for the breach. Ishiguro et al. (2007) find statistically significant reactions in around 10 days after the news reports and observe that the reaction to news reports of the cyber attacks is slower in the Japanese stock market than in the US market. Gordon et al. (2011) conduct the analysis over two distinct sub-periods and found that the impact of information security breaches on stock market returns of firms is significant. In particular, attacks associated with breaches of availability are seen to have the greatest negative effect on stock market returns.

On the other hand, it is interesting to note that voluntary disclosure concerning information security seems to be positively related to stock price of firms (Gordon et al., 2010).

There is limited data available on the costs of cyber-crime for securities markets. A number of studies have calculated costs of cyber-crime to society as a whole, suggesting figures between $388 billion to $1 trillion so far. However, costs may vary considerably by segment and sector, making it difficult to extrapolate general results across all securities market actors.

Some studies state that the information security breaches could be quite costly to firms. In particular, there are potential explicit and implicit costs to firms due to these breaches (Iheagwara et al., 2004; Kerschbaum et al., 2002).

Some surveys show that information security breaches cause significant financial losses for firms. Moreover, understanding the true impact of cyber attack on the stock market returns is crucial to decide the investments in information security activities. In this regard, Gordon and Loeb (2002) present an economic model that determines the optimal amount to invest to protect a given set of information. They suggest that to maximize the expected benefit from investment to protect information, a firm should spend only a small fraction of the expected loss due to a security breach.

In general, there are a large number of studies dealing with information security breaches (Dos Santos et al., 1993; Oates, 2001; Gordon and Loeb, 2002; Garg et al., 2003; Gordon et al., 2003a; Ettredge and Richardson, 2003; Hovav and D'Arcy, 2003; Ko and Dorantes, 2006; Andoh-Baidoo and Osei-Bryson, 2007; Kannan et al., 2007; Anderson and Moore, 2007; Eisenstein, 2008; Kahn and Roberds, 2008; Shackelford, 2008; Winn and Govern, 2009; Geers, 2010; Kundur et al., 2011; Brockett et al., 2012; Shackelford, 2012), but literature related to the financial sector is still limited.

Yet, in the financial sector, cyber-crime is becoming increasingly important. A 2012 PWC survey ranked cyber-crime as the second most commonly reported type of economic crime for financial sector organisations; in a 2012 survey by Marsh and Chubb, 74% of financial services respondents categorized cyber-crime as a high or very high risk; and a 2013 Verizon report on data breaches noted that more than one third of all breaches reported in the year of 2012 affected financial organizations.

For securities markets specifically, cyber threats are evident. Now markets are becoming increasingly digitized, with sensitive data and critical processes being moved to computer-based platforms connected to a vast cyberspace.

Also financial processes have been transformed by technology and continue to evolve. But there is a very real possibility that the industry's digital dependency could have material impacts for individual financial institutions and even develop into systemic concerns.

Cyber-attacks could be disruptive for the financial system. It is potentially aimed to choke financial services; steal or damage information, money supply and markets; damage the capability of the private sector to ensure functioning of the economy; and severely damage investor confidence.

In general, cyber-criminals in the financial system look for financial gain. They could be the following types of subjects:

- Thieves or fraudsters;
- Hactivists motivated by a political deal;
- Cyber spies, stealing political or economic secrets;
- Nation states or terrorist groups;
- Insiders;
- Individuals.

Financial services have long been a target for cybercriminals, but the threat has changed over the last few years. Furthermore, in the financial system cyber-attacks are generally more sophisticated than ever, with attacks coming from not only fraudsters but political activists aiming to disable financial institutions.

Cybercriminals have broadened their activities and are waging long-term, sophisticated campaigns known as advanced persistent threats, aimed at gathering and stealing companies' intellectual property or data and customer information. Additionally, as previously said, the financial services sector has come under fire from political activists, some of whom have already attacked banks' and exchanges' Internet presence.

In particular, cyber risk is a big threat in the banking sector.

Digital technology has transformed the way we do business, especially within banking. This digital dependency represents an opportunity but, at the same time, could foster cyber crime. It is a crucial issue because of the negative effects of cyber attacks, among others, the financial losses and the reputational risk. In addition, banks should consider their vital role, as critical infrastructures.

The targeted intrusion into a bank's system is often perceived as the greatest threat due to the malicious actor's ability to not only steal data but modify or delete it. By exploiting software, hardware or human vulnerabilities hackers can gain administrative control of networks which, if abused, could cause catastrophic consequences. If publicised, network security breaches can affect share prices, cause irreparable reputational damage and impact on the stability of the wider financial market.

The economic effects of cyber-attacks can reach far beyond simply the loss of financial assets or intellectual property. There are costs associated with loss of client confidence, the opportunity costs of service disruptions, "cleaning up" after cyber incidents and the cost of increased cyber security. More and more, damage to brand and reputation in the aftermath of an attack is perceived as a critical risk to firms. In addition, as a key enabler of economic and social development, the banking sector needs to think about the critical infrastructure nature of its operations.

Nevertheless, innovation is crucial to the survival of the banking industry. A collaborative approach is essential to success; a shared view on priorities and a clear understanding of regulatory expectations would help banks to better develop their strategies and controls.

A number of prominent figures and experts highlight the increasing scale of the risks posed by cyber-crime in the financial sector, and the urgency faced. Cyber-crime in the financial system is, in fact, a substantial risk, so political institutions have a stake in keeping the global financial systems stable, relying on the idea of mutually assured destruction.

In conclusion, it is important to point out that cyber-security measures in securities markets, and in particular in financial system, should be proactive as well as reactive, in order to anticipate potential vulnerabilities.

THE CYBER RISK MANAGEMENT IN DEVELOPED AND EMERGING MARKETS: A SUMMARY

Cyber-attacks are considered as one of the most serious economic and national security challenges now facing governments around the world. In fact, cyber-attacks were ranked fifth among the top five global risks in terms of likelihood in 2014 World Economic Forum's annual *Global Risks* report.

Developed nations but also emerging markets suffer from cyber risk. The issue for the developed countries is important especially for international companies with emerging market branches that may be more vulnerable. Cyber risk for the emerging economies is more important if we consider the extent to which information technology is entwined with their development and in particular the internationalisation process of their multinational enterprises.

An emerging market is a country with an economy and stock market in the early phases of development. Coupled with changing business requirements, speed to market pressures, expansion into emerging markets, business innovation requirements and budget cuts, the challenge for managing cyber risk is significant.

The threats and trends within emerging and developed markets are similar, but the way they are approched should be quite different, including the types of security products and services that take priority. It is, therefore, important to examine the state of the art, including different information security regulation implemented across developed and emerging markets.

The evaluation of the information security regulation across the countries is a really important issue. The need for this kind of regulation is strong, considering the spread of Internet: over 2.7 billion people use it (ITU, 2013).

Then, cybercrime rates are on the rise: it affects 1.5 million people every day in the world. The 2012 Norton Cybercrime Report shows that the highest rates of cybercrime victims are found, respectively, in Russia (92%), China (84%) and South Africa (80%)

In general, developed nations, such as United States and Germany, have stable regulation, while emerging markets, such as China and India, have published their information security regulation recently.

Information security regulation is being developed in different ways (Johnson et al., 2014). Moreover, it is focused on different aspects. Some countries specify security goals while others consider a risk management approach. The implementation of information security regulation also depends on the culture and industrial development characterizing the individual nations.

In China, for example, there are limitations in regards to the freedom of the use of internet and, at the same time, there are large measures to protect data. However, the implementation of the regulation is vague.

Indian government considers cyber security as really important to maintaining its infrastructures. India provides clear definitions (e.g. personal data) but there are not guidelines for protecting data. Regulation is recent and it is goal oriented.

With reference to the developed countries, the European Union aims to harmonize the legal situation in the Member States. As a consequence, the national legislation is influenced by EU-directives. The EU provides a regulatory framework also concerning the cyber risk and, in particular, to achieve a high level of cyber security.

Also in the United States there is a strong regulation. Moreover, companies that violate the rules are punished by applying substantial fines. The goal is to promote the risk management processes and ensure security compliance.

In conclusion, cyber crime is a serious threat for all economies. The frequency and severity of cyber-attacks on businesses and organizations across the world have exploded in recent years. Nevertheless, in general, companies' level of protection is not high. Some reasons could be the following: cyber attacks are difficult to detect and, above all, cyber security is a cost-saving and not a revenue-generating measure.

Furthermore, it is not a static situation. The vulnerability of critical sectors to information security breaches could increase because of the increasing reliance on computer networks. It is, therefore, necessary that national internet protocols and information security regularization become more strong and effective (Lewis, 2002). Moreover, the cooperation among nations might be really good for defeating cyber attacks.

CYBER SECURITY AND CYBER INSURANCE

Cyber security presents a critical challenge for businesses, institutions and governments. They need, in fact, to protect their own data from competitors and cybercriminals and to safeguard the personal data of their customers, clients, patients, employees, and suppliers.

Awareness of cyber-based risks in different sectors is gradually increasing.

As explained in the previous paragraph, cyber risk has been at least partially addressed in some regulations around the world, taken up through practical industry-wide initiatives and captured in a number of reports and surveys. World leaders and experts have also acknowledged the cyber-threat to society and the economy. Finally, governments are elevating cyber-related risks into a national security issue. Hence, cyber-based threats are being recognized more generally as constituting a top economic risk. As a consequence, cyber security threats are becoming one of the most important risks for the insurance industry.

As is well known, insurance is a risk industry that analyzes good data in order to evaluate, comprehend and mitigate the risks. With the increasing severity and frequency of cyber-attacks and data breaches worldwide, the demand for cyber-specific insurance is growing.

Cyber-insurance can be defined as a risk management technique via which network user risks are transferred to an insurance company, in return for the insurance premium.

Figure 1 shows the development of cyber insurance over time in the United States and in Europe.

Figure 1. Historical development of cyber insurance
Source: Guy Carpenter

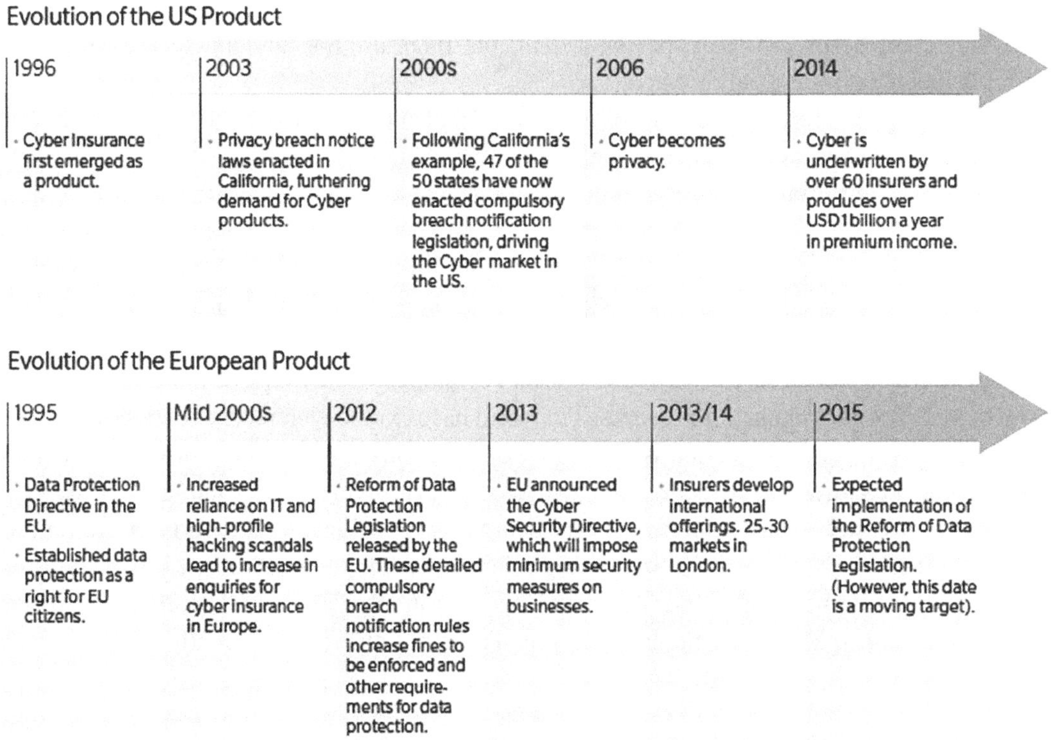

Evolution of the US Product

1996	2003	2000s	2006	2014
· Cyber Insurance first emerged as a product.	· Privacy breach notice laws enacted in California, furthering demand for Cyber products.	· Following California's example, 47 of the 50 states have now enacted compulsory breach notification legislation, driving the Cyber market in the US.	· Cyber becomes privacy.	· Cyber is underwritten by over 60 insurers and produces over USD1 billion a year in premium income.

Evolution of the European Product

1995	Mid 2000s	2012	2013	2013/14	2015
· Data Protection Directive in the EU. · Established data protection as a right for EU citizens.	· Increased reliance on IT and high-profile hacking scandals lead to increase in enquiries for cyber insurance in Europe.	· Reform of Data Protection Legislation released by the EU. These detailed compulsory breach notification rules increase fines to be enforced and other requirements for data protection.	· EU announced the Cyber Security Directive, which will impose minimum security measures on businesses.	· Insurers develop international offerings. 25-30 markets in London.	· Expected implementation of the Reform of Data Protection Legislation. (However, this date is a moving target).

Marsh and Chubb (2012) estimate the US cyber insurance market was worth USD1 billion in gross written premiums in 2013 and could reach as much as USD2 billion this year. The European market is currently a fraction of that, at around USD150 million. Estimates see the European market reaching a size of EUR700 million to EUR 900 million by 2018.

According to McAfee (2014), though in its infancy, the market's potential is vast with cyber-crime costing the global economy about USD445 billion every year.

The recent 2015 Marsh benchmarking trends report on cyber insurance reveals that interest in cyber insurance continues to increase. The report found that the number of the firm's clients who sought to purchase this type of coverage increased by 21 percent from 2012 to 2013. Media reports of serious data breaches have undoubtedly prompted more companies to buy cyber coverage of USD100 million or more compared to the prior year. Since traditional insurance products often do not cover damages resulting from an incident like a computer breach, specific cyber liability insurance may be necessary.

Traditional insurance products often do not cover damages deriving from a computer breach, but specific products have been created. These specific covers normally include, among others, the following events: data privacy, regulations breaches, network business interruption, cyber extortion and identity theft.

However, companies are uncertain of how much coverage to acquire and whether their current policies provide them with protection. One of the roots of the uncertainty stems from the difficulty in quantifying potential losses because of the dearth of historical data for actuaries and underwriters to model cyber-related losses.

Current cyber-insurance markets are moderately competitive and specialized. The most prominent amongst them is information asymmetry between the insurer and the insured, and the interdependent and correlated nature of cyber-risks.

Information asymmetry has a significant negative effect on most insurance environments, where typical considerations include inability to distinguish between users of different (high and low risk) types, i.e., the so called adverse selection problem, as well as users undertaking actions that adversely affect loss probabilities after the insurance contract is signed, i.e., the so called moral hazard problem. The challenge due to the interdependent and correlated nature of cyber-risks is particular to cyber-insurance and differentiates traditional insurance scenarios, concerning, for example, car or health insurance, from the former.

The aim of cyber-insurance is to enable individual users to internalize the externalities in the network so that each user optimally invests in security solutions, thereby alleviating moral hazard and improving network security. In traditional insurance scenarios, the risk span is quite small (sometimes it spans only one or two entities) and uncorrelated, thus internalizing the externalities generated by user investments in safety, is much easier.

Cyber-insurance policies have become more comprehensive as insurers better understand the risk landscape and specific business needs. More specifically, cyberinsurers are addressing what used to be considered insurmountable problems (e.g., the above mentioned adverse selection, asymmetric information and moral hazard) that could lead to a failure of this market solution.

Cyber insurance produces, therefore, a number of advantages. First, cyber-insurance would result in higher security investment, increasing the level of safety for information technology infrastructure. Second, cyber-insurance can facilitate standards for best practices as cyberinsurers seek benchmark security levels for risk management decision-making. Third, the creation of an IT security insurance market will result in higher overall societal welfare.

Hence, the development of cyber insurance is necessary, but IT security and cybercrime prevention is also important. In this regard, securities market regulators should strengthen the following activities related to cyber crime:

- Updating/implementing regulation and standards (in collaboration with other authorities);
- Identifying and providing guidance on best practice, principles and/or frameworks;
- Building, partaking in and promoting information sharing networks;
- Acting as a repository of knowledge for securities market participants to tap into.

Moreover, since the cyber risk is changing, provisions and regulations have to be flexible and adapt to it. Furthermore, it should promote information sharing.

Finally, the authors share the following possible remedies to counter cyber risk proposed by Tendulkar (2013):

- Harmonization of different approaches to cyber crimes across country and support efforts in emerging markets;
- Facilitation of information sharing on cyber attacks;
- Provision of a repository of knowledge for securities market participants;
- Development of principles for cyber security and resilience and for regulation to deter cyber criminals;
- Consideration of emerging response guidelines to deal with large-scale cyber attacks on securities markets.

CONCLUSION

The growth of the internet has been a big social and technological change. It is a massive force for good in the world in the way it drives growth, reduces barriers to trade, and allows people to communicate and co-operate. At the same time the increasing dependence on cyberspace has brought the risks that key data and systems can be compromised or damaged.

Cyber risk poses a particular challenge for governments, institutions and companies.

In order to combat cyber crime, nations are adopting Internet protocols and information security regulations increasingly detailed and effective. Political and economic institutions are exposed to big cyber risks. For this reason, the attention to the issue has grown in recent years and considerable progress has been made, in terms of identifying and tackling cyber attacks. Finally, even the private companies suffer from cyber attacks. The negative consequences may be different, just think of the following: lower sales revenues, higher expenses, decrease in future profits and dividends, worse reputation, reduction in the market value.

The reduction in market value, in addition to the potential reputational loss, may be significant, even for the financial sector and, in particular, for the banks. Moreover, the issue is really important considering that these institutions are "critical infrastructures".

Moreover, the use of digital technologies is increasing in all economic sectors and cyber attacks are becoming increasingly sophisticated.

In light of this situation, prevention and detection alone are not sufficient. Robust *cyber-security*, in terms of detection and prevention and *cyber-resilience*, that is the ability to continue functions and/or bounce back quickly during and after an attack, are important factors in mitigating impacts from cyber-crime. In addition to this, there is the possibility of resorting to *cyber-insurance*.

ACKNOWLEDGMENT

We express our appreciation to the Prof. R. Baldoni, whose contribution to the analysed topic was of great significance.

REFERENCES

ACE. (2013). *Emerging risks barometer*. European Risk Briefing. Retrieved from http://www.acegroup.com/de-de/assets/ace_emerging_risks_barometer_2013.pdf

Acquisti, A., Friedman, A., & Telang, R. (2006). Is there a cost to privacy breaches? An event study. In *Proceedings of the 27th International Conference on Information Systems* (December 2006). Paper 94. Retrieved from http://aisel.aisnet.org/icis2006/94

Allen, F., & Santomero, A. M. (1997). The theory of financial intermediation. *Journal of Banking & Finance, 21*(11-12), 1461–1485. doi:10.1016/S0378-4266(97)00032-0

Allen, F., & Santomero, A. M. (2001). What do financial intermediaries do? *Journal of Banking & Finance, 25*(2), 271–294. doi:10.1016/S0378-4266(99)00129-6

Anderson, R., & Moore, T. (2007). Information Security Economics – and Beyond. In A. Menezes (Ed.), *Advances in Cryptology – Crypto 2007* (pp. 68–91). Berlin: Springer. doi:10.1007/978-3-540-74143-5_5

Andoh-Badoo, F. K., & Osei-Bryson, K. M. (2007). Exploring the characteristics of internet security breaches that impact the market value of breached firms. *Expert Systems with Applications, 32*(3), 703–725. doi:10.1016/j.eswa.2006.01.020

Bhattachrya, S., & Thakor, A. V. (1993). Contemporary banking theory. *Journal of Financial Intermediation, 3*(1), 2–50. doi:10.1006/jfin.1993.1001

Brockett, P. L., Golden, L. L., & Wolman, W. (2012). Enterprise cyber risk management. In J. Emblemsvåg (Ed.), *Risk management for the future – Theory and cases* (pp. 319–340). Rijeka: InTech.

Campbell, K., Gordon, L., Loeb, M., & Zhou, L. (2003). The economic cost of publicly announced information security breaches: Empirical evidence from the stock market. *Journal of Computer Security, 11*, 431-448.

Cashell, B., Jackson, W. D., Jickling, M., & Webel, B. (2004). *The Economic Impact of Cyber-Attacks. Report for United States Congress*. Washington, DC: CRS.

Cavusoglu, H., Mishra, B., & Raghunathan, S. (2004). The effect of Internet security breach announcements on market value: Capital market reactions for breached firms and Internet security developers. *International Journal of Electronic Commerce, 9*(1), 69–104.

Cohen, F. (1997a). Information system defences: A preliminary classification scheme. *Computers & Security, 16*(2), 94–114. doi:10.1016/S0167-4048(97)88289-2

Cohen, F. (1997b). Information systems attacks: A preliminary classification scheme. *Computers & Security, 16*(1), 29–46. doi:10.1016/S0167-4048(97)85785-9

Cohen, F., Phillips, C., Swiler, L. P., Gaylor, T., Leary, P., Rupley, F., & Isler, R. (1998). A cause and effect model of attacks on information systems. *Computers & Security, 17*(1), 211–221. doi:10.1016/S0167-4048(98)80312-X

Dos Santos, B. L., Peffers, K., & Mauer, D. C. (1993). The impact of information technology investment announcements on the market value of the firm. *Information Systems Research, 4*(1), 1–23. doi:10.1287/isre.4.1.1

Eisenstein, E. M. (2008). Identity theft: An exploratory study with implications for marketers. *Journal of Business Research, 61*(11), 1160–1172. doi:10.1016/j.jbusres.2007.11.012

Ettredge, M. L., & Richardson, V. J. (2003). Information transfer among Internet firms: The case of hacker attacks. *Journal of Information Systems, 17*(2), 71–82. doi:10.2308/jis.2003.17.2.71

Garg, A., Curtis, J., & Halper, H. (2003). Quantifying the financial impact of IT security breaches. *Information Management & Computer Security, 11*(2), 74–83. doi:10.1108/09685220310468646

Geers, K. (2010). The Challenge of Cyber Attack Deterrence. *Computer Law & Security Report, 26*(3), 298–303. doi:10.1016/j.clsr.2010.03.003

Gordon, L. A., & Loeb, M. P. (2002). The economics of information security investment. *ACM Transactions on Information and System Security, 5*(4), 438–457. doi:10.1145/581271.581274

Gordon, L. A., Loeb, M. P., & Lucyshyn, W. (2003). Sharing information on computer systems security: An economic analysis. *Journal of Accounting and Public Policy, 22*(6), 461–485. doi:10.1016/j.jaccpubpol.2003.09.001

Gordon, L. A., Loeb, M. P., & Sohail, T. (2010). Market value of voluntary disclosures concerning information security. *MIS Quartely, 34*(3), 567–694.

Gordon, L. A., Loeb, M. P., & Zhou, L. (2011). The impact of information security breaches: Has there been a downward shift in costs? *Journal of Computer Security, 19*(1), 33–56.

Gupta, M., Chaturvedi, A. R., Mehta, S., & Valeri, L. (2000). The experimental analysis of information security management issues for online financial services. In *Proceedings of The twenty-first international conference on Information systems* (pp.667-675).

Hovav, A., & D'Arcy, J. (2003). The impact of denial-of-service attack announcements on the market value of firm. *Risk Management & Insurance Review, 6*(2), 97–121. doi:10.1046/J.1098-1616.2003.026.x

Iheagwara, C., Blyth, A., & Singhal, M. (2004). Cost effective management frameworks for intrusion detection systems. *Journal of Computer Security, 12*(5), 777–798.

International Telecommunications Union (ITU). (2013), *ICT facts and figures.* Retrieved from https://www.itu.int/en/ITU-D/Statistics/Documents/facts/ICTFactsFigures2013-e.pdf

Ishiguro, M., Tanaka, H., Matsuura, I., & Murase, I. (2007). *The effect of information security incidents on corporate values in the Japanese stock market.Workshop on the Economics of Securing Information Infrastructure.* Arlington.

Johnson, J., Lincke, S. J., Imhof, R., & Lim, C. (2014). A comparison of International Information Security Regulation. *Interdisciplinary Journal of Information. Knowledge and Management, 9,* 89–116.

Kahn, C. M., & Roberds, W. (2008). Credit and identity theft. *Journal of Monetary Economics, 55*(2), 251–264. doi:10.1016/j.jmoneco.2007.08.001

Kannan, A., Rees, J., & Sridhar, S. (2007). Market reaction to information security breach announcements: An empirical analysis. *International Journal of Electronic Commerce, 12*(1), 69–91. doi:10.2753/JEC1086-4415120103

Kerschbaum, F., Spafford, E. H., & Zamboni, D. (2002). Using embedded sensors and detectors for intrusion detection. *Journal of Computer Security, 10*(1-2), 23–70.

Ko, M., & Dorantes, C. (2006). The impact of information security breaches on financial performance of the breached firms: An empirical investigation. *Journal of Information Technology Management, 17*(2), 13–22.

Kundur, D., Feng, X., Mashayekh, S., Liu, S., Zourntos, T., & Butler-Purry, K. L. (2011). Towards modelling the impact of cyber attacks on a smart grid. *International Journal of Security and Networks, 6*(1), 2–13. doi:10.1504/IJSN.2011.039629

Lewis, J. A. (2002). Assessing the risks of cyber terrorism, cyber war and other cyber threats. *National Criminal Justice, 200114,* 1–12.

MacKinlay, A. C. (1997). Event studies in Economics and Finance. *Journal of Economic Literature, 35*(1), 13–39.

Marsh, & Chubb. (2012). *Cyber Risk perceptions: An industry snapshot, Cyber Survey.* Retrieved from http://www.asecib.ase.ro/cc/articole/Cyber%20Survey%20report_v4.pdf

Marsh. (2015). *Benchmarking trends: as cyber concern broaden, insurance purchases rise.* Retrieved from http://usa.marsh.com/Portals/9/Documents/BenchmarkingTrendsCyber8094.pdf

McAfee. (2014). *Net losses: Estimating the Global Cost of Cybercrime. Economic Impact of Cybercrime II.* Retrieved from http://www.mcafee.com/jp/resources/reports/rp-economic-impact-cybercrime2.pdf

Norton. (2012). *Norton Cybercrime Report.* Retrieved from http://now-static.norton.com/now/cn/pu/images/Promotions/2012/cybercrimeReport/2012_Norton_Cybercrime_Report_Master_FINAL_050912.pdf

Oates, B. (2001). Cyber Crime: how technology makes it easy and what to do about it. *Information Systems Security, 9*(6), 1-6.

Pennathur, A. K. (2001). "Clicks and bricks": e-Risk Management for banks in the age of the Internet. *Journal of Banking & Finance, 25*(11), 2013–2123.

Power, R. (2002). CSI/FBI 2002 Computer Crime and Security Survey. *Computer Security Issues and Trends, 18*(2), 7–30.

PWC. (2012). *Fighting Economic Crime in the Financial Services Sector.* Retrieved from https://www.pwc.com/gx/en/economic-crime-survey/pdf/fighting-economic-crime-in-the-financial-services-sector.pdf

PwC. (2013). *Information Security Breach Survey.* Retrieved from https://www.pwc.co.uk/assets/pdf/cyber-security-2013-exec-summary.pdf

Shackelford, S. J. (2008). From Nuclear War to Net War: Analogizing Cyber Attacks in International Law. *International Law, 27*(1), 191–251.

Shackelford, S. J. (2012). Should Your Firm Invest in Cyber Risk Insurance? *Business Horizons, 55*(4), 349–356. doi:10.1016/j.bushor.2012.02.004

Swiss Re. (2013). *Emerging risk insights.* Retrieved from http://www.stopumts.nl/pdf/Zwitserland%20Swiss%20Reinsuranse%202013.pdf

Tendulkar, R. (2013). *Cyber-crime, Securities Markets and Systemic Risk.* Working Paper of the IOSCO Research Department and World Federation of Exchanges. Madrid, Spain.

Verizon. (2013). *Data Breach Investigations Report.* Retrieved from http://www.verizonenterprise.com/resources/reports/rp_data-breach-investigations-report-2013_en_xg.pdf

Winn, J., & Govern, K. (2009). Identity theft: Risks and challenges to business of data compromise. *Journal of Science Technology & Environmental Law, 28*(1), 49–63.

World Economic Forum. (2014), *Global Risks 2014* (9th ed.). Retrieved from http://www3.weforum.org/docs/WEF_GlobalRisks_Report_2014.pdf

KEY TERMS AND DEFINITIONS

Cyber Crime: A harmful activity executed by one group through computers, IT systems, and/or the internet and targeting the computers, IT infrastructure, and internet presence of another entity.

Cyber Espionage: The use of computer networks to gain illicit access to confidential information, held by a government or other organization.

Cyber Extortion: An attack, or threat of attack, against an enterprise, coupled with a demand for money to avert/stop the attack.

Cyber Risk: One of the following categories of attack: hacking/Denial of service attacks, data theft by third parties and staff, operational error, business interruption, accidental loss, computer fraud and violation of customer privacy/data security breach.

Cyber Spying: A form of cybercrime in which hackers target computer networks in order to gain access to profitable information.

Cyber Terrorism: A premeditated, politically motivated attack against information, computer systems, computer programs, and data which results in violence against non-combatant targets by sub-national groups or clandestine agents.

Emerging Risk: A newly developing or changing risk that is difficult to quantify and could have a major impact on society and industry.

Chapter 15
The Value of Personal Information

K.Y Williams
Walden University, USA

Dana-Marie Thomas
Walden University, USA

Latoya N. Johnson
Walden University, USA

ABSTRACT

Many cyber-attacks that result in data loss can be prevented if the target of the cyber-attack is properly prepared, has the necessary and latest defenses in place, and is constantly monitoring for attacks and intrusions. Whether those cyber-attacks occur as a result of user error; network issues (password files being created and distributed to a list of people); direct assaults (direct intrusion via a designed hack, system flaw, or exploitation of a known network/software issue); or due to an insider-threat (giving a password to a trusted co-worker who then uses it for other means) one aspect of prevention that must be addressed is the need for better security and additional layers of protection on the data that resides on the servers and in computing systems. With up-to-date protocols, reduced access to the system, and compartmentalization of information, it is possible to reduce the amount and type of data that is lost in many cyber-attacks. This chapter explores five types of information that are targeted during cyber-attacks, and discuss why this information is of importance.

INTRODUCTION

With each cyber-attack the amount and type of data that hackers are retrieving is increasing with more vicious, blunt force, direct attacks, and in the accuracy and efficiency of the attacks. Government agencies have noticed that during the past decade the increase in the information targeted by hackers has grown from what was only information found on servers in government agencies to now include information from servers of financial systems and corporate entities. With this increase of cyber-attacks, the nature of the stolen information has increased to include more specific, personal information.

DOI: 10.4018/978-1-5225-0808-3.ch015

In the past many individuals, organizations, academic institutions, companies, and government agencies generally thought that one individual alone was usually responsible for as attack, and in the past this may have been the case. However, it is no longer plausible to think that a sole individual is responsible for the substantial number of hacks that occurred over the past decade. In fact, it is far more reasonable to think that larger groups of individuals numbering from three to ten (at least) are responsible for the attacks that have occurred on the different companies, financial entities, and government agencies, and depending on the sophistication and complexity of the system, the number of people involved only grows. Interestingly more direct well-coordinated cyber-attacks targeted towards an individual, organization, academic institution, company, and government agency are no longer scarce, and they are becoming commonplace.

With the increase in the number of cyber-attacks, it seems that hackers may have obtained and secured diverse funding sources to support the cyber-attacks. With renewed funding, computational resources, networking, and multimedia/storage resources, hackers are able to achieve the goal(s) of their attacks with more accuracy and efficiency than in previous years. By utilizing the underlying nature and blind spots within digital systems and having a familiarity with the encryptions used within digital systems, advanced coding, and general knowledge of the flaws within operating systems and servers, hackers are finding it easier and easier to access the targeted systems. This makes the timing and type of attack increase with more efficiency, and with each attack it leaves many of the targets even more vulnerable than expected.

As the number of security breaches increase, hackers not only are able to explore systems with each attack, but also may leave ways to get back into a system for future use. With each intrusion into the system, the information that hackers target range from personal to financial to intellectual in nature. Because the type of information obtained during an attack can vary, it is important to keep in mind that the intent of the attack may be based on the motivation of the person or organization who intends to use the information obtained by the hackers, and not necessarily the hackers themselves if it is done for the benefit of a third party. Private information such as Personal Identifying Information (PII), Personal Health Information (PHI), and private data is valuable in a very particular market and to select groups of people/buyers. Financial Information, Credit Information, and Credit History Information will have a different market, such as others who may have a desire of to gain financially, in the immediate future, or the long term. However, intellectual property and discovery information have a very different value and interest to the right company, buyer, or agency. Additionally cyber-attacks and security breaches that target these types of information hold value if the right combination of information is placed together to create a profile or idea of a particular person, or if the goal is to gain financially from a security breach. This chapter explores these types of information, discusses how the information can be used to compromise individuals, organizations, academic institutions, companies, government agencies, and then explores how financial institutions can be affected by such intrusions.

BACKGROUND

Intrusions into Personal, Private, and Professional Lives

Nothing is impenetrable. If someone designed or built a computer system or network, then it is possible for someone else to penetrate, circumvent, cripple, dismantle, or occupy the system. No one in the computer industry, information storage industry, or technology development industry wants to think of cyber-attacks, unwanted intrusions, or security breaches occurring as it will become a nightmare to investigate, report, and analyze the breached systems when these attacks do occur. However when they occur various checks must occur to ensure that the potential for them to occur in the future is reduced. Cyber-attacks on individuals, organizations, corporations, government agencies, financial institutions, and academic institutions occur and recent events within the last decade would give anyone the impression that those attacks occur on a daily basis, or that they are becoming more and more common place. These data breaches have increased in number and frequency as a result of the improvements in technology, the innovations and strides made within technology and wireless communication, and with the increased capabilities of remote and wireless networks. With each new capability and system access, such innovations make it easier for hackers to gain access to more secure systems. Having personal and private computers, smartphones, home security systems, and televisions that have wireless connections connected to the internet through a private network does not mean that it is secure even though it is on a private network. It only means that they are networked to the same system and convenient to the owner. Therefore, it is not surprising that these advances have also affected corporate security.

At the time of writing of this manuscript, two highly publicized and very detailed cyber-attacks occurred on Sony Pictures Entertainment and Sony Gaming System affecting their servers and data networks. With these types of cyber-attacks, Sony Pictures Entertainment security systems were breached and approximately 100 TBs of data/information was taken from their servers (Robb, 2014). Information in the form of unreleased motion pictures, incomes of the executive employees, PII, and detailed financial information of the company was placed on the Internet by a group called Guardians of Peace (Robb, 2014). In addition to the leaked movies from Sony Pictures Entertainment, the group responsible for the hack also released employee data/information and warned employees that their "family will be in danger." This also was accompanied with additional demands in regards to not releasing a movie that portrayed the Democratic People's Republic of Korea leader Kim Jong-un in a negative light (Robb, 2014). This is just one example of how the goal of the intrusion is related to the type of the information stolen when a system is hacked.

Private networks are not only vulnerable to cyberattacks, but they have also been hacked to allow intruders to enter into private systems where they have been able to take control of an automobile (CBS, 2014), air traffic control systems (Cooper, 2015), and nuclear power plants (Kwaak, 2015). Such incidents are not a representation of the normal home systems, but with each system coming online as a result of wireless connections to any network, it allows for additional ways for intruders to enter and penetrate our levels of privacy to include our cars, homes, finances, and personal communication devices. Recent hacks of several manufactures of webcams by a Russian group showed that many users of the different systems and services use the manufactures' passwords to not only setup up the system, but also they retained the manufactures' default password after installing the system. This made it easy for the group to gain access to private systems and then exploit them based on the information. The group then showed the world how users are not making themselves safe or safer based on the use of manufacturers' passwords and their inability to change basic features and system passwords (Kottasova, 2014).

A further explanation into the types of commonly hacked information and how they are related to the goal of the hacker (or the hacker's client) may help the system and network engineers better equip their infrastructures to thwart cyber-attacks.

MAIN FOCUS OF CHAPTER

Intrusions into Personal, Private Lives

Private information includes Personal Identifying Information (PII), Personal Health Information (PHI), and private data and holds value for different reasons. Eleanor Meux (1994) stated that data that includes PII such as "demographic (e.g., race, gender, age) and clinical (e.g., diagnoses, procedure)" data that can be linked to financial information should be considered confidential as it becomes of value. This information becomes of value not only to the person whose information is contained within the documents, but also to individuals that could benefit from knowing about said data within the documentation. Most documents that contain such information usually include social security numbers and dates of birth.

Research published on the use of PII and the use of the information when acquired via cyber-attacks revealed that it can be used to create a false identity and to commit fraud only under the disguise of another individual (i.e., identity theft). Additionally these results have shown that PII is valuable in a very particular market and to select groups of people/buyers. From this research several other things have become apparent in terms of risks. Research into the use and acquisition of PHI exposed that information containing personal health information has been used to deny individuals health insurance or coverage based on pre-existing, and could be used in gaining treatment for illnesses based on the information of a person with health insurance. Within the software and web community many times programmers and developers do not take security into consideration at every step and stage of the development process, therefore many issues can arise after the deployment of a website or a software suite of programs. However security of medical and clinical data (Chen, et. al. 2009) and personal information (Landi & Rao, 2003) is necessary at each stage of development of software, websites, and web applications. Neame (2013) reiterated that sharing of health records can be done effectively and in a private manner, and goes on to share how "a method of verifying authenticity, integrity, and authorships is required, which can be provided using a public key infrastructure (PHI) for crytopgraphy" a sentiment previously stated by Steinbrook (2008).

Financial Information

Credit Information and Credit History Information is another form of information targeted during cyber-attacks. This can have a lasting effect on individuals when issues are not resolved immediately and in the proper manner. The three credit agencies that monitor the actions of individuals usually rely on information submitted from companies that have accounts associated with individuals by demographic information (name, age, and income) and social security numbers. Because this type of PII can be acquired via cyber-attack it becomes easier for someone to assume the identity of an individual and make purchases in another person's name. If only demographic and social security information is used by the credit agencies then it becomes impossible for a person to correct the errors or purchases if they are not made immediately aware of the issues. Similar to financial institutions, credit institutions offer constant credit monitoring as an option (and usually after credit incidents have occurred); therefore credit incidents can go unnoticed until an individual applies for credit or obtains a copy of his or her credit report.

This type of information usually has a different market and interest to others who may have an idea of wanting to gain financially via larger purchases that can go unnoticed or undiscovered. When information of this type is captured it is easily identifiable and usable in different systems and in the establishment of other identities. Information in the form or emails, text messages, photos (Sang, Ling, & Alam, 2012) and credit card information can be easily captured by hackers via cyber-attack and card skimmers. Sang, et al., (2012) outlined how security measures can be used to encrypt this information and also how information within text format can be encrypted and hidden with double-random phase encoding.

Value attributed to financial information has also shown that the right information can be used to instantly affect the bank accounts and credit accounts of individuals from various financial institutions. With constant monitoring of debit/credit activity being an option for bank accounts as opposed to the standard package of a bank account, this lapse in security makes it easier for a hacker with the proper financial information to recreate a debit card or credit card containing stolen credit/bank information. This type of financial gain can be traced to various locations and purchases without giving the actual identity of the individual or group who stole the information, but it should generate information on who may have used the information and in what manner.

Intrusions into Professional Lives

Intellectual Property in the way of innovation, invention, software and application (Apps) development has the potential for increased financial gain. Regardless of who developed the information, having information or the discovery of information can be of value to any interested individual, corporation, agency, or institution – if they are the right company, buyer, or agency. In many cases, the gain of the type of information may be proprietary, and this type of information may be accessed via different means than the normal cyber-attack or in addition to a cyber-attack. Intellectual property and discovery information may be acquired via cyber-espionage or corporate espionage (see other manuscript). The loss of such information due to a cyber-attack becomes costly to the company, individual, agency, or institution in terms of legal fees, court time, and trade agreements. However by encrypting the information with the use of double-random phase encoding methods (Sang, et al., 2012) it is possible to add an additional layer of security onto the information that will allow for more security on systems where proprietary information resides.

With all of the information that can be gained and the value that is contained within each form of information, there are various ways that someone can use the information for present and future gain. Therefore one must ask the questions: *Once information is in hand, what can be done with it?* Additional questions include: *Will someone be able to construct an identity or re-construction an identity based on the information? Is it possible to falsify information or reproduce records for another individual?*

When faced with the following two questions, *will someone be able to construct an identity or re-construction an identity based on the information,* and *is it possible to falsify information or reproduce records for another individual,* one must think about the value of the information to others, not to themselves. Once hackers have personal information in hand, any number of things can occur and can be done with the information. The limits are only at the whims of the person who is using the information and his or her intentions. If a hacker sells the information to someone who is looking to conduct any fraudulent actions then the use of the person's demographic information, SSN, and salary can be used to recreate an identity and begin to purchase items based on the person's identity and credit information. Opening additional credit accounts and making purchases using a person's identity can go undetected if the person is not aware of the actions for at least one week; however, the actions can be stopped by paying attention to ones credit on a routine bases. If a hacker sold the personal health information of someone who has a very good health insurance plan to someone who needs medical attention, then the recipient would be able to receive medical treatment and healthcare for personal medical illnesses that they normally would not have been able to be treated for based on their own health insurance.

Reconstruction of an identity is not as difficult as one would assume mainly because various electronic entities do not communicate with each other, and different data systems and databases do not have access to information that other systems may have, (*i.e.,* banking and financial institutions usually do not have access to medical records). Therefore a person who lives in Washington, D.C. may be able to have their personal health information duplicated and used by someone in Birmingham, AL in an effort for the person to obtain medical treatment for an illness, but a financial institution would not be aware of the intrusion. However if the person used the stolen personal financial and personal health information to duplicate an identity, debit or credit card, and try to obtain medical treatment for an illness, then the financial institution would be aware of the duplication. The financial institution would alert the person that someone may have tried to use a debit or credit card with their information in another location that where they normally use their debit or credit card, but it does not mean that the financial institution would alert other authorities or health care providers or insurance companies that a potential breach is occurring or have occurred.

Value in Each Type of Information

Different forms of risks exist: intrusions into personal privacy, loss/acquisition of PII and/or PHI, financial loss, loss of credit/changes in credit, denial of service, data reduction, data duplication, data loss, loss of physical and intellectual property, and/or breaches of personal and network security. However, these security risks can be reduced by having improved security measures, reducing activity and access to private networks, establishing password update and reminder measures, adding additional authentication methods, and improving on identification and authentication methods.

The thought that hackers do not exist or that the average person is not a target is slim in regards to the amount of information that is leaked and how it can affect an individual. Within any security or law enforcement agency that provides protection for each of these agencies/systems – police, government, intelligence, or industry – members of the security field usually have a clear idea of the type of person(s) that are responsible for the incidents based on digital signatures, known identity/aliases, language structure/coding style, or confirmation of identity for known offenses. Many agencies have information on prior offenses and people that have hacked their systems in the past. For instance, the FBI's list of 10 most wanted cyber criminals (as of December 14, 2014) (Pagliery, 2014) included:

- Nicolae Popescu
- Dumitru Daniel Bosogioiu
- Evgeniy Mikhailovich Bogachev
- The Chinese Army Five
- Alexsey Belan
- Peteris Sahurovs
- Artem Semenov
- Alexandr Sergeyevich Bobnev
- Carlos Enrique Perez-Melara, and
- Noor Aziz Uddin

Each of these individuals and/or group is wanted for various crimes and carries rewards ranging from no reward to $1 Million USD. Each of the named cyber criminals allegedly committed crimes that ranged from writing malicious spyware that affected consumers on public websites such as personal and private information on dating sites, to defrauding government agencies, companies or everyday customers of bank information, payments, or PIN (personal identification numbers) for ATM transactions. The type of crime does not simply reflect large crimes that affect only one type of entity or large organizations or companies, but it also ranged to affecting the everyday costumer of companies such as Loews, Walmart, Home Depot, J.C. Penney, and Sears.

Hackers who have perpetuated such crimes began with simply learning how to code, and the ability to code (or writing in code), which can be gained by proper education, being self-taught or instinctually. Coding can be outsourced to private companies, individuals, or as a recently as December 5, 2014 even convicted criminals (Fink & Segall, 2014). Fink and Segall (2014) states that convicted criminals with no direct computer access are being taught and trained to code while thy complete their incarceration periods. For example the inmates of San Quentin State Prison are being trained to code as a means of trying to prepare them for a life outside of prison, these prisoners are being trained with the hopes of allowing them to gain a set of skills that should help them reduce recidivism and give the prisoners a hope for a better life and job prospects outside of prison. Recidivism rates for convicted felons are particularly high for repeat offenders. However, equipping a convicted felon with a set of skills that can affect a large number of people's personal information, personal health information, and credit information can be seen as a potential hazard and risk. The convicted felon may be considered a risk for individuals and companies who would employ the individuals once they are released from prison as other members of society would see the individuals as having a larger propensity for using the skills gained to create more sophisticated crimes in the future, especially given the value in each of the types of information that can be obtained during a cyber-attack.

PII

Personal Identifying Information (PII) holds a wealth of information. PII such as demographic information (age, race, income, ethnicity, address, SSN, and salary) allows for many data managers and data manipulators to be able to reconstruct or duplicate the identity of a person if they possessed the right sequence and type of information. Research shows this type of information is valuable and necessary for identity theft and identity reconstruction. Meux (1994) suggested that information available in discharge records and discharge databases that contain SSN should be encrypted as it contains personal identifiers. The researcher developed a Record Linkage Number encryption algorithm that would allow the encryption of SSN so that databases could be released to the necessary agencies that require records of discharge information without releasing the SSN. It is not unheard of that systems are compromised for various types of information, as this information can easily assist criminals in creating false identities. However, other forms of information are just as valuable as PII. When this information is coupled with financial information then identity reconstruction becomes possible, and at that point only physical/health information complete with biometric data would be a means for correctly identifying individuals when disputes arise over proper identification. Systems and services have reported how such information as PHI and PII can be invaluable for the use of identity duplication and identity reconstruction.

PHI

Personal Health Information (PHI) is invaluable when used as a means to identify an individual, as a way to get medical treatment for an ailment, or when used to extort money from an individual that would otherwise wish to keep certain health information private. PHI can be used to properly identify an individual who may have been assaulted, murdered, or may be living under an assumed identity. Having the medical and health information of the individual can rule out individuals or properly identify the individual that is using the information. Individuals who may not have medical/health insurance or wish to be treated for an ailment may assume the identity of an individual who does have the same ailment and is being treated for the same ailment. In this case, having the PII and PHI of the individual can assist a person in getting the necessary treatment for the ailment. In many instances physicians do not retain photographs of individuals or transmit identifiable information along with records from one medical facility to another; therefore, it becomes easier for a person to assume the identity of someone when they have the necessary information for identity theft. Many individuals wish to keep certain information private as the stigma associated with various diseases tend to cause others to wonder about the potential for the individual to accomplish a task or question their ability to perform the duties of a position. The need to keep information private increase when it can result in the loss of a position, the loss of wages as a result of illnesses, or potentially a change in career as a result of various types of diagnoses. Therefore, it becomes imperative that an individuals' health information should remain private.

Guan, Zhang, and Ji (2013) maintains that privacy of medical data can and should be made secure and private as early as preschool in order to protect and students' privacy and to remove stigmas associated with certain ailments. Therefore, they developed an algorithm that protects PHI of preschoolers' privacy as it is "unnecessary for education authorities to know the identities of the children." They suggest the use of a public key cryptosystem to secure the medical health data.

Financial Information

In terms of financial information, it is not unheard of for a financial institution to have information removed from a system; however, the layers of authentication needed to get to the financial information makes it more difficult to infiltrate than to receive the information from a different source. Take for instance some of the most publically known data hacks that occurred with regard to information from customers that has affected and implicated financial institutions. Such hacks included the penetration of Home Depot, Target, Sony, TJX, and Heartland – five of the biggest ever credit card hacks compiled and reported by Jose Pagliery and Julianne Pepitone of CNNTech (Pagliery & Pepitone, 2014), include:

1. Home Depot had to investigate whether customer data in the form of debit and credit cards were lost as a result of a hack to their payment/electronic charge system. It is estimated that more than 40 million customers' information was lost. This can lead to a reduction in many aspects of the corporation in the way of customer trust, store foot-traffic, revenue, and stock prices.
2. Heartland Payment Systems (Heartland) was hacked in 2008 and reported data loss for 130 million customers. Heartland processes credit card payments for companies that use VISA, MasterCard, and American Express. This type of data loss is one of the largest in history due to the number of people affected and the companies it affected.

3. In 2005, TJX, which includes stores such as T.J. Maxx and Marshalls, lost the data of 94 million customers to a data breach that went unnoticed. Within this breach, customer credit card information was also retrieved and stolen from the company computer system. The exact nature of the breach was not clear to the customers that were affected.
4. Although Sony has had several public breaches in the past five years, two of the most well-known occurred in 2011 and 2014. In 2011, Sony PlayStation Network use of the media streaming service Qriocity investigated an "external intrusion" that put customers' information at risk. Later Sony Online Entertainment placed personal information at risk not credit card information which affected 77 million customers. The 2014 hack of the aforementioned system suggested that there was North Korea Regime involvement, which resulted in a 100TB of information being leaked to the public.
5. During the 2013 holiday season Target was targeted and infiltrated. This theft included data for 40 million cards that were used between November 27, 2013 and December 15, 2013. Within this theft numerous safeguards and alarms within their system were reported to have been triggered but ignored.

Timing of conflicts and intrusion within any system is very important and costly with any system. Whether that intrusion is in the form of a data breach, a reduction in services, a denial of services, an unwanted intrusion, an access of the system, or data leak, the use of the system and having access to the system after an attack leaves the institutions vulnerable. Use of the system and timing of the system intrusion can result in loss of the system for future use. Axelrod and Iliev (2014) discuss the timing of cyber conflicts and how resources and use of resources can be timed to determine when resources should be used and how they can be exploited.

If one was to review the data breach of Target 2013 it is possible to see how using this information could have been optimized based on the mathematical modeling of Axelrod and Iliev. Because of the holiday period a massive amount of information could have been gathered and taken between the days of Black Friday and Christmas Eve of 2013. Using information and sale data available within the company reports and normally reported during the holiday period should and could show spending patterns of the customers that can be used in planning and implementing a targeted attack. With proper planning and targeting, a well targeted attack could have impacted the system more than what was intended based on the reports of the cyber-attack. This type of data loss is expanded upon in the companion chapter located within this volume, titled: *Cyber-Threat Detection in Corporate and Cyber-Espionage*.

University of Maryland Economics graduate student Calvin Wang, states that 2015 will be a year of increased cyber-attacks simply from the trends within the global market. With an eye and ear for Macroeconomics and Policies governing trade agreements, Wang expects a large increase in cyber-attacks that will start to target the trade industry. Additionally he hypothesizes that more hacks will focus on privacy violations and global prosperity and loss of intellectual property and financial hacks. It is common belief that in a time of crisis, it seems that it becomes plausible for a company and individuals to steal rather than to conceive their own brilliant idea.

Ideally one considers economic and social trends that would be affected based on an increase in cyberterrorism. However it is necessary to think about the effect on the micro and macro scales as well. National Security within every country will play a part in how the economy will be affected, not only locally, but also internationally as other nations are also entangled and intertwined. This could lead to a larger effect than one could imagine, especially as it relates to trade, finance, and industrial finance in the form of lending, banking, savings, and networks that are linked to affected targets.

No doubt, it becomes clear how an increase in cyber-attacks would have an effect on the system, and it would become problematic for victims and markets that are the target of the cyber-attacks. Unfortunately, the cyber-attacks will get worse with the constant networking and connections that use and rely upon advanced technology and wireless connections. The heady dependence on wireless access and networking for convenience makes it easier for hackers to have access to private computers, personal information that is in public domains, general consumer information that resides in purchasable databases, spending/purchasing habits and information within the infrastructure of places of employment.

Credit Information

Credit Information and PII are necessary for identity reconstruction and identity theft. In these instances it is necessary to have an idea of the person's credit history and credit information when assuming the identity of an individual. With a person's PII any criminal can obtain a copy of a credit report of the intended target. This information can be used to establish credit at another location and also compromise the credit of an individual in the future based on purchases, credit cards, and bank information that the perpetrator may have at his (or her) disposal. However, this is not limited to just assuming an identity and making purchases but also to reproducing the credit history of another individual as one's own. Therefore one must ask, *"How long before the credit agencies become the target?"*

With the right intrusion method, credit agencies and their methods for thwarting threats to their system can become a target for hackers that wish to insert identities based on the information obtained by others. Many times for identity thief to be successful one identity is duplicated for the personal use of another; however, in the case of identity insertion a false identity can be created and placed into a system when using information that may be realistic in nature. Credit companies can become the target of cyber-attacks for other reasons. With major credit agencies the information that is contained within the agency is not consistent across other credit agencies; therefore, the information may not be duplicated accurately across agencies. The leading credit agency may be the target and information loss could or would not be the only outcome. In addition to information loss and duplication, the outcome could be the insertion of information into the system. Credit ratings and credit score alterations could affect the future of an individual for years if undetected.

Private Data/Information

It is not surprising that various laws have been passed pertaining to the exposure and release of private information such as pictures, emails, letters, videos, contact lists, and personal information as these types of information can be (and usually are) invaluable to the right buyer. Having private information that many people do not know and usually would not share can be detrimental to a person's career, reputation, company portfolio, or finances. Using these types of data, encryption can play a large role in how this data is reduced in value due to the amounts of computer power that would be needed to break the encryption.

Data encryption of emails has been used by government agencies for years within the US and in other countries; however, the encryption of photos is not a practice that personal handheld devices or smartphones use when storing information or when sending photos or information to others. The use of encryption algorithms that are user specific and smartphone specific can be an additional feature that is used in the establishment of the operating system of the phone and in the communication network.

Current personal computers use security and encryption algorithms to lock and protect computers, but once someone have access to the computer they have access to all of its contents unless there are password protected. This is similar to the passwords and protections on smartphones and handheld devices. Although the user has the ability to encrypt the material on the systems, not every user wishes to use passwords for each area of their phone as it would be inconvenient and time consuming to the user.

Intellectual Property

Inspiration and innovation does not always happen at a desk, in a company or research lab during the hours of 9 AM – 5PM. True inspiration and innovation happens when someone least expects it and in a manner when they are not prepared for it to occur. The use of ideas and theories that come from the inspiration and the innovation leads to intellectual development and planning that becomes of value to employers, research groups, and companies that find it useful and of interest. This innovation leads to intellectual property for the individual and becomes the property of the company if the person is employed to create such innovation in the course of their position.

Within the current digital and data driven age, wireless communications, computer systems, and application development are all important areas for intellectual property and idea development. Such development can be done within an individual's home on a personal computer or laboratory computer and continued within the workplace with the help of others. Such innovation usually means that someone has information in a less secured area than what was originally intended as development of the idea may have begun in a personal and not a professional area. Therefore, the intellectual property of the individual can be acquired from cyber-attacks of the personal accounts of individual computers of people within the various research and scientific fields.

Once the Intellectual Property or corporate information is found and it is determined to be of value, its use can assist in financial gain by an individual or organization with very little effort on the part of the hacker. In order for the hacker to understand the information and determine that they have the correct information, they would have to have inside information on what information they are looking for or to gain access to the entire contents of the computer or server where the information is stored, and then copy the entire data system. Once the information has been retrieved it would become of value back to the owner/developer and also to others that would like to acquire the information. This information can be used to leverage financial information, existing information from the developer or the researcher, or to achieve an end that was not originally intended by the developer as they may be forced to assist in other endeavors based on their knowledge and experience.

Acquisition of the new information can be sold or licensed for usage to other companies or agencies based on the type of information. The companies of interest or parties involved in the hack would benefit from the information and then gain based on the information retrieved and acquired from the cyber-attack. The result of the cyber-attack could be to gain help to advance research that may be already underway within the area, only it may have stalled or seemed impossible to achieve based on the knowledge of the parties involved in the development. Having a different perspective on the area or information on the area can improve and move the research goals in the field forward in the area. Thus, the prospective from an individual within the field and their innovative ideas and inspiration in the field would allow one area of research and innovation to progress that would not have progressed without the additional information.

When acquiring information that comes from a cyber-attack, the acquisition, collection, compression, encryption, transport, and storage of large data that can be found on company servers is not be an easy task to accomplish. Although it is possible to store information from a personal computer on a small system, the storage of information from a larger system requires additional storage space that is not as simple as an external hard drive. In order to acquire, collect, compress, encrypt, transport, and store the information, the complete task requires that the information be processed and secured via a tested mechanism that will ensure that the data is retrievable after the process and that it is unharmed during the processing. However testing these processes requires having large data sets for this process to be perfected. Researchers like Brinkman et al. (2009) used large scale electrophysiology data to illustrate this process and encryption to show how medical data would undergo this process. This process shows that the acquisition, collection, compression, encryption, transport, and storage of information as a result of a cyber-attack of a personal and corporate system would allow the most informed and astute hacker to be able to penetrate the networking system of a company, acquire the information of value, and move it as needed to buyers or parties of interest.

SOLUTIONS AND RECOMMENDATIONS

Having the right protections in places for sensitive information is important and necessary when one compares the result of a data loss and what can happen with the information to the cost of that will be attributed to the company's negligence in security measures.

Recommendations Based on Information Currently Available

Individuals, organizations, academic institutions, companies, and government agencies that have access to individuals PII, PHI, financial information, intellectual property, and other sensitive material should have better security on the servers that contain the information. Protections, safeguards, detection methods, and constant surveillance should be standard with each system and within the security department. Each of the entities and companies that have access to personal information of consumers should have better means of communication between agencies and to the media in regards to what was taken, as well as alerts that include information tracking and automated communications used for alerting security officers of unwanted intrusions. Breaches of a personal computer or a personal network are a means of direct targeting of an individual that can be for any number of reasons; however, when individuals are targeted for personal or intellectual property it becomes difficult to determine if the information taken belonged to a particular person or to a company. In the case of information that belongs to a company, the company's security measures should be in place to establish what occurred, when it occurred, how much information was taken, and what are the potential ramifications for the breach.

Constant review of the triggers and surveillance methods that are already in place and used within the security departments of companies that have access to consumers' personal and financial information is necessary when companies have access to the personal data that is targeted for financial gain. This constant monitoring can reduce the likelihood that a breach can be successful and it can reduce the amount of information taken if a breach occurs. Constant monitoring of the systems can lead to a reduction in the time it takes to disable networks and systems when they are under attack, and it will also reduce the amount of information that would be stolen during an attack.

Constant credit monitoring should be a standard part of any financial institutions account features for all types of accounts. Usually in data breaches one of the major forms of support that companies offer to victims of data breaches is "free credit monitoring" for a pre-determined period of time. These services can range in price and level of service. Although this is effective in reducing the possibility of identity thief or identity duplication it is not 100% effective to safeguard against the complete duplication of the identity. Identity duplication can be reproduced simply by being in the physical presence of a person to make them the victim of identity thief. Additionally, financial institutions that rely on credit monitoring as a practice should also include verification of identity and cross-communications with agencies that can be affected by the breach of information and the hack that can and may have occurred.

Unfortunately, following these recommendations are only the beginning. Because of the type of information that can be obtained through cyber-attacks, trying to get the information necessary to fully analyze scenarios that have resulted in intrusions often comes with the possibility of having to access information that is protected under other confidentiality laws that would require multiple layers of consent. Furthermore, publishing information on research could provide potential hackers with the opportunity to circumvent recommendations before they can be implemented. Thus, with the constant evolution of technology and while trying to maintain the integrity and confidentiality of others involved, it is necessary to consider any other areas that may require improvement.

Areas of Improvement for Security

Evidence and research is needed on data security, newer means of protection on data systems and data networks, and the development of a knowledge repository inclusive of instructions and known methods that work to safeguard material and systems from intrusion. These ideas can lead to the development and dissemination of information that can assist individuals who are not the most technologically savvy to safeguard their personal computers against cyber-attacks that can potentially lead to data loss.

Means for evaluating how many people change passwords and what is done to remind individuals to change passwords on a regular basis. Examples of this is most commonly seen in universities, companies, and government agencies, as they try their best to constantly update Acceptable Use Agreements as it pertains to users of the computing systems. Moist organizations have users update their passwords on a regular basis based on the networking systems and the strategies that companies use to remind their users; consequently, users who do not follow these guidelines find it difficult to login, use, or navigate their company's systems as many systems will lock user accounts for non-compliance. This is quickly becoming a standard operating procedure for those who try to stay ahead of hackers attempting to penetrate the company computer systems, and networks; or trying to obtain the passwords that users may have been assigned based on insider information, because it becomes easier for a cyber-attack to occur if the users have not changed or updated their passwords on a regular basis. Therefore it is not uncommon that more systems are now requiring that users update their passwords on a regular basis to make it more difficult to obtain the passwords created by users.

Most systems that are in place now require users to have at least two forms of authentication, and various components when creating a password. Current requirements include: two capitalized letters, two numbers, two lower case letters, two special characters, at least ten letters in length, and not previously used within the last year. This is now becoming the normal method for password changes and part of the Acceptable Use Agreements as every person that is non-compliant or late in changing this information becomes a liability to the organization. Non-compliance with this process can inadvertently allow intruders to have access to the system.

Research into the private financial systems: (a) Financial/Banking Industry Intrusions and (b) Credit Agencies. Information has not been published in these areas as a result of privacy policies and banking/financial institutions privacy statements. However, since cyber-attacks may be able to cripple, dismantle, affect the infrastructure of a company, or potentially affect the infrastructure of our economy, these areas should be analyzed from various aspects – on the micro scale and; on the macro scale, both nationally; and globally. It is possible that financial institutions have already analyzed these types of scenarios on each of these scales and from various flashpoints that include an agricultural and cultural crisis; changes in the European Trade and Economic Market; volatility within the current Russian economy; different aspects of banking, lending, and stock exchanges that are located and housed on Wall Street; and individual banks collapsing on a micro/macro scale. Additional analysis and D-Day scenarios exist for various contingencies and economic fall-outs from these scenarios; nevertheless, this information would be considered proprietary and should never be made public, printed, disseminated, or acknowledged; however these theoretical instances should be studied. This is not uncommon or unexpected and the repercussions that can occur as a result of this information being made public could be disastrous for any individual, agency, company, country, or nation. However, prevention and safeguards must be in place for any type of economic/financial failure, otherwise a domino effect may occur as a result of a collapse of one (or several) economic systems. With the collapse of one system, it is possible to see how other foreign markets and businesses associated with the market would be affected and could lead to an economic and financial crisis for other agencies, companies, countries, or nations.

CONCLUSION

As previously stated, with each intrusion into the system, the information that hackers target ranges from personal to financial to intellectual in nature. Because the type of information obtained during an attack can vary, it is important to keep in mind that the intent of the attack may extend beyond the hacker's desire for financial gain and include the motivation of the person or organization who intends to use the information obtained by the hackers if it is done for the benefit of a third party. Once the different forms of information are in hand, what can be done with the information can range from:

A. Identity Construction/Re-construction
B. Falsification/Reproduction of vital and financial records
C. Financial Lost that can be immediate or in the future
D. Loss of Property that can occur on a private, personal, and/or intellectual level, or
E. Medical Fraud

Identity Construction/Reconstruction

With the right information, any number of things can occur in regards to identity construction and reconstruction. Individuals who are skilled in identity construction and reconstruction can use the information to create false identities of individuals that are deceased, create identities for older individuals from records of children, and even recreate the same identity of an individual in another state.

Falsification/Reproduction of Vital and Financial Records

Falsification of vital and financial records or the reproduction of vital and financial records is routinely done as a means to change the identity of an individual or to swap identities. Individuals who would desire to swap identities typically do so to deter law processes and procedures from occurring or not to be identified by law enforcement authorities.

Financial Lost

Any information that is taken from an individual in an attempt to committee fraud can and may result in financial lost to the individual if financial institutions are not constantly monitoring the transactions of their customers. With constant credit monitoring, bank alerts, and transaction verification implemented in financial institutions, it can be difficult for customers to have transactions occur without their notification.

Loss of Property that can occur on a private, personal, and/or intellectual level

Physical properties in the form of land, homes, of automobiles are usually tracked via hard copy documents that are not normally part of a cyber-attack. However, recent changes to procedures in some financial institutions has led to certain transactions that were traditionally performed through hard copies alone being transitioned to electronic systems, such as mortgage trading between banks, thereby leaving potential opportunities for cyber-attacks. Furthermore, intellectual property that is in form of digital records or data that is proprietary to a company that resides on personal or private networks and serves are able to be retrieved by cyberattacks. Showing ownership and tracking the location of this information once it has left the environment that it was conceived and developed is a difficult task and should security measures that track proprietary information should be possible.

Medical Fraud

Using the information of an individual who has medical insurance is not a new phenomenon. Individuals have been willing and knowingly used the medical and health insurance information of friends and family in the past to obtain medical care, prescription medicine, and medical treatment in the time of crisis. However, the use of such information is considered medical fraud and has become an increasing area of potential business for hackers who have clients that are interested in obtaining information on individuals with particular medical illnesses.

There are a number of outcomes that can be derived from these different pieces of valuable information that is listed and outlined within this chapter, and the manner in which the information is used will have an effect on an individual that can be lasting and goes well beyond the immediate instances that are listed above. These effects can have a rippling and crippling effect that depends of the level of severity of actions by the people that perpetrated the crime or cyber-attack, and the amount of information that the hackers acquired during the cyber-attack. Additionally the impact on the company systems should not be overlooked or disregarded as a result of the loss of information. Having access to information pertaining to an individual not only poses a personal risk to the individual but also to the personal credit, career, financial status, or credit history for years, and it can affect the person's employer – if additional information in the way of employer user accounts and passwords are also acquired. If the employer is a national agency or government entity, then the security implications can be gravely impacted. Each of these actions can be committed by any criminal, and can be committed with very little information.

REFERENCES

Axelrod, R., & Iliev, R. (2014). Timing of cyber conflict. *Proceedings of the National Academy of Sciences of the United States of America*, *111*(4), 1298–1303. doi:10.1073/pnas.1322638111 PMID:24474752

Brinkmann, B. H., Bower, M. R., Stengel, K. A., Worrell, G. A., & Stead, M. (2009). Large-scale electrophysiology: Acquisition, compression, encryption, and storage of big data. *Journal of Neuroscience Methods*, *180*(1), 185–192. doi:10.1016/j.jneumeth.2009.03.022 PMID:19427545

Chen, D. Q., Chen, W. B., Soong, M., Soong, S. J., & Orthner, H. F. (2009). Turning Access (TM) into a web-enabled secure information system for clinical trials. *Clinical Trials*, *6*(4), 378–385. doi:10.1177/1740774509338228 PMID:19625330

Cooper, A. (2015, March 2). *Air Traffic Control System Vulnerable to Cyberattack*. Retrieved from http://www.cnn.com/2015/03/02/politics/cyberattack-faa-air-traffic-control-hacking/

Egan, M. (2014, December 22). *Thank you Sony! Cybersecurity Stock Soar*. Retrieved from http://money.cnn.com/2014/12/22/investing/sony-cybersecurity-stocks/

Fan, L. J., Wang, Y. Z., Jin, X. L., Li, J. Y., Cheng, X. Q., & Jin, S. Y. (2013). Comprehensive Quantitative Analysis on Privacy Leak Behavior. *Plos One, 8*(9). DOI:10.1371/journal.pone.0073410

Guan, S. P., Zhang, Y., & Ji, Y. (2013). Privacy-Preserving Health Data Collection for Preschool Children. *Computational and Mathematical Methods in Medicine*. Doi:10.1155/2013/501607

Interactive, C. B. S. (2015, February 6). *Car Hacked on 60 Minutes*. Retrieved from http://www.cbsnews.com/news/car-hacked-on-60-minutes/

Kottasova, I. (2014, November 20). *Russian Website Streams Thousands of Private Webcams*. Retrieved from http://money.cnn.com/2014/11/20/technology/security/hacked-web-cameras-russia/

Kwaak, J. S. (2015, March 17). *North Korea Blamed for Nuclear-Power Plan Hack*. Retrieved from http://www.wsj.com/articles/north-korea-blamed-for-nuclear-power-plant-hack-1426589324

Landi, W., & Rao, R. B. (2003). *Secure De-identification and Re-identification*. Proceedings of AMIA 2003 Symposium.

Meux, E. (1994). Encrypting Personal Identifiers. *Health Services Research*, *29*(2), 247–256. PMID:8005792

Neame, R. (2013). Effective sharing of health records, maintaining privacy: A practical schema. *Online Journal of Public Health Informatics*, *5*(2), 217. doi:10.5210/ojphi.v5i2.4344 PMID:23923101

Pagliery, J. (2014, November 18). *FBI's 10 Most Wanted Cyber Criminals*. Retrieved from http://money.cnn.com/gallery/technology/security/2014/11/18/fbi-cyber-most-wanted/

Pagliery, J., & Pepitone, J. (2014, September 5). *Five of the Biggest-Ever Credit Card Hacks*. Retrieved from http://money.cnn.com/gallery/technology/security/2014/09/05/biggest-hacks/

Robb, D. (2014, December 22). *Sony Hack: A Timeline*. Retrieved from http://deadline.com/2014/12/sony-hack-timeline-any-pascal-the-interview-north-korea-1201325501/

Rooney, B. (2014, December 5). *Hackers Threaten Sony Employees Families*. Retrieved from http://money.cnn.com/2014/12/05/news/sony-threatened-by-hackers/

Stelter, B. (2014, December 14). *Sony Lawyers tell Media to Stop Reporting on Material Stolen by Hackers*. Retrieved from http://money.cnn.com/2014/12/14/media/sony-hack-lawyer-media/

Wallace, G. (2015, February 15). *Hackers Stole from 100 banks and Rigged ATMS to Spew Cash*. Retrieved from http://money.cnn.com/2015/02/15/technology/security/kaspersky-bank-hacking/

ADDITIONAL READING

Baker, D. B., Masys, D. R., Jones, R. L., & Barnhart, R. M. (1999). Assurance: The power behind PCASSO security. *Journal of the American Medical Informatics Association*, 666–670. PMID:10566443

Breiger, R. L., Boorman, S. A., & Arabie, P. (1975). Algorithm for Clustering Relational Data with Applications to Social Network Analysis and Comparison with Multidimensional-Scaling. *Journal of Mathematical Psychology*, *12*(3), 328–383. doi:10.1016/0022-2496(75)90028-0

Cho, Y. C., & Pan, J. Y. (2014). Hybrid Network Defense Model Based on Fuzzy Evaluation. *Scientific World Journal*. Doi:10.1155/2014/178937

Cimino, J. J., Socratous, S. A., & Clayton, P. D. (1995). Internet as Clinical Information-System - Application Development Using the World-Wide-Web. *Journal of the American Medical Informatics Association*, *2*(5), 273–284. doi:10.1136/jamia.1995.96073829 PMID:7496876

Doreian, P. (1980). On the Evolution of Group and Network Structure. *Social Networks*, *2*(3), 235–252. doi:10.1016/0378-8733(79)90016-9

Fink, E., & Segall, L. (2014, December 5). *Hire a Coder Behind Bars*. Retrieved from http://money.cnn.com/2014/12/05/technology/coding-san-quentin/

Frank, O. (1978). Sampling and Estimation in Large Social Networks. *Social Networks*, *1*(1), 91–101. doi:10.1016/0378-8733(78)90015-1

Gil, S., Kott, A., & Barabasi, A. L. (2014). A genetic epidemiology approach to cyber-security. *Scientific Reports*, *4*, 5659. doi:10.1038/srep05659 PMID:25028059

Guo, X. F., Zhang, J. S., Khan, M. K., & Alghathbar, K. (2011). Secure Chaotic Map Based Block Cryptosystem with Application to Camera Sensor Networks. *Sensors (Basel, Switzerland)*, *11*(2), 1607–1619. doi:10.3390/s110201607 PMID:22319371

He, H., Fan, G. T., Ye, J. W., & Zhang, W. Z. (2013). A Topology Visualization Early Warning Distribution Algorithm for Large-Scale Network Security Incidents. *Scientific World Journal*. Doi:10.1155/2013/827376

Hripcsak, G., Cimino, J. J., & Sengupta, S. (1999). WebCIS: Large scale deployment of a Web-based clinical information system. *Journal of the American Medical Informatics Association*, 804–808. PMID:10566471

Kim, J., Lee, D., Jeon, W., Lee, Y., & Won, D. (2014). Security Analysis and Improvements of Two-Factor Mutual Authentication with Key Agreement in Wireless Sensor Networks. *Sensors (Basel, Switzerland)*, *14*(4), 6443–6462. doi:10.3390/s140406443 PMID:24721764

Lee, Y., & Paik, J. (2014). Security Analysis and Improvement of an Anonymous Authentication Scheme for Roaming Services. *Scientific World Journal*. Doi 10.1155/2014/687879

Luo, G. C., Peng, N. D., Qin, K., & Chen, A. G. (2014). A Layered Searchable Encryption Scheme with Functional Components Independent of Encryption Methods. *Scientific World Journal*. Doi:10.1155/2014/153791

Morse, R. E., Nadkarni, P., Schoenfeld, D. A., & Finkelstein, D. M. (2011). Web-browser encryption of personal health information. *Bmc Medical Informatics and Decision Making, 11*. Doi:10.1186/1472-6947-11-70

Oh, J. Y., Yang, D. I., & Chon, K. H. (2010). A Selective Encryption Algorithm Based on AES for Medical Information. *Healthcare Informatics Research*, *16*(1), 22–29. doi:10.4258/hir.2010.16.1.22 PMID:21818420

Peng, N. D., Luo, G. C., Qin, K., & Chen, A. G. (2013). Query-Biased Preview over Outsourced and Encrypted Data. *Scientific World Journal*. Doi:10.1155/2013/860621

Sang, J., Ling, S. G., & Alam, M. S. (2012). Efficient Text Encryption and Hiding with Double-Random Phase-Encoding. *Sensors (Basel, Switzerland)*, *12*(10), 13441–13457. doi:10.3390/s121013441 PMID:23202003

Wright, A., & Sittig, D. F. (2007). Encryption characteristics of two USB-based personal health record devices. *Journal of the American Medical Informatics Association*, *14*(4), 397–399. doi:10.1197/jamia. M2352 PMID:17460132

Zhang, W. P., Chen, W. Y., Tang, J., Xu, P., Li, Y. B., & Li, S. Y. (2009). The Development of a Portable Hard Disk Encryption/Decryption System with a MEMS Coded Lock. *Sensors (Basel, Switzerland)*, *9*(11), 9300–9331. doi:10.3390/s91109300 PMID:22291566

Zhou, Q., Yang, G., & He, L. W. (2014). A Secure-Enhanced Data Aggregation Based on ECC in Wireless Sensor Networks. *Sensors (Basel, Switzerland)*, *14*(4), 6701–6721. doi:10.3390/s140406701 PMID:24732099

KEY TERMS AND DEFINITIONS

Breach: The act of breaking or failing to observer a law, agreement, or code of conduct.

Credit History: An electronic or hardcopy record of a consumer's ability to repay their debts with a demonstrated responsibility in repaying debts in a timely fashion as determined by the creditor.

Credit Information: Information about a person, business, company, or institution to pay is creditors or suppliers.

Cyber-Attack: The use of electronics to attempt the intrusion, delay, damage, or destruction of a computer network or system.

Data Leak: The unauthorized transfer of classified information from a computer or datacenter to the outside world.

Data Loss: An error condition in information systems in which information is destroyed by failures or neglect in storage, transmission, or processing.

Financial Information: Records that outline the financial activities of a business, an individual or any other entity.

Intrusion: The act of intruding or the condition of being intruded upon; an inappropriate or unwelcomed addition.

Personal Health Information (PHI): Also referred to as protected health information, generally refers to demographic information, medical history, test and laboratory results, insurance information and other data that is collected by a health care professional to identify an individual and determine appropriate care.

Personal Identifiable Information (PII): Any data that could potentially identify a specific individual.

Prevention: The action of stopping something from happening or occurring.

Protection: The action of protecting, or the state of being protected.

This work was previously published in National Security and Counterintelligence in the Era of Cyber Espionage edited by Eugenie de Silva, pages 161-180, copyright 2016 by Information Science Reference (an imprint of IGI Global).

Chapter 16
How Private Is Your Financial Data?
Survey of Authentication Methods in Web and Mobile Banking

Vidya Mulukutla
State University of New York – Buffalo, USA

Manish Gupta
State University of New York – Buffalo, USA

H. R. Rao
State University of New York – Buffalo, USA

ABSTRACT

The ease and convenience of Internet Banking or e-banking has made it the most preferred way for customers as well as the banking industry alike. The fact that e-banking enables remote accessibility of a customer's account translates to round-the-clock service from the bank and has made this mode of operation a success in every sense. The starting and most important point for which would be the authentication to customer's financial data. This chapter sheds light on the different authentication mechanisms that could be followed as per the situational demands taking into consideration the various threat environments and possible vulnerabilities in the system. The advantages and disadvantages arising out of different authentication mechanisms are presented with the possible attack scenarios enumerated. An overview of the personal computer environ and the mobile environ are discussed. The chapter will be invaluable for managers and professionals in understanding the current authentication landscape.

INTRODUCTION

The online banking is a service provided by many banks to their customers to access their account from anywhere with a computer and Internet connection with them (Online Banking, 2010). The users prefer this service as they can save time by accessing their bank transaction through the Internet from home

DOI: 10.4018/978-1-5225-0808-3.ch016

or any place. The factors that drive accelerated growth of banking on the Internet are as listed below (Hutchinson & Warren, 2003):

- Increase the demand of customers.
- With more and more players in the market, there is increasing competition to stand out and satisfy customer needs.
- In order to cut down on costs and maintain high levels of efficiency.
- Relaxation of regulations in the financial services market world-wide.

With increase in fraud and identity theft, the banking sector is constantly on its toes and is struggling a lot with the authentication issues. The authentication of the user is of utmost importance as fraud should be avoided on this service and bank should also ensure that only authorized person accesses the account. Though the banks have taken keen interest in developing secure authentication mechanisms for the users, the fraud is still growing and the improvement in the authentication processes are much needed. At present banks follow different methods to secure their service.

Authentication is a process of verifying that the right person is provided access when requested (Authentication, 2007). Using the authentication we can ensure that the right person is provided with exact identity such as driving license, passport etc to show that he/she is the authorized person to hold those identity cards. There are different types of authentication methods available to authorize a person. The person once verified using those methods are permitted to access the particular resource where the authentication is required. The access control is a term where the authorized person is provided with authorization to access particular factor in the web resources which can be granted or declined as per the service provider (control, 2010).

The authentication can be provided through many methods and authentication is an essential factor in banking sectors to provide complete security to the online banking service. Banks are investing more in providing security to their online banking services. However, with the lack of robust authentication mechanisms for users who access their accounts from multiple number of devices, be it personal computers or shared computers or mobile devices and from any corner of the world, all efforts to make the network secure can turn out futile. For a really long time, passwords were the most common and a de-facto standard for authentication. With recent changes in the stakes and increasing value of underlying information, users are required to remember longer and more complex passwords while also requiring them to change them frequently. This has led to more insecurity and inconvenience (see for example, Bunnell et al., 1997; Furnell et al, 2000; Pond et al, 2000, Bishop & Klein, 1995); and alternative and more secure methods of authentication have made their way in the mainstream. There are different types of authentication methods and each had their unique qualities in providing authentication. There many different issues that are faced by the banking sectors in the online banking and are described in detail in this paper.

AUTHENTICATION: BACKGROUND

Authentication is a process where one has to prove his identity. A user can be authenticated to the server by means of providing identity in the form of username and authenticating by means of a password.

Further mechanisms can be added to strengthen security. Reliable customer authentication is imperative for financial institutions engaging in electronic banking (Gupta et al,, 2004). In today's online financial services environment, authentication is the bedrock of information security. Simple password authentication is the prevailing paradigm, but its weaknesses are all too evident in today's context (Gupta et al, 2008). The authorization is a term which is provided to identify whether the identified person is authorized to enjoy the service. This is verified based on the records that are maintained in the database and it should match the identification provided by the person. Authorization is like the boarding pass that is used to board airplanes. The access control is another term relevant in this context, which refers to varying level of access to different users depending on their ability to prove their identity, by means of controls enforced by the system. The service provider has the full rights to grant or denied the access level to the user. In general, means controlling the full access of the user (control, 2010). There are many different methods are used to provide a secure authentication.

Need for Authentication

The delivery of the services through the publicly accessible infrastructure (i.e Internet) has increased to a great level. The transactions in the e-commerce are done using the Internet as medium and the provider cannot see the user as he/she may be from anywhere in the world. So the service providers should ensure that only the right person is accessing the right account. To identify that, the authentication of the users is essential to perform the transactions through Internet as it's an open network and anyone can access it. (Liang & Wang, 2005). Authentication is provided by the concept of cryptography using the encryption and decryption technique. The basic authentication can be provided by the user's password. The authentication can be created only when the user submits any authentication code like passwords when requested (Liang & Wang, 2005).

The corporate world has now started to use the web technology to improve their operations and they use the Internet as the medium. The corporations have also started to share confidential information to their users through the Internet. Some organizations are even operating their servers from one place to another using the remote accessing technique and which needs a high secure authentication so that the data can be transferred within the certain authenticated groups. Most of the organizations use the intranet and hence they need to secure their web server and only the authorized persons can access the server and authentication method provides a good security (Byron, 2003). "In an April 2002 report, the FBI/ Computer Security Institute (CSI) noted that ninety percent of respondents (primarily large corporations and government agencies) detected computer security breaches within the last twelve months. As in previous years, the most serious financial losses occurred through theft of proprietary information and financial fraud. (Byron, 2003)".

With increasing amount of sensitive information being shared over the internet and advancements in technologies, there are more ways in which intruders are finding way to penetrate into systems leading to fraudulent activity. To overcome this issue the authentication process is created and using this process the right person alone is allowed to access the right resources. A secret code (passwords, PINS etc) are provided to the users and so they can access only using those access codes and so that the organization can have only the authorized persons accessing their intranet and this reduces the fraud to a higher extent (Byron, 2003).

Types of Authentication

The authentication is provided differently by different web servers and all servers have their own authentication methodology and properties for authentication. The authentication in general can be classified into eight types and are as follows,

1. Basic authentication,
2. Client certificates and Server certificates,
3. Digest authentication,
4. Integrated authentication,
5. Customized authentication with HTTP module,
6. Pass through authentication,
7. Windows integrated authentication, and
8. URL authentication.

Basic Authentication

The basic authentication type means where the user name and passwords are requested and when entered data are sent in a format with the full document as normal text and only the user name and password are encoded. The passwords are encoded and this provides the basic authentication to the user's data. It's the user's responsibility to remember the password and also its properties like case sensitive etc. The user will enter the data to the application when requested by the servers and the entered data are stored in the server. Later when the user access the application, the data that are requested by the server and when the user enters the data are being matched by the saved data and finally the user is allowed to access the application only if the data matches the stored data in the server. This is the method followed in the basic authentication technique (Magalhaes, 2001). While passwords, still, are the most authentication mechanism, extensive research has shown that passwords have their own inherent security issues (Morris & Thompson, 1979). And when complex passwords provide some respite in that regard, they pose a bigger usability concern (Adams & Sasse, 1999; Gaw & Felten; 2006)), so different mechanisms for authentication needs to be investigated and implemented (Herley & Oorschot, 2012).

Client Certificates and Server Certificates

- **Client Certificates:** The authentication in this type is performed such that the server requests the client to provide the client certificate before the client request to connect to the service provider. After the client sends the certificate the server checks with the earlier stored details about the client and matches it. If the details provided matched, then it request the service provider the details about the client and it provides the certificates that are supplies earlier from the service provider to the client. After the client accepts that certificate and ensures that he is getting the response from the correct service provider and not a fraud, he/she provides the details and then after matching with those details it allows the client to connect the service provider (Magalhaes, 2001).
- **Server Certificates:** The service providers have to register their server certificates with the ISA servers when they obtain the server. The client when trying to connect to the service provider will

be provided with the certificate that will be used for verifying the client. The client accepts the certificate means the ISA server will link the client and the service provider. Thus authentication is made and both the client and server can ensure that they are working with the authorized persons (Magalhaes, 2001).

Digest Authentication

This is advanced version of the basic authentication where the user's data is sent in the encrypted form using the hashing methodology whereas in the basic methodology the data is transferred unencrypted. In the digest authentication it provides more security as the encryption and also hash (message digest) makes the data more secure so that intruders cannot decipher the text that are transferred in the Internet. The hash strings added will easily locate the place, computer's details, username and domain. More security is available than to the basic authentication methodology (Magalhaes, 2001).

Integrated Authentication

This is another type where we are able to get more security as the exchange of the username and passwords among the service provider and the client is not done and so the intruders can't trace any details. This scenario is very similar to federation identity management where Identity and access management systems are used by online service providers (SP) to authenticate and authorize users to services based on access policies (Gupta & Sharman, 2008). The verification in this authentication type is provided in such a way that use of the inbuilt challenge/response authentication protocol. The IE 5.5 (and above) that comes with Microsoft Windows operating system has the inbuilt authentication protocol which verifies the certificate and provides a reliable authentication to transaction (Magalhaes, 2001).

Customized Authentication with HTTP Module

The authentication is provided faster than the web method in this type. The ASP.NET will create series of events and all the events perform their operation till the verification is made and this will be complete in a quick manner than that of the web method. The data can be edited even after the request is on progress and this helps the users more easier and convenient way to get accessed (Liu, 2004).

Pass through Authentication

This type of authentication occurs when the ISA server passes the clients information to the server and this is provided for both the incoming and outgoing web requests. The following are the steps involved in pass-through authentication:

1. The request to the server from the client is made through the web server.
2. The web server request for the authentication code and type the server supports.
3. The client provides the required authentication code and it will be directed by the web servers to the appropriate service providers.
4. The response from the service providers will be taken into account and then the client is made to communicate with the service providers directly.

Windows Integrated Authentication

This is another type which is similar to basic authentication but also an advanced version of it. In this type the authentication is provided based on the hashing algorithm. This type is used in most organizations where the intranet is used and they want to control the access. This authentication helps in providing good access control inside the organization (Liu, 2004).

URL Authentication

This is another type of authentication such that it based on the verification done using the ASP.NET. Here when the client provides the authentication code the server checks for the occurrence of the username in the database. It will scroll top-down the database till it obtain the username in the database and then it checks for authentication code and then provide access to the client (Liu, 2004).

Methods of Authentication

The authentication can be provided by means of three different methods based on the authentication technique and the human nature and are as follows:

- **What You Have:** The physical cards that the user has and use it to prove his identity. This includes the tokens, smart cards, pass cards, etc.
- **What You Know:** These are known to the user only. This can be obtained only by forcing the user and only if the user wishes can be provided. This includes passwords, PIN, pass phrases, etc.
- **What You Are:** This can be obtained only from the user's physical appearance and characteristics. This term differs from all the individuals. This includes all Biometrics, DNA, etc (Kay, 2005).

Authentication Techniques

The authentication which is provided to obtain more security for accessing certain services through Internet had follows various methods of authentication technique. Each authentication technique had its own unique properties and each provide authentication in different forms. Using a combination of these have also been researched and shown to have mixed results (Wimberly & Liebrock, 2011; Gormon, 2003) There are many different techniques in the authentication and some techniques are as follows:

- Usernames and passwords,
- PIN,
- Identifiable picture,
- One-time password,
- Swipe card,
- Token,
- Biometric,
- Keyboard rhythm, and
- OTP Scratch card.

Usernames and Passwords

The usernames and passwords authentication technique is the first and old technique where the user will be provided with unique username and a secret phrase known as the passwords. These data's are stored in the database and are verified all times when the user enters the information. The password can be numeric, alphabetic, symbols etc based on the service provider's terms and conditions. This is the basic, common technique but a weak technique to provide authentication. The user provides the username and then the existence of the username in database is to be verified and if available the password is requested from the user. The user then enters the secret phrase and then after checking with the database it allows the user to access and hence the authentication is provided (Thigpen, 2005). A recent research (Vance, 2010) shows that about 5000 passwords constitute around 20% of all passwords. At the same time complex password requirements such as long passwords using special characters and numbers, frequent forced changes present usability issues and challenges (Enleman et al., 2013; Karole et al., 2011; Weiss and Deluca, 2008; Kamnduri et al., 2011; Zezschwitz, 2013) which take direct toll on productivity and satisfaction, something financial companies want to avoid at any cost. This paves way for multiple factor authentication mechanisms, but that is also fraught with issues. Some of the recent studies have shown that multiple factor authentication are difficult and cumbersome to use for users, while being complex and expensive for companies (Bauer et al., 2007; Bonneau et al., 2012; Braz and Robert, 2006; Gunson et al, 2011; Sabzevar & A. Stavrou, 2008; Strouble et al., 2009).

PIN (Personal Identification Number)

The PIN is another technique which is similar to that of passwords but contains only numeric terms and it should be kept in secret. The PIN is a four digit number and it's used mostly in the Automated Teller Machine (ATM) to identify the personal identification. If the user enters the wrong PIN a certain number of times, his/her account gets locked automatically. The number of combinations for guessing the PIN number are high so it is not easy to guess and so a safer method and its used as the authentication method in ATMs at present (Thigpen, 2005).

Identifiable Picture

This is another technique of authentication which is provided by means of using the picture. This system is used as a subsidiary term for entering passwords and personal identification numbers. The user is provided with a picture when he registers his account and so that the user can easily remember the picture. When the user needs to access the account many pictures are provided as choice and the user has to select the appropriate picture and after that access will be granted only if the correct picture is identified (Thigpen, 2005). This technique has matured a lot in today's technological environment (see for example: Renaud, 2009; Komanduri and Hutchings, 2008; Wiedenbeck et al., 2005; Chiasson et al., 2008).

One-Time Password

This is the advanced form of the passwords that overcome the vulnerable that are in the basic authentication techniques. The user enters the password once and they are associated with many hashing techniques and the data are then exchanged with the server and will be stored. So when user tries to connect multiple times the hash technique helps to identify the password and so it will be more secure and the user can avoid changing the passwords many times (Thigpen, 2005).

Swipe Card

The swipe card's data is stored in an encrypted form and has magnetic strip that is used to read the data. The best example for the swipe cards are credit and debit cards. The user can swipe this card and transactions are made based on the information provided in the magnetic strips. The possibility of fraud is more in this card as the card can be theft and duplication of the magnetic strip can be made this result in misuse of the card (Thigpen, 2005).

Token

The token is the device that is provided to the user and the user will physically submit the device which provides authentication. The tokens can be classified into three types:

- **USB Token:** The device can be connected to the system directly and the software is not needed. The device requests for a password upon connecting to the machine which gives it a double authentication (Authentication Techniques, 2006).
- **Smart Card:** This is another device, which is of similar form factor as of a credit card and contains small microprocessor. The user inserts the card into the appropriate reader and the inbuilt identity provides the basic information about the user and after checking the details the user provides a password to authenticate (Authentication Techniques, 2006).
- **Password Generating Token:** This is a token where the token itself generates a new password after every use of the old password. The token generates the OTP (One Time Password) or the unique pass code each time and ensures that the password is not used consequently. The generated password is provided by the token and the user will enter his existing username and password and then enters the newly generated OTP. This provides a higher degree of strength to the authentication process. This technique is more secure than other token (Authentication Techniques, 2006).

Biometric

Another attractive method of authorization or identification is using the biometrics, which has been suggested to have shown increased security (Normalini and Ramayah, 2012). "Biometrics are automated methods of identifying a person or verifying the identity of a person based on a physiological or behavioral characteristic (Podio & Dunn, 2001)". A biometric typically refers to a feature or characteristic measured from a biological body. Biometric authentication systems use these features to distinguish users and for establishing an identity. Some of the most common biometrics used include fingerprints, retina, iris, voice, face, hand, etc (Jain et al., 1998; Jain et al, 2006). Bioemteric technology is already playing an increasingly important role on banking environments for authentication (Venkatraman & Delpachitra, 2008)

The biometrics will be compared between the enrolled data and the currently captured data. The identification mode of this technique will search for the captured data with the central database and finally the exact data of the user that has been enrolled earlier will be matched and provided using the

"One-to-Many Matching" technique. The verification mode is that when the user provides the data the captured data is identified using the "One-to-One technique" matching. There are many different forms of biometric test forms available like fingerprint recognition, face recognition, voice recognition, retinal scan, signatures, Iris feature etc.

- **Fingerprint Recognition:** This is an interesting method of authentication where the user's finger print is recognized. Each and every individual had their unique finger print and this technique had followed earlier by the law and order of the government. At present they are stored using the finger print reader machines and stored electronically and used when ever needed. Each finger had different form of prints and even the difference can be found among twins and so the individual can be identified easily. This is a good replacing technique than entering the passwords (Podio & Dunn, 2001).
- **Face Recognition:** In this technique the facial image of the user is identified and accordingly the identification is obtained. The user's face has been recognized using some inexpensive cameras where the image of the face in the visible spectrum is captured. It can be done using the IR (Infrared) of facial heat image. Even though the user changed his appearance the user's hair properties and facial expressions will never change and this provides the proper identification of the user (Podio & Dunn, 2001).
- **Voice Recognition:** This is another technique to authenticate such that the user's voice is used as the identification code for verification. The user had to register the voice to the service providers while the authentication is initially made and when ever needed the user has to speak (ex: the user can say his/her name) and the voice will be matched with the voice in the database. The requirement for this system to execute is need of the system and voice recognizing software. The software calculates the user's vocal track and the characteristics that are present in the user's voice and finally it will be matched when the user used them finally. The main drawback of this process is that if the user affected with any throat related problem, the system cannot able to recognize the voice and the access cannot be provided until the reset in done.
- **Iris Recognition:** This feature provides identification using the featured iris of the eyes which is a colored portion that covers the pupil in the eyes. Each and every individual had their unique difference in their iris and this is recognized by the system and can able to identify the exact match for that iris. Both the verification and identification is done easily using this method and the increase in this type of technique is increasing at recent trends. Nowadays many users are using contact lens and eyeglasses and at present the teat of the iris can be done even with that. This system also provides good identification of the users.
- **Hand and Finger Geometry:** This is an old method for more than about twenty years and in this method the user's hand characteristics are analyzed. The characteristic includes the length, width, surface, thickness etc. The distance among the fingers are calculated and used to later identification. This system is tough to handle and need more space when compared to other biometrics technique and so the usage of this technique is reducing (Podio & Dunn, 2001).

Digital Signature

This is a process where the user's signature is used to identify the person. The user can enroll the signature digitally and the pressure, angle and modes used to create that signature is calculated and stored. So when the user need to authenticate using the signature the characters of the signature is analyzed with the enrolled one and matched and finally the access will be provided if it matched with the existed signature.

Keyboard Rhythm

This technique is followed in some workplaces where the user's usage of the keyboard is calculated and accordingly the authentication is provided to the user. The pressure the user uses the keyboard, the time needed to strike between the keys used by the user is calculated and accordingly the authentication is provided. This is also a different technique that is used in some workplace to reduce unauthorized access of the system (Thigpen, 2005).

OTP Scratch Card

The scratch card is a low expensive card that contains the numbers arranged in rows and column format like grids. The number of the grids in the card is recognized. The user when use this card will enter the username and password first time and then will enter the randomly generated passwords that are created by the scratch card with the numbers in it. This is easy for the user to carry as he can place it in wallets and the drawback of this method is that the physical misuse and theft of the product (Authentication Techniques, 2006).

ROLE OF AUTHENTICATION IN ONLINE BANKING

Nowadays the usage of the Internet banking has increased a lot and the possibility of fraud also increased. Since many users started to use the online banking and also the intruders increased in order to hack the users details and to steal the money from others account without their knowledge. Because of this problem many users stopped using these services from the banks. It's bank's responsibility to provide users the account security and so banks prefer to authenticate the user so that they can ensure that only the right person is using the appropriate account. Attacking the banks server had started to occur often and the banks are pushed to authenticate their users (CEPIS, 2007).

Some banks provide authentication based on the 'Two Factor Authentication' which has two basic authentication factors. The security is more essential factor in banks and they depend only on the two factor authentication and are as follows,

- What the user knows (PIN, Password, Pass phrases),
- What the user has (Smart cards, Tokens, etc).

Most of the banks use only the username and password or pass phrase as their authentication factor over the Internet. The users are requested to provide the PIN/Passwords/Passphrase when they try to access the online banking. These are used as the basic authentication term in online banking. If the security provided to be more means then the bank will provide with extra hardware security devices like tokens along with the password provided to the users. The authentication factor provided are implemented in the following ways and are as follows:

- One-time password approach,
- Certificate based approach,
- Time based password approach.

Certificate Based Approach

In this approach a certificate is provided along with the password to the user. The certificates are software token that is installed inside a USB or any Smart card device and it should be provided by the user. The bank server will execute the card along with the passwords provided and will be used for the authentication purpose.

One-Time Password Approach

This is another method where the passwords are provided to the user by the server and can be used only once for a transaction and after single use, it expires. The user will have to request new password for next attempt to login. The passwords that are created temporarily are termed as TAN's (Transaction Authorization Numbers). There are three types of TAN's and are iTAN (TAN's distributed in lists), eTAN (TAN's created using special hardware devices) and mTAN (Tan created through mobile phones). The operation of the TAN's are represented in Figure 1. The iTAN process is also described in the figure which is done using the lists for each TAN request. The same approach is followed in the eTAN and mTAN where the SMS messages and other media devices are used as the medium of transaction; and these are successfully deployed at many Ausrian and German banks (Wiesmaier et al, 2004).

Time-Based Password Approach

This is another method which is more secure than the one-time password approach. The operation is similar to that of one-time password approach but there will be certain time limit provided to it such

Figure 1. Authentication – TAN approach
(CEPIS, 2007).

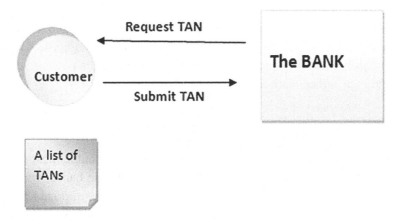

that after the password is generated it will be there only for certain time after that it will expire. This is created with a design that the hackers cannot have sufficient time to calculate the codes and so it will be more secure (CEPIS, 2007).

INTERNET BANKING: ISSUES

In recent trends, the use of the Internet in the organization had increased to higher extend and many organizations follow Internet as their major business medium. Similarly the banking sector also introduces the Internet banking to their customers as an easier method to perform their transactions. Since a greater portion of population now uses Internet, the amount of information on Internet has exploded, securing which has become a major issue in the Internet banking (OCC, 1999). Some of the issues in the Internet banking are as follows,

- Authentication,
- Trust,
- Non-repudiation,
- Privacy, and
- Availability.

Authentication

Another issue in the Internet banking is the Authentication. The banking operations performed through Internet must be well authenticated with the provider and the user. The bank should provide more care for authenticate their users. In general, the bank uses the encryption and decryption technique to transfer the authentication code where the public key and private key are used for the authentication. Later on the passwords used as codes are transferred and now they are using biometric identification codes are used as latest form of authentication codes.

Trust

This is another issue in Internet banking. Since the transactions are made through the Internet, authentication service provider for Internet i.e, Certificate Authority is essential and it's a trust oriented part that the bank relies on the third party for their security. The certificate authorities provide the "Digital Signatures" which helps in providing good security with good mix of the preventive, detective and corrective controls to provide authentications.

Non-Repudiation

The participation by both the sender and receiver in transferring their authentication codes are undeniable proof and this is one of the issues in the Internet banking. While banks, which technically have dedicated Internet connections, are at risk of being perpetrated by unauthorized personnel, electronic banking system users face greater risks due to the remote accessibility and therefore, more exposure of sensitive information. Therefore, it becomes a cardinal rule for banks to ensure non-repudiability by means of attestation by a third party, who holds the identity certificates, the identities of the sender and receiver. (Fatima, 2011)

Privacy

This is consumer issue in the Internet banking. Consumers in the Internet banking should be provided more security and their privacy in more essential such that the customer should rely on their security services.

Availability

This is a major part that user expects from the service providers. The service should be provided all times and no inconvenient should be faced by the customers from the bank's service. The service should be provided to the customers twenty hours a day and seven days a week. The customer should be comfortable with all sort of service provided by the Internet banking service providers.

Authentication Issues in Online Banking

Due to the volume of sensitive information handled by banks, it is always under pressure to uphold the privacy of its customers from perpetrators. As is commonly quoted, 'Human is the weakest link', which is what makes user authentication one of the most important vulnerable areas to be taken care of by banks. There are various ways in which web applications could be subjected to attack. Below listed provide a broad categorization of the same:

- Online Channel Breaking Attacks.
- Offline Credential Stealing Attack.
- Software based Attacks.
- Phishing.
- Data Breaches.

Online Channel Breaking Attacks

This is a system where the intruders attack web application of banks. The intruders will never aim to obtain the user's credential instead they try to hijack the information that was transferred between the user and the bank, which is seen in the cookie information. The intruders will watch the transactions and also will intercept the messages from the client and the server and will record the authentication codes used by the user. The intruders will make use of those cookies and may access that account as an authenticated user. This is one way of attacking the authentication of the online banking. Most of the intruders are using this methodology to attack the bank servers (Weigold, 2006). Two examples of online attacks that can render Public Key Infrastructure (PKI) inefficient are Cross-site Scripting Attack and Cross-Site request forgery.

Offline Credential Stealing Attacks

This is another type of attack that is faced by the banking sector. This attack is performed when the system is placed in offline mode. The system is hacked by means of miscellaneous software that contains viruses and Trojan horses. This viruses and Trojan horses will get rooted into the system and will be used to store the confidential data is processed by the system and is then provided to the attackers. The hackers install software through un-trusted sites and downloads from the Internet. (Weigold, 2006).

Software Based Attacks

Usually, banks use software based protection for their servers. Banks use software protection rather than the hardware-based protection because former is cheaper (Yang, 1997). There are many drawbacks in this system and are as follows,

1. The encryption algorithm used to encrypt the data in these software based protection system can be attacked by the attackers.
2. Direct approach of trying the combination of the possible occurrence of the PIN can be calculated by the attackers.
3. Hacking the bank's server and accessing all the confidential data.
4. Hacking client's personal computers through miscellaneous programs.

Phishing

This is a process where the fake websites like bank's website, financial institution website or government websites are created to and fraud users into revealing confidential data such as passwords and access codes; and then to access their accounts to indulge in fraud. There are many organizations that are affected by phishing websites created by the attackers. Many e-commerce organizations are still trying to reduce the effect of these phishing websites attacks. "There are several different types of phishing attacks including misleading e-mails, man-in-the-middle, URL obfuscation, page content overriding, malware phishing, key loggers and screen grabbers, session hijackers, web Trojans, IP address manipulation, and system reconfiguration attacks (Williamson, 2006)". While organizations try to track and bring down these fake websites creation, the perpetrators continuously invent new ways to phish. In year 2005 alone, the number of phishing sites almost quadrupled (Williamson, 2006).

A recent survey (APWG, 2013) shows that about 77% of all phishing attacks in the first half of 2013 targeted the financial sector. One of the most common technical countermeasures for protection against phishing that has been adopted by many financial services firms is use of Extended Validation Secure Socket Layer (EV SSL). EV SSL is used for server-client mutual authentication and for also encryption of data in transmission. It also facilitates verification of certificate on the servers by furnishing more information such as company location, corporate name and a registration number for the server website (CA, 2012). However, it has also been shown that this method is also vulnerable to phishing (Marlinspike, 2009). Another method is to show customer-selected image at the time of any online interaction with the company, usually at the time of login. Bank of America's SiteKey is an example of such technique(BOA,

2014). According to a survey by Anti Phishing Working Group(APWG-1, 2012; APWG-2, 2012), the average lifetime of phishing sites has gone down from 46 hours in 2011 to 26 hours in 2012, while their number had climbed from 50,298 to 89,748. Another recent solution against phishing is based on black lists maintained and published by leading browser companies such as Google Chrome's Safe Browsing, Microsoft Internet Explorer's Phishing Filter and the Phishing Protection by Mozilla Firefox (Mozilla, 2014; Google, 2014)

Data Breaches

This is another type of attack that is used to obtain users confidential information. The Internet is used as the medium and the users are provided with names of famous organizations to provide different offers and terms. There are billions of records of personal and private information stored and processed by universities, healthcare institutions, businesses, government agencies and other entities for providing services and products. The personal information stored include social security numbers, credit card numbers, data of birth, driver license number, addresses and much more. Risks from unintended disclosure of personal information include privacy risks and risks from potential identity theft frauds. The damages done from these risks alone already cost billions of dollars in detection and remediation (Hasan & Yurcik, 2006). There are several organizations, for-profit and non-profit that has been actively engaged in maintaining the incidents of security breaches. There also have lot of organizations that suffered a breach and have disclosed it to mass media (Attrition.org, 2009; Tehan, 2005). Privacy Rights ClearingHouse (PRC, 2009) estimates that around 100 million records containing sensitive personal information have been compromised over last few years. The users are lured into entering Credit Card details, Social Security Number, Date of Birth etc that is stolen by the attackers. The users tend to provide the information as the links seem to be coming from banks, high level financial organizations, big organizations etc. After the trap is successful, the stolen information is used to launch fraudulent activities (Williamson, 2006).

FRAUD PREVENTION STRATEGIES

The fraud in the Internet banking has become common and prevention has become more essential and banks have to take precautionary steps to perform the process without fraud (BITS, 2003). ACFE defines fraud as "the use of one's occupation for personal enrichment through the deliberate misuse or application of the employing organization's resources or assets". Companies and individuals lose billions of dollars every year to various types of fraud (Levi & Burrows, 2008; Chan et al., 1999; Chen et. al., 2006; McAlearney, 2008). The proceedings from these frauds helps fund organized crime, international trafficking, and even cross-border terrorist financing (McAlearney, 2008). There are three different stages where strategies are followed to prevent the fraud and some are provided below:

- Application process,
- Application Authentication,
- After application approval.

Application Process

- **Limit Timeframes:** This process is implemented when the application is filled up by the customers and it is provided with time limit so that it will be closed before the provided time and application should be finished by the user within the provided time.
- **Provide a Secure Channel:** This is provided to the user immediately so that the user can verify provided details and also check for any intruders or intercept of the data.
- **Create an Audit Trail:** This feature will automatically record the user's IP address and time for the further references.

Application Authentication

- **Use a Real Time Process:** This is created to verify whether the provided details by the user are accurate. It also verifies the details provided by the user during applying through online and the user should register to the concern authority before applying.
- **Ask "In Wallet" Question:** The wallet questions are the one of the confidential question where the user can provide like social security number, driving license number and date of birth etc where the intruders can hack these wallets but don't know whether they are applying for a new application or an existing application.
- **Use "Out-of Wallet" Questions:** This is automatically generated questions asked to the user about the exact value of the monthly chargers to be paid. So that the intruders can be avoided if wrong details are provided.
- **Use of "Out-of Credit" Questions:** These are about the personal questions about the user apart from the credit of the account. This also secures the server from the intruders.
- **Provide Standard Field Variation:** This is to ensure that whether the user is using the application correctly.
- **Verify Application Data:** The user details are verified with the central database and the information provided is correct and to ensure the user also that he/ she enters only the correct information.

After Application Approval

- **Wait for Funding Prior to Opening an Account:** The waiting time is provided by the financial institutions for the user to enter the PIN numbers in ATM centers so that perpetrators would not be able to identify the code within the provided time.
- **Require That a Signed Application on File:** The user's signature is verified with the signature recorded in the database and so that unauthorized users cannot misuse the user's checks or any other transactions.
- **Require Customer Authentication to be Completed in the Branch or through Customer Call Centers:** The information about the user is to be recorded earlier in the particular branch where the user operates the accounts. If not the information should be registered either through the customer call centers.
- **Implementing Manual Fraud Screening on Initial Deposits:** The image that is captured when the check is dropped and the machine also captures the image of the person who deposits the initial amount and it can be helpful to avoid unauthorized access to the account.

SYSTEMS AND SOLUTIONS TO ATTACKS IN ONLINE BANKING

The online banking should be provided with high security so that the attacks in the authentication of the Internet banking can be stopped and the server can be secured (Yang, 1997). The solutions are provided by means of the two terms namely,

- Software based security system, and
- Hardware based security system.

Software Based Security System

In this system the authentication is based on the software programs. Encryption is the main method used to encrypt the code. Encryption is a technique where the data is jumbled and can be retrieved using some shared secret. This process needs both the public key and private key. In one method only one key is used by both the client and server where both for encryption and decryption the key is used (symmetric encryption). The second method is that using a private key and public key (asymmetric encryption). The public key should be made available to both the client and the server. The data can be transferred using the public key in the public domain but retrieved by means of the private key. This method is more secure than that of first encryption method. The encryption methodology can be classified in to four classifications such as Digital signatures, Secure Electronic Transactions, Pretty good privacy and Kerberos (Yang, 1997).

- **Digital Signatures:** A digital signature is used to identify the sender by the receiver using the signature placed along with the messages. The private key is used to encrypt and the public key to decrypt. The user's signature is used as the private key in this case. Only the user can create the signature and it is difficult to copy the signature.
- **Secure Electronic Transactions (SET):** This is another method based on the software to create a secure card which can be used to do the payments in Internet. These cards are provided with the world wide accessible terms such as Visa Master Card, IBM, Microsoft, Netscape communication corp, Verisign. The online bank transaction can be done securely using the SET technology. RSA public key encryption technique is used in this method. The digital signature is created using a unique public and private key. A digital signature is provided with the data and it encrypted using some hashing techniques. The encrypted data will be sent along with the user's private key which helps to provide users identity to the bank so that the receiver can get the details of the sender. The receiver uses the hashing algorithm to generate the messages and should match the old one.
- **Pretty Good Privacy (PGP):** This is another method where its functions are based on the combination of the public key algorithm and private key algorithm. No transmitted channel medium is required for this technique. The received public key can be decrypted with the user's private key and so the identity of the sender can be verified. This method also provides more security for the data transfer.
- **Kerberos:** This is a private key encryption technique. It creates an encrypted data packet called ticket and it will be transferred through Internet. The tickets are used to identify the user and the tickets can be transferred only between Kerberos servers. The private keys are shared between the two systems.

Hardware Based System

It is another more secure form of exchanging data over Internet and comprises physical devices which are expensive and difficult to handle. There are many hardware based systems and most common is the Smart card and MeChip (Yang, 1997).

- **Smart Card:** This card is mechanically designed with the programs and chips are inbuilt and it can store data related to the user's personal identification terms. The user can use this card when needed to retrieve the information. The virus can affect this card but this will be used mostly in outdoors and the Internet usage cannot be made in this card.
- **MeChip:** This is a device that is connected using the USB port of a personal computer. The information that needed to be sent in a secure manner is added to the device, which transfers the data and checks the status of the transmission.

Comparison of Authentication Techniques

In this section, we present a comparison of different authentication methods that are most commonly used. Table 1 presents a summary of the comparison based on handling (support and maintenance from user standpoint), cost (to the company) and security of the solution. As we can see, tokens and OTP scratch pads are the most difficult methods for support and for handling (more from a convenience standpoint). Biometrics has the most costs in terms of implementing a solution and on-going maintenance. However, there are several methods that score "High" on security or on authentication strength including biometrics, which has the highest score.

Table 1. Comparison of authentication techniques

S. No.	Technique	Handling	Cost	Security
1	Username & Passwords	Easy	Nil	Average
2	PIN	Easy	Nil	Average
3	Identifiable picture	Easy	Nil	Moderate
4	One-Time Password	Moderate	Nil	Moderate
5	Swipe Card	Easy	Low	Average
6	Tokens	Hard	Medium	High
7	Biometric	Easy	High	Very High
8	Keyboard Rhythm	Moderate	Medium	Moderate
9	OTP Scratch Card	Hard	Medium	Moderate
10	Digital Signatures	Easy	Medium	High
11	Secure Electronic Transactions (SET)	Easy	Medium	High
12	Pretty Good Privacy (PGP)	Moderate	Medium	High
13	Kerberos	Easy	Medium	High
14	Smart Cards	Easy	Low	Moderate
15	MeChip	Moderate	Medium	Moderate

AUTHENTICATION IN MOBILE BANKING

Mobile phones, today, provide many more luxuries that they did not provide a few years ago. From the basic functionality of making and receiving calls to sending emails to making transactions, mobile devices have made lives, both personal and professional, more convenient and much easier. The constantly evolving mobile environment calls for more functionality where mobile phones are increasingly becoming reflections of the personal computers implying more storage and processing capabilities. Mobile phones are thus, a miniature portable version of personal computers (Ben-Asher et al., 2011). As mobile phones increasingly become an indispensable commodity, enriching user experience is key which is achieved by means of creating rich mobile applications which in turn need to be supported by developing powerful mobile operating systems that have capabilities of running the applications in the most efficient manner. While these platforms may draw a parlance from existing desktop operating systems, they introduce a gamut of security mechanisms relevant to the mobile landscape. (Singh, 2012)

As much as mobile phones may derive functionality from traditional personal computers, they offer a different perspective in terms of usage. While personal computers are used over a long continuous stretch of time, mobile phones are accessed intermittently for more number of times and shorter periods whenever there is the need, for example, an email notification. This introduces an additional security mechanism to authenticate the device multiple number of times as compared to a personal computer. Being the handy devices that they are, the idea of security in a mobile phone overwhelms users as it is perceived to hinder convenience and ease of usability. A recent study notes that, more than 30% of mobile phone users do not use a PIN on their phones. On the contrary, there is increasingly a large amount of high value data being stored on mobile devices; with mobile payment and money transfer applications as well as enterprise data becoming available on mobile devices (Riva, et. al., 2012). In this context it is pertinent that the banking industry acquaints itself with the security aspect of the mobile environment in order to avoid ramifications that could be detrimental to stakeholders. In the digital world where impersonation is the gravest form of security breach, non-repudiation, which means the identity of the sending and receiving party is attested by an authorized third party, is a prudent step towards keeping intruders and illegal activities at bay (Fatima, 2011).

Methods of Authentication in Mobile Banking

There are a few common and very widely used methods of authentication in mobile banking environment including (but not limited to):

1. Basic Password Authentication System,
2. Implicit Password Authentication System,
3. Multi-factor Authentication System,
4. Progressive Authentication System, and
5. Client Server Authentication System.

Basic Password Authentication System

The basic password authentication system is the traditional means of authentication, where the user is required to register a username and password which is used for every instance of authenticating to the system. In order to make the application resistant to brute force attacks and simple dictionary attacks, character restrictions and specifications are set on the password. For instance, the application may accept passwords only if they satisfy the criteria of – 8 characters in length, alphanumeric and at least one special character. The user's session is timed such that it expires/logs the user out when the application is idle for some time. The session idle time after which the user is force logged out can be set according to the severity of the application. Additional layer of protection could be added by the system by means of remembering the device from which the user generally logs in and send out an email or SMS for any unusual activity.

- **Benefits:**
  - If the system implements strong password policy, the application is secure from brute force attacks or simple dictionary attacks.
  - It is the easiest to implement among authentication methods.
- **Drawbacks:**
  - Unless there is strong server security, the database that stores all passwords could be compromised.
  - Due to the difficulty in remembering or keying in the password, most users save the password in the device, which can make it a vulnerability in the case of a stolen device or borrowed device.

By providing just a single layer of security, the system could be vulnerable to several other threats which are attempted to be overcome by some of the methods discussed next.

Implicit Password Authentication System

Know Your User

The user logs in with the basic username and password. Subsequently, the server picks a couple of questions (the number of questions depends on the level of service requested) out of the 10-20 questions selected by the user out of 100-200 standard questions in the bank's database during the registration process. For example, the user may choose the following questions:

- The name if the city you were born?
- The name of the breed of your pet animal?
- Date of birth?

The server creates and henceforth associates every question to images where the answers can implicitly be implied from the corresponding images. Every question chosen by the user, triggers a randomly selected image from the authentication space which is presented to the user as a challenge. The user is expected to navigate his/her way through the image to get the answer that is embedded in the image. For instance, the server may present the user with a geographical map. The user should correlate to Question 1. If Los Angeles is the city the user was born, he needs to click on North America. It will then zoom into North America where the user can choose Los Angeles. Every other time the user wants to authenticate to the server, a different question may be presented or if the same question repeats, a different scenario is presented. Hence, an outsider cannot make sense of the authentication scheme, as it is a fuzzy system. Also, session keys could be generated from the correct clickable area in the image in order to ensure there are no static keys that can give leeway to intruders. (Almuairfi, Veeraraghavan, & Chilamkurti, 2011)

- **Benefits:**
  - ◦ This authentication method helps secure the application from shoulder surfing and screen dump/screen capture attacks.
  - ◦ Due to the implicit nature of the authentication, only a legitimate user can make sense of the challenge posed by the server and therefore decode it to gain access to perform an authorized transaction through the application.
- **Drawbacks:**
  - ◦ A drawback of implementing this method of authentication could be that the system could ask a very easy question at the time of registration – an alphanumeric question – and ask the user to key in the answer through a graphical keyboard (Almuairfi et al., 2011)

Audio and Haptic Cues

While the audio modality has been considerably explored, authentication by means of haptic cues is a less trodden path and may gain more momentum given its implicit nature and thus the security it has to offer. Based on tactile feedback technology, haptic cues take advantage of the sense of touch by decoding the pressure or force, vibrations or any mechanical association of the user to the device, which is unique to the user.

There is a PIN lock system and the PIN is derived from a set of tactile or audio cues. The PIN is, therefore, a sequence of the audio and haptic cues. Accordingly, the size of the cues and length of the PIN can be changed. (Bianchi, et. al, 2011)

- **Benefits:**
  - ◦ The system employs cues, which cannot be interpreted or seen due to the fact that they are observation resistant and more importantly unique to every user.
  - ◦ Protects from shoulder surfing.

Multifactor Authentication Systems

Traditional M-Banking Process

In the basic traditional M-Banking process, the client side presents a request. Subsequently, the server side transfers the message containing the On-Time-Password (OTP) to the client side. An authentic user who is in possession of the device will receive the OTP and therefore, key in the correct OTP to the server side. In order to avoid hacking or spoofing, the OTP should be verified from the webpage of the server side for non-repudiation (so that the OTP is actually sent from the authentic server side), after which, the client side will register/input the OTP on the webpage of the server side. The server side then checks for validity of the OTP. The transaction is accepted or rejected depending on the validity of the OTP. (Tsai, Chen, & Zhuang, 2012)

- **Benefits:**
  - Unless the right device is possessed, the OTP cannot be accessed and hence unauthorized transactions cannot be made.
  - Also, the OTP is valid for a limited time and therefore cannot be reused making it immune to replay attacks.
- **Drawbacks:**
  - A stolen device can help gain unauthorized access into the system.
  - Also, man-in-the-middle attacks could be successfully done if the OTP is not strongly encrypted.

Authentication Using OTP and Biometric

This authentication is similar to the traditional two-factor authentication discussed above up until the point where the OTP is sent to the server side. An extra layer of defense is added in this case - if the OTP sent is valid, the server sends one more request to client for biometric information. If the information sent is correct, the user can perform the transaction. This model can be modified and implemented towards progressive authentication, which is discussed later in the chapter. (Tsai et al., 2012)

Authentication Using TIC

TIC Authentication: TIC authentication is the technique used to verify both the user and the ongoing transaction. A TIC code is used to certify that the right person has initiated the current transaction and that it is a legitimate user who is trying to access his/her account. TIC codes are:

- Issued by the Bank or Financial institution to its customers.
- An 8 bit or 16 bit Pseudo randomly generated code which is assigned to the customers.
- May be a complicated digit sequence or combination of numeric and alpha numeric characters.

So, Multifactor Authentication can be used to verify the user and the transaction by using the following steps:

1. **Web-Based Basic Authentication:** First, a basic traditional authentication – username/password based protocol – is required to gain initial access into the system by proving one's identity to the web server.
2. **TIC Authentication:** Once authentication to the web server is successful using the basic username/password, a TIC code is demanded from the user. The TIC code is decrypted at user end and the user then inserts the one time TIC code that helps in uniquely identifying his/her transaction and thereby proving his/her identity to the web Authentication server.
3. **SMS Confirmation:** An extra layer of defense is added by means of an SMS confirmation in order to confirm one's financial transaction. The web Authentication server sends an SMS to the web user for confirmation of the transaction made. The strength of security of the system also depends on the security of the messages sent by SMS and WAP, which are encrypted. The transaction can be confirmed by the user by means of replying to the SMS with a 'YES' or a 'NO'. This helps in further ensuring the authenticity of transactions made every single time.

Mobile phones cannot handle the highly computation intensive nature of Public Key Infrastructure. Therefore, PKI can be used to encrypt the symmetric key while the entire data that can simply be encrypted using the symmetric key.

- **Benefits:**
  - The two-way authentication protocol addresses several of the shortcomings of the Secure Electronic Transmission. Data is always in an encrypted form making the information that is vital to a user highly secure and available to the merchant in an encrypted form.
- **Stolen Device:** In the case of a stolen device, despite the intruder having the user's password he cannot surpass the extra layers of authentication, as the TIC code is also encrypted whose key is known only to the valid user.
- **Man-in-the-Middle Attack:** The fact that there is no unencrypted data sent over untrusted network at any stage during the authentication process protects and secures the system from man-in-the-middle attacks. Additionally, the benefit of having OTPs which expire in a timely fashion making them available for only one single transaction (Tiwari et al., 2011).

Bio-Cryptography: Combination of Biometrics and Cryptography

Biometrics and cryptography could be used in combination in a way that they could complement each other and derive the best of both worlds. The fingerprint biometric is used to generate a cryptographic key, by means of employing it to work with the Elliptical Curve Cryptography (ECC) public key cryptography. The key retrieval process is thus protected by means of fingerprint verification. A successful fingerprint authentication results in generation of correct keys.

The basic idea is to transfer the locally matched fuzzy vault index to the central server for biometric authentication using the PKI which offloads the computation demand to the central server. The keys generated are dynamic as they change for every biometric authentication while the minutia details are never exposed externally, Vulnerability risk is further notched down as the establishment of symmetric session keys does not need a conventional key exchange process.

RSA is the most widely accepted standard in the industry. However, owing to the computational demands posed, ECC which offers the same security strength as RSA but with smaller key sizes, is employed in the mobile environment, where small memories and lower computational capacities are expected.

Recent significant research outcome on bio- cryptographic includes bio hashing, cancelable template, fuzzy extractor and fuzzy vault.

- **Benefits:** Secures application from:
  - **Trojan Horse Attack:** Even in the worst case scenario where the attacker compromises the private key of the PKI which has been stored in the mobile device, it does not help break the system as the attacker has to surpass the biometric authentication at the central server in the first place. Also, the cryptographic key being generated from the biometric information which is unique to every user makes it unpredictable. Furthermore, it is not stored at either mobile client side or server side.
  - **Brute Force Attack:** No static key stored in hardware - Both genuine minutiae and chaff points can be used to generate the session key.

- ○ **Biometric Template Attack:** Increasing the total number of minutiae from the usually collected 10-20 or increasing the difficulty for attackers to capture the minutiae information are two possible solutions.
- ○ The other attacks from which this method can secure the system are Transmission channel attack – ECC algorithm provides security that RSA algorithm provides; Replay attack – adoption of timestamps; Man-in-the-middle attack – use of Public Key Infrastructure (PKI) and truly random session keys generated from biometrics (Xi et al., 2011).

Progressive Authentication Methods

Graded Security

Graded security is a means of granting graduated access to a user. Graded security can be seen from two different perspectives: One way of which is user-based access control where access is granted on the basis of role held by the user often described in a hierarchical manner – guest-user to super- user. Second, graded security can be seen as a content- based system. In this case, access is provisioned on the basis of content alone. The user is required to authenticate to the system every single time he/she is to be provided with content requested with no overlap to other content thus making each content accessible independently only. (Ben-Asher et al., 2011)

Implicit Password Authentication

This method of authentication has been described earlier in the chapter, which could be used to provide graded security. The user would be granted with the initial level of access when he authenticates to the system with username and password which could be sent as plain text. As per the level of access required, the system might choose relevant questions that have been registered by the user during the time of registration process.

Progressive Authentication by Means of Sensors

Mobile systems can progressively authenticate (and de-authenticate) users by constantly collecting cues about the user, such that at any point in time the user is authenticated with a certain level of confidence. Several authentication signals are used. Sensors such as the voice recognition or haptic cues can be used to establish knowledge about the user and henceforth pose authentication challenges to gain access to critical information. In order to extend the validity of the user and avoid cases wherein, an illegitimate user is exploiting a session that has been idle for hours. This method can make the best use of the technological advancements in the mobile environment. With mobile phones being increasingly networked, proximity and motion sensors can be used to detect whether the phone is next to another device of the same user where he is currently authenticated and active.

- **Benefits:**
  - ○ This approach makes the authentication overhead lower and proportional to the value of the content being accessed.

- **Drawbacks:**
  - There is inherent noise in sensing data as well as energy and performance constraints. If sensor streams are the only source used for detection, the system is likely to suffer a high number of false rejections (inability to recognize the owner) or cases of unauthorized accesses.
  - Moreover, it is a challenging task to process the sensor data and run the inference stack on a mobile device. Continuously recording data from the sensors can drain the battery of the mobile phone at faster rate (Riva et al., 2012).

Client-Server Authentication

In order to cryptographically protect the communication channel between the client and server, e-commerce applications employ a secure sockets layer/ transport layer security protocol. The server side authenticates itself to the client using a public key certificate and so should the client. One disadvantage of this pre-shared key based approach is that every server needs to generate and securely distribute a key-bearing token to every user, which is likely to be a significant burden in practice. Another disadvantage is its poor scalability. Therefore, Transport Layer Security-Session Aware user authentication (TLS-SA) using a GAA (General Authentication Architecture) bootstrapped key is a viable approach. The scheme employs a GAA-enabled user device with a display and an input capability (e.g. a 3G mobile phone) and a GAA-aware server, and binds the user authentication process to the TLS session without modifying the operation of TLS. A GAA bootstrapped session key is used in the computation of the user authentication code, there is no need to generate and securely distribute a key-bearing token to every user (Chen et. al., 2011). The main benefit is that it secures application from Man-in-the-middle attacks.

CONCLUSION

The security of the bank operations is essential, more so when the intensity and frequency of attacks is higher than ever. So, the need of authentication in a secure manner is more essential than ever. There are many different authentication techniques available and each has its own unique properties in providing authentication. The online and mobile banking which is now used worldwide has more useful functions than ever, but the growth in fraud and identity theft shows failure in securing the information. Authentication has emerged to be the one of the most vital pieces of strengthening security and ensuring privacy of financial date. The chapter presented several authentication methods and the solutions to some potential types of attacks, for both web banking and mobile banking. We discussed our survey of different authentication issues, some of the most important factors in selecting an authentication mechanism. The discussions and conclusions in the chapter can be used by managers and security professionals in understanding different approaches to authentication and will aid them during the decision making process.

REFERENCES

Adams, A., & Sasse, M. (1999). Users are not the enemy. *Communications of the ACM, 42*(12), 41–46. doi:10.1145/322796.322806

Almuairfi, S., Veeraraghavan, P., & Chilamkurti, N. (2011). *IPAS: Implicit password authentication system*. Paper presented at the Advanced Information Networking and Applications (WAINA), New York, NY.

APWG. (2012a) Anti-phishing working group. *Global Phishing Survey*. Retrieved 1ˢᵗ August, 2012 from http://docs.apwg.org/reports/APWG_GlobalPhishingSurvey_1H2012.pdf

APWG. (2012b). Anti-phishing working group. *Global Phishing Survey*. Retrieved 1ˢᵗ August, 2012 from http://docs.apwg.org/reports/APWG_GlobalPhishingSurvey_2H2012.pdf

APWG. (2013). Anti-phishing working group. *Global Phishing Survey*. Retrieved 1ˢᵗ August, 2012 from http://docs.apwg.org/reports/APWG_GlobalPhishingSurvey_1H2013.pdf

Attrition.org. (2009). Retrieved from 3ʳᵈ March, 2013 from Attrition.org http://attrition.org/security/dataloss.html

Authentication. (2007, June 4). Retrieved 3rd April, 2010 from www.searchsecurity.techtarget.com

Authentication Techniques. (2006, January 10). Retrieved 3rd April, 2010 from www.sheshunoff.com: http://www.sheshunoff.com/ideanet/index.php?itemid=204&catid=4

Bauer, L., Cranor, L. F., Reiter, M. K., & Vaniea, K. (2007). Lessons learned from the deployment of a smartphone-based access-control system. In *Proceedings of the 3rd Symposium on Usable Privacy and Security* (pp. 64-75). ACM.

Ben-Asher, N., Kirschnick, N., Sieger, H., Meyer, J., Ben-Oved, A., & Möller, S. (2011). On the need for different security methods on mobile phones. In *Proceedings of the 13th International Conference on Human Computer Interaction with Mobile Devices and Services*. Academic Press.

Bianchi, A., Oakley, I., Kostakos, V., & Kwon, D. S. (2011). The phone lock: Audio and haptic shoulder-surfing resistant PIN entry methods for mobile devices. In *Proceedings of the Fifth International Conference on Tangible, Embedded, and Embodied Interaction* (pp. 197-200). Madeira, Portugal: Academic Press. doi:10.1145/1935701.1935740

Bishop, M., & Klein, D. V. (1995). Improving system security via proactive password checking. *Computers & Security*, *14*(3), 233–249. doi:10.1016/0167-4048(95)00003-Q

BITS. (2003, April). *Fraud prevention strategies for internet banking*. Retrieved 3ʳᵈ April, 2010 from http://www.bits.org/downloads/Publications%20Page /mointernetwp.pdf

BOA. (2014). *Bank of America SiteKey*. Retrieved 6ᵗʰ June 2013 from https://www.bankofamerica.com/privacy/online-mobile-banking-privacy/SiteKey.go

Bonneau, J., Herley, C., van Oorschot, P. C., & Stajano, F. (2012). The quest to replace passwords: A framework for comparative evaluation of web authentication schemes. In *Proceedings of IEEE Symposium on Security and Privacy* (pp. 553 – 567). IEEE. doi:10.1109/SP.2012.44

Braz, C., & Robert, J.-M. (2006). Security and usability: the case of the user authentication methods. In *Proceedings of the 18th International Conferenceof the Association Francophone d'Interaction Homme-Machine* (pp. 199 – 203). ACM. doi:10.1145/1132736.1132768

Bunnell, J., Podd, J., Henderson, R., Napier, R., & Kennedy-Moffat, J. (1997). Cognitive, associative, and conventional passwords: Recall and guessing rates. *Computers & Security, 16*(7), 645–657. doi:10.1016/S0167-4048(97)00008-4

Byron, B. (2003, August 1). *The need for authentication & authorization*. Retrieved on 3rd April, 2010 from http://www.redbooks.ibm.com/abstracts/tips0266.html?Open

CA. (2012). *Guidelines for the issuance and management of extended validation certificates*. Retrieved from www.cabforum.org

CEPIS. (2007, October 27). *Authentication approach for online banking*. Retrieved 3rd April, 2010 from http://www.cepis.org/files/cepis/20090901104203_Authentication%20approaches%20for%20.pdf

Chan, P. K., Fan, W., Prodromidis, A. L., & Stolfo, S. J. (1999). Distributed data mining in credit card fraud detection, data mining. *IEEE Intelligent Systems & their Applications, 14*(6), 67–74.

Chen, C., Mitchell, C. J., & Tang, S. (2011). SSL/TLS session-aware user authentication using a GAA bootstrapped key information security theory and practice. In *Security and privacy of mobile devices in wireless communication* (pp. 54–68). Springer.

Chen, R. C., Chen, T. S., & Lin, C. C. (2006). A new binary support vector system for increasing detection rate of credit card fraud. *International Journal of Pattern Recognition, 20*(2), 227–239. doi:10.1142/S0218001406004624

Chiasson, S., van Oorschot, P. C., & Biddle, R. (2008). Lecture notes in computer science: Vol. 4734: Graphical password authentication using cued click points. Springer.

Control, A. (2010). *Authentication, authorization and access control*. Retrieved 3rd April, 2010 from http://eregie.premier-ministre.gouv.fr/manual/howto/auth.html

Egelman, S., Sotirakopoulos, A., Muslukhov, I., Beznosov, Z., & Herley, C. (2013). Does my password go up to eleven? The impact of password meters on password selection. In *Proceedings of the SIGCHI Conference on Human Factors in Computing Systems* (pp. 2379-2388). ACM. doi:10.1145/2470654.2481329

Fatima, A. (2011). E-banking security issues--Is there a solution in biometrics? *Journal of Internet Banking & Commerce, 16*(2), 1–9.

Furnell, S. M., Dowland, P. S., Illingworth, H. M., & Reynolds, P. L. (2000). Authentication and supervision: A survey of user attitudes. *Computers & Security, 19*(6), 529–539. doi:10.1016/S0167-4048(00)06027-2

Gaw, S., & Felten, E. W. (2006). Password management strategies for online accounts. In *Proceedings of the 2nd Symposium on Usable Privacy and Security* (pp. 44–55). Academic Press. doi:10.1145/1143120.1143127

Google. (2014). *Google safe browsing*. Retrieved from http:///www.google.com/chrome/intl/ko/more/security.html

Gunson, N., Marshall, D., Morton, H., & Jack, M. (2011). User perceptions of security and usability of single-factor and two-factor authentication in automated telephone banking. *Computers & Security, 30*(4), 208–220. doi:10.1016/j.cose.2010.12.001

Gupta, M., Lee, J., & Rao, H. R. (2008). Implications of FFIEC guidance on authentication in electronic banking. In Handbook of research on information security and assurance. Hershey, PA: IGI Global.

Gupta, M., Rao, H. R., & Upadhyaya, S. (2004, July-September). Electronic banking and information assurance issues: Survey and synthesis. *Journal of Organizational and End User Computing, 16*(3), 1–21. doi:10.4018/joeuc.2004070101

Gupta, M., & Sharman, R. (2008, December). Dimensions of identity federation: A case study in financial services. *Journal of Information Assurance and Security, 3*(4), 244–256.

Hasan, R., & Yurcik, W. (2006). A statistical analysis of disclosed storage security breaches. In *Proceedings of 2nd International Workshop on Storage Security and Survivability* (StorageSS '06). Academic Press. doi:10.1145/1179559.1179561

Herley, C., & Oorschot, P. C. V. (2012). A research agenda acknowledging the persistence of passwords. *IEEE Security and Privacy, 10*(1), 28–36. doi:10.1109/MSP.2011.150

Hutchinson, D., & Warren, M. (2003). Security for internet banking: A framework. *Logistics, Information, &. Management, 16*(1), 64–73.

Jain, A., Bolle, R., & Pankanti, S. (Eds.). (1998). Biometrics: Personal identification in networked society. Dordrecht, The Netherlands: Kluwer.

Jain, A. K., Ross, A., & Pankanti, S. (2006). Biometrics: A tool for information security. *IEEE Transactions of Information Forensics and Security, 1*(2), 125–143. doi:10.1109/TIFS.2006.873653

Karole, A., Saxena, N., & Christin, N. (2010). A comparative usability evaluation of traditional password managers. In *Proceedings of the 13th International Conference on Information Security and Cryptology* (pp. 233-251). Springer-Verlag.

Kay, R. (2005, April 4). *Biometric authentication*. Retrieved 3rd April 2010 from http://www.computerworld.com/s/article/100772/Biometric_Authentication?taxonomyId=17&pageNumber=1

Komanduri, S., & Hutchings, D. (2008). Order and entropy in picture passwords. In *Proceedings of Graphics Interface*. Academic Press.

Komanduri, S., Shay, R., Kelley, P. G., Mazurek, M. L., Bauer, L., & Christin, N. et al. (2011). Of passwords and people: Measuring the effect of password-composition policies. In *Proceedings of ACM CHI Conference on Human Factors in Computing Systems* (pp. 2595 – 2604). ACM.

Levi, M., & Burrows, M. (2008). Measuring the impact of fraud in the UK: A conceptual and empirical journey. *The British Journal of Criminology, 48*(3), 293–318. doi:10.1093/bjc/azn001

Liang, W., & Wang, W. (2005). *A quatitative study of authentication & QoS in wirless IP network*. Retrieved 8th April, 2010 from http://www.ece.ncsu.edu/netwis/papers/05LW-INFOCOM

Liu, S. (2004, February). *Authentication in ASP.NET web servers*. Retrieved from 3rd March 2010 from http://progtutorials.tripod.com/Authen.htm

Magalhaes, R. M. (2001, November 19). *Understanding ISA's different types of authentication*. Retrieved 3rd April 2010 from www.isaserver.org/tutorials/Understanding_ISAs_different_Authentication_types.html

Marlinspike, M. (2009). *New tricks for defeating SSL in practice, Blackhat*. Retrieved 21st April, 2011 from https://www.blackhat.com/presentations/bh-dc-09/Marlinspike/BlackHat-DC-09-Marlinspike-Defeating-SSL.pdf

McAlearney, S. (2008, August 7). TJX data breach: Ignore cost lessons and weep. *CIO Magazine*.

Morris, R., & Thompson, K. (1979). Password security: A case history. *Communications of the ACM*, *22*(11), 594–597. doi:10.1145/359168.359172

Mozilla. (2014). *Phishing protection: Design documentation, Mozila Wiki*. Retrieved from https://wiki.mozilla.org/Phishing_Protection:_Design_Documentation

Normalini, M. K., & Ramayah, T. (2012). Biometrics technologies implementation in internet banking reduce security issues? In *Proceedings of International Congress on Interdisciplinary Business and Social Sciences 2012* (ICIBSoS 2012) (vol. 65, pp. 364–369). Academic Press. doi:10.1016/j.sbspro.2012.11.135

O'Gorman, L. (2003, December). Comparing passwords, tokens, and biometrics for user authentication. *Proceedings of the IEEE*, *91*(12), 2019–2040. doi:10.1109/JPROC.2003.819605

OCC. (1999, October). *Internet banking*. Retrieved 3rd April, 2010 from http://www.occ.treas.gov/handbook/intbank.pdf

Online Banking. (2010). Retrieved 3rd April, 2010, from http://www.investorglossary.com/online-banking.htm

Podio, F. L., & Dunn, J. S. (2001). *Biometric authentication technology*. Retrieved 3rd April, 2010, from http://www.itl.nist.gov/div893/biometrics/Biometricsfromthemovies.pdf

Pond, R., Podd, J., Bunnell, J., & Henderson, R. (2000). Word association computer passwords: The effect of formulation techniques on recall and guessing rates. *Computers & Security*, *19*(7), 645–656. doi:10.1016/S0167-4048(00)07023-1

PRC. (2009). *A chronology of data breaches reported since the choicepoint incident (list)*. Privacy Rights Clearinghouse. Retrieved January 24th 2010 from http://www.privacyrights.org/ar/ChronDataBreaches.htm

Renaud, K. (2009, February). On user involvement in production of images used in visual authentication. *Journal of Visual Languages and Computing*, *20*(1), 1–15. doi:10.1016/j.jvlc.2008.04.001

Riva, O., Qin, C., Strauss, K., & Lymberopoulos, D. (2012). Progressive authentication: Deciding when to authenticate on mobile phones. In *Proceedings of the 21st USENIX Security Symposium*. USENIX.

Sabzevar, A. P., & Stavrou, A. (2008). Universal multi-factor authentication using graphical passwords. In *Proceedings of IEEE International Conference on Signal Image Technology and Internet Based Systems*. IEEE. doi:10.1109/SITIS.2008.92

Singh, K. (2012). Can mobile learn from the web. In *Proceedings of IEEE Computer Society Security and Privacy Workshops, WPSP '12*. IEEE.

Strouble, D., Schechtman, G., & Alsop, A. S. (2009). Productivity and usability effects of using a two-factor security system. In *Proceedings of the Southern Association for Information Systems Conference* (pp. 195-201). Academic Press.

Tehan, R. (2005, December 16). *Personal data security breaches: Context and incident summaries.* Congressional Research Service Report for Congress.

Thigpen, S. (2005, July 17). *Banking authentication methods.* Retrieved 3rd April, 2010 from http://www.infosecwriters.com/text_resources/pdf/ Authentication_Methods_For_Banking.pdf

Tiwari, A., Sanyal, S., Abraham, A., Knapskog, S. J., & Sanyal, S. (2011). A multi-factor security protocol for wireless payment-secure web authentication using mobile devices. In *Proceedings of IADIS International Conference on Applied Computing*. IADIS.

Tsai, C., Chen, C., & Zhuang, D. (2012). Trusted m-banking verification scheme based on a combination of OTP and biometrics. *Journal of Convergence, 3*(3), 23–30.

Vance, A. (2010). If your password is 123456, just make it hackme. *New York Times*. Retrieved 15th March, 2010 from http://www.nytimes.com/2010/01/21/technology/21password.html

Venkatraman, S., & Delpachitra, I. (2008). Biometrics in banking security: A case study. *Information Management & Computer Security, 16*(4), 415–430. doi:10.1108/09685220810908813

Weigold, T. K. (2006, March/April). *Secure internet banking and authentication*. Retrieved 3rd April 2010 from http://www.zurich.ibm.com/pdf/csc/SecureInternetBanking Authentication.pdf

Weiss, R., & De Luca, A. (2008). Passshapes: Utilizing stroke based authentication to increase password memorability. In *Proceedings of the 5th Nordic Conference on Human-Computer Interaction*. Academic Press. doi:10.1145/1463160.1463202

Wiedenbeck, S., Waters, J., Birget, J., Brodskiy, A., & Memon, N. (2005, July). PassPoints: Design and longitudinal evaluation of a graphical password system. *International Journal of Human-Computer Studies, 63*(1-2), 102–127. doi:10.1016/j.ijhcs.2005.04.010

Wiesmaier, A., Fischer, M., Karatsiolis, E. G., & Lippert, M. (2004). *Proceedings of the 2005 International Conference on Security and Management*. Retrieved from arxiv.org/pdf/cs.CR/0410025

Williamson, G. D. (2006). Enhanced authentication in online banking. *Journal of Economic Crime Management, 42*(2).

Wimberly, H., & Liebrock, L. M. (2011). Using fingerprint authentication to reduce system security: An empirical study. In *Proceedings of IEEE Symposium on Security and Privacy* (pp. 32–46). IEEE. doi:10.1109/SP.2011.35

Xi, K., Ahmad, T., Han, F., & Hu, J. (2011). A fingerprint based bio-cryptographic security protocol designed for client/server authentication in mobile computing environment. *Security and Communication Networks, 4*(5), 487–499. doi:10.1002/sec.225

Yang, Y.-J. (1997). *The security of electronic banking*. Retrieved 3rd April, 2010, from http://csrc.nist. gov/nissc/1997/proceedings/041.pdf

Zezschwitz, E., De Luca, A., & Hussmann, H. (2013). Survival of the shortest: A retrospective analysis of influencing factors on password composition. In *Proceedings of Human-Computer Interaction*. Academic Press.

KEY TERMS AND DEFINITIONS

Authentication Factor: One of three possible factors – something the user knows (knowledge), something user possesses (possession) and something user is (behavioral).

Authentication: Verifying user's assertion of its identification through credentials.

Authorization: Verifying user's privileges to a system.

Identity Federation: Asserting user's identification information to a trusting partner for purpose of user's identification and authorization.

Identity Management Architecture: Design of identity system for managing credentials and entitlements for users of covered systems.

Identity Management System: A system for managing user identities and related privileges.

Multiple Factor Authentication: An authentication system that is based on more than one factor or authentication.

Password Management: Managing users' passwords for purpose of authentication.

Role Management: Managing user's roles for purpose of authorization and entitlements.

Single Sign On: Use of a single set of credentials to provide access to multiple systems and applications.

This work was previously published in the Handbook of Research on Emerging Developments in Data Privacy edited by Manish Gupta, pages 170-197, copyright 2015 by Information Science Reference (an imprint of IGI Global).

Chapter 17
Cyber–Crimes against Adolescents:
Bridges between a Psychological and a Design Approach

Filipa da Silva Pereira
University of Minho, Portugal

Marlene Alexandra Veloso de Matos
University of Minho, Portugal

Álvaro Miguel do Céu Gramaxo Oliveira Sampaio
Polytechnic Institute of Cávado and Ave, Portugal

ABSTRACT

At young ages there is an increase in reports of intimidation, harassment, intrusion, fear, and violence experienced through Information Technologies (IT). Hacking, spamming, identity theft, child pornography, cyber bullying, and cyber stalking are just few examples of cyber-crimes. This chapter aims to contribute, from a psychological and design perspective, to an integrative viewpoint about this complex field of cyber-crime. In this chapter, the most common types of cyber-crimes, epidemiological data, and the profiles of cyber victims and aggressors' are approached. The studies that identify the factors contributing to IT misuse and to growing online vulnerability, principally in adolescents, are also discussed. Likewise, the central explanatory theories for the online victimization and the risk factors for victimization and perpetration online are addressed. Finally, some cyber-crime prevention strategies are anticipated, in particular among young people, seeking to provide clues to the consolidation of recent policies, namely at the digital design level.

INTRODUCTION

During the last 15th years, the Internet and the other ITs have radically transformed the world, mainly in terms of communication and social interaction. In areas such as science, education, health, public administration, commerce and the development of the global net, the Internet offers an unmatched variety

DOI: 10.4018/978-1-5225-0808-3.ch017

of benefits. Therefore, information technologies turn out to be a communication tool deep rooted in the quotidian of world population. This applies especially to youths who present high indices of utilization and digital skills (Haddon, Livingstone & EU Kids Online network, 2012; Madden, Lenhart, Cortesi, Gasser, Duggan, Smith & Beaton, 2013). In this way, it is not surprising, as IT imposes as a mean of mass communication, the increase in reports of harm, intimidation, harassment and violence experienced through IT: experiences commonly known as cyber-crime (Dempsey, Sulkowsk, Dempsey & Storch, 2011).

Cyber-crime is a concept that integrates a set of activities related to the use of telecommunications networks for criminal purposes (Kraemer-Mbula, Tang & Rush, 2013) and it is described in the Portuguese law nº 109/2009 of 15th of September. It can comprises a diversity of (1) anti-social activities, such as those supported by computers (e.g., sending spam, malware) and (2) offenses aimed at a specific target (e.g., cyber stalking, cyber bullying) (Kim, Jeong, Kim & So, 2011). To accomplish cyber-crime activities, there are a variety of manipulation techniques (e.g., bribe, threat) and different ways through which Internet users can find themselves involved in risk behaviors (e.g., contact with strangers, the sharing of personal information) (Whittle, Hamilton-Giachritsis, Beech & Collings, 2013). However, the Portuguese penal code only contemplates as cyber-crime, anti-social activities supported by computer (material damages of technical content). In contrast to what happens in the United States, for example, cyber stalking or cyber bulling is not criminalized in the Portuguese law as a criminal offense, being only possible to criminalize individual actions that make up this form of persistent persecution and harassment (e.g., threats, identity theft and invasion of privacy).

The Internet turned into a space in which the more traditional crimes may take new forms and prosper in a totally immaterial environment (Clarke, 2004). The criminal activities that previously required the physical presence of his actors, in a place and specific time, are now possible independently of the physical location or time (Reyns, 2013). Because of this, the mysticism that surrounds the cyberspace and the anonymous nature of Internet means that individuals with reduced likelihood to start a criminal act in the real context (e.g., children and adolescents) can easily began to have a high probability to do so in the online context (McGrath & Casey, 2002).

As acknowledged previously, with the diffusion of IT, there is a tendency for cyber-crime to increase, both in its frequency as in the sophistication of the acts and techniques to commit it. However, it is not possible to eradicate this side of the online world. Thus, the solution is to investigate those new forms of cyber aggression in order to understand, control and minimize potential forms of cybernetic victimization and their impact (physical, mental and social health loss) (Marinos et al., 2011).

Despite cyber-crime being looked at with a growing scientific interest, this has not been sufficiently reflected from the psychological approach, which may have an important role in understanding the key factors that allow an early identification of features and enables the prediction of the course and evolution of these behaviors.

Cyber-crime is substantially different from traditional crimes, since it benefits from the timelessness, the possibility of anonymity and the absence of a restricted space (Yar, 2005). There are several theories that have been developing explanations about cyber-crime, including the routine activity theory (Cohen & Felson, 1979), the general theory of crime (Gottfredson & Hirschi, 1990) and the social learning theory (Skinner & Fream, 1997).

After exploring the cyber victims and aggressors' profiles, we address the main contributions of the above-mentioned theories for the understanding of the data related to cyber aggressors and cyber victims. The recognition of the steps implicated on cyber-crime and the conditions that facilitate it, permits allows the development of preventive actions towards cyber-crime (Clarke, 2004).

This chapter is organized as follows: the first part describes the literature background about cyber-crime in general population, specifically against IT devices and against IT users. Part two analyzes cyber-crime against adolescents, discussing common cyber-crimes typologies and targets, and risk factors for cyber victimization in adolescence are also discussed. Subsequently, various issues and controversies are discussed (e.g., strengths and weaknesses) related to psychological and digital approaches to cyber-crime against adolescents. The role of the victim, the offender, the digital environment, and the importance of parental involvement in cyber-crime prevention are problematized. Finally, solutions and future directions to achieve enhanced security of adolescents are addressed.

BACKGROUND

The Norton cyber-crime report (2011), carried out by Symantec-Norton, concludes that more than 2/3 of online adults (69%) were victims of cyber-crime throughout their lives, which is equivalent to more than a million victims per day and 14 victims per second. In 2012 the Norton Cyber-crime Report documented a worsening incyber victimization to 18 victims per second. At the same time, during the year of 2010, cyber-crime grew 337% in Portugal and in Spain, which corresponds to nine million cyber-attacks (Kasperksy Lab, 2010). The most common targets are, according to the aforementioned study, men between 18 and 31 years, who access the Internet often via cell phone.

According to Bossler and Holt (2010), sending malicious software (e.g., spam, malware) is the most common type of cyber-crime. Their study shows that 37% of American college students (N=573) have experienced this type of victimization during the year of 2009. More specifically, 16.8% was a target of password theft; 9.8% experienced the improper access to their computer data and 4.4% was victim of credit card theft through electronic means. In relation to these forms of theft, invasion and misuse, spamming, phishing and hacking are the three most common ways to acquire sensitive data (e.g., usernames, passwords, banking information) towards financial gain and scams (e.g., obtain goods and services or sell information to other cyber aggressors) (Kraemer-Mbula et al., 2013). The number of spammers has grown exponentially and the new trend points to the growing use of social networking sites (e.g., Facebook, MySpace) for the diffusion of indiscriminate messages, inducing Internet users to access web pages with malware (e.g., virus, worms, Trojan horses, spyware) (Kraemer-Mbula et al., 2013). In turn, phishing is a sophisticated form of spam that appears many times through an email of an apparent reliable entity. Hacking happens when a non-authorized person breaks into a computer (Holt, 2007). This last strategy is generally known as cyber terrorism and is achieved through the application of specific tools that requires superior programming skills to the earlier mentioned forms of digital crime (Kraemer-Mbula et al., 2013).

Despite the existence of various anti-virus software, encryption and fraud detection, the ENISA Threat Landscape Report (Marinos, 2013) assumes that we are witnessing a growing proficiency, sophistication and effectiveness by cyber criminals that outweigh the protection and preventive mechanisms. In addition, the current literature has pointed to the combination of online methods (e.g., through Trojans, phishing, hacking) with offline methods (e.g., intercepting mail and bank documents, verification of the victims personal garbage) for accessing private information and for the execution of identity theft and other frauds, which may indicate more effectiveness and extent of the illegal practices committed (Kraemer-Mbula et al., 2013).

Considering its consequences, data from the Norton cyber-crime annual report (2012) indicate that the cost of cyber-crimes supported by computer has as principal aggressors and targets adults' population and it ascends to 110 billion dollars annually. It illustrates the vast business and economic impact of this emerging phenomenon. Besides adults, the "actors" can also be children and adolescents, especially when we talk about the forms of cyber-crime against the person and/or their dignity (e.g., cyber stalking, cyber bullying and harassment) and it can result in important emotional and social implications at the individual level). The EU Kids Online network (2013) concluded that about 15 to 20% of online adolescents have reported significant levels of discomfort and threat regarding this form of cyber-crime experience. Because some adolescents achieve offline encounters with strangers and are targets of cyber bullying and/or cyber stalking, they are becoming more likely to experience a greater impact (Almeida, Delicado & Alves, 2008; Bocij, 2004; Haddon et al., 2012; Helsper, Kalmus, Hasebrink, Sagvari & Haan, 2013). Still, it is especially pertinent to point out that not all risk means negative experiences or damage to the adolescent: it depends on the individual and social factors such as self-confidence, acquired skills and mediation held, and prior experiences of victimization and / or perpetration in the cyberworld (Smahel, Helsper, Green, Kalmus, Blinka & Ólafsson, 2012; Vandoninck, d'Haenens & Roe, 2013).

In that context, online harassment (e.g., cyber stalking, cyber bullying) is a form of cyber-crime that involves sending threatening or sexual messages through email, instant messaging services or posts in online chats (Bocij, 2004; Fisher, Cullen & Turner, 2002) and it can lead victims to feel fear, emotional and psychological stress, equivalent to harassment and persecution experienced in the real world (Finn, 2004). In Bossler and Holt's study (2010), online harassment was the second most common form of victimization experienced by college students (18.8%). However, the complexity of the phenomenon and the different settings and samples taken in the study of online harassment are some of the obstacles to reliable comparison of the online harassment incidence and to understand the phenomenon. The fact that this crime occurs in the virtual environment, guided by anonymity, innovation and versatility of the strategies of intrusion used, makes the understanding of online harassment and the study of the profiles of cyber victims more complex (Wolak, Mitchell & Finkelhor, 2007; Pratt, Holtfreter & Reisig, 2010).

After the explanation of the two bigger forms of cyber-crime and respective targets this chapter presents some contributions, which are focused on cyber-crime against people as an emerging topic of concern, especially among adolescents. The type of crime (against the person and their dignity), the population, the psychological and emotional damage, as well as the invisibility of this cyber-crime typology in the Portuguese penal code, justify the relevance of this approach focus. We also expect to contribute to the acknowledgement of the necessity to develop effective strategies at the preventive level.

CYBER-CRIME AGAINST ADOLESCENTS

Adolescence is a phase that is characterized by the need for sexual and moral maturity as well as the construction of identity (Subrahmanyam, Greenfield & Tynes, 2004). The complexity involved in understanding oneself leads to an increased curiosity on specific topics (e.g., sexuality) and to the need of adolescents to extend their interpersonal relationships (e.g., make new friendships with peers or adults) and to explore multiple social and relational contexts. As a result, their social activity and exposure to different interpersonal relationships is greater (Subrahmanyam et al., 2004). In order to broaden these opportunities for socialization and development, adolescents have joined cyberspace (as a complement to the real world), specifically social networks.

Concerning the American reality, the study of Pew Internet & American Life (Madden et al., 2013) concludes that one in four adolescents, between the ages of 12-17 (*N*=802) are "cell-mostly" internet users; they mostly go online using their phone instead of using some other device such as a desktop or laptop computer. Ninety-five of these adolescents used the Internet during 2012, 78% had a cell phone, and almost half (47%) of them own smartphones (Madden et al., 2013). In Europe, studies with adolescents suggest similar results. The network EU Kids Online (2011) concluded that 93% (N=25142) of European adolescents (9-16 years) access the Internet at least once a week and 60% access all, or almost every day, and the average daily time spent online is 88 minutes. The study also documents that 59% of adolescents are registered in a social network and within those active users, 26% have the profile in public mode. The most popular networks are Facebook and Twitter, but new types of social networks continue to arise and some, like Instagram or Pinterest, begin to engage many members. In Portugal, for example, 54% of adolescents use the Internet daily and about half of the adolescents above 11 years old have reported signs of Internet overuse (the second highest value in European terms) (Smahel et al., 2012). Smahel et al. (2012) also revealed that Portugal is one of the countries where more adolescents access the Internet in their bedrooms (67% vs. 49% of the European average) and where fewer parents access the Internet (30%), noting that youth population is the one that masters the use of IT. Based on these data, it is evident the great vulnerability of adolescents towards victimization and perpetration of negative behaviors in the virtual environment (Bilic, 2013; Wolak, Mitchel & Finkelhor, 2006, 2007).

The Internet seems to be a virtual laboratory and a stage for a series of developments and transformations in the process of construction of adolescents' identity (Palfrey & Gasser, 2008). One of the reasons for this increasing membership and digital enhancement may be the fact that adolescents perceived too many restrictions in the real world (e.g., need for physical confrontation, geographical and temporal limitation) and/or feel rejected by the social and cultural patterns prevailing in offline world (e.g., on the sexuality theme) (Palfrey & Gasser, 2008). Adolescents need to be constantly connected to their peers may also cause a greater adherence to IT and the establishment of an increasingly positive attitude about cyberspace. However, recent estimates on Internet usage habits suggest that adolescents are sharing an increasing amount of information at different public virtual environments (Madden et al., 2013). Based on these data, and bearing in mind that the virtual environment assigns a greater fragility to information disclosed (e.g., increases the potential for manipulation, falsification and misuse), it is understandable the greater vulnerability of these adolescents to the online victimization (Bilic, 2013; Wolak et al., 2006, 2007).

So, recent estimates on adolescence cyber-crime indicate that this is a growing and transversal problem (Marinos, 2013; Marinos et. al, 2011; Madden et al., 2013; Mitchell, Finkelhor, Jones & Wolak, 2010; Wolak et al., 2007) that may take different forms and involve several Internet resources (e.g., chat rooms, social networks, email) and mobile devices (e.g., image or text messages) (Child Exploitation and Online Protection Centre [CEOP], 2013; Haddon et al., 2012). However, there are still few studies on cyber-crime that answer the question of "how" and "why". Therefore the next section presents an analysis of predominant online risks among adolescents, seeking to answer the question: How do the conditions of access and use, as well as the cyber activities, constitute risk factors for adolescent cyber victimization?

Common Cyber-Crimes Typology and Targets

About 5722 (N=25000) European adolescents (9-16 years) already experienced one or more online risks, being Portugal one of the European countries associated with a moderate use and an incidence rate of low-risk online (Helsper et al., 2013). According to the EU Kids Online project, the risk exposure to sexual explicit material (e.g., pornography) seems to be the most common European threat (4 out of 10 adolescents have already experienced it). These data are in accordance with the previous European and international literature (CEOP, 2013; Wolak, Mitchell & Finkelhor, 2004; Wolak et al., 2007; Marcum, 2008). In addition, the viewing of violent content (e.g., maltreatment of animals or people, real murders, torture) seems to be experienced in a proportion of 1 in every 3 adolescents. Being the target of cyber bullying and cyber stalking, for example, comes in the fourth place (in a proportion of 1 in every 5/6 online adolescents), followed by being a target of unwanted sexual comments, reported by 1 in every 10 adolescents in Germany, Ireland and Portugal. Finally, scheduling offline meetings with someone whose adolescent just met online (another adolescent or adult) seem to be one of the less common risks (1 in every 11 adolescents) (Helsper et al., 2013). This victimization sorting is also the ranking of the most reported concerns by online adolescents – biggest concern to the exposure to inappropriate content, while they are less worried about the possibility of offline meetings with someone unknown – which may go against the trend of many parents and digital prevention professionals (which typically care more about the risk of contact with strangers) (Livingstone, Kirwil, Ponte & Staksrud, 2013).

On the basis of these data, it is possible to conclude that, once online, children and adolescents have high probability to find potentially disturbing material and expose themselves to violent and/or sexual content. These data must be analyzed in the light of the literature and studies on multiple victimization in childhood and youth (e.g. Finkelhor, Ormrod & Turner, 2007), taking an intersectional approach (e.g. Berguer & Guidorz, 2009). Studies in this field indicate a significant percentage of children who experience multiple types of victimization and suggest the cumulative risk of the disadvantaged children and young people (Finkelhor et al., 2007). The intersections of some disadvantage conditions (poverty, lower socioeconomic status, lower education) and socio-demographic characteristics (lower age, being a girl) may potentiate the risk of cumulative victimization in cyberspace. Girls, for example, are slightly more likely to use chat rooms and other communication platforms, being more easily targeted by unwanted messages and/or unpleasant questions (by strangers online) about their personal life. On the other hand, boys tend to play more online and show a greater tendency for the involvement in risk situations (e.g., hacking) and to the exposure to violent or pornographic content (Livingstone & Haddon, 2009; Helsper et al., 2013). Boys also seem to be more likely to achieve offline meetings with individuals who they only met over the Internet (Livingstone & Haddon, 2009). Similarly, it is important to highlight that, although older adolescents with a higher socioeconomic status can get access more often and longer to a greater number of IT, the experience of cyber-crime seems to be higher among younger adolescents with social disadvantages (Livingstone & Haddon, 2009). Such vulnerability is due to the fact that online victimization is related to the adolescents' digital literacy skills, which in turn also relate to the socio-economic level of the household and their respective countries' development (Livingstone & Haddon, 2009; Palfrey & Gasser, 2008). Older adolescents, who belong to more educated households and digitally more developed societies (e.g., United States) have greater probability to present digital literacy rates (e.g., possess greater knowledge and skills), which gives them a higher capacity of online risk management and of problem solving. These competencies are sustained by the formal (e.g., through schools) and informal (e.g., parenting) educational systems, which often teach safety skills to adolescents and emphasize their critical judgment. Instead, younger adolescents who belong to aggregates and to digitally less-developed countries tend to have lower literacy rates, lacking the number of teachers and guardians that are able to transmit the skills required for the use, management and prevention of the online risk (Palfrey & Gasser, 2008).

Once cyber-crime in adolescence is a complex and dynamic concept, encompassing a variety of ambiguous and controversial ways, it has not been easy to know the phenomenon of cyber-crime against adolescents as a whole neither to determine objective and static cyber victimization profiles (Marcum, 2008). Thus, it becomes necessary to develop more investigations in this area, as individuals and society give evidence of their digital development.

Factor Risks for Cyber Victimization in Adolescence

Despite the rise of cyber-crime threats, the understanding and explanation of cyber-crime is still at an embryonic stage of development, since there are limited investigations available with research focus on the adolescent phase and/or that privilege sufficiently comprehensive methodological approaches (e.g., quantitative and qualitative, with victims and offenders) for the understanding of cyber-crime. However, some authors have examined some risk factors – at situational, at peers and at individual levels - that may explain the greater vulnerability of adolescents (Helsper et al., 2013; Mitchell, Finkelhor & Wolak, 2003, 2007; Wolak et al., 2004; Ybarra, Mitchell, Finkelhor, & Wolak, 2007). Through the analysis of these factors and the exploitation of their interaction, we intended to provide a better understanding of the complexity of the adolescent victimization in the online world, and to compete for the opportunity to act in a preventive and increasingly effective way.

Cyber Lifestyles-Routines

Marcum (2008) examined how the online routine activities affect the probability of adolescents becoming online victims. According to this study, the sharing of personal information (e.g., name, address and pictures) is one of the risk factors that best predict the online victimization of adolescents. These results were consistent with other empirical studies that concluded that adolescents who spend more time online, participating in a wide range of online activities (e.g., social networks, chat rooms, games) and discussing sexual matters with virtual contacts, are also the most likely to encounter a online hazard (Helsper et al., 2013; Mitchell et al., 2007; Wolak et al., 2007; Ybarra et al., 2007; Sengupta & Chaudhuri, 2011). Virtual environments frequented by adolescents also seem to predict an increased predisposition to this victimization. More specifically, adolescents between 9 and 16 years of age (N=9904) are commonly subjected to inappropriate content (e.g., violent, pornographic), mainly due to surfing in video sharing websites, such as Youtube (32%). The general sites (29%) and the social networking sites (13%) and online games (10%) also appear to provide a greater risk of exposure to inappropriate material (Livingstone et al., 2013). On the other hand, chat rooms and other communication platforms tend to be often associated with the experience of unwanted contact by unknown users (43%) and the risk of conducts related to interpersonal violence (27%) (e.g., cyber bullying, cyber stalking, sexting) (Livingstone et al, 2013). This is precisely the principle supported by the routine activities theory (Cohen & Felson, 1979): the achievement of certain routine activities and the frequency of certain virtual environments are factors that may explain the victim's exposure and, consequently, the greater vulnerability to cyber victimization (Eck & Clarke, 2003). Risk opportunities arise when a motivated offender intersects, in an unprotected environment (e.g., no filters, blocking the window, low parental mediation) with a vulnerable target (Cohen & Felson, 1979). The fact that Internet broke through adolescents' lifestyles increased the process of changing their daily routine activities the likelihood of adolescents intersects with a motivated cyber offender. The fact that digital literacy at certain ages, parents-children generations and households could still be very incipient and/or uneven increases the likelihood of online surfing under low protection. Consequently, criminal opportunities multiply in adolescent population. Although the cyber victim and offender may never have interacted in the same physical place, the integrity of these theories would be ensured by the offender-victim interaction within a virtual unprotected network. However, it is pertinent to note that adolescents' vulnerability to cyber victimization does not result only from the simple convergence of the vulnerable target, the motivated offender and of the unprotected environment. In fact there are no data that support the suggestion that only just adolescents spend long periods of time online, and share information about them. Nevertheless, the risks that adolescents face is substantial (Palfrey & Gasser, 2008). As a result, there is a need to explore additional risk factors associated with potentially deviant peers or friends and individual psychological characteristics.

Deviant Behaviors and Association with Deviant Peers

The risky lifestyles, including the practice of crimes based on computer misuse (e.g. hacking), crimes against people (e.g., cyber stalking, cyber bullying) and the association to deviant cyber peers have been considered important risk factors for the increased experience of cyber-crime (Bossler, Holt & May, 2012). More specifically, the fact that adolescents had some friends who occasionally become involved in piracy crime or other illegal behaviors seem to increase the likelihood of these to also become involved in cyber-crime activities as an aggressor (Hollinger, 1997. Thus, there is a process of social learning and behaviors' imitation, as advocated by the social learning theory (Skinner & Fream, 1997). The prolonged coexistence with deviant peers leads to a constant exposure to criminal practices and to the possibility of transmission and learning criminal strategies. Access to cyber-crime software (e.g., hacking) is also facilitated, by a kind of social reinforcement between these peers to commit cyber-crime. Such cyber-crime is often assumed as legitimate and necessary (Bossler & Holt, 2009, 2010). However, this contact with the criminal world could have two mainly consequences: 1) the proximity to motivated cyber aggressors, and 2) the reduction of individual protection of adolescent (increasing the vulnerability to be a potential target). In the same context, the practice of offline and/or online harassment against other peers or individuals can also increase the risk of the offender become a cyber-crime victim. Given a previous harassment experience, some victims may exhibit high levels of reactive aggression, being able to carry out retaliatory attacks, through IT, against their aggressor (Sontag, Cleman, Graber & Lyndon, 2011; Ybarra et al., 2007). We can witness, in this case, that the roles overlap between victim and aggressor. For this reason, although there are certain factors that may be more related to victimization or online perpetration, it is not correct to dichotomize the standardization of risk factors, since the fact that a person became a victim may also explain the practice of cyber-crime (Jennings, Piquero & Reingle, 2012).

Socio-Psychological Characteristics

Livingstone et al. (2011) and Wolak et al. (2004) concluded that adolescents with psychological problems (e.g., depression, isolation), with relationship problems with parents and/or friends and belonging to minority groups (e.g., gay groups), are more likely to face the risk of contacts and grooming.

The personality traits, still incipient, and the socio-psychological characteristics also seem to influence the way adolescents interact with the online world (Olson, Daggs, Ellevold & Rogers, 2007). In particular, low self-confidence and self-esteem and poor social competence and problem solving, present a greater vulnerability for adolescents to be manipulated and to respond in accordance with the motivations of cyber aggressors, even developing strong emotional ties with their cyber aggressors (Livingstone & Helsper, 2007). These individual characteristics are advocated by the general theory of crime (Gottfredson & Hirschi, 1990). This theory conceptualizes crime as a result of low self-control, and there is a set of studies that corroborate this relationship (Buzzell, Foss & Middleton, 2006; Higgins, 2005; Higgins, Fell & Wilson, 2006; Higgins & Makin, 2004). Being adolescence a phase of development of the ability to control impulses, digital media can be a potentially dangerous tool.

In the online world, the metrics that matter to adolescents are how many "friends" they have on their social profile, how many comments they can attract to their Facebook wall and who is saying what and to whom, via the Internet (Palfrey & Gasser, 2008). This means that adolescents are focused on being accepted and on expanding their relations and competencies, regardless of the risk (e.g., sharing of private information). Accordingly, and regarding to the general theory of crime referred above, low self-control (characteristic of this age) leads to the adolescents tending to act impulsively (e.g., in order to achieve benefits and instant gratification), without reflecting sufficiently on potential risks and consequences of their actions (e.g., contact from strangers, legal punishment or retaliation attacks) (Bossler & Holt, 2010). Similarly, the low tolerance can lead to frustration among adolescents, with the complexity of many digital security devices (e.g., jammers of Windows, alarm systems), ending with the not regular update of these devices or even installing them at all (Schreck, 1999). The same is true, for example, in social networks, in which definitions of privacy and security are too complex and demanding for younger users. As a result, they surf the Internet unprotected, increasing their vulnerability to criminal victimization (Bossler & Holt, 2010; Forde & Kennedy, 1997).

Another individual characteristic of adolescents is the zeal for privacy. When they use IT and interact with content and virtual contacts, one of the normal procedures of adolescence is therefore to avoid any controls or parental supervision. However, the absence of monitoring and parental mediation is a risk factor that adds to the previously stated (Livingstone & Haddon, 2009; Marcum, 2008; Wolak et al., 2004).

As above mentioned, the type of online activities, the type of peers and the personal characteristics of adolescents' vulnerability are important components in order to understand the cyber victimization. Additionally, cyber-crime can be a "normal" and common experience in the daily life of adolescents, due to the growing need for adherence to new activities and exploration of new experiences of freedom, allowed by the virtual environment (Haddon, Livingstone, & EU Kids Online network, 2012). The investigation of risk factors based on lifestyles, peers, individual characteristics and routine activities of individuals is therefore crucial, and can provide important insights for designing situational prevention initiatives for the different types of cyber-crime against adolescents (Reyns, Henson & Fisher, 2011).

ISSUES, CONTROVERSIES, PROBLEMS

According to the presented information, the online victimization seems to be due not only with psychological and developmental characteristics but also with to the preferences and choices of the activities that adolescents do while they are online.

However, this assumption should not be reflected as a problem of the victims (i.e., was the victim that exposed herself too much) (Clarke, 2004). In fact, some forms of cyber-crime can effectively take place even if the victim is provided with digital protection systems (e.g., antivirus, antispyware and firewall). That is why the principle of the routine activity theory is subject to empirical controversy. If, from one point of view, Choi (2008) argues that the use of digital protection decreases the probability of a computer be target by malware, on the other, Reyns et al. (2011) state that, in the case of cyber stalking, for example, this method is not fully effective in protecting targets against unwanted contacts and threats. The same is also corroborated by Marcum (2008). In addition, some young people, because they are digital natives or because they have superior knowledge of technology, can alter security settings and/or filter preferences that their parents, teachers or educators have defined for their safety (e.g. against pornography). At the level of exposure of adolescents to pornography and other inappropriate content, one must still point out that often these experiences happen because the adolescents are looking for them. Although parents, educators and professionals in the field can choose to believe otherwise, a set of studies has documented that about a third of American adolescents (10-17 years) who were exposed to pornography were in fact looking for it (e.g., Wolak et al., 2007). The same is also true in the real world. How many adolescents did the educators surprise while viewing, on their own initiative, a magazine or a porno video?

Exposure to risk during adolescence is therefore a common reality, necessary and inevitable, extensible to the virtual world and the real world. Often, adolescents do not perceive these risks as an adverse situation, but as an opportunity to promote a moral development experience, and sexual identity.

However, experiences in the virtual world can differ from experiences in the real world, because: 1) the immaterial nature of cyberspace, 2) to the reduced probability of mediators (e.g., parents and educators) between the adolescents and the experience, 3) to the increased diversity of information available. While in the physical world educators may feel safer about the kind of content that adolescents have access, in cyberspace this awareness may be diminished. In addition, it is much easier to access disturbing information via the Internet, maximizing the chances of unwanted criminal victimization. The fact that cyberspace is a place where users can present themselves often in the form of an avatar (fictional character), or an anonymous user, leads to greater behavioral disinhibition, characterized by a greater sense of freedom, creativity, relaxation and sense of impunity (Blais, Craig, Pepler, & Connolly, 2008). Such characteristics may thus substantiate the greatest difficulty in reducing the online impulses and a greater propensity of adolescents, including female, to engage in socially objectionable activities (e.g., of cyber bullying, cyber stalking, identity theft), either as targets or as cyber aggressors (Finkelhor, Mitchell, & Wolak, 2000; Alexy, Burgess, Baker, & Smoyak, 2005; Curtis, 2012). Finally, we highlight that the impact of physical experiences can be confined and restricted to a time and a specific space, while the online victimization (e.g., cyber stalking, cyber bullying) tends to have uncontrollable proportions by the victim and being witnessed by dozens or thousands of users (e.g., colleagues, relatives, strangers). Take as an example the sharing of private information or victimization by cyber bullying: from the moment that the information and the insults are disseminated by IT, the adolescent has no control over its proportion, about who gains access to information and how it is being interpreted by others. In this way, the online environment can maximize the diffusion and impact of victimization, transforming the victim perception about these experiences.

Several studies have been documented the importance of parental involvement for the promotion of online safety of adolescents, for the critical use of ICT and for the crime prevention (Marinos, et al., 2011; Wolak et al., 2004; Whittle et al., 2013; Hertz & David-Ferdon, 2011; Livingstone & Haddon, 2009; Sengupta & Chaudhuri, 2011; Helweg-Larsen, Schütt & Larsen, 2012). The aim is not to implement a restrictive mediation or authoritarian posture, which limits access to information or freedom of exploration and expression of young people. On the contrary, it is intended to adopt a parental mediation that is fair and moderate (e.g., parents as a source of information and support before, during and after the online surfing) (Helpser et al., 2013, Marinos, et al., 2011). Teaching safety skills to adolescents, as well as instrumental tasks and/or information seems to be a crucial protective factor that helps adolescents to develop their digital and safety skills (Livingstone & Haddon, 2009). Teaching technological skills to professors and parents will be also necessary in order to overcome differences in the level of knowledge between themselves and the adolescents (Marinos, et al., 2011).

Regarding the difficulty in controlling impulses by adolescents while they are online, it is also important to reflect on that issue. Bossler e Holt (2010) in their study with university sample concludes that, while the low self-control has been associated with cyber-crime where the individual is the specific victim (e.g., cyber stalking, information theft); the same is not the case when individuals were victim of cyber-crime based on computer misuse (e.g., malware, identity theft). Consequently, the static vision that any cyber-crime (based on the specific target choice and on a random choice) is always a product of disadvantage and that people involved in cyber-crime present difficulties in terms of psycho-cognitive (e.g., low self-control), economics (e.g., membership of disadvantaged households) and/or social (e.g., isolation) skills, must be rejected (Clarke, 2004; Palfrey & Gasser, 2008). In contrast, this viewpoint can also be adopted when we are dealing with the scenario of perpetration (versus victimization) by an adolescent. Regarding an adolescent as a hacker or cyberbullying aggressor, for example, this cannot be also explained by adolescents' disadvantage but rather by the presence of sophisticated digital skills and higher social status among peers. The social learning theory approach strengthens this last idea focused on perpetration behaviors. Certain types of cyber-crime perpetration result of learning procedures, pursuit techniques, specific and advanced computational programming and monitoring, being the adolescents also taught motive, means and specific rationalizations that legitimize the practice of cyber-crime (Fox, Nobles & Akers, 2011; Skinner & Fream, 1997). In some cases, adolescents are extremely capable of assessing the risks and the potential consequences of their actions in the online environment, acting informed, conscious and controlled.

Another perspective that should be abandoned is the idea that all cyber aggressors (adolescents or adults) begin their online browsing with the goal of finding criminal opportunities (Clarke, 2004). In fact, the existence of many available criminal opportunities can easily attract people in general to commit situational crimes, whether they had the motivation or not. Take as an example the number of available literature – through books, journals, and websites – which enables, either children or adolescents or adults, to have a fast learning about new forms of cyber-crime to those who occasionally had access to this type of information. In this field, we must also point out that some risks and criminal opportunities that adolescents are daily exposed do not result necessarily from the characteristics of the context, the peers or the individual. Sometimes these results are caused by the way the digital design itself is built and how the designers design the use of virtual resources. The design of social networks (which contains thousands of adolescent users), for example, contains specific fields that encourage the sharing of a large amount of personal information. However, these pages can hardly guarantee the total privacy of user identity, or even the stability of the information disclosed. Although sometimes adolescents create their virtual identities thinking in a private and secure environment, the truth is that, due to the need for conservation and users attraction, the digital design allows the contact with unknown users, as well as the location (fast and free) of the social profiles, from the search engines available on the Web. This enables the rise of improper access to personal information, the augmented exposure to crime and the decrease of the notion of privacy and security. Everything that could be "our" is attainable by thousands of users, inhabitants of this global village that is the Internet.

SOLUTIONS AND RECOMMENDATIONS

Cyber-crime is common in modern society and in most cases committed by individuals who are socially integrated.

Towards digital protection of adolescents, we ought to invest more in the awareness of digital protection measures, complemented by a parental balanced mediation. Contrary to the notion of restriction, there is a need for a creative use, proactivity, consciousness and informed criticism of IT by the adolescents. In this way, the importance of initiatives of the academic community is reinforced (e.g., Social Adventure Project), such as telecommunications initiatives (e.g., New Project Genesis, index analysis of cyber-crime-Norton Cyber-crime Index), organizational (e.g., DADUS project, safer Internet Centre, SeguraNet project, MiudosSegurosNa.Net project) and the media, all of whom have developed important advances in online security and promotion of good practices of adolescents, without limiting their activities online.

Since the lower educational level and the lower socio-economic status are associated with higher levels of risk, it is recommended to investment in awareness and education to families, schools and less privileged neighborhoods, in order to increase competence in the use of the Internet and in the understanding of its risks. Schools present a leading role in digital education, as they may present resources greater than those of their parents, being therefore in a privileged position to educate adolescents in an effectively and efficiently way (Livingstone & Haddon, 2009). These forms of awareness should be adapted as new risks arise (e.g., via cell phone or other platforms of content generated by users), addressing both cyber-crimes types (based on computer and crimes against people). The ultimate goal should be the infusion of this knowledge in the general population (especially among the most vulnerable group, but also among the others). In this way, it prevails the need to redesign the current pedagogical proposal remains, to ensure the inclusion of a couple of hours centered on digital education. These hours could be included in an existing discipline or a curriculum unit set up for this purpose. With regard to the curriculum, these should focus on the development of digital skills, critical thinking and decision-making of adolescents, as well as the ethical, legal and safe use of digital media. This is the approach advocated in the CyberSmart Australian program. Nevertheless, we must recall the importance of preparing the teacher through awareness-raising and specific training on the subject. In this way they will be able to bring knowledge to the classroom and effectively prepare students for the new model of society: the digital society.

Regarding the cyber-crime prevention against adolescents, it is recommended to redesign the interface basing it on the video-sharing sites, online games, social networks and chat rooms. Since technology evolution, the economy, politics and culture shape the processes of diffusion and use of Internet, these digital protection mechanisms should also be the constantly developed and evaluated. A multidisciplinary perspective (e.g., psychology, criminology, economics, demographics, design) during the construction, implementation and evaluation of the effectiveness of the prevention strategies used is also crucial (Clarke, 2004).

One important role is had by the designers. Designers use their knowledge to understand the needs of users and the technologies available, to develop new products, systems or services that satisfy the needs and desires of consumers (Press & Cooper, 2003). Crime is one factor that occurs within this process. In many cases the ineffectiveness of designers to anticipate the vulnerability of their creations to crime or the use of those creations to commit criminal acts means that individual victims and society in general have to deal with a legacy of opportunities for crime (Ekblom, 1997). Therefore, it seems that designers belong to the group of professionals who are better placed to address crime issues. Pease

(2001) observes that designers are trained to anticipate several issues: the needs and desires of users, environmental impacts, ergonomic aspects, etc. As such they are the best placed to anticipate the criminal consequences of products and services and make easier to gain the technological race against crime. As such, design can be used as a tool to prevent crime, incorporating features in potential targets that transform the criminal event in a less attractive act for criminals and therefore breaking the criminal event. This could be done with a variety of mechanisms that need to be addressed during the design development phase (Ekblom & Tilley, 2000). Towards reducing criminal opportunities, Cornish and Clark (2003) have proposed 5 main techniques that are based on: (1) the increasing of the effort, (2) the increasing of the risk, (3) on reducing the rewards, and (4) reducing provocations and (5) on removing excuses. These main techniques present 25 sub techniques all focused on breaking the criminal event. These techniques have already been applied in the design field trough the Design Against Crime initiative (Design Council, 2002, 2003). Although this initiative had the focus on the real world, some studies had made particular correlations to the virtual environment (Wooton, Davey, Cooper & Press, 2003). One particular study by Wooton et al. (2003) had developed the crime life-cycle model to help and encourage designers to implement preventive measures in their creations. This model, that divides the criminal event in 10 phases, describes ways to address the crime, before, during and after the criminal event. Additionally, in the context of cyber-crime, Verma et al. (2012) have proposed several techniques to prevent crime that is in line with the concept of preventing crime trough design. These techniques are centered in measures to reduce opportunities through the use of authentication technologies, adequate language and placing alerts. Nevertheless, digital design, far from security software development, can also, create intuitive and secure virtual environments, by developing clean and not dubious virtual spaces. Accordingly, the digital manipulation of criminal opportunities can certainly decrease the motivation for crime, the rewards and increase the likelihood of identifying the potential cyber aggressor (causing changes in the criminal behavior).

In sum, the criminal prevention must focus not only on individuals, but also on interaction routines, design interfaces and on the control structures and incentives that are applied on digital users.

FUTURE RESEARCH DIRECTIONS

The subject of cyber-crime against adolescents has not yet been sufficiently explored in all its dimensions, although currently there is a growing body of national (e.g., Project Adventure, SeguraNet, DADUS Project, Internet Segura), European [e.g., EU Kids online network, Inform to Prevent Project (LEAD), ENISA, ClickCEOP button] and international studies (e.g., CyberSmart, Pew Internet & American Life Project) which focus their attention on IT use. More scientific studies are needed to estimate the extent and severity of this phenomenon in order to create specific structures to give appropriate answers to the needs of adolescents' victims of cyber-crime.

This domain, stresses the importance of participants selection be random and held in the community itself (versus clinical specimen or forensic), being also useful to opt for a decoded language and enhance the collection of data online, with adolescents. This investigator attitude will enable a better overall understanding of cyber-crime and provide a higher availability of teenagers to get involved in this kind of studies. In regard to ethical guidelines, it will be required to provide immediate answers aimed to the resources of the community, whenever an adolescent is in online risk.

Exploratory interviews with adolescents who are cyber aggressors and/or cyber victims are needed. Future investigations should focus on integrated and complementary methodologies (use of qualitative and quantitative design), as well as a constant dialogue between research and action. This will provide a greater insight into the motivations, the dynamics and the context of the occurrence of cyber-crime. An additional advantage would be the knowledge and understanding of existing problems in terms of digital design and difficulties and/or needs of victims when they are using the Internet. In addition, it becomes pertinent to investigate strategies that are more effective in responding to different types of online risk.

Based on this knowledge, the role of the primary sector (e.g., at the awareness campaigns level) may be more focused and efficient. Being Portugal one of the European countries in which the parental mediation is based on the application of restrictive measures on Internet access (Helsper et al., 2013), there is a need for further promotion of awareness-raising actions, among parents and educators: 1) a greater awareness for the potential that IT provide to education and psycho-social development of adolescents, and 2) improved skills for active parental mediation (e.g., through parental involvement).

We must reflect on the prevention of cyber-crime in general and on the online victimization in particular, since for example, there are currently more than 1 million Portuguese homes that already have mobile Internet access in which a few clicks stand between adolescents and adult content.

National initiatives such as the National Commission for Data Protection (e.g., through the Project DADUS, the creation of "Quiz na ótica do utilizador" and the self-assessment questionnaire of identity theft), the APAV (e.g., through its online page aimed at the safety of young people) and of the SeguraNet (e.g., through their activities, awareness-raising, promotion of videos and games), for example, must be valued and expanded. It becomes therefore important to continue to invest in the construction and dissemination of electronic platforms to support the population, as well as in the construction of specific guidelines for the self-assessment of risk. These are the current best practices which allow testing the knowledge of the general population and the level of awareness on how to use the computer and Internet services.

CONCLUSION

In recent decades society has seen profound changes in how to deal and conceptualize crime. Similarly to traditional crime, cyber-crime has brought with it a series of risks, insecurities and problems of social control, becoming a true test of social order and government policies, as well as a challenge for civil society, democracy and human rights (Garland, 2001). In this sense, this chapter is helpful to understand the social and psychological elements relevant to the domain of cyber-crime.

Empirical data indicates that cyber-crime can be a common experience in online adolescents' routine, due to the growing need to engage in new activities and explore new freedom experiences, allowed by the virtual environment (Haddon et al., 2012). Also, the economic and individual impact of this emerging phenomenon is being documented.

The type of online activities, the type of peers, and the personal characteristics of adolescents' vulnerability are components that can help understanding cyber victimization. However, it is important to remember that, despite some risk factors (e.g., online exposure, criminal association) and recommendations (e.g., information and awareness-raising) that were presented in this chapter are transversal to all age groups, socio-psychological characteristics that adolescents present make them a peculiar group. Adolescents are a risk group with needs (e.g., information, guidance) and specificities (e.g., developmental level) that are a priority at the intervention level. In this sense, further investigation of risk factors based on lifestyles, peer network, individual characteristics and an individual's routine activities is crucial, as it can provide important insights for designing situational prevention initiatives for the various types of cyber-crime against this specific and priority group: adolescents (Reyns, at al., 2011).

Nevertheless, the addressed controversies highlight that there is no single understanding for cyber-crime against adolescents. There is the increasingly need to conceptualize cyber-crime against adolescents as a product of interaction of the existing theoretical perspectives and of a multitude of intrinsic and extrinsic risk factors. This chapter advocates the necessity of field agents (e.g., psychologists, criminologists, digital designers) to conceptualize cyber-crime as a complex phenomenon that requires an integrative approach of different areas of knowledge.

As cyber-crime is transcultural, it also requires the effort of establishing more cyber-crime research partnerships between different countries, as well as a judicial and criminal recognition, in order to increase the success of the investigation and discourage the practice of this type of crime by its criminalization.

REFERENCES

Alexy, E., Burgess, A., Baker, T., & Smoyak, S. (2005). Perceptions of cyberstalking among college students. *Brief Treatment and Crisis Intervention*, *5*(3), 279–289. doi:10.1093/brief-treatment/mhi020

Almeida, A. N., Delicado, A., & Alves, N. A. (2008). *Crianças e internet: Usos e respresentações, a família e a escola*. Unpublished doctoral dissertation, Instituto de Ciências Sociais da Universidade de Lisboa, Lisbon.

Berguer, M. T., & Guidorz, K. (2009). Intersectional approach. Chapel Hill, NC: The University of North Carolina Press.

Bilic, V. (2013). Violence among peers in the real and virtual world. *Paediatrics Today*, *9*(1), 78–90. doi:10.5457/p2005-114.65

Blais, J., Craig, W., Pepler, D., & Connolly, J. (2008). Adolescents online: The importance of internet activity choices to salient relationships. *Journal of Youth and Adolescence*, *37*(5), 522–536. doi:10.1007/s10964-007-9262-7

Bocij, P. (2004). *Cyberstalking: Harassment in the internet age and how to protect your family*. Westport, CT: Praeger.

Bossler, A. M., & Holt, T. J. (2009). On-line activities, guardianship, and malware infection: An examination of routine activities theory. *International Journal of Cyber Criminology*, *3*(1), 400–420.

Bossler, A. M., & Holt, T. J. (2010). The effect of self-control on victimization in the cyberworld. *Journal of Criminal Justice*, *38*(3), 227–236. doi:10.1016/j.jcrimjus.2010.03.001

Bossler, A. M., Holt, T. J., & May, D. C. (2012). Predicting online harassment victimization among a juvenile population. *Youth & Society*, *44*(4), 500–523. doi:10.1177/0044118X11407525

Buzzell, T., Foss, D., & Middleton, Z. (2006). Explaining use of online pornography: A test of self-control theory and opportunities for deviance. *Journal of Criminal Justice and Popular Culture*, *13*(2), 96–116.

Child Exploitation and Online Protection Centre (CEOP). (2013). Threat assessment of child sexual exploitation and abuse 2013. London, UK: Child Exploitation and Online Protection Centre.

Choi, K. C. (2008). Computer crime victimization and integrated theory: An empirical assessment. *International Journal of Cyber Criminology, 2*(1), 308–333. Retrieved September 1, 2010, from http://cyber.kic.re.kr/data/Kyungchoiijccjan2008.pdf

Clarke, R. V. (2004). Technology, criminology and crime science. *European Journal on Criminal Policy and Research, 10*(1), 55–63. doi:10.1023/B:CRIM.0000037557.42894.f7

Cohen, L. E., & Felson, M. (1979). Social change and crime rate trends: A routine activity approach. *American Sociological Review, 52*(August), 170–183.

Cornish, D. B., & Clarke, R. V. (2003). Opportunities precipitators and criminal dispositions: A reply to wortley's critique of situational crime prevention. In M. J. Smith & D. B. Cornish (Eds.), *Theory and practice in situational crime prevention* (pp. 41–96). New York, USA: Criminal Justice Press.

Curtis, L. (2012). *Virtual vs. reality: An examination of the nature of stalking and cyberstalking.* (Unpublished doctoral dissertation). San Diego State University, San Diego, CA.

Dempsey, A., Sulkowsk, M., Dempsey, J., & Storch, E. (2011). Has cyber technology produced a new group of peer aggressors? *Cyberpshycology, Behavior, and Social Newtworking, 14*(5), 297–301. doi:10.1089/cyber.2010.0108 PMID:21162661

Design Council. (2002). *Evidence Pack. DAC case studies*. London, UK: Design Council.

Design Council. (2003). *Think thief: A designer's guide to designing out crime*. London, UK: Design Council.

Eck, J. E., & Clarke, R. V. (2003). Classifying common police problems: A routine activity approach. *Crime Prevention Studies, 16*, 7–39.

Ekblom, P. (1997). Gearing up against crime: A dynamic framework to help designers keep up with the adaptive criminal in a changing world. *International Journal of Risk. Security and Crime Prevention, 2*(4), 249–265.

Ekblom, P., & Tilley, N. (2000). Going equipped. *The British Journal of Criminology, 40*(3), 376–398. doi:10.1093/bjc/40.3.376

Finkelhor, D., Mitchell, K., & Wolak, J. (2000). *Online victimization: A report on the nation's youth (6-00-020)*. Alexandria, VA: National Center for Missing & Exploited Children. Retrieved May 10, 2011, from http://www.unh.edu/ccrc/pdf/jvq/CV38.pdf

Finkelhor, D., Ormrod, R. K., & Turner, H. A. (2007). Poly-victimization: A neglected component in child victimization. *Child Abuse & Neglect, 31*, 7–2. doi:10.1016/j.chiabu.2006.06.008 PMID:17224181

Finn, J. (2004). A survey of online harassment at a university campus. *Journal of Interpersonal Violence, 19*(4), 468–483. doi:10.1177/0886260503262083 PMID:15038885

Fisher, B. S., Cullen, F. T., & Turner, M. G. (2002). Being pursued: Stalking victimization in a national study of college woman. *Criminology & Public Policy*, *1*(2), 257–308. doi:10.1111/j.1745-9133.2002. tb00091.x

Forde, L. W., & Kennedy, D. R. (1997). Risky lifestyles, routine activities, and the general theory of crime. *Justice Quarterly*, *14*(2), 265–294. doi:10.1080/07418829700093331

Fox, K. A., Nobles, M. R., & Akers, R. L. (2011). Is stalking a learned phenomenon? An empirical test of social learning theory. *Journal of Criminal Justice*, *39*(1), 39–47. doi:10.1016/j.jcrimjus.2010.10.002

Garland, D. (2001). *The culture of control. Crime and social order in comtemporary society*. Chicago, IL: University of Chicago Press.

Gottfredson, M. R., & Hirschi, T. (1990). *A general theory of crime*. Standford, UK: Standford University Press.

Haddon, L., Livingstone, S., & EU Kids Online network. (2012). *EU Kids Online: National perspectives*. London, UK: EU Kids Online.

Helsper, E. J., Kalmus, V., Hasebrink, U., Sagvari, B., & Haan, J. (2013). *Country classification: Opportunities, risks, harm and parental mediation*. London, UK: EU Kids Online, London School of Economics & Political Science.

Helweg-Larsen, K., Schütt, N., & Larsen, H. B. (2012). Predictors and protective factors for adolescent internet victimization: Results from a 2008 nationwide Danish youth survey. *Acta Paediatrica (Oslo, Norway)*, *101*(5), 533–539. doi:10.1111/j.1651-2227.2011.02587.x PMID:22211947

Hertz, M. F., & David-Ferdon, C. (2011). Online aggression: A reflection of in-person victimization or a unique phenomenon? *The Journal of Adolescent Health*, *48*(2), 128–134. doi:10.1016/j.jadohealth.2010.11.255 PMID:21257110

Higgins, G. E. (2005). Can low self-control help with the understanding of the software piracy problem? *Deviant Behavior*, *26*(1), 1–24. doi:10.1080/01639620490497947

Higgins, G. E., Fell, B. D., & Wilson, A. L. (2006). Digital piracy: Assessing the contributions of an integrated self-control theory and social learning theory using structural equation modeling. *Criminal Justice Studies*, *19*(1), 3–22. doi:10.1080/14786010600615934

Higgins, G. E., & Makin, D. A. (2004). Self-control, deviant peers, and software piracy. *Psychological Reports*, *95*(3), 921–931. doi:10.2466/pr0.95.3.921-931 PMID:15666930

Hollinger, R. C. (1993). Crime by computer: Correlates of software piracy and unauthorized account access. *Security Journal*, *4*, 2–12.

Holt, T. J. (2007). Subcultural evolution? Examining the influence of on- and off-line experiences on deviant subcultures. *Deviant Behavior*, *28*(2), 171–198. doi:10.1080/01639620601131065

Jennings, W. G., Piquero, A. R., & Reingle, J. M. (2012). On the overlap between victimization and offending: A review of the literature. *Aggression and Violent Behavior*, *17*(1), 16–26. doi:10.1016/j. avb.2011.09.003

Kaspersky Lab. (2010). *Kaspersky security bulletin. Malware evolution 2010.* Retrieved October 21, 2013, from http://www.securelist.com/en/analysis/204792161/

Kim, W., Jeong, O.-R., Kim, C., & So, J. (2011). The dark side of the internet: Attacks, costs and responses. *Information Systems, 36*(3), 675–705. doi:10.1016/j.is.2010.11.003

Kraemer-Mbula, E., Tang, P., & Rush, H. (2013). The cybercrime ecosystem: Online innovation in the shadows. *Technological Forecasting and Social Change, 80*(3), 541–555. doi:10.1016/j.techfore.2012.07.002

Livingstone, S., & Haddon, L. (2009). *EU Kids Online: Final report.* London, UK: EU Kids Online, London School of Economics & Political Science. Retrieved August 10, 2012, from http://www.lse.ac.uk/media@lse/research/EUKidsOnline/EU%20Kids%20I%20(2006-9)/EU%20Kids%20Online%20I%20Reports/EUKidsOnlineFinalReport.pdf

Livingstone, S., & Helsper, E. J. (2007). Taking risks when communicating on the internet: The role of offline social–psychological factors in young people's vulnerability to online risks. *Information Communication and Society, 10*(5), 619–644. doi:10.1080/13691180701657998

Livingstone, S., Kirwil, L., Ponte, C., & Staksrud, E. (2013). *In their own words: what bothers children online? with the EU Kids Online Network.* London, UK: EU Kids Online, London School of Economics & Political Science. Retrieved August 10, 2012, from http://www.lse.ac.uk/media@lse/research/EUKidsOnline/EU%20Kids%20III/Reports/Intheirownwords020213.pdf

Madden, M., Lenhart, A., Cortesi, S., Gasser, U., Duggan, M., Smith, A., & Beaton, M. (2013). *Teens, Social Media, and Privacy.* Washington, DC: Pew Research Center's Internet & American Life Project. Retrieved September 10, 2013, from http://www.pewinternet.org/Reports/2013/Teens-Social-Media-And-Privacy.aspx

Marcum, C. D. (2008). Identifying potencial factors of adolescent online victimization for high school seniors. *International Journal of Cyber Criminology, 2*(2), 346–367.

Marinos, L. (2013). *ENISA Threat Landscape 2013. Overview of current and emerging cyber-threats.* Greece, Athens: European Union Agency for Network and Information Security. Retrieved January 30, 2014, from http://www.enisa.europa.eu/activities/risk-management/evolving-threat-environment/enisa-threat-landscape-2013-overview-of-current-and-emerging-cyber-threats

Marinos, L., et al. (2011). *Cyber-bullying and online grooming: Helping to protect against the risks. A scenario on data mining / profiling of data available on the Internet.* Greece, Athens: European Network and Information Security (ENISA). Retrieved January 30, 2014 from https://www.enisa.europa.eu/activities/risk-management/emerging-and-future-risk/deliverables/Cyber-Bullying%20and%20Online%20Grooming

McGrath, M., & Casey, E. (2002). Forensic psychiatry and the internet: Practical perspectives on sexual predators and obsessional harassers in cyberspace. *Journal of the American Academy of Psychiatry and the Law Online, 30*(1), 81–94. PMID:11931372

Mitchell, K., Finkelhor, D., & Wolak, J. (2003). The exposure of youth to unwanted sexual material on the internet: A national survey of risk, impact and prevention. *Youth & Society, 34*(3), 3300–3358. doi:10.1177/0044118X02250123

Mitchell, K., Finkelhor, D., & Wolak, J. (2007). Youth internet users at risk for the more serious online sexual solicitations. *American Journal of Preventive Medicine, 32*(6), 532–537. doi:10.1016/j.amepre.2007.02.001 PMID:17533070

Mitchell, K. J., Finkelhor, D., Jones, L. M., & Wolak, J. (2010). Use of social networking sites in online sex crimes against minors: An examination of national incidence and means of utilization. *The Journal of Adolescent Health, 47*(2), 183–190. doi:10.1016/j.jadohealth.2010.01.007 PMID:20638011

Olson, L. N., Daggs, J. L., Ellevold, B. L., & Rogers, T. K. (2007). Entrapping the innocent: Toward a theory of child sexual predators' luring communication. *Communication Theory, 17*(3), 231–251. doi:10.1111/j.1468-2885.2007.00294.x

Palfrey, J., & Gasser, U. (2008). *Digital born. Understanding the first generation of digital natives*. New York, NY: Basic Books.

Pease, K. (2001). *Cracking crime through design*. London, UK: Design Council.

Pratt, T. C., Holtfreter, K., & Reisig, M. D. (2010). Routine online activity and internet fraud targeting: Extending the generality of routine activity theory. *Journal of Research in Crime and Delinquency, 47*(3), 267–296. doi:10.1177/0022427810365903

Press, R., & Cooper, M. (2003). *The design experience*. Chichester, UK: John Wilet and Sons.

Reyns, B. W. (2013). Online routines and identity theft victimization: Futher expanding routine activity theory beyond direct-contact offenses. *Journal of Research in Crime and Delinquency, 50*(2), 216–238. doi:10.1177/0022427811425539

Reyns, B. W., Henson, B., & Fisher, B. S. (2011). Being pursued online: Apllying cyberlifestyle-routine activities theory to cyberstalking victimization. *Criminal Justice and Behavior, 38*(11), 1149–1169. doi:10.1177/0093854811421448

Schreck, C. J. (1999). Criminal victimization and self-control: An extension and test of a general theory of crime. *Justice Quarterly, 16*(3), 633–654. doi:10.1080/07418829900094291

Sengupta, A., & Chaudhuri, A. (2011). Are social networking sites a source of online harassment for teens? Evidence from survey data. *Children and Youth Services Review, 33*(2), 284–290. doi:10.1016/j.childyouth.2010.09.011

Skinner, W. F., & Fream, A. M. (1997). A social learning theory analysis of computer crime among college students. *Journal of Research in Crime and Delinquency, 34*(4), 495–518. doi:10.1177/0022427897034004005

Smahel, D., Helsper, E., Green, L., Kalmus, V., Blinka, L., & Ólafsson, K. (2012). *Excessive internet use among European children*. London, UK: EU Kids Online, London School of Economics & Political Science. Retrieved December 11, 2012, from http://www.lse.ac.uk/media@lse/research/EUKidsOnline/EU%20Kids%20III/Reports/ExcessiveUse.pdf

Sontag, L. M., Clemans, K. H., Graber, J. A., & Lyndon, S. (2011). Traditional and cyber aggressors and victims: A comparison of psychosocial characteristics. *Journal of Youth and Adolescence, 40*(4), 392–404. doi:10.1007/s10964-010-9575-9 PMID:20680425

Subrahmanyam, K., Greenfield, P. M., & Tynes, B. (2004). Constructing sexuality and identity in an internet teen chat room. *Journal of Applied Developmental Psychology, 25*(6), 651–666. doi:10.1016/j.appdev.2004.09.007

Symantec Corporation. (2011). *2011 Norton cybercrime report.* Retrieved October 15, 2013, from http://now-static.norton.com/now/en/pu/images/Promotions/2012/cybercrime/assets/downloads/en-us/NCR-DataSheet.pdf

Symantec Corporation. (2012). *2012 Norton cybercrime report.* Retrieved October 15, 2013, from http://now-static.norton.com/now/en/pu/images/Promotions/2012/cybercrimeReport/2012_Norton_Cybercrime_Report_Master_FINAL_050912.pdf

Vandoninck, S., d'Haenens, L., & Roe, K. (2013). Online risks: Coping strategies of less resilient children and teenagers across Europe. *Journal of Children and Media, 7*(1), 60–78. doi:10.1080/17482798.2012.739780

Verma, M., Hussain, S., & Kushwah, S. (2012). Cyber law: Approach to prevent cybercrime. *International Journal of Research in Engineering Science and Technology, 1*(3), 123–129.

Whittle, H., Hamilton-Giachritsis, C., Beech, A., & Collings, G. (2013). A review of online grooming: Characteristics and concerns. *Aggression and Violent Behavior, 18*(1), 62–70. doi:10.1016/j.avb.2012.09.003

Wolak, J., Mitchell, K., & Finkelhor, D. (2004). Internet-initiated sex crimes against minors: Implications for prevention based on findings from a national study. *The Journal of Adolescent Health, 35*, 11–20. doi:10.1016/j.jadohealth.2004.05.006 PMID:15488437

Wolak, J., Mitchell, K., & Finkelhor, D. (2006). *Online victimization of children: Five years later.* Washington, DC: National Center for Missing and Exploited Children.

Wolak, J., Mitchell, K., & Finkelhor, D. (2007). Unwanted and wanted exposure to online pornography in a national sample of youth internet users. *Pediatrics, 119*, 247–257. doi:10.1542/peds.2006-1891 PMID:17272613

Wootton, A. B., Davey, C., Cooper, R., & Press, M. (2003). *The crime lifecycle: Generating design against crime ideas.* Salford, UK: The University of Salford.

Yar, M. (2005). The novelty of "cyber-crime": An assessment in light of routine activity theory. *European Journal of Criminology, 2*(4), 407–427. doi:10.1177/1477370805056056

Ybarra, M., Mitchell, K., Finkelhor, D., & Wolak, J. (2007). Internet prevention messages: Targeting the right online behaviors. *Archives of Pediatrics & Adolescent Medicine, 161*(2), 138–145. PMID:17283298

KEY TERMS AND DEFINITIONS

Adolescence: Stage of human development that marks the transition between childhood and adulthood. According to the UN this phase extends between 15 and 24 years of age, while the World Health Organization defines adolescents as the individual who is between 10 and 20 years of age.

Criminal Victimization: To have been the target of some sort of crime that can cause discomfort and damage.

Cyber Bullying: A form of violence that involves the use of IT to commit repeated and intentional hostile behavior against a peer of the same context of the cyber victim.

Cyber Stalking: Default behavior implemented repeatedly and intentionally that is not desired by the target(s), with the use of IT. Some of the behaviors include routine and seemingly harmless actions (e.g., posting on Facebook, sending email), but also unambiguously intimidating actions (e.g., sending threatening messages, identity theft).

Digital Design: Focuses on the design of digitally mediated environments and experiences. It is centered in the development of digital platforms, web and mobile products.

Harassment: Unpleasant and unwanted behaviors that someone is repeatedly subject to, during a given period of time.

Online Risk: Likelihood of anyone being exposed to a danger or adverse situation, during navigation in the virtual world.

This work was previously published in the Handbook of Research on Digital Crime, Cyberspace Security, and Information Assurance edited by Maria Manuela Cruz-Cunha and Irene Maria Portela, pages 211-230, copyright 2015 by Information Science Reference (an imprint of IGI Global).

Chapter 18
Privacy Dangers of Wearables and the Internet of Things

Scott Amyx
Amyx McKinsey, USA

ABSTRACT

This chapter identifies concerns about, and the managerial implications of, data privacy issues related to wearables and the IoT; it also offers some enterprise solutions to the complex concerns arising from the aggregation of the massive amounts of data derived from wearables and IoT devices. Consumer and employee privacy concerns are elucidated, as are the problems facing managers as data management and security become an important part of business operations. The author provides insight into how companies are currently managing data as well as some issues related to data security and privacy. A number of suggestions for improving the approach to data protection and addressing concerns about privacy are included. This chapter also examines trending issues in the areas of data protection and the IoT, and contains thought-provoking discussion questions pertaining to business, wearables/IoT data, and privacy issues.

INTRODUCTION

Data privacy concerns are not new, but they are taking on an increased urgency as more wearable and Internet of Things (IoT) devices are used in commercial, public, and private settings. While companies may be partially addressing enterprise, consumer, and employee concerns about data privacy and collection, it is difficult to be completely prepared for the ubiquity of connected sensors that will rapidly become part of everyday life. This lack of preparedness can be seen in the innumerable data breaches that have resulted in lost consumer confidence, damaged reputations, stolen confidential business insights, identity theft, and litigation.

Technological solutions, such as firewalls and antivirus software, provide only part of the solution to the challenge of successfully managing wearables and IoT data. A change in the approach to data security on devices and on corporate servers (or in the cloud) is foundational to success: privacy must be a priority, and enterprises that engage in positive privacy practices will offer a unique differentiation

DOI: 10.4018/978-1-5225-0808-3.ch018

in the market. As argued below, companies that are serious about protecting data need to incorporate privacy into their business models, promote a culture of privacy in the workplace, empower a Chief Privacy Officer, become involved in standards-based consortiums, and develop an enhanced privacy policy that is easy to understand. All connected devices need to have software/encryption protections and enterprise storage of data needs to be secure and maintained.

BACKGROUND

The advent of the Internet of Things (IoT), sometimes referred to as the Internet of Everything (IoE), and wearables has had a tremendous impact on consumer and enterprise concerns about privacy. The IoT consists of any object that can be connected to a network, and wearables are clothing, jewelry, or accessories that can collect and transmit data about the wearer. The IoT is driven by M2M (machine to machine) telemetry, and although some consider these two terms to be interchangeable, there are important differences (see Polsonetti, 2015). In this work, the term IoT will be used to refer to objects, in or upon which sensors can be placed, and which allows them to connect to a network.

Benefits and Drawbacks

Wearables and the IoT come with a number of benefits and drawbacks. The benefits of these devices can be seen in the data they supply. Ubiquitous connected sensors and devices constantly recording, transmitting, and sending data create an enormous opportunity for businesses to generate detailed consumer profiles to improve marketing campaigns and engender increased revenue through targeted advertising. The data derived from IoT devices can also improve productivity in the workplace, as the monitoring of certain activities can give insight to management while enhancing innovation, cooperation, and safety practices at the individual and team levels. (For example, IoT sensors on equipment can indicate when a machine is being placed under great stress and may suffer a malfunction that endangers employees.) The utilization of data is beneficial on multiple levels: studies have shown that companies that are data-driven make more money than their counterparts, since more data yields increased insight and control (McAfee & Brynolfsson, 2012).

However, the ubiquity of the IoT and wearables creates serious privacy concerns, both for companies and for consumers. The theft of corporate secrets damages investment in R&D, brand image and corporate reputation, and revenue. The theft of an individual's data can not only harm the person, but it can also damage the company responsible for managing the data. For example, when Experian suffered a cyberattack that resulted in the data theft of 15 million T-Mobile customers, both companies had lawsuits filed against them (Larson, 2015).

The unfortunate truth facing most companies is that few wearables and IoT devices are secure. In fact, it is difficult to keep up with the evolving security needs of the technology, much less the protection of the massive quantities of data being gathered. Wearables and the IoT are therefore particularly large targets for data leaks or theft, and will continue to be so. This type of data is not confined merely to that given out by commercial fitness devices, such as name, location, step count, or heart rate. IoT devices and wearables are available for industrial, municipal, medical, and private use. Connected devices, such as those that monitor employee activities or those that regulate insulin pumps, broadcast a tremendous amount of data. The events described below show that a number of companies are not adequately addressing data privacy concerns; changes need to be made in order to preserve and promote corporate viability in the era of ubiquitous connected devices.

One industry study by Symantec (Symantec Security Response, 2014) showed that wearables data could be harvested by using a simple, commercially-available device (a Raspberry Pi computer). The data the researchers were able to collect did not have to be stolen from the devices, and the information that was collected included individual names, birthdays, passwords, and serial numbers. The researchers were able to monitor individuals based on the hardware addresses broadcasted by the IoT devices; indeed, the Symantec team also noted that 20% of the apps they reviewed did not make an attempt to hide or protect the data being collected, that is, they did not encrypt the data *at all*.

The enterprise management of consumer data in general must take into account the safety, perceptions, and abilities of the individuals providing the data. Managers need to be aware of the methods for managing the IoT and wearables in the workplace, and directly address the most effective means of utilizing them. The effects of poorly managing customer and enterprise data can be far-reaching. Since the impact of data security is so broad, complete end-to-end solutions are needed: suggestions for such solutions are described later in this chapter.

Consumer Privacy Concerns

Pew Research has shown that Americans are very concerned with privacy, and this concern took on a new fervor after Edward Snowden released government documents about the NSA's spy programs (Rainie & Madden, 2015). Hartman (2004) noted that over 90% of those surveyed about privacy issues want the government to legislate protections, even as a distrust of the government grows. Average citizens used to enjoy a degree of anonymity, but that is rapidly disappearing as data collection and aggregation increase.

Increasing disregard of an individual's privacy in the US is particularly troubling, as alarms are being raised about data abuse in the form of harassment for non-criminal issues; the public backlash that arose from the IRS misuse of tax information is one example of the snowballing concern over privacy (Goldfarb & Tumulty, 2013). In 2014, the Internal Revenue Service (IRS) disclosed that the agency had been targeting certain groups applying for tax-exemptions based on their perceived political affiliations. IRS workers were asked to flag certain keywords for non-profit organizations; a number of these key words were tied to perceived political views. It was also found that the IRS was also using donor lists from non-profits for audits (Judicial Watch, 2015).

Wearables and the IoT have a greater ability to collect even more detailed information about individuals, and this data can be combined with easily-obtainable identifying information to create a surprisingly in-depth picture of a single person's lifestyle, purchasing habits, belief systems, and social interactions. Indeed, Sweeney (2000) showed that only five pieces of information were actually required to uniquely identify approximately 87% of the population; pieces of information that can easily be obtained from a number of sources, including unsecured wearables and IoT devices.

Businesses that collect wearables and IoT data should be concerned about data privacy, since the last few years have been host to a large number of high-profile thefts of private data, including personal information, business emails and confidential information, and health and insurance records. Identity theft continues to be of particular concern to consumers (Finklea, 2014). The Bureau of Justice Statistics shows that ID theft is on the rise, and the cost of attempting to recover one's reputation is high (Bureau of Justice Statistics, 2011).

For businesses to get a better understanding of the best approach to privacy, it is important to view data security from the consumer's standpoint. Motti and Caine (2014) highlighted the particular concerns users had about wearable data privacy:

- **Infringing on the privacy of non-users:** Wearable device data can be synced online with social networks, revealing information about others. In many cases, this information is being sent automatically.
- Confidential information may be displayed on screens, giving others access to non-public data.
- Consumers do not have control over who views their information.
- **Surveillance and Sousveillance:** Outside intrusion into daily life though monitoring can be particularly worrisome; these types of monitoring are often associated with malicious intent.
- Head-mounted devices that collect audio and video information can provide an incredibly broad range of extremely personal data about others. Advances in facial recognition software make this a particularly serious concern.
- Clandestine audio or video recording.
- **Right to Forget:** There are some events in life that are best left in the past or that consumers want to forget; data, however, can be stored for a very long time, so consumers are worried that they may be penalized for a past event or mistake.

These issues are being addressed in some fashion or to some degree by corporations that develop wearables and IoT devices, but there is little industry cohesion. No enterprise is completely addressing all of these customer needs. Data breaches and leaks damage corporate reputations and brand images (Ponemon, 2011), and potentially expose businesses to customer distrust, new legislative actions and possible lawsuits. All of these concerns are related to fear---fear that personal information will be revealed to those not originally granted access, that more information is being secretly gathered than was originally agreed upon, or that multiple sources of data are being aggregated to develop in-depth individual profiles for malicious purposes. Consumers, however, have good reason to fear.

Data Breaches and Consumer Confidence

Data breaches have an effect on consumer confidence, and ignoring this effect comes with significant risks. It is important to understand that the repetitive nature of data breaches has caused a shift in public sentiment. There is a significant backlash to the gathering of data, and companies that deal with the IoT and wearables need to understand its foundation.

For companies that create or utilize wearable or IoT devices, security needs to be end-to-end: the device needs to be secure (e.g., the design of the device should take into consideration a safety measure in case it is lost or stolen, such as password protection), the data transmissions need to be secure (encrypted), the company culture needs to promote privacy protections (e.g., privacy policies and the promotion of privacy in the workplace), and the storage methods (whether at the company itself or in the cloud) need to be secure. Unfortunately, few companies use an end-to-end approach for privacy management--- though to be fair, it is difficult to provide such an approach. For example, one of the first end-to-end solutions on the market was TRUSTe's, which was launched in November of 2014 (TRUSTe, 2014).

The 2013 release of top-secret records showed that the NSA, and other spy agencies, was gathering large quantities of information about regular citizens through the PRISM program (Greenwald, 2013). The government, however, was not the only bogeyman. The records also revealed that nine large companies were helping aggregate information about consumers. Microsoft, Yahoo, Google, Facebook, PalTalk, AOL, Skype, YouTube, and Apple were all implicated.

This shock was soon followed by the revelations about the Facebook psychology experiment, which it executed on its unknowing users in violation of the rules of research conduct. In 2014, it was revealed that Facebook was modifying the news feeds of some of its users (about 700,000 accounts). The company wanted to investigate the impact of social media on users' moods by manipulating the number of positive or negative items available for view. While there was a significant uproar over the company's experiment, Facebook did point to its "terms of service" agreement, indicating that the experiment was considered within the scope of its interactions with users (Goel, 2014). Some users, however, felt that the company had violated what is considered a basic tenet of academic research: the informed consent[1] of participants.

While there are few hard numbers on the backlash over the NSA issue, it has been reported that almost 50% of the Facebook users that left after the experiment quit due to privacy concerns (Woolaston, 2013).

Large data breaches at companies are particularly damaging to the public trust, and have resulted in significant damage to the corporations themselves. In 2013, Target, for example, admitted the loss of at least 70 million records on its website while Home Depot in 2014 confessed that at least 53 million email addresses from its databases had been stolen. UPS admitted a breach in 2014, as did numerous other companies including Neiman Marcus, Dairy Queen, Goodwill, Kmart, and Staples (Hardekopf, 2015).

Wearables and IoT devices are also increasingly pushing into the realm of medicine. These devices provide targeted but highly personal information about a patient's well-being and needs. Since these types of devices tend to be more invasive than a wellness product, there is a great need to provide extremely secure environments for the data. However, hospitals, like other companies, have experienced dangerous "data hemorrhages" that have resulted in the dissemination of millions of patient records containing highly personal information (Johnson, 2009). The US Department of Health and Human Services maintains a breach report on the numerous data issues found at healthcare service providers[2]. Recent examples of data breaches include attacks on Healthfirst's patient portal (affecting 5,300 patients) and UCLA Health (affecting 4.5 million people); employee carelessness and outright theft were also responsible for the dissemination of personal information (Jayanathi, 2015).

Wearables, IoT, and the Workplace

The temptation to use the IoT to monitor every facet of a business is attractive, especially when small productivity gains in a number of areas can result in additions to revenue, reduced time to value, and positive, lasting change (LaValle, Lesser, Shockley, Hopkins, & Krushwitz, 2010). Should managers watch employees more? There are important reasons to utilize wearables and IoT devices in the workplace. Fraud prevention, cutting down on wasted time ("cyber loafing", or using company time to surf the internet), and fending off potential lawsuits are all reasonable explanations for the expansion of employee monitoring. There are also safety, productivity, and revenue gains to be derived from increasing monitoring in the workplace.

Employees are getting used to the idea of some type of monitoring at work, although most of the monitoring may come in more conventional forms than wearables or IoT sensors (such as cameras, ID badges with chips for access, and specialized software). Hartman (1999) noted that over 20 million employees were subject to some type of digital monitoring as long ago as 1993, and that number has grown as businesses find new ways to use technology to enhance productivity.

Wearables or IoT sensors placed on the body might, however, draw a different reaction from workers, since the addition of such devices to a person might seem extremely intimate or invasive. The other downside to monitoring comes as a link to productivity gains. Martin and Freeman (2003) noted that studies indicated productivity gains from monitored workers were often linked to high stress and poor health outcomes for those workers; greater stress on individual health led to missed working days and higher incidents of work-related injuries, such as carpal tunnel syndrome. Workers who see the monitoring as micro-management or distrust will not feel valued and may take action against what is viewed as tyrannical oversight. This is no small problem in regards to corporate data security--- a majority of data breaches (about 59%) are the result of employee or insider actions from within the company. Unhappy, careless, or misinformed employees are frequently responsible for theft or data loss, as shown through a UK government-backed research study (Bradley & Vaizey, 2015).

Enterprise Perceptions

Numerous companies have failed to integrate privacy concerns into their overall operations. Part of the issue lies in business perceptions. Technology is frequently seen as the answer to solving data issues, but purely technological solutions cannot address all of the complications related to data management and storage. Another issue is that companies frequently only *react* to data breaches: they do not have adequate safeguards in place to begin with.

Popular myths among small business include the idea that they are too minor to attract notice or that only companies with online payment exposure are at risk., Bradley & Vaizey (2015) noted, however, that small companies are particularly interesting targets for data thieves because they frequently operate on a shoestring budget but may have access to vast quantities of unsecured consumer data. The same study showed that that the leadership at such firms often indicates that there is not enough money to tackle the security issues or do not know how to begin to address security issues dealing with privacy and data.

Large companies may have more secure technological systems in place to protect data, but these systems are not necessarily completely adequate. This can be seen in the case of JP Morgan Chase: the company did not utilize a "common" two-step authentication measure that led to a massive data heist (Goldstein & Perlroth, 2015). Large companies face the increased chance of a data breach since they make such inviting targets, not just to disgruntled employees or domestic hackers, but also to foreign thieves. FBI director James Comey once famously noted that: "There are two kinds of big companies in the United States. There are those who've been hacked by the Chinese and those who don't know they've been hacked by the Chinese" (Quoted in Cook, 2014).

Another common misperception is that technology can solve privacy issues. For example, many companies have invested in antivirus software, firewalls, and other technology-based solutions. Unfortunately, IT departments tend to be small, and protecting data does not simply involve stopping a malicious attack from the outside. Companies may provide some server-side data protection, but may not be equipped to protect the actual wearable device in the hands of the consumer, or the IoT device with the employee.

Many data breaches occur from inside companies themselves, but even without inside help, data theft can occur at any stage of the gathering, sending, or retrieving process for wearables and IoT devices. For example, CISCO routers were hacked with malicious software ("SYNful"), so the firewalls and antivirus protections at companies or organizations made little difference in the data harvesting; the data thefts had apparently been going on for at least a year and had affected government and private organizations on three continents (Auchard, 2015). As noted earlier, not all wearables and IoT devices make use of security functions on the actual device or during the transmission of the data.

While the majority of companies have privacy policies and may take some steps to protect data through technological methods, such as firewalls or antivirus software, few have a comprehensive approach that affects every level of the organization and sets privacy as a foundational, driving principle. A multi-pronged approach is therefore needed for developing more reliable systems for data protection.

ISSUES, CONTROVERSIES, AND PROBLEMS

Two significant challenges have collided with privacy concerns. It appears that some companies are not taking data security seriously. This is particularly dangerous in light of the fact that the IoT and wearables sector is exploding. Many companies have at least some technology solutions in place to protect server-side data, as well as privacy policies that limit enterprise exposure to consumer litigation. However, these solutions are not adequate to address the immense data collecting abilities and ubiquity of the IoT.

Privacy must be central to a company's policies and activities at every level. It is clear that companies (and government organizations, for that matter) are not providing adequate protections for the data to which they currently have access, so it is unlikely that any company is prepared for the heightened protections needed for the data derived from IoT devices and wearables. Data theft is on the rise, and enterprises that use or provide wearables or IoT devices need to lead with privacy in order to survive and thrive. A number of specific concerns arise from these two challenges.

Limited IT/Security Budgets

As margins tighten and companies are belt-tightening, it can become difficult to focus on something as ephemeral-sounding as security---after all, there is no direct return on Investment (ROI) for any particular security implementation. This way of thinking is particularly dangerous in the area of the IoT and wearables, since these devices will be collecting data on a massive scale. There needs to be a significant alteration in the approach to data security. As seen in Motti and Caine's (2014) research, data privacy is valued for a broad range of reasons, but all of the reasons are related to a basic understanding of human nature. Extremely-limited IT budgets are not benefitting the company's bottom line if they result in a breach that causes customer flight or a loss of corporate secrets.

Increased Use of Wearables and IoT Sensors

Statistics on wearables and the IoT show the incredible growth and projected market worth. For example, the value of the market in 2018 was projected to be almost double what it was in 2015, about $12.6 billion (Statista, 2015). Few other sectors can match such growth, especially in light of the sluggish economy and recovery after the GFC of 2008. CISCO estimated that over 50 billion connected devices will be online by 2025, each one adding to a mind-boggling collection of data that will be transmitted, stored, and analyzed by a global army of private companies and public organizations.

While it is not surprising that advanced nations, such as the US, UK, Australia, and South Korea are speeding towards massive IoT implementations, it might come as a shock that African nations and other less-developed counties are quickly becoming a new market for connected devices (Nyambura-Mwaura, 2015). Wearables and the IoT are global issues, and companies of all sizes need to address the privacy issues related to them before suffering corporate setbacks and government regulation.

ENTERPRISE SOLUTIONS TO PRIVACY CONCERNS

A significant problem linked to data breaches lies in corporate approaches to privacy. Some industry leaders are beginning to address these issues, but these few advocates and processes are not adequate in addressing the realities of ubiquitous computing.

Technology Solutions

Many businesses use common technological safeguards for data, such as antivirus software and firewalls. They are also utilizing different forms of encryption to ensure safety. For example, public key encryption is currently considered a particularly useful option for protecting data. Public key encryption uses two "keys": a public one and a private one. Public key encryption can be useful in creating safer transactions, but it is not foolproof. Multiple safeguards are required to effect a reasonable technological solution to data breaches. However, a purely technological approach is inadequate since most breaches are caused by insiders: securing data therefore requires an examination of human nature (Anderson, 2001).

Monitoring and Company Culture

Using workplace monitoring can provide productivity gains, but it needs to complement a solid corporate culture that shows a respect for employee privacy. There are companies successfully implementing monitoring systems, but it can be difficult to draw the line between helpful data collection and stressful micromanagement that leads to disgruntled employees. In addition, not all work lends itself well to monitoring, for example creative activities such as design, programming, research, or modeling.

Research has shown that monitoring can result in stressed, unhealthy or angry employees (Holman, Chisick, & Totterdell, 2002) unless proper feedback and a solid, respectful company culture exists (Chalykoff & Kochan, 1989). While constant or excessive monitoring can lead to a host of problems, targeted, anonymous monitoring that provides employees support and feedback has shown to be useful--an indicator that company culture is vital to the successful implementation of any project. Employees perform best when they feel that the business is concerned about their well-being as well as protecting the privacy of the employees. It can, however, be difficult to effectively create a culture of privacy in the workplace, and this leads to employees who are either misinformed or do not care about privacy. This is where corporate leadership could play a key role in firming up enterprise security.

Leadership sets the tone for the company culture, so getting employees to engage in a greater understanding and compliance with data security involves management that perceives value in the person. Seijts and Crim (2006) showed that employees "reward" leaders with better engagement in the workplace when leaders can "connect", or show how they value employees. This same study highlighted a key problem in dealing with employees: a staggering 54% of them simply show up and do their job, while 17% are actively disengaged. Since most data breaches occur from within the company, leadership needs to move to create a significantly different environment.

Privacy Policies

The implementation of updated privacy policies is probably one of the lowest cost options for targeting security issues. However, many of these existing policies are extensive and employ legal jargon; they are confusing or simply seemed targeted at protecting the enterprise at the cost of the consumer. Much of the language can be opaque and open to interpretation (Dehghantanha, Udzir, & Mahmod, 2010). On the other hand, it is better to have a policy than not. The Symantec researchers who showed that large amounts of personal data could simply be harvested with some inexpensive hardware were discouraged to find that 52% of the apps they investigated did not have a privacy policy (Symantec Response, 2014).

Spending More, but Not Enough

While limited IT budgets are a common lament for small and mid-sized companies as well as for startups, it does not mean that no money is being thrown at security issues. In fact, businesses are spending more money on IT security than ever before. Gartner reported that in 2014, more than $71.1 billion was spent by companies to protect their computer systems from attack and expected this to increase as companies begin to take security issues more seriously (Gartner 2014). It is doubtful that these companies are taking into consideration the upcoming wave of IoT devices and wearables.

How much money should be spent on security and privacy solutions? Finding the right amount to spend is not easy, but the funding issues for computer security probably have more to do with what is referred to as the "wait-and-see" approach to data breaches---one that has cost businesses and consumers billions (Gordon, Loeb, & Lucyshin, 2003). For example, Google stepped up its investment in the protection of user data, but only after it was revealed that the company participated in the US government's information dragnet (Timberg, 2013).

Dealing with Exposed Security Flaws

Individuals and security firms are beginning to act independently to reveal security flaws in consumer products. While this can be beneficial in uncovering serious data leaks before a crisis, not all companies are responding in an appropriate manner. Enterprises have been poorly managing data hacks by "white hat hackers". For example, in 2012, a team of University of Southern California researchers built an app that could control a Volkswagen vehicle's computer systems remotely---an extremely dangerous flaw in the system design. Volkswagen sued—and obtained—a two-year injunction that forced the researchers into silence (Solon, 2013).

Volkswagen's response to the security issue is not unique. White hat hackers do not steal data and are commonly acting in the public's interest, but habitually end up facing lawsuits or jail time for their work (Jackson Higgins, 2014). The Digital Millennium Copyright Act (DMCA) and the Computer Fraud and Abuse Act (CFAA) are often utilized to bring charges against white hat hackers instead of attacking and fixing the security problem.

Little can be gained from attempting to prevent tinkering with consumer products with legalese, either. GM, for example, issued a statement that indicated that consumers who purchase their vehicles are "leasing" the software in them, opening up any tampering with the system to corporate legal action (Bigelow, 2015). Using lawsuits to shut down those who highlight serious security flaws is counterproductive and dangerous. These types of approaches also damage corporate reputation and brand image, since the public will associate the enterprise with a lack of concern for the public good.

FALLOUT FROM SECURITY BREACHES

The "wait-and-see" attitude cannot survive in the age of wearables and the IoT---companies need to address security issues and lead with privacy. By tackling these issues head-on, it may be possible to avoid or diminish the problems associated with the fallout from security breaches and data theft. Failing to deal with privacy concerns now means that companies will have to deal with losses in areas like revenue, resources, and brand recognition, as discussed below.

Loss of Revenue and Resources

The most notable outcome of failing to focus on privacy or data security issues comes in the form of lost revenue and wasted resources. Some companies have had bank accounts hacked or credit cards stolen, just as consumers have. Others suffer from the loss of secret or proprietary information that could have led to market domination. One example of this loss is the data theft that occurred at US Steel. US Steel had developed a proprietary pipe for extraction, which would have positioned the company well to take advantage of the US fracking boom. However, there was a sudden influx of Chinese pipe into the market, and the pipe was amazingly like that provided by US Steel---except it was priced to undercut the American company's product. The issue was brought to the attention of the US government and charges were eventually laid against a team of Chinese hackers. However, as the hackers are all foreign nationals, little can be done to undo the damage or reclaim the lost revenue (Talbot, 2015).

US Steel is not the only company who has suffered at the hands of foreign "black hat hackers". Westinghouse Electric Co. (Westinghouse), U.S. subsidiaries of SolarWorld AG (SolarWorld Allegheny Technologies Inc. (ATI), the United Steel, Paper and Forestry, Rubber, Manufacturing, Energy, Allied Industrial and Service Workers International Union (USW), and Alcoa Inc., have all brought charges against data thieves to little effect (US Department of Justice, 2014).

Breaches at companies are common, and it is possible to perform damage assessments. It is almost impossible to know how much information has already been obtained from unsecured wearable devices---but it is likely a large amount, considering that many computer professionals are well-aware of the security deficiencies of wearables.

For example, wardriving is the act of driving around and noting wireless access points (which are either hardware or software that allow a company's wearable or IoT devices to connect to the internet)—and it is not illegal (Hurley, 2004). The instructions for setting up a simple system can be readily found in computer security books or websites. Many wardrivers are simply experimenting and mean no harm, but there is no way to ensure that every person who starts harvesting user data is harmless. If an individual working on her network certification can scoop up unencrypted wearables or IoT data, so can competitors.

Damage to Brand Recognition and Corporate Image

In a bustling global economy, brand image and corporate reputation provide an edge over competitors. However, when it appears that a company has a lax approach to data security or that the consumer is not of central concern, the enterprise image and reputation suffer damage---and it is not always clear how long the problem will persist in the mind of the consumer. The high-profile data losses at Target have cost the company its coveted place as a leading mid-market retailer: a serious loss considering that then US First Lady Michelle Obama herself gave the company a boost by publicly shopping there. When Target customers were first made aware of the data breach, the company's profits fell about 50% in the quarter immediately after the breach, and the quarter after that showed a further 30% decrease in profits (McGrath, 2014).

Costly Lawsuits and Legal Actions

The joke about America being the "land of the lawsuit" is not particularly amusing, especially since data privacy issues are resulting in more legal actions against companies. While suffering the loss of revenue and reputation are serious enterprise considerations, lawsuits are quickly becoming one way to punish companies that do not take care of data privacy. A list called the "Top 20 Government-imposed Data Privacy Fines Worldwide" collated by the International Association of Privacy Professionals, (IAPP, 2014) shows that Apple received fines totaling $32.5 million dollars, Google received fines of $22.5 million, and Cignet health $4.3 million. Government regulating bodies are getting more involved in legal actions as well. The US Federal Trade Commission (FTC) is now actively addressing complaints that corporations are not providing enough security for consumer data, or lack appropriate privacy protections. For example, mobile device/app maker HTC failed to protect data and was successfully sued by the FTC on behalf of the public (FTC, 2013).

Increased Business Regulation and Legislation

Governments are beginning to broach privacy issues. Europe's Right-to-Forget laws, originally created to allow a second chance for convicted criminals who had served their sentences, were foundational to legal cases against Google; the company lost a key lawsuit from a man who wanted his past mistakes stripped from the search engine's results. Other suits are beginning to gain momentum as governments wrestle with managing the "right to know" with the "right to forget". These legal actions are only the beginning trickle of a tsunami of problems, and increased government oversight is fast becoming a popular topic among consumers.

Increasing government regulation is costly and intrusive, with the potential to severely limit consumer and enterprise protections from unwanted or unmerited red tape or legal actions. Doing business in a global economy means that foreign regulation is as important as domestic. For example, European data privacy concerns are already enshrined in treaties and in its proposed constitution: For example the Data Protection Directive 95/46/EC(European Commission, 1995) and Article II-68 (Protection of Personal Data: see Fuster, 2014). Business leaders also need to be aware of domestic legislation that is currently in the works to address the data privacy issues experienced by consumers. For example, a US senate subcommittee report, " (US Senate, 2014) that investigated online advertising and data usage clearly indicated that the senators felt companies are not responsibly providing data protections for consumers. One of the recommendations of the subcommittee was that

... the FTC should consider issuing comprehensive regulations to prohibit deceptive and unfair online advertising practices that facilitate or fail to take reasonable steps to prevent malware, invasive cookies, and inappropriate data collection delivered to Internet consumers through online advertisements. (p. 9)

What would be considered deceptive or unfair? What would the subcommittee consider "reasonable steps"? Would these issues be settled by how much money a company spends on security, or would there be a list of regulations requiring compliance? While it may not be clear exactly where the lines are drawn for advertising security, it is clear that the subcommittee is interested in increasing regulation. Stringent regulation creates difficult hurdles for businesses to overcome. Currently, there is no single set of federal guidelines concerning data privacy, but states and regulators have a broad range of rules.

The US National Association of Manufacturers (NAM) reported that regulations in the manufacturing sector alone cost about $20,000 a year per employee, and about $10,000 per employee in other sectors. Small businesses were suffering from these costs and were shouldering a heavier burden than larger, more established companies----they were responsible for a cost of about $35,000 a year per employee. The report showed that this cost tallies to about $2.028 trillion for businesses, and is comparable to about 20% of the average company's payroll (NAM, 2014). Additional regulation, especially that added to a small or mid-sized company, could be catastrophic.

SOLUTIONS AND RECOMMENDATIONS

The clearest path towards effectively managing data privacy concerns is to deal with them directly and to consider privacy as one of the key aspects of doing business. Privacy should be a part of the leadership directives, the company culture, the brand image and reputation, and should be implemented throughout the organization's technological approach. Protecting privacy differentiates a company in an evolving market. Moving past compliance to leadership is increasingly becoming important.

Privacy as a Foundation

Privacy should be a foundational tenet of every enterprise, especially as wearables and the IoT advance into every aspect of life. Leadership needs to develop a comprehensive approach and strategy for implementing privacy at every level of the enterprise. Business plans need to incorporate privacy, and mission statements should make it clear that the consumer, employee, and corporate data are being managed safely with a high regard for confidentiality. Since managers and other corporate officials set the tone for privacy management, top-level policy must prioritize data security, safety, and a concern for the individuals involved, both employees and customers.

It is important to see data protection in light of market differentiation: customers are more likely to appreciate an enterprise's product and services if they feel safe using them. Driving privacy commitments through *visible* leadership is one way that leadership can promote a respect for data security and privacy. Targeted employee monitoring solutions can be used in the workplace, with reasonable limits for data use. It is here that particular approaches such as data anonymization can play a simple yet effective role. Data anonymization involves collecting data that is stripped of identifying markers. For example, it can be used in an entire department in order to harvest useful information that can guide safety and productivity decisions without targeting a particular individual.

Company culture can make or break privacy policies and security implementations. Employees are always acting as representatives for the corporate brand as long as they are employed by the company. While non-disclosure agreements (NDAs) and other agreements attempt to prohibit employee divulgence of corporate information, the ubiquity of anonymous chat rooms and social media sites guarantee that not every worker will worry about dismissal for a disclosure. Showing employees the seriousness of data protection and then modeling the behavior creates employee-ambassadors that spread the word about a company's commitment. Company culture should incorporate the ideas of security and privacy. This includes promoting the idea that there are real people behind the data and that these individuals can suffer harm if privacy protections are not implemented or executed well. Promoting a culture of understanding is fundamental to success and getting employees to empathize with those whose data they manage is key to driving a positive culture. Leaks that occur from carelessness can be addressed through policies on data handling and through encouraging employees through incentive programs.

Involving customers in data privacy is important as well. Engaging customers through targeted communications, advertising, and conversations with company representatives can help bolster privacy and security. Customers that engage with the company on issues of privacy can then garner a better understanding of their own role in protecting their data. They also become exposed to the corporate approach to their data privacy, and this enhances the corporate image. For example, Disney uses a wristband with customer data on it that allows for access to its parks and attractions; the consumer knows what information is being gathered upfront. The company has noted that the wristbands are popular and have resulted in increased attendance (Palmeri, 2016).

Chief Privacy Officer (CPO)

A major recommendation is to create, and empower, a Chief Privacy Officer. Creating a position and a department that focus on privacy issues and data security concerns reveals a real commitment to protect consumers. The creation of the department enhances the corporate management of data security and privacy in three ways: the department can solely focus on security needs, it shows employees how valued privacy is, and it creates a positive view of the company in the eyes of the public. The department can also work with the IT department to make sure that the software and hardware concerns are being addressed in a timely manner. The CPO can manage continuing education so that employees are always current about privacy and security needs and concerns.

Privacy by Design Framework

A strong commitment to implanting secure measures at every stage of data management or transmission is vital. Implementing privacy into the corporate vision and business plan will help managers set reasonable targets for ongoing security updates and costs. One framework that is particularly useful is Privacy By Design, developed by Dr. Ann Cavoukian, who was one of the Information and Privacy Commissioners of Ontario. The framework stresses seven key supports[3]:

1. Proactive not reactive; preventative not remedial,
2. Privacy as the default setting,
3. Privacy embedded into design,
4. Full functionality – positive-sum, not zero-sum,

5.   End-to-end security,
6.   Visibility and transparency – keep it open,
7.   Respect for user privacy – keep it user-centric.

Clearly, this framework addresses the privacy concerns raised by Motti and Caine. By implementing a proactive, end-to-end strategy to protect data, it is possible to reduce the number of areas where data breaches occur.

Industry Self-Regulation

The best way to ensure data security and the standardization of protocols is to work with others in the same industry. Companies involved in the IoT and wearables are uniquely positioned to have a powerful impact on the direction of privacy standards. A number of industry organizations already exist that support standardization, protection, and advancement of secure devices and sensors. By supporting and becoming involved in these consortiums, businesses can ensure that they are not only in compliance with the law, but also that they are truly affording their customers the best in data security: belonging to, and taking an active part in, a consortium also enhances a company's brand image and reputation as a leader in data security issues.

Some of the better-known consortiums are:

- The AllSeen Alliance (allseenalliance.org) is one of the largest groups, and its framework is based on AllJoyn (an open source project created by Qualcomm Innovation Center, Inc.). Its members include companies like Microsoft, Qualcomm, Sony, ADT, AT& T, Cisco, Honeywell, and Haier.
- The Open Interconnect Consortium (openinterconnect.org) is dedicated to the principles of open source standardization. Its board of directors includes representatives from Samsung, Intel, Cisco, and GE.
- Industrial Internet Consortium (industrialinternetconsortium.org) is another non-profit consortium that targets the framework and direction for IoT devices. It was started by industry leaders AT&T, Cisco, GE, IBM, and Intel, and its membership includes hundreds of companies.
- OASIS (oasis-open.org) is supported by Microsoft and IBM, with sponsorships from a broad range of companies, including Adobe, Boeing, the US Department of Defense, Verisign, and Nokia.
- The Eclipse Foundation (eclipse.org) is working on creating a framework for the IoT. Google, IBM, Red Hat, Oracle, and SAP are all members.

Privacy Policies

In order to get the most out of privacy policies, the policies need to be easy to understand and include several levels that clarify or add detail about the enterprise's and consumer's rights and responsibilities. Privacy policies need to address some of the most difficult questions posed about IoT and wearable data. The policies should explain exactly what types of data are being gathered from devices and indicate the reasons for the data collection. How the data will be used, who will have access to it, and how long it will be stored all need to be included in the policy. Corporate privacy policies should be designed with opting out as the initial customer choice. Making privacy policies clear can be challenging, but it can be done.

A drill-down approach to content is best: the policy is first explained in simple, succinct language. Additional paragraphs can provide greater detail or legal terminology. One example of a customer-focused policy comes from Facebook. Facebook's Privacy Checkup tool is simple to understand and allows a granular level of privacy settings.

Managing Data Breaches

Data breaches will eventually happen on large and small scales. Corporate policy needs to address these issues with clearly defined steps and protocols. For in-house data security issues, the problem needs to be identified and fixed as soon as possible. For leaks of enterprise or consumer data outside of the organization, the company needs to have a public method for notifying the public, apologizing for the breach, explaining the situation, as well as its severity and expected outcomes. The steps the company is taking to remedy the problem should also be included.

Consumers may no longer want their data stored on a company's systems, but that may not be possible. Offering to remove identifying consumer data is one option, or creating a policy with a reasonable time limit for the data erasure is another. The nature of the data should be taken into consideration, as well. For example, if the database is storing personal health data along with a consumer's address and identifying information, the enterprise has the responsibility to consider the customer's privacy over the enterprise use of the data. Non-user data that appears in the database should be deleted; devices should not gather non-user data.

Employee Work-Related Data

Employee data collected while on the job may be anonymized, but what happens to that data when the employee leaves the company? Employees are concerned that data collected about them at work will be used against them for future employment. One option is to view employee data as having the same tenure as the employee. Employee data should be considered to be on loan for the duration of the employment; after an employee leaves or is terminated, the data must be erased as well.

DATA STORAGE

Data storage and management must take into consideration a variety of solutions. Data anonymization, which is the stripping or encrypting of identifying data, makes the storage of that data safer. Data minimization refers to only gathering and using exactly the type of data needed for a wearable or IoT device to effectively provide the service it needs to. For example, if a health wristband needs to show how many steps a user has taken, does it also need to collect the user's location? The data should then be removed after it has served its purpose.

Data Vaults and Private Clouds

Two secure storage approaches are currently garnering attention: the data vault, which is a kind of architecture that allows for the owner's control of the data, and the private cloud, which is set up behind the company's firewall and allows for enterprise control of data. Data vaults would allow for the maximum in user control while still permitting companies to take advantage of certain types of information; of course, these types of storage options would significantly reduce the amount of data that may be available to businesses. One business that is successfully using data vaults is. Consumers are able to manage access to data such as insurance information, prescriptions, and other types of healthcare data (Singer, 2012).

Businesses that find value in the cloud may want to go with their own private cloud, since it offers the same types of ease-of-use and services as a typical cloud service. Fujitsu notably uses a private cloud to allow for better data management. The company has 170,000 employees, and expects significant cost savings from adopting a private cloud (Fujitsu, 2012).

Local Data Storage and Home Automation Hubs

Local data storage in wearables and connected homes can deliver the benefits of the cloud, but do not transmit data over an Internet connection. Users of local data storage can securely access and manage their information, so these options operate in a somewhat similar fashion to a data vault---outside access would be limited to those the owner allows. Some wearable and IoT devices can also provide local storage solutions. One example of this type of wearable is the ReVault smartwatch: it allows for auto-synchronization across all of the user's devices while safely storing all private information.

IoT devices in the home provide a particularly tricky field for data collection, but newer technologies, such as the home automation system, are creating value for consumers and businesses. A home automation system stores and manages data within the home environment, such as data about energy usage or temperature regulation; this data collection can include data gathered from wearables. More on this emerging technology can be found elsewhere (e.g. LaMarche, Cheney, Roth, & Sachs, 2012; Samsung, 2016).

FUTURE RESEARCH DIRECTIONS

The possibilities for research in the areas of enterprise privacy approaches, data collection and aggregation, and wearables and the IoT are limitless, but there are a few key areas that are quickly evolving into viable fields of interest.

- Increasing litigation and consumer demands may curb or even result in the cessation of data collection for some enterprises. Who will determine the limits of the rights/responsibilities related to personal data?
- Emerging trends in data security include increasing attacks from both foreign domestic hackers on small and mid-sized businesses that utilize or sell wearables or IoT devices. Domestic wearables data breaches are likely to be the domain of local data thieves and corporate saboteurs for the near future due to the ease of data harvesting in public areas. How can companies address multiple threats, and how can they handle these situations when litigation may not be an option?
- Companies will need to face the increasing chance of both cyber terrorism and actual physical acts of terrorism. This type of aggression is already occurring in the US military: soldiers' family information gleaned from social or government sites has been used by foreign nationals to threaten military families in the US (Fantz, 2015). How will companies approach overall security for their customers and employees?

- Open source solutions will increasingly be used to provide enhanced security for small and mid-sized companies. What approaches can businesses use to engage open source solutions?
- What newer methods of data analysis can help limit the amount of data gathered and stored? These methods need to focus on and revise assumptions of consumer behavior in order to create better models and profiles.
- Greater government involvement is inevitable, as well as a push for global standards and protocols for data protection and consumer privacy rights. How can enterprises take the lead in effectively managing government involvement?

CONCLUSION

This chapter examined the challenges facing managers in regard to the increasing amounts of data derived from wearables and IoT devices. It offered insight into some of the questions concerning data rights, privacy, and solutions. Decision-makers and leaders need to make data security and privacy a foundational part of their business plan in order to protect enterprise and consumer data, enhance brand image and reputation, prevent lawsuits, and promote freedom from excessive legislation.

The IoT and wearables allow for massive amounts of data aggregation, but consumers are increasingly wary of the storage and use of this data. Past data breaches have proven that consumer fears about data misuse and abuse are well-founded. Companies that sell or use wearables or IoT devices will face data security issues at some point in their lifespan, regardless of the size or nature of the business. With this in mind, enterprises need to engage privacy directly through concerted leadership directives. They also need to design and implement a corporate culture that values privacy and the people involved, create a privacy officer position (or department), establish clearly-defined policies that provide for security, and methods for addressing breaches. Businesses need to get involved in consortiums and use data storage solutions that give the most protection to consumer, employee, and enterprise data.

DISCUSSION POINTS

Consumer Privacy

Consumers are willing to turn over some types of data when they see value in the return. However, the return on that data is typically temporary, while the aggregated data from devices can be stored permanently. What types of policies can be developed to help consumers understand the trade-offs? How can a company show its commitment to privacy? How should a company manage privacy issues in light of a lawsuit?

People in advanced countries are becoming acclimated to the idea of extensive monitoring and data collection. How will that affect enterprise data security? Should consumers have the right to demand access to enterprise databases if it is believed it would be in the public interest? Is a constantly monitored consumer the best kind of customer, or do people who know they are being watched behave differently than those who don't know they are being watched?

Employee Privacy

Monitoring some work activities can cut costs and boost productivity. Could monitoring be damaging creative problem solving, since thinking about a solution is rarely quantifiable? Will employee monitoring affect the quality of applicants that apply for positions at a company? Will monitoring encourage employee fraud, either through skirting the tracking of the device or direct tampering?

Collecting employee data can give insights into corporate functioning, but it also creates a profile of an individual worker. How can employees be protected from the creation of a detailed personal profile? Should they be? How much control should enterprises have over employee data? What happens to a company when employee data gathered from monitoring becomes public knowledge?

Enterprise Security

Most data breaches occur due to employee behavior, either through a misuse or malicious use of protections or policy. How might a company's policies currently address issues related to malicious use of data? Are there levels of malicious use that are managed in different ways? How do successful enterprises work to impede misuse of data through accident or carelessness? How effective are policies in addressing employee use of data?

Cost is a motivating concern in all data privacy issues, but it is extremely difficult to quantify data security's return on investment (ROI). How should companies determine security budgets? Should these budgets be explained at all levels of the organization? How much information should employees have about security issues? Would costs affect consumer perceptions of the company?

QUESTIONS

- How should managers approach data management/privacy?
- How will their approach affect the enterprise and consumer?
- Do companies really need to spend a lot on security, or does the size of the company (or type of data gathered) affect its likelihood of getting hacked?
- Wearable owners may be sharing their data, and that of others, unwittingly. Should companies have the right to track all wearable data?
- Who owns this data?
- What happens when a customer no longer uses the product?
- What are corporate responsibilities for the data privacy?
- How can these issues be managed in social, private, and work contexts?
- How can managers deal with employee rights and wearables?
- How long will data be stored, and what rights do companies and users have?
- What rights do other individuals have?
- How does location disclosure affect others? How does it relate to tracking or protecting others?
- How can companies head off data privacy issues and protect their image?

REFERENCES

Anderson, R. (2001). Why information security is hard - an economic perspective.*Seventeenth Annual Computer Security Applications Conference*. DOI: doi:10.1109/ACSAC.2001.991552

Auchard, E. (2015, September 16). Cisco router break-ins bypass cyber defenses. *Reuters*. Retrieved from http://www.bbc.com/news/technology-28602997

Bigelow, P. (2015, May 20). General Motors says it owns your car's software. *Autoblog*. Retrieved from https://www.gov.uk/government/news/cyber-security-myths-putting-a-third-of-sme-revenue-at-risk

Bureau of Justice Statistics. (2011, November 30). *Identity Theft Reported by Households Rose 33 Percent from 2005 to2010*. Retrieved from http://www.bjs.gov/content/pub/press/itrh0510pr.cfm

Chalykoff, J., & Kochan, T. (2006). Computer-Aided Monitoring: Its Influence On Employee Job Satisfaction And Turnover. *Personnel Psychology*, *42*(4), 807-834. 10.1111/j.1744-6570.1989.tb00676.x

Cook, J. (2014, October 6). FBI Director: China Has Hacked Every Big US Company. *Business Insider*. Retrieved from http://www.businessinsider.com/fbi-director-china-has-hacked-every-big-us-company-2014-10

Cyr, B., Horn, W., Miao, D., & Specter, M. (2014). *Security Analysis of Wearable Fitness Devices (Fitbit)*. Massachusetts Institute of Technology. Retrieved from https://courses.csail.mit.edu/6.857/2014/files/17-cyrbritt-webbhorn-specter-dmiao-hacking-fitbit.pdf

Dehghantanha, A., Udzir, N. I., & Mahmod, R. (2010). Towards a Pervasive Formal Privacy Language. In *Advanced Information Networking and Applications Workshops (WAINA), 2010 IEEE 24th International Conference* (pp. 1085-1091). DOI: doi:10.1109/WAINA.2010.26

European Commission. (1995). *Directive 95/46/EC of the European Parliament and of the Council*. Retrieved from http://eur-lex.europa.eu/legal-content/en/TXT/?uri=CELEX:31995L0046

Fantz, A. (2015, March 23). As ISIS threats online persist, military families rethink online lives. *CNN*. Retrieved from http://www.cnn.com/2015/03/23/us/online-threat-isis-us-troops

Federal Trade Commission. (2013, July 2). *Enforcement Case Proceedings in the Matter of HTC America Inc*. Retrieved from https://www.ftc.gov/enforcement/cases-proceedings/122-3049/htc-america-inc-matter

Finklea, K. (2014, January 16). Identity Theft: Trends and Issues. *Congressional Research Service*. Retrieved from https://www.fas.org/sgp/crs/misc/R40599.pdf

Fujitsu Limited. (2012, January 19). *Fujitsu Uses Private Cloud for Communications Platform to Integrate Global Communications*. Retrieved from http://www.fujitsu.com/global/about/resources/news/press-releases/2012/0119-02.html

Fuster, G. G. (2014). *The Emergence of Personal Data Protection as a Fundamental Right of the EU*. Cham, Switzerland: Springer International. doi:10.1007/978-3-319-05023-2

Gartner. (2014). *Gartner Says Worldwide Information Security Spending Will Grow Almost 8 Percent in 2014 as Organizations Become More Threat-Aware*. Retrieved from http://www.gartner.com/newsroom/id/2828722

Goel, V. (2014, June 29). Facebook Tinkers with Users' Emotions in News Feed Experiment, Stirring Outcry. *New York Times*. Retrieved from http://www.nytimes.com/2014/06/30/technology/facebook-tinkers-with-users-emotions-in-news-feed-experiment-stirring-outcry.html?_r=0

Goldfarb, Z., & Tumulty, K. (2013, May 10). IRS admits targeting conservatives for tax scrutiny in 2012 election. *The Washington Post*. Retrieved from http://www.washingtonpost.com/business/economy/irs-admits-targeting-conservatives-for-tax-scrutiny-in-2012-election/2013/05/10/3b6a0ada-b987-11e2-92f3-f291801936b8_story.html

Goldstein, M., & Perlroth, N. (2015, March 15). Authorities Closing In on Hackers Who Stole Data From JPMorgan Chase. *The New York Times*. Retrieved from http://www.nytimes.com/2015/03/16/business/dealbook/authorities-closing-in-on-hackers-who-stole-data-from-jpmorgan-chase.html

Gordon, L. A., Loeb, M. P., & Lucyshin, W. (2003). Information Security Expenditures and Real Options: A Wait-and-See Approach. *Computer Security Journal*, *19*, 2. Retrieved from http://papers.ssrn.com/sol3/papers.cfm?abstract_id=1375460

Greenwald, G. (2013, June 6). NSA collecting phone records of millions of Verizon customers daily. *The Guardian*. Retrieved from http://www.theguardian.com/world/2013/jun/06/nsa-phone-records-verizon-court-order

Hardekopf, B. (2015, January 13). The Big Data Breaches of 2014. *Forbes*. Retrieved from http://www.forbes.com/sites/moneybuilder/2015/01/13/the-big-data-breaches-of-2014/

Hartman, L. P. & Bucci, G. (1999). The Economic and Ethical Implications of New Technology on Privacy in the Workplace. *Business and Society Review*. DOI: 10.1111/0045-3609.00021

Holman, D., Chisick, C., & Totterdell, P. (2002). The Effects of Performance Monitoring on Emotional Labor and Well-Being in Call Centers. *Motivation and Emotion*, *26*(1), 57-81. Retrieved from http://link.springer.com/article/10.1023/A:1015194108376

Hurley, C. (2004). *WarDriving: Drive, Detect, Defend: A Guide to Wireless Security*. Rockland, MD: Syngress Publishing.

Jackson Higgins, K. (2014, October 21). White Hat Hackers Fight For Legal Reform. *Dark Reading (Information Week)*. Retrieved from http://www.darkreading.com/white-hat-hackers-fight-for-legal-reform/d/d-id/1316838

Jayanathi, A. (2015, September 1). 19 latest healthcare data breaches. *Becker's Health IT & CIO Review*. Retrieved from http://www.beckershospitalreview.com/healthcare-information-technology/19-latest-healthcare-data-breaches.html

Johnson, M. E. (2009). Data Hemorrhages in the Health-Care Sector. In R. Dingledine & P. Golle (Eds.), Lecture Notes in Computer Science: Vol. 5628. *Financial Cryptography and Data Security* (pp. 71–89). doi:10.1007/978-3-642-03549-4_5

Judicial Watch. (2015, July 22). *New Documents Show IRS Used Donor Lists to Target Audits*. Retrieved from http://www.judicialwatch.org/press-room/press-releases/judicial-watch-new-irs-documents-used-donor-lists-to-target-audits

LaMarche, J., Cheney, K., Roth, K., & Sachs, O. (2012). *Home Energy Management: Products & Trends*. Fraunhofer Center for Sustainable Energy Systems Marco Pritoni, Western Cooling Efficiency Center. Retrieved from http://cdn2.hubspot.net/hub/55819/docs/lamarcheetal_2012_aceee.pdf

Larson, E. (2015, October 7). T-Mobile, Experian Sued Over Data Hack Affecting 15 Million. *Bloomberg*. Retrieved from http://www.bloomberg.com/news/articles/2015-10-07/t-mobile-experian-sued-over-hack-on-15-million-customers

LaValle, S., Lesser, E., Shockley, R., Hopkins, M. S., & Krushwitz, N. (2010). Big Data, Analytics and the Path From Insights to Value. *Sloan Review, Winter Research Feature*. Retrieved from http://sloanreview.mit.edu/article/big-data-analytics-and-the-path-from-insights-to-value

Martin, K. & Freeman, R. E. (2003). Some Problems with Employee Monitoring. *Journal of Business Ethics*, *43*(4), 353-361.

McAfee, A., & Brynolfsson, E. (2012, October). Big Data: The Management Revolution. *Harvard Business Review*. Retrieved from https://hbr.org/2012/10/big-data-the-management-revolution/ar

McGrath, M. (2014, February 26). Target Profit Falls 46% On Credit Card Breach And The Hits Could Keep On Coming. *Forbes*. Retrieved from http://www.forbes.com/sites/maggiemcgrath/2014/02/26/target-profit-falls-46-on-credit-card-breach-and-says-the-hits-could-keep-on-coming/

Motti, V. G., & Caine, K. (2014). Users' Privacy Concerns About Wearables: impact of form factor, sensors and type of data collected [PDF]. *Financial Cryptography and Data Security Proceedings*. Retrieved from http://fc15.ifca.ai/preproceedings/wearable/paper_2.pdf

Nyambura-Mwaura, H. (2014, November 6). Africa fast off blocks in adopting Internet of Things - industry group. *Reuters*. Retrieved from http://www.reuters.com/article/2014/11/06/africa-tech-idUSL6N-0SW5O920141106

Palmeri, C. (2016, January 10). Why Disney Won't Be Taking Magic Wristbands to Its Chinese Park. *Bloomberg*. Retrieved from http://www.bloomberg.com/news/articles/2016-01-10/why-disney-won-t-be-taking-magic-wristbands-to-its-chinese-park

Polsonetti, C. (2015). Know the Difference Between IoT and M2M. *Automation World*. Retrieved from http://www.automationworld.com/cloud-computing/know-difference-between-iot-and-m2m

Ponemon Institute. (2011, November). *Reputation Impact of a Data Breach U.S. Study of Executives & Managers*. Retrieved from https://www.experian.com/assets/data-breach/white-papers/reputation-study.pdf

Rainie, L., & Madden, M. (2015, March). Americans' Privacy Strategies Post-Snowden [PDF]. *Pew Research*. Retrieved from http://www.pewinternet.org/files/2015/03/PI_AmericansPrivacyStrategies_0316151.pdf

Seijts, G., & Crim, D. (2006). What Engages Employees the Most, or the Ten Cs of Employee Engagement. *Ivey Business Journal*. Retrieved from http://iveybusinessjournal.com/publication/what-engages-employees-the-most-or-the-ten-cs-of-employee-engagement/

Shahnazarian, D., Hagemann, J., Aburto, M., & Rose, S. (2013). *Informed Consent in Human Subjects Research*. Office for the Protection of Research Subjects (OPRS), University of Southern California. Retrieved from oprs.usc.edu/files/2013/04/Informed-Consent-Booklet-4.4.13.pdf

Singer, S. (2012, December 8). Company envisions vaults for personal data. *New York Times*. Retrieved from http://www.nytimes.com/2012/12/09/business/company-envisions-vaults-for-personal-data.html

Solon, O. (2013, August 14). VW Has Spent Two Years Trying to Hide a Big Security Flaw. *Bloomberg Business Review*. Retrieved from http://www.statista.com/statistics/259372/wearable-device-market-value/

Sweeney, L. (2000). *Simple Demographics Often Identify People Uniquely*. Retrieved from http://data-privacylab.org/projects/identifiability/paper1.pdf

Symantec Security Response. (2014, July 30). How safe is your quantified self? Tracking, monitoring, and wearable tech. *Symantec*. Retrieved from http://www.symantec.com/connect/blogs/how-safe-your-quantified-self-tracking-monitoring-and-wearable-tech

Talbot, D. (2015, June 10). Cyber-Espionage Nightmare. *MIT Review*. Retrieved from http://www.technologyreview.com/featuredstory/538201/cyber-espionage-nightmare/

Timberg, C. (2013, November 6). Google encrypts data amid backlash against NSA. *Washington Post*. Retrieved from http://www.washingtonpost.com/business/technology/google-encrypts-data-amid-backlash-against-nsa-spying/2013/09/06/9acc3c20-1722-11e3-a2ec-b47e45e6f8ef_story.html

TRUSTe. (2014, November). *Beta Program for TRUSTe Data Privacy Management Platform Commences at Full Capacity*. Retrieved from https://www.truste.com/about-truste/press-room/beta-program-truste-data-privacy-management-platform-commences-full-capacity/

US Department of Justice. (2014). *U.S. Charges Five Chinese Military Hackers for Cyber Espionage Against U.S. Corporations and a Labor Organization for Commercial Advantage*. Retrieved from http://www.justice.gov/opa/pr/us-charges-five-chinese-military-hackers-cyber-espionage-against-us-corporations-and-labor

US Senate. (2014). *Online Advertising and Hidden Hazards to Consumer Security and Data Privacy*. Retrieved from https://otalliance.org/system/files/files/resource/documents/report_-_online_advertising_hidden_hazards_to_consumer_security_date_privacy_may_15_20141.pdf

Woolaston, V. (2013). Facebook users are committing 'virtual identity suicide' in droves and quitting the site over privacy and addiction fears. *UK Daily Mail*. Retrieved from http://www.dailymail.co.uk/sciencetech/article-2423713/Facebook-users-committing-virtual-identity-suicide-quitting-site-droves-privacy-addiction-fears.html

ADDITIONAL READING

Martin, K. (2015). Understanding Privacy Online: Development of a Social Contract Approach to Privacy. *Journal of Business Ethics*. doi:10.1007/s10551-015-2565-9

Martin, K., & Freeman, R. (2013). The Separation of Technology and Ethics in Business Ethics. *Journal of Business Ethics*, 53(4), 353–364http://link.springer.com/article/10.1023/B:BUSI.0000043492.42150.b6. RetrievedSeptember262015. doi:10.1023/B:BUSI.0000043492.42150.b6

Mun, M., Hao, S., Mishra, N., Shilton, K., Burke, J., Estrin, D.,... Govindan, R. (2010). *Personal Data Vaults: A Locus of Control for Personal Data Streams*. Presented at ACM CoNEXT 2010, November 30 – December 3 2010, Philadelphia. Available from http://www.remap.ucla.edu/jburke/publications/Mun-et-al-2010-Personal-Data-Vaults.pdf

Pa Pa, Y., Suzuki, S., Yoshioka, K., Matsumoto, T., Kasama, T., & Rossow, C. (2015, August 10). IoT-POT: Analysing the Rise of IoT Compromises. Retrieved September 26, 2015, from https://www.usenix.org/system/files/conference/woot15/woot15-paper-pa.pdf

Ryan, M. (2013, August 13). Bluetooth: With low energy comes low security. Retrieved September 26, 2015, from https://www.usenix.org/conference/woot13/workshop-program/presentation/ryan

Shilton, K. (2009, November). Four Billion Little Brothers?: Privacy, Mobile Phones, and Ubiquitous Data Collection. *Communications of the ACM*. 52,11, (pp. 48-53). DOI: 10.1145/1592761.1592778

KEY TERMS AND DEFINITIONS

Black Hat Hacker: A professional software and/or hardware thief who works to infiltrate systems for malicious purposes.

Cloud: Also "the cloud", referring to cloud-based computer services, or internet-based computing services.

Data Vault: A type of secure data storage.

Home Automation Hub: A central device that manages all of the IoT sensors or wearable devices in a localized area, usually a home.

Internet of Things: Objects that have embedded sensors that can connect to a network.

M2M: Machine-to-machine technologies, a term that is used to refer to a system that allows wired and wireless devices or networks to communicate.

Open Source: Free (or inexpensive) source code that is made available to anyone to copy and use.

Right to Forget: A key component of the European privacy laws that allows user information to be removed from certain Internet pages, such as search pages.

Wearables: Any object or piece of clothing with an embedded sensor or computer that can be connected to a network.

White Hat Hacker: A software and/or hardware professional who purposely tests or infiltrates systems to expose flaws in the name of the public good.

ENDNOTES

[1]   For more on informed consent, see the publication by the Office for the Protection of Research Subjects (OPRS), USC. (Shahnazarian, Hagemann, Aburto, and Rose, 2013)

[2]   The report can be found at ocrportal.hhs.gov/ocr/breach/breach_report.jsf).

[3]   see privacybydesign.ca and http://www.ipc.on.ca/images/Resources/7foundationalprinciples.pdf.

Chapter 19
User Authentication Based on Dynamic Keystroke Recognition

Khaled Mohammed Fouad
Benha University, Egypt

Basma Mohammed Hassan
Benha University, Egypt

Mahmoud F. Hassan
Benha University, Egypt

ABSTRACT

Biometric identification is a very good candidate technology, which can facilitate a trusted user authentication with minimum constraints on the security of the access point. However, most of the biometric identification techniques require special hardware, thus complicate the access point and make it costly. Keystroke recognition is a biometric identification technique which relies on the user behavior while typing on the keyboard. It is a more secure and does not need any additional hardware to the access point. This paper presents a developed behavioral biometric authentication method which enables to identify the user based on his Keystroke Static Authentication (KSA) and describes an authentication system that explains the ability of keystroke technique to authenticate the user based on his template profile saved in the database. Also, an algorithm based on dynamic keystroke analysis has been presented, synthesized, simulated and implemented on Field Programmable Gate Array (FPGA). The proposed algorithm is tested on 25 individuals, achieving a False Rejection Rate (FRR) about 4% and a False Acceptance Rate (FAR) about 0%. This performance is reached using the same sampling text for all the individuals. In this paper, two methods are used to implement the proposed approach: method one (H/W based Sorter) and method two (S/W based Sorter) are achieved execution time about 50.653 ns and 9.650 ns, respectively. Method two achieved a lower execution time; the time in which the proposed algorithm is executed on FPGA board, compared to some published results. As the second method achieved a small execution time and area utilization so it is the preferred method to be implemented on FPGA.

DOI: 10.4018/978-1-5225-0808-3.ch019

1. INTRODUCTION

The word "Biometric" is an ancient Greek word which referees to bio means "life" and metric means "measure" (Babaeizadeh et al., 2015). Biometric authentication supports three important factors of information security system. These factors are authentication, identification, and non-repudiation (Smith et al., 2013). Authorization and Authentication (Emam, 2013) are kind of security and privacy issues of biometric authentication system. However, a lot of research discussed this problem and tried to introduce many solutions to decrease the gap among security, authentication and security environment which prevents the spread of that technology. Biometrics (Jaiswal et al., 2011) is a set of technologies based on the measurement of unique behavioral or physical characteristics for the purpose of identifying or authentication an individual (Bandara et al., 2015).

Biometric authentication systems (BAS) are believed to be the effective technologies compared to the traditional authentication methods such as passwords, tokens and PINs (Tin, 2015) that failed to keep up with the challenges presented because they can be stolen or lost (Babaeizadeh et al., 2015), this means infirm security system. Authentication types can be classified under three different security field (Liu et al., 2001) such as Table 1 shows an overview of different authentication approaches:

- **Something you Know:** Something only you remember like password, PIN, or a piece of personal information such as (where are you born?) and knowledge approaches.
- **Something you Have:** Something only you possess such as a Smart card, Card key or a token approaches like a secure – ID card.
- **Something you Are:** Some biometric property.
- **Combinations:** (Multiple factors)

Biometric authentication classifications consist of two types Physical and behavioral biometrics (Jaiswal et al., 2011) as shown in Figure 1

- **Physiological Biometrics:** Based on data derived from direct measurement of a part of the human body and relies on something the users are such as fingerprint (Cao, 2013), iris (LI, 2015), face (ACO, 2015; Ghanavati, 2015), hand geometry (Guo, 2012), retina (Kochetkov, 2013; Javier et al., 2013) as well as Palm prints (Lee, 2012; Wu et al., 2013) recognitions.
- **Behavioral Biometrics:** Based on the user's behavior such as signature (Shah et al., 2015), voice (Rudrapal, 2012) and keystroke dynamics (Babich, 2012).

Table 1. Overview of different authentication approaches

Approach	Advantage	Disadvantage	Example
Knowledge	Effortless High acceptance	Forgotten Shoulder spoofing	Password, PIN
Token	Cheap Simple deployment	Lost, theft	Smart Card
Biometrics	Deter sharing Unique Unforgettable	Cost Invasive	Fingerprint, Voice, Keystroke

Figure 1. Classification of Biometric Authentication

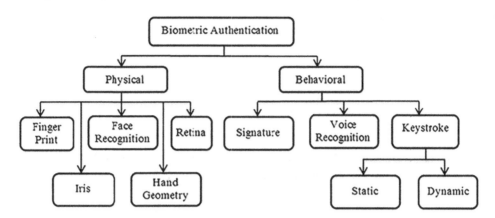

Personal identification methods are the most common mechanisms for authentication in may security systems; however, it is not a secure way for authenticating users. Moreover, most of the biometric identification techniques (Babich, 2012) require special hardware, thus the complexity of the access point and make it costly to the ordinary users or even to the companies. Keystroke dynamics (Rupinder et al., 2014; Monrose et al., 1999; Messerman et al., 2011; Peacock et al., 2004; Bergadano et al., 2002) is a biometric identification technique which depends on user behavior while typing on a computer keyboard (Kaur et al., 2013). It is more secure and does not need any special hardware to the access point.

Dynamic keystroke is the most apparent sort of biometrics available on computer components, but it has not yet led to real hardware security applications. However, keystroke dynamics can be an actual tool to access the computer resources and other related applications. In this paper, an algorithm based on keystroke dynamics has been chosen to be implemented in hardware. The proposed algorithm (Pettey et al., 2014) converts to a VHDL (V: Very High-Speed Integrated circuit, HDL: Hardware Description Language) (Ashenden, VHDL cookbook), then successfully synthesized, simulated and implemented on the Spartan-3E XC3S1600E (Spartan-3, 2015; MicroBlaze, 2007) FPGA (Field Programmable Gate Array) with the programming Xilinx tool ISE Web Pack 9.2i to discuss the possibility of implementation keystroke dynamics in hardware such as the others biometric authentication techniques.

The paper objectives are studying a new measurement biometric technique depend on individuals unique manner while typing on the keyboard called keystroke dynamics as a biometric authentication system and compare between this technique and the other biometric identification methods to discuss its merits and disadvantages.

An algorithm explains the user authentication through keystroke dynamics method is converted to VHDL then load this design to Spartan-3E XC3S1600E to be implemented on FPGA. This research illustrates that dynamic keystroke system can be implemented in hardware with acceptable execution time 9.650ns, the maximum frequency that the system can work with it, comparing to the other biometric identification systems such as (Iris, fingerprints, face, hand geometry, etc.,) which achieved a more execution time than the proposed design.

The performance of the biometric authentication system is measured through the following definitions:

- **False Rejection Rate (FRR):** Represents the percentage to reject incorrectly a legitimate user as a result of some variation in his normal type of typing (Tin, 2015) and can be calculated as the following Equation (1).

$$\text{FRR}\left(\%\right) = \frac{\text{No. of false rejected}}{\text{total No. of legal authentiction attempts}} \tag{1}$$

- **False Acceptance Rate (FAR):** Represents the percentage of incorrectly acceptance the user Impostors as a legitimate user. This type of error is caused by cheating and imitation on the system (Hassan et al., 2013) and can be calculated as the following Equation (2).

$$\text{FAR}\left(\%\right) = \frac{\text{No. of false\ accepted}}{\text{total No. ofimpostor authentication attempts}} \tag{2}$$

- **Equal Error Rate (EER):** Represents the percentage of the overall accuracy of the security system against other systems. It may be also referred to as Crossover Error Rate (CER) (Joyce et al., 1990).

The following Figure 2 has shown the relation between FER and FRR. These graphs "work against each other", so you must select the work point of the system at a location, where it will perform adequately, considering all parameters of the particular installation. Generally, the devices, by default, are set to the EER (Equal Error Rate) point, which is the intersection of the FAR and FRR curves. Whether this is good for a particular application or not depends on a large number of factors.

Figure 2. FAR and FRR relationship

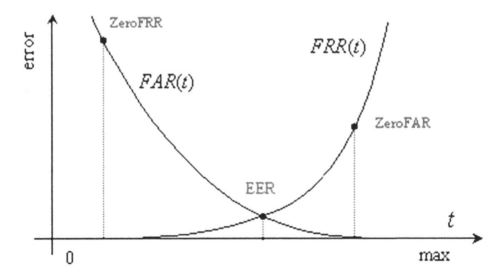

ZeroFAR: denotes FRR when FAR=0

ZeroFRR: denotes FAR when FRR=0

2. RELATED WORK

Cloud computing providers faced a challenge for the confidential contents of the customers. Providers should handle potentially millions of customers and this presents a challenge of security (Carlin & Curran, 2011).

This research is discussed to cover all aspects of biometrics authentication methods implemented in hardware and software. There is a lot of research also tried to make a hardware implementation of many biometric identification systems on FPGA or DSP such as the following. In (Giacometto et al., 2011) proposed an implementation of an algorithm characterization and correlation of templates created for biometric authentication based on iris texture analysis programmed on FPGA.

The authentication based on processes like characterization methods based on frequency analysis of the sample and achieved high accuracy of 96.52% and time of 16.11 ms. Wakil et al., (2015) presented an FPGA-based architecture for fingerprint recognition by using Xilinx System Generator which can be further implemented on all Xilinx FPGA gave high accuracy and can be used for high-security issues. Gayathri et al., (2013) proposed and improved fast thinning algorithm for Fingerprint Image implemented in MATLAB and simulation results of Xilinx ISE and Modelsim.

Based on two modules (binarization module and thinning module) their Experimental results showed that the algorithm is more efficient than the refereed algorithm systems according to the proposed architecture results.

Fatt et al., (2009) have presented a Digital Signal Processor (DSP) implementation of the iris verification algorithm. Using hamming distance method to extract the iris features based on texture analysis. Experiment results showed that the approach has achieved high accuracy of 98.62% and time of 198.96 ms. Kannavara et al., (2009) have presented a local-global (LG) graph methodology for iris-based biometric authentication. The global graph of the presented test image was compared with the global graph of the stored reference image and achieved high accuracy of 92% and time of 0.0149 ms. Poinsot et al., (2001) proposed a biometric system combines two modalities Palmprint and face. Hardware implementation of the Texas instrument digital signal processor and Xilinx FPGA platforms using Hamming distance algorithm and score fusion then have time 0.4 ms.

Liu et al., (2006) have proposed a hardware implementation based on FPGA for an iris biometric processor. By this solution, a reduction of the processing time is obtained and security levels of the whole system are increased due to the reduction of software involved and achieved high accuracy of 88% and time of 2.725 ms.

Rakvic et al., (2009) have provided novel hardware implementations which enabled us to discover that three key portions of an iris recognition algorithm can be parallelized. The main result is that the implementation on a modest sized FPGA is approximately 9.6, 324, and 19 times faster than a state-of-the-art in their research and achieved a time of 0.002 ms. Vijayalami et al., (2012) have presented a generic, flexible parallel architecture, which is suitable for all ranges of object detection applications and image sizes. The proposed architecture implemented the AdaBoost-based detection algorithm, which is one of the most efficient object detection algorithms and achieved minimum period 15.30 ns.

Zhao et al., (2009) have described an embed iris recognition system for the personal identification they used only one DSP core which completed image acquisition, image processing, and communication with the peripheral circuits. The model system not only reduced costs, shorten the development cycle. It also provided a good running platform for the high-speed image processing achieved a time of 471.56 ms. Vatsa et al., (2009) have presented an accurate non-ideal iris segmentation using the modified Mumford-Shah functional. Depending on the type of abnormalities to be encountered during image capture, a set of global image enhancement algorithms was applied to the iris image.

While this enhances the low-quality regions, it also added undesirable artifacts in the original high-quality regions of the iris image achieved an accuracy of 97.21% and 1.82 ms.

In Hu et al., (2010) have showed a study of Iris Identification in authentication techniques. Most modern iris recognition systems were deployed on traditional sequential digital systems, such as simple DSPs and data matched one by one, which wasted much time. In their study, iris matching considered the executed portion of a modern iris recognition algorithm parallelized on an FPGA system demonstrated a 22 times speedup of the parallelized algorithm on the FPGA system when compared to simple DSPs and got out 32 us and this is a great time different.

Ting-Yi et al., (2012) have proposed a graphical-based password keystroke dynamic-based authentication system for touch screen mobile devices. A user enters the graphical password through a human–computer interface therefore the user's keystroke features would not be affected if the user used different devices. The experiment results are reduced EER to 6.9% when the pressure feature was used in the proposed system compared with related algorithms in mobile devices and achieved EER about 12.2% in the graphical-based password KDA proposed system.

Giot et al., (2015) have proposed several benchmark datasets for keystroke dynamics in the literature. They differed in a lot of ways and the performance of the algorithms under evaluation. The review analysis is showed a great disparity in the acquisition protocol, the population, the passwords complexity and the performance (the relative difference of 76% between the EER on the worst and best algorithms performing datasets with the same authentication technique).

Dougan and Curran (2012) have examined the capability of one type of attacks named as "Man-in-the-Browser attacks" and the method; which can be used by this attack, to be executed. They also descried the data interaction techniques of these attacks, and methods which could be used for fudging security. Finally, the authors proved the effectiveness of counter- Man-in-the-Middle strategies, and showed how could be estimated upon what could these attacks tell us about the Internet environment.

Montalvão et al., (2015) have addressed three publicly available datasets were used to empirically and answered to many questions. Their results about all subjects tended to write a given password in a similar rhythm was more strongly related to the sequence of characters itself than to the subject (user-independent rhythm profile) should not be regarded as a threat to biometric applications and they noticed that two habituation phenomena, through both short-term and long-term rhythmic pattern convergences toward the former mentioned central rhythmic pattern.

Xuan et al., (2012) have proposed approach consists of two stages, a training stage and an authentication stage. In the training stage, a set of orthogonal bases and a common feature vector are periodically generated from keystroke features of a legal user's. In the authentication stage, the current feature vector of keystroke was projected onto the set of orthogonal bases and the distortion of the feature vector between its projections was obtained. User authentication is implemented by comparing the slope correlation degree of the distortion between the common feature vector with a threshold determined periodically using the recent impostor patterns. Experimental results are showed that the proposed method achieved a better performance in terms of FAR and FRR in comparison with some recent methods.

The mathematical approaches to keystroke analysis can be divided into the following techniques (Statistical and Neural Networks). These techniques are not all the existing methods but they explained the terminology of summary of the main research approaches of keystroke such as:

1. **Statistical Approach:** Statistical methods of keystroke dynamics are the most common study thoroughfare within that field. The basic statistical features like the median, mean and standard deviation (Modi et al., 2006; Revett et al., 2006; Revett et al., 2005) of keystroke timings were used because this method is low overhead, ease of implementation and the simplicity
2. **Neural Networks:** Is a technique that emulates the biological artificial neuronal network (ANN) for information processing. ANN has used the timing features between successive keystrokes. These keystroke timings are computed through the network comparator to validate the data, in order to determine whether the user is authentic or not (Uzun & Bicakci, 2012).

Table 2 illustrates each approach (statistical or neural network) of the studies since (1990 until 2014), classification of the keystroke (static or dynamic) used in this study, number of the participated users and the percentage of FAR and FRR values.

Table 2. Summary of the main research approaches of keystroke

Study	Mathematical Techniques			Users	FAR (%)		FRR (%)	
Joyce & Gupta (1990)	Static	Statistical		33	0.25		16.36	
Leggett et al. (1991)	Dynamic	Statistical		36	12.8		11.1	
Brown & Rogers (1993)	Static	Neural Network		25	0		12.0	
Bleha & Obaidat (1993)	Static	Neural Network		24	8		9	
Napier et al (1995)	Dynamic	Statistical		24	3.8 (Combined)			
Obaidat & Sadoun (1997)	Static	Statistical	Neural Network	15	0.7	0	1.9	0
Monrose& Rubin (1999)	Static	Statistical		63	7.9 (Combined)			
Cho et al., (2000)	Static	Neural Network		21	0		1	
Ord & Furnell (2000)	Static	Neural Network		14	9.9		30	
Bergadano et al. (2002)	Static	Statistical		154	0.01		4	
Guven & Sogukpinar (2003)	Static	Statistical		12	1		10.7	
Sogukpinar & Yalcin (2004)	Static	Statistical		40	0.6		60	

continued on following page

Table 2. Continued

Study	Mathematical Techniques		Users	FAR (%)	FRR (%)
Yu & Cho (2004)	Static	Neural Network	21	0	3.69
Gunetti & Picardi (2005)	dynamic	Neural Network	205	0.005	5
Clarke & Furnell (2007)	Static	Neural Network	32	5 (Equal Error Rate)	
Lee & Cho (2007)	dynamic	Neural Network	21	0.43 (Average Integrated Errors)	
Grabham et al., (2008)	Static	Statistical	30	15	0
Campisi et al., (2009)	Static	Statistical	30	EER: 13	
Douhou et al., (2009)	Static	statistical	1254	16	1
Davoudi et al., (2009)	Static	Statistical	21	0.14	1.59
Giot et al., (2009)	Static	Statistical	16	EER: 4.28	
Killourhy et al., (2010)	Static	Statistical	51	EER: 7.1	
Samura et al., (2011)	Static	Statistical	189	0.01	3
Kaneko et al., (2011)	Static	Statistical	51	EER: 0.84	
Singh et al., (2011)	Static	Statistical	20	2	4
Rahman et al., (2011)	Static	Statistical	50	EER: 10	
Xi et al., (2011)	Static	Statistical	186	1.65	2.75
Johansen (2012)	Static	Statistical	42	--	--
Monaco et al., (2013	Static	Machine Learning	40	Accuracy: 88.2	
Trojahn et al., (2013)	Static	Machine Learning	152	4.19	4.59
Gascon et al., (2014)	Static	Machine Learning	300	--	--
Jain et al., (2014)	Static	Machine Learning	30	EER: 10.5	
Nisha et al., (2014)	Static	Neural Network	--	Accuracy: 93.5	
Wankhede et al., (2014)	Static	Neural Network	--	4.8	3.1
Draffin et al., (2014)	Static	Neural Network	13	14	2.2

3. METHODOLOGY FRAMEWORK

Firstly, the developed software, using Java language, is an easy-to-use programming language that can be embedded in the header of your web pages. It can enhance the dynamics and interactive features of your page by allowing you to perform calculations, check forms, add special effects, customize graphics selections and create security passwords. Firstly, the developed software is using to capture the user keystroke features while typing. The output of this stage is each digraph of the user password with its duration time. This information is used for the next step.

Secondly, Xilinx ISE-9.2i is utilized for the synthesis, simulation, implementation, place/route and finally for area analysis processes. Regarding the power consumption estimations, we make use of the XPower estimator provided by Xilinx.

4. PROPOSED ALGORITHM

The proposed system consists of two phases. Enrollment phase and Log in phase, as Figure 3 shown, each phase satisfied a part of the authentication phase to test the ability of the system described in the proposed algorithm to distinguish users while they are typing their password.

Figure 3. Architecture of the proposed algorithm

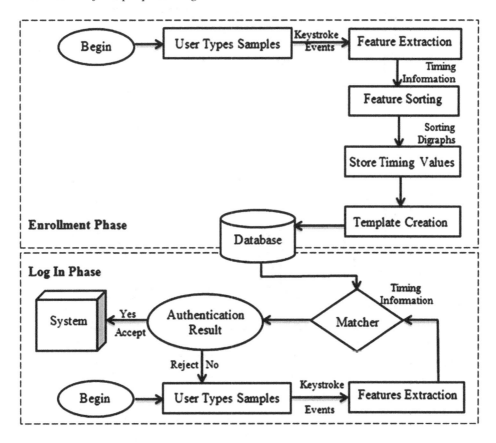

5. ENROLLMENT PHASE

A user asked to type four samples to create his templates for further comparison. Figure 4 shows the hardware architecture of the enrollment phase, after the user typed the four samples they are stored in 256*8 RAMs as a matrix, bubble sorter used for sort them ascending according to their duration times then stored them in database, the finite state machine (FSM) used to find the distance metrics between

Figure 4. Hardware architecture of the Enrollment Phase

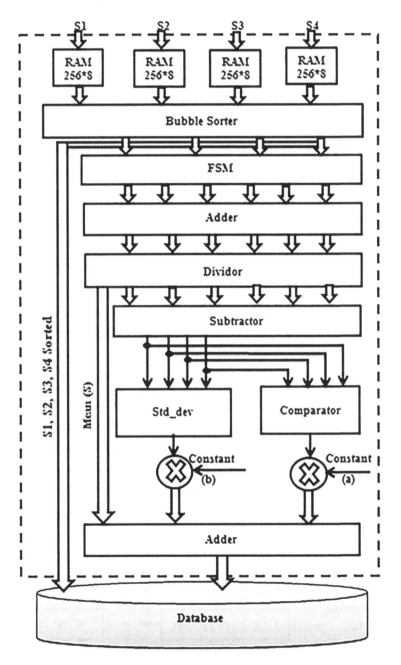

samples, adder and divider to find the normalized distance between the samples, comparator to find the maximum value of the distances MAX_d (S) then multiply it with constant (a), the standard deviation module used to find Std_d(S) then multiply it with constant (b) and finally stored the obtained results in the database for coming calculations.

The registration stage consists of many block diagrams such as Figure 5 shown. A user asked to type four samples to create his templates for further comparison.

1. **Key Input Device:** The sensor of the keystroke authentication system is the existing keyboard so there is no need to additional hardware like other biometric authentication techniques. Users are allowed to generate their own keystrokes containing uppercase characters, lowercase characters, numbers and also special characters that mean there isn't any restriction on the user password.

2. **Feature Extraction:** The password used to produce the template is the word "authenticate". The user is free to write any word and there isn't avoid any capitals letters (hence, the shift key had to be used), smalls letters plus the space, the full stop, the comma, the apostrophe and the return keys so there isn't any restriction to type the password. All the users participating in the experiments were native speakers of Arabic and may be not familiar with the language of the text they were typing that written in English. They were also some of them is familiar with English, and used to typing English words and sentences. Features are extracted while the user pressed and released keys. There are many algorithms used to find the keystroke features such as the digraph durations

Figure 5. Block Diagram of the Enrollment Phase

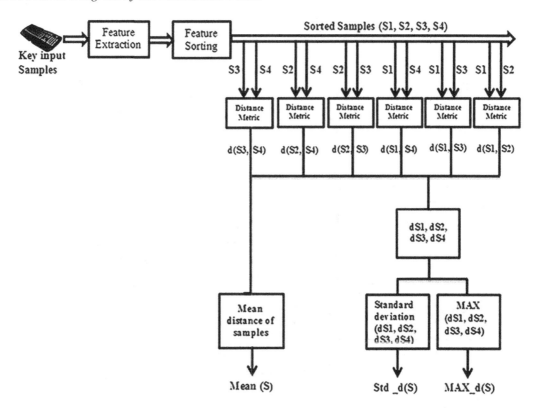

(The elapsed time between the depression of the first and of the second key). Therefore, the feature extraction outputs each digraph the users typed and its duration in milliseconds, for other more feature extraction algorithms you can see (Hassan et al., 2013).

3. **Feature Sorting:** Is used to sort the obtained from the feature extraction block to output the sorted digraphs ascending according to its duration times. Feature sorter is implemented using two methods. Method one used hardware based sorter and method two used software based sorter.

4. **Distance Metric:** Find the shared element between the two samples to measure the distance (d) between them then computes the sum of the distances between the position of each element in sample one (S1) and the position of the same element in sample two (S2) then divided by $\dfrac{N^2}{2}$ If N is even, $\dfrac{\left(N^2-1\right)}{2}$ If N is odd where N is the shared element between the two samples (S1 and S2) as Bergadano et al., 2002 illustrated in their algorithm.

If the user types the password such as the word "authenticate". It is considered sample one then type it again to generate sample two to find the distance metric (d) between S1 and S2 such as the following calculations in Figure 6.

N=11 is odd, so divide the summation of (d) by $\dfrac{\left(N^2-1\right)}{2}$ to find the normalized distance d (S1, S2).

Figure 6. Distance metric of two typing samples of the same text

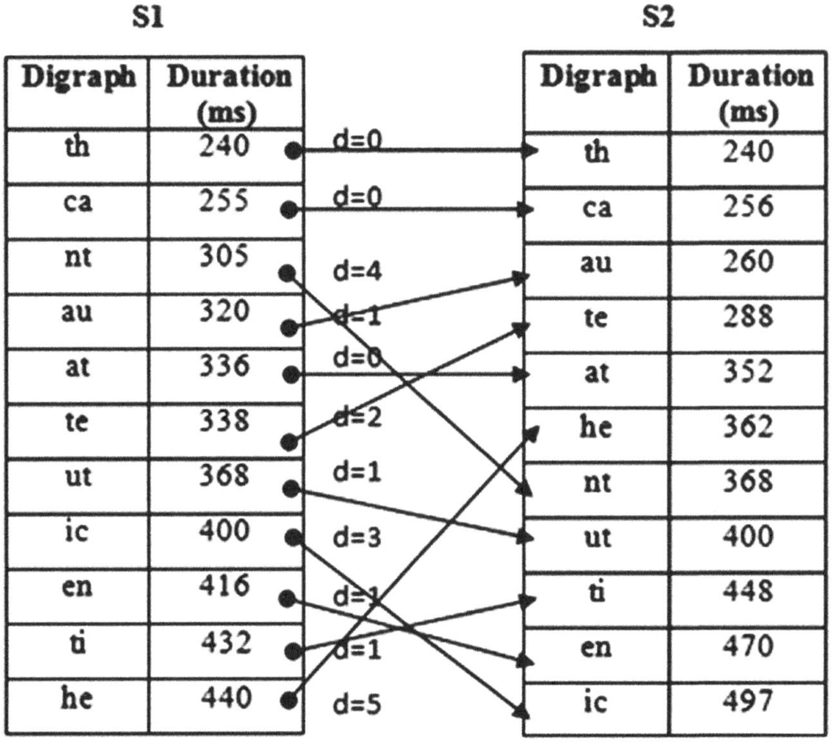

S1			S2	
Digraph	**Duration (ms)**		**Digraph**	**Duration (ms)**
th	240	d=0	th	240
ca	255	d=0	ca	256
nt	305	d=4	au	260
au	320	d=1	te	288
at	336	d=0	at	352
te	338	d=2	he	362
ut	368	d=1	nt	368
ic	400	d=3	ut	400
en	416	d=1	ti	448
ti	432	d=1	en	470
he	440	d=5	ic	497

$$d\left(S1, S2\right) = \frac{0+0+4+1+0+2+1+3+1+1+5}{60} = \frac{18}{60} = 0.3$$

Digraph is the major feature used in keystroke dynamics (Kim et al., 2012). the digraph duration times are utilized between the press times of two consecutive keys. in this research, the procedure for measure the similarity between two samples or degree of disorder described in (Bergadano et al., 2002) 256x8 matrix in which rows and columns are assigned to ASCII code corresponds to each digraph in the samples and its duration time.

A user asked to type four samples (S1, S2, S3, and S4). The normalized distances from samples captured of user "A" are d (S1, S2), d (S1, S3), d (S1, S4), d (S2, S3), d (S2, S4), d (S3, S4) that are calculated as the previous example. Let mSxyz be the mean distance of samples x, y and z of user "A" such as mS123 and find such as the following Equation (3).

mS123 = [d (S1, S2) + d (S1, S3) + d (S2, S3)] / 3   (3)

For each of the four samples, compute the mean distance of that sample with respect to the other samples of user "A" to find (dS1, dS2, dS3, dS4) such as Equation (4)

dS1= |[d(S1,S2)+d(S1,S3)+d(S1,S4)]/3−mS234| (4)

For each of the four samples, compute the mean distance of that sample with respect to the other samples of user "A" to find (dS1, dS2, dS3, dS4) such as equations below

dS1=|[d(S1,S2)+d(S1,S3)+d(S1,S4)]/3−mS234| (5)

dS2=|[d(S2,S1) +d(S2,S3)+d(S2,S4)]/3−mS134| (6)

dS3=|[d(S3,S1) +d(S3,S2)+d(S3,S4)]/3−mS124| (7)

dS4=|[d(S4,S1)+d(S4,S2)+d(S4,S3)]/3−mS123| (8)

5.   **MAX_d (S):** Find the maximum value of the distances from samples (S1, S2, S3, and S4) captured from the previous section illustrates in the following Equation (9).

MAX_d (S)=MAX (dS1, dS2, dS3,dS4)   (9)

6.   **Mean Distance between Samples:** Find m(S) as the following calculation shows to find the mean distances between the users "A" input samples as equation shown below.

m(S)=[d(S1,S2)+d(S1,S3)+d(S1,S4)+d(S2,S3)+d(S2,S4) +d(S3, S4)]/6   (10)

7.   **Standard Deviation:** Find the standard deviation as equation explains.

Std_d(S) = standard deviation (dS1, dS2, dS3, dS4).

$$Std\_d(S) = \sqrt{\frac{\sum[d(S) - m\_d(S)]}{N}}$$ (11)

where, Std_d(S) is the standard deviation

d(S) is each value in the population
m_d(S) is the mean value of [d(S1),d(S2),d(S3),d(S4)]
N is the number of the values (the population)

5.1. Log In Phase

The user types a new sample X in web page to capture the digraphs duration times, sorted using the sorter, then find the normalized distances between samples (S1, S2, S3, S4) which stored in the database and the new sample X as illustrates in Figure 7 to find d (X, S1), d (X, S2), d (X, S3) and d (X, S4) then find Md (X, S) and as equation shows.

Md(X,S) =[d(X,S1)+d(X,S2)+d(X,S3)+d(X,S4)]/4 (12)

Figure 8 shows the hardware architecture used for the log in phase and how to compare between the new sample X and the stored profile of the user and output the authentication results to accept the user to be the legal person or reject the user to aces the system.

Figure 7. Block diagram of the log in phase

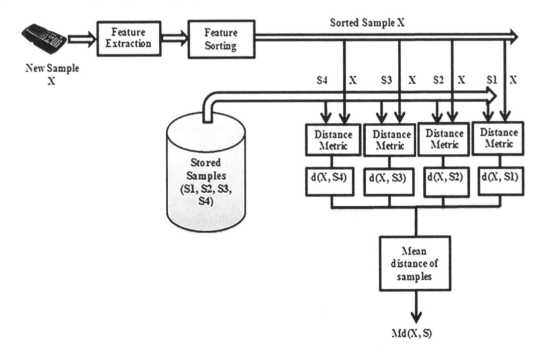

Figure 8. Hardware architecture of log in phase

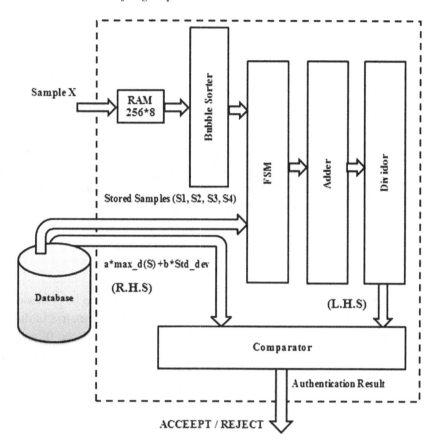

6. AUTHENTICATION RESULT

Accept the user which typed the sample X to be the same user who typed the four samples before and had already stored profile in the database if and only if Equation (13) satisfied the authentication results, where (a) and (b) are two constant chosen to vary the threshold of acceptance/rejection balance to have more or less stringent requirements. If L.H.S >= R.H.S the user is rejected and if L.H.S < R.H.S the user is accepted after the log in phase to be the legal user.

$$Md(X,S) < m(S)+a*MAX\_d(S)+b*Std\_d(S) \tag{13}$$

In this paper, there are two methods created to find the distance metric between two samples. The following sections explain method one and method two works in detail and how the whole proposed design affected by using each method. Comparing between two methods in work, architecture, results and the better method is chosen to compare between this paper results and the other results in the hardware implementation of biometric authentication methods and this will be in the following section.

6.1. Method One (H/W based Sorter)

In this method, a developed application used to capture the samples digraphs and their durations without sorting then enter this information to H/W-based sorter which used to sort the output feature extraction then find the distance between two samples using distance metric module as a Figure 9 illustrates.

6.1.1. Feature Extraction

In method one, feature extractor used a developed application to type the password and output each digraph of the password as long with its duration in milliseconds. If there is a repeated digraph, the mean of them is used. Figure 10 shows the flowchart to capture the user key input samples then shows the computed dynamics keystroke, i.e. each digraph with its duration. Result from this block can be send to any other input such as the H/W based sorter block.

6.1.2. Feature Sorting

After showing the computed dynamic keystroke from the previous step, the H/W based sorter starts to sort the timing information data by using two steps. The first step is to load matrix of duration time into ram1 when write enable (wr= 1) then read from ram1 when write enable (wr= 0) and load matrix of digraph into ram2 then read digraph from ram2 if the duration is completed then if other thing happed do nothing, as the Finite State Machine (FSM) procedures in Figure 11.

The second step is to use the bubble sorter algorithm to sort the digraph ascending according to its duration time as the pseudo algorithm in Table 3

Figure 9. Block diagram of method one

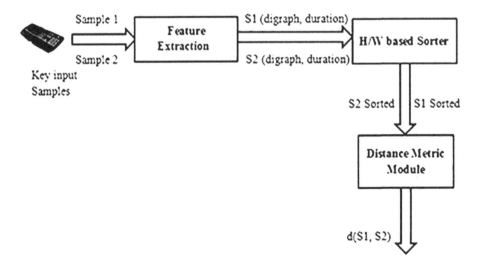

Figure 10. Feature extraction flowchart

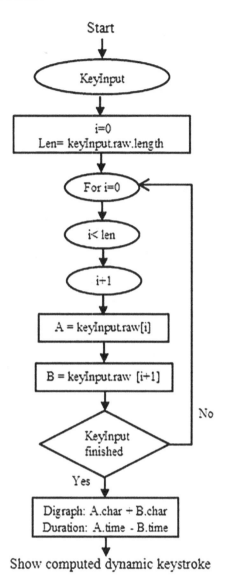

6.1.3. Distance Metric

In this block the distance metric between two samples is calculated as illustrated before in section 4. On the average, the distance metric between two samples of the same user are expected to be smaller than the distance metric between two samples of different users. It may be that d (S1, S2) = 0 for two different samples of the same user, while in fact it also sometimes happen that d (S1, S2) > d(X1, Y2) if S1 and S2 belong to the same user while X1 and Y2 belong to different users but it may be happened because the way an user types on the keyboard may vary according to different factors conditions, such as stress, weariness and tiredness. So always 0 < d (S1, S2) < 1, whereas d (S1, S2) =1 if the distance metric between two given samples of the same user are absolutely diverge and vary each other.

Figure 11. Finite State Machine Procedures

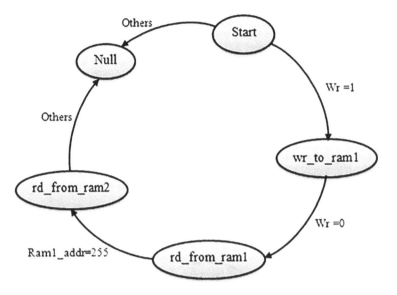

Table 3. Pseudo code for bubble sorter

Algorithm 1: bubble sorter module Algorithm
Input: Duration into ram1
Input: Digraph into ram2
Output: Sort the digraphs ascending according to its durations
1: Interface duration into ram1
2: Interface digraph into ram2
3: FSM procedures
4: if ram1_addr > 1 and ram1_out /= x"00" then
5: ram2_addr:= ram2_addr + 1
6: if ram2_addr:= count and state:= rd_from_ram2 then
7: end if
8: end if
9: read from ram2
10: if reset_addr:= 1 then
11: ram2_addr:= count
12: elsif state:= rd_from_ram2 then
13: if ram2_addr /= 0 and enable:= 1 then
14: ram2_addr:= ram2_addr -1
15: end if
16: end if
17: digraph_out:= ram2_out
18: duration_out:= ram1_out

6.2. Method Two (S/W based Sorter)

In this method, another developed application used to capture the samples digraphs and their durations, then sort feature extraction then enter this information to distance metric VHDL module between two samples as Figure 12 illustrates.

Figure 12. Block diagram of method two

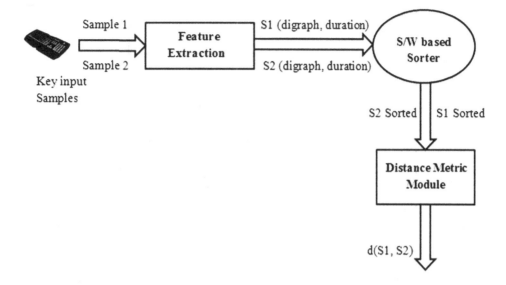

6.2.1. Feature Extraction

In method two, the feature extractor is also used a developed application as method one and the outputs from this block used as the inputs to the next block.

6.2.2. Feature Sorting

In method two, the feature sorter is used software based sorter and outputs depend on a developed application that captures the key inputs password from the user and outputs a sorted matrix contains on each digraph ascending according to its duration in milliseconds as the flowchart in Figure 13 shown.

6.2.3. Distance Metric

For method two, the calculation to find the distance metric between two samples is the same as method one. So in this method the developed application used to capture and feature extraction between samples then sort them ascending according to its duration then the hardware program (Xilinx ISE-9.2i) used to find the distance metric between samples and complete all design.

7. EXPERIMENTAL RESULTS

Two methods provide different resource of Slices and LUTs. The proposed algorithm used by second method consumes fewer slices compared with first method. Slices number in FPGA is more important in power consumption than LUTs because each slice contain two LUPs and two FFs. In each slice they are two LUTs and two FFs, during the PAR, ISE software put all necessary LUTs close to each other for minimum propagation of data, for that some LUT inside slice not used and in some slice only FFs is

Figure 13. Flowchart to sort digraph durations

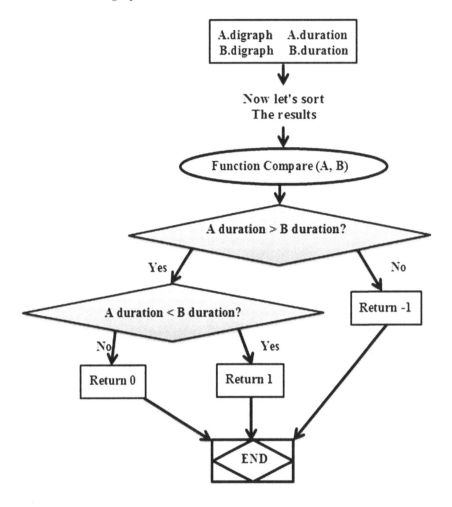

used without LUT so the number of LUTs cannot be calculated manually, therefore the LUTs could be less than Slices and vice versa. Table 4 shows that method two is better than method one for consuming Slice and LUTs.

Following are results of the "Timing Summary" section for two methods are as Table 5 and Table 6 shown from the Place and Route Report, which lists the constraints in this design and whether they were met or not. Digital synchronous signals/clocks always have a setup and hold time.

- **Clock Positive Slack:** Is a measure of how much the design exceeded its constraints. Negative slack is a measure of how much the design failed in realizing its goals.
- **Setup Time:** The amount of time the synchronous input must be stable before the active edge of the clock. Setup means time for the signal to prepare and method one achieved the best case equal to 10.750 ns for method one and 9.056 ns for method two.
- **Hold Time:** The amount of time the synchronous input must be stable after the active edge of the clock and means "time to process" and is equal to 1.072 ns and 1.390 ns, respectively for method one and two.

Table 4. FPGA Slices and LUTs Comparison

Resource	Slices	LUTs
Method one (H/W based Sorter)	125/14,752	193/29,504
Method two (S/W based Sorter)	41/14,752	74/29,504
Improvements %	0.84	1.19

Table 5. Timing constraints of method one

Met	Constraint	Check	Worst Case Slack	Best Case Achievable	Timing Errors	Timing Score
Yes	Autotime spec constraint for clock net clk_BUFGP	SETUP HOLD	N/A 1.072ns	10.750ns	N/A 0	0 0

Table 6. Timing constraints of method two

Met	Constraint	Check	Worst Case Slack	Best Case Achievable	Timing Errors	Timing Score
Yes	Autotime spec constraint for clock net clk_BUFGP	SETUP HOLD	N/A 1.390ns	9.056ns	N/A 0	0 0

The smaller the setup time, the faster the system can run so; the second method is faster than the first method and the time difference = 10.750 – 9.056 = 1.694 ns.

- **Worst Case Slack:** Is the difference between constraints and best case achievable and must not exceed the constraint clock. For example: In method one, if the constraint clock period = 11.822 ns and the best case achievable = 10.750 ns, then the worst case slack = 11.822 −7.899= 1.072 ns. Due to the positive value of the worst case slacks the ISE software produces zero timing error and zero timing score.

After a comparison between two methods, the conclusion showed that second method is faster than first method with difference time 10.750 - 9.056 = 1.694 ns, lower device utilizations, lower clock report and timing constraints so second method used for further design and implement the rest of the proposed design as long with method two because it is lower results than first method and contribute to the reduction of hardware resources.

There isn't any over-mapping for any of the resources used in the FPGA, allowing the implementation of the hardware architecture of keystroke dynamics in the chosen FPGA device. Memory blocks of dual RAMs (used 20 of the 36 available) and MULT 18*18SIOs (employee 28 of the 36 available) and number of Slices for programmed hardware architecture uses 1% of the available FPGA slices, showing that the hardware implementation of keystroke dynamics has significant resource consumption due to the number of operations that have to be performed. The Spartan-3E XC3S1600E FPGA is on the Xilinx MicroBlaze (Spartan-3, 2015; MicroBlaze, 2007) Development Kit, this development board has an external memory RAM: DDR SDRAM with 64 Mbyte, 50 MHz and 66 MHz clock oscillators, ports: HDMI, 10/100 Ethernet PHY, Onboard USB-based FPGA, serial, expansion, Four slides switches, Eight discrete LEDs and Four push-button switches, etc. (Spartan-3, 2015)

8. SIMULATION RESULTS

Xilinx ISE 9.2i is used for the simulation. The design simulation results of the proposed algorithm are addressed in Figure 14 and Figure 15.

Figure 14 shows the snapshot of the inputs illustrating each four samples (digraph, duration) for creating the user template's profile then the new sample X added to be distinguished if the user "A" who typed the four samples which stored in the database to be the same user who typed the X sample as discussed in the previous chapter.

Figure 15 shows the snapshot of the outputs results after comparing the template of the user with his new log in sample.

Comparing the results obtained from left hand side L.H.S = m (X, S), after substitution values of (a) and (b) which are given in Table 7 to find the summations of the right hand side R.H.S = [m(S)+a*MAX_d (S)+b*Std_d (S)]. Finally, the comparison will be between two values as the Figure 14 shown R.H.S = 35560 and L.H.S = 32000, showing that the authentication phase was successfully satisfied and the value of L.H.S < R.H.S so the user who typed sample "X" is the same user who typed the four samples before and already get his template profile in database.

Figure 14. Simulation Snapshot of Inputs

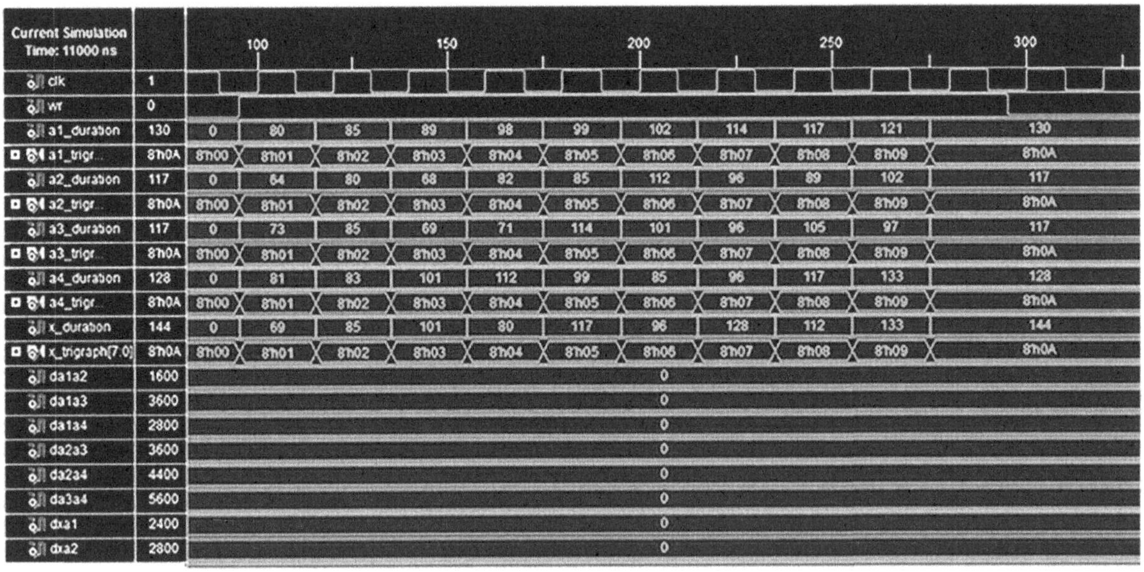

Figure 15. Simulation Snapshot of Outputs

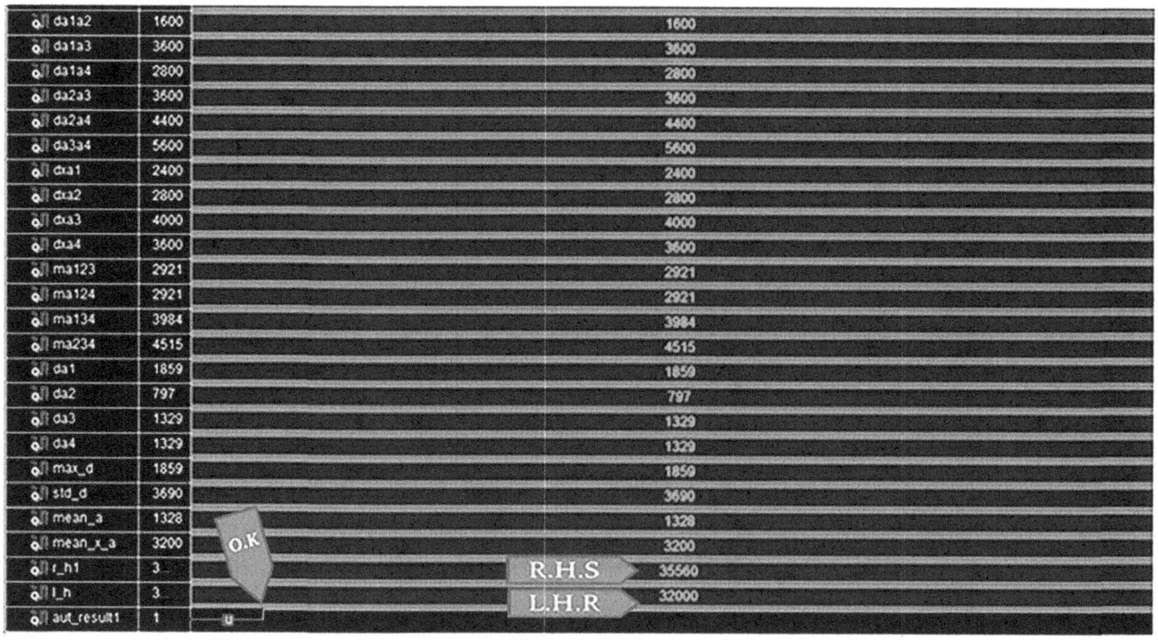

Table 7. Results of user authentication

Value of (a) Value of (b)	a = 1 b = 1.5	a = 1 b = 1.75	a = 1.5 b = 0
Successful attacks (out of 25) Failed legal connections (out of 25)	1 1	1 0	2 1
FRR	4%	4%	8%
FAR	4%	0%	4%

9. SYNTHESIS RESULTS

Much information obtained from synthesis report such as Device utilization summary as Table 8 shown. Timing Summary as Table 9 shown which obtained after loading the design to Xilinx ISE 9.2i.

- **Minimum Period:** The proposed design achieves minimum period 6.955ns (4.895ns logic, 2.060ns route) means (70.4% logic, 29.6% route) and the used frequency is 143.781MHz
- **Minimum Input Arrival Time Before the Clock:** The proposed design achieves minimum input arrival time 5.249ns (2.691ns logic, 2.558ns route) which means (51.3% logic, 48.7% route).
- **Maximum Output Required Time After the Clock:** The design achieves maximum output time before the clock 40.055ns (30.557ns logic, 9.498ns route) means (76.3% logic, 23.7% route).
- **Total Memory Usage:** Tells how much memory was used by each of the processes and in the design experiment it is equal to 223476 kilobytes.

Table 8. Device utilization summary of the proposed design

	Used	Available	Utilization
Logic Utilization			
Total Number Slice Registers	**551**	**29,504**	**1%**
Number used as Flip Flops	471		
Number used a Latches	80		
Number of 4 input LUTs	1,099	29,504	3%
Logic Distribution			
Number of occupied Slices	752	14,752	5%
Number of Slices containing only related logic	752	752	100%
Number of Slices contain unrelated logic	0	752	0%
Total Number of 4 Input LUTs	**1,286**	**29,504**	**4%**
Number used as logic	1,099		
Number used as route-thru	171		
Number used as shift registers	16		
Number of bonded IOBs	54	250	21%
Number of block RAMs	20	36	55%
Number of GCLKs	1	24	4%
Number of MULT18X18SIos	28	36	77%
Total equivalent gate count for design	**1,326,556**		

Table 9. Timing summary of the proposed design

Timing Summary	Proposed Design
Minimum period	6.950 ns
Maximum Frequency	143.781MHz
Minimum input arrival time before clock	5.249ns
Maximum output required time after clock	40.055ns
Maximum combinational path delay	No path found
Total memory usage	223476 kilobytes

10. IMPLEMENTATION RESULTS

After synthesis, then run design implementation, which converts the logical design into a physical file format that can be downloaded to the selected target device (Xilinx Spartan 3E-XC3S1600E Development System) From Project Navigator, after running the implementation process in one step, or run each of the implementation processes separately as Table 10 shows.

Comparison between implementation dynamic keystroke described in this thesis and other existing implementation of biometric authentication methods will be explained in Table 11 such as the hardware used in each research, the algorithms used and the time obtained to implement each biometric authentication technique.

Table 10. Timing constraints of the proposed design

Met	Constraint	Check	Worst Case Slack	Best Case Achievable	Timing Errors	Timing Score
Yes	Autotimespec constraint for clock netclk_BUFGP	SETUP HOLD	N/A 0.910ns	9.650ns	N/A 0	0 0

Table 11. Comparison between the implementation hardware described in this research and other existing hardware implementations for other biometric authentication techniques

Reviewed Article	Hardware	Algorithm	Biometric Authentication Technique	Time (ms)
Proposed Design (method one)	FPGA (Spartan-3e XC3S1600E) CLK: 143.781MHz	Degree of disorder	Keystroke Dynamics	50.653ns
Proposed Design (method two)	FPGA (Spartan-3e XC3S1600E) CLK: 143.781MHz	Degree of disorder	Dynamic Keystroke	9.950ns
Giacometto et al.,	FPGA(Virtex 5, LX50T) CLK: 100MHz	Frequency correlation using FFT	Iris	16.11
Fatt et al.,	ADSP-BF561 EZ-KIT LITE CLK: 600MHz	Hamming Distance	Iris	198.96
Gayathri et al.,	FPGA (Virtex 5, xc5vlx30) CLK: 550 MHz	Euclidian Distance	Iris	0.0149
Poinsot et al.,	FPGA (Virtex-5 CLK: 175 MHz	Hamming distance and score fusion.	Palmprint and face	0.4
Liu et al.,	FPGA (Virtex4, sx family) CLK: 53.53MHz	Hamming Distance	Iris	2.725
Rakvic et al.,	FPGA(Stratix IV) CLK: 500 MHz	Hamming Distance	Iris	0.002
Vijayalami et al.,	FPGA (Spartan-3E) CLK:65.432MHz	AdaBoost	Face	15.30 ns
Zhao et al.,	DSP (TMS320DM642) CLK: 720MHZ	- -	Iris	471.56
Vatsa et al.,	CPU, Pentium IV CLK: 3.2 GHz	Hamming Distance	Iris	1.82

Figure 16 and Figure 17 are shown the frequency used and the execution time in this research and other techniques, illustrating that the execution time for method two is the lowest time comparing other biometric authentication systems.

11. POWER CONSUMPTION ANALYSIS

Power consumption for the proposed design is estimated by using the XPower Estimator spreadsheet as shown in Figure 18. The XPower Estimator (XPE) spreadsheet is a power estimation tool used in the pre-design and pre-implementation phases of a project. XPE assists with architecture evaluation such

Figure 16. Comparison between proposed design frequency and related methods

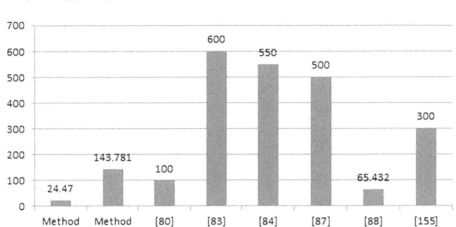

Frequency(MHz)

Figure 17. Comparison between proposed design time and related methods

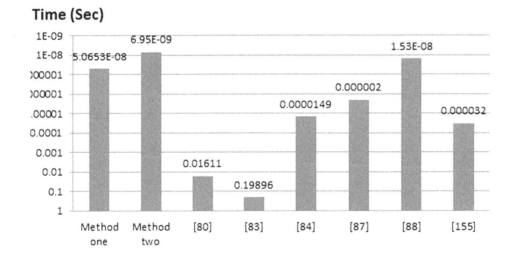

Time (Sec)

as device selection, power supply components and thermal management components specific for your application. XPower Estimators are a set of Excel spreadsheets that can be found on the Web at Xilinx website. The spreadsheets support all Xilinx FPGAs. Total power in an FPGA or any semiconductor device is the sum of two components. From quick logic's application notes for static power and dynamic power in FPGA's:

- **Power Basics:** The total power usage of an FPGA device can be broken down to total static power and total dynamic power. Static power is associated with DC current while dynamic power is associated with AC current.

Figure 18. Estimate power consumption for proposed design by using XPE

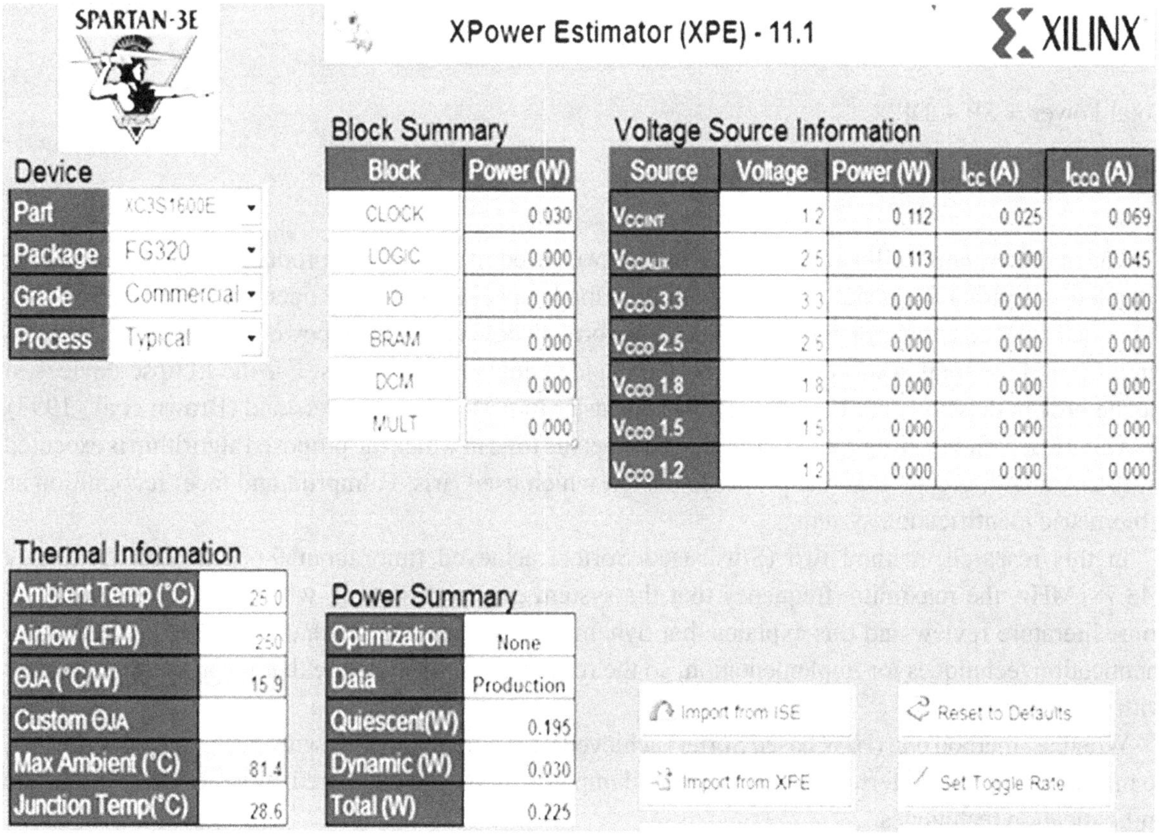

- **Static Power (Quiescent Power):** FPGA static power is proportional to the static current ICC. The current that flows regardless of gate switching (transistor is ON "biased" or OFF "unbiased"). DC power dissipation can be estimated by the worst-case equivalent equation. In this research, the static power obtained is about 0.195 W

SP = VCC * ICC, For Eclipse devices VCC = 2.5 V and ICC = 0.140 mA.

SP = (2.5V)*(0.140mA) = 0.350 mW

- **Dynamic Power (Active Power):** The FPGA dynamic is related to the active current ICC. The current that flows when switching takes place (transistor ON "biased" and responds to small-signals). The AC power dissipation can be estimated by the worst-case equivalent equation. In this research, the dynamic power is about 0.030 W

DP = VCC *ICC

ICC [active] = C*(dVcc/dt)

$DP = Vcc*C \ (dVcc/dt)$

$DP = f*C*Vcc^2$

$Total \ Power = SP + DP$

$Total \ Power = 0.195+0.030 = 0.225 \ W$

The above equations illustrate that dynamic power is equivalent to the product of the maximum (or intended) operating frequency, the total switching load capacitance and the operating voltage. The total dynamic power consumption for any FPGA can be broken down to the total power utilized by the internal circuitry and the total power consumed by the device's inputs and outputs. For the Eclipse devices, it can be broken down further to make calculation easier to perform and understand (Brown et al., 1993)

Many researches had dissipated an execution time; the time in which the proposed algorithm is executed on FPGA board, greater than the proposed design which used (iris, Palmprint and face) recognition as a biometric identification system.

In this research, method two (S/w based Sorter) achieved time about 9.650ns with frequency 143.781MHz, the maximum frequency that the system can work with it, which is a lower time than some literature review and this explains that dynamic keystroke is faster than the other biometric authentication techniques for implementation, so the research results illustrate that it can be implemented with minimum time.

Whereas, method one (H/W based Sorter) achieved time about 50.653ns with frequency 24.470MHz, so method two is the preferred one to be used and implemented to be compared with the others biometric authentication techniques.

12. CONCLUSION AND FUTURE WORK

Authentication in cloud computing requires a systemic view because the security will be constructed along a faraway. Authentication is a very important issue that refers to determine if the individual is the legal person who accesses to his rented portion. In this research, dynamic keystroke as a biometric authentication technique applied to cloud computing technology has been suggested. The proposed algorithm concerned with keystroke technique and its procedures to distinguish the true user was discussed in details. The proposed algorithm has been synthesized, simulated and implemented in the Xilinx Spartan-3E FPGA using VHDL with Xilinx tool ISE Web Pack 9.2i and achieves a time 9.650 ns. This research tries to proof that dynamic keystroke as a biometrics algorithms can be implemented in hardware. The algorithm calculation optimized in order to reduce and overcomes the problem of floating point number. It demonstrates that the operations can be performed with integer numbers without any significant changes in the obtained details.

The following contributions have been achieved; developed application is created to capture the user keystroke samples and the results are each digraph of the user password with its duration times, and sorting duration times ascending according to its duration times and these outputs give to the Xilinx ISE 9.2i software. The proposed design based on the degree of disorder converted to VHDL to be implemented using Spartan-3E XC3S1600E device. The proposed algorithm is synthesized using Xilinx ISE 9.2i software. The design is loaded to Xilinx Spartan-3E on a FPGA. Simulation and implementation of the proposed design achieves time about 9.650ns; the time in which the proposed algorithm is executed on FPGA board and frequency 143.781 MHz, the maximum frequency that the system can work with it. Comparing several existing implementation algorithms of other authentication techniques is figured out the time execution of the proposed design. The results show dynamic keystroke as a biometric identification system can be implemented with minimum time.

There are many tracks of research worthy to follow up in the future. It is expected that improving the proposed design in this research to create a big database included several samples of many users and when any user tried to access the system distinguishes him and specifies exactly, who is this user among the registered participants. Also designing about continuous dynamic keystroke algorithm can be implemented in hardware using many others FPGA.

ACKNOWLEDGMENT

The authors would like to thank the anonymous reviewers and the editor for the constructive and helpful comments and suggestions.

REFERENCES

Ashenden, P. (2006). *The VHDL cookbook* (1st ed.).

Avnet Memec, Inc., (2011). Spartan-3E FPGA Starter Kit Board User Guide, UG230 Version 1.2.

Babaeizadeh, M., Bakhtiari, M., & Mohammed, A. (2015). Authentication Methods in Cloud Computing: A Survey, Research Journal of Applied Sciences. *Engineering and Technology*, *9*(8), 655–664.

Babich, A. (2012). *Biometric authentication, types of biometric identifiers* [Bachelor's Thesis Programming in Business Information Technology].

Bandara, H., Ravindra, S., Silva, P., & Weerasinghe, P. (2015). The Universal Biometric System, *Proceedings of theInternational Conference on Advances in ICT for Emerging Regions*, Colombo, Sri Lanka

Barrero, M., Javier, G., & Julian, F. (2013). Efficient software attack to multimodal biometric systems and its application to face and iris fusion. *Pattern Recognition Letters*, *36*, 243–253. doi:10.1016/j.patrec.2013.04.029

Bergadano, F., Gunetti, D., & Picardi, C. (2002). User authentication through keystroke dynamics. *ACM Transactions on Information and System Security*, *5*(4), 367–397. doi:10.1145/581271.581272

Bleha, S., & Obaidat, S. (1993). Computer user verification using the perceptron. *IEEE Transactions on Systems, Man, and Cybernetics*, *23*(3), 900–902. doi:10.1109/21.256563

Brown, M., & Rogers, J. (1993). User Identification via keystroke characteristics of typed names using neural networks, Studies. *International Journal of Man-Machine*, *39*(6), 999–1014. doi:10.1006/imms.1993.1092

Campisi, P., Maiorana, E., Bosco, M. L., & Neri, A. (2009). User Authentication Using Keystroke Dynamics For Cellular Phones. *IET Signal Processing*, *3*(4), 333–341.

Cao, K., Liaojun, P., Jimin, L., & Jie, T. (2013). Fingerprint classification by a hierarchical classifier. *Pattern Recognition Letters*, *46*(12), 3186–3197. doi:10.1016/j.patcog.2013.05.008

Carlin, S., & Curran, K. (2011). Cloud Computing Security. *International Journal of Ambient Computing and Intelligence*, *3*(1), 14–19. doi:10.4018/jaci.2011010102

Cho, S., Han, C., Han, D., & Kim, H. (2000). Web-based keystroke dynamics identity verification using neural network. *Journal of Organizational Computing and Electronic Commerce*, *10*(4), 295–307. doi:10.1207/S15327744JOCE1004_07

Clarke, L., & Furnell, M. (2007). Advanced user authentication for mobile devices, *Network Research Group, School of Computing, Communication and Electronic, University of Plymouth. Computers & Security*, *26*(2), 109–119. doi:10.1016/j.cose.2006.08.008

Davoudi, H., & Kabir, E. (2009). A New Distance Measure for Free Text Keystroke Authentication. *Proceedings of the 14th International CSI Computer Conference*, Tehran, Iran (pp. 570–575). doi:10.1109/CSICC.2009.5349640

Dougan, T., & Curran, K. (2012). Man in the Browser Attacks. *International Journal of Ambient Computing and Intelligence*, *4*(1), 29–39. doi:10.4018/jaci.2012010103

Douhou, S., & Magnus, J. R. (2009). The Reliability of User Authentication through Keystroke Dynamics. *Statistica Neerlandica*, *63*(4), 432–449.

Draffin, B., Zhu, J., & Zhang, J. (2014). *Passive User Authentication through Micro-Behavior Modeling of Soft Keyboard Interaction, LNCS* (Vol. 130, pp. 184–201). Springer International Publishing. doi:10.1007/978-3-319-05452-0_14

Emam, A. (2013). Additional Authentication and Authorization using Registered Email-ID for Cloud Computing. *International Journal of Soft Computing and Engineering*, *3*(2), 110–113.

Fatt, R. N. Y., Haur, T. Y., & Ming, M. K. (2009). Iris verification algorithm based on texture analysis and its implementation on DSP. *Proceedings of the International Conference on Signal Acquisition and Processing DSP*, Kuala Lumpur (V*ol. 2*, pp. 198 – 202). doi:10.1109/ICSAP.2009.9

Gascon., Uellenbeck, S., Wolf, C., & Rieck, K. (2014). Continuous Authentication on Mobile Devices by Analysis of Typing Motion Behavior. *Proceedings of the GI Conference Sicherheit*, Vienna.

Gayathri, S., & Sridhar, V. (2013). An improved fast thinning algorithm for fingerprint image. *International Journal of Engineering Science and Innovative Technology*, *2*(1), 264–270.

Ghanavati, B. (2015). Designing a new face recognition system robust to various poses. *Journal of mathematics and computer science*, *15*, 32-39.

Giacometto, F., Vilardy, M., Torres, C. O., & Mattos, L. (2011). Template characterization and correlation algorithm created from segmentation for the iris biometric authentication based on analysis of textures implemented on an FPGA. *Journal of Physics*, *274*(1).

Giot, R., Dorizzi, B., & Rosenberger, C. (2015). A Review on the Public Benchmark Databases for Static Keystroke Dynamics. *Computers & Security, Elsevier, 55*, 46–61. doi:10.1016/j.cose.2015.06.008

Giot, R., El-Abed, M., & Rosenberger, C. (2009). Keystroke Dynamics Authentication for Collaborative Systems. *Proceedings of theIEEE International Symposium on Collaborative Technologies and Systems*, Baltimore, Piscataway (pp. 172–179).

Grabham, J., & White, M. (2008). Use of a Novel Keypad Biometric for Enhanced User Identity Verification. *Proceedings of theIEEE International Conference on Instrumentation and Measurement Technology*, Victoria, British Columbia, Canada (pp. 12–16). doi:10.1109/IMTC.2008.4546995

Gunetti, D., & Picardi, C. (2005). Keystroke analysis of free text. *ACM Transactions on Information and System Security, 8*(3), 312–347. doi:10.1145/1085126.1085129

Guo, J., Hsien, H., Yun-Fu, L., Jie-Cyun, Y., Mei-Hui, C., & Thanh-Nam, L. (2012). Contact-free hand geometry-based identification system. *Expert Systems with Applications, 39*(14), 11728–11736. doi:10.1016/j.eswa.2012.04.081

Guven, A., & Sogukpinar, I. (2003). Understanding users' keystroke patterns for computer access security. *Computers & Security, 22*(8), 695–706. doi:10.1016/S0167-4048(03)00010-5

Hassan, S., Selim, M., & Zayed, H. (2013). User Authentication with Adaptive Keystroke Dynamics. *International Journal of Computer Science Issues, 10*(4), 127–134.

Hu, Z., & Xie, M. (2010). Iris biometric processor enhanced module FPGA-based design. *Proceedings of theSecond International Conference on Computer Modeling and SimulationICCMS '10* (Vol. 2, pp. 259 – 262). IEEE Browse Conference Publications.

Jain et al. (2014). Passcode Keystroke Biometric Performance on Touchscreen is Superior to that on Hardware Keyboards. *International journal of Research in computer applications and information technology, 2*(4), 29–33.

Jaiswal, S., Bhadauria, S., & Jadon, R. (2011). biometric: Case study. *Journal of Global Research in Computer Science, 2*(10), 19–48.

Johansen, U. (2012). Keystroke Dynamics on a Device with Touch Screen [Master's Thesis Science in Information Security].

Joyce, R., & Gupta, G. (1990). Identity authentication based on keystroke latencies. *Communications of the ACM, 33*(2), 168–176. doi:10.1145/75577.75582

Kaneko, Y., Kinpara, Y., & Shiomi, Y. (2011). A Hamming Distance like Filtering in Keystroke Dynamics. *Proceedings of the9th Annual International Conference on Privacy, Security and Trust* (pp. 93–95). doi:10.1109/PST.2011.5971969

Kannavara, R., & Bourbakis, N. (2009). Iris biometric authentication based on local global graphs, an FPGA implementation. *IEEE transaction On Computational Intelligence for Security and Defense Applications*.

Kaur, M., & Virk, R. (2013). Security system based on user authentication using keystroke dynamics. *International Journal of Advanced Research in Computer and Communication Engineering, 2*(5), 11–21.

Kim, M., Jeong, H., & Choi, E. (2012). Context-aware platform for user authentication in cloud database computing. *Proceedings of theInternational Conference on Future Information Technology and Management Science & Engineering* (*Vol. 14*, pp. 170-176).

Kochetkov, A. (2013). Cloud-based biometric services: just a matter of time. *Biometric Technology, 5,* 8–11.

Lee, H., & Cho, S. (2007). Retraining a keystroke dynamics based authenticator with impostor patterns. Department of Industrial Engineering, Seoul National University, Computers & Security, Republic of Korea, 26(4), 300-310.

Lee, J. (2012). A novel biometric system based on palm vein image, *Department of Electrical Engineering. Chinese Naval Academy, 33*(12), 1520–1528.

Leggett, J., Williams, G., Usnick, M., & Longnecker, M. (1991). Dynamic identity verification via keystroke characteristics. *International Journal of Man-Machine Studies, 35*(6), 859–870. doi:10.1016/S0020-7373(05)80165-8

LI, Y. (. (. (2015). Iris recognition algorithm based on MMC-app, *International Journal of Signal Processing. Image Processing and Pattern Recognition, 8*(2), 1–10. doi:10.14257/ijsip.2015.8.2.01

Liu, J., Sanchez, R., Lindoso, A., & Hurtado, O. (2006). FPGA implementation for an iris biometric processor. *Proceedings of theIEEE International Conference on Field Programmable Technology,* Bangkok (pp. 265 – 268).

Liu, J., Sanchez, R., Lindoso, A., & Hurtado, O. (2006). FPGA implementation for an iris biometric processor. *Proceedings of theIEEE International Conference on Field Programmable Technology,* Bangkok (pp. 265 – 268).

Liu, S., & Silverman, M. (2001). Practical Guide to Biometric Security Technology. *ITS Pro IEEE, 3*(1), 27–32. doi:10.1109/6294.899930

Messerman, A., Mustafic, T., Camtepe, S., & Albayrak, S. (2011). Continuous and non-intrusive identity verification in real-time environments based on free-text keystroke dynamics, *Proceedings of the International Joint Conference on Biometrics,* Washington, DC (pp. 1-8). doi:10.1109/IJCB.2011.6117552

MicroBlaze. (2007, December 5). Development Kit Spartan-3E 1600E Edition User Guide.

Modi, S., & Elliott, S. (2006). Keystroke dynamics verification using a spontaneously generated password. *Proceedings of theIEEE International Carnahan Conference on Security Technology (ICCST '06),* Lexington, KY, USA (pp. 116–121). doi:10.1109/CCST.2006.313439

Monaco, V., Bakelman, N., & Charles, C. (2013). Keystroke Biometric Studies on Password and Numeric Keypad Input. *Proceedings of theEuropean Intelligence and Security Informatics Conference* (pp. 204–207).

Monrose, F., & Rubin, D. (1999). Keystroke dynamics as a biometric for authentication.

Montalvão, J., Freire, E., Bezerra, M. Jr, & Garcia, R. (2015). Contributions to empirical analysis of keystroke dynamics in passwords. *Contributions to Empirical Analysis of Keystroke Dynamics in Passwords, Pattern Recognition Letters, 52*, 80–86. doi:10.1016/j.patrec.2014.09.016

Napier, R., Laverty, W., Mahar, D., Henderson, R., Hiron, M., & Wagner, M. (1995). Keyboard user verification: Toward an accurate, efficient and ecological valid algorithm. *International Journal of Human-Computer Studies*, *43*(2), 213–222. doi:10.1006/ijhc.1995.1041

Nisha, J., & Anto Kumar, R. (2014). User Authentication Based on Keystroke Dynamics. *International Journal of Engineering Research and Applications*, *4*(3), 345–349.

Obaidat, M., & Sadoun, B. (1997). Verification of computer users using keystroke dynamics. *IEEE Transactions on Systems, Man, and Cybernetics. Part B, Cybernetics*, *27*(2), 261–269. doi:10.1109/3477.558812 PMID:18255865

Ord, T., & Furnell, S. (2000). User authentication for keypad-based devices using keystroke analysis [MSc Thesis]. University of Plymouth, UK.

Peacock, A. K. X., & Wilkerson, M. (2004). Typing patterns: A key to user identification. *IEEE Security and Privacy*, *2*(5), 40–47. doi:10.1109/MSP.2004.89

Pettey, C., & Meulen, R. (2008). Gartner says contrasting views on Cloud computing is creating confusion, *Gartner Symposium/ITxpo, Orlando*. Retrieved from http://www.gartner.com/newsroom/id/766215

Poinsot, A., Yang, F., & Brost, V. (2011). Palmprint and face score level fusion: Hardware implementation of a contactless small sample biometric system. *Optical Engineering (Redondo Beach, Calif.)*, *50*(2), 1–12. doi:10.1117/1.3534199

Rahman, K. A., Balagani, K. S., & Phoha, V. (2011). Making Impostor Pass Rates Meaningless: A Case of Snoop-forge-replay Attack on Continuous Cyber-Behavioral Verification with Keystrokes. Proceedings of the IEEE Computer Society Conference on Computer Vision and Pattern Recognition Workshops (pp. 31–38). doi:10.1109/CVPRW.2011.5981729

Rakvic, R., Ulis, B., Broussard, R., Ives, R., & Steiner, N. (2009). Parallelizing Iris Recognition. *IEEE Transactions On Information Forensics and Security*, *4*(4), 812–823. doi:10.1109/TIFS.2009.2032012

Revett, K., deMagalh˜aes, S., & Santos, H. (2005). Password secured sites-stepping forward with keystroke dynamics, *International Conference on Next Generation*, (pp. 1-6)

Revett, K. deMagalh˜aes, S., & Santos, H. (2006). Enhancing login security through the use of keystroke input dynamics. In Advances in Biometrics, LNCS (Vol. 3832, pp. 661-667).

Revett, K., deMagalh˜aes, S., & Santos, H. (2007). On the use of rough sets for user authentication via keystroke dynamics. *Proceedings of the 13th Portuguese Conference on Progress in Artificial Intelligence* (pp. 145–159). doi:10.1007/978-3-540-77002-2_13

Rudrapal, D., Debbarma, S., & Debbarma, N. (2012). Voice Recognition and Authentication as a Proficient Biometric Tool and its Application in Online Exam for P.H People. *International Journal of Computers and Applications*, *39*(12), 5–12.

Rupinder, S., & Narinder, R. (2014). Comparison of various biometric methods. *International Journal of Advances in Science and Technology*, *2*(I), 24–30.

Samura, T., & Nishimura, H. (2011). Keystroke Timing Analysis for Personal Authentication in Japanese Long Text Input. *Proceedings of the50th Annual Conference on Society of Instrument and Control Engineers* (pp. 2121–2126).

Shah, A., Khan, M., & Salam, A. (2015). An appraisal of off-line signature verification techniques. *International Journal of Modern Education and Computer Science, 7*(4), 67–75. doi:10.5815/ijmecs.2015.04.08

Singh, S., & Arya, V. K. (2011). Key Classification: a New Approach in Free Text Keystroke Authentication System. *Proceedings of the 3th IEEE of Pacific-Asia Conference on Circuits, Communications and System*, Wuhan.

Sogukpinar, I., & Yalcin, L. (2004). User identification at login via keystroke dynamics. *Journal of Electronic and Electrical Engineering, 4*(1), 995–1005.

Tin, H. (2015). The performance evaluation for personal identification using palmprint and face recognition. *Proceedings of theInternational Conference on Image Processing, Singapore* (pp. 39-44), *Electrical and Computer Engineering*

Ting-Yi, C., Cheng-Jung T., & Jyun-Hao, L. (2012). A Graphical-based Password Keystroke Dynamic Authentication System for Touch Screen Handheld Mobile Devices. *The Journal of Systems and Software, 85*(5), 1157–1165.

Trojahn, M., Arndt, F., & Ortmeier, F. (2013). Authentication with Keystroke Dynamics on Touchscreen Keypads - Effect of different N-Graph Combinations. *Proceedings of the3th International Conference on Mobile Services, Resources and Users* (pp. 114–119).

United States Government Accountability Office (ACO). (2015). Facial recognition technology. *Subcommittee on Privacy, Technology and the Law, Committee on the Judiciary, U.S. Senate.*

Uzun, Y., & Bicakci, K. (2012). A second look at the performance of neural networks for keystroke dynamics using a publicly available dataset. *Computers & Security, 31*(5), 717–726. doi:10.1016/j.cose.2012.04.002

Vatsa, M., Singh, R., & Noore, A. (2008). Improving iris recognition performance using segmentation, quality enhancement, match score fusion and indexing. *IEEE Transactions on Systems, Man, and Cybernetics. Part B, Cybernetics, 38*(4), 1–15. doi:10.1109/TSMCB.2008.922059 PMID:18632394

Vijayalami & Obulesu, B. (2012). Hardware implementation of face detection using AdaBoost algorithm. *Journal of Electronics and Communication Engineering, 1*(2), 93–102.

Wakil, Y., Tariq, S. G., Humayun, A., & Abbas, N. (2015). An FPGA-based minutiae extraction system for fingerprint recognition. *International Journal of Computers and Applications, 111*(12), 31–35. doi:10.5120/19592-1362

Wankhede, S. B., & Verma, S. (2014). Keystroke Dynamics Authentication System Using Neural Network. *International Journal of Innovative Research and Development, 3*(1), 2014.

Wu, K., Jen-Chun, L., Tsung-Ming, L., Ko-Chin, C., & Chien-Ping, C. (2013). A secure palm vein recognition system. *Journal of Systems and Software, 86*(11), 2870–2876. doi:10.1016/j.jss.2013.06.065

Xi, K., Tang, Y., & Hu, J. (2011). Correlation Keystroke Verification Scheme for User Access Control in Cloud Computing Environment. *The Computer Journal, 54*(10), 1632–1644. doi:10.1093/comjnl/bxr064

Xilinx, I. S. E. (2007). *9.2i Software Manuals.* Constraints Guide and Development System Reference Guide.

Xilinx, Inc. (2003). DSP Design Flows in FPGA Tutorial Slides.

Xilinx, Inc. (2007). System Generator for DSP User Guide', Release 9.2.01.

Xilinx Inc. (2008). System Generator for DSP', User Guide, Release 10.1. Retrieved from www.xilinx.com

Xilinx: Spartan-3 Generation Configuration User Guide. (2015). Extended Spartan-3A, Spartan-3E, and Spartan-3 FPGA Families UG332, Version 1.7.

Xilinx tool ISE Web Pack 9.2i website. (n. d.). Retrieved from http://www.xilinx.com/webpack/classics/wpclassic/

Xuan, W., Fangxia, G., & Jian-feng, M. (2012). User Authentication via Keystroke Dynamics based on Difference Subspace and Slope Correlation Degree. *Digital Signal Processing, 22*(5), 707–712. doi:10.1016/j.dsp.2012.04.012

Yu, E., & Cho, S. (2004). Keystroke dynamics identity verification - its problems and practical solutions. *Computers & Security, 23*(5), 428–440. doi:10.1016/j.cose.2004.02.004

Zhao, X., & Xie, M. (2009). A practical design of iris recognition system based on DSP. *Proceedings of theInternational Conference of Intelligent Human-Machine Systems and Cybernetics* (*Vol. 1,* pp. 66-70). doi:10.1109/IHMSC.2009.25

This work was previously published in the International Journal of Ambient Computing and Intelligence (IJACI), 7(2); edited by Nilanjan Dey, pages 1-32, copyright 2016 by IGI Publishing (an imprint of IGI Global).

Index

Printed in the United States
By Bookmasters